Handbook of Spelling

ABOUT THE EDITORS

Gordon Brown is a senior lecturer in cognitive science at the University of Wales, Bangor, but is shortly to take up the appointment of Professor of Psychology at the University of Warwick, UK. He has carried out research in several areas of cognitive psychology and cognitive science, especially connectionist modelling and experimental studies of reading, spelling, developmental dyslexia and short-term memory.

Nick Ellis is a reader in psychology at the University of Wales, Bangor. His main research interests concern applied cognitive psychology—understanding and improving human cognition—particularly with regard to development and disorders of reading, spelling, and short-term memory, second language acquisition, imagery, and implict and explicit learning and memory.

Handbook of Spelling
Theory, Process and Intervention

Edited by

GORDON D. A. BROWN and NICK C. ELLIS
University of Wales, Bangor, UK

JOHN WILEY & SONS
Chichester · New York · Brisbane · Toronto · Singapore

Other Wiley Editorial Offices

John Wiley & Sons, Inc., 605 Third Avenue,
New York, NY 10158-0012, USA

Jacaranda Wiley Ltd, 33 Park Road, Milton,
Queensland 4064, Australia

John Wiley & Sons (Canada) Ltd, 22 Worcester Road,
Rexdale, Ontario M9W 1L1, Canada

John Wiley & Sons (SEA) Pte Ltd, 37 Jalan Pemimpin #05-04,
Block B, Union Industrial Building, Singapore 2057

Library of Congress Cataloging-in-Publication Data

Handbook of spelling : theory, process, and intervention / edited by
　　Gordon D. A. Brown and Nick C. Ellis.
　　　　p.　cm.
　　Includes bibliographical references and index.
　　Ellis, Nick C.
　　ISBN 0-471-94342-8
　　1. English language—Orthography and spelling—Handbooks, manuals,
　　etc.　2. English language—Orthography and spelling—Study and
　　teaching.　I. Brown, Gordon D. A.
　　PE1143.H26　1994　　　　　　　　　　　　　　　　　92-33921
　　421′.52—dc20　　　　　　　　　　　　　　　　　　　　CIP

British Library Cataloguing in Publication Data

A catalogue record for this book is available from the British Library

ISBN 0-471-94342-8

Typeset in 10/12pt Times by Dobbie Typesetting Ltd, Tavistock, Devon
Printed and bound in Great Britain by Bookcraft (Bath) Ltd

Contents

List of Contributors

JESUS ALEGRIA
Laboratoire de Psychologie experimentalle, Universite libre de Bruxelles, 117 Av. Adolphe Buyl, B-1050-Brussels, Belgium

CHRISTOPHER BARRY
Department of Psychology, University of Wales College of Cardiff, Cardiff CF1 3YG, UK

LYNETTE BRADLEY
Department of Psychology, University of Oxford, Oxford OX1 3UD, UK

GORDON D. A. BROWN
Department of Psychology, University of Wales, Bangor, Gwynedd LL57 2DG, UK

RUTH CAMPBELL
Department of Psychology, Goldsmiths' College, University of London, London SE14 6NW, UK

ALFONSO CARAMAZZA
Department of Psychology, Silsby Hall, Dartmouth College, Hanover, NH 03755, USA

NICK C. ELLIS
Department of Psychology, University of Wales, Bangor, Gwynedd LL57 2DG, UK

HENRYKA M. EVANS
Department of Psychology, University of Dundee, Dundee DD1 4HN, UK

ANGELA J. FAWCETT
Department of Psychology, University of Sheffield, Sheffield S10 2TN, UK

UTA FRITH
MRC Cognitive Development Unit, 17 Gordon Street, London WC1H 0AH, UK

DAVID W. GLASSPOOL
Department of Psychology, University College London, Gower Street, London WC1E 6BT, UK

PIPPA J. GLOVER
Department of Psychology, University of Wales, Bangor, Gwynedd LL57 2DG, UK

NATA K. GOULANDRIS
National Hospitals College of Speech Sciences, Chandler House, 2 Wakefield Street, London WC1N 1PG, UK

RICHARD HANLEY
Department of Psychology, University of Liverpool, Liverpool, UK

GEORGE HOUGHTON
Department of Psychology, University College London, Gower Street, London WC1E 6BT, UK

LAURA HUXFORD
Cheltenham and Gloucester College of Higher Education, The Park, Cheltenham GL50 2RH, UK

JANICE KAY
Department of Psychology, Washington Singer Laboratories, University of Exeter, Exeter, UK

CAROLYN LENNOX
Peel Board of Education, 3700 Dunrankin Dr, Mississauga, Ontario L4T 1V9, Canada

KATHRYN LINK
Department of Psychology, Silsby Hall, Dartmouth College, Hanover, NH 03755, USA

RICHARD P. W. LOOSEMORE
Department of Psychology, University of Warwick, Coventry CV4 4AL, UK

ELAINE MILES
Dyslexia Unit, University of Wales, Bangor, Gwynedd LL57 2DG, UK

T. R. MILES
Dyslexia Unit, University of Wales, Bangor, Gwynedd LL57 2DG, UK

DAVID MOSELEY
School of Education, 4th Floor, Ridley Building, Claremont Place, Newcastle-upon-Tyne NE1 7RU, UK

PHILIPPE MOUSTY
Laboratoire de Psychologie experimentalle, Universite libre de Bruxelles, 117 Av. Adolphe Buyl, B-1050-Brussels, Belgium

RODERICK I. NICOLSON
Department of Psychology, University of Sheffield, Sheffield S10 2TN, UK

ANDREW OLSON
Department of Psychology, University of Birmingham, Birmingham B15 2TT, UK

RICHARD K. OLSON
Department of Psychology, University of Colorado, Boulder, Colorado 80309-0345, USA

PHILIP J. SCHOLFIELD
Department of Linguistics, University of Wales, Bangor, Gwynedd LL57 2DG, UK

RUTH SCOTT
Faculty of Education, Brock University, St Catherines, Ontario L2S 3A1, Canada

PHILIP H. K. SEYMOUR
Department of Psychology, University of Dundee, Dundee DD1 4HN, UK

TIM SHALLICE
Department of Psychology, University College London, Gower Street, London WC1E 6BT, UK

LINDA S. SIEGEL
The Ontario Institute for Studies in Education, 252 Bloor Street West, Toronto, Ontario M5S 1V6, Canada

MARGARET J. SNOWLING
Department of Psychology, University of Newcastle-upon-Tyne NE1 7RU, UK

REBECCA TREIMAN
Department of Psychology, Wayne State University, 71 W. Warren Avenue, Detroit, Michigan 48202, USA

DALE M. WILLOWS
Department of Special Education, The Ontario Institute for Studies in Education, 252 Bloor Street West, Toronto, Ontario M5S 1V6, Canada

BARBARA W. WISE
Department of Psychology, University of Colorado, Boulder, Colorado 80309-0345, USA

Foreword

UTA FRITH

According to some estimates a reasonably literate person has at least 50 000 words at their fingertips. How are these words represented in the mind? How are we able to call on them at an instant's notice? How do we learn their orthographic patterns and remember them for a lifetime? The letter-by-letter sequence of the word we want to write seems to be there just when we need it. We don't have to think about it. The puzzle of spelling is only made more puzzling when we think about breakdowns in this process. Even the best speller has moments of uncertainty and may fail on some occasions to retrieve the right spelling. But what is particularly challenging is the case of the poor speller who can *not* do precisely that which the good speller does so effortlessly: the poor speller finds it difficult, first to learn the spellings of words, and, second, to retrieve them when needed. Here is a short extract from a piece written by a self-confessed poor speller who, incidentally, was an excellent reader.

> The bane of my young life was the know-all teachers and pontificating adults who said: "If you don't know how to spell a word look it up in the dictionary". But when I wrote "comming", or, "untill" or "thier" it looked OK to me . . . Why look up a word if it looks perfectly all right? Other teachers thought lots of reading would somehow rub correct spellings in—I read more . . . than anyone else in my class. That certainly doesn't work for me. I was 18 before I could spell "does" correctly every time, but by 15 I know it was a word I had to check every time I wrote it. I still have a list of words I need to look up—"resources", "Britain", "maintenance", "receive", "guarantee". Every poor speller needs such a list to cut down on the dreadful embarrassment.

Fortunately, the word processor revolution has liberated the poor speller, but it has also raised expectations of written work to a new level of perfection. Spelling continues to be of concern to teachers, and now *everyone* is expected to have a good command of written language. With spell checkers, the pedantic speller can no longer take unwarranted pride in his achievements, and the poor speller is spared much pain. In some sense, the misery has gone out of spelling but not the mystery. The questions I have posed at the beginning still need to be answered. To my delight, I find that this new *Handbook of Spelling*, brilliantly put together by Gordon Brown and Nick Ellis, already offers some of the answers that I feared might still be a long way away.

A most exciting advance of the new work on spelling is in tackling the difficult question of "representation", that is what words in the mind might actually be like. Put simply, the very attractive and plausible answer is that words are represented simultaneously at different levels, in different modalities, using such units as phoneme, rime, grapheme, word, and so forth. Spelling knowledge may then be a reflection of the goodness of the mapping between these levels.

The other difficult question tackled in this book is about the "process", that is what actually happens when we produce a spelling. Both questions, what sort of representations, and what sort of process, can be advanced within the powerful theoretical framework of connectionism. Connectionism provides a tool that allows testable hypotheses about spelling representation and process to be realized as computational models. As Brown and Ellis say in their lucid introduction, computational models allow the systematic exploration of the properties and predictions of a model that may not be possible when models are simply described verbally. I wholeheartedly agree.

A new insight from this work that I found particularly exciting relates to the learning of spelling. How does the young child acquire spelling competence? Many suggestions have been made, but none so far have gone unchallenged. It now seems possible that an elegantly simple model may work, namely that one and the same processing mechanism operates throughout spelling development. Stage-like transitions of behaviour may only be a surface phenomenon which may result from the interaction of an unchanging process with changing representations. The way I understand this is that a child might have holistic representations (CAT) and various piecemeal representations of words (C-AT, C-A-T) available simultaneously. At first this would lead to conflicting pressures to develop spelling rules—spelling rules being mappings between levels of representations. (Later on, of course, for the skilled speller, the mappings are clear and cohesive between all levels.) This sort of explanation could solve some contradictions in existing developmental studies, which claim varying precedence of one type of strategy over another. The fact of the matter may be that if children have different representations available, then it is simply not possible, or rather not yet possible, to predict which spelling rules (low-level or high-level) will be developed first.

Spelling, in its very artificiality compared to, say, speaking, can provide a rare glimpse into the mind's machinery. The normal, effortless ease of spelling, achieved after effortful learning can lead us to think about the possibility of complex internal programs which govern the action of writing. It is obvious, on reflection, that the letter-by-letter sequence of a word must be specified "in the mind", for the word to be spelled out on paper. In other words, the existence of an invisible cognitive level is forcefully suggested. It could well be that the alphabetic code, and our everyday use of it, has contributed to the development of cognitive psychology itself. Future historians of science might consider that research on the humdrum activity of reading and spelling occupies a key position in the progress of modern psychology. (But not just because psychologists have to read and write a lot!)

The visible and lasting trace of the written form of language provides a model for the understanding of spoken language. The alphabetic system, that staggering invention of *Homo sapiens*, is a system that makes speech visible phoneme by phoneme. Thus, the relevance of spelling to speech cannot be overestimated. Indeed, the connection of speech and spelling at the phoneme level is a crucial factor in the understanding of dyslexia. However, this handbook does not only consider spelling problems in dyslexia, but also in other conditions, such as deafness.

When, about 15 years ago, I edited a volume on "cognitive processes in spelling", the then flourishing information processing models were ripe for application to the process of spelling and for explaining disorders of spelling. The types of exploration that were made possible by these models have been remarkably fruitful. However, the more recent connectionist models have dramatically changed the theoretical outlook. The time has indeed come for a new collection of research papers. This handbook contains such a collection. Moreover, it is not just an update, nor just a much needed stock-take of a vigorously growing field. What emerges is a much more coherent view of the field. This grand view is laid out before us in the introduction. Gordon Brown and Nick Ellis reveal the hidden layer beneath the rich and varied selection of research reviews. The organization of the book into sections concerned with linguistics, development, disorder, computational models, and remediation, covers highly relevant areas all of which can be drawn together in mutually enhancing ways. Thus, we learn, from abnormal development, facts that are vital to our understanding of normal development, and vice versa. What is particularly impressive, is that, as the introduction shows, computational models can now inform all these areas.

Handbooks are useful to the student and to the specialist. They provide an authoritative introduction and summary of a particular topic. This handbook will certainly do this, and will become a constant reference for anyone studying processes that underpin the everyday activities of reading and spelling. Perhaps it will also be used by the curious reader who wonders why he can't spell as easily as others. I think that the self-confessed poor speller whose remarks I quoted earlier (who also happens to be a well-known educationalist and editor) would be fascinated by this volume. He would learn that there are many different types of spelling disorder, and he would find that there are people who can spell astoundingly well, while being rather limited in most other aspects of language ability. He would learn about the intricate course of early reading and spelling development in young children; and he would marvel at the complexity of the neural networks that might well be needed in order to sustain the mental lexicon. Lastly, he would be cheered by the many positive attempts to improve the teaching of spelling.

Spelling has always afforded a privileged window into the mind, and spelling errors are a magnifying glass in that window. There is still much to be discovered by further study. Of course, the mystery of spelling is nowhere more striking than in English orthography. Here we have a natural experiment that allows us to unravel components of the otherwise deeply opaque spelling process. How are English spellings—as opposed to any other spellings—represented in the mental lexicon? (Of course, we could ask the same for other fascinating orthographies, such as French, Norwegian, or German.)

I like to think that there are lessons in English spelling, lessons in archaeology, syntax, then lessons on diction, accent, and vocal delivery; even lessons on the aesthetics of letters and letter combinations. Think of names such as Pall Mall which simply wouldn't be the same without the insistent doubling of ascenders. Perhaps what we need is the spelling spotters' special book of English spelling. There would be contributions from historians, linguists, educationists and psychologists, as well as from atrocious spellers and from those who can spot a spelling error a mile away. It is fascinating to speculate on the history of English spelling as an evolutionary process. Here too we find extinction (no more æ ligatures), archaic remnants (lam-b, with a once pronounced b), survivors (victuals not vittels), oddities (gaol), migrants (yacht), and newly emerging patterns (kwiksave). Thus spelling also affords a window into history.

I wish this handbook every success. I hope it will inspire many students of cognitive and developmental psychology. If this book makes them think about what it means to represent words in the mind and, by association, what it means to represent ideas in the mind, it will have succeeded splendidly. What I wish for the editors is that they will be asked, some time in the future, to provide a foreword to a new handbook on spelling. Moreover, I hope that they will be as lucky as I was when asked to write this foreword: to be given the unique pleasure of introducing a volume of work that one can truly admire.

London
March 1994

Part I

Background

1

Issues in Spelling Research: An Overview

GORDON D. A. BROWN AND NICK C. ELLIS

University of Wales, Bangor

Spelling research is a growth area. Once the "poor relation" of research in reading, spelling has received increasing attention as a research topic in the last decade, both in its own right and as a process now clearly seen to be related in important ways to reading development.

The research reviewed and reported in this book provides an up-to-date overview of theoretical and applied research on spelling. The chapters describe both new theoretical models of spelling and overviews of the application of research to the remediation of spelling problems. We use this introductory chapter to draw out and link the themes that run through the various chapters. We begin by highlighting some of the main theoretical and practical conclusions that have emerged from the recent work on spelling. Have there been substantial advances in our theoretical understanding of spelling, and have better models of spelling led to improvements in the range and quality of remedial techniques available for children with spelling problems? We believe the research described in the present volume enables us to give a confident "yes" in response to these questions.

We then show how "representation" and "process" issues can be linked in terms of recent theoretical advances. Finally, this introduction gives a brief description of each of the chapters contained in the book. Readers who wish to locate chapters concerned with particular topics should turn to this section, which is titled "Organization of the book".

Handbook of Spelling: Theory, Process and Intervention. Edited by G. D. A. Brown and N. C. Ellis.
©1994 John Wiley & Sons Ltd.

PROGRESS IN SPELLING RESEARCH

In summarizing "progress" we take as our landmark the influential collection of papers edited by Uta Frith and published in 1980 under the title *Cognitive Processes in Spelling*. Although research on spelling predates that volume (indeed, as Chapter 10 by Willows and Scott in the present volume points out, many issues of contemporary concern were raised in a perhaps surprisingly familiar form by Orton over half a century ago), Frith's collection was the first to draw together a large collection of papers that adopted the tools and methods of cognitive psychology in an attempt to gain a better understanding of the processes underlying normal and impaired spelling. Important questions for the present chapter, then, concern the developments that have taken place over the intervening decade or so.

First of all, has the amount of research on spelling increased relative to that on reading? Certainly there have been many books and collections of papers on spelling published over the past decade and a half (e.g. Gregg & Steinberg, 1980; Hartley, 1980; Peters, 1985; Read, 1986; Snowling, 1985; Sterling & Robson, 1992; Treiman, 1993). But has there been an increasing *proportion* of research effort devoted to spelling as indexed by the number of spelling-related research articles appearing in psychological and educational journals? Bibliometric analysis suggests that this is indeed the case. Figure 1.1 shows the ratio of papers on reading to papers on spelling published in each year since 1974. Although we used a relatively crude measure, simply adding up the numbers of papers published in each calendar year with "reading" or "spelling" appearing either as a keyword or in the title or abstract, the results obtained are sufficiently robust to support the suggestion that the ratio of research in reading to that in spelling has changed, from the mid-1970s, when about 15 articles on reading appeared for each paper on spelling, to the early 1990s, with about seven articles on reading appearing for each one on spelling. Indeed, a good straight-line fit can be made to the data in Figure 1.1 ($R^2 = 0.71$) on the basis of which we can predict that spelling research will overtake reading research in about 300 years; or more specifically, in the latter part of the year 2304!

Despite this increasing amount of research effort devoted to the cognitive processes involved in spelling, there continues to be a much larger volume of published research on reading than on spelling. Furthermore, as Barry points out in Chapter 2, a greater proportion of the published literature on spelling (as compared with reading) is concerned with the normal and impaired *development* of spelling. Why is this? As Barry (this volume) and others have suggested, part of the explanation may be found by considering methodological factors. Much of the early research on reading made use of simple tasks like lexical decision or single word naming, as it is a straightforward task to present words visually on a computer screen and measure the time required to name the word or recognize it as a word. However, it is much less easy to examine the processes involved in skilled adult spelling, for it is difficult to devise methodologies for examining the speed of spelling production time (see Glover and Brown, this volume, Chapter 9). Thus it has been more difficult to examine the influence of factors such as word frequency or sound–spelling regularity on skilled adult spelling than on reading. This can also account for the greater proportion of spelling research that has examined the normal and impaired development of spelling, for error data can

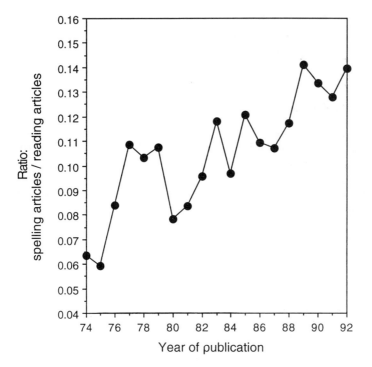

FIGURE 1.1   Ratio of number of academic journal articles on spelling to number on reading, 1974–1992.

be obtained from the relevant subject populations. Some of the methodological limitations on the study of spelling are now being removed, however—for example, the wider availability of computer-based techniques for analysing auditory stimuli and responses has led to new studies of spelling reaction times (e.g. Kreiner, 1992; Glover and Brown, this volume, Chapter 9). These and other developments may permit the study of a wide range of variables on spelling time.

There are, of course, other possible reasons for the relative dearth of spelling research compared to that on reading. The winds of educational fashion change, and this can lead to differential emphasis being placed on spelling and reading ability. In addition, in today's society an inability to read quickly and fluently is undoubtedly more of a handicap than a spelling-specific problem. Most adults spend much more time reading than they do writing.

Thus there are several considerations that can lead to an increased relative emphasis on spelling research. First, the development of new methodological techniques permits cognitive processes in spelling to be studied in ways similar to those used to investigate reading for many years. Second, any re-emphasis on "traditional teaching methods" in educational practice (as is currently happening within the United Kingdom) may result in increased demand for applied research into appropriate teaching methods. Third, and of more theoretical interest, there is an increasing realization that the processes of learning to read and learning to spell are intimately related, as evidenced by the research discussed in several chapters of the present volume. There are now good theoretical reasons for believing that the developmental process of learning to read will not be understood without a concomitant understanding of spelling development, and this is likely to lead to an increased research focus on reading and spelling as they develop together (see, e.g., Chapter 8 by Ellis in the present volume).

What Theoretical Issues Remain the Same?

Although most of the issues raised in the Frith (1980) volume are still with us today (e.g. the importance of phonology; the processing strategy of good readers who are poor spellers; the availability of two different routines for spelling), new ones have arisen. Our purpose in the present section is to review the extent to which the same theoretical issues remain with us, whether new issues and approaches have arisen and what progress has been made on important outstanding questions.

Information-Processing Models of Spelling

The dual-route model of spelling asserts that there are two different mechanisms by which the spelling of a word can be produced. One is the "assembled" or "sound-to-spelling translation" or "non-lexical" routine, which encodes information about the correspondences between sound patterns and spelling patterns. This "route" can be used to produce spellings for nonwords and unfamiliar words, but cannot be used to spell words such as *yacht* that are not spelled in a way that is predictable given the sound–spelling rules of English. The second route by which spellings may be produced is the "lexical" or "direct" or "addressed" route, which can be used to access store information about the spellings of known words directly. In Chapter 2, Barry reviews the operation of, and evidence for, dual-route models of spelling. Although the dual-route approach has been refined and extended over the last decade and further evidence has been adduced in support of it, the model is still recognizably similar in form to the models used in 1980 to interpret spelling data.

However, much progress has resulted from the integration of the dual-route approach with developmental models of spelling, reading and dyslexia. The idea that there exist two separate mechanisms for deriving spellings fits readily with the suggestion that the mechanisms may develop at different times and that the relative use of each may be under strategic control (see Ellis, this volume, Chapter 8). Furthermore, it raises the possibility that developmental disorders of reading and spelling may be characterized in terms of an over-reliance on one of the two routes. Thus Frith (1985) suggests that classic developmental dyslexia can be characterized as an inability adequately to develop an alphabetic reading strategy, such a strategy being based on a spelling-to-sound translation routine for reading.

Thus the dual-route approach has important conceptual links with the idea that children pass through different developmental "stages" in spelling development, and that impaired spelling development can be characterized in terms of inability to pass beyond a particular stage. These approaches were around in 1980, and have proved both useful and influential in the intervening years. In addition, as Barry documents, additional neuropsychological data have been gathered and have been interpreted in support of the dual-route framework. However, it does seem that the dual-route approach must be augmented if it is to accommodate the full richness of developmental spelling data. First of all, there is evidence that the two routes do not always function independently (see Chapter 2 by Barry and Chapter 6 by Snowling), and as Snowling also points out, the information-processing demands of a task can influence spelling accuracy considerably.

Furthermore, the traditional dual-route framework is limited in that so far it has failed to provide a complete causal explanation for *why and how* the causal transition between stages is achieved. Although Frith (1985) showed how changes in spelling strategy could be causally linked to changes in reading strategy, and Ellis (e.g. this volume, Chapter 8) has expanded on the nature of these developmental interactions, we still lack a mechanistic explanation of the emergence of different strategies within orthographic or phonological domains at given developmental stages.

One marked change in recent years is the advent of computational models of spelling development within a "connectionist" framework. These provide a radical alternative to "dual-route" and "stage" models of spelling development, for they can embody claims such as (a) one mechanism can be used to spell both regular and irregular items and (b) just one process can give rise to different apparent developmental stages. We turn to these below. Before doing so, however, we consider whether the dual-route framework can account for other "basic phenomena" that have assumed central importance in recent spelling reseach.

One such set of findings concerns the importance of phonology in spelling development. It has been clear for many years that the exact nature of children's representations of the phonological structure of the language profoundly influences the nature of their errors in the early stages of spelling development, and evidence for this is documented extensively in the present collection (see most chapters, but especially Chapter 4 by Treiman, Chapter 5 by Lennox and Siegel, and Chapter 6 by Snowling). Current formulations of the dual-route model implicitly involve an important role for phonological representations, as the development of sound-to-spelling translation rules will be constrained at all stages by the quality of phonological representations that are available to be mapped onto orthography—clearly a rule that /ei/ is commonly spelled a_e cannot be acquired unless a phonological representation of /ei/ exists. However, dual-route models typically do not provide a detailed specification about how the proposed rules operate or how the outputs from the two different routines are combined to produce a single orthographic output. Thus, as Snowling and others argue, current dual-route models cannot yet do justice to the detailed and specific spelling error patterns that have been studied in children. Furthermore, as the chapters by Snowling, by Lennox and Siegel, and by Seymour and Evans as well as others argue, the constant interaction between the different sources of knowledge that are brought to bear on the spelling process must be explained.

In summary, a recurrent theme in recent research is the rejection of the notion of progression through a clear sequence of separate stages towards a more interactive approach where several different knowledge sources interact in parallel to constrain the operation of the spelling output mechanisms. Methodological advances have also led to confirmation of specific hypotheses. Longitudinal studies carried out by Ellis and others, in combination with Frith's own theoretical analyses (e.g. Frith, 1985), have confirmed the importance of spelling in the development of reading (see Chapter 8 by Ellis and Chapter 20 by Bradley and Huxford).

A Task Analysis Approach: Representations and Strategies

Much evidence for the importance of developing phonological representations is reviewed in this book. In this section we discuss the consequences of this for the processing strategies that will be available at different developmental stages—an important question which has received less explicit attention in the literature is exactly *how* the available phonological and orthographic representations constrain the strategies available for reading and spelling. A consideration of the nature of the task facing the child as he or she attempts to relate phonological and orthographic representations at different and incompatible levels can help in understanding the different strategies that are available at different stages as well as the pressure to develop new levels of representation in both phonological and orthographic domains.

In recent experimental studies of reading development, there has been some controversy concerning the order in which spelling-to-sound correspondences at different levels of analysis are used by children. Many models of skilled adult reading assume that spelling–sound correspondences at several levels are used (e.g. Shallice & McCarthy, 1985; Patterson & Morton, 1985; Brown, 1987), but there is disagreement about which develop first. Thus Goswami (1993; see also Goswami, 1986), on the basis of a study of analogical transfer by children, argues that rime-based spelling-to-sound correspondences are among the first to be used because these are the most relevant phonological units that children possess initially that can be used to link to orthographic patterns. In contrast, Coltheart and Leahy (1992; cf. also Laxon, Masterson & Coltheart, 1991; Marsh *et al.*, 1981) argue, on the basis of developmental studies of word and nonword reading, that children initially read using low-level spelling-to-sound correspondences, at the level of graphemes and phonemes, and that only later do they develop correspondences at higher levels as they become aware of sub-lexical units larger than the grapheme. Thus there continues to be controversy about just how developing phonological representations will constrain the reading strategies that can be applied at different stages of development.

A similar question can be asked in the case of spelling. There is abundant evidence, reviewed throughout this volume, that phonological representations are the crucial determinant of spelling. Given this, how does the nature of the phonological and orthographic representations available to the child determine the kinds of sound-to-spelling correspondences that are learned and used at different developmental stages? More specifically, do children begin to spell using high-level (e.g. rime-based) sound–spelling correspondences or lower-level (e.g. phoneme–grapheme) correspondences?

It is helpful to approach this issue by considering the conflicting levels of representation in the different modalities. In terms of phonological representations, there is considerable evidence that the first sub-lexical representations to develop are onsets and rimes (see, e.g., Chapter 4 by Treiman). We assume for present purposes that phonological representations at the whole-word level can be treated as "given". In the case of written words, however, the "input" provides whole-word units and (more or less saliently, depending on the particular task facing the child) letters.

Thus, when children attempt to make connections between sound patterns and print they are faced with the impossible task of mapping between incompatible representations. Initially they have no "orthographic rime" letter-cluster units that can be made to correspond with phonological rime units, and they have no phoneme representations that can be mapped onto letter units. To learn to spell, then, the child must not only realize that there is some connection between orthographic and phonological forms, but must develop representations that allow mapping between orthography and phonology at compatible levels.

Two general considerations follow from this fact. First, there will in each domain be pressure to develop representations at a level corresponding to the level already existing in the other domain. For example, the availability of letter-level representations in the orthographic domain will encourage the development of equivalent phoneme-level representations that can be mapped onto letters and graphemes, and the availability of rime-level units in the phonological domain will encourage the development of corresponding orthographic letter-cluster units that can be mapped onto them (Goswami, 1993; cf. also Ehri, 1980). There is already ample evidence for the role of literacy acquisition in developing low-level phonological representations (see, e.g., Chapter 8 by Ellis in the present volume) but the development of new levels of orthographic representation in response to available phonology has been less well investigated (although cf. Goswami, 1993). Second, the availability of different kinds of spelling-to-sound and sound-to-spelling strategy can be considered in terms of the levels of representation that are available. Thus, for example, phoneme–grapheme or grapheme–phoneme rules cannot be used if there are no phoneme-level representations, and rime-level rules cannot be developed if there are no orthographic rime units. Some possible constraints are summarized in Table 1.1. This outlines the different sound-to-spelling and spelling-to-sound correspondence that could potentially be used depending on the availability of appropriate representations; of course, it is not necessarily the case that rules that make use of particular levels of representation will be developed or used as soon as the relevant representations are available—it is theoretically possible that representations of orthographic rimes and phonological rimes are both available even when rime-based correspondences are not used for spelling and/or reading (this can also explain asymmetries between strategies used in reading and in spelling).

Thus Table 1.1 is not intended to represent a model of spelling and reading development; rather, it is a schema of how *rules* may be constrained by *representations*. In the case of both orthographic and phonological domains, we assume that there are essentially three causal influences leading to the formation of different levels of representations. These are:

- The levels of representation that are effectively "given" by the input (or by explicit teaching)
- The levels of representation that are developed in response to the need to store representations of a large number of orthographic or phonological wordforms as economically as possible.
- The levels of representation that are developed in one domain because the existence of representations at that level in the *other* domain focuses the search

TABLE 1.1 Links between available levels of orthographic and phonological representation and theoretically possible translation routines.

Phonological representations	Source of new phonological representations	Orthographic representations	Source of new orthographic representations	Possible levels of spelling-to-sound translation[a]	Possible levels of sound-to-spelling translation[a]
Whole word	Early spoken language	Whole word Letters	Printed words	Word → word	Word → word
Whole word Onsets and rimes (Letter names)	Pressure to store phonology more economically Rhyming games (Explicit teaching)	Whole word Letters	Alphabet teaching	Word → word Letters → assembled letter names	Word → word Letter names → letters Rimes → letters
Whole word Onsets and rimes Letter names Phonemes	Explicit teaching Pressure to develop phonemic representations to map onto graphemes	Whole word Letters		Word → word Letters → assembled letter names or sounds	Word → word Letter names → letters Rimes names → letters
Whole word Onsets and rimes Letter names Phonemes		Whole word Sub-lexical clusters (e.g. orthog. rimes) Letters	Reading experience Pressure to develop orthog. units to map onto phonol. rimes	Word → word Letters → assembled letter names Orthog. rimes → phonol. rimes	Word → word Letter names → letters Rimes → letters Rimes → orthog. rimes

[a]The fact that a given translation routine is theoretically available does not mean it will be used in practice.

for, construction of and attention to equivalent-level representations in the first domain

We should note that the second of these has received relatively little attention in the literature on spelling and reading development. However, the need to develop economical representations for the storage of wordforms is likely to be an important one. Consider, for example, the case of orthographic letter clusters corresponding to orthographic rimes. Particularly where high-frequency monosyllabic words are concerned, there is much redundancy in the orthographic endings of words—thus many words end in -ing or -ave or -and, for example (Stanback, 1992). The development of an increasingly large written vocabulary, on the basis of reading experience, is likely to lead to the formation of units to represent frequently occurring clusters such as these, for it will be far more economical to recognize and represent these common sub-lexical orthographic patterns as units rather than storing the orthography of every word separately and in full. Note that this effect could occur even if there was no requirement to map orthography onto phonology. It is therefore quite separate from the third item above, which could motivate the development of orthographic rime representations for quite a different reason—i.e. the need to search for and create orthographic representations that reliably correspond to existing phonological rime representations. Thus, for example, if a child has a phonological representation for the rime /Int/, and is faced with the task of finding some orthographic input pattern that reliably predicts this rime, this may lead to development of a recognition unit for the orthographic pattern *int* (Goswami, 1993).

The important point to note is that there are various different forces acting to encourage the development of both orthographic and phonological representations at a variety of levels. These include the relatively well-investigated pathway from spelling to phonological awareness to reading, but also the computational demands of representing a large vocabulary as efficiently as possible. The role of explicit instruction in grapheme–phoneme correspondences may also be important in encouraging the development of phoneme-level representations (Morais, 1991). It is not possible to decide the relative importance of these factors *a priori*, but they must be understood if we are to comprehend the causal chain of development in its full complexity. For example, it is not clear to what extent orthographic rime-level units will develop because of influence from preexisting rime-level phonological representations and to what extent they will develop simply due to the need to represent the orthographic forms of many English words in as economical a form as possible.

In any case, the kinds of sound-to-spelling or spelling-to-sound translation procedures that can be learned will be constrained by the levels of representation available. It is not possible to use rime-level spelling-to-sound correspondences until orthographic as well as phonological rime representations have been developed, or grapheme–phoneme and phoneme–grapheme correspondences until representations of both phonemes and graphemes are available. These constraints are illustrated in Table 1.1.

The development of representations will be motivated both by the need to establish correspondences between sound and print and by the other considerations adduced above. This is likely to lead to a complex interactive development of sub-skills, as repesentations make the establishment of correspondences possible and the development of correspondences in turn motivates the development of representations. Furthermore, high-level phonological sub-lexical representations (e.g. rimes) will tend to encourage the development of correspondingly high-level orthographic units *at the same time as* the "given" low-level (letter) orthographic units encourage development of corresponding low-level phonological units (e.g. phonemes).

Because of the parallel operation, during development, of these different (and sometimes conflicting) pressures to develop different levels of representation, it is not possible to predict *a priori* whether low-level or high-level sound-to-spelling rules will be developed first. This is a matter for empirical investigation. For example, it is not clear whether or not the causal link emphasized by Goswami (phonological rimes → development of orthographic rimes) will be more powerful or have developmental primacy over the causal link (letters → development of phonemic representations) that other researchers have focused on. Indeed, it seems likely that both will develop in parallel, as the mechanisms that are trying to establish correspondences between the domains of orthography and phonology make use of whatever piecemeal representations are available at any given time. Thus the debate as to which develop first may be misplaced, and the evidence that is found in favour of the earlier development of either high- or low-level correspondences may depend on the nature of the task used to investigate the issue.

Computational Models of Spelling

In this section we briefly review the use of computational techniques in the modelling of reading and spelling development, for this marks a major change in recent years. The last 5 years in particular have seen the advent of a new class of "connectionist" models of reading development, and three of the papers in this book represent some of the first attempts to apply similar techniques to the modelling of spelling development. These models are all sufficiently explicit to be implemented in the form of computer programs. Implementing models in this way permits the systematic exploration of the properties and predictions of a model in a way that may not be possible when the models are simply verbally described. The connectionist approach, and advantage of computational modelling in general, are reviewed in Chapter 16 by Brown and Loosemore. Here we simply outline some of the main theoretical issues where connectionist models of spelling may result in a change in perspective or may provide a computational-level explanation for phenomena which may otherwise be difficult to explain satisfactorily.

The importance of representation

It is clear from the research mentioned above and reviewed and reported throughout this book that the nature of available phonological representations is a crucial determinant of spelling performance. However, connectionist models of reading have enabled us to gain more of a computational-level understanding of these issues. The important and influential connectionist model of reading described by Seidenberg and McClelland (1989a; see also Seidenberg, 1989; Seidenberg & McClelland, 1989b;

Patterson, Seidenberg & McClelland, 1989) represented the orthographic and phonological forms of words in terms of the "triples" of letters or phonemes they contain. Thus a word such as _have_ (where _ is a start-or-end symbol) would be represented by activating a group of simulated artificial neurons standing for _ha, a group standing for hav, a group standing for ave and a group standing for ve_, but not groups of artificial neurons standing for (e.g.) sav or vah. In this way a unique pattern of activity can be used to represent the orthography of each English word, and the simplified artificial neurons used for this representation can be linked up to a separate population of neurons that represent the phonology of English words in a similar fashion. The network can then learn connection strengths between its artificial neurons such that, when presented with a pattern of activity corresponding to (e.g.) the orthographic input have, it can learn to produce the pattern of activity corresponding to the correct pronunciation of the word. Seidenberg and McClelland showed that their reading model can learn to read both regular and irregular words, and can assign plausible pronunciations to nonwords.

Although the model accounts for an impressively wide variety of data from lexical decision and single word naming tasks, it has been criticized for its inability to read nonwords as well as humans are able to (Besner et al., 1990). More recent work has investigated the effect of providing connectionist reading models with different input and output representations. This work has shown that the performance of a network on nonwords relative to both regular and irregular words can be substantially improved by providing the model with more specific or local orthographic and phonological representations at differnet levels (e.g. Bullinaria, 1993; Phillips & Hay, 1992; Norris, 1993; Plaut, McClelland & Seidenberg, 1992). These models use input and output units that stand either for individual letters or phonemes or higher-level units such as orthographic rimes.

What this computational work suggests is that, in the case of reading, the provision of appropriate phonological representations has a much greater effect on nonword reading than on the reading of either regular or irregular words. This is of considerable psychological interest for at least three reasons. First of all, there is now considerable evidence from several studies that dyslexic children are selectively impaired on nonword reading when compared with control non-dyslexic children who are matched on word-reading ability (Rack, Snowling & Olson, 1992). However, it has proved more difficult to demonstrate that dyslexic readers are selectively impaired on processing any particular type of word. Second, there is ample evidence (reviewed and discussed in many of the present chapters) that dyslexia is associated with impaired phonological representations, as indexed by dyslexics' difficulty in performing tasks that require manipulation of the sound structure of English (e.g. phonemic awareness tasks). The computational work helps us to understand this association in a concrete way: the availability of good phonological (and orthographic?) representations has a greater effect on nonword reading than on the reading of either regular or irregular words. Thirdly, nonword reading can be seen as a test of the ability of a reading mechanism to generalize to new items (e.g. unfamiliar words). Thus the selective deficit in nonword reading that is associated in connectionist models with inadequate phonological representations can be seen as illustrating the fact that explicit teaching, with feedback, can lead to the successful learning of both regular and irregular items, and that the inadequate phonological representations will primarily be evidenced in a relative inability to generalize the knowledge thus acquired to previously unseen items.

The discussion above has been primarily concerned with reading. Will the same conclusions apply to spelling development? There is some evidence that this is indeed the case. Brown, Loosemore and Watson (1993), using similar procedures to those employed to model reading by Seidenberg and McClelland (1989a,b) and Plaut, McClelland and Seidenberg (1992), found that a connectionist model of spelling was selectively disadvantaged on nonword spelling, compared to the spelling of both regular and irregular words, when it was provided with less explicit phonological and orthographic representations. Thus in spelling, as in reading, the results from connectionist modelling support empirical research in underlining the importance of representations, particularly in the case of nonword spelling.

Olson and Caramazza (Chapter 17 in the present volume) have also shown that connectionist modelling can be used to demonstrate the inadequacy of particular representations in accounting for data that require the assumption of sub-lexical structure in an orthographic output buffer. This work, which we summarize in more detail below, provides a further illustration of the role that connectionist modelling is coming to play in aiding our understanding of the constraints on possible models of the spelling process.

The sequential nature of spelling

The operation of the sequential processes involved in producing a sequence of letters is generally left somewhat underspecified in most current cognitive models of spelling. However, the connectionist model of spelling output processes described by Houghton and his colleagues in the present volume (Chapter 18) examines the serial ordering of spelling output from an explicitly computational perspective. One plausible mechanism for producing serially ordered behaviour in any domain requires the suppression of the representation that causes an item to be produced immediately after the item in question has been output. This avoids perseveration—when an item in a set of candidate items for output is the most highly activated, that item will be outputted and its representation will then be strongly inhibited so that other items can succeed in the competition to be the next outputted item. Problems arise when the same item must be outputted twice in succession, and an extra mechanism must be introduced to accommodate this when it is required. This leads to an independent computational motivation for the special treatment of "geminates" (doubled consonants in a word's spelling). This is of considerable psychological relevance, for Caramazza and his colleagues have adduced considerable evidence from the study of neuropsychological patients that doubled letters are indeed treated in a special way (see, e.g., Chapter 14 by Link and Caramazza in the present volume). Houghton et al. show that the computational mechanism that was developed to account for serial order effects generally can give a good account of much of the relevant psychological data. It is difficult to see how these data could have been completely understood without the adoption of an explicitly computational perspective.

Spelling deficits in developmental dyslexia

A widespread view of developmental dyslexia, following Frith (1985), is that dyslexia involves a failure to make a successful transition to a stage of using alphabetic processing—spelling-to-sound and sound-to-spelling translation procedures. This type of account makes two distinct predictions—first, that dyslexia should be associated with a particular problem in reading or spelling nonwords (for nonword processing requires the application of correspondence-based procedures, given that lexical knowledge is unavailable) and, second, that dyslexia should be associated with reduced effects of sound-to-spelling or spelling-to-sound regularity (for such effects must indicate the use of procedures that are sensitive to the relevant regularities). As we stated above, there is ample evidence that dyslexics do indeed show impaired nonword processing (in both reading and spelling) and this has been taken as evidence for impaired phonological processing in these subjects. However, studies have generally failed to find evidence for reduced effects of spelling-to-sound or sound-to-spelling regularity in dyslexic children when their performance is compared with that of reading age or spelling age matched controls (Brown & Watson, 1991), and these studies have sometimes been taken as evidence against the suggestion that dyslexia involves a specific impairment in phonological processing and in support of the idea that dyslexics utilize the same processing strategies as normal children but are delayed in their acquisition of them. The connectionist model of spelling described by Brown and Loosemore in the present volume (Chapter 16) provides an alternative perspective on this problem, for they find that reducing the computational resources available to a system during learning has a detrimental effect on the spelling of nonwords relative to words while leaving the sound-to-spelling regularity effect intact. Thus a general, quantitative change in the model (reducing its computational resources during learning) can lead to a pattern of behaviour (selective deficit on nonword processing) that has hitherto been taken as evidence for the use of qualitatively different strategies in dyslexic children. The co-occurrence of a selective nonword processing deficit and preserved regularity effects is something that would be difficult to explain without adopting a computational perspective.

Developmental stages and causal transitions

In the early part of this chapter we suggest that dual-route and "stage" models of spelling have some difficulty in providing causal explanations of why transitions between developmental stages occur within a processing domain, although they have been successful in explaining the reciprocal interactions between reading and spelling at different stages of development. Connectionist models provide a radical alternative to the suggestion that different processing strategies are involved at different developmental stages. Rather, they implicitly assume that essentially the same processing mechanisms are employed throughout development, although the database (e.g. the size of the vocabulary) over which they operate may change. Such models have proved successful in explaining the developmental changes that have previously been taken as evidence for "stage-like" development in a wide range of psychological domains (Plunkett & Sinha, 1992) and future research is needed to investigate the possibility that similar explanations of stages of spelling development will be possible. It is likely, however, that more detailed models of developmental changes in orthographic and phonological representations will be needed to enable this progress. The central point here is that connectionist models hold out the possibility that stage-like transitions in behaviour may result from the application of unchanging processing strategy to changing representations—it may be misleading to assume that the processing strategies themselves undergo any developmental change.

Remediation

We suggested above that many of the theoretical issues that concerned spelling researchers in 1980 are still around today, although one substantial change in theoretical approaches has come from attempts to build computational models of the spelling process; attempts which have led to new insights concerning the nature of spelling mechanisms. We now turn to the question of remediation of spelling problems. Here, we suggest, there has been substantial progress in recent years. Two of the theoretical developments mentioned above have been particularly important in the development of remedial programmes: first, the increasing realization of the importance of phonological representations in learning to spell and, second, increasing understanding of the important relationship between learning to spell and learning to read. In addition, recent years have seen reports of several carefully conducted evaluation studies. A number of important studies of the effect of remediation have been undertaken (see, for example, Chapter 20 by Bradley and Huxford) and these have shown that achievable levels of intervention can lead to improvements in children's spelling performance that are certainly worthwhile. Furthermore, the advent of sophisticated computer-based methods of remediation (see Chapter 23 by Wise and Olson and Chapter 24 by Nicolson and Fawcett) has allowed new approaches to remediation to be developed and evaluated. These are described in more detail below. For now, we simply emphasize the point that theoretical developments in our understanding of the processes involved in learning to spell have led to significant and worthwhile improvements in the range and success of remedial techniques that are available and there is every reason to be optimistic that this process will continue as new theoretical advances feed into educational intervention programmes.

It is noteworthy that the advances in practical application reviewed in this book have largely arisen from research conducted and interpreted within the dual-route and developmental stage approaches described above. It will be interesting in future years to see what impact is made by the new computational approaches to spelling. Connectionist models can, for example, be used to make predictions about what kinds of input will lead to the fastest learning of the phonology → orthography mapping system, either in a system that is damaged after learning or in one that has reduced computational resources or impaired representations throughout the course of learning.

ORGANIZATION OF THE BOOK

The book is divided into parts. The first one or two chapters in each part provide reviews of much of the relevant literature; and subsequent chapters present more detailed descriptions of research in a subset of the relevant area.

Background

Part I, the "background" section of the book, contains material useful to understanding the remainder of the contributions. Barry provides a comprehensive summary of the dual-route model of spelling and evidence for it, based on a consideration of the English spelling system and empirical studies. In such models there are two different routines by which a spelling can be derived—a "lexical" route, which involves retrieval of a known word's spelling from an orthographic lexicon, and an "assembled" route, used to assemble spellings on the basis of some variety of sound-to-spelling translation procedure. These are assumed to be separable, in that they can be selectively impaired by brain damage, although they need not function independently in normal spellers. Barry considers in detail how the observed nature of errors produced by brain-damaged patients can motivate revisions to models of normal spelling and goes on to consider how the lexical route can itself be fractionated.

Scholfield provides a linguistic perspective in the next chapter. He describes ways in which linguists attempt to understand the structure, systems and rules that are relevant to our understanding of writing systems. Through consideration of the different types of writing system that exist and the ways they have evolved, he shows that it is possible to explain the origin of many of the ambiguities in the English sound–spelling mapping system. Indeed, adoption of the linguistic perspective reveals that the spelling system is not as irrational as might at first appear. In the course of establishing some of the deeper and non-obvious regularities in the English spelling system, this chapter suggests some new hypotheses for psychologists to test.

The Development of Spelling

Part II contains chapters that are primarily concerned with the development of spelling. Treiman shows that children's spelling errors can be understood in terms of the phonological knowledge they bring to the task of learning to spell, and examines the role of letter-name knowledge and awareness of orthographic regularities developed as a consequence of exposure to print. She focuses particularly on the importance of the onset–rime distinction as a representational principle that affects early spelling, and on the observation that errors may reflect children's phonological representations rather than inadequate translation procedures. Lennox and Siegel also emphasize the point that many different skills are involved in learning to spell. After a review of stage models and the use of error analysis, they suggest that it is inappropriate to view spelling development in terms of a stage-like sequence—rather, children will use all the stages available to them for spelling at any given time. They also review their research, which has investigated processing differences between good and poor spellers matched for spelling level, and show that the rich set of resulting data suggests that poor spellers do use qualitatively different spelling strategies—i.e. their spelling is "deviant" rather than simply "delayed".

Snowling presents further evidence, from a range of populations, that existing stage-type models fail to do justice to the range and complexity of difficulties faced by the beginning speller. At any given stage in early spelling, children will make use of a variety of sources of spelling knowledge depending on the task context and the phonetic characteristics of the items to be spelled. In particular, the information-processing demands of the task will determine the spelling strategies that will be used—for example, it was found that children produced fewer phonetically plausible errors in spontaneous writing than in single-word dictation. Dual-route models need to be extended to account for the effects of information-processing limitations as well as interactions between lexical and phonological processes. The role of output phonology is also discussed in the context of a detailed single-case study. Finally, Snowling argues that more explicit descriptions of the spelling process are needed to motivate the design of improved remediation programmes.

Seymour and Evans are particularly concerned with how individual differences can be accounted for by models of spelling, and describe a new and highly interactive model. They propose that a "letter sequence generator" is constrained in its operation by many different knowledge sources, and that logographic and alphabetic processes can develop in parallel. Employing their model as a framework, the relative importance of different knowledge sources in the spelling of different individuals can be examined by looking at lexicality effects, and the authors do this using data from a large population of subjects. This analysis points to some interesting differences between reading and spelling, for it reveals that words have a greater advantage than nonwords in reading than in spelling. It is argued that the lack of universal lexicality effects in spelling may be problematic for some specific connectionist models of spelling which predict that words will generally be less error-prone than nonwords.

Ellis examines stage theories of the development of spelling and reading, the interaction between the two developmental processes, in the light of evidence from several recent longitudinal studies. Ellis argues that longitudinal methods are best able to answer some of the critical questions concerning the relation between different developmental stages in spelling and reading. He shows that (a) early awareness of the phonological structure of language is a good predictor of subsequent literacy; but (b) phonological awareness (PA) seems more related in early development to spelling than to reading, and training in PA first affects the development of spelling rather than reading; (c) the acquisition of PA through spelling engenders development of an alphabetic strategy of reading; and (d) later acquisition of orthographic knowledge through reading promotes orthographic spelling. However, these data also suggest some additions and qualifications: (i) there are different facets of PA, an early implicit awareness of syllables and rhyme and a later sophisticated explicit ability at segmentation at the level of phonemes, and even very early reading seems to capitalize on this implicit phonological awareness, which plays a role in the logographic reading otherwise characterized as being primarily visual in nature; (ii) experience in alphabetic spelling and reading promotes more analytic and explicit phonological awareness at sub-syllabic levels; (iii) although experience with reading allows the child to abstract knowledge of orthographic sequences which can then be applied in spelling, it seems that this is happening not just with mature readers who are solidly at an orthographic stage of reading, but also even with first-grade children at the beginnings of literacy. Thus use of longitudinal studies has enabled the confirmation and extension of aspects of the cognitive process models described earlier.

In the final chapter in Part II, Glover and Brown describe some results they have obtained using a new methodology to assess spelling production time as well as error rates. They show that examination of latencies to spell words permits the investigation of strategies used by skilled adult spellers who make few errors and whose spelling performance cannot therefore be examined in detail using error analysis. They demonstrate that the method can be used to test predictions of a connectionist model of spelling about how a word's sound-to-spelling characteristics should influence the ease with which it can be spelled, and that these predictions are upheld. Glover and Brown suggest that the spelling production time methodology may be used to test more fine-grained predictions about the processes involved in skilled, error-free spelling as well as incorrect spelling. In particular, reaction time techniques may be useful in understanding how information from different sources (e.g. lexical and phonological information) is combined over time.

Abnormal Spelling Processes

Part III of the book contains chapters that focus on abnormal spelling processes. Willows and Scott open with a comprehensive overview of past and present spelling disabilities research and the relation of this work to research on reading disabilities. They show that many of the issues that concern today's researchers were anticipated many decades ago by Orton and others. They focus particularly on the interrelations between reading and spelling and the study of good readers who are poor spellers, concluding that there is little reliable evidence that these constitute a distinct subgroup of spellers who use qualitatively different strategies. They also describe the considerable methodological problems associated with assessing nonword spelling and draw attention to possible differences between oral and written spelling processes.

Alegria and Mousty adopt a cross-linguistic perspective. They show that in French, as in English, only a proportion of words can be correctly spelled using sound-to-spelling translation procedures and that multiple sources of constraint are brought to bear on the spelling process. They describe the results of a study in which they examined the success of normal and disabled children at using different types of sound–spelling correspondence units, in order to examine the use of different sources of information developmentally. Explicitly taught rules were found to be important in the spelling of the young children in particular.

Siegel describes a single-case study of a hyperlexic child who has very advanced reading and spelling skills compared to general cognitive ability or high-level language comprehension. She reviews the (relatively rare) reported cases of hyperlexics with advanced spelling skills, and on the basis of these and her own results argues that hyperlexia indicates the possible independence or "modularity" of lower-level skills such as spelling from higher-level cognitive and language comprehension processes. Thus, she argues, hyperlexia provides evidence against some of the more interactive views that have been proposed in the literature—good phonological processing and rote memory skills can lead to spelling that is very successful relative to higher-level comprehension ability.

Campbell reviews studies on spelling in deaf children. Because such children lack normal phonological forms to map onto orthographic representations, they provide an alternative methodology for examining the importance of phonological representations. Campbell finds that several studies have discovered no effects of sound-to-spelling regularity in deaf children, although paradoxically such children do seem to be able to make use of speech-sound-to-letter mappings. However, it appears that some of the earlier studies suffer from methodological problems, and that it can be shown the deaf children do demonstrate effects of sound-to-spelling regularity and exhibit other evidence that indicates reliance on phonological processing. This suggests that even deaf children do make use of phonological information, thus providing further evidence for the importance of phonological information in spelling.

Link and Caramazza are concerned with whether current models of spelling will generalize to different orthographies or if the models will need to be extended to accommodate the fact that different writing systems relate the written spoken and semantic forms of words in very different ways. A central feature of the model that Caramazza and his co-workers have been developing over many years is a "graphemic output buffer", the existence of which is supported by the observation of certain error types that are observed independently of the modality of input or output and also independently of the type of material to be spelled. They review evidence that complex structural information must be represented in the output buffer—for example, information about whether a letter is a consonant or a vowel may be available even if the exact identity of the letter is not. In the present chapter they examine the ability of an extended model to account for data from other orthographic systems, specifically those of Arabic and Mandarin Chinese. Following a detailed consideration of the relevant features of these orthographies, they conclude that some features of Mandarin Chinese do challenge the model, in that some of the model's features do not receive any independent computational motivation from that language. Thus the model may need to be modified to account for spelling in other languages.

In the subsequent chapter, Kay and Hanley also consider the output buffer and the extent to which the structural information represented therein can be assumed to be the same across different languages. After setting out criteria that suggest an impairment of the graphemic buffer in brain-injured patients and a review of data from several patients who are assumed to have impairments of the buffer, they test one of their own, English patients (who meets these criteria) in order to assess whether the conclusions about the structure of the graphemic output buffer, which have been drawn primarily on the basis of the Italian-speaking patients investigated hitherto, will generalize to English-speaking patients. In their English-speaking patient Kay and Hanley failed to find evidence for the same type of consonant–vowel structure that has been apparent in the data from Italian-speaking patients and conclude that the system may be structured differently in patients of different languages, reflecting differences in the spelling systems of those languages.

Computational Models

In the first chapter of Part IV, which contains chapters on computational models of spelling, Brown and Loosemore begin with an introduction to connectionist models of spelling and discuss reasons why adopting a computational approach can lead to insights into the spelling process that could not be obtained in any other way. All three chapters in Part IV illustrate this point in different ways. The connectionist model described by Brown and Loosemore learns to associate representations of word pronunciations with representations of the corresponding orthographic forms. The model successfully learns to spell both regular and irregular items, but learns words that contain irregular or unusual sound-to-spelling correspondences more slowly. Words containing sound–spelling correspondences that are both common and regular are learned first and spelled most quickly. Brown and Loosemore also describe experiments that test the predictions of the model regarding which words will be spelled most accurately by children of different ages and the empirical results are shown to be consistent with these predictions. Limiting the computational resources of the model leads to a selective deficit in spelling nonwords along with preserved effects of sound-to-spelling regularity, and this is put forward as an explanation of some of the paradoxical aspects of dyslexic spelling problems.

Olson and Caramazza describe a connectionist model of spelling (NETspell). They are particularly concerned to investigate the relative role of learning procedures and the representations over which they operate in determining the empirical behaviour of a spelling system. They show that there are many empirical phenomena that point to the importance of sub-lexical structural representations in the spelling process, and suggest in particular that supra-segmental representations are required if all the generalizations necessary for spelling can be supported. They use connectionist modelling to demonstrate the inadequacy of a model without lexical or supra-segmental representations—a detailed analysis of their network's performance (both the errors that it makes and the way it is solving the task of spelling) shows that implausible errors produced by the network reflect limitations of its representations. They also highlight the problem of understanding network performance, and the danger that reproducing some aspect of behaviour may not amount to an explanation of that behaviour if it cannot be understood exactly how the network is producing its output.

Houghton, Glasspool and Shallice describe a complementary model, also within a computational framework. They are concerned with output processing—how is the serially ordered output of a sequence of letters achieved in the spelling process? As they point out, the problem of serial order is not solved in a plausible way in existing connectionist models of reading and spelling. Houghton *et al.* consider error data both from normal subjects' errors and from patients assumed to have impairments of the orthographic output buffer. They demonstrate that many features of the human error data can be explained by a consideration of how serially ordered output can be produced computationally. Their model gives a good account of much of the data taken as evidence for orthographic buffer impairment and in particular provides an independent computational explanation for special treatment of geminates, as discussed earlier in this introduction. Note that the Houghton model is complementary to the other two computational models described in Part IV, in that it is primarily concerned with output processes rather than with how sound–spelling correspondence information is learned or represented.

Remediation

The fifth and final part of the book is concerned with the application of theory to practice—how can spelling difficulties be remediated in the light of the theoretical understanding currently available? Goulandris provides a helpful and accessible summary of some selected empirical findings of particular importance to our understanding of spelling and assesses their practical implications for teaching practice. She reviews the importance of pronunciation; awareness and perception of speech sounds and knowledge of sound–letter correspondences. Some practical implications that she finds are that (i) fostering phonological skills is good; (ii) spelling is important for developing early alphabetical skills; and (iii) teaching children to link sound patterns in words with spelling patterns can be highly effective. Goulandris also describes practical teaching techniques and reports a single-case study of remediation using multi-sensory procedures.

Bradley and Huxford also review evidence for the importance of phonological skills and the use of phonological cues in early spelling. They describe a variety of research conducted by themselves and others showing that children's performance on phonological tasks (such as rhyme and alliteration judgement tasks) is related to spelling ability. They then describe some training studies that produced impressive results—with only a few hours of training it was possible to obtain useful gains in spelling age in trained children as compared with appropriate control groups. This provides further evidence for a causal link between phonological skills and spelling as well as illustrating a bridge between theory and practice.

Miles and Miles make the point that the remediation of spelling cannot be considered independently of the remediation of reading. They highlight early work by Hinshelwood and by Orton, finding points of agreement and disagreement between these researchers. Miles and Miles question some of the assumptions involved in current research. They caution against drawing close comparisons between developmental and acquired dyslexia and also argue that an emphasis on subtypes derived from the study of acquired disorders or an emphasis on individual children may not be useful for understanding remediation. It is particularly important to take into account differences in teaching that individual children may have received. Miles and Miles also discuss the implications for remediation of recent work suggesting that dyslexia may be associated with a selective impairment in the transient visual system and consider the implications of another recently reported possibility: that dyslexia may involve a general deficit in automaticity.

Moseley is concerned with the relation between theory and practice in spelling teaching. He reviews data concerning the rate of spelling development and the cognitive demands of the spelling task. After outlining characteristics of good and poor spellers and the consequences of impaired spelling, he describes some of his own research on the visuo-spatial correlates of spelling. This research finds an association between spelling and spatial visualization that is independent of vocabulary size. Moseley reviews many practical techniques for teaching spelling, and research on their effectiveness. He reports the results of an intervention study of his own and describes a course devised for dyslexic and generally poor spellers. This produced significant gains in spelling ability in a relatively short time and provides further evidence that carefully thought out remedial programmes can undoubtedly be highly effective.

The final two chapters are both concerned with the use of computer-based remedial techniques. Wise and Olson begin by reviewing some of the possible advantages associated with the use of computers in teaching spelling. These include the individual pacing of learning; repeated practice; and the ready provision of immediate feedback. As do other contributors to the present volume, they emphasize the important point that spelling instruction may be useful for remediating deficits in reading and review evidence that teaching spelling does indeed lead to improvements in reading as well. On the basis of a review of previous research, they assess the advantages and disadvantages of different types of computer program and examine the crucial question of whether the use of computers is in itself really beneficial. They then describe their own project which uses computer-based-speech and report carefully controlled studies suggesting that speech feedback is used by students and may sometimes be useful. Nicolson and Fawcett describe their own computer-based system for children learning to spell. Their method is based on the application of insights from the cognitive psychology of skill acquisition and computer support for such acquisition. They also report the results of a study of their own, and conclude that computer-based remediation techniques can indeed be useful.

ACKNOWLEDGEMENTS

This work was supported by a grant to both authors from the Medical Research Council (UK) and by a grant to the first author from the Economic and Social Research Council (UK). We are grateful to Rachael Deavers for helpful discussion.

REFERENCES

Besner, D., Twilley, L., McCann, R. S. & Seergobin, K. (1990). On the association between connectionism and data: are a few words necessary? *Psychological Review*, **97**, 432–446.

Brown, G. D. A. (1987). Resolving inconsistency: a computational model of word naming. *Journal of Memory and Language*, **23**, 1–23.

Brown, G. D. A., Loosemore, R. & Watson, F. L. (1993). Normal and dyslexic spelling: A connectionist approach. Manuscript submitted.

Brown, G. D. A. & Watson, F. L. (1991). Reading in developmental dyslexia: a connectionist approach. In M. Snowling & M. Thomson (Eds), *Dyslexia: Integrating Theory and Practice*. Oxford: Whurr.

Bullinaria, J. (1993). Neural network models of reading without Wickelfeatures. Unpublished manuscript, University of Edinburgh.

Coltheart, V. & Leahy, J. (1992). Children's and adults' reading of non-words: effects of regularity and consistency. *Journal of Experimental Psychology: Learning, Memory, and Cognition*, **18**(4), 718–729.

Ehri, L. (1980). The development of orthographic images. In U. Frith (Ed.), *Cognitive Processes in Spelling*. London: Academic Press.

Frith, U. (1980). Unexpected spelling problems. In U. Frith (Ed.), *Cognitive Processes in Spelling*. London: Academic Press.

Frith, U. (1985) Beneath the surface of developmental dyslexia. In K. E. Patterson, J. C. Marshall & M. Coltheart (Ed.), *Surface Dyslexia*. Hillsdale, NJ: LEA.

Goswami, U. (1986). Children's use of analogy in learning to read: a developmental study. *Journal of Experimental Child Psychology*, 42, 73–83.

Goswami, U. (1993). Towards an interactive analogy model of reading development: decoding vowel graphemes in beginning reading. *Journal of Experimental Child Psychology*, 56(3), 443–475.

Gregg, L. W. & Steinberg, E. R. (Eds) (1980). *Cognitive Processes in Writing*. Hillsdale, NJ: Erlbaum.

Hartley, J. (Ed.) (1980). *The Psychology of Written Communication*. London: Kegan Paul.

Kreiner, D. (1992). Reaction time measures of spelling: testing a two-strategy model of skilled spelling. *Journal of Experimental Psychology: Learning, Memory and Cognition*, 18(4), 765–776.

Laxon, V., Masterson, J. & Coltheart, V. (1991). Some bodies are easier to read: the effect of consistency and regularity on children's reading. *Quarterly Journal of Experimental Psychology*, 43, 793–824.

Marsh, G., Friedman, M. P., Welch, V. & Desberg, P. (1981). A cognitive-developmental approach to reading acquisition. In T. G. Waller & G. E. MacKinnon (Eds), *Reading Research. Advances in Theory and Practice*, Vol. 3. New York: Academic Press.

Morais, J. (1991). Metaphonological abilities and literacy. In M. Snowling & M. Thomson (Eds), *Dyslexia: Integrating Theory and Practice*. Oxford: Whurr.

Norris, D. (1993). A quantitative model of reading aloud. Unpublished manuscript.

Patterson, N. E. & Morton, J. (1985). From orthography to phonology: an attempt at an old interpretation. In K. E. Patterson, J. C. Marshall & M. Coltheart (Eds), *Surface Dyslexia*. Hillsdale, NJ: LEA.

Patterson, K. E., Seidenberg, M. S. & McClelland, J. L. (1989). Connections and disconnections: acquired dyslexia in a computational model of reading. In R. G. M. Morris (Ed.), *Parallel Distributed Processing: Implications for Psychology and Neurobiology*. Oxford: Oxford University Press.

Peters, M. L. (1985). *Spelling: Caught or Taught? A New Look*. London: Routledge & Kegan Paul.

Phillips, W. A. & Hay, I. M. (1992). Computational theories of reading aloud: multi-level neural net approaches. Technical report CCCN-13, Stirling University.

Plaut, D. C., McClelland, J. L. & Seidenberg, M. S. (1992). Reading exception words and pseudowords: are two routes really necessary? Paper presented at the Annual Meeting of the Psychonomic Society, St Louis, MO, November 1992.

Plunkett, K. & Sinha, C. (1992). Connectionism and developmental theory. *British Journal of Developmental Psychology*, 10, 209–254.

Rack, J. P., Snowling, M. J. & Olson, R. K. (1992). The nonword reading deficit in developmental dyslexia: a review. *Reading Research Quarterly*, 27(1), 29–51.

Read, C. (1986). *Children's Creative Spelling*. London: Routledge & Kegan Paul.

Seidenberg, M. S. (1989). Visual word recognition and pronunciation: a computational model and its implications. In W. Marslen-Wilson (Ed.), *Lexical Representation and Process*. Cambridge, Mass: MIT Press/Bradford Books.

Seidenberg, M. S. & McClelland, J. L. (1989a). A distributed, developmental model of word recognition and naming. *Psychological Review*, 96, 523–568.

Seidenberg, M. S. & McClelland, J. L. (1989b). Visual word recognition and pronunciation: a computational model of acquired skilled performance and dyslexia. In A. Galaburda (Ed.) *From Reading to Neurons*. Cambridge, Mass: MIT Press/Bradford Books.

Shallice, T. & McCarthy, R. (1985). Phonological reading: from patterns of impairment to possible procedures. In K. C. Patterson, J. C. Marshall & M. Coltheart (Eds), *Surface Dyslexia: Neuropsychological and Cognitive Studies of Phonological Reading*. Hillsdale, NJ: LEA.

Snowling, M. J. (1985). *Children's Written Language Difficulties*. Windsor: NFER-Nelson.

Stanback, M. L. (1992). Syllable and rime patterns for teaching reading: analysis of a frequency-based vocabulary of 17,602 words. *Annals of Dyslexia*, **42**, 196–221.

Sterling, C. M. & Robson, C. (1992). *Psychology, Spelling and Education*. Bristol, PA: Multilingual Matters.

Treiman, R. (1993) *Beginning to Spell*. Oxford: Oxford University Press.

2

Spelling Routes (or Roots or Rutes)

CHRISTOPHER BARRY

University of Wales College of Cardiff

How, on hearing a spoken word, do we manage to produce it in writing? For languages with alphabets there are two major ways we might logically perform this dictation task. On hearing a spoken word we might (a) retrieve its spelling from a lexical store, or (b) construct its spelling using sound-to-spelling correspondences. (It is also possible that we might be able to do both.) I shall refer to these two methods as the "lexical" and the "assembled" spelling "routes", respectively. By a spelling "route", I mean a sequence of cognitive processing components (or systems) which may be considered to be isolable (at least to some extent) from other systems. The lexical route retrieves spellings of known words from a learned repository, which I shall refer to as the "orthographic output lexicon". The assembled route constructs spellings by applying some form of sub-word sound-to-spelling conversion.

In this chapter, I shall first consider the constraints imposed upon spelling words in English by the nature of its orthography, i.e. its system of representing sounds in spellings. I shall then discuss some issues following from the dual-route model of spelling, the skeleton of which was presented above. In a brief review of the major cognitive neuropsychological evidence for the existence of the lexical and assembled spelling routes, I will argue that these two routes are separable, in that brain damage can selectively impair one while leaving the other relatively intact. I shall then consider proposals that, although separable in this sense, these two processes need not function independently in normal spellers. Finally, I shall also suggest that the lexical route can itself be fractionated and propose that there may be separate semantically mediated and solely lexical routes involved in the retrieval of the spellings of known words.

Handbook of Spelling: Theory, Process and Intervention. Edited by G. D. A. Brown and N. C. Ellis.
©1994 John Wiley & Sons Ltd.

ENGLISH ORTHOGRAPHY

The relationships between the sounds and the spellings of English words are notoriously inconsistent. This inconsistency is well known from the study of reading skills, where, indeed, it is almost gleefully utilized in the construction of stimulus material for experiments. Researchers have studied the recognition and reading of: homophones, such as *rain*, *rein* and *reign*; pseudohomophonic nonwords that sound identical to words, such as *rane* and *wurd*; words (and nonwords) containing inconsistently pronounced segments, such as *cove*, *love* and *move*; and very many forms of irregular words, from "typically divergent" words, such as *head* (Shallice, Warrington & McCarthy, 1983), down to the downright exception words, such as *yacht* and *colonel*. Such inconsistency and irregularity certainly compromise the efficiency of any non-lexical means of pronouncing English words correctly: if we were to rely on assembling a pronunciation using some form of spelling-to-sound conversion, we might read *hint* correctly but we would certainly stumble over *pint*. However, as foreigners struggling to master the language are often profoundly dismayed to discover, spelling English is even less straightforward than reading it! What is frequently suspected (e.g. Seymour & Porpodas, 1980), but appears to be less formally appreciated, is that English sound-to-spelling correspondences are considerably more inconsistent than spelling-to-sound relationships. This asymmetry of irregularity results from the orthographic–phonological relationships of vowels, as I shall now illustrate.

In reading, spelling-to-sound correspondences are characterized by one-to-many mappings. However, the most common ("regular" or "major") phonological correspondences of most spellings tend to occur in the *majority* of words and there are generally only few alternative ("irregular", "minor" or "exception") correspondences. For example, the regular phonological correspondence of the spelling pattern *ea* is /iː/ (as in *eat* and *peach*), because this is the one that occurs in the large majority of words; there are only relatively few words with the irregular correspondences of /ei/ (in *great*) and /e/ (in *sweat*).

In spelling, sound-to-spelling relationships are generally characterized by one-to-*very many* mappings. For the majority of vowels, there exist a large number of fairly commonly occurring spelling patterns and the most common spelling correspondence does not necessarily occur in the majority of words. For example, the vowel /ou/ is spelled in 13 different ways in English words, as in *dole*, *droll*, *bowl*, *coal*, *toe*, *folk*, *soul*, *owe*, *sew*, *dough*, *mauve*, *brooch* and *yeoman* (and even more if we were to include *comb*, *ohm* and *beau*). In a computational analysis of the spelling patterns of vowels in monosyllabic and some disyllabic words, Barry and Seymour (1988) found that for the "long" vowels and diphthongs the most common spelling correspondence occurs in less than 70% of words (and, indeed, on average for these vowels, in less than 50% of words). For example, for /ou/, the most common spelling pattern (*o-e*) occurs in 32% of words, the second most common (*o*) occurs in 26% and *ow* and *oa* occur in 16% and 15% of words respectively. Barry and Seymour used the term "contingency" rather than "regularity" to refer to the widely distributed nature of English sound-to-spelling associations. They defined contingency in terms of the frequency with which spelling patterns represent vowel sounds in words. So, both *o-e* and *o* are the high-contingency spellings of /ou/, whereas the rarer spellings *oa*, *oe*, etc., are its low-contingency spellings.

Most vowel phonemes have many spelling correspondences. Furthermore, it will be generally true that more than one of these spellings will be phonologically plausible; for example, Venezky (1970) shows that /ou/ is the major phonological correspondence of three spellings: *o-e*, *ow* (in a final position) and *oa*. There are about 20 vowel phonemes in English but there are many more spelling patterns used to represent vowels, including: the simple forms *a, e, i, o, u* (and *y*); all these followed, after a consonant, by a final *e* (as in v<u>o</u>te); the digraphs *ae, ai, ea, ee, ei, ia, ie, io, oe, oo, ou, ue* and *ui*; and many other forms such as *aw, ew, ow, oy, ey, ay, er, ur, ir, ar, are, air, ear, igh* and even *ough*. As there are more spelling patterns of vowels than there are vowel phonemes (and as many spelling patterns have more than one phonological correspondence), it follows that sound-to-spelling correspondences are necessarily inconsistent and will, in the main, also be more inconsistent than spelling-to-sound correspondences. Furthermore, we could say that there exists a "double dissociation" between contingency in spelling and regularity for reading. Table 2.1 gives some examples showing the stark lack of correspondence between sound-to-spelling and spelling-to-sound correspondences. Whereas many words are "regular" for both reading and spelling (and there are some old stalwarts that are clearly "irregular" for both), there also exist two "dissociations":

1. Some words contain low-contingency (i.e. rarely occurring) spellings which are nevertheless phonologically plausible; as such they are "exceptional" for spelling, but perfectly regular for reading. For example, in Barry and Seymour's analysis, the vowel /i:/ is spelled as e + consonant + e (as in *theme*) in only 3.6% of words and yet Venezky (1970) identifies /i:/ as the major phonological correspondence of the spelling pattern *e-e*.
2. There are some words which (at least for some speakers) contain high-contingency spellings but are actually *irregular* for reading. In received pronunciation (RP), there are a small number of words with the vowel /u/, for example *wool, full, could* and *wolf* (as opposed to the "longer" vowel /u:/, in *stool* and *fool*). Barry

TABLE 2.1 The "Double Dissociation" of reading regularity and spelling contingency.

	For reading	
	Regular	Irregular
For spelling		
High-contingency	*Beef, leaf* /i:/ → *ea* (40%) or *ea* (39%) Both *ea* + *ee* → /i:/	*Book, wool* /u/ → *oo* → /u:/ (for received pronunciation only)
Low-contingency	*Thief, theme* /i:/ → *ie* (6%) or *e-e* (4%) Both *ie* + *e-e* → /i:/	*Ski, key*
	Soap, soul /ou/ → *oa* (15%) or *ou* (1%) Both *oa* + *ou* (medial) → /ou/	*Mauve, brooch*

and Seymour analysed 54 words containing /u/ and found that its most common spelling pattern is *oo* (as in *foot* and *good*), which accounted for 65% of words, and the second most common spelling, accounting for 26% of words, is *u* (as in *full* and *push*). The low-contingency spellings were *ou* (in *could*, *should* and *would*) and *o* (*wolf* and *woman*). According to Venezky, the major phonological correspondence of *oo* is /u:/, as in *boot* and *spook* (rather than *book*), and the major phonological correspondence of U is /ʌ/, as in *hut* (rather than as in "to '*put*' something in its place"). So, for RP speakers, there can be *no* phonologically plausible spellings of words with /u/!

Spelling English is a considerably more troublesome task than reading it. Spelling English words using correspondences that related vowels to their most common spelling would be intolerably unreliable for words with long vowels and diphthongs. It may be somewhat more reliable for the so-called "short" vowels, where Barry and Seymour have shown that the most common spelling correspondences occur in 90% or more of words, but there typically exist many different "exception" spelling patterns. For example, /i/ is spelled *i* (as in *it*) in 97% of words, yet it is also spelled as in *cyst*, *build*, *sieve* and *women*. Similar exceptions may easily be found for the generally consistent correspondences of consonants (e.g. initial /k/ as in <u>c</u>at, <u>k</u>ite and <u>ch</u>ord). Spelling English words non-lexically would be substantially more unreliable than reading them non-lexically.

So far, in considering the statistical regularities between sounds and spellings in English, I have concentrated on vowels, i.e. individual phonemes. It is not clear to what extent the inconsistency of sound-to-spelling correspondences would be reduced appreciably by considerations of the correspondences of multi-sound units, particularly those of "rimes" (see Treiman, 1986). Rimes are the phonologically defined terminal vowel-consonant clusters of words (such as -/i:m/) and two words rhyme when they share the same terminal rime (such as *te<u>am</u>* and *th<u>eme</u>*). Whereas most vowels are spelled in many different ways, most rimes are spelled in considerably fewer patterns. For example, the vowel /ei/ is spelled in 12 ways, with *a-e* being the most common (occurring in 43% of words) and *ai* being the second most common (occurring in 20% of words). However, the rime /ein/ is spelled with only four different patterns (as in *cane*, *gain*, *deign*, *rein*— but there are many homophones); furthermore, the most common spelling of /ein/ is *ain* and not the lexically most frequent spelling of the vowel /ei/, which is *a-e*. If the assembled spelling system used the spelling correspondences of rimes rather than the correspondences of vowels (as computed from the lexicon as a whole), then we should expect people to spell nonwords more often with the most common spelling of its rime rather than of its vowel. (For instance, we should expect people to spell /tein/ more often as *tain* than as *tane*.) Although their nonword spelling experiment was not designed as an explicit test of this hypothesis, Barry and Seymour performed a *post hoc* analysis of their data to compare two categories of nonwords: (i) those like /tein/ for which the most common spelling of their rhyming words is not the lexically most common spelling of the vowel; and (ii) those others where the most common spelling of their rhyming words is also the lexically most common spelling of the vowel. They found no significant difference between the number of lexically most common spellings produced for two categories of nonwords. (They found that /tein/ was spelled as *tane* by 55% of their subjects but as *tain* by only 38%.) They concluded that people "utilize sound-to-spelling contingencies abstracted from the lexicon as a whole rather than only from the subset of rhyming words to generate their nonword spelling" (p. 26).

THE DUAL-ROUTE MODEL OF SPELLING PRODUCTION

The previous section has shown how difficult it would be to spell English words correctly (or even particularly consistently) using an assembled spelling system alone. Indeed, this difficulty has been taken as a justification for the necessity of a lexical spelling system for English: how else, the argument runs, could we spell *yacht* correctly apart from retrieving some word-specific spelling knowledge (i.e. using a lexical route)? It is then only a small further step to propose that, given the great inconsistency of English orthography, we use *only* a lexical spelling system and do not rely at all upon the operation of any assembled spelling system. However, it cannot be that people *never* use the assembled route because they occasionally produce phonologically plausible misspellings. For example, Wing and Baddeley (1980) list many such errors—which they call "convention" errors—in their corpus of the spelling errors in written examination scripts (e.g. *properganda, sensative, occurance*, etc.)—and these, shockingly, from candidaits applying for entrence to Camebridg! Such errors suggest that there is at least some contribution of an assembled spelling system in normal writing. It is also true that normal writers can produce spellings for new words and nonwords. This, and the fact that such new spellings tend to be phonologically plausible, may be taken as support for the idea that we can call upon an assembled spelling route. The combination of this pair of notions, namely (i) that we *must* have a lexical system to cope with the vagaries of English and (ii) that we *can* use an assembled system to spell new items (and seem to show an effect of assembled spelling in some of our misspellings), has come to motivate the dual-route model of spelling production.

In the dual-route theoretical framework, two major spelling routes are assumed to operate in parallel (see Figure 2.1): the lexical (or word-specific) route retrieves spellings of known words from an orthographic lexicon, and the assembled route constructs spellings using some form of sub-word sound-to-spelling conversion process.

The lexical route operates by the retrieval of spellings of known words stored in the orthographic output lexicon, a permanent memory structure which acts as the repository for our knowledge of word spellings. Known words could be spelled by the lexical route, but it would not work directly for any new words or the nonwords (such as *vot*) much beloved by psychologists. In the task of spelling to dictation, a spoken word would be recognized and then would activate its corresponding representation in the orthographic output lexicon, either via the word's meaning or via its output phonology (in a spoken word production system). A lexical route is all that could be used for languages with scripts such as Chinese, in which, essentially, each word has its own unique character, in the form of an "ideogram".

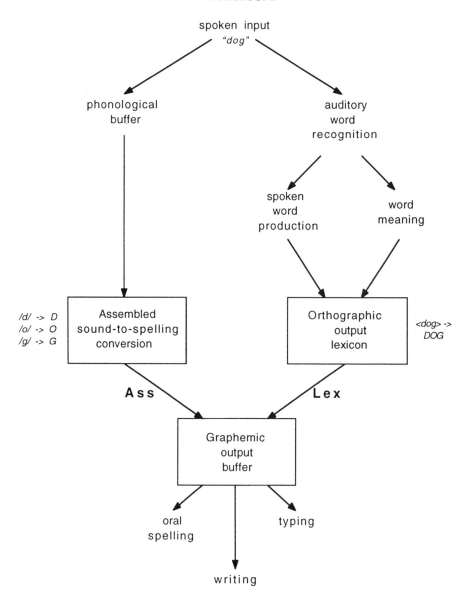

FIGURE 2.1   The Dual-Route Model of spelling production.

The assembled route operates by the application of knowledge of how the
constituent sounds of words are conventionally produced in spelling. In the dictation
task, the phonological form of a spoken item would be held in a phonological
temporary buffer (which may be akin to the "articulatory loop" of short-term
memory) and segmented in some way in order to apply a process of sound-to-spelling
conversion. The assembled route would be reliably correct only for words with
"regular" sound-to-spelling correspondences; it would produce phonologically

plausible misspellings for irregular words (and English contains very many such words). The assembled route might spell *vot* plausibly (as *vot*) and spell *hot* correctly, but it would not spell *yacht* correctly, as this would require some lexically-specific knowledge. Indeed, it would most probably spell *yacht* as *yot* as, in effect, it treats everything as if it were a nonword. (Note that nonwords must be spelled by the assembled route *ex hypothesi* because they involve *sub-word* sound-to-spelling conversion.) An assembled route would be able to spell words quite efficiently in languages with "shallow" (or phonologically regular) sound-to-script associations. This would be true for many syllabic-based scripts (such as some Indian languages) and also for some alphabetic scripts, such as Italian and Welsh.

Once a spelling has been either lexically retrieved or assembled, it is deposited in a presumed graphemic output buffer (GOB), which holds spellings while output processes are being prepared and implemented. Output can be in writing or in oral spelling or in typing or however else we wish to do it.

It is fair to say that the dual-route model has established itself as the orthodox theoretical conception of the processes subserving spelling in English, although more recent connectionist accounts (see, for example, Brown & Loosemore, this volume, Chapter 16) may be mounting a substantive challenge to its modular framework. There are a number of issues following the adoption of the dual-route model which have not been fully resolved, and I shall now consider five pertinent theoretical questions.

1. What is the relative contribution of the two routes to normal spelling production? If there is a "race" between the two routes, then it is possible that one is effectively relied upon more than the other. For English, it would not be unreasonable to suppose that the lexical route is either faster or more dependable than the assembled route, which would ensure that most spellings of words are produced by the lexical system, with the assembled route being used only as a "back-up" when attempting to produce rare or new words. If there is some form of cooperation between the two routes, then it is unclear how any discrepancies are to be resolved if they offer different spellings for the same item. (What would be the outcome of any duel between the dual routes?)

2. Can the lexical route operate for all words? It may be possible that only some words are stored in the lexicon and that the assembled route is used to generate the spellings of other words. Words stored lexically might include those which are very frequently used and/or those which have produced difficulty in the past (probably irregular words). Note that this view also commits us to the position that, in order to have normal correct spelling of all words, then both routes need to be operating optimally.

3. How, exactly, does the lexical route operate and, in particular, what form of orthographic representations does it use? Are words stored in the lexicon as *whole units*, or might it be the case that only the "irregular" (i.e. "difficult") *portions* of words are stored? When spelling the (increasingly frequent) exception word *yacht*, it is quite possible to imagine the misspelling *yaht*, rather than *vot*, an error which would reflect what Ellis (1982) calls "partial lexical knowledge". Could it be the case that only the spellings of vowels are stored lexically, as these are the elements which are generally spelled so inconsistently in English words? Note

that if we were to grant that only portions of the spellings of words are stored in the lexicon, then we would be forced to propose quite complex functional interaction between the two routes: the correct and complete spelling of a word (e.g. *mauve*) would necessarily require the lexical retrieval of the spelling of its vowel (e.g. *au-e*), plus the contribution of the assembled route (/m/ = *m* and /v/ = *v*), followed by a fairly intricate integration of these spelling elements. Furthermore, if spelling words necessarily requires the cooperative interaction between the two routes, then it would not be possible to spell properly if either of the two routes were somehow disabled.

4. How exactly does the assembled spelling route operate? A major contrast is between rule-based and lexical analogy conceptions of the operation of assembled spelling. The assembled route is frequently referred to as a "non-lexical" spelling route and is often characterized as applying phoneme-to-grapheme correspondence (or PGC) rules. However, some authors who refer to a "PGC" route appear not to have considered the implications of proposing a conversion mechanism based on phonemes in particular rather than simply on "sounds" in general and it is quite possible that rules could operate at a variety of levels including combinations of sounds (e.g. /ng/ → *ing*), as suggested by Baxter and Warrington (1987, 1988). In contrast to rule-based theories, assembled spelling could operate by a process of lexical analogy. If we were required to spell the nonword *pog*, an analogy process might involve the activation of the spellings of words with similar sounds, perhaps all those that end in /ɔg/ and all those that begin with /pɔ/. From these activated spellings, we should be able to somehow synthesize a possible spelling. There are obviously clear difficulties for procedures such as this, especially when it comes to specifying the precise means by which a spelling is actually synthesized (or chosen), as it is highly likely, given the inconsistency of English, that there will be more than one likely candidate emerging from all those activated. (Spelling *pog* might be straightforward, as all words ending in /ɔg/ are spelled − *og*, and virtually all words beginning with /pɔ/ are spelled *po-*. Spelling /kiːk/, however, would be more tricky: the initial consonant may be spelled as *c* or *k*, the vowel may be spelled as *ee*, *ea*, *e-e* or *ie*, and the terminal consonant may be spelled as *k* or even *que*, as in *clique*.) All possible lexical analogy models of assembled spelling require the activated spellings of similar words to be segmentable into sub-word collections of letters. This is not contentious, but what should be the cause of more careful reflection is the accompanying claim that stored orthographic representations of words must be segmentable along lines which correspond to phonological dimensions. It is, of course, possible that the orthographic representations of words are coded along (or marked for) essentially phonological dimensions, but is there any independent body of direct evidence to compel us to accept such a claim? Also, for some words, the assigning of segmented orthographic elements to phonological features is ambiguous. Is the vowel of the inordinately useful word *yacht* spelled *a* or *ach*? (Some letters are not merely "silent", they can be downright bothersome.) In addition, it must not be forgotten that lexical analogy models require the stored orthographic representations of *all* known words to be available. As such, they would seem to carry the implicit belief that spelling words does not normally involve the process of assembled spelling.

It would be very strange to imagine that, in order to spell a particular word, we activate the spellings of similar words in order to synthesize (or "pool") something to produce, rather than simply producing its own activated stored spelling!

5. Do the two routes interact in their normal operation? The possibility that there might exist some degree of functional interaction between the lexical and assembled spelling routes has already been mentioned. There are a number of possible views of such functional interaction and one clearly articulated model, proposed by Nolan and Caramazza (1983), will be discussed later.

SUPPORT FOR THE DUAL-ROUTE MODEL OF SPELLING PRODUCTION

It seems to me that there are three principal sources of support (and so converging motivations) for the dual-route model as an explanatory framework for spelling in adults. The first is the logical plausibility for dual spelling systems, based upon observations of our spelling competence and supported by arguments of the kind rehearsed when considering the nature of English orthography. That we can spell many frankly irregular words correctly and can manage to spell new words and nonwords is certainly consistent with the notion that we have at our disposal both a lexical and an assembled spelling system. Furthermore, the fact that we may sometimes misspell words in a phonologically plausible fashion indicates that we may sometimes rely upon assembled spelling.

The second motivation for the dual-route model comes from the view that spelling somehow "follows" reading, in two respects: (i) in the acquisition of literacy skills in children, the mastery of spelling is generally subsequent to reading having been well established; and (ii) the study of spelling has tended to follow in the wake of the considerable research activity devoted to reading and has wished to capitalize on its corresponding theoretical progress. The dual-route model of word recognition and reading aloud has proved to be a useful and productive framework in which to interpret a large body of data from skilled adult readers, children and people with various forms of reading difficulty, including patients with acquired dyslexia (e.g. Coltheart, 1985). Indeed, given that reading may be said to have both ontogenic and intellectual primacy, we can see that the dual-route model of spelling production has been adapted—*mutatis mutandis*—from the corresponding model of reading.

The third and perhaps the most persuasive empirical support for the dual-route model of spelling production has come from studies of spelling impairments in neurological patients (with forms of acquired central dysgraphia). The 1980s witnessed considerable interest in the study of spelling impairments. Much of this activity has embraced the enthusiasm for the detailed single case studies of relatively "unusual" (and rarely presenting) patients which has characterized the study of impairments in a wide range of language skills, but most particularly in acquired dyslexic disturbances of reading. In cognitive neuropsychology, evidence from single case studies of neurological patients is used to test and inform theories of normal processing. As an enterprise, cognitive neuropsychology entails a reciprocal relationship between theories of normal cognitive processes and investigations of acquired disorders of those processes. On the one hand, data from neurological patients are used to test theories of normal processing (and may be taken to suggest new hypotheses concerning the organization of normal functioning). If, as a result of brain damage, a patient shows a dissociation between their ability to perform two tasks of equivalent difficulty (i.e. that they can perform one task fairly normally while another is substantially impaired), then this may be interpreted within a model of normal processing by proposing that there exist two separable processing systems (or modules) which are responsible for the tasks. On the other hand, patterns of specific impaired and preserved abilities of particular neurological patients are interpreted within models of normal processing: the performance observed is presumed to reflect selective breakdown of (or functional dissociation between) separable, normal processing systems.

The results of the patients under review all indicate varieties of acquired dysgraphia. Their impairments of literate production (dysgraphia) are "acquired" in the sense that their spelling problems are assumed to have been caused by their neurological damage in adulthood and that they were previously "normal", competent spellers. Note that it may be possible to obtain "documentary" proof that the patients were able to write correctly before their neurological damage, by consulting any extant texts they have produced. (As it is seldom possible to have access to a patient's premorbid reading abilities, the study of dysgraphia may be easier than that of dyslexia in this regard.)

In providing explanatory cognitive accounts of written language production, it is important to distinguish between impairments of spelling and writing. I shall use the term "spelling" to refer to the central ability to retrieve or to assemble an orthographic representation, that is, a coded sequence of letters. I shall use the term "writing" to refer to the means whereby this orthographic code is translated into the production of ink marks on paper. Writing may be seen as one of many ways to produce (or output) a spelling; other output systems include oral spelling (i.e. saying the names of letters), typing and arranging scrabble letter tokens. Patients with acquired *central* dysgraphia have impaired spelling, in that their errors are essentially the same whatever output modality is used. Patients with a solely *peripheral* dysgraphia show deficits specific to one output mode, typically writing (in which they may produce variously poorly formed letters); their spelling ability as tested in other output modalities can remain intact.

Before discussing the patterns of dissociations found in patients with varieties of acquired central dysgraphia, it is worth mentioning that such neuropsychological evidence has played a fairly weighty role in the specification of theories of *normal* spelling ability. The last decade has seen more research on impairments of spelling (and on the analysis of spelling errors in children) than on normal *correct* spelling production in competent spellers. This is quite unlike the situation for the study of reading, where data from patients with varieties of acquired dyslexia have tended to complement a larger body of experimental evidence directed towards our understanding of the details of normal reading performance. The reason for this difference is undoubtedly the methodological difficulty of studying normal (adult) spelling production directly and in real time, where reliable measures of latency are considerably harder to take (and to interpret) than for word recognition, reading aloud and various word comprehension tasks. Thus, the dual-route model of spelling has been supported most persuasively by the erroneous spelling performance of patients with disorders of spelling competence, and in particular by the dissociations observed within patients with phonological and surface dysgraphia.

Phonological Dysgraphia

Shallice (1981) described a patient, PR, who showed a selective impairment of spelling nonwords. PR was able to spell words quite successfully; indeed, he correctly spelled 91.3% of 622 words, but he was able to spell only 18% of 50 nonwords. (Note that a "correct" spelling for a nonword is anything deemed to be phonologically plausible.) It must be stressed that PR could both repeat spoken nonwords before he attempted to write them and remember them for the duration of his spelling attempts. For example, on a test with 60 nonwords, he could repeat 56 immediately, write only 16 but report 46 when asked 10 seconds later. This shows that his spelling impairment cannot be due to any problem of auditory recognition or of holding phonological information sufficiently long to implement assembled spelling. It is also the case that he had no general problems with written nonwords, as he was able to read aloud 72% of printed nonwords.

PR could not spell all words correctly. Shallice examined the possible effects of both word frequency and concreteness on his word spelling performance. For high-frequency words, he was 100% correct on those above the median in rated concreteness and 92% correct on those below the median. For low-frequency words, he was correct for 96% concrete and 80% abstract words. He would therefore only seem to be troubled by rare, abstract words. PR was no worse on "irregular" than regular words, but was significantly worse spelling function words (62% correct) than high-frequency content words (98% correct). In a further test, he was required to first repeat a spoken function word and then to write it. He was able to repeat all 50 of the words but "failed to write 17 of them".

In spelling words, PR reported that he was "transcribing from an inner 'screen' on which he sees the word" (p. 418). However, I am not convinced that this is a valid account of the mode of operation of the lexical route. (Can we spell backwards as easily as naming letters in reverse order from words we are looking at? I think not.) What appears to me to be more insightful is PR's report of his strategy for spelling nonwords, as this seems to be supported by his behaviour. PR commented that when he attempted to spell nonwords, he often used a word as a mediator. For example, he spelled *sim* as *sym* and reported that he had thought of, and used as an analogy, the word *symbol* (which is an irregular word as /i/ is only very rarely spelled *y* in English words). This analogy strategy often led PR to produce errors, however, as in *na* spelt as *gn* (via *gnat*). It may be possible that PR was using what remained of his impaired assembled spelling route, in which lexical knowledge is *normally* consulted within some form of analogy process. However, it is equally possible that PR was using a lexical analogy strategy in order to *compensate* for his primary deficit of normally rule-based assembled spelling.

Shallice's report of PR was the first description of a case of phonological dysgraphia, not, we must presume, because it is a new affliction but rather that until a theoretical motivation to do so (as provided by the dual-route framework, coming from work on reading impairments), it would have been unlikely that nonwords would have been given to anyone who could spell words successfully and so it would not have been detected. Since Shallice's study, other similar patients have also been reported. Bub and Kertesz (1982a) report the case of MH, who could spell 79% of words correctly but who was only able to spell one of 29 nonwords. MH was also more accurate at written than spoken naming, which could be seen as another example of "non-phonological" spelling. Roeltgen, Sevush and Heilman (1983) have reported a further four patients with impaired nonword writing. I saw a phonological dysgraphic patient (who sadly died before testing was completed) who was able to correctly spell 84% of high-frequency words, 72% of low-frequency words, but only 3% of even the most simple nonwords, where her errors were rather strange (e.g. *vout → foxet, brut → busthy*).

The manifest interpretation of phonological dysgraphia in terms of the dual-route model is that the assembled spelling route has been damaged (as evidenced by patients' substantially impaired nonword spelling), but the lexical route remains intact (and so they spell words correctly and show no effect of sound-to-spelling irregularity). Precisely how phonological dysgraphics retrieve lexical spellings may be open to some debate. Figure 2.1 shows two sub-routes to the orthographic output lexicon as being available, via word meaning or via word phonology. The suggestion of a small effect of concreteness on PR's spelling accuracy for words may indicate that the semantic route is involved.

Exactly what part of the assembled route is impaired in phonological dysgraphia is also not always entirely clear. It would seem to me that the assembled route logically entails three component functions: (i) the phonological segmentation of the item to be spelled; (ii) the application of sound-to-spelling correspondence; and (iii) the integration of the orthographic elements provided by these conversion procedures, which will be especially necessary for the "final-*e*" spellings of vowels (e.g. /ei/ = *a-e*). Shallice (1981), however, considered only two components, "the segmenting of the overall sound into smaller units and the writing of individual speech sounds" (p. 422), and concluded that both were impaired in PR, although no explicit tests of phonological segmentation (such as phoneme deletion or individual sound comparison tasks) were reported.

Surface Dysgraphia

From the point of view of theoretical development (if not from that of the patients involved), 1981 was a "good" year for acquired dysgraphia. In addition to the first report of phonological dysgraphia by Shallice, there was also the first detailed report of an apparently "complementary" disorder, which I shall call "surface" dysgraphia. Beauvois and Dérouesné (1981) reported the French patient RG, whom they referred to as a case of "lexical agraphia". RG was quite able to spell nonwords; indeed, in the majority of cases, he produced the most economical orthographic renderings for phonemes (e.g. *o* and not *eau* for /o/). He was much better with words with "regular" than with "ambiguous" sound-to-spelling correspondences (93% vs 67% correct), and even worse with "very irregular" (i.e. exception) words (only 36%

correct). Furthermore, he tended to spell ambiguous and irregular words in a phonologically plausible fashion: he omitted silent letters (*habile → habil*), he substituted graphemes with identical phonemic realizations (*souk → souc*) and "regularized" words with very rare correspondences (*monsieur → messieu*).

Hatfield and Patterson (1983) report an English surface dysgraphic patient, TP, who also spelled more regular than irregular words (64% vs 27%) and produced many phonologically plausible but incorrect spellings (e.g. *flood → flud, biscuit → bisket, mortgage → morgage*). TP also produced homophone confusion errors, even when in disambiguating sentences: asked to "spell *pale*, as in 'She turned pale at the news'", TP wrote *pail* (which indicates another form of "phonological spelling"). TP was also 93% correct on a set of words claimed to have only a single phonologically plausible spelling, such as *thing*.

Other surface dysgraphics have been reported by Roeltgen and Heilman (1984), Goodman and Caramazza (1986) and Goodman-Schulman and Caramazza (1987). Baxter and Warrington (1987) reported a very clear surface dysgraphic case, KT, who produced many clear errors (such as *clay → clai*) and who appeared to spell words in an extremely similar fashion to how normal subjects spell nonwords, see Barry (1988) for a commentary.

The interpretation of surface dysgraphia within the dual-route model is that there is an impairment of the lexical spelling route. The stored orthographic representations of words are unable to be retrieved and so the patients are forced to rely upon the operation of their intact assembled spelling route, which produces phonologically plausible errors. It may be worthy of note that many "normal" spellers produce similar misspellings which also reflect an over-reliance upon assembled spelling due to imprecise (or absent) lexical knowledge.

All the surface dysgraphic patients so far reported have been able to spell at least some irregular words correctly, which shows that not all lexical orthographic representations have been rendered unavailable. Goodman and Caramazza (1986) presented their patient MW with words with high or low probabilities of being produced by phoneme-to-grapheme correspondence rule (i.e. "regular" and "irregular" words) and within each category there were words of high and low frequency of occurrence. For both oral and written spelling, they found that MW was virtually perfect with all high-frequency words, but that for the low-frequency words he was significantly worse for the irregular than the regular words. The fact that MW showed surface dysgraphic performance only for low-frequency words suggests that he had a deficit in addressing lexical spelling representations and that access to such representations is determined by frequency.

Not all surface dysgraphic spelling errors are phonologically plausible. (Indeed, as noted above, there can be no phonologically plausible spelling for the vowel /u/.) Some errors reflect what Ellis (1982) calls "partial lexical knowledge", such as TP's errors *yacht → yhagt* and *sword → sward*. These errors suggest that some, but incomplete, lexical orthographic information about a word may be available (for example that the word *yacht* contains the letter *h* somewhere). This suggests that the surface dysgraphic deficit of retrieval of lexical orthography may not be an "all-or-none" one.

FUNCTIONAL INTERACTIONS BETWEEN
THE DUAL ROUTES IN ENGLISH

The dissociations found in (and the claimed double dissociation between) phonological and surface dysgraphia provide strong neuropsychological support for the *separability* of the lexical and the assembled spelling routes: neurological damage seems to be able to selectively impair one distinct processing route and leave the other relatively intact. Phonological dysgraphic patients have an impaired assembled route but a preserved lexical route, and surface dysgraphics have an impaired lexical route and so spell by their preserved assembled route. However, the notion of the functional *independence* of the two routes, especially in normal spellers—who possess both—is a separate question. There are a number of possible operational relationships between the lexical and the assembled spelling routes, and I shall now consider two major ones: the contribution of the lexical route to the process of assembled spelling, and the claim that the assembled spelling system is necessary for the normal (and efficient) spelling of words.

Lexical Influences on Assembled Spelling

At one extreme, it might be suggested that there is not a separate assembled spelling route at all. It might be considered that normal spellers, when required to produce spellings which do not already exist in their lexicons, actually use some process of lexical analogy: like Shallice's patient PR, they might activate a similar sounding word (or words) and adapt these spellings to produce a new one. In an important paper, Campbell (1983) found that a previously heard word could bias normal subjects' spellings of rhyming nonwords. For example, people who heard *sweet* and then /pri:t/ tended to spell the nonword as *preet*, whereas people who heard *treat* followed by /pri:t/ tended to spell it as *preat*. Campbell concluded from these lexical priming effects that "skill at assigning letters to sounds *never* becomes independent of lexical skill in adult readers" (p. 153).

Barry and Seymour (1988) looked at how people spell nonwords in both a priming task (like that used by Campbell) and a free-spelling task in which only nonwords were presented. They confirmed that nonword spelling could indeed be lexically primed; for example, /toup/ was spelled as *toap* significantly more often following the presentation of the priming word *soap* than when the nonword was presented alone. However, Barry and Seymour also found that nonword spellings (in both their priming and free-spelling tasks) were strongly determined by sound-to-spelling *contingency* (a variable that reflects spelling "regularity"). People in both tasks produced significantly more high-contingency (i.e. common or "regular") than low-contingency (i.e. rare or "irregular") spelling patterns for the vowels in the nonwords. For example, the nonword /pi:m/ was spelled as *peam* or *peem* (with the two most common spelling patterns for the vowel /i:/) more often than as *peme* or *piem* (which contain phonologically plausible but very rarely occurring spelling patterns for /i:/). Barry and Seymour proposed a model of assembled spelling in which a set of probabilistic sound-to-spelling correspondences relate vowel phonemes to weighted lists of alternative spelling patterns, which are ordered by sound-to-spelling contingency.

They suggested that these correspondences are abstracted from lexical knowledge but are represented (and may be implemented) separately from it (i.e. as an assembled spelling route). They further proposed that the selection of a spelling pattern from such lists is *normally* open to lexical influence (as demonstrated by the lexical priming effects). This model suggests that lexical priming effects upon nonword spelling can be interpreted within a dual-route model of spelling production, in which the two routes are in functional interaction, rather than within a single "lexical analogy" model.

Is Assembled Spelling Involved in the Normal Spelling of Words?

The dissociations observed in phonological dysgraphic patients are impressive but are not absolute: no patient has been reported with "perfect" (i.e. 100% correct) word spelling and completely obliterated (i.e. zero%) nonword spelling. There are a number of possible reasons for this. Perhaps the most mundane is that the patients never knew all the "words" the experimenter considered to be words, although this is unlikely to be the case for PR's difficulties with function words. (Indeed, it may also be possible that patients "know" some of the nonwords as meaningful units, and it is indeed always possible that, for example, *pog* is the name of someone's pet cat, or, like *bonk*, has assumed a significance which has passed the innocent experimenter by.) Alternatively, it might be proposed that faultless spelling of words requires some contribution of the assembled route. One of the possible forms of functional interaction between the two routes (as previously mentioned) may be readily eliminated: the overall accuracy of word spelling by phonological dysgraphics would appear to be too high to support the notion that only portions of the spellings of all words are stored lexically and that the assembled route is necessary to "flesh out" the remainder.

It is also possible that the correct production of at least *some* words might require some contribution of the assembled route. The data from PR could be taken to suggest that the assembled route is necessary for the efficient production of function words (and/or low-frequency abstract words). In fact, such a proposal takes the exact form of an argument advanced by Patterson (1982) when considering the phonological dyslexic patient AM, who could read about 90% of words but only 12% of nonwords. AM's word-reading errors including both "derivational" errors (e.g. *think → thinking* and *applaud → applause*) and some "function word substitution" errors (e.g. *he → when* and *in → an*). Patterson reasoned that AM's impairment of phonological recoding of print (as evidenced by his nonword reading deficit) was functionally implicated in his word-reading problems. In particular, she advanced the hypothesis that phonological recoding is necessary for the correct reading of bound morphemes and function words. Note that this is based on AM's association of impairments, namely that he cannot do phonological recoding *and* he makes particular word-reading errors. However, Funnell (1983) subsequently reported a phonological dysgraphic patient, WB, who could read 85% of the words presented to him but only one of the 30 nonwords. Although WB made some derivational errors, he made more visual errors (eg *theme → scheme*). He was no worse on words with affices than monomorphemic words and not especially worse on function words. There can, therefore, exist a dissociation between impaired phonological recoding and derivational errors, thus refuting Patterson's hypothesis: phonological recoding is *not* necessarily required for reading affices and function words. In general, the development of theory in cognitive neuropsychology proceeds by the study of dissociations of function rather than finding association of deficits (i.e. that a patient is impaired on two functions). Such associations, which may be due to brain damage to two functionally separate systems whose neurological substrates are anatomically close, are considered to provide only "provisional" evidence: cognitive neuropsychologists take dissociations (even though these tend to be seldom absolute) to be stronger evidence for theories of the functional architecture of normal processing. The data from phonological dysgraphia can be taken to support the notion that the lexical and the assembled spelling routes are effectively separate but that their neural substrates happen to be anatomically close, so that the effects of brain damage (which is always accidental and "messy") have not been completely selective.

Phonological dysgraphics can spell many words but have a pronounced deficit in spelling nonwords. This indicates that an entirely intact assembled route is not essential for word spelling. However, it remains the case that nonword spelling is never completely abolished in phonological dysgraphics, so it may be impossible to completely rule out the possibility that the assembled route exerts some influence on word spelling. Nolan and Caramazza (1983) have advanced a theory in which assembled spelling is proposed to be functionally necessary for correct word spelling. Nolan and Caramazza's model is predicted upon the assumption that orthographic information, held in the graphemic output buffer (GOB), "is subject to decay . . . unless the representations stored in the buffer are periodically refreshed" (p. 320). They suggest that the contents of the GOB are refreshed by the assembled spelling route. The orthographic representation of a word to be spelled is placed in the GOB and, simultaneous with this, the word's corresponding phonological representation is activated and placed in a phonological output (or response) buffer, which temporarily holds, but is also assumed to be able to rehearse, phonological codes. The representation in the GOB, which is assumed to decay fairly rapidly, is then refreshed by information in the phonological buffer via the assembled route, which Nolan and Caramazza conceive of as a phoneme-to-grapheme conversion (PGC) process.

Nolan and Caramazza report the case of the English-speaking deep dysgraphic patient VS, who produced semantic errors to words in dictation (see later) and was unable to spell nonwords. However, VS also produced various *visual* (non-phonological) writing errors. These include single-letter substitutions (e.g. *ground → grourd*), omissions (e.g. *circle → cicle*) and additions (e.g. *torch → storch*), as well as transposition errors (e.g. *problem → promble*) and some "gap" errors in which VS left spaces within a written production for missing letters (e.g. *streng-h*). In order to interpret these graphemic errors, Nolan and Caramazza make two proposals: (i) because VS had severely impaired assembled spelling, as shown by her nonword spelling deficit, she was unable to refresh the graphemic representations held in the GOB; and (ii) because information held in the GOB is normally subject to decay, writing errors involving the loss of both specific letter identity and letter position information would be expected.

I must confess that I am unconvinced by this theory, and I shall now present what I see are the conceptual problems with it. First, the pivotal premise of the Nolan and Caramazza model is that representations held in the GOB are normally subject to inefficient decay. Now, as the major function of the proposed GOB is to hold graphemic representations to support normal writing—a process that is necessarily extended over time—it seems very strange to me that this should be the case. Why should the system proposed to be primarily responsible for holding spellings to sustain normal writing be unable to do so without the aid of another supplementary system? Nolan and Caramazza's argument from VS's performance seems to be that her neurological damage has removed the "stabilizing" support of a normally error-prone system. For me, this is counter-intuitive but, more importantly, there is no direct evidence to support such a notion. An alternative account of VS's graphemic writing errors would be that she had impairments to *both* the PGC system and a normally efficient and adequately durable graphemic buffer which limited the effective "life" of the representations held within it.

The second problem I have with their model is that, even if we concede that the GOB is subject to decay, then why should the assembled spelling system be the source of its refreshment? A more plausible suggestion would be to rely upon an unambiguous source of refreshment, such as the repeated activation (of the same information) by the system which deposited the graphemic representation in the GOB in the first place. For English words, this could only be served reliably by the orthographic lexicon. Indeed, it appears to me that if the PGC system were to be used to refresh GOB representations, this would produce more problems than it would solve. To appreciate this, a brief consideration of how the PGC system might actually refresh decaying representations in the GOB is required. Nolan and Caramazza claim that the decaying information held within the GOB places constraints upon what information (generated by the PGC system) it accepts. They acknowledge, as they put it, "the vagaries of English orthography" and assume that the PGC system can generate a number of different spelling patterns. They do not specify precisely how these are generated, but the view I favour of the operation of the assembled system is the Barry and Seymour (1988) model mentioned before. This claims that, for any particular phoneme, a number of orthographic alternatives are made available, ordered by their sound-to-spelling contingency. For example, the vowel /i:/ would probably generate (in order) at least the following correspondences: *ea*, *ee*, *ie* and *e-e* (which are the most common and phonologically plausible spellings). Nolan and Caramazza say that the PGC system "must consult the information in the Graphemic Buffer [the GOB] to determine which alternative is appropriate" (p. 322). This presumably occurs by the matching of the decaying graphemic information with the alternatives generated by the PGC system; for example, if the representation for the word *beef* had decayed to *be--*, then *ea* or *ee* would match and so could refresh such partial information whereas *ie* would not be "accepted".

However, a major problem now arises: without an explicit theory of how the fragmentary graphemic representations determine which PGC-generated spelling alternative will refresh them, it is unclear why the procedure would not often accept a partially matching but incorrect spelling, which would then result in the production of a phonologically plausible misspelling. For example, if the representation for *street* decayed to *stre--*, it should, presumably, be refreshed by the PGC-generated *streat* just as often as by *street*. This process should be particularly troublesome for irregular words, where the decaying graphemic representation would be expected to frequently accept an incorrect but a more commonly occurring spelling pattern that shares common letters. This argument holds for all words with inconsistent vowels with digraphic correspondences that share common letters, of which there are many cases; for example, if *soap* decayed to *so--*, it might be expected to be incorrectly refreshed as *sope* or *sowp*.

This reasoning therefore seems to lead to the conclusion that any refreshing by assembled spelling could only result in error-free spelling of words if the decaying graphemic information placed fairly rigorous constraints upon the refreshing spellings it accepted. This produces a clear paradox: the assembled refreshing system could only work without error if the information stored in the GOB had not actually decayed to a level where it would confuse similar spelling patterns. The representations of different (but similar) spellings held would need to be easily distinguishable, and this, of course, fundamentally undermines the necessity for any contribution of assembled spelling to normal word spelling production.

LEXICAL ROUTES TO THE ORTHOGRAPHIC OUTPUT LEXICON

As in the dual-route model of reading, there may be subdivisions within the lexical spelling system (i.e. different lexical routes to the orthographic output lexicon). Figure 2.2 shows three major possible routes from the auditory input lexicon (the system which recognizes heard words) to the orthographic output lexicon as could be used for the dictation task and I shall now review the neuropsychological evidence for these.

Semantically Mediated Spelling

There must be a connection from the auditory input lexicon to the semantic system to permit the comprehension of heard words. There must also be a route from the semantic system to the orthographic output lexicon to permit normal writing; this may exist as a direct connection although it is also possible that our normal writing involves activation of the phonology of words before activating their spelling. The neuropsychological evidence for the semantically mediated route (which I have labelled L-sem in Figure 2.2) comes from cases of "deep dysgraphia" (Newcombe and Marshall, 1980; Bub and Kertesz, 1982b; Nolan and Caramazza, 1983), which may be considered to be the spelling parallel of deep dyslexia. Deep dysgraphic patients are unable to spell nonwords, are more accurate spelling concrete than abstract words, and make semantic errors in dictation (e.g. *yacht* → *boat*). For example, Bub and Kertesz's patient JC could repeat all words and nonwords correctly, could read all words and 85% of nonwords, and showed good comprehension. She was able to write only 5% of nonwords and only between 33% and 45% of abstract words (and only 30% of function words), but was able to correctly spell between 75% and 80% of

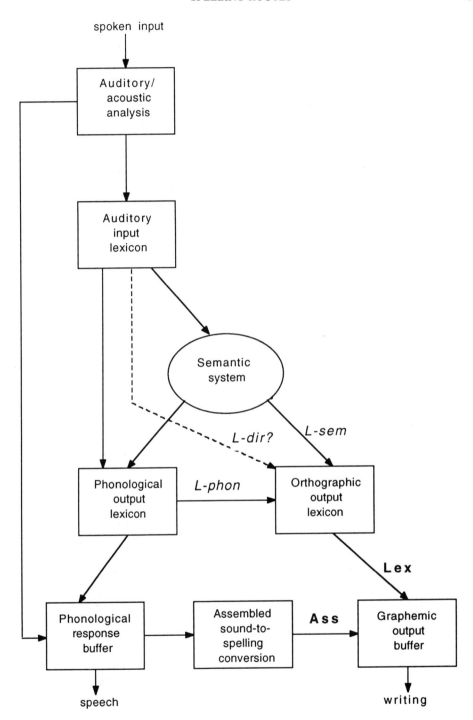

FIGURE 2.2   Routes to the orthographic output lexicon.

concrete words. She also produced clear semantic errors in dictation, including *time → clock*, *desk → chair* and *sky → sun*.

The interpretation of this complex pattern of performance is as follows. The patients cannot be spelling by the assembled route, as they cannot produce nonwords and show no effect of sound-to-spelling regularity. The fact that they produce semantic errors (and show a concreteness effect) suggests that they must be spelling by the semantic route (L-sem). As in deep dyslexia, there are two possible explanations for semantic errors: either there may be some deficit in the semantic system itself or there may be some instability in the mapping between the semantic system and the output lexicon, so that a semantic representation may result in the activation and subsequent production of an incorrect but related item. Bub and Kertesz's JC made no semantic errors in either reading or oral repetition and so her semantic errors in spelling must be due to an impairment of transmission of information from the semantic system to the orthographic output lexicon. In contrast, Nolan and Caramazza's patient VS also made semantic errors in reading.

Spelling Via the Phonological Output Lexicon

Once a word has been recognized by the auditory input lexicon, its output phonology can be activated, either directly or via the semantic system. There is a connection from the phonological output lexicon to the orthographic output lexicon (labelled L-phon in Figure 2.2), by which a word's spoken form can activate its spelling. The phonology of a homophone (e.g. /greit/) would activate *both* its entries in the orthographic output lexicon (namely *grate* and *great*) and contextual information, from the semantic system transmitted directly to the orthographic output lexicon (by L-sem), would be necessary to select the appropriate spelling. If the orthographic output lexicon were to be disconnected from direct contact with the semantic system but received information from the route via the phonological output lexicon, then there would be occasional homophone substitutions in writing: *great* might be produced when *grate* would have been correct. Roeltgen, Rothi and Heilman (1986) have reported five patients who make such errors. The patients showed no particular disadvantage for either nonwords or irregular words but all produced homophone substitution errors. They were given homophones to spell which were clearly disambiguated by simple context sentences, for example "Spell /not/ as in 'He is *not* here'." The patients wrote the homophone of the target between 24% and 42% of trials. Importantly, many of these homophones have low-contingency (or irregular) spellings, indicating that they must have been lexically retrieved rather than assembled. For example, when doe was written as *dough*, it is highly unlikely that the correspondence /ou/ = *ough* (which occurs in less than 1% of words) would have been supplied by the assembled spelling route.

Rapcsak and Rubens (1990) have reported a similar patient. The patient could spell 29/30 regular words, 27/30 irregular words, 26/30 nonwords and 30/30 function words (and was no different from five neurologically intact control subjects matched for age and education level). However, the patient was impaired in a task in which homophones were presented in disambiguating sentences: he was correct on only 17/30 homophones (57%), compared with 28/30 (93%) by controls, and spelled (correctly) the semantically inappropriate homophone on the remainder. The patient demonstrated intact comprehension of the homophones (as tested by a spoken sentence to picture matching test). Further, the length and complexity of the disambiguating sentences in the spelling task were equal to or less than those of a test of auditory comprehension on which the patient performed normally. The patient therefore understood both the homophones and the sentences.

The interpretation of the homophone substitution errors is that the route from the semantic system to the orthographic output lexicon (L-sem) is functionally severed. The patients were spelling by the route from the phonological output lexicon to the orthographic output lexicon (L-phon), which sometimes produces the "wrong" spelling of a homophone. It might be expected that either the most frequent or the most recently produced of the two activated spellings would be selected again, but, unfortunately, the variables of word frequency and repetition have not been explored systematically in the case studies of the patients who make homophone substitutions.

Lexically "Direct" Spelling?

Although most researchers have not entertained such a notion, it may be possible that a "*direct*" connection exists between the auditory input lexicon and the orthographic output lexicon (labelled L-dir? in Figure 2.2). One interesting patient who is relevant to this possibility is Patterson's (1986) GE. Sadly, GE had very many impairments: he could not speak, repeat, read aloud, decide if spoken words rhymed or decide if spoken words (e.g. *friend* and *mate*) had the same meaning. However, GE was between 60% and 70% correct writing words to dictation. It is clear that GE was not spelling by the assembled route: he could spell only 34% of nonwods "correctly" and showed no effect of sound-to-spelling regularity on his accuracy of spelling words. Although not shared by Patterson, my interpretation of GE's spelling is that it was unlikely to be generated by the semantic route (as his comprehension was rather poor) and did not involve the phonological output lexicon (as his speech was very poor and he made only three homophone substitutions when spelling 80 homophones). Therefore, by exclusion, he was spelling by the direct route from the auditory input lexicon to the orthographic output lexicon!

The proposal that hearing a word directly activates its spelling is a fairly contentious one. It is difficult to find any direct evidence for such a direct route (and, indeed, the fact that many people find spelling such a difficult activity appears to speak against such a possibility), but two sources of data merit some consideration. First, there are some (rare) patients with "word meaning deafness" (see Ellis, 1984; Kohn & Friedman, 1986), who can write words they are unable to understand (indicating that the spoken word has not activated any semantic representation, thus rendering unavailable any semantic spelling route). The assembled route is unlikely to be responsible for their spelling as they can produce at least some irregular words. Although their spelling could be generated by the route via the phonological output lexicon, thcy have not been reported to produce homophone substitutions. Therefore, it is at least possible that they were spelling by the lexically direct route. The second line of evidence worth mentioning is the effect of orthography in auditory rhyme judgements in normal subjects. Seidenberg and Tanenhaus (1979) found that people performed rhyme decisions on spoken words reliably *faster* if the two words were spelled similarly (e.g. *cot–hot*) than if they were spelled with different patterns (e.g. *yacht–hot*). They also found that people were *slower* to respond to non-rhymes with similar spellings (e.g. *dead–bead*) than to non-rhymes with different spelling patterns (e.g. *fed–bead*). Effects of spelling in an essentially phonological task (which could, after all, be performed reliably by some non-lexical means, as we can easily decide if spoken nonwords rhyme) are intuitively surprising. The effects surely suggest that the orthographic representation of words can be activated implicitly (as the presence of non-rhymes with similar spellings, like *mint–pint*, might be expected to dissuade people from activating spelling in this task) and very quickly (as Seidenberg and Tanenhaus's mean rhyme decision latencies were typically less than 650 ms, with over 95% accuracy).

A direct (and automatic) route from the auditory input lexicon to the orthographic output lexicon might help to explain both the results of some patients and the data from normal subjects in the auditory rhyme decision task. Katz and Deser (1991) report a dysgraphic patient with extremely poor spelling production who, like normal subjects, showed an orthographic facilitation effect in rhyme decisions on spoken words. This suggests that the patient's deficit affected the production rather than the integrity of lexical orthographic representations. If only what is implicit could become effortlessly explicit, then overt spelling might become less frustrating. A recent survey (reported in the *Independent* newspaper of November 12, 1992) found that only 27% of 1000 adults questioned could correctly spell *accommodation*. The direct route to the orthographic output lexicon should activate the knowledge that this troublesome word is spelled with two *c*s and two *m*s; people may be able to spell, but counting is another problem.

REFERENCES

Barry, C. (1988). Modelling assembled spelling: convergence of data from normal subjects and "surface" dysgraphia. *Cortex*, **24**, 339–346.

Barry, C. & Seymour, P. H. K. (1988). Lexical priming and sound-to-spelling contingency effects in nonword spelling. *Quarterly Journal of Experimental Psychology*, **40A**, 5–40.

Baxter, D. M. & Warrington, E. K. (1987). Transcoding sound to spelling: single or multiple sound unit correspondence? *Cortex*, **23**, 11–28.

Baxter, D. M. & Warrington, E. K. (1988). The case for biphoneme processing: a rejoinder to Goodman-Schulman. *Cortex*, **24**, 137–142.

Beauvois, M.-F. & Dérouesné, J. (1981). Lexical or orthographic agraphia. *Brain*, **104**, 21–49.

Bub, D. & Kertesz, A. (1982a). Evidence for lexicographic processing in a patient with preserved written over oral single word naming. *Brain*, **105**, 697–717.

Bub, D. & Kertesz, A. (1982b). Deep agraphia. *Brain and Language*, **17**, 146–165.

Campbell, R. (1983). Writing nonwords to dictation. *Brain and Language*, **19**, 153–178.

Coltheart, M. (1985). Cognitive neuropsychology and the study of reading. In M. I. Posner & O. S. M. Marin (Eds), *Attention and Performance XI*. Hillsdale, NJ: LEA.

Ellis, A. W. (1982). Spelling and writing (and reading and speaking). In A. W. Ellis (Ed.), *Normality and Pathology in Cognitive Functions*. London: Academic Press.

Ellis, A. W. (1984). Introduction to Byrom Bramwell's (1897) case of word meaning deafness. *Cognitive Neuropsychology*, **1**, 245–258.

Funnell, E. (1983). Phonological processes in reading: new evidence from acquired dyslexia. *British Journal of Psychology*, **74**, 159–180.

Goodman, R. A. & Caramazza, A. (1986). Dissociation of spelling errors in written and oral spelling: the role of allographic conversion in writing. *Cognitive Neuropsychology*, **3**, 179–206.

Goodman-Schulman, R. & Caramazza, A. (1987) Patterns of dysgraphia and the nonlexical spelling process. *Cortex*, **23**, 143–148.

Hatfield, F. M. & Patterson, K. E. (1983). Phonological spelling. *Quarterly Journal of Experimental Psychology*, **35A**, 451–468.

Katz, R. B. & Deser, T. (1991) . Distinguishing representation deficits and processing deficits in a case of acquired dysgraphia. *Quarterly Journal of Experimental Psychology*, **43A**, 249–266.

Kohn, S. E. & Friedman, R. B. (1986). Word-meaning deafness: a phonological–semantic dissociation. *Cognitive Neuropsychology*, **3**, 291–308.

Newcombe, F. & Marshall, J. C. (1980). Transcoding and lexical stabilization in deep dyslexia. In M. Coltheart, K. Patterson & J. C. Marshall (Eds), *Deep Dyslexia*. London: Routledge and Kegan Paul.

Nolan, K. A. & Caramazza, A. (1983). An analysis of writing in a case of deep dyslexia. *Brain and Language*, **20**, 305–328.

Patterson, K. E. (1982). The relationship between reading and phonological coding: further neuropsychological observations. In A. W. Ellis (Ed.), *Normality and Pathology in Cognitive Functions*. London: Academic Press.

Patterson, K. E. (1986). Lexical but nonsemantic spelling? *Cognitive Neuropsychology*, **3**, 341–367.

Rapcsak, S. Z. & Rubens, A. B. (1990). Disruption of semantic influence on writing following a left prefrontal lesion. *Brain and Language*, **38**, 334–344.

Roeltgen, D. P. & Heilman, K. M. (1984). Lexical agraphia: further support for the two-system hypothesis of linguistic agraphia. *Brain*, **107**, 811–827.

Roeltgen, D. P., Rothi, L. G. & Heilman, K. M. (1986). Linguistic semantic agraphia: a dissociation of the lexical spelling system from semantics. *Brain and Language*, **27**, 257–280.

Roeltgen, D. P., Sevush, S. & Heilman, K. M. (1983). Phonological agraphia: writing by the lexical–semantic route. *Neurology*, **33**, 755–765.

Seidenberg, M. S. & Tanenhaus, M. K. (1979). Orthographic effects on rhyme monitoring. *Journal of Experimental Psychology: Human Learning and Memory*, **5**, 546–554.

Seymour, P. H. K. & Porpodas, C. D. (1980). Lexical and non-lexical processing of spelling in dyslexia. In U. Frith (Ed.), *Cognitive Processes in Spelling*. London: Academic Press.

Shallice, T. (1981). Phonological agraphia and the lexical route in writing. *Brain*, **104**, 412–429.

Shallice, T., Warrington, E. K. & McCarthy, R. (1983). Reading without semantics. *Quarterly Journal of Experimental Psychology*, **35A**, 111–138.

Treiman, R. (1986). The division between onsets and rimes in English syllables. *Journal of Memory and Language*, **25**, 476–491.

Wing, A. M. & Baddeley, A. D. (1980). Spelling errors in handwriting: a corpus and a distributional analysis. In U. Frith (Ed.), *Cognitive Processes in Spelling*. London: Academic Press.

Venezky, R. L. (1970). *The Structure of English Orthography*. The Hague: Mouton.

3

Writing and Spelling: The View from Linguistics

PHILIP J. SCHOLFIELD

University of Wales, Bangor

SOME BASIC DISTINCTIONS

Casual commentators on spelling often come up with observations such as:

In words like "hate", the "e" makes the preceding "a" long

or

English is not a very phonetic language

To the linguist, both these statements exhibit some confusion. One of the first principles of linguistics has always been the insistence on care regarding the distinction between speech and writing in language. In the first statement we see this is not explicitly taken, since the "e" must be being referred to as a written letter but the "long 'a'" is a sound (in many accents of English a diphthong rather than a long vowel, in fact). To clear up such statements, linguistics adopt the convention that words or bits of words cited in written orthography should be marked as such either by being underlined/italicized or by being enclosed in angle brackets 〈 〉. We shall adopt the latter convention. Anything cited as sounds should be in a recognized phonetic or phonemic transcription and placed between square brackets or slashes (the former

Handbook of Spelling: Theory, Process and Intervention. Edited by G. D. A. Brown and N. C. Ellis.
©1994 John Wiley & Sons Ltd.

for phonetic transcription, the latter for phonemic). We shall use the latter, since natural writing systems rarely reflect detailed differences of sound that would require phonetic transcription. In revised form, then, we might now say:

> In words like ⟨hate⟩, the ⟨e⟩ indicates that the preceding ⟨a⟩ is pronounced as /eɪ/.

It must be noted that talking in terms of "vowels" and "consonants" is equally ambiguous as both terms are regularly applied to both sounds and letters. The terms "vocoid" and "contoid" are available as differential terms for the sound, but not universally exploited.

Another insistence of linguistics is on the careful distinction between a language and the writing system used to write it. The second statement fails to make this, as no natural language *per se* can be more or less phonetic. None lacks sounds adequate for efficient communication. It is only writing systems that could be said to vary in this respect, particularly alphabetic ones, and this should be made clear in the wording. Additionally, as already indicated, it is phonemes rather than more specific phonetic units that letters usually correspond to (more or less well). More prosaically, then, the linguist might say:

> In the English writing system, letters correspond to phonemes less straightforwardly than in some other alphabets.

or

> The English alphabet is less phonemic than many others

Beyond emphasizing the *difference* between sound and writing, linguists also point to the *primacy* of the former. It soon becomes apparent in the study of writing that writing is attached to a language relatively more loosely than its sounds or grammar or even much of the vocabulary. Many languages lack a writing system altogether, and in those that have one, ontogenetically it is learnt later by speakers than other aspects. Furthermore, writing is far more amenable to conscious reform or replacement; writing systems spread round the world largely independently of languages—witness not just the variety of unconnected languages now using some version of the roman alphabet, but also how arabic writing, for example, has been adapted at various times to write as disparate a set of languages as Urdu, Turkish, Swahili and Malay.

THE LINGUISTIC PERSPECTIVE

It is something of a paradox that linguists, who, when considering questions of syntax or vocabulary, often use only data actually or potentally occurring in writing, at the smaller-scale levels of analysis typically focus on the sounds of language to the exclusion of letters, etc. Even if (as I shall do) we include as linguists language scholars such as Diringer and Gelb who might well not so label themselves, the body of purely linguistic work on writing and spelling is relatively sparse. I exclude from this account the small number of psycholinguists and applied linguists who *have* interested themselves in writing, as their focus would not be so clearly distinguishable from that of psychologists and educationalists.

A consequence of this is that, though there does exist a distinctive linguistic approach to writing systems, it is not as elaborated in theoretical constructs, terminology and so forth as its obvious partner, phonetics/phonology, which deals with sounds. Furthermore, while much work by linguistic phoneticians these days is indistinguishable from what might be done by workers in neighbouring disciplines such as physics, computer science and psychology, there are no obvious "grapheticians" of whom the same could be said. In so far as linguists have thought about the wider connections of the study of writing, it tends to be more on the socio-side, specifically in relation to the birth, death and spread of writing systems in history, and the matter of spelling and writing system reform and its success (or lack of it).

What then *is* the distinctive linguistic perspective on writing systems, spelling, etc.?

In a nutshell, what centrally interest linguists are the notions of structure, system and rules in language. In the area of writing this means primarily focusing on ways of capturing regularities in the correspondences between written symbols— "graphemes"—and other linguistic units. Here graphemes may be letters (in an alphabet), or so-called "characters" (in Chinese writing), or whatever visual shapes function as distinct units in a writing system. The "linguistic units" may be individual sounds (phonemes), groups of sounds, or some other units such as morphemes. In documenting these regularities, linguistics make explicit various assumptions and formulate rules in a variety of ways, with a variety of terminology, some traditional (e.g. "alphabet") and some novel (e.g. "grapheme"). In general, the rules proposed are mostly varieties of correspondence rule relating graphemes and other kinds of unit, rigorously stated and in all-or-none fashion. Those formulated with directionality, starting from some linguistic unit and detailing what graphemes represent those units on what occasions, may appropriately be called spelling rules.

Something clearly missing from this approach is much focus of attention on the substance of writing—the actual visible marks which often form the main fascination for the casual observer and clearly play some role in real-life learning and use of writing. To the linguist, what is important about writing is the values graphemes have, not what they look like, which is usually seen as somewhat accidental and uninteresting. As De Saussure noted in a famous analogy, what is crucial to the game of chess is the rules for how the pieces move, not their shape or material, which could be anything provided a bishop differs in *some* visible respect from a knight, and so forth. In fact, linguists have been rather purer in their resolve here than in the study of sounds, where phoneticians very much pursue the *substance* of sounds besides phonologists who focus on the system/rule aspects.

A note is in order here on terminology. Some do employ the terms "graphetics" and "graphology" when talking about writing, in analogous senses to "phonetics" and "phonology" when talking about sounds. Thus in "graphetics", one might study the visual shapes of graphemes (which may differ in different printed or handwritten styles), how they are written (e.g. compulsory stroke order in handwriting) and possibly how they are perceived (by human or machine). In graphology, one identifies the set of distinctive symbols used in a writing system and studies their sound or other values, their permissible combinations, and so forth. But these terms have not gained wide popularity. In part, perhaps, this is because of the wider currency of the term "graphology" in everyday use labelling the study of handwriting, particularly with an eye to predicting personality traits, something which a linguist would regard as, if anything, an offshoot of graphics, analogous to the study of individual voice quality by phoneticians.

On the whole, if one wishes to mark the difference between writing as visual shapes and writing as correspondence rules, it tends to be done by referring to the former as a script and the latter as a writing system (or orthography), though this terminological distinction is not universally adhered to. Thus, for instance, one might say that the English writing system may be written in a number of visual styles such as "italic script", "cursive script", etc.

The rule-focused interest of the linguist manifests itself in various modes, some of which we take up below.

Descriptive: the aim is simply to describe the correspondence rules for the writing system of a particular language at some period (current or not) as elegantly and economically as possible.

Contrastive: the aim is to compare two or more writing systems, identifying similarities and differences.

Typological: the aim is to establish what general kinds of rule system exist/have ever existed and categorize writing systems accordingly, often with an eye to generalizing about whether particular types of language seem to favour particular types of writing system.

Historical/diachronic: the aim is to trace the development of writing from its origins to the present-day writing systems observable in use, with particular attention to any discernible irreversible progression from one kind of rule system to another.

In all this a word of warning is in order, particularly for the psychologist. Often linguists' rules *appear* to be saying something directly about what people actually do when using language. If a linguist offers some rules about what sounds the letters of the English alphabet correspond to, he/she can easily be construed as offering a model of one step in the reading process. Indeed, he/she can be construed as supporting the view that people do in fact read by decoding words letter by letter, that "phonics" is therefore the best approach to teaching reading, and so forth. However, this is not usually how the linguist intends them. Rather, he/she is interested simply in language and writing as an object, about which some generalizations can be made. Typically, he/she will deal only with rules in the standard language, and in a depersonalized form (e.g. rules for spelling all words may be considered regardless of the fact that real speakers only know subsets of them). Usually the best generalizations are arrived at by breaking the written word up into smaller units that are matched with some other linguistic units, but this is purely on the basis of economy of description, elegance and other general scientific principles. The linguist will not typically claim any psychological reality for his rules or conduct empirical studies to support them.

As a consequence, if psychologists (or psycholinguists) think that linguists' rules make interesting bases for hypotheses to test about what actually goes on in the reading or writing process, or learning to read and write, it is up to them to test them and prove their psychological reality. Indeed, for the psychologist probably the main use of the linguistic view of writing, apart from perhaps tidying up a few concepts and supplying some basic terminology, *is* as a source of such hypotheses. But the relevance of the linguist's statements to actual human processing *cannot* be taken as established *a priori*. Indeed, there is plenty of evidence that real speakers do not necessarily store and process language in what to the linguist would be the most economical way (e.g. fluent readers may well not process every letter of a word using sound-to-letter correspondence rules even when writing in a much more regular alphabetic system than English, but rather draw on a large stock of whole-word visual images).

TYPES OF WRITING SYSTEM

One achievement of linguists and allied language scholars has been the establishment of an overall picture of types of writing system. Nowadays, with Sampson, usually four main types are recognized, based on the kinds of correspondence between graphemes and other linguistic units that are involved. Of course, typology is also possible based on the visual appearance of symbols used in writing systems, for example by analysis of the repertory of kinds of stroke shape needed to write the symbols in a particular script, but this has not proved very interesting to linguists. The basic systems one can recognize are:

1. Logographic. Here in principle each written symbol corresponds to a morpheme— the minimal meaningful unit of language, which may be a simple word or part of word, for example the elements we write as ⟨happy⟩, ⟨pillow⟩, ⟨un-⟩ or ⟨-ing⟩ in English. In the purest form nothing about the graphemes reflects sounds at all, so if English were written this way there would be no strokes as part of the symbol for ⟨happy⟩ systematically recurring in that for ⟨pillow⟩ reflecting the /p/ sound they have in common. The only rules that are economical to make relate some visual symbol as a whole to some morpheme. In such a system typically a morpheme is represented by the same grapheme wherever it appears, with whatever variation in its pronunciation, and morphemes that have the same sound but quite different meanings ("homophones") are written differently.

The remaining three types of writing are called "phonographic", because the graphemes are all linked to sounds in some way:

2. Syllabic. In such a system the graphemes basically match up with syllables— typically vowel + consonant combinations. If English were so written it would have unrelated symbols for syllables like /pɪ/ and /hæ/ which it would string together to write words—so ⟨happy⟩ and ⟨pillow⟩ would each be spelt with two symbols, that for /pɪ/ occurring in both.
3. Alphabetic. Here in simplest form each grapheme corresponds to a phoneme. We shall look at this type in more detail later. However, one point that should be made clear from the start is that what linguists will regard as graphemes in an

alphabetic writing system are not necessarily identical with "letters". For instance, it is easy to demonstrate that ⟨ll⟩ and ⟨ch⟩ function as distinct graphemes from ⟨l⟩, ⟨c⟩ and ⟨h⟩ in Welsh writing. Not only do they have clearly different sound values from their parts, but dictionaries put words beginning with ⟨ch⟩ in a separate list after those beginning with ⟨c⟩, and paragraphs designated by letters on an official form run ⟨a⟩, ⟨b⟩, ⟨c⟩, ⟨ch⟩, ⟨d⟩, ⟨dd⟩. In English writing such "digraphs" are not so institutionally demarcated, but they are nonetheless recognizable. Indeed, some would recognize three graphemes for ⟨ch⟩—by virtue of its corresponding respectively to /k/, /tʃ/ and /ʃ/ in words like ⟨chaos⟩, ⟨chair⟩, ⟨champagne⟩. Graphemes may even be discontinuous sequences of letters, as English ⟨a-e⟩ representing /eɪ/ in ⟨hate⟩.

4. Featural. Here the basic graphemes match up with sound components rather than whole phonemes. If English were written this way it might, for instance, write the /m/ sound with a symbol analysable into two minimal graphemes, one of which occurred also in the symbol for /b/ and the other in the symbol for /n/. Thus the graphemes would effectively be writing sound components like "articulation involving the two lips" and "nasal sound".

It is hard to find completely pure examples of the above systems. Most existing writing systems are "transitional", in the sense of being poised somewhere between two of the above. Thus, though modern Chinese writing is usually classified as logographic, it has some syllabic features. The writing system of modern Hindi, though usually classed as an alphabet, retains some traits typical of a syllabic system.

What is more unexpected perhaps is to see "mixed" systems, i.e. more than one writing system used at once. This is the case with modern Japanese writing. In essence, parts of some words (the roots of content words of Japanese or Chinese origin) are written with logographic symbols (called "kanji"), while the remaining words and parts of words are written in syllabic symbols (called "kana").

THE EVOLUTIONARY HISTORY OF WRITING

Unlike language as a whole, writing can be traced and documented more or less from its origin to the present day. Fascinating accounts are available (e.g. by Diringer, 1968 and Gelb, 1952) rich with details of the historical, cultural and social concomitants of the development of writing and illustrations of the changes in its visual appearance. This cannot be recapitulated here. To the linguist the key area of interest is the origin and subsequent evolution of the various correspondence types, some issues relating to which are now mentioned.

Whether or not one believes that writing was only invented once (the "monogenesis" question), the earliest writing clearly was "iconic" in substance and logographic in system, i.e. the symbols were pictorial, resembling typical referents of the morphemes or words they wrote. A (stylized) picture of a man (or a distinctive part of a man!) was the written symbol for the morpheme meaning "man", and so forth. Now where writing is representational in appearance, it can be hard to distinguish from "picture language" (or what some call "ideography"— idea writing), which linguists would be at pains to distinguish from "writing proper". The former occurs where one or more pictures or diagrams are used to convey a message, but with no established correspondence existing between specific pictures (or bits of them) and specific words or other units of language. The message conveyed could be put into words in a variety of ways, just as with contemporary sign languages. "Picture language" as against "picture writing" is used today, for example when one draws a sketch map to show someone how to get somewhere, or decodes a road sign showing bent figures moving across a road as variously saying "Watch out for old folk", "Beware of senior citizens crossing", etc.

Though the details are unclear, it is widely assumed that some use of pictures in "picture language" mode preceded the first true writing. The great innovation was the association of specific pictures with specific words. It was probably made first in ancient Sumeria, the original home of Abraham and today the no-fly zone of southern Iraq. From here on, while the pictures rapidly become unrecognizable as such, there seems to have been a reasonably consistent trend in the development of the system aspect of writing: logographic ⟩ syllabic ⟩ alphabetic (⟩ featural in one instance only—Korean). Changes occurred more often in the process of a writing system being adopted and adapted to write a different language than as developments accompanying the same language. Today some writing systems evidence little change from the first stage of this development (e.g. Chinese), others evidence having moved on to the syllabic stage (e.g. Japanese kana), but most approximate the alphabetic stage (e.g. various versions of the roman alphabet and arabic writing). There is some agreement that the development of the alphabet only occurred once, around 1000 BC, with credit shared between Semitic inhabitants of what is now the Holy Land and Lebanon and the Greeks. Modern alphabets or near-alphabets are descendants of (or copies from descendants of) either the Greek or early Semitic alphabets.

THE HISTORICAL DEVELOPMENT OF THE ENGLISH WRITING SYSTEM

The writing associated with the English language has changed considerably both in appearance and system since the arrival of the Anglo-Saxons in the fifth century AD. Visually the angular upper case runes resemble little the neat lower case of the Old English "insular hand", and both these and the more flowery "Gothic hand" of Middle English produce letter shapes that are often distant from their modern counterparts. But as usual what interests the linguist is the development of the *system*. Here too, though at all periods English writing would be classed as alphabetic, dramatic changes have occurred, far beyond what might be expected from the slight changes in membership of the set of letters constituting the alphabet at different periods of English. The following account is of necessity simplified and selective, attempting to illustrate the essential features through relatively uncomplicated examples (see Scragg, 1974, Chapters 1–5 for the standard account).

From the Arrival of the Anglo-Saxons to the
Norman Conquest: Old English

Old English (OE) writing, whether in the form of runic or roman script (which we confine discussion to here), seems to have approximated quite closely what some would regard as the ideal for an alphabet—one-to-one correspondence between graphemes and phonemes. It used some letters that are not familiar today, such as ⟨æ⟩ for /æ/ (the vowel sound of modern ⟨hat⟩). And some letters that we do recognize today were used in different values, for example ⟨c⟩ on occasion wrote /tʃ/ (the initial sound of in modern ⟨chop⟩), but never an /s/ sound. However, this should not distract one from the considerable simplicity of the system. Thus there were (as far as we know) no silent letters. ⟨hring⟩ "ring" was actually pronounced with an /h/ and a /g/ as /hring/; ⟨mæsse⟩ "mass" corresponded to a sound shape /mæsse/ with lengthened /ss/ and the ⟨e⟩ on the end pronounced. There were a few digraphs, such as ⟨sc⟩ uniformly used to write the /ʃ/ sound as in ⟨scip⟩ "ship".

The irregularities then are relatively few. There was one marked case of two alternative letters being used for the same sound: ⟨þ⟩ and ⟨ð⟩ could be used more or less at the whim of particular writers in particular instances to write the /θ/ phoneme, as in ⟨þynne⟩ or ⟨ðynne⟩ "thin". There were more cases of the reverse—one letter having more than one sound value. For example, ⟨c⟩ in some words corresponded to /k/, in some to /tʃ/. This is often predictable from the adjacent vowel—the former correspondence holding with low and back vowels, the latter with high front ones. Thus ⟨catt⟩ "cat" writes the sound /katt/; ⟨munuc⟩ "monk" /munuk/; but ⟨cidan⟩ "chide" /tʃiːdan/ and ⟨brec⟩ "breeches" /bretʃ/. There are, however, some exceptions, such as ⟨cene⟩ writing /keːne/ "keen". More sweepingly, vowel graphemes represented both short and long vowels of a given quality: ⟨god⟩ was written for both /god/ "god" and /goːd/ "good". Vowel length is generally not predictable on the basis of any surrounding sounds in OE.

Being a reasonably "pure" alphabetic system, if words sounded different (barring instances of correspondences like those in the last paragraph), they would be written differently, regardless of any morphological connection. Thus OE writes ⟨smæl⟩ "small" (singular) but ⟨smalu⟩ "small" (plural), changing the vowel letter used in the stem because the quality of the first vowel sound was a different one in the plural, even though the same root morpheme is present. Contrast the lack of spelling difference in comparable modern English cases like ⟨child⟩–⟨children⟩.

Conversely, if two words sounded the same they were written the same, despite being quite unrelated in meaning. For example, ⟨ær⟩ was written for two quite different words, /æːr/ "brass" and /æːr/ "before". Contrast again modern English practice (e.g. ⟨heir⟩ and ⟨air⟩). However, by the tenth century, which marks the high point of the OE writing system, there was (as in modern English) little variation in how a given wordform was spelt; where variants are recorded they usually reflect different dialectal pronunciations of the word, not different ways of writing one and the same sound shape. The speculation would be that the system was a little harder for the reader than the writer/speller.

From the Norman Conquest to the
End of the Middle Ages: Middle English

In any language there are sound changes constantly in progress, and by the Norman Conquest some sounds of many words had changed or begun to change. At first the spelling changed accordingly. Thus the word for "home" in OE was pronounced /hɑːm/ (sounding like modern ⟨harm⟩), in early Middle English (ME) /hɔːm/ (with the vowel sound of modern English ⟨born⟩). In due course the spelling changed from ⟨ham⟩ to ⟨hom⟩. An /h/ sound before a consonant was lost, so we see OE ⟨hlid⟩ "lid" replaced by the spelling ⟨lid⟩. The sounds /i/ and /y/ existed as distinct phonemes in early OE, the latter sounding like the ⟨ue⟩ of modern French ⟨rue⟩, and were written as ⟨i⟩ and ⟨y⟩ respectively. However, they merged into /i/ in late OE/early ME. As a result we see OE ⟨hyll⟩ "hill" coming to be written ⟨hill⟩.

A more complicated change concerns the sounds [f] and [v], which were clearly variants of one phoneme in OE, and so logically both written with one letter—⟨f⟩. Simplifying slightly, the [v] sound could be thought of as at that period just a variant of [f] that occurred in certain environments, such as between vowels—so ⟨finger⟩ and ⟨cræft⟩ when spoken contained the [f] variant, ⟨drifen⟩ and ⟨ofer⟩ the [v] one. By ME these two sounds had, through a variety of means, come to be recognized as separate phonemes /f/ and /v/, as they are in English today. Along with this the letter ⟨v⟩ (also written ⟨u⟩ at this period) was adopted from Latin to write the latter and the ⟨f⟩ retained for the former (with the ultimate exception of ⟨of⟩). Thus a one-grapheme–one-phoneme system was largely maintained.

In OE words were borrowed from other languages—notably Latin (in a church context) and Old Norse (the language of the Danes/Vikings, who, of course, settled in parts of northeastern England such as York). These were adopted without great effect on the sounds or spelling of OE. After the Conquest, however, there was an increasing influx of French words into English, many containing unfamiliar sounds or sound combinations. Thus French words like ⟨vanite⟩ "vanity" contained a /v/ sound in a position where it would not have occurred in OE, and written with the ⟨v/u⟩ letter. Such loans were typically adopted with little change to the French pronunciation and spelling and no doubt helped to promote both the sound and spelling changes described at the end of the last paragraph. Again words like ⟨chois⟩ "choice" contained a diphthongal sound new to English. In this instance, its spelling was adopted direct from French. By contrast, words like the French ⟨danger⟩ contained a nasalized vowel in authentic pronunciation. On first appearance in English they were typically written with the novel spelling ⟨aun⟩, as ⟨daunger⟩, which suggests that for a time an effort was made to approximate the French pronunciation with a diphthongal /aun/ sound. An indirect effect of borrowing is seen in the appearance of ⟨sch⟩ replacing OE ⟨sc⟩ to write /ʃ/. This probably occurred to avoid a situation where ⟨sc⟩ wrote two alternative sounds when loans from French were made in which ⟨sc⟩ represented the sound combination /sk/ (as indeed it had in early OE before /sk/ became /ʃ/ in English), for example ⟨scars⟩ "scarce".

A related area of change involved the adoption of new conventions for letter–sound correspondences, and sometimes new letters or digraphs, from Latin, French or elsewhere, in instances where *no* innovations in the sounds were involved at all.

In some cases this removed a shortcoming of the OE system. For example, the ⟨ch⟩ digraph was introduced to write the /tʃ/ sound and the Latin ⟨th⟩ slowly replaced the OE ⟨þ⟩ and ⟨ð⟩. In others there was, eventually, a straight replacement of the OE convention. For example, the sound combination /kw/, which had been written in OE quite regularly with the sequence of letters ⟨c⟩ + ⟨w⟩ in words like ⟨cwic⟩ "quick", came to be written with the French digraph ⟨qu⟩. Such replacements, though in a sense "unnecessary", did not greatly alter the complexity of the writing system, once completed.

If these changes had been the only ones, the ME version of the English alphabet would have had a system in essence much like the OE one, simply adjusted to the fact that the sounds being written were different in some words and some different correspondence conventions had been adopted.

However, what makes the alphabet as used for ME much more complicated than that for OE (with knock-on effect on modern English writing) is the growth of a plethora of variant spellings for the same sound. In part this is due to not all sound changes being dealt with as quickly or neatly as so far suggested, in part to unresolved competition between rival conventions for writing certain sounds. The ultimate reason for this "anarchy" seems to be largely the fact that written English, which in the late centuries before the Conquest had become the instrument of a centralized English government, had this function taken over by French and Latin for several centuries under the Normans, and so became somewhat marginalized and open to uncontrolled differentiation.

Repercussions of a sound change we can illustrate by returning to the merger of the /i/ and /y/ sounds mentioned above. This led not just to words previously written with a ⟨y⟩ being written with an ⟨i⟩, but also the reverse as the two letters competed as ways of writing one sound. So we find the word for "lid" written ⟨lyd⟩ as well as ⟨lid⟩, though it had never contained the /y/ sound. In fact, there was a prolonged period when most words with an /i/ sound, whether coming from OE words with /i/ or /y/ in or borrowed from French, occurred with either letter used—for example ⟨happi⟩, ⟨syx⟩, ⟨ryver⟩, ⟨choys⟩, ⟨symply⟩, as well as ⟨happy⟩, ⟨six⟩, ⟨river⟩, ⟨chois⟩, ⟨simply⟩. An additional influence here no doubt was the fact that the same interchangeability existed in medieval Latin writing. A few words like ⟨gipsy⟩/⟨gypsy⟩ still exhibit this uncertainty today.

Other major sources of variant spellings arising similarly after mergers or losses of sounds include the following. Long consonants came to sound identical with single ones; there ensued extensive competition of double and single consonant spellings. Many short vowel sounds at the ends of words were lost leading to extensive variant spellings of words with and without a final written ⟨e⟩. Thus ⟨lidd⟩, ⟨lide⟩, ⟨lidde⟩ are all recorded variant spellings of ⟨lid⟩, though this word had never had a double consonant or final vowel as part of its sound shape. The practice of paying copyists by length may have encouraged use of the longer variants!

In some instances spelling variation consequent on sound change already existed in French and this was borrowed into ME along with loan words. The classic example involves initial ⟨h⟩. Though the sound /h/ had already disappeared in French, many words retained alternative spellings with it still there—for example ⟨able⟩/⟨hable⟩, ⟨onour⟩/⟨honour⟩, ⟨orrible⟩/ ⟨horrible⟩. Forms both with and without the silent ⟨h⟩

appear also in ME, and in some cases "spelling pronunciation" eventually restored the /h/ to the word's sound shape.

A slightly different source of complexity arising from sound change was where an OE sound changed differently in different regions of Britain, and was consequently written differently in different areas. In the unstandardized ME era of English writing, variant spellings of this sort often entered the general repertoire of variant spellings that writers far afield felt able to draw on, whether or not they also borrowed the corresponding regional pronunciation. Thus, for example, the OE /y/ sound became /u/ rather than /i/ in the West Country, and so went on to become /ʌ/ (the vowel of words like ⟨cup⟩ in modern received pronunciation). But we find the word for "hill" written ⟨hull⟩ as well as ⟨hill⟩ and ⟨hyll⟩, even where the writer would only have said the word as /hil/. In modern ⟨busy⟩ a spelling of this origin survives today, while in ⟨crutch⟩ (from OE ⟨crycc⟩) both the western spelling *and* pronunciation have become standard.

Further complexity was created by simple rivalry of different conventions where no real sound change was involved. For instance, there were numerous rivals to ⟨sch⟩ as the first major replacement of the OE ⟨sc⟩ spelling of /ʃ/ (which as a sound has remained unchanged from late OE to today). We can see some in the spellings recorded for the word for "fish" (OE ⟨fisc⟩), which appears as ⟨fiss⟩, ⟨fich⟩, ⟨fix⟩ as well as the commoner ⟨fisch⟩ and ⟨fish⟩. Multiply these by the ⟨i⟩/⟨y⟩, final vowel and double consonant variations already mentioned and a staggering array of variants are possible for this simple word. In fact, not all possible combinations are recorded, but a good selection are found—for example ⟨fisse⟩, ⟨fyssh⟩, ⟨fishsh⟩ and even ⟨fischsch⟩!

Also witness the case of how to write the long vowel sounds, as in the word for "home" (ME /hɔːm/). Following the OE convention, we find the spelling ⟨o⟩, just as for a short vowel. But another convention in competition was to double the vowel letter. Thus beside ⟨hom⟩ we find the spelling ⟨hoom⟩, plus of course ⟨home⟩ and ⟨hoome⟩. The range of variant spellings of vowels was often not only similar for short and long vowel sounds of a given quality but also overlapped that of vowels of different qualities. Even in this simple example we can see this: the word for "hum", which had an /u/ vowel sound in ME, could also be written ⟨home⟩. Similarly, the words we now write as ⟨sock⟩, ⟨soak⟩ and ⟨suck⟩, with respectively /o/, /oː/ and /u/ vowel sounds in ME, had the shared variant spelling ⟨soke⟩. Thus in the end the proliferation of multiple spellings of specific phonemes resulted also in the existence of multiple pronunciations for a given grapheme.

In instances where a French convention competed with an English one for writing the same sound, often there was prolonged coexistence of difference conventions, with a predominance of the French convention to write words recently borrowed from French. An example here is the practice of writing the /s/ sound with ⟨c⟩ rather than OE ⟨s⟩. The ⟨c⟩ spelling was standard in some French words such as ⟨grace⟩ and ⟨cite⟩ "city", but not others such as ⟨chois⟩. At first it was a common variant in ME only for such words when borrowed, but it later spread to other words of French origin, so the spelling ⟨choice⟩ entered the ring. The ⟨c⟩ even spread to some native English words, so ⟨ice⟩ appeared beside ⟨ise⟩/⟨yse⟩ (OE ⟨is⟩).

It must be noted, however, that since the variety of ways of writing a given sound was on the whole a matter of free variation, in the sense of being up to the preference of the particular writer, the multiplicity of spellings presumably created more problems for the reader than the writer. A point also worth making is that the lack of morphemic reference of the writing system remained as in OE, despite the range of variant spellings available. Homophones were not systematically distinguished: ⟨mete⟩, ⟨mett⟩, ⟨meet⟩, ⟨meete⟩ are all ME spellings of *either* the word for "flesh" *or* the word for "to encounter". Indeed, as we have seen, many words that were *not* complete homophones were not distinguished either.

The Tudor and Stuart Periods: Early Modern English

With the re-emergence of English as the language of government, the invention of printing in the fifteenth century and the spread of education, there began to be interest in standardizing and simplifying the writing system again. However, the revival of interest in classical scholarship, and a desire to "fix" the system regardless of sound change (just as Latin spelling has been fixed), had the effect of adding yet further complexity to the correspondences between sounds and letters.

Towards the end of the ME period a major change known as the "Great Vowel Shift" affected a whole range of English vowel sounds. However, unlike in previous centuries, new spellings did not emerge reflecting the changes. Thus, for example, the long /i:/ sound of a word like ⟨mil⟩ "mile" moved on to become a diphthong /əi/ (with the first element sounding like the first sound in modern ⟨about⟩). But spellings with ⟨ei⟩ or ⟨ai⟩ attempting to reflect the new sound are rarely recorded. In one way this stopped further complexity arising, since if ME custom continued the new spelling would simply have been added to the range already there, and not replaced ⟨mil⟩, ⟨mile⟩, ⟨myle⟩, etc. Confusion would have been great since around the same time the long /e:/ sound of a word like ⟨mel⟩/⟨meal⟩/⟨mele⟩ "time for food" moved to become /i:/, so spellings like ⟨mil⟩ might have started appearing for this word too. Again we do not find this happening. However, this development, or lack of it, did lead ultimately to the modern situation where English vowel letters often represent sound values quite unlike those of the same letters in other systems based on the roman alphabet.

Where sound changes led to mergers of sounds previously separate, the situation was different. As in previous centuries, this often produced more spelling variants. For instance, the aspirated "w" sound usually written with ⟨wh⟩ (and still heard in some Scottish accents) began to be replaced by an ordinary /h/ sound in words like ⟨who⟩, ⟨whom⟩ and by an ordinary /w/ sound more generally (e.g. in ⟨when⟩). Consequently we see not only spellings like ⟨ho⟩ and ⟨wen⟩ but also ⟨whome⟩ for ⟨home⟩ which had only ever had an /h/ sound initially, and ⟨whelk⟩ for ⟨welk⟩, which had only ever had the unaspirated /w/ sound.

Borrowing of new words continued, especially from Latin and Greek and contemporary French. On the whole this did not involve new sounds for the English writing system to deal with, as they were adapted to the English pronunciation of the time. However, they were often adopted without adjustment of the spelling conventions. Thus, for example, French ⟨machine⟩ instanced ⟨ch⟩ writing the /ʃ/ sound, rather than /tʃ/. Latin ⟨chorus⟩ contained ⟨ch⟩ writing a /k/. Though such conventions tended not to spread much beyond the words they had been borrowed with (unlike French conventions in ME), they naturally added to the overall complexity of both grapheme-to-sound and sound-to-grapheme correspondences.

Another consequence of the new scholarship of the period was the interest in tracing the origins of English words. This was often followed by the creation of new spellings for words which (supposedly) reflected better their older forms. This was particularly common for words of French origin which had entered English in ME. In effect spellings were borrowed from the past, so they often reflected features of the words' former pronunciation that were no longer current. A typical example is the spelling ⟨debte⟩/⟨debt⟩ which arose beside the spellings ⟨det⟩ and ⟨dette⟩ inherited from ME. The new spelling reflects the fact that the word is ultimately traceable to Latin ⟨debitum⟩, though the /b/ sound had gone from it before it reached English, via borrowing from French. The ME-based spelling actually reflected the contemporary pronunciation better. Similarly, compare etymologized spellings ⟨receipt⟩, ⟨salmon⟩ and ⟨phantasy⟩ with ME ⟨receite⟩, ⟨samoun⟩ and ⟨fantasy⟩.

Some learned spellings of this sort were, of course, based on misunderstandings of a word's history. Thus ⟨scissors⟩ and ⟨anchor⟩ beside inherited spellings ⟨sisoures⟩ and ⟨ancour⟩ show added letters not supported by today's knowledge of the history of these words. However, the learned spellings, misconceived or not, often overtook the older ones and even in some cases led to the words having their sound shapes altered to suit the new spelling. Examples are: ⟨corpse⟩, ⟨falcon⟩, ⟨admiral⟩ and ⟨throne⟩, which had been pronounced in ME in accordance with the ME spellings ⟨corse⟩, ⟨faucon⟩, ⟨amiral⟩ and ⟨trone⟩. Where such spelling pronunciation did not ensue, the net effect of the new etymologizing spellings was, of course, to make yet more complex the correspondences of English, by proliferating instances of "silent" letters in specific words.

In contrast with the preceding trends, the Early Modern English (ENE) period also saw a deliberate move to reform English spelling, argued for in various ways by scholars and schoolmasters of the time. The main goal was perceived as being to reduce the variant spellings acceptable for any given word to just one—a goal which with few exceptions like ⟨jail⟩/⟨gaol⟩ and ⟨judgment⟩/⟨judgement⟩ has been achieved today. However, this goal of simplification is not at all the same as that of getting back to a system with more or less one-to-one grapheme–phoneme correspondences. The latter tends to achieve the former automatically (witness the OE system), but the reverse does not hold at all. In fact, a major difference of opinion developed in the late sixteenth century between scholars like Hart, an early phonetician, who wanted reform more in the direction of restoring one-to-one letter correspondence with phonemes, and ones like Mulcaster, a schoolmaster, who wanted appeal to sound to be moderated by "reason and custom".

It was the latter view which prevailed, and we can see in published lists of recommended spellings the ways in which reason and custom manifested themselves. For instance, preference was nearly always given to the learned alternative spelling, where one existed, rather than any of the inherited ones, which were often closer to the sound, because it was typically better known in the period when this fixing of spelling was occurring. Nor was there any effort to adjust recent foreign loans to English spelling (e.g. to replace ⟨machine⟩ with ⟨masheen⟩), as this would have involved total abandonment of the customary spelling of the time. Otherwise, definitive spellings were selected from those in use for any given word with *some* eye to which represented the sounds most directly (look again at the examples above with attention to which variant "won" in each case). An important new element in all this was the policy of picking different spellings for words which sounded the same (i.e. avoiding homophones becoming homographs)—for example ⟨hole⟩ and ⟨whole⟩, where both spellings were available at the time for both words. In some cases words that had developed variant senses that had drifted apart eventually had different variant spellings fixed on different senses, thus tangibly splitting the word into two—for example ⟨flower⟩ and ⟨flour⟩.

Along with the above, some rules familiar today did begin to become established. One of interest in connection with variation we have looked at earlier was the restriction of final silent ⟨e⟩ to spellings of words with a long vowel or diphthong sound. Another was the limitation of doubled final consonant letters to just a few (including ⟨l⟩, which Mulcaster liked doubled for decorative reasons), though medial consonant doubling was left less systematic (cf. ⟨pity⟩ with ⟨ditty⟩). A third was the solution of the ⟨i⟩–⟨y⟩ variation, with the former usually being preferred medially in words and the latter finally. As can be seen, these were all limitations and rationalizations of contemporary practices, not radical breaks from tradition. But the net effect of the way in which unique spellings were chosen for words was to make the system harder for the writer/speller than it had been at any time before, leaving English writing with many more graphemes per phoneme (in different words) than the reverse. It is at this period that the long history of recorded complaint about people's bad spelling begins!

Printers also favoured the limitation of spelling variation, and would typically not print exactly the spellings provided by an author in his or her manuscript. This helped popularize standard spellings, though for a time they actually perpetuated some variation for purely mechanical purposes. When typesetting they were unable to fine-tune spacing to achieve right justification of text, as on today's word processor, and instead would use variant spellings with double consonants and/or final ⟨e⟩ to achieve this when required. Apart from this, the choice of variants favoured by printers tended to be in line with the suggestions of the pedagogical reformers. For commercial reasons, they too were inclined to go along with what was likely to be most acceptable to the public.

By 1700 with few exceptions today's British English spellings had already been fixed on. In America, Webster's reforms had some minor effects later (e.g. ⟨labor⟩ versus British ⟨labour⟩). Of course, words have continued to be borrowed into English, usually without much modification to their spelling, and so introduced more variety of correspondences in specific words, for example ⟨cafe⟩ and ⟨sake⟩ "Japanese wine" evidence final ⟨e⟩ not used as a mute indicator of preceding vowel quality. Also sound change has continued to affect the English language but this is no longer reflected in any way by the writing system. One example is loss of the /r/ sound in certain positions in received pronunciation, for example ⟨fear⟩, ⟨firm⟩. Another is the reduction of vowels in unstressed syllables in words like ⟨abolition⟩, where the second vowel sound now has the /ə/ quality (like the first vowel of ⟨about⟩), not the /ɒ/ sound in ⟨abolish⟩, where the corresponding vowel is stressed.

Of course, from Hart onwards there have always been individuals and bodies interested in more or less radical reform of the English writing system. In recent times

Shaw and the Simplified Spelling Society stand out (see Scragg, 1974, Chapter 6 for a review, and Sampson, 1985, Chapter 10). Since there seems little prospect of any of their proposals having any effect, I shall not discuss them here. In any case, there is a prevailing view among linguists that the system is not as bad as it seems, unless one allows oneself to formulate rules only in the naivest way—see the following.

THE ENGLISH WRITING SYSTEM TODAY

One kind of "explanation" of the current English writing system is the preceding, historical, one that traces how the correspondences have come to be how they are. However, linguists attempting to describe the rules of language at any given period usually aim to do so "synchronically"—that is, without reference to what is known of earlier history. The best explanation of the English writing system of today in this approach is that with the best generalizations that can be found to relate together today's spellings and other relevant linguistic units of English and the fewest exceptions that just have to be listed. We consider here how such accounts could be formulated in linguistic unit-to-grapheme direction rather than the reverse (which in fact is more favoured in published accounts of English writing). Indeed, this is the harder direction, as may be guessed just from the fact that, for the historical reasons seen above, English today has around 45 phonemes but over 100 graphemes (on Wijk's (1966) analysis).

Synchronic accounts are likely to be of more immediate interest to psychologists than historical ones since one usually assumes that ordinary speakers/writers of languages do not have details of history available to them when formulating or using any psychological rules. However, we shall see that the history of writing is by no means irrelevant to understanding some of these synchronic accounts. We here consider the four main kinds of approach that linguists suggest, in characteristically idealized form (see further Sampson, 1985, Chapter 10). They differ in essence in what kind of linguistic unit is taken as the most useful starting point for generalization and what they are prepared to assume as being "there" to exploit in synchronic descriptions. It is worth noting that what constitutes an "irregular" spelling is entirely dependent on such choices.

The Surface Phonemic Approach

This approach in its purest form would take as starting point simply the phonemic representation of English words (in received pronunciation for the UK) and look for the best phoneme-to-grapheme rules that could be formulated to predict a word's spelling from it. The assumption is that English writing is simply a version, albeit a poor one, of a pure alphabetic system like the Spanish or Old English alphabet.

In order to achieve the best generalization possible, rules in such an account are usually allowed to be formulated not only with reference to features of sound (neighbouring phonemes/ syllables/ stress, etc.) but also to surrounding letters. "Consonant letters are doubled after the spellings of short vowel sounds in the middle of a word" is an example of the former; "'i' before 'e' except after 'c'" illustrates the latter. The latter rule, of course, assumes that it is somehow already known that a ⟨c⟩ occurs in the spelling; like all rules that refer to other letters in their specification, it has no predictive power for the spellings of particular words without some sound-to-grapheme rules having been first applied in order to supply part of the spelling.

Within this approach there is room for a wide range of detailed choices about how to formulate rules—especially how "delicate" it is cost-effective to make them. For example, the medial consonant doubling rule as given above would predict correctly ⟨merry⟩, ⟨rabbit⟩, ⟨pretty⟩ but have many exceptions such as ⟨very⟩ and ⟨habit⟩, and with medial /v/ the exceptions far outnumber the spellings that follow this rule. One might therefore decide it is preferable to make the rule a little more complicated, and so reduce the number of exceptions to be listed, by saying "Consonant letters other than ⟨v⟩ are doubled after short vowels in the middle of a word". In this formulation ⟨never⟩ is regular and ⟨navvy⟩ is not, while with the original, simpler, rule the reverse is the case.

Among spellings that no amount of contortion can predict without listing in this approach are: where silent consonant letters should be written—for example in ⟨knee⟩ and ⟨condemn⟩; how /s/ is written—for example ⟨sit⟩ and ⟨university⟩ but ⟨city⟩ and ⟨electricity⟩; how /ə/ is written—for example the first vowels of ⟨canal⟩ and ⟨condemn⟩; how /iː/ is written—for example ⟨meat⟩ but ⟨meet⟩. The last illustrates another common source of considerable difficulty. Both ⟨ee⟩ and ⟨ea⟩ are very common as spellings of /iː/ and it is not obviously "natural" to pick on either as the "rule" and list words with the other as the "exceptions".

Questions for the psychologist to answer with this approach include what precise rules of this sort might be psychologically real in people (more or less delicate, with greater or lesser reliance on rote-learnt lists) and whether or not real people do not also use rules with more sophisticated bases such as those below. Also, of course, real people would not necessarily have RP or standard US phonemic representations available to start from, but regionally accented ones or, in the case of children and foreign learners, partial and "erroneous" ones.

The Deep Phonological Approach

This approach exploits some analysis of English sounds that recognizes a "deeper" level than phonemes (the original being that of Chomsky & Halle, 1968). The assumption is that a morpheme has (normally) *one* basic sound shape that is not exactly like that of all, or perhaps any, of its surface phonemic manifestations in words. As part of an overall account of English, linguists who use this approach will list morphemes in their deep sound shapes initially, and formulate phonological rules to turn the deep shapes into surface forms similar to the phonemic ones. This entire apparatus is (in principle) justified on the usual grounds of economy and so forth without regard to writing or history. The proposal is then made that the spelling rules of English are much simpler and can make better predictions if we assume that what they are representing are the sounds in the deep rather than surface representations of morphemes.

An example will make this clear. The word with surface sound shape /kəndɛm/ could only be looked at and have its spelling considered in isolation by the surface phonemic approach, which cannot then readily predict either the ⟨n⟩ on the end of the written form or the fact that the first vowel is written as ⟨o⟩ and not ⟨a⟩, for example. However, in the present approach it will be considered in relation to the full set of words that contain the same morphemes—including especially /kɒndəmneɪʃən/—and a deep sound shape established from which simple phonological rules can predict the surface sound shapes of all members of the set. Obviously this is done in such a way that the same phonological rules will be applicable to large numbers of deep sound shapes and will successfully turn them into surface forms. In the present example it is simplest to suppose that the deep shape is something like /kɒndɛmn/ and propose rules that when not stressed /ɒ/ or /ɛ/ become /ə/, and when word final /n/ after another consonant is lost. A deep shape without a final /n/ would not work because phonological rules could not then be formulated to predict generally where the /n/ should be added—compare /kənfɜːm/ but /kɒnfəmeɪʃən/ (not /kɒnfəmneɪʃən/). If we then consider spelling, it is apparent that the spelling of (surface) /ə/ and the silent ⟨n⟩ in ⟨condemn⟩ are readily predictable from correspondence rules that start from the deep phonological shape.

On similar lines, this approach allows deep sound shapes to be formulated from which one can predict many vowel spellings that the surface approach cannot, and a good many silent consonants. It may appear to some that the reason for this is that the linguist has "cheated" and drawn on knowledge of history (e.g. vowel reduction sound changes) in establishing his deep sound shapes and phonological rules in what is supposed to be a synchronic account. The deep sound shapes often resemble the surface sound shapes we know morphemes to have had centuries ago, and since English spelling stopped changing in the seventeenth century it is not surprising that the deep shapes are a better starting point to predict spelling from. However, when this approach is used strictly, it in fact *only* uses evidence for the deep forms which is "there" synchronically in the variant surface forms of the same morpheme, and this does not in every case lead to the deep shapes and the phonological rules simply recapitulating history.

Still, it is true that usually deep phonology does follow history. The reason is that historical sound changes very often do not affect a sound in *every* environment in which it appears. For example, vowels change often just when stressed, or when unstressed or when preceded by some other sound, etc. So if a given morpheme with a certain vowel appears in words in both stressed and unstressed circumstances, after a stress-conditioned sound change the different occurrences of the morpheme sound slightly different but retain evidence of the history in their synchronic variation.

The corollary of this is that where sound changes were unconditioned or where a morpheme does not happen to crop up in different words both in and out of the key environment for a sound change, history will not be synchronically recoverable and spellings may be no more predictable than in the surface approach. Thus the silent ⟨k⟩ of ⟨know⟩ is predictable because it is sounded in ⟨acknowledge⟩, so a deep sound shape with a /k/ can be reconstructed for this morpheme. The silent ⟨k⟩ in ⟨knee⟩ cannot, because this morpheme does not survive in any word where it has a /k/ sound, so there is no synchronic phonological evidence on which to reconstruct a deep phonological shape with a /k/.

Another problem for this approach is that though it can often explain why the same morpheme has the same spelling even when it sounds slightly different, it cannot always predict what that constant spelling will be. The deep sound shapes for ⟨condemn⟩ and ⟨fear⟩ will contain /n/ and /r/ respectively because these are sounded in other words where these morphemes crop up, so the silent ⟨n⟩ and ⟨r⟩ are predictable. However, the spelling of the past tense morpheme is not so easy. Often a deep shape /d/ is supposed to underlie the /d/, /t/ and /ɪd/ sounds it has in ⟨strolled⟩, ⟨walked⟩ and ⟨trotted⟩, which makes the ⟨e⟩ of the spelling ⟨ed⟩ hard to predict. Finally, this approach cannot explain some spelling *differences* where uniformity would be expected—for example ⟨abolish⟩ but not ⟨abolishion⟩.

Questions for the psychologist here include that of whether the whole notion of deep sound shapes and phonological rules has any reality in real people's minds, and, if it does, whether it embraces all the examples for which linguists use it to predict the spelling. For instance, do all speakers of English actually know the word ⟨acknowledge⟩, and if so, do they recognize the morpheme ⟨know⟩ in it or not? What is the deep phonological shape of this morpheme for a child for whom the answers are negative?

The Polysystemic Approaches

This approach could start from sounds in the manner of either of the preceding approaches, but adds the key idea that the English writing system should not be analysed as if it is one system with one integrated set of correspondence rules but rather several systems used in and out of each other. In this respect it regards English writing as like Japanese writing, except that there the different systems use different sets of graphemes (immediately distinct visually) while in English the same letters are used and only some digraphs like ⟨ae⟩ are overtly peculiar to one system.

The simplest version would say broadly that English morphemes or words can be divided into classes (beyond phonologically defined ones), and that different spelling rules apply to morphemes or words of different classes. Making this assumption, each set of rules should be simpler and require fewer exceptions to be listed than one overall set. The classes of items often distinguished in this approach are: content/lexical morphemes (roots of nouns, verbs, adjectives and adverbs) versus function/grammatical ones (articles, prepositions, plural and tense inflections, etc.); proper names versus common words; Germanic words versus Greco-Latinate words, versus recent foreign words. Often classifications like this are appealed to in combination with each other and with phonological considerations, both deep and surface, as we shall see in the example rules below.

Some examples of rules that exploit this are as follows. In one-syllable personal surnames, final single-consonant sounds are spelt double in cases where they would be spelt single elsewhere: for example ⟨Mann⟩, ⟨Judd⟩ versus ⟨Bowman⟩, ⟨man⟩, ⟨dud⟩. Apparent exceptions ⟨inn⟩ and ⟨add⟩ are covered by a rule that states that content words have a spelling with a minimum of three letters: cf. grammatical words like ⟨in⟩ and ⟨at⟩. In Germanic words /s/ is written ⟨s⟩, in Greco-Latinate ones ⟨c⟩ before ⟨e⟩, ⟨i⟩, ⟨y⟩, though still with many exceptions, only some of which can be explained by further generalization. In the first syllable of disyllabic Germanic words short vowels have to be followed by two written consonants (except in the case of ⟨v⟩), in Greco-Latinate words only one: for example ⟨pretty⟩, ⟨rabbit⟩ and ⟨ferry⟩ versus ⟨city⟩, ⟨habit⟩ and ⟨very⟩. (See further Vallins, 1954, Chapter 3, though his account is partly historical).

One issue with this approach, as with the deep phonological one, is whether history has been brought in surreptitiously in the germanic versus Greco-Latinate versus foreign kind of classification. Clearly there is synchronic evidence in English that justifies classification of words as grammatical or not and so forth, but is there any for this seemingly etymological classification, useful though it clearly is in formulating rules, because of the way English spelling has come to be how it is? There certainly are *some* independent ways in which this can be supported: for instance, germanic words (of Old English or Old Norse origin) are usually shorter than Greco-Latinate ones (of ME/ENE origin borrowed either directly from classical languages or via French). They have certain sounds occurring in them more often (e.g. /h/), may be marked by containing distinctively Germanic suffixes like ⟨-er⟩ and ⟨-ly⟩ versus Greco-Latin ⟨-ical⟩, ⟨-ity⟩, etc., are often less formal and tend to convey meanings in the semantic "core" of English (e.g. they are function words, the numbers, words for basic parts of the body, animals and natural phenomena). However, these are probabilistic indicators, and not sufficient to successfully classify every word of English correctly, in the historical sense, even if optimally exploited. For instance, ⟨ditty⟩ is actually of Greco-Latin origin but on the above criteria might be classed on balance as Germanic (and indeed its double consonant is a Germanic spelling). So there is the possibility of words being synchronically different from their true etymology. For the psychologist, the question would be, of course, whether speakers of English exploit the indicators at all, and so whether any such classification has any psychological reality, and if so whether it is exploited or exploitable when it comes to spelling.

Something that confuses the issue further is that some words that every synchronic evidence (other than spelling) would probably suggest to be Germanic are written with Greco-Latin spellings. Such are ⟨mice⟩ and ⟨ice⟩, for historical reasons mentioned above. In this framework, then, these are irregular spellings. An alternative version of the polysystemic approach (see Albrow, 1972) would say rather that one should work purely with system-defined classes. That is, one identifies multiple spelling systems for English and classes of words (or parts of words) to which the systems apply *without* regard for any independent synchronic evidence for Germanicness, etc., of words. In that case, one just refers to the systems as "system 1", "system 2" and so forth, and whatever words (or parts of words) are spelled according to a particular system belong to the corresponding class. Thus ⟨mouse⟩ and ⟨sit⟩ would belong to the class that one system of spelling rules applies to and ⟨mice⟩ and ⟨city⟩ to another, and it is purely coincidental that most words in one system turn out to be Germanic, etc. If psychologically real, such a classification could only be operative for a word after speakers have seen how to spell it, however, since it does not incorporate any way of predicting which class a word belongs to until one knows how it is spelled.

The Morphemic Approach

This approach starts from the premise that English writing is, at least to some degree, logographic, and hence that spelling rules that start only from sounds in some way will necessarily be inadequate. To the extent that this is true, English writing is an exception to the general trend of writing systems to develop historically away from logographicity and towards alphabeticity. The policies adopted in the ENE spelling fixing era put this trend into reverse.

In a very limited area English writing is fully logographic. Symbols like ⟨5⟩ and ⟨%⟩ do not represent the sounds of the morphemes they write at all. And, like Chinese characters used by Japanese, they are used abroad to write translationally equivalent morphemes with no sound similarity—for example ⟨5⟩ in Greece writes the sound shape /pende/.

The most obvious way in which English writing more generally can be seen as "writing morphemes" is in its treatment of homophones. It is much more common for them to be written differently, as ⟨meat⟩ but ⟨meet⟩, than for them to be written the same, as ⟨pen⟩ "animal enclosure" and ⟨pen⟩ "writing instrument", which is what would be universal in a surface phonemic alphabet like that of Old English. In some cases the preceding three approaches can predict the different spellings. Thus ⟨sign⟩ is predictable beside ⟨sine⟩ because the former alternates with ⟨signature⟩, indicating a deep /g/, and the latter, with no such related forms, has the surface regular spelling ⟨i-e⟩ for the /ai/ diphthong. Spellings like ⟨in⟩ beside ⟨inn⟩, ⟨I⟩ beside ⟨eye⟩ are partly predicted by the polysystemic approach, which generalizes that non-grammatical words are written with a longer spelling than function words. The former have normally at least three letters, the latter may have only two or one. However, a great many differences of spelling between homophones are explicable only by the basic principle of logographic writing, that different morphemes with distinct meanings have to be written differently—for example ⟨meet⟩ and ⟨meat⟩.

In the other key respect English is also extensively but not fully logographic. Where a morpheme has different sound shapes that are related phonologically, they tend to be written the same (as also predicted by the deep phonological approach). However, where (rarely) a morpheme has more than one separate family of sound shapes representing it, they are spelled differently. Take the plural morpheme, which crops up in many words in one of three phonologically related sound shapes /-s/, /-z/ and /-ɪz/. These are all written with an ⟨s⟩, as in ⟨cats⟩, ⟨dogs⟩ and ⟨horses⟩. However, unrelated plural sound shapes are written differently, reflecting their sound, as in ⟨oxen⟩, ⟨sheep⟩, ⟨men⟩, ⟨gladioli⟩. In a fully logographic system the same written symbol would be used regardless of sound wherever the plural morpheme was present.

The morphemic approach is not viable for the linguist as a substitute for the first three approaches to English spelling. To embrace it exclusively would mean that no reference could be made to sounds at all in trying to describe English spelling, and a lot of generalization would be lost. Even with homophones it is not the case that there is *nothing* about the spelling ⟨meet⟩ that reflects its sound, or even nothing about the ⟨ee⟩ bit of it that relates to /iː/, and that it is purely an arbitrary graphic shape for this morpheme. Its best place is combined with the preceding approaches as a principle that where multiple alternative spellings exist, different ones will be exploited for different homophonous morphemes. However, from the psychologist's point of view, it is not impossible to imagine real people operating widely with whole-word visual images of words' spellings *as if* they were simply logographic, and disregarding the phonographic information contained in them.

To conclude, in describing writing systems such as the English alphabet, linguists are inclined to want to limit assumptions rigorously and see how much generalization can be extracted with the minimum given, and will attempt "all-or-none" rule systems with lists of exceptions. They are not very good at combining approaches eclectically and probabilistically. The challenge remains to establish which approaches or combinations of approaches resemble anything exploited or exploitable by the human mind, in combination, no doubt, with the visual factors that linguists usually entirely overlook.

REFERENCES

Albrow, K. H. (1972). *The English Writing System: Notes Towards a Description*. London: Longman, for The Schools Council.

Chomsky, N. & Halle, M. (1968). *The Sound Pattern of English*. New York: Harper and Row.

Diringer, D. (1968). *The Alphabet*. London: Hutchinson.

Gelb, I. J. (1952). *A Study of Writing*. Chicago: University of Chicago Press.

Sampson, G. (1985). *Writing Systems*. London: Hutchinson.

Scragg, D. G. (1974). *A History of English Spelling*. Manchester: Manchester University Press.

Vallins, G. H. (1954). *Spelling*. London: Andre Deutsch.

Wijk, A. (1966). *Rules of Pronunciation for the English Language*. London: Oxford University Press.

Part II

Spelling Development

4

Sources of Information Used by Beginning Spellers

REBECCA TREIMAN

Wayne State University, Detroit

A child of six, writing about her birthday party, might produce the following: WE KEND THE HAOS FOR THE PRTE. WE AT KACK. (In this example and throughout this chapter, children's spellings are in upper-case letters.) Translated, the meaning is, "We cleaned the house for the party. We ate cake." This passage exemplifies some of the typical characteristics of beginning writing. First-graders who are encouraged to write on their own may produce spellings such as these (Treiman, 1993); so might younger children who start to write before receiving formal classroom instruction (Read, 1975). Beginners are often correct on short, frequent words such as *we* and *the*, especially if the words are regularly spelled. However, beginning writers produce many errors. In the example, *cleaned* is spelled as KEND, *party* as PRTE and *cake* as KACK. Why do children write these words in these particular ways? What sources of information do children use when they spell? These are the questions addressed in this chapter.

The study of children's spelling errors can shed light on the knowledge that children bring with them to the spelling task and the way in which they apply this knowledge. The understanding gained from a detailed study of children's errors provides a basis for theories of spelling and spelling development. Similarly, analyses of children's "miscues" have helped illuminate the nature of the reading process (Goodman, 1967) and naturally produced errors have been an important source of information in understanding the acquisition of spoken language. Any theory of spelling development

Handbook of Spelling: Theory, Process and Intervention. Edited by G. D. A. Brown and N. C. Ellis.
©1994 John Wiley & Sons Ltd.

must be able to explain the errors that beginning spellers make and how these errors change with experience. Thus, in addition to discussing the factors that influence children's spelling errors, I consider the implications of the findings for our views of spelling development.

The focus of this chapter is on normally developing children who are learning to read and write in English. I briefly mention possible implications of the results for cross-linguistic studies but have little to say about research in languages other than English. Readers who are interested in children's spelling in other languages may consult Read (1986) and Alegria and Mousty (this volume, Chapter 11). The research to be reviewed deals primarily with children in kindergarten and first grade, about 5 and 6 years old. Research with precocious younger children who start to write without formal classroom instruction is also mentioned. These age groups are chosen, in part, because it is beginners who make the most spelling errors. Studies of young children are particularly important because they shed light on the knowledge and skills that children bring with them to the spelling task. Although English spelling continues to be a problem for many children into the later school grades and even into adulthood (see Carlisle, 1988; Fischer, Shankweiler & Liberman, 1985; Templeton & Scarborough-Franks, 1985), it is young children who are the focus of attention here.

To understand the demands of writing acquisition, it is important to understand the nature of the English writing system. Our writing system is, to a first approximation, an alphabet. Each phoneme in a spoken word is represented with a grapheme (a letter or group of letters) in the corresponding printed word. For example, the /k/ of *clean* (/klin/) is conventionally spelled as *c*, the /l/ as *l*, the /i/ as *ea* and the /n/ as *n*. Given that the English writing system represents the sound structure of the language, the characteristics of children's phonological or sound systems would be expected to affect their spelling. For example, if children treat initial /kl/ as a single unit rather than a sequence of two units, they may spell it with a single grapheme (e.g. *c* or *k*) rather than a sequence of two graphemes (e.g. *cl* or *kl*). The role of phonology in children's spelling errrors is discussed in the first section of this chapter. I ask what phonological abilities children bring with them to the spelling task and how their phonological knowledge affects the spellings that they produce.

In addition to knowing about the phonological forms of spoken words, beginning spellers also know about the names of letters. In the United States and many other English-speaking countries, children learn letter names from an early age. For example, middle-class American kindergarteners can typically recite the alphabet. Shown a letter, at least an upper-case one, they can usually say its name (Mason, 1980). One would expect children to take advantage of their experience with letter names when they spell. For example, children might symbolize the /i/ of *clean* with the letter that has this name, *e*, rather than with the conventional *ea*. They might spell the /ɑ/ and /r/ of *party* with single *r*, the letter whose name matches this sequence of phonemes, rather than with the conventional *ar*. In the second section of this chapter, I discuss the role of letter names in children's early spelling errors. Interactions between letter-name knowledge and phonological knowledge are also considered.

In English, the links between phonemes and graphemes are not one-to-one. Many phonemes have more than one possible spelling. For instance, /k/ may be spelled as *c* (as in *clean*), *k* (as in *kite*) or *ck* (as in *back*), among other possibilities. For /k/ and other phenomes, context can help spellers to decide on an appropriate grapheme. English words never begin with *ck*, so the /k/ of *kite* could not be spelled as *ck*. The grapheme *ck* only occurs in the middles or at the ends of words, as in *packet* or *pack*. Children's understanding of such orthographic regularities is considered in the third section of this chapter. Do children learn, from their exposure to printed words, that *ck* occurs in the middles and at the ends of words but not at the beginnings of words?

The final section of the chapter considers the implications of the results for our views of spelling and its development. I review various ideas about spelling and spelling development and discuss the influences of phonology, letter-name knowledge and orthographic knowledge in the context of these views.

PHONOLOGY

In English, the spelling of a word reflects its phonological structure. For example, the spoken form of *clean* contains four phonemes—/k/ followed by /l/ followed by /i/ followed by /n/. A child who does not know the conventional printed form of the word can none-the-less produce a plausible spelling by consulting the word's phonological structure. To do this, the child can analyze the word as a sequence of phonemes and use a grapheme to represent each phoneme. A spelling constructed in this way may turn out to be correct. This will probably be the case when the word's spelling is highly regular. If the spelling is wrong, as it may be for a less regular word, it will generally be a reasonable error. For example, a child may misspell *clean* as *klean*. A child who can apprehend the phonemic structure of the spoken word should not produce errors such as *kean* (in which one phoneme, /l/, is not represented) or *kealn* (in which two phonemes /l/ and /i/, are represented in the wrong order).

Apprehending the phonemic structure of spoken words involves a degree of explicit linguistic awareness that is not required for everyday speaking and listening. When we converse, we typically pay attention to the meanings of words rather than their sounds. Gaining the ability to focus on sounds requires a good deal of time and practice. Although adults are able to segment spoken words into phonemes, many children cannot perform complete phonemic analyses of spoken words at the time they begin to write. As a result, they make predictable types of spelling errors.

To understand how difficulties in analyzing spoken words into phonemes can cause spelling errors, it is necessary to discuss the development of phonological awareness. The first steps in the developmental sequence occur well before children go to school, as children become able to divide spoken words into syllables. Evidence of children's awareness of syllables was provided by Treiman and Zukowski (1991), using a word pair comparison task. The task was presented with the aid of a puppet. The puppet was said to like pairs of words that had some of the same sounds in them. The puppet disliked words that did not share any sounds. All of the word pairs were presented in spoken form; no printed words were shown to the children. In the syllable condition of the study, the puppet was said to like pairs of words such as *hammer* and *hammock*, which share a syllable at the beginning. The puppet also liked word pairs such as *compete* and *repeat*, which share a syllable at the end. Pairs such as *delight* and *unique* or *plastic* and *heavy* were not pleasing to the puppet. After hearing several examples of word pairs that the puppet did and did not like, the child heard a series of pairs and judged whether the puppet liked each one. Treiman and Zukowski (1991) tested three groups of children—preschoolers (mean age 5 years, 1 month, tested the summer before they were to enter kindergarten), kindergarteners (mean age 5 years, 9 months, tested between January and March of the school year) and first-graders (mean age 7 years, 0 months, also tested between January and March). Nearly all of the children succeeded in the syllable comparison task. All of the preschoolers, 90% of the kindergarteners and all of the first-graders reached a preset criterion of six consecutive correct responses. Even among preschoolers and kindergarteners, almost half of the children made no errors at all. These results, together with other findings (Fox & Routh, 1975; Hardy, Stennett & Smythe, 1973; Leong & Haines, 1978; Liberman et al., 1974; Treiman & Baron, 1981), show that children are relatively good at segmenting spoken words into syllables.

What of the ability to divide syllables into smaller linguistic units? English syllables are composed of two primary units, an onset and a rime. The onset is the initial consonant or consonant cluster of the syllable, such as the /kl/ of /klin/. The rime consists of the vowel and any following consonants, such as the /in/ of /klin/. The rime in turn is composed of a vocalic peak and a consonantal coda. (See Treiman, 1989 for a detailed discussion of the internal structure of English syllables.) Many children can segment monosyllabic words into onsets and rimes before they enter first grade. Evidence for this claim comes from the study of Treiman and Zukowski (1991). In addition to the syllable condition described above, this study included an onset/rime condition and a phoneme condition, to be described later. Each child participated in one of the three conditions. The children in all conditions received the same general instructions. However, the words that the puppet liked differed across conditions. In the onset/rime condition, the puppet's favored words shared an onset, as with *plank* and *plea*, or a rime, as with *spit* and *wit*. The disfavored words shared neither of these linguistic units, as with *twist* and *brain* or *rail* and *snap*. Performance in the onset/rime condition improved with age and schooling, with 56% of the preschoolers, 74% of the kindergarteners and 100% of the first-graders reaching criterion. Thus, although the onset/rime task was harder than the syllable task, many children could do it before the time at which they would be taught to read and write.

Further evidence of children's sensitivity to onsets and rimes comes from studies by other investigators that document children's sensitivity to rhyme and alliteration (Bowey & Francis, 1991; Calfee, Chapman & Venezky, 1972; Kirtley *et al.*, 1989; Knafle, 1973, 1974; Lenel & Cantor, 1981; Maclean, Bryant & Bradley, 1987; Stanovich, Cunningham & Cramer, 1984). With monosyllabic words, rhyming words are those that share a rime and alliterative words are those that share an onset.

Some onsets and rimes are only a single phoneme. For example, the onset and rime of /ti/ (*tea*) are one phoneme each. In such cases, an analysis of the syllable at the onset/rime level is equivalent to an analysis of the syllable at the phoneme level. In other cases, onsets and rimes are more than one phoneme. The onset of /klin/ (*clean*) contains two phonemes, as does the rime. With such words, children must segment the onset and rime units if they are to reach the phoneme level. Many kindergarteners and preschoolers have difficulty performing such fine-grained analyses. Consider the results from the phoneme condition of the Treiman and Zukowski (1991) study. Here, half of the word pairs that the puppet liked shared one phoneme of a two-phoneme onset cluster. It was always the first consonant that was shared, as in *blue* and *brave*. The other favorite word pairs shared one phoneme of a vowel–consonant rime, always the final consonant. For example, the puppet liked *smoke* and *tack*, which both end with /k/. Only 25% of the preschoolers and 39% of the kindergarteners succeeded in this phoneme comparison task. Such results suggest that children who can break syllables into onsets and rimes may still have trouble analyzing at least some complex onsets and rimes into their component phonemes.

Preschool and kindergarten children have similar difficulties in other tasks that require them to subdivide complex onsets and rimes (Barton, Miller & Macken, 1980; Bowey & Francis, 1991; Kirtley *et al.*, 1989; Treiman, 1985a, 1993; Treiman & Weatherston, 1992). For example, they have more trouble recognizing that /flo/ begins with /f/ than that /fo/ or /fol/ begin with /f/ (Treiman, 1985a). A given phoneme, /f/, is harder to recognize when it is part of a complex onset than when it is an onset on its own.

By the middle of first grade, all of the children tested by Treiman and Zukowski (1991) succeeded in the phoneme comparison task. However, children's ability to analyze complex onsets and rimes into phonemes is not perfected by this time. Tasks that require children to focus on the *second* consonants of two-consonant onsets (unlike the phoneme comparison task of Treiman & Zukowsi, 1991, which involved the *first* consonants of cluster onsets) continue to be difficult. For example, Bruck and Treiman (1990) tested a group of first- and second-graders (mean age 7 years, 5 months) who scored at least at grade level on standardized reading and spelling tests. In an auditory deletion task, the experimenter pronounced a nonword such as /floi/. She asked the children to remove the first sound and to say the remaining nonword. Several demonstration and practice trials were given, showing the children that the correct answer was /loi/. When children attempted the task on their own, though, they tended to say /oi/, removing the entire onset, rather than /loi/, removing just the first consonant of the onset. The children's error rate was a striking 62%. In another version of the auditory deletion task, children were asked to omit the second consonants of initial clusters while retaining the first consonants. Given /floi/, they were to say /foi/. Children did much better on this task, in which only the first consonant of the cluster was retained (28% errors), than on the task in which only the second consonant of the cluster was retained (62% errors). These results, together with those of Treiman (1985a), show that even children of 7 and 8 have a tendency to treat onset clusters as units. Moreover, the second consonant of a two-consonant initial cluster seems to be less salient than the first, as attested by the greater difficulty of the task in which only the second consonant of the cluster was retained.

Several conclusions may be drawn from this survey of the development of phonological awareness. First, this development is a long and gradual process. It begins well before children go to school and does not reach a plateau until they have been in school for some years. Relatedly, most children do not have easy or automatic access to the level of phonemes when formal reading and spelling instruction begins (the start of first grade for most American children). Many children can segment spoken syllables into onsets and rimes at this time. However, some of these children have trouble decomposing complex onsets and rimes into phonemes.

Given this background on the nature and development of phonological awareness, we may consider how children's segmentation skills affect their spelling. As mentioned earlier, one way to spell a word is to divide it into phonemes and to symbolize each phoneme with a grapheme. If children cannot achieve a complete phonemic breakdown of a word, they are likely to misspell it. We would expect specific links between phonemic segmentation and spelling such that those features of words that prove difficult in segmentation tasks also prove difficult in spelling.

We have seen that initial consonant clusters are one stumbling block in the development of phonemic awareness. Children often treat onset clusters as units rather than sequences of phonemes. These difficulties with initial clusters in spoken words are reflected in children's spellings. Treiman (1985b, 1991, 1993) analyzed the classroom writings of 43 first-graders. These children's teacher favored whole-language and language-experience approaches to the teaching of reading and writing. The children were encouraged to write on their own each day. The teacher did not explicitly correct the misspellings in children's independent writings; indeed, she did not tell the children the correct spelling of a word even if they asked. Writings produced from the beginning of the school year until near the end were collected and analyzed. The resulting collection of 5617 spellings included 390 attempts to spell words beginning with two-consonant clusters. The majority of the attempts (71%) were composed of a grapheme that could legally represent the first consonant of the cluster followed by a grapheme that could legally represent the second consonant of the cluster, as in *cl* or *kl* for /kl/. The next most common type of spelling (23%) was illegal. It consisted of a legal spelling of the first consonant but no representation of the second consonant. Examples are *k* for /kl/, as in KEN for *clean*, and *p* for /pr/, as in PINSOS for *princess*. Thus, first-graders sometimes fail to spell the second phonemes of onset clusters. These errors, I suggest, reflect a difficulty in apprehending the internal structure of the clusters.

To confirm and extend the findings of the naturalistic study, a series of experiments was undertaken (Treiman, 1991). The children in the experiments were kindergarteners and first-graders. These children produced errors such as FOY for the nonword /floi/ even after they had just repeated the nonword correctly. Thus, second-consonant omission errors do not reflect simple mispronunciation. Children who spelled /floi/ as FOY generally knew that *l* makes the sound /l/. They could usually spell /loi/ with initial *l*. Thus, errors such as FOY for /floi/ do not reflect simple ignorance of the letter *l* or of its sound. Perhaps most strikingly, some children continued to spell /floi/ as FOY even after spelling /foi/ as FOY and even after being shown that they had spelled two different-sounding words alike. Thus, errors such as FOY for /floi/ can be very persistent. In other studies, too, onset clusters have been found to cause difficulty for inexperienced spellers (Bruck & Treiman, 1990; Marcel, 1980; Miller & Limber, 1985; Shankweiler, 1992). In all of these studies, the second consonants of initial clusters were more susceptible to omission than the first consonants.

Children differ from one another in their tendency to omit the second consonants of onset clusters. As Treiman (1991) showed, some first-graders and kindergarteners make these errors at high rates. Others rarely or never do so. Similarly, children vary in their performance on phonemic awareness tasks involving onset clusters in spoken words. To our knowledge, only one published study, that of Bruck and Treiman (1990), has looked for a relation between the two skills by giving spelling tasks and phonemic awareness tasks to the same children. Bruck and Treiman (1990) found a significant though modest correlation between omissions of the second consonants of initial clusters in spelling and errors in an auditory recognition task involving the second consonants of initial clusters ("Does /floi/ contain /l/?").

There are thus two kinds of evidence for a connection between phonological awareness and the spelling of onset clusters. First, errors in spelling and errors in phonemic awareness tasks show similar patterns. In both cases, children have special difficulty with the second consonants of onset clusters. Second, children who have particular difficulty accessing the second consonants of initial clusters in an auditory recognition task seem more likely to omit these consonants when they spell. These findings show that certain spelling errors reflect limitations in children's phonemic segmentation abilities. Some children misspell *clean* as KEN because they have trouble apprehending the internal structure of the /kl/ onset. These children spell the cluster as a single unit, with *k*, rather than dividing it into two phonemes and using one grapheme for the first phoneme and another grapheme for the second phoneme.

Misspellings such as *k* for /kl/ and *p* for /pr/ reflect limitations in children's phonemic awareness. Some first-graders have trouble apprehending the internal structure of onset clusters, preferring instead to treat the clusters as single units. As a result, they make predictable spelling errors. The case of onsets is by no means unique. Other frequent misspellings also reflect limitations in phonemic awareness. For example, inexperienced spellers make errors on final consonant clusters as well as initial ones. They may misspell *send* as SED, *sink* as SEK, or *milk* as MIK (Marcel, 1980; Read, 1975; Treiman, 1993). These errors seem to occur because children treat the vowel and the following sonorant consonant (i.e. liquid or nasal) as a unit for purposes of spelling. They have trouble segmenting /ɪl/ into /ɪ/ and /l/ and /ɛn/ into /ɛ/ and /n/. However, because there has been less research on children's segmentation of vowel–final cluster units than their segmentation of initial clusters, the link between phonemic awareness and spelling of final clusters requires further investigation.

In most of the examples discussed so far, phonologically based spelling errors happen to be omissions. For example, children omit the *l* of *clean*, the *k* of *skip* and the *n* of *hunt*. Errors that are motivated by phonological factors may also be substitutions. For example, children who do not omit the second consonant of *sky* altogether may spell it as *g* instead of *k*, as in SGIE (Treiman, 1985c, 1993). This error reflects the phonological properties of this consonant. Being unaspirated (i.e. not pronounced with a following puff of air), the consonant is similar to sounds in the /g/ category. Some children apparently assign the consonant to /g/ rather than /k/ for this reason. As another example, children may spell the vowel of *house* with *ao*, reflecting the two-part or diphthongal nature of the vowel (Treiman, 1993).

Omission errors such as omission of *k* in *skip* and substitution errors such as use of *g* for the *k* of *sky* give us insight into children's phonological systems. The former error reveals children's difficulties in apprehending clusters as sequences of phonemes. The latter error reveals differences between children's representations of phonemes in clusters and adults'. As Shankweiler and Lundquist (1993, p. 187) state, "it is chiefly through their writing, and not through their reading, that children reveal their hypotheses about the infrastructure of words".

It is often thought that English-speaking children's difficulties in learning to spell stem from the irregularity of the English writing system. The many attempts that have been made to reform the system all rest on this assumption. However, children often misspell even highly regular words such as *slip*, *hunt* and *milk*. Although irregularity as manifested in words such as *said* and *come* is one source of difficulty in learning to spell in English (see Treiman, 1993), it is not the only one. Even regular words can cause trouble when they contain phonological features such as consonant clusters.

LETTER NAMES

Children bring their existing knowledge and skills to whatever new task confronts them. This is as true for spelling as it is for the other tasks that children encounter at school. As we have seen, children's preexisting phonological knowledge plays an important role in their spelling. Another source of knowledge that children use in spelling, and the one that is the focus of this section, is letter names. Most middle-class American children are very familiar with the names of the letters before they start to write words. They know that /e/, /bi/, /si/ and so on are the names of English letters. They know what most, if not all, of the letters look like. Children may therefore use their knowledge of letter names to gain entrance into the writing system.

The preschool children studied by Read (1975), who began to write before receiving formal instruction in spelling or reading, did just this. According to Read (1975), these children typically learned to recognize and name letters when they were 2 years old. Some time later, the children realized that a letter, such as *b*, usually spells a phoneme that occurs in the name of the letter, such as /b/. For example, a boy named Bob might learn to spell his name. From this, he might infer that *b* stands for /b/, the first phoneme of the letter's name, /bi/. The child would then apply this insight to spell words. Indeed, many of the vowel errors in Read's (1975) study reflected the names of letters. Children spelled *clean* with *e* rather than *ea*, *my* with *i* rather than *y*, and so on.

It is perhaps not surprising that the children in Read's (1975) study used the names of letters to spell words. Not having received formal instruction in spelling or reading and not knowing the conventional spellings of a large number of words, these children did not have many other ways to spell new words on their own. However, it is not only precocious preschoolers who are influenced by the names of letters when they spell. The first-graders studied by Treiman (1993) showed many of the same phenomena reported by Read (1975). These first-graders frequently spelled /e/, /i/, /ai/ and /o/ with the letters that have these names—*a*, *e*, *i* and *o*, respectively. They spelled *birthday* as BRTA, *happy* as HAPE, *bike* as BIK, and *blow* as BO. Similar vowel errors have been reported by other investigators (Beers, Beers & Grant, 1977).

Letter-name knowledge led the children in Treiman's (1993) study to omit vowel graphemes as well as misspell them. Omission errors occurred when children symbolized a sequence of phonemes with the consonant letter whose name matched the entire sequence. For example, children sometimes spelled *car* as CR, representing the group of phonemes /ɑ/ and /r/ with the single letter *r*. Similarly, children sometimes spelled *help* HLP. In these cases, children used a consonant letter to symbolize an entire vowel–consonant sequence. They did not represent the vowel phoneme and the consonant phoneme with separate graphemes, as conventional English does.

Interestingly, these errors were found for some letters but not others. In the study of Treiman (1993), letter-name errors occurred at a significant rate for *r*, *l*, *m* and *n*. When a spoken word contained a sequence of phonemes that matched the name of one of these letters, children omitted the vowel reliably more often than expected on the basis of other factors. Thus, children were more likely to delete the vowel of *park* (a vowel that occurs in a letter-name context, /ɑr/) than the vowel of *pork* (where /or/ is not a letter name). Children were more likely to omit the vowel of *help* (/ɛl/ being the name of *l*) than the vowel of *milk* (/ɪl/ not being the name of an English letter). The rate of letter-name spellings appeared to be especially high for *r* as compared with *l*, *m* and *n*, but the difference was not significant. For many other letters, including *s*, *p* and *t*, letter-name spellings were not observed. The vowel of *mess* was not omitted at an especially high rate, even though it and the following consonant together constitute the name of a letter (*s*). Nor was the second vowel of *happy* omitted especially often, even though it and the preceding consonant form the name of an English letter (*p*). Treiman's (1993) results suggest, then, that some sequences of phonemes are more susceptible to letter-name spellings than others.

To confirm these observations, Treiman (in press) carried out a series of experiments with preschool, kindergarten and first-grade children. In the experiments, children were asked to spell stimuli containing various types of letter-name sequences. Examples are /gɑr/ (which contains the name of *r*), /zɛl/ (which contains the name of *l*), /hɛs/ (which contains the name of *s*) and /tib/ (which contains the name of *t*). Almost all of the stimuli were nonwords, ensuring that children could not spell the stimuli based on knowledge of their conventional spellings. The children in some of the experiments spelled the nonwords using pencil and paper. The children in other studies used moveable letters to make the task easier. Another important feature of the experiments is that children's knowledge of letter names was checked. In line with previous reports of good letter-name knowledge in middle-class American children (e.g. Mason, 1980), all of the first-graders and the great majority of the kindergarteners knew the names of the letters that were included in the stimuli, although many of the preschoolers did not. Any child who did not know the letter names was dropped from the study.

The results of Treiman's (in press) experiments confirm that letter-name sequences differ in their susceptibility to single-consonant spellings. For kindergarteners and first-graders, letter-name spellings were most common for nonwords such as /gɑr/, which contain the name of *r*. Indeed, the kindergarteners in one experiment made errors such as GR for /gɑr/ at a rate of 61%. Although letter-name spellings for *r* were not as frequent in the other experiments, letter-name errors were always more numerous for *r* than for other letters. After *r*, the consonant most likely to elicit letter-name spellings was *l*. Other consonant letters were less susceptible to omission, including letters with vowel–consonant names such as *m*, *n* and *s* and letters with consonant–vowel names such as *t*, *p* and *k*.

Why are some consonant letters more likely to elicit letter-name spellings than others? Treiman (in press) suggested that the observed differences stem from the phonological properties of the letters' names. Consider the names of *r*, *s* and *t*. Recall that *r* led to many letter-name spellings in both the classroom data (Treiman, 1993) and the experiments (Treiman, in press), while *s* and *t* did not. Children have difficulty analyzing the name of *r*, /ɑr/, into its component phonemes. From a linguistic point of view, the /ɑ/ and /r/ are closely bound. Indeed, some linguists maintain that the /r/ is part of the syllable's peak together with the vowel (Selkirk, 1982). If children have difficulty apprehending the internal structure of the /ɑr/ unit, they may spell the entire unit with the letter that is suggested by the letter name. In contrast, the phonemes in the name of *s* are less closely joined. Although the phonemes form a rime, the vowel is the peak and the consonant is the coda. Thus, even though children know that /ɛs/ is the name of a letter, they are unlikely to spell /ɛs/ with *s* because they can analyze this relatively simple rime into a vowel followed by a consonant. Similarly, children have little tendency to spell /ti/ with single *t*. This is because the /t/ of /ti/ forms one linguistic unit, an onset, while the /i/ forms another unit, a rime. Children's ability to divide syllables into onsets and rimes causes them to treat /ti/ as a sequence of phonemes rather than a single unit.

If the preceding arguments are correct, children's tendency to use letter names in spelling is mediated by the phonological properties of the letter names themselves. Some letter names are easy to analyze into phonemes whereas other letter names are harder to analyze. These differences affect children's tendency to use the names of letters as guides to spelling. The interaction between letter-name knowledge and phonological knowledge means that the study of children's use of letter names in spelling turns out to illuminate the nature of children's phonological knowledge. The results also have some more practical implications, suggesting that teaching children to analyze syllables into phonemes should help to eliminate errors such as CR for *car*.

As discussed earlier, children sometimes misspell words that are highly regular. This can happen when the words contain phonological complexities such as consonant clusters. Similarly, children's use of letter names can cause them to misspell even regular words. *Tar* and *bar* would be classified as regular by any reasonable criterion, yet beginners are prone to misspell these words as TR and BR. Although some of children's spelling errors reflect the inconsistent phoneme–grapheme correspondences of English as observed in words such as *said* and *come*, not all of children's errors can be explained in this manner.

To summarize, children bring their knowledge of letter names to bear on spelling. They sometimes analyze a spoken word into phonemes and use the names of letters in decidng how to spell one or more of the phonemes. This can happen with vowel phonemes that match the name of an English letter. Errors such as *e* for the *ea* of *cleaned* or *i* for the *y* of *my* often arise for this reason. In other cases, children fail to perform a complete phonemic analysis of the spoken word. With *car*, they may stop with /k/ plus /ɑr/ instead of /k/ plus /ɑ/ plus /r/. Because /ɑr/ is a familiar letter name, children may write the word as CR or KR.

ORTHOGRAPHY

Even before children begin to read and spell on their own, they have a good deal of experience with print. Children in a literate society see words on street signs, cereal boxes and food cans. They see words in books and newspapers. In some preschools and kindergartens, objects in the classroom are also labeled. With the start of formal reading instruction, children receive even more exposure to print. In this section, I discuss what children learn about orthography from their experience with printed words and how this knowledge affects their spelling.

English words are not random sequences of graphemes. The graphemes pattern in certain ways, with some of the patterns reflecting the phonological constraints of English. For example, printed words do not begin with *bw* because spoken words do not begin with /bw/. Other constraints are purely orthographic. For example, *ck* occurs in the middles and at the ends of words, as in *packet* and *pack*, but not at the beginnings of words. The ban against initial *ck* does not reflect a ban against initial /k/; many words begin with /k/ spelled as *k* or *c*. Rather, the non-occurrence of initial *ck* is an orthographic feature of English. Venezky (1970) has described a number of such orthographic patterns. To give another example, there are predictable alternations between digraphs (two-letter graphemes) ending in *y*, such as *ay* and *oy*, and digraphs ending in *i*, such as *ai* and *oi*. Digraphs ending in *y* generally occur before vowels and at the ends of words, as in *mayor* and *boy*. Digraphs ending in *i* usually appear before consonants, as in *maid* and *coin*. Similar alternations are found for digraphs ending in *w*, such as *ow*, and those ending in *u*, such as *ou*. The former usually occur before vowels and at the ends of words, as in *power* and *how*; the latter usually occur before consonants, as in *ouch*. Other orthographic patterns involve doublets (two-letter spellings in which the two letters are identical). Certain letters, such as *e* and *l*, occur as doublets. Other letters, such as *v* and *i*, rarely double.

Do beginning spellers appreciate these orthographic patterns? If so, they may make errors such as KACK for *cake* which conform to the positional constraints on *ck*. They should make few errors such as CKAK for *cake*, which violate the constraints. Using the classroom data, Treiman (1993) asked whether first-graders honor the orthographic patterns of English. For each pattern that was investigated, the first-graders usually, although not always, followed the pattern. Consider, as one example, the results for *ck*. The children used this digraph 38 times when it was not a part of a word's correct spelling. They used the digraph at the beginning of a word only twice. The digraph was used in the middle of a word 11 times, as in MRCKUT for *market*, and at the end of a word 25 times, as in BICK for *bike*. Apparently, the children had begun to pick up the restriction against initial *ck*. Interviews with the children's teacher confirmed that this restriction, like the other orthographic patterns studied, was not formally taught in school. The children probably discovered the pattern on their own from seeing words such as *sick* and *package* but not *ckan*.

As another example, consider the alternation between digraphs ending in *i* and *y* and digraphs ending in *u* and *w*. As discussed earlier, digraphs ending in *i* and *u* usually appear before consonants, whereas digraphs ending in *y* and *w* usually occur before vowels and at the ends of words. Treiman (1993) examined errors that contained one of the digraphs in question where the digraph did not occur in the word's conventional spelling. Errors were classified as either honoring or violating the orthographic pattern. For example, SEILF for *self* honors the pattern because it has a digraph ending in *i* before a consonant; PLEW for *play* is also legal because it has a digraph ending in *w* at the end of a word. Errors that violate the orthographic pattern include AI for *a*, which has a digraph with final *i* at the end of a word, and EWT for *it*, which has a digraph with final *w* before a consonant. Errors which followed the graphemic pattern significantly outnumbered errors which violated it. In addition, there was another important finding. The *i/y* alternation has fewer exceptions in conventional English than the *u/w* alternation. Exceptions to the *i/w* alternation include the common words *you* and *down*. Correspondingly, children's adherence to the pattern was significantly greater for *i* and *y* than for *u* and *w*. This difference strengthens the view that exposure to print rather than explicit teaching is the important factor in the learning of orthographic patterns. It is unlikely that an adult would point out a rule to a first-grader but then tell the child that the rule has more exceptions in one case than another.

Compliance with the orthographic constraints tended to be greater during the second half of first grade than during the first half. Even during the first half of first grade, though, the children showed some knowledge of the patterns. This is an important finding because it suggests that children begin learning about the orthographic structure of their language from an early age.

Thus, children pick up the patterns in the printed words that they see. They notice the types of letter sequences that make up these words. They notice that some letters and letter groups occur in certain positions but not in others. Such learning may even begin before children are able to read and spell words on their own. Once children start to write, their spellings tend to honor the orthographic patterns that they have observed.

SUMMARY OF FINDINGS ON SPELLING ERRORS

To summarize, we may return to the writing sample at the beginning of this chapter: WE KEND THE HAOS FOR THE PRTE. WE AT KACK. (We cleaned the house for the party. We ate cake.) Several of the errors in this sample occur for phonological reasons. KEND for *cleaned* is an example. The omission of *l* in this error reflects the strong bond between the consonants in the syllable–initial cluster. The vowel substitution in HAOS for *house* is also phonologically motivated. Other errors in the sample are driven by the names of English letters. The vowel substitutions in KEND for *cleaned*, AT for *ate* and KACK for *cake* reflect, in part, the child's knowledge of the names of *e* and *a*. The spelling of *party* as PRTE is especially interesting. The child uses a letter-name spelling for the sequence /ar/ while spelling the sequence /ti/ with two separate graphemes (her choice for /i/ being influenced by letter-name knowledge). The child's different treatment of /ar/ and /ti/ reflects the greater cohesiveness of /ar/ than /ti/. Thus, PRTE is a more likely misspelling of *party* than PART. Finally, KACK for *cake*, although incorrect, conforms to the orthographic patterns that the child has picked up from her experience with print. The child uses *ck* at the end of the word rather than at the beginning, making KACK a more likely error than CKAK.

As this discussion shows, careful analyses of the knowledge that children bring with them to the spelling task, including phonological, letter-name and orthographic knowledge, can help to show why children make the errors that they do. Such analyses can also show what children need in order to spell better. For example, the child who produced the above sample needs help in analyzing initial clusters and groups of vowels followed by /r/ into phonemes.

IMPLICATIONS FOR VIEWS OF SPELLING AND SPELLING DEVELOPMENT

Traditionally, learning to spell in English was considered a matter of rote visual memorization. Children were thought to memorize the letters in words that they saw and to reproduce the letter sequences when attempting to spell the words. In this view, spelling a word is similar to recalling a string of letters or digits from an arbitrary memorized sequence. Indeed, Jensen (1962) and others argued that spelling and memorization show the same type of serial position curve, with more errors in the middle positions of the sequence than at the beginning or the end. Traditional classifications of spelling errors (e.g. Spache, 1940) rest on this view of spelling as visual memorization. In such systems, errors are classified as omissions, substitutions or reversals relative to the correct spelling of the word. For example, TR for *tar* and TG for *tag* both involve omission of *a*.

The traditional view of spelling, ignoring as it does the phonological foundations of spelling and the role of letter-name knowledge, is insufficient to explain many of the patterns in beginners' spelling errors. On the traditional view, omissions of *a* should be equally common in words like *tar* and words like *tag*, assuming that children have equal exposure to the two types of words. This is because *a* is the second letter of a three-letter sequence in both cases. As we have seen, though, children are more likely to omit *a* in words like *tar* than words like *tag*. The difference reflects children's use of letter-name knowledge in spelling, together with the phonological cohesiveness between /ɑ/ and /r/. As another example, the traditional view predicts similar omission rates for the *l* of *clean* and the *l* of *alone*. But the omission rates are not similar for the two types of words: they are substantially higher for *clean*. The difference stems from the words' phonological forms. The phoneme corresponding to *l* is the second consonant of an onset cluster in *clean* but a singleton onset (the onset of the second syllable) in *alone*.

Although orthographic knowledge has a place in the traditional view of spelling, this knowledge is word-specific. According to the traditional view, children memorize the sequence of letters in each word. They do not learn general patterns that apply to more than one word at a time, such as the positional restriction on *ck* or the alternation between digraphs ending in *i* and *u* and digraphs ending in *y* and *w*. If learning to spell is a matter of rote, word-by-word memorization, children would not be expected to pick up such patterns. As we have seen, however, children learn these patterns at an early age and without explicit instruction. The view of spelling as rote visual memorization needs to be rethought.

More recent views of spelling include two different routes or processes (e.g. Ellis, 1982). The first process, which involves rote, word-by-word memorization, is similar to that envisaged by the traditional view of spelling and thus is subject to the same problems. The second process is more creative. Here, spellers construct the spelling of a word from its phonological form. As a result, they may err on phonemes that have more than one possible spelling, choosing *k* rather than *c* for the initial /k/ of *cake*, for example. The results reviewed here, together with Read's (1975) findings with preschoolers, show that phonology plays an important role in children's early attempts to spell. Errors must be classified by reference to the phonological forms of words as well as by reference to their conventional spellings. Only by viewing errors from a phonological perspective can we understand why omissions of *l* are more common in *clean* than *alone* and why omissions of *a* are more common in *tar* than *tag*.

Within dual-route models, the variable that has been of most interest to researchers has been the regularity of phoneme–grapheme correspondences. Other things being equal, phonemes that have many possible spellings are harder than phonemes that have few spellings (Treiman, 1993). Other things being equal, irregular words such as *said* are harder than regular words such as *sail* (e.g. Treiman, 1984, 1993; Waters, Bruck & Seidenberg, 1985). However, regularity is not the *only* factor that affects children's ability to construct spellings for words. Even regular words cause difficulty when they are phonologically complex. Thus, *slip* is hard for many young children because of the initial consonant cluster. Regular words can also be difficult to spell when a phoneme is not spelled with the letter whose name matches the phoneme. Thus, *hate* causes trouble because the vowel is symbolized with *a* followed by final *e* rather than the single *a* that is expected under a letter-name system. These findings imply that a language that had one-to-one links between phonemes and graphemes would not necessarily be simple to spell. Cross-linguistic studies of spelling development must consider the phonological properties of languages and their systems of letter names as well as the relations between phonemes and graphemes.

The view of spelling as rote memorization and the dual-route theory are meant to apply to both children and adults; they are not true developmental theories. Edmund Henderson and his students and colleagues at the University of Virginia have proposed a theory of spelling development to deal with the changes that take place as children learn to spell. This theory is based on their own observations of schoolchildren and on Read's (1975) findings with preschoolers who began to write before receiving formal instruction in spelling or reading. In the Virginia view, children go through a series of stages in learning to spell. During the various stages, children use qualitatively different types of strategies to spell. (For more detailed discussion of the stages than I am able to provide here, see Henderson & Beers, 1980 and Templeton & Bear, 1992.) During the early stages, the sounds of words are the primary influence on children's spelling. Children progress from representing only some of the segments in spoken words to representing all of the segments. However, the Virginia researchers have not provided a complete picture of *which* segments tend to be omitted during the early phases of spelling development. The results reviewed here confirm that phonology plays an important role in beginning spelling. They further show that children's failures to represent segments are not random. Some segments are more likely to be omitted than others, often for phonological reasons.

The University of Virginia researchers also grant an important role to letter names. Indeed, children in the early stages of learning to spell are thought to symbolize *any* phoneme or sequence of phonemes that matches the name of a letter with the corresponding letter, using a consistent letter-name strategy (Gentry, 1982). The results reviewed here suggest that this claim is too broad. Letter-name spellings are more common for *r*, say, than for *t*. The differences reflect the phonological properties of the letters' names. The interactions between phonological knowledge and letter-name knowledge are not captured by the Virginia theory.

According to the Virginia researchers, children in the early stages of learning to spell string letters together without regard to orthographic conventions (Gentry, 1982). They are as likely to use *ck* at the beginnings of words as at the ends. The results reviewed here speak against this view. They suggest that children notice the orthographic patterns in printed words from the very beginning. Even in the first half of first grade, children are more apt to use *ck* at the ends of works than at the beginnings. Thus, orthographic knowledge is not a late addition to the sources of knowledge used by spellers. It is involved from the beginning.

Existing theories, therefore, do not provide a complete picture of the sources of information that children use to spell. The research reviewed here suggests that children do not rely just on one type of information. From the beginning, children take advantage of what they know about the phonological forms of spoken words, the names of letters and the sequences of letters that make up printed words. If this is true, spelling is unlikely to progress through a series of qualitatively distinct stages in which different sources of knowledge are used. Development should be more continuous, reflecting gradual improvements in children's phonological and orthographic knowledge.

In order to develop a comprehensive theory of spelling development, we must collect further information about children's spelling. We must learn more about the abilities that children bring with them to the spelling task, including their phonological capabilities and limitations, their knowledge of letter names and their knowledge of print. Individual differences in spelling will be traceable, in part, to differences in background knowledge. Finally, we must learn more about how the various sources of information that are used in spelling work together.

ACKNOWLEDGEMENTS

Preparation of this chapter was supported by NSF Grant SBR-9020956. It was written while the author was on sabbatical leave at the Medical Research Council Applied Psychology Unit, Cambridge, England. Thanks to Marie Cassar, Jennifer Gross and E. Daylene Richmond-Welty for their comments on an earlier draft of the chapter.

REFERENCES

Barton, D., Miller, R. & Macken, M. A. (1980). Do children treat clusters as one unit or two? *Papers and Reports on Child Language Development*, **18**, 93–137.

Beers, J. W., Beers, C. S. & Grant, K. (1977). The logic behind children's spelling. *Elementary School Journal*, **77**, 238–242.

Bowey, J. A. & Francis, J. (1991). Phonological analysis as a function of age and exposure to reading instruction. *Applied Psycholinguistics*, **12**, 91–121.

Bruck, M. & Treiman, R. (1990). Phonological awareness and spelling in normal children and dyslexics: the case of initial consonant clusters. *Journal of Experimental Child Psychology*, **50**, 156–178.

Calfee, R. C., Chapman, R. S. & Venezky, R. L. (1972). How a child needs to think to learn to read. In L. W. Gregg (Ed.), *Cognition in Learning and Memory*. New York: Wiley, pp. 139–182.

Carlisle, J. F. (1988). Knowledge of derivational morphology and spelling ability in fourth, sixth, and eighth graders. *Applied Psycholinguistics*, **9**, 247–266.

Ellis, A. W. (1982). Spelling and writing (and reading and speaking). In A. W. Ellis (Ed.), *Normality and Pathology in Cognitive Functions*. London: Academic Press, pp. 113–146.

Fischer, F. W., Shankweiler, D. & Liberman, I. Y. (1985). Spelling proficiency and sensitivity to word structure. *Journal of Memory and Language*, **24**, 423–441.

Fox, B. & Routh, D. K. (1975). Analyzing spoken language into words, syllables, and phonemes: a developmental study. *Journal of Psycholinguistic Research*, **4**, 331–342.

Gentry, J. R. (1982). An analysis of developmental spelling in GNYS AT WRK. *The Reading Teacher*, **36**, 192–200.

Goodman, K. (1967). Reading: a psycholinguistic guessing game. *Journal of the Reading Specialist*, **6**, 126–135.

Jensen, A. R. (1962). Spelling errors and the serial-position effect. *Journal of Educational Psychology*, **53**, 105–109.

Hardy, M., Stennett, R. G. & Smythe, P. C. (1973). Auditory segmentation and auditory blending in relation to beginning reading. *Alberta Journal of Educational Research*, **19**, 144–158.

Henderson, E. H. & Beers, J. W. (Eds) (1980). *Developmental and Cognitive Aspects of Learning to Spell: A Reflection of Word Knowledge*. Newark, DE: International Reading Association.

Kirtley, C., Bryant, P., Maclean, M. & Bradley, L. (1989). Rhyme, rime, and the onset of reading. *Journal of Experimental Child Psychology*, **48**, 224–245.

Knafle, J. D. (1973). Auditory perception of rhyming in kindergarten children. *Journal of Speech and Hearing Research*, **16**, 482–487.

Knafle, J. D. (1974). Children's discrimination of rhyme. *Journal of Speech and Hearing Research*, **17**, 367–372.

Lenel, J. & Cantor, J. (1981). Rhyme recognition and phonemic perception in young children. *Journal of Psycholinguistic Research*, **10**, 57–67.

Leong, C. K. & Haines, C. F. (1978). Beginning readers' analysis of words and sentences. *Journal of Reading Behavior*, **10**, 393–407.

Liberman, I. Y., Shankweiler, D., Fischer, F. W. & Carter, B. (1974). Explicit syllable and phoneme segmentation in the young child. *Journal of Experimental Child Psychology*, **18**, 201–212.

Maclean, M, Bryant, P. & Bradley, L. (1987). Rhymes, nursery rhymes, and reading in early childhood. *Merrill-Palmer Quarterly*, **33**, 255–281.

Marcel, T. (1980). Phonological awareness and phonological representation: investigation of a specific spelling problem. In U. Frith (Ed.), *Cognitive Processes in Spelling*. London: Academic Press, pp. 373–403.

Mason, J. M. (1980). When do children begin to read: an exploration of four year old children's letter and word reading competencies. *Reading Research Quarterly*, **15**, 203–227.

Miller, P. & Limber, J. (1985). The acquisition of consonant clusters: a paradigm problem. Paper presented at the Boston University Conference on Language Development, Boston, MA.

Read, C. (1975). *Children's Categorization of Speech Sounds in English*. NCTE Research Report No. 17. Urbana, IL: National Council of Teachers of English.

Read, C. (1986). *Children's Creative Spelling*. London: Routledge & Kegan Paul.

Selkirk, E. O. (1982). The syllable. In H. Van der Hulst & N. Smith (Eds), *The Structure of Phonological Representations (Part II)*. Dordrecht: Foris, pp. 337–383.

Shankweiler, D. (1992). Surmounting the consonant cluster in beginning reading and writing. Paper presented at the annual meeting of the American Educational Research Association, San Francisco, CA.

Shankweiler, D. & Lundquist, E. (1993). On the relations between learning to spell and learning to read. In R. Frost & L. Katz (Eds), *Orthography, Phonology, Morphology, and Meaning*. Amsterdam: Elsevier, pp. 179–192.

Spache, G. (1940). A critical analysis of various methods of classifying spelling errors, I. *Journal of Educational Psychology*, 31, 111–134.

Stanovich, K. E., Cunningham, A. E. & Cramer, B. (1984). Assessing phonological awareness in kindergarten children: issues of task comparability. *Journal of Experimental Child Psychology*, 38, 175–190.

Templeton, S. & Bear, D. (1992). *Development of Orthographic Knowledge and the Foundations of Literacy*. Hillsdale, NJ: LEA.

Templeton S. & Scarborough-Franks, L. (1985). The spelling's the thing: knowledge of derivational morphology in orthography and phonology among older students. *Applied Psycholinguistics*, 6, 371–390.

Treiman, R. (1984). Individual differences among children in spelling and reading styles. *Journal of Experimental Child Psychology*, 37, 463–477.

Treiman, R. (1985a). Onsets and rimes as units of spoken syllables: evidence from children. *Journal of Experimental Child Psychology*, 39, 161–181.

Treiman, R. (1985b). Phonemic analysis, spelling, and reading. In T. Carr (Ed.), *New Directions for Child Development: The Development of Reading Skills*. San Francisco: Jossey-Bass, pp. 5–18.

Treiman, R. (1985c). Spelling of stop consonants after /s/ by children and adults. *Applied Psycholinguistics*, 6, 261–282.

Treiman, R. (1989). The internal structure of the syllable. In G. Carlson & M. Tanenhaus (Eds), *Linguistic Structure in Language Processing*. Dordrecht: Kluwer, pp. 27–52.

Treiman, R. (1991). Children's spelling errors on syllable–initial consonant clusters. *Journal of Educational Psychology*, 83, 346–360.

Treiman, R. (1992). The role of intrasyllabic units in learning to read and spell. In P. B. Gough, L. Ehri & R. Treiman (Eds), *Reading Acquisition*. Hillsdale, NJ: Erlbaum, pp. 65–106.

Treiman, R. (1993). *Beginning to Spell: A Study of First-Grade Children*. New York: Oxford.

Treiman, R. (in press). Use of consonant letter names in beginning spelling. *Developmental Psychology*.

Treiman, R. & Baron, J. (1981). Segmental and analysis ability: development and relation to reading ability. In G. E. MacKinnon & T. G. Waller (Eds), *Reading Research: Advances in Theory and Practice*, Vol. 3. San Diego, CA: Academic Press, pp. 159–197.

Treiman, R. & Weatherston, S. (1992). Effects of linguistic structure on children's ability to isolate initial consonants. *Journal of Educational Psychology*, 84, 174–181.

Treiman, R. & Zukowski, A. (1991). Levels of phonological awareness. In S. A. Brady & D. P. Shankweiler (Eds), *Phonological Processes in Literacy*. Hillsdale, NJ: LEA, pp. 67–83.

Venezky, R. L. (1970). *The Structure of English Orthography*. The Hague: Mouton.

Waters, G. S., Bruck, M. & Seidenberg, M. (1985). Do children use similar processes to read and spell words? *Journal of Experimental Child Psychology*, 39, 511–530.

5

The Role of Phonological and Orthographic Processes in Learning to Spell

CAROLYN LENNOX

Peel Board of Education, Mississauga, Ontario

LINDA S. SIEGEL

Ontario Institute for Studies in Education, Toronto

Learning to spell involves the integration of several skills. These include knowledge of phonological representations, grammatical and semantic knowledge, as well as the formulation of analogies with words in visual memory and the knowledge of orthographic rules and conventions (Bradley & Bryant, 1981; Bruck & Treiman, 1990; Gough, Juel & Griffith, 1992; Henderson & Templeton, 1986; Marsh et al., 1980; Moats, 1991; Siegel & Heaven, 1986; Siegel & Ryan, 1988; Stanovich & West, 1989; Wagner & Torgesen, 1987; Waters, Bruck & Malus-Abramowitz, 1988). The research on spelling indicates that these skills are mediated primarily by two different processes. One is a phonological process in which spelling is based on the application of the grapheme–phoneme correspondence rules of English and the other is based on a visual process in which lexical analogies can be facilitated through a process of direct lexical access (Ehri & Wilce, 1980; Frith, 1985).

This chapter will address the following issues in terms of this developmental process conceptualization of spelling:

1. How spelling develops in normal spellers
2. What spelling processes are used in learning to spell by both good and poor spellers

Handbook of Spelling: Theory, Process and Intervention. Edited by G. D. A. Brown and N. C. Ellis.
©1994 John Wiley & Sons Ltd.

3. Whether poor spellers merely lag behind good spellers in their spelling or whether they use qualitatively different processes to spell
4. Whether poor spellers who differ in their reading skills use similar or different strategies in spelling

The primary purpose of this chapter is to review the findings from the research in each of the above areas. An additional purpose is to add more specific information about the nature of phonological and orthographic processes used in spelling.

DEVELOPMENTAL SPELLING MODELS

A methodological approach used to determine spelling strategies employed by children has been an analysis of misspellings (see Cook, 1981, for a review). An analysis of children's misspellings reveals whether or not the children apply information about grapheme–phoneme conversion rules in spelling. A phonological strategy, in which phonological rules are used, or a visual strategy, in which the spelled word visually resembles the target word, or a combination of these strategies can be used in spelling. It is possible to distinguish between these alternatives by scoring misspellings according to the degree to which the misspelling approximates the "sound" of the word (phonological strategy) or how well it visually matches the target word (visual strategy). If the child produces a misspelling with "sounds like" the target word, then the child has produced a "phonological misspelling" and is able to use phonological rules. If, on the other hand, the misspelling shows little evidence of phonological matching, then the child has produced a "non-phonological misspelling" and does not use phonological rules. Similar assumptions are made in scoring the child's misspellings according to visual-matching rules.

The findings of studies on spelling, while providing some clear guidelines, are difficult to interpret in certain areas, as they have differed in terms of sample size, tests used to identify spelling and reading levels, and the composition of comparison groups. However, the results do clearly support the importance of phonological processing in the development of spelling. These conclusions come from studies that investigated good and poor spellers, as well as spellers who vary in their reading abilities (Bradley, 1988; Bruck & Waters, 1988; Cromer, 1980; Finucci et al., 1983; Perin, 1982; Waters, Bruck & Seidenberg, 1985).

One cannot be certain that the strategy used by a child to produce a misspelling is the same as the strategy used to produce a correct spelling. However, the use of error analysis is based on the assumption that an analysis of errors provides clues as to the strategy used in spelling. As Read (1986) has indicated, children's non-standard spellings "provide a window on their spelling processes, their notions of writings and (as it turns out) their judgments of speech sounds" (Read, 1986, p. 2). He indicates that non-standard spellings are valued for what they can tell us about psycholinguistic processes (see also Cook, 1981).

A developmental model of spelling in which stages of emergence of spelling skills are noted has been outlined by a number of investigators (Brown, 1990; Gentry, 1982; Henderson & Templeton, 1986). The model proposed by this group of researchers includes an initial precommunicative stage in which children experiment with language symbols; a semiphonetic stage (grades 1 and 2) in which children learn about sound–symbol associations and about left to right progression; a phonetic stage (grades 3 and 4); and a fourth transitional stage (grades 4–6) in which spellers become more knowledgeable about spelling rules and develop a visual strategy. In stage five, they suggest that spellers demonstrate an extensive knowledge of English spelling and recognize spellings because they "look right".

Frith (1980, 1985) also proposed a model of the development of literacy skills. Three stages in the spelling process were outlined. These involve an initial logographic stage in which spelling is restricted to a few rote words; an alphabetic stage in which decoding takes place; and a final or orthographic stage in which spelling becomes independent of sound and lexical analogies may be used.

A model was suggested by Marsh et al. (1980). Marsh and his colleagues proposed an initial strategy that involves sequential phonemic encoding, in which the child is successful in decoding simple consonant–vowel–consonant (CVC) patterns. The child at this stage is required to process the entire word, and in doing so, the child builds up a visual representation of the word in memory. The child then develops the use of a hierarchical encoding strategy which is based on conditional rules. They suggest that this strategy develops more slowly than the sequential phonemic encoding strategy. Marsh and his colleagues also suggested that performance is quite good by the fifth grade, but that some rules are not mastered until adulthood. They noted that "the more experienced subject may (then) switch from a phonemic encoding strategy in spelling unfamiliar words to a strategy based on analogy with known words in visual memory".

These models of spelling development have two major factors in common. The first factor is that each of these models posits a stage of phonological analysis, followed by a stage in which spelling is based on lexical analogies. For example, a coding strategy based on phonological analysis has been called a phonetic stage by Brown (1990), an alphabetic stage by Frith (1985) and sequential and hierarchical encoding by Marsh et al. (1980). Concerning the stage in which spelling is based on lexical analogies, Brown's (1990) research indicates that spellings are recognized because they "look right". Similarly, Frith (1985) suggests that spelling becomes independent of sound at this time and lexical analogies are used. Marsh et al. (1980) also suggest that there is a shift from the phonemic encoding strategy to a strategy based on analogy. In all of these models, visual memory at this stage is seen as a primary component. A second factor that these models share in common is the notion that children learn to spell in a series of stages. Marsh et al. (1980) proposed that this developmental shift occurs around grade 5. They postulated that at this time better spellers might switch from a phonological strategy to a strategy based on analogy with visual characteristics of the word. This stage corresponds to Frith's (1985) orthographic stage and to Brown's (1990) stage 5.

We investigated this developmental shift hypothesis: the hypothesis that at the grade 5 level (approximately 10–11 years of age), spellers shift from a spelling strategy in which phonological cues are primarily used to a strategy based on analogy with visual characteristics of a word (Lennox & Siegel, 1993b). Our results suggested that phonological and visual skills in spelling develop in a continuous manner from the early years through to adolescence, although changes in the *relative use* of phonological strategies or strategies based on the use of visual memory skills can be seen in normal spellers (see also Marsh *et al.*, 1980; Moats, 1991). At any given time, children will use all of the strategies available to them to spell. As children become older and gather more knowledge upon which to base their spelling decisions, visual memory skills and use may be more evident, as children have more experience with print upon which to draw. In a similar vein, Marsh *et al.* (1980) actually provide evidence that children use analogies in their judgement of words for grade 2, but that they do not appear to use their actual spelling until much later. This finding suggests that the ability to actually use analogy in their judgements is present from an early age. As Goswami (1992) points out, the stages are not distinct in practice and the distinction between the stages is too simplistic. Goswami and Bryant (1992), drawing on an earlier study by Goswami (1988), argue that young children are in fact able to use analogies to words learned earlier.

There are important connections between the use of visual and phonological cues in learning to spell. As children decode words, they put the words into visual memory and are able to build on knowledge of words in order to spell other words, through a system of analogy. Analogy to a word in visual memory is therefore dependent upon earlier phonological skills, and can only proceed if phonological skills have been developed and used successfully. The use of analogy involves both sensitivity to the sound of the word as well as matching it, or components of it, to a word in visual memory. Gough and Walsh (1991) found that children who could read pseudowords (presumably read with reference to grapheme–phoneme conversion rules) could also read exception words (presumably read with word-specific knowledge). According to Gough, Juel and Griffiths (1992), this finding suggests that reading and spelling are based on knowledge of the cipher (the translation of print to spoken words) but that specific lexical knowledge is also needed. Neither alone is sufficient.

Information about spelling development is also provided by studies that have examined the effects of early phonological development on spelling. This research has demonstrated that the ability to segment sounds and to produce rhymes is an important predictor of spelling development (Bradley & Bryant, 1981). It is important to determine the specific nature of this connection between phonological awareness and spelling development. Goswami (1988, 1992) argues that the effect of early sound segmentation skill is not just on the child's ability to sound out individual letters (although this is important), but also on the child's ability to use analogies between spellings based on larger phonological units, or rhymes such as *en* in *hen* and *pen*.

In summary, children begin to learn the phonological and visual skills necessary for spelling from the initial stage of learning. They gradually accumulate skills and, when they have a large enough store of knowledge, use these skills in their spelling.

DEVELOPMENT OF SPELLING IN GOOD AND POOR SPELLERS

Much of the research concerning the development of spelling in poor spellers has compared poor spellers who were also poor readers with good spellers who were good readers. This research generally concludes that children with reading and spelling disabilities display a poorer understanding and use of phonological information in their spelling than do normally achieving children (Bruck & Waters, 1988; Cromer, 1980; Finucci *et al.*, 1983; Lennox & Siegel, 1993a,b; Perin, 1982). There is some contradictory evidence, though (Holmes & Peper, 1977; Nelson, 1980), and this can be explained by methodological considerations (Finucci *et al.*, 1983). However, it may not be correct to assume that the processes used in spelling by normally achieving children are similar to those used by children with learning disabilities.

Very little is known about how spelling develops in good and poor spellers, regardless of whether or not a reading problem exists. Some information can be abstracted from studies by Bruck and Waters (1988), Frith (1980) and Waters, Bruck and Seidenberg (1985) in which comparisons were made between good and poor spellers. Both groups were also good readers. A third group, students who are poor readers and poor spellers, was also included in these studies.

Frith (1980) studied children in the age range 11–13 years. She found that good spellers who were also good readers as well as poor spellers who were also good readers had an overwhelming majority of phonological misspellings. That is, both good and poor spellers who were also good readers used a greater proportion of phonologically accurate, albeit unconventional, spellings than did poor readers and spellers when they incorrectly spelled a difficult word. There was a significant difference between these groups and the group that included poor readers and poor spellers. The group of poor readers and spellers produced an almost equal proportion of phonological and non-phonological errors. Waters, Bruck and Seidenberg (1985) studied children in grades 3 and 4 and also found that good readers and spellers produced more phonologically accurate misspellings than poor readers and spellers. However, contrary to Frith's findings, they found that poor spellers, regardless of reading comprehension level, had weaker knowledge of sound–symbol correspondences and were less systematic in their use of them in spelling. In other words, they found that good and poor spellers who were also good readers performed differently from one another, with the poor spellers who were also good readers performing more like the children who were both poor readers and poor spellers. Bruck and Waters (1988), using a decoding measure of reading ability, examined the spelling of students at grade 3 and grade 6. They used two different systems for scoring the phonological accuracy of a misspelling. The first system (unconstrained system) resulted in coding words as phonologically spelled if they sounded like the target word by application of sound–spelling association rules (e.g. *kat* for *cat*; *educat* for *educate*). The second system (constrained system) was more stringent and involved the same grapheme-correspondence rules, as well as the adherence to rules of letter combinations or positions which dictate the sounds of the letters. For example, *educat* would be scored as a phonologically accurate rendition of the target word *educate* in the unconstrained system, but not according to the constrained system. The results for the grade 3 and grade 6 students indicated, again in contrast to the earlier findings of Frith (1980), that poor spellers, regardless of reading decoding ability, performed significantly differently from good spellers on the constrained measure of phonological accuracy, producing fewer phonological misspellings. However, when more rudimentary sound–symbol association rules were examined, the results of the analysis for the grade 3 data failed to reach significance, although grade 6 children who were poor spellers–good readers resembled good spellers who were also good readers, thus similar to the pattern reported by Frith (1980).

To investigate phonological and orthographic development in a larger number of good and poor spellers and to extend the research across several spelling grades, we examined the development of spelling in 234 good spellers and 186 poor spellers from age 6 to 16 (Lennox & Siegel, 1993a,b). The spelling errors of these children were analysed according to the scoring scheme designed by Bruck and Waters (1988). In this scheme, each misspelling was scored three times: first according to whether the misspelling used simple grapheme–phoneme correspondence rules, second according to the child's use of more complex phonological position rules, and third according to the degree to which it visually matched the target word. On both measures of phonological errors, we also found that good spellers consistently used phonological rules more adequately than age-matched poor spellers who were poor readers. That is, the good spellers made a greater percentage of errors in which some attempt was made to match the letters to sounds than did poor spellers. As well, age-matched good spellers also consistently made more errors that were closer visual approximations to the target word. Our research indicated that good spellers had a better grasp of grapheme–phoneme rules and how to apply them, as well as a better ability to remember and use knowledge of the visual configuration of the target word in their spelling. In English, knowledge of sound–symbol association rules alone does not indicate that the student will choose the correct orthographic representation of the word. We also found that poor spellers who were good readers produced as many phonologically based errors as good spellers who were good readers. This result was similar to Frith (1980), and to Bruck and Waters (1988) for the phonological–unconstrained analysis.

Our findings are different from Waters, Bruck and Seidenberg (1985) and this can likely be explained by the fact that we used a decoding task to define reading ability, while Waters and her colleagues used a reading comprehension test. Our findings partially support those of Bruck and Waters (especially for the unconstrained phonological analysis). Our different findings can likely be explained by the widely different sample size, in which our larger sample made it possible to detect differences.

Goswami (1992) noted that children who are developing spelling skills use different strategies than children who are proficient spellers. She draws on the work of Bryant and Bradley (1980) as well as Ehri (1980, 1991) to suggest that proficient spellers use information gained from reading in their spelling. Bryant and Bradley found that 6- and 7-year-old children could spell phonologically regular words that they could not read, but that by age 10 spelling and reading came to be better integrated. This work suggested to Bryant and Bradley (1980) and to Goswami (1992) that, as children developed literacy skills, they used different strategies to read and spell. They suggested that children primarily used visual skills in their reading and phonological skills in their spelling, but that these skills came to be integrated as they became more proficient. Gough, Juel and Griffith (1992) investigated Bryant and Bradley's findings and argued that, in fact, there is a consistency between strategies used by children to read and spell. They suggest that this consistency is based on what they call the cipher, that is, the system by which printed words are pronounced. However, the work of both groups of researchers suggests that phonological skills as well as orthographic skills need to be used for proficient spelling.

Stanovich and West (1989) investigated the reading and spelling of college undergraduates. They found that a measure of exposure to print predicted variance in spelling ability, even after they partialled out differences in phonological coding ability. That is, exposure to print provided information to the student, beyond phonological information, that was helpful in spelling. Information used in spelling was derived from the word structure (see also Templeton & Scarborough-Franks, 1985). These results are consistent with Goswami (1992) and suggest that proficient spellers integrate visual and phonological information.

Our finding that good and poor spellers had an almost equal proportion of visual errors at spelling grade 2 is consistent with Frith's (1985) logographic stage, in which she posits that beginning spellers rely on visual cues and patterns. We found, however, that by the time the good speller reaches grade 3, he/she is performing differently from the poor speller. While the good speller, as most of the previous research has indicated (Frith, 1985; Hendersen & Templeton, 1986; Marsh *et al.*, 1980), is spelling phonologically, the poor speller seems to be relying on visual memory skills in spelling difficult words. These differences persist until the children have reached a spelling grade level 6. By grade 6, the good and poor spellers begin to use visual and phonological cues to a similar extent. That is, the proportions of phonological misspellings and the proportions of visual misspellings are approximately equal for good and poor spellers in grade 6. The finding that the good spellers use visual cues as frequently as poor spellers in grade 6 is consistent with Frith's (1985) orthographic stage, in which automaticity and flexibility are important and in which lexical analogies are frequently used. Bryant and Bradley (1980) and Barron (1980) postulated a "principle of associative symmetry" in the development of literacy skills. They suggested that beginning spellers primarily use phonological cues and that, as the speller becomes more experienced, this specificity declines and memory for visual chunks and analogy is used more frequently. Our findings support this model. Treiman (1984) examined the spelling of grade 3 and 4 normally achieving spellers and concluded that "the ability to use (spelling–sound correspondences) is a more important determinant of ability to spell regular words than is the ability to use word-specific associations" (p. 470). Juel, Griffith and Gough (1986) also provide evidence concerning the importance of spelling–sound correspondence rules (what they call the cipher) in the development of literacy skills.

In conclusion, the use of phonological rules increases over time for both good and poor spellers. In the early years, good and poor spellers do somewhat better with rudimentary sound–symbol association rules than with the more complex rules that include position contraints, but phonological misspellings using simple grapheme–phoneme correspondence rules as well as those also using position rules are produced equally as often once the children have attained a grade 6 spelling level. Good spellers at all ages display a better understanding of phonological rules and orthographic patterns than poor spellers, and more frequently use a phonological as opposed to a visual approach to spelling. However, it must be stressed that, while it may be useful to conceptualize the development of spelling as a series of stages, these stages are not distinct. In fact, our research suggests that both phonological analysis skills and skills based on visual memory and analogy to known words develop continuously and in tandem. What may appear to characterize a particular stage is, in reality, a preponderance of use of one or other strategy, rather than use of one strategy in an absolute sense.

DEVELOPMENTAL LAG/DEVIANCE MODEL

The findings of the research comparing good and poor spellers matched for age indicate that the groups differ in terms of prevalence of types of errors at various ages. However, this analysis does not address the question of whether poor spellers are delayed or deviant when compared to good spellers. In order to answer this question, it is necessary to match the groups in terms of their spelling ability, measured by spelling level on a spelling test. If older poor spellers show a similar pattern of scores to younger good spellers at the same age, it can be concluded that the difference between the age-matched groups is due to a developmental delay. In other words, a young poor speller, when he/she is older, will likely attain the spelling skills demonstrated currently by a spelling level matched good speller. On the other hand, if older poor spellers display a different pattern of scores to younger good spellers at the same spelling level, it can be concluded that poor spellers display deviant spelling patterns: that is, poor spellers use different strategies from good spellers in their spelling, and these differences are not due to maturation alone. This finding would suggest that poor spellers use different strategies to spell and display a different pattern of development of spelling skills, rather than a developmental lag or immaturity.

However, an important distinction should be made between pattern of phonological error (phonological pattern) and pattern of strategy or process used in spelling (strategy pattern). In terms of the phonological pattern, studies that have used a spelling grade match indicate that younger good spellers, matched with older poor spellers, show a similar pattern of use of complex phonological rules (Bruck & Treiman, 1990; Invernizzi & Worthy, 1989; Lennox & Siegel, 1993a; Moats, 1983; Nelson, 1980). In other words, poor spellers attained complex phonological rules involving positional rules more slowly than good spellers, but the two groups showed a similar sequence in acquiring such rules. However, Lennox and Siegel (1993a) found, in a comparison of good and poor spellers matched according to spelling grade, that, on a measure of rudimentary sound–symbol associations, good spellers at all spelling levels produced significantly more phonological matches than poor spellers. These findings were similar to those of others who also investigated the use of phoneme–grapheme correspondence rules (Bruck & Treiman, 1990; Rohl & Tunmer, 1988). That is, this research suggested that when children are matched according to spelling grade level, good and poor spellers successfully master the same complex phonological rules that involve positional constraints. However, poor spellers who attain the same level of ability as good spellers continue to experience difficulty in using simple sound–symbol associations.

There are few data available concerning the most frequently used strategy or process in spelling. To address this question, we examined children's misspellings for information concerning how frequently information about the visual representation of the word was successfully used. We found that older poor spellers at spelling grade levels 3 and 5, matched with younger good spellers at the same spelling grade levels, more frequently produced misspellings that were close visual matches to the target word than did good spellers. These data provided an indication of differences between the groups. The most compelling evidence concerning strategy pattern, however, came from an examination of children's misspellings according to whether their errors were more frequently phonological (that is, they made phonological matches but incorrect spellings) or visual, that is, were close visual matches to the target word (Lennox & Siegel, 1993a). The results of this more direct comparison indicated that poor spellers at spelling grades 3, 4 and 5 more frequently used a visual strategy rather than a phonological strategy, while the reverse pattern was true for the good spellers. These data suggested that poor spellers, because of poor phonological skills, are more likely to successfully use their visual memory skills for the form of a word in their spelling.

These results are similar to the observations made by Siegel (in press) of the performance of reading disabled and normally achieving children on an orthographic task. The children who were reading disabled were also poor spellers, and the normally achieving children were good spellers. The children were presented with two pseudowords, one of which contained a letter combination that never occurs in English (e.g. *filv–filk*). The children were asked to indicate which one could be a word. On this task the reading disabled group (poor spellers) performed *more accurately* than reading level matched normally achieving children (good spellers). These results suggested that the poor spellers were probably using a visual route to read and had good visual memory skills.

In summary, our results (Lennox & Siegel, 1993a) suggest that older poor spellers attain a similar level of spelling ability with young good spellers through the use of orthographic conventions such as visual matching (in which visual memory skills are employed) and phonological position rules, rather than, as is the case with good spellers, the use of simple sound–symbol association rules as well as more complex orthographic rules. Our research suggests that good and poor spellers use different strategies to spell. In a similar vein, Juel, Griffith and Gough (1986) collected longitudinal data on word recognition, spelling, reading comprehension and writing as children went from the first to the second grade. They investigated the degree to which progress in each of these areas was related to phonemic awareness, spelling–sound knowledge and lexical knowledge. The authors found that children with good and poor spelling–sound knowledge who attained average reading comprehension scores at the end of the first grade did so in qualitatively different ways. Juel *et al.* (1986) suggested that children with poor spelling–sound knowledge succeeded in memorizing relevant visual cues. Children who possessed good spelling–sound knowledge seemed to use this knowledge in their reading. Juel *et al.* (1986) concluded that there are "code" readers, who rely primarily on visual cues, and "cipher" readers, who also use letter–sound information.

Three sets of results suggest that poor spellers use different spelling strategies from good spellers. First, our finding that poor spellers at spelling grade levels 3, 4 and 5, matched with younger good spellers according to spelling grade, produced more visual than phonological errors while the reverse pattern was true for good spellers suggests that poor spellers display a deviant developmental pattern in learning to spell, rather than a developmental lag or immaturity. As well, poor spellers at spelling grades 3 and 5 made more visually accurate matches than good spellers at the same spelling grade level, while poor spellers at other grade levels were equally as proficient as good spellers at producing a visual match to the target word. Finally, when matched according to spelling grade, good and poor spellers were equally as proficient in the use of higher-level phonological rules that involved positional constraints. However, poor spellers at all grade levels had more difficulty than grade-matched good spellers in producing accurate phonological matches to the target word. Poor spellers, when compared with good spellers, displayed a deviant developmental pattern in learning to spell, with a greater success in the reliance on visual memory skills than on phonological analysis.

In summary, good spellers use their good phonological processing skills in spelling while poor spellers show a different pattern, primarily using visual memory strategies in spelling difficult words.

DIFFERENCES BETWEEN SPELLERS AS A FUNCTION OF READING ABILITY

Phonological information is used by young children for both spelling and reading (Waters, Bruck & Seidenberg, 1985). Therefore, it would be expected that there is a group of children characterized by good spelling and reading skills and that, in fact, is the case. Phonological skills used for spelling are more complex and ambiguous than those used in reading (Bruck & Waters, 1988; Frith, 1980). For example, there may be several ways to spell a word (only one of which is conventionally correct) so that the speller has to choose one alternative out of several possibilities. However, there is usually only one way a given configuration of letters sounds. Children with good spelling abilities are likely also to have good reading abilities. A group of children with poor reading and poor spelling skills can also be identified. If children do not understand and use phonological skills sufficiently well enough to read, they will not have the more complex phonological skills for spelling. There are few, if any, children who are good spellers and poor readers. However, a subgroup of children characterized by good reading and poor spelling abilities has been identified (Bruck & Waters, 1988; Frith, 1980; Lennox & Siegel, 1993b; Rourke, 1981; Siegel & Feldman, 1983; Siegel & Heaven, 1986). We will refer to these children as having mixed reading and spelling abilities.

The results of the studies that have compared these groups have been somewhat inconsistent (Bruck & Waters, 1988; Frith, 1980; Waters, Bruck & Seidenberg, 1985) and these differences can probably be explained by differing tests used to determine reading level, differing age groups studied and differing sample sizes. We investigated the spelling of these groups from grade 2–5 and found, consistent with Frith (1980) and Nelson and Warrington (1974), and partially with Bruck and Waters (1988), that children who had mixed reading and spelling skills performed similarly to good readers and spellers in terms of proportion of phonological errors.

In explaining the finding that both good readers and spellers and the mixed group displayed a higher percentage of phonological errors than poor readers and spellers, Frith (1980) suggested that the precise nature of the deficit could be elucidated by comparing the reading strategies of the good readers and spellers with those of the mixed group. In a comparison of the groups, she found that good readers and spellers read by complete analysis of the letters while the mixed group attended only to partial cues. She argued that children with mixed reading and spelling abilities used a visual approach to reading, attending only to partial cues. She indicated further that the deficits of children who were poor readers and spellers were primarily the result of a language deficit, while the deficit displayed by the group with mixed reading and spelling abilities was of a different nature. Reading by partial cues would not provide the opportunities for learning about orthographic rules (see also Stanovich & West, 1989). She hypothesized therefore that the deficit of the group with mixed reading and spelling abilities involved an ignorance of the English Orthographic system that lay beyond phonological analysis. Ehri (1991) also provides evidence that the subjects with good reading but poor spelling skills lack knowledge of the orthographic system, so that they have difficulty choosing the conventional spelling when there are two plausible alternatives. Our results support this hypothesis.

We conducted a detailed examination of the reading and spelling skills of good readers and spellers (Good), poor readers and spellers (Poor) and good readers–poor spellers (Mixed). The children were divided into groups on the basis of their performance on the Wide Range Achievement Test—Revised (WRAT-R, Jastak & Wilkinson, 1984). Children were classified as good readers and spellers (Good) if they attained a score on the reading and spelling subtests of the WRAT-R above the 30th percentile. They were classified as poor readers and spellers (Poor) if they attained scores on the reading and spelling subtests below the 25th percentile. They were classified as good readers–poor spellers (Mixed) if they attained a score on the reading subtest above the 30th percentile and on the spelling subtest below the 25th percentile. The children were administered a variety of standardized tests and experimental tasks to measure reading and spelling. They were then matched on spelling grade level and the groups compared.

The following reading tasks were used:

Regular and Exception Words

The children were asked to read a list of 36 regular and 36 exception words (Baron, 1979). The pronunciation of the regular words follows the letter–sound correspondence rules of English; the exception words do not. Examples of regular words include *cut*, *gave*, *few*, *nice*; exception words include *put*, *have*, *sew*, *police*.

Reading of Pseudowords

The children were administered the Reading of Symbols subtest of the GFW Sound–Symbol Test (Goldman, Fristoe & Woodcock, 1984), in which they were required to read pronounceable non-words such as *bim*, *rayed*, *neap*, *toaf*, *cedge*.

Phonological Task

These tasks (Siegel, 1986) were adapted from one designed by Olson *et al.* (1985). In each of these tasks there were 26 trials in which two stimuli were presented for each trial. Chance level performance was 13 correct. For the phonological task, the child was required to specify which of two visually presented pseudowords (*kake–dake*, *joak–joap*) sounded like a real word.

Experimental Pseudoword Task

The children were presented with 32 regular and irregular pseudowords, some of which could be read by grapheme–phoneme conversion (GPC) rules or by analogy to a real word. For example *bave* could be read as *bav* or by analogy to *have*.

Analogy Reading Task

The children were asked to read a list of 18 pseudowords that could be read either by analogy or by GPC rules (Siegel & Geva, 1990). For example, words included *puscle*, *fody*, *risten*.

The following spelling and orthographic tasks were used:

Spelling of Nonwords

The children were administered the Spelling of Symbols subtest of the GFW Sound–Symbol Test. The child was asked to write pseudowords that were read aloud by the examiner, such as *tash*, *plen*, *etbom*, *spong*. Any acceptable phonological equivalent was scored as correct. For example, the sound of *imbaf* could be spelled *imbaf* or *imbaff*. Before spelling the word, the child was asked to repeat it to ensure that he or she had heard it correctly. Mispronunciations were corrected.

Orthographic Awareness Task

This task investigated the ability to recognize legal and illegal orthographic combinations of English letters. The task was a two-choice one in which the children were presented with 17 pairs of pronounceable pseudowords, one of which contained a bigram that never occurs in an English word in a particular position and the other one of which contained an orthographic string that does occur in English. Examples included *filv–filk*, *make–moje*, *vism–visn* and *powl–lowp*. The children were told that neither was a real word but their task was to specify which one "could be a word" or "looks like a word".

Visual Task

Olson *et al.* (1985) developed a task that investigates the visual processing route. The child was presented with a real word and a pseudohomophone (e.g. *rain–rane*, *boal–bowl*) and had to select the correct spelling. In this task, both choices sounded exactly the same, so that visual memory for the orthography of a word had to be used; phonological processes were not helpful in this case because sounding out the words would produce identical responses to each word.

The results of the reading tasks are shown in Table 5.1. For all of the phonological reading tasks, the Good group performed similarly to the Mixed group. Both groups

TABLE 5.1   Means on the reading and phonological tasks as a function of spelling grade level.

	Good RS		Mixed RS		Poor RS	
	M	N	M	N	M	N
Regular words[a] Grades 3 & 4	28.8	56	32.2	17	29.7	27
Irregular words[a] Grades 3 & 4	26.4	56	30.7	17	27.4	27
Pseudoword reading (GFW)[a] Grades 3 & 4	31.16	43	35.0	11	22.4	27
Pseudoword reading task[b]						
Grade 2	82.6	7	85.4	13	53.6	49
Grade 3	89.9	9	91.8	8	73.1	38
Grade 4	90.1	6	92.9	7	83.0	7
Analogy reading task[b]						
Grade 2	72.2	7	73.1	13	32.4	47
Grade 3	75.3	9	79.2	8	57.5	38
Grades 4 & 5 combined	84.3	18	84.4	15	67.6	12
Phonological task[b] Grades 2 & 3 combined	69.2	11	78.8	8	56.4	49

[a]Number correct.
[b]Per cent correct.

performed significantly better than the Poor group. The results were similar for the regular and irregular word reading tasks, as well as for the reading of pseudowords, the phonological task, and the experimental pseudoword task.

The findings for the analogy reading task were as expected. The Good and Mixed groups performed similarly on this task, except at the oldest spelling grades, while the Poor group performed at a lower level. At older ages the Mixed group performed at a lower level than the Good group, indicating that they may have more difficulties using lexical analogies.

The findings for the spelling and orthographic tasks are shown in Table 5.2. The findings for the spelling of nonwords task (GFW) were similar to the previous phonological tasks. The Good group performed in a manner similar to the Mixed group, while the Poor group performed more poorly than the other groups.

On the visual task, Mixed and Good groups performed similarly, while the Poor group obtained lower scores. This task requires the child to use visual memory for the orthography of a word, and highly frequent words are used. The Mixed group, matched with the Good group according to spelling grade level, were older than the Good group. They had therefore more exposure to print and to real words. Consequently, it was not surprising that the Good and Mixed groups, who were able

TABLE 5.2   Means on the spelling tasks as a function of spelling grade level.

	Good RS		Mixed RS		Poor RS	
	M	N	M	N	M	N
Orthographic task 1[a] Grades 2 & 3 combined	81.9	13	74.5	21	73.8	79
GFW pseudoword[b] spelling Grades 3 & 4						
combined	20.8	43	23.7	12	14.2	25
Visual task[a] Grades 2 & 3 combined	90.2	11	92.8	8	79.3	51

[a]Mean per cent correct.
[b]Mean number correct.

to read at approximately the same level, attained similar scores on this task. The Poor group, who were impaired in their reading and spelling ability and who therefore had not been exposed to as many words, attained lower scores on this task.

On the other hand, the results for the orthographic awareness task were different from the previous results. On this task, the Good group performed better than either the Poor group or the Mixed group. The older Mixed group could not use their memory of real, overlearned words, as in the visual task, to complete this task. For this task, as opposed to the visual memory task, the good readers and poor spellers had to remember components of the real words and use this information in recognizing pseudowords. Frith (1980) provided evidence to suggest that the Mixed group read by partial cues. Reading by partial cues would suggest that the visual memory skills of the Mixed group would be sufficient to permit recognition of real words, such as in the visual memory task. However, when the task requires visual memory for components of words read, the Mixed group have difficulty. These results suggested that the visual memory skills of the Mixed group were similar to those of the Poor group and worse than those of the Good group.

The results indicate that the Good and Mixed groups do better than the Poor group on phonological tasks that involve reading regular and irregular words, pseudowords, and in using analogy for the sound of a previously learned word. The Good and Mixed groups also do better than the Poor group on a pseudoword spelling task, which involves phonological skills because direct lexical access cannot be used as there are, by definition, no lexical entries for pseudowords. These results are also consistent with a more direct examination of the children's actual spelling, in which Good and Mixed groups use phonological matching rules more frequently in their spelling errors than do poor readers and spellers (Lennox & Siegel, 1993b). However, the Mixed group performed similarly to the Poor group on the orthographic awareness task. In summary, children with mixed reading and spelling abilities appear to have similar phonological skills to and more deficient visual memory skills than normally achieving children.

CONCLUSIONS

We can conclude the following about the development of spelling:

1. Phonological skills are of primary importance in the development of spelling.
2. In children with normal spelling abilities, visual skills gained through exposure to print develop in tandem with phonological skills but are not used until the more advanced stages, when the use of analogy is common.
3. Poor spellers have difficulty with the use of phonological skills and rely on their visual memory skills and orthographic conventions rather than more rudimentary phonological skills.
4. Poor spellers who are also good readers have an advantage over poor spellers who are poor readers in that they are able to use phonological skills more readily in their spelling.
5. Although poor spellers who are also good readers are able to successfully use their phonological knowledge to spell a word, they have more difficulty than good

readers and spellers in then choosing the correct orthographic representation of that word from among the phonologically accurate alternatives. Therefore, poor spellers who are good readers appear to have deficits in visual memory and a lack of awareness of the orthographic patterns of the English language.

ACKNOWLEDGEMENTS

The research described in this chapter was supported by a grant to L. S. Siegel from the Natural Sciences and Engineering Council of Canada. This chapter was prepared while L. S. Siegel held a Senior Research Fellowship from the Ontario Mental Health Foundation. The authors wish to thank Letty Guirnela for secretarial assistance.

REFERENCES

Baron, J. (1979). Orthographic and word-specific mechanisms in children's reading of words. *Child Development*, **50**, 60–72.
Barron, R. W. (1980). Visual and phonological strategies in reading and spelling. In U. Frith (Ed.), *Cognitive Processes in Spelling*. Toronto: Academic Press, pp. 195–213.
Bradley, L. (1988). Making connections in learning to read and to spell. *Applied Cognitive Psychology*, **2**, 19–31.
Bradley, L. & Bryant, R. E. (1981). Visual memory and phonological skills in reading and spelling backwardness. *Psychological Research*, **43**, 193–199.
Brown, A. (1990). A review of recent research in spelling. *Educational Psychology Review*, **2**, 365–397.
Bruck, M. & Treiman, R. (1990). Phonological awareness and spelling in normal children and dyslexics: the case of initial consonant clusters. *Journal of Experimental Child Psychology*, **50**, 156–178.
Bruck, M. & Waters, G. (1988). An analysis of the spelling errors of children who differ in their reading and spelling skills. *Applied Psycholinguistics*, **9**, 77–92.
Bryant, R. E. & Bradley, L. (1980). Why children sometimes write words which they do not read. In U. Frith (Ed.), *Cognitive Processes in Spelling*. Toronto: Academic Press, pp. 355–370.
Cook, L. (1981). Misspelling analysis in dyslexia: observation of developmental strategy shifts. *Bulletin of the Orton Society*, **31**, 123–134.
Cromer, R. F. (1980). Spontaneous spelling by language disordered children. In U. Frith (Ed.), *Cognitive Processes in Spelling*. Toronto: Academic Press, pp. 405–421.
Doehring, D. G. (1984). Subtyping of reading disorders: implications for remediation. *Annals of Dyslexia*, **34**, 205–216.
Ehri, L. (1980). The development of orthographic images. In U. Frith (Ed.), *Cognitive Processes in Spelling*. London: Academic Press, pp. 311–338.
Ehri, L. (1991). The development of reading and spelling in children: an overview. In M. Snowling & M. Thompson (Eds), *Dyslexia: Integrating Theory and Practice*. London: Whurr, pp. 63–79.
Ehri, L. & Wilce, L. (1980). The influence of orthography on readers' conceptualization of the phonemic structure of words. *Applied Psycholinguistics*, **1**, 371–385.
Finucci, J. M., Isaacs, S., Whitehouse, C. C. & Childs, B. (1983). Classification of spelling errors and their relationship to reading ability, sex, grade placement and intelligence. *Brain and Language*, **20**, 340–355.
Frith, U. (1980). Unexpected spelling problems. In U. Frith (Ed.), *Cognitive Processes in Spelling*. Toronto: Academic Press, pp. 495–515.

Frith U. (1985). Beneath the surface of developmental dyslexia. In K. E. Patterson, J. C. Marshall & M. Coltheart (Eds), *Surface Dyslexia*. London: Routledge & Kegan Paul.

Gates, A. I. & McKillop, A. S. (1962). *Gates-McKillop Reading Diagnostic Tests*. New York: Teacher's College Press.

Gentry, J. R. (1982). An analysis of developmental spelling in GNYS at WRK. *Reading Teacher*, **36**, 192–200.

Goldman, R., Fristoe, M. & Woodcock, R. W. (1984). *GFW Sound-Symbol Tests*. Circle Pines, MN: American Guidance Service.

Goswami, U. (1988). Orthographic analogies and reading development. *Quarterly Journal of Experimental Psychology*, **40A**, 239–268.

Goswami, U. (1992). Annotation: phonological factors in spelling development. *Journal of Child Psychology and Psychiatry*, **33**, 967–975.

Goswami, U. & Bryant, P. (1992). Rhyme, analogy and children's reading. In P. Gough, L. Ehri & R. Treiman (Eds), *Reading Acquisition*. Hillsdale, NJ: LEA, pp. 49–63.

Gough, P. B. & Walsh, M. A. (1991). Chinese Phoenicians, and the orthographic cipher of English. In S. A. Brady & D. P. Shankweiler (Eds), *Phonological Processes in Literacy: A Tribute to Isabelle Y. Liberman*. Hillsdale, NJ: LEA, pp. 199–209.

Gough, P. B., Juel, C. & Griffiths, P. (1992). Reading, spelling and the orthographic cipher. In P. Gough, L. Ehri & R. Treiman (Eds), *Reading Acquisition*. Hillsdale, NJ: LEA, pp. 35–48.

Henderson, E. H. & Templeton, S. (1986). A developmental perspective of formal spelling instruction through alphabet, pattern, and meaning. *The Elementary School Journal*, **80**, 305–316.

Holmes, D. L. & Peper, E. J. (1977). Evaluation of the use of spelling error analysis in the diagnosis of reading disabilities. *Child Development*, **48**, 1708–1711.

Invernizzi, M. & Worthy, J. (1989). Spelling errors of learning disabled and normal children across 4 grade levels of spelling achievement. *Reading Psychology*, **10**, 173–188.

Jastak, S. & Wilkinson, G. (1984). *The Wide Range Achievement Test—Revised*. Wilmington, Delaware: Jastak.

Juel, C., Griffith, P. & Gough, P. B. (1986). Acquisition of literacy: a longitudinal study of children in first and second grade. *Journal of Educational Psychology*, **78**, 243–255.

Lennox, C. & Siegel, L. (1993a). The development of phonological rules and visual strategies in good and poor spellers. Manuscript submitted for publication.

Lennox, C. & Siegel, L. (1993b). Visual and phonological spelling errors in subtypes of children with learning disabilities. *Applied Psycholinguistics*, **14**, 473–488.

Marsh, G., Friedman, M., Welch, U. & Desberg, P. (1980). The development of strategies in spelling. In U. Frith (Ed.), *Cognitive Processes in Spelling*. Toronto: Academic Press, pp. 339–353.

Moats, L. C. (1983). A comparison of the spelling errors of older dyslexic and second grade normal children. *Annals of Dyslexia*, **33**, 121–139.

Moats, L. C. (1991). Spelling disability in adolescents and adults. In A. M. Bain, L. L. Bailet & L. C. Moats (Eds), *Written Language Disorders: Theory into Practice*. Austin, TX: Pro-Ed, pp. 23–42.

Nelson, H. D. (1980). Analysis of spelling errors in normal and dyslexic children. In U. Frith (Ed.), *Cognitive Processes in Spelling*. Toronto: Academic Press, pp. 475–493.

Nelson, H. E. & Warrington, E. K. (1974). Developmental spelling retardation and its relation to other cognitive abilities. *British Journal of Psychology*, **65**, 265–274.

Olson, R., Kliegl, R., Davidson, B. J. & Foltz, G. (1985). Individual developmental differences in reading disability. In T. G. Waller (Ed.), *Reading Research: Advances in Theory and Practice*, Vol. 4. New York: Academic Press, pp. 1–64.

Perin, D. (1982). Spelling strategies in good and poor readers. *Applied Psycholinguistics*, **3**, 1–14.

Read, C. (1986). *Children's Creative Spelling*. London: Routledge & Kegan Paul.

Rohl, M. & Tunmer, W. E. (1988). Phonemic segmentation skill and spelling acquisition. *Applied Psycholinguistics*, **9**, 335–350.

Rourke, B. P. (1981). Neuropsychological assessment of children with learning disabilities. In S. B. Filskov & T. S. Bell (Eds), *Handbook of Clinical Neuropsychology*. New York: Wiley, pp. 453–478.

Siegel, L. S. (1986). Phonological deficits in children with a disability. *Canadian Journal of Special Education*, **2**, 45–54.

Siegel, L. S. (in press). Phonological processing deficits as the basis of developmental dyslexia: implications for remediation. In G. Humphries & J. Riddoch (Eds), *Cognitive Neuropsychology and Cognitive Rehabilitation*. Hove, UK: LEA.

Siegel, L. & Feldman, W. (1983). Nondyslexic children with combined writing and arithmetic difficulties. *Clinical Pediatrics*, **22**, 241–244.

Siegel, L. S. & Geva, E. (1990). Reading by analogy or rules: a comparison of poor and normal readers. Unpublished manuscript.

Siegel, L. S. & Heaven, R. K. (1986). Categorization of learning disabilities. In S. J. Ceci (Ed.), *Handbook of Cognitive, Social and Neuropsychological Aspects of Learning Disabilities*, Vol. 1. Hillsdale: NJ: LEA, pp. 95–121.

Siegel, L. S. & Ryan, E. B. (1988). Development of grammatical sensitivity, phonological, and short-term memory skills in normally achieving and learning disabled children. *Developmental Psychology*, **24**, 28–37.

Stanovich, K. & West, R. (1989). Exposure to print and orthographic processing. *Reading and Research Quarterly*, **24**, 402–433.

Templeton, S. & Scarborough-Franks, L. (1985). The spelling's the thing: knowledge of derivational morphology in orthography and phonology among older students. *Applied Psycholinguistics*, **6**, 371–390.

Treiman, R. (1984). Individual differences among children in spelling and reading styles. *Journal of Experimental Child Psychology*, **37**, 463–477.

Wagner, R. K. & Torgesen, J. K. (1987). The nature of phonological processing and its causal role in the acquisition of reading skills. *Psychological Bulletin*, **101**, 192–212.

Waters, G. S., Bruck, M. & Malus-Abramowitz, M. (1988). The role of linguistic and visual information in spelling: a developmental study. *Journal of Experimental Child Psychology*, **45**, 400–421.

Waters, G. S., Bruck, M. & Seidenberg, M. (1985). Do children use similar processes to read and spell words? *Journal of Experimental Child Psychology*, **39**, 511–530.

Woodcock, R. W. (1973). *Woodcock Reading Mastery Tests*. Circle Pines, MN: American Guidance Service.

6

Towards a Model of Spelling Acquisition: The Development of Some Component Skills

MARGARET J. SNOWLING

University of Newcastle-upon-Tyne

Learning to write in an orthography such as English is a considerable undertaking. When young children first begin to write, the motor demands of the task are themselves challenging and a great deal of effort goes into the production of the first recognizable words. As well as coordinating their motor movements, children draw on their visual experience of printed words, they work out how to translate spoken words into written form and they learn about the convention that words are written from the left to the right with spaces in between. Considering the complexities of these various processes, it is not unreasonable to expect that it will take 4–5 years to master the basics of the spelling system, and the task of learning exceptional spellings inevitably continues into adulthood.

Current models of spelling have generally failed to recognize the information-processing demands of the task, especially for the novice. This chapter will put forward the view that models of spelling development that stress the stage-like passage of a child through qualitatively different phases in which different strategies are involved do not capture the range of difficulties that young children are likely to encounter before they can spell proficiently. Similarly, models which separate lexical and phonological processes in spelling do not recognize the dependence of one kind of strategy upon another during development. We shall argue that from the earliest stages of development, children use a variety of sources of knowledge in spelling, all to different levels of proficiency, and the extent to which they are successful depends

Handbook of Spelling: Theory, Process and Intervention. Edited by G. D. A. Brown and N. C. Ellis.
©1994 John Wiley & Sons Ltd.

upon processing demands; their spelling will normally be better when they are writing single words than when they are composing a "story", their letter–sound translation skills will be better when tested in isolation than when used in a situation where they also have to segment and to memorize components of spoken words.

Stage models of literacy development have focused on the progression of the child from writing in a rudimentary, impressionistic way, through a period of what might be described as phonetic transcription, to a stage when he or she can spell all types of word with great facility using morphemic knowledge (e.g. Ehri, 1991; Marsh *et al.*, 1980). According to Frith (1985), the beginning reader is largely unable to write because, at this stage, the cues used for reading will not support the writing process. Put simply, children are reading using partial cues; this means that they might recognize *gentleman* because it is a long word starting with *g*, and *jelly* because of the double *l*. Spelling, however, requires full cues and would be grossly inaccurate if it were to proceed using the information extracted during reading, i.e. *jelly→ll*. Thus, in the early "logographic" phase, the child might write a few whole words from memory but, by and large, will not spell.

Frith (1985) argues that it is in fact the need to write that transforms the child's approach to print. Thus, rather than using a logographic spelling strategy, the child starts to spell using a strategy of sound–letter translation, signalling entry to the alphabetic phase of development. Once the child becomes aware of the relationships between letters and sounds, this knowledge will be applied to the reading process, greatly increasing the child's reading competence. At a later stage, the child moves into the orthographic phase, when both reading and spelling are automatic and independent of sound. The child makes this transition first for reading and then for spelling. Once in this final stage, the speller is familiar with orthographic conventions, including the morphemic relationships between words.

Within Frith's framework, children with specific learning difficulties experience problems in moving between the phases. Hence, a child with phonological processing problems typically finds it difficult to move into the alphabetic phase (Snowling, Stackhouse & Rack, 1986), while another child, perhaps with visual problems, will be unable to move into the orthographic phase (Goulandris & Snowling, 1991). Still other individuals, described by Frith (1980) as "group B" spellers, are good readers in the orthographic phase but they remain alphabetic spellers and spell phonetically.

While it is useful theoretically to characterize spelling difficulties in this way, such gross explanations do not capture the range of spelling problems that can be experienced by children during the acquisition phase, nor do they provide sufficiently explicit descriptions to prescribe remedial programmes. If this is to be possible, it is necessary to develop a theory of spelling development that is cast in processing terms. In addition, we believe from our observations of young children spelling that they draw upon diverse knowledge and use a wide range of strategies, albeit imperfectly, from the outset. It therefore seems to be important to develop theories of spelling that are interactive and less stage-like in their conception. To this end we will discuss some sets of data that we have collected from young children learning to spell and also from developmental dyslexics. We hope these data will be mutually informing and provide some of the basic building blocks for such a theory.

EXPLORATIONS OF CHILDREN'S SPELLING

Emergent Spelling and the Case of Consonant Clusters

Preliterate children most commonly adopt a "scribble" mode of written communication. In addition, they may know how to write their own name. Soon after this, some children begin to write parts of the words they can read, for example one child we saw recently wrote *oo* for *roof* and also produced a mixture of first letters and pictograms to depict words. However, in exceptional circumstances, some precocious spellers will also produce non-conventional forms. Read (1971) studied the writings of a group of preschool children who had received no formal instruction, though they knew their letters. He found that many of these children's spellings were rough approximations to the phonological forms of the words. For example, they wrote *chrubl* for *trouble* and *chan* for *train*. On the face of it, these naive attempts were a long way from their targets, but closer examination indicated that they may be phonetically acceptable attempts that are "uncontaminated" by orthographic experience.

Evidence for this view was provided by some studies in which Read (1973) showed that, while 5- and 6-year-olds consider words beginning with [tr] to sound similar to words beginning with [tʃ], 7- and 8-year-olds classify words beginning with [tr] together with words beginning with [t]. The younger children seemed to be treating the onsets of these words as single sounds while the older children appeared to be able to decompose the cluster /tr/ into /t/ and /r/. Arguably, it is reading experience that brings about this change in children's perception of the sounds of spoken words. As Goswami and Bryant (1990) have argued, the ability to segment spoken words into phonemic segments is critical for spelling development. However, phoneme awareness is usually not acquired before children go to school. It is most likely that the ability to segment words phonemically is a consequence of learning to read and of observing that the letter or graphemic segments of printed words correspond to the speech segments of spoken words. Thus, before children learn to read, their use of phonological spelling strategies is limited. It was for this reason that some of the young children studied by Read produced very unusual written forms.

One aspect of young children's spelling that has attracted considerable interest is the difficulty they experience in writing words that contain consonant clusters (Marcel, 1980; Read, 1975; Snowling, 1982; Treiman, 1985, 1991). It is not uncommon to hear a child segment a word into onset and rime units, for example *pram*→[pr-am] and then to see them write *pam*, or *tent*→[t-ent] and then to write *tet*. Indeed, Treiman (1985) reported that some 27% of the spelling errors made by a class of first-grade children on words containing word–initial clusters stemmed from failure to represent one or more phonemes of the cluster. The omitted phoneme tended to be the second phoneme in the case of two-phoneme clusters such as *bl* and *sn* and the third phoneme in the case of three-phoneme clusters such as *spr*.

In Treiman's study, children also show a marked tendency to omit one of the phonemes from clusters in word-final position (e.g. *bak* for *bank*). Similar evidence that we have collected suggests that this tendency may persist for some time longer than the tendency to reduce initial clusters (Snowling, 1982). In this study, we investigated the ability of normal and dyslexic readers to spell nonwords containing nasal clusters, for example *nent, pank* and *randle*. Nonword stimuli were chosen to minimize the potential influence of lexical knowledge in this experiment. The children ranged in spelling age from 6 to 9 years and the two groups were closely matched. At the start of the experiment, we provided the children with a printed sheet containing the initial parts of the nonwords. In each case the initial consonant or consonants and the medial vowel were supplied and the children's task was to complete the spelling after they had heard the target nonword.

All possible nasal endings were tested in the experiment and each nasal spelling was tested three times in the context of the different nonwords. The complete set of experimental stimuli included nonwords ending in the singletons *n, m* and *ng* and in the following nasal clusters: *nt, nk, mp, nd, ns, nse, nce, nch* and *nge*. We also included nonwords containing nasal clusters in medial position preceding syllabic [1] (*ntle, nkle, mple, ndle, ngle, mble*). Our first hypothesis was that nasal singletons would be transcribed more accurately than nasal clusters. Secondly, we predicted that nasal clusters in medial position, preceding syllabic [1], would be the most difficult to spell because, in processing terms, the addition of syllabic [1] means there are more components to this task.

Since there was no significant difference between the performance of the dyslexic readers and the control children who were matched on spelling age, we shall focus on the data from the normal group for present purposes and consider the extent to which the phonetic characteristics of the stimuli affected performance.

Three different types of error were possible: the nasal in the cluster could be misrepresented (*blen* for *blem*), the other consonant in the cluster could be incorrect, *hend* for *hent*, or there could be a problem in transcribing syllabic [1] (*stemper* for *stemple*). Examination of the error corpus indicated that 85% of the errors were with respect to the nasal segments. A much smaller proportion, some 12%, affected other consonants and a negligible 3% affected syllabic [1]. Furthermore, some 87% of the nasal errors were omissions and only 13% involved substitutions. These were made primarily by children with a spelling age less than 9 years who tended to represent [ŋ] as *n*. The phonemes [n] and [m] were never confused. As predicted, nasals were relatively easier to spell in isolation and nasal clusters were harder to spell in medial than in final position.

In most English accents, nasals are less perceptible in clusters where they precede unvoiced stops (e.g. *bent*) than when they precede voiced stops (e.g. *bend*). We therefore predicted that nasals preceding unvoiced stops would be omitted more frequently than nasals preceding voiced stops. The relative difficulty of the various nasal spellings is shown in Figure 6.1. Although these data were not amenable to statistical analysis, there was some support for our hypothesis. In the case of medial nasal clusters following syllabic [1], the nasals preceding voiced stops were easier to spell than in those preceding unvoiced stops. Thus, nonwords ending in *-ngle, -ndle* and *-mble* were easier to spell than those ending in *-nkle, -ntle* and *-mple*. However, the difference between word-final clusters ending in voiced stops and those ending in unvoiced stops was not significant. Our other findings were that word-final nasal clusters were of approximately equivalent difficulty to nasal + fricative endings (*-ns, -nse, -nce*) and overall, the clusters containing affricates caused the most difficulty (*-nge, -nch*).

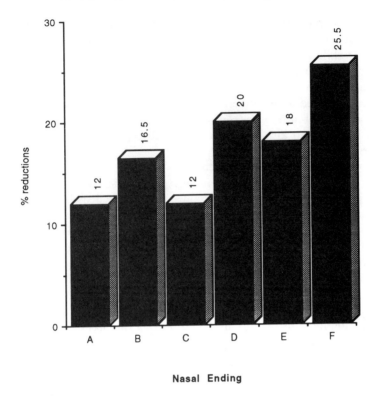

FIGURE 6.1 Spelling reduction errors across different nasal endings. A, Nasal alone; B, Voiced stop/fricative; C, Unvoiced stop; D, Affricate; E, Voiced stop + [l]; F, Unvoiced stop + [l].

These data add to the body of evidence showing that children have difficulty spelling nasal clusters in the early years of school and that their difficulty is related to the perceptual salience of the nasal in the cluster. Read (1975) offered the explanation that young children regard nasals as features of the vowel and therefore omit them from their spellings of clusters. When the nasal precedes a voiced stop, it is more likely to be perceived as distinct from the vowel, and therefore more likely to be retained (e.g. *bend*). Although we did not find this tendency with word-final nasal clusters in our completion task, we did demonstrate the effect when nasal clusters occurred in medial position prior to syllabic [l]. These results led us to wonder whether an additional factor affecting the children's performance was the information-processing demands of the task.

Our reasoning was as follows. In order to spell a nonword, a child has to hold its phonological form in memory while segmenting the phonemic components in preparation for the process of phoneme–grapheme translation. It is, of course, probable that children will begin writing before they have completed the segmentation processes. If children are provided with a "stem" to complete, as they were here, this cuts down on the memory demands of the spelling task. This manipulation may explain why our results do not replicate those of Read (1975) and Marcel (1980), who reported an increased tendency to omit nasals prior to unvoiced stops in free spelling. Of interest was the finding that when memory demands were increased by the need also to transcribe syllabic [1], the voiced/unvoiced effect was observed.

Sarah Dodd and I decided to extend this work to examine children's competence in spelling a wider range of consonant clusters. We elicited the spellings of a set of 36 words in two contexts, once in response to a dictated spelling test and once in spontaneous writing. All of the words contained consonant clusters; half were of one and half of two syllables in structure. Three types of cluster were examined in this experiment, nasal clusters (hand, sandal), plosive + approximant clusters (green, greedy) and s-clusters (post, toaster).

Thirty children aged between 7 and 10 years participated in the study. The children were all normal readers and were grouped into three reading ability bands (reading age 7, 8 and 9 years). In the first part of the experiment, the children wrote the 36 words containing consonant clusters following auditory presentation of the randomized list. In the second part of the experiment (which took place on a separate day), they listened to a story that had been created to include the target words. They were then presented with a series of pictures depicting episodes from the story and were asked to write the story out, taking care to mention everything that happened in it.

The accuracy with which the children spelled the consonant clusters improved with age ($F(2,27) = 12.43$, $p < 0.001$) and was correlated with their reading skill ($r(28) = 0.69$, $p < 0.01$). Furthermore, clusters were transcribed more accurately in one- than two-syllable words ($F(1,27) = 93.4$, $p < 0.001$). This finding is consistent with the hypothesis that the information-processing demands of the spelling task influence spelling performance. Although the processes involved in spelling one- and two-syllable words are similar, we would suggest that two-syllable words pose greater memory demands than one-syllable words because, when producing them, one syllable must be held in working memory while the other is processed. The need to hold one syllable in memory leaves a beginning speller with insufficient attentional resource to segment and transcribe consonant clusters that can be spelled accurately in less demanding contexts.

The children's ability to spell the words containing the different consonant clusters is shown in Table 6.1. There was a main effect of cluster type ($F(2,54) = 4.02$, $p < 0.05$), nasal clusters being easier to transcribe than fricative s-clusters. This finding must be qualified, however, because the nasal clusters were all final clusters, while half of the s-clusters and all of the plosive clusters were in initial position. When spelling nasal clusters there was a tendency to omit the first consonant (the nasal), but this tendency was not noted in the spellings of fricative or plosive clusters. These tendencies were reversed when spelling of the second consonant in the cluster was examined. Here there was a much greater tendency for omissions in the case of plosive and fricative clusters than in nasal clusters.

TABLE 6.1   The number of consonant clusters spelled correctly in one- and
two-syllable words (Max. = 6).

Cluster type	One syllable	Two syllables
Nasal		
Mean	3.5	2.6
SD	(2.7)	(2.4)
Plosive		
Mean	2.8	2.5
SD	(2.0)	(2.3)
Fricative		
Mean	2.6	2.0
SD	(2.1)	(2.2)

Many of the younger children found the free writing task difficult and therefore
we decided to score only the spellings of those children who had attempted at least
10 of the target words. We compared performance on the different consonant clusters
in free writing with performance of the same children in the dictated spelling condition.
On the face of it, the pattern of performance was similar despite the greater processing
demands imposed by the free writing task. However, further assessment of the spellings
that were made in the two situations in terms of their phonetic accuracy revealed
some interesting differences. While some 53% of the spelling errors made on the
spelling test were phonetically acceptable, only 35% of those committed in the
spontaneous writing situation were phonetically accurate.

A number of conclusions can be drawn from this study. The results support previous
work indicating that young children find it difficult to spell consonant clusters and that
the difficulty is, at least in part, related to the phonetic context in which the cluster
occurs. Nasal clusters in final position were easier to spell than fricative or plosive
clusters in initial position, where there was a tendency for the second consonant in the
cluster to be omitted (e.g. *spade→sade*; *drink→dink*). A further finding was that children
spelled fewer clusters in two-syllable than in one-syllable words (e.g. they were more
likely to spell the *gr* correctly in *green* than in *greedy*). The most obvious explanation of
this finding is that, when processing demands are higher, say when two syllables have
to be transcribed, there is a greater tendency for children to apply a more superficial
phonetic segmentation of the word before writing it down. The finding that spellings
were less phonetically accurate in the free-writing condition is also consistent with this
view. The very important influence of information-processing demands on children's
spelling performance cannot be accounted for by current stage models of development.
We view this as one of their most serious limitations. Furthermore, processing models
that stress the separation of lexical and phonological spelling strategies (e.g. Ellis &
Young, 1988) oversimplify the components of the phonological spelling process and
are unable, in their present form, to account for the acquisition process.

Children's Use of Lexical Knowledge in Spelling

The studies involving the spelling of consonant clusters have emphasized children's
use of phonological spelling strategies and the difficulties that they have with these

for some time after they have adopted an "alphabetic" approach. It is important to make clear, however, that these are not the only strategies upon which they must rely. As noted above, many theorists have argued that there are at least two ways in which spellings can be generated. One is via a direct route accessing lexical knowledge and the other is via a phonological route utilizing phoneme–grapheme correspondences. So far, we have been mainly concerned with the operation of the phonological route in children. However, even though young children have relatively little lexical knowledge in the beginning stages, observation suggests that what they have they make use of from time to time in conjunction with their phonological skills. For instance, Bissex (1980), observing her young son writing, noted that he remarked how one word such as *look* could be altered to *book* by substituting a letter. This spontaneous remark suggests that once a child has acquired a limited store of spellings, he or she will use this knowledge in their attempts to generate new words.

The process that involves spelling new words according to the orthographic patterns of known words has become known as spelling "by analogy". Using lexical information (the orthography of a known word) together with knowledge of the phonological similarity between a familiar word and an unfamiliar word, a plausible spelling for a new word can be derived without recourse to sequential phoneme–grapheme rules. Campbell (1983) showed that adults make use of lexical information in their spelling in a study in which participants listened to a series of words and nonwords and were instructed, on the basis of a lexical decision, to write only the nonwords. Target nonwords all had at least two alternative orthographic representations, for example [spi:z] could be spelled *speeze* or *speese*. Each target nonword was preceded by a real word that rhymed with it. These were chosen to prime one of the alternative spellings, for example *cheese* primed the spelling *speese*, *sneeze* primed *speeze*. Campbell (1983) found that the adults' choice of spelling pattern was highly influenced by the orthography of the word that had primed it.

In an extension of this study, Barry and Seymour (1988) showed that when spelling nonwords, adults appear to be sensitive to the frequency with which vowel phonemes are represented by alternative spelling patterns. According to Barry and Seymour, it is possible to differentiate between high and low sound-to-spelling contingency patterns. When a particular letter string is the most common way of representing a vowel sound, it can be referred to as having high sound-to-spelling contingency. In contrast, a letter string that is used rarely to represent a particular vowel sound can be said to have low sound-to-spelling contingency.

Barry and Seymour (1988) found that spellers tend to choose the spelling patterns with high sound-to-spelling contingency to represent vowels in a free spelling test. However, spellers are also sensitive to the frequency with which they see different spelling patterns. According to Barry and Seymour, individuals derive a system of sound-to-letter mappings, weighted according to the frequency of occurrence of each plausible alternative. Over and above this, lexical priming can override the selection of a spelling pattern that has been generated by the probabilistic sub-lexical routine (see also Burden, 1989).

Marsh *et al.* (1980) were the first investigators to discuss children's use of lexical analogies in spelling. In their study, the children were asked to spell pseudowords which were analogues of exception words, for instance *jation*, *zoldier*, *wength* and *cuscle* as in *nation*, *soldier*, *length* and *muscle*. Seven-year-old children in second grade were unable to spell the nonwords by analogy to the irregular words, and only a third of 10-year-olds (fifth-graders) managed to do so. It was only when Marsh and his colleagues tested college students that more than half of the group demonstrated the ability to spell by analogy. Marsh and his colleagues concluded that children do not make use of analogical spelling strategies before the age of 10. However, it should be noted that the words from which the pseudowords were described were all fairly difficult and presumably acquired relatively late by children learning to spell.

Nonetheless, Campbell (1985) found similar results to Marsh *et al.* (1980) in a parallel study to the one she had carried out with adults. Using the modified lexical decision paradigm, she instructed children to write down any nonwords that they heard in a mixed list of words and nonwords. The nonwords were preceded by regular or irregular word primes. Children who had a reading age below 11 years experienced a much weaker priming effect than children with a reading age of 11, whose performance was similar to that of adults.

The studies of Marsh and his colleagues and of Campbell might tempt one to believe that, during the early school years, children rely heavily upon phonological spelling strategies and do not make use of lexical knowledge. However, such a hypothesis does not square with observations of children's spontaneous use of analogies. Moreover, a strong advocate of the view that young children make use of lexical knowledge in spelling is Goswami (1988). In her experiments, children were taught the spelling of a clue word such as *beak*. This clue word then remained visible while the children were told that it might help them to construct the spelling of an unfamiliar word, for example *bean* or *peak*. Goswami (1988) found that young children could spell words by analogy to the words they had just learned with some proficiency. In short, in this experimental situation, beginning spellers demonstrated that they could use analogies in their spelling much earlier than supposed by Marsh and Campbell.

Spelling by Analogy: An Experimental Study

Goswami's work demonstrates that if children's attention is drawn to the orthographic structure of words, they can make use of orthographic analogies to produce novel words. Recently, Nata Goulandris and I set out to clarify the extent to which children can make use of *preexisting* lexical knowledge in this way. We used the nonword spelling paradigm of Campbell (1985) and, following Barry and Seymour (1988), investigated the extent to which young children are aware of the probabilities of occurrence of different spelling patterns to represent vowel sounds (sound-to-spelling contingency).

Forty children, all normal spellers, ranging in age from 6 years, 11 months to 9 years, 8 months participated in the experiment. The children were told that they would hear a list of words and nonwords and that they were to write only the nonwords, spelling them so that anyone reading the spelling would know exactly how to pronounce them. Each nonword was preceded in the list by a word prime that either rhymed with it (and could be spelled by analogy) or was unrelated, producing a neutral context.

The primes in our study consisted of 10 pairs of rhyming words. One of the words in each pair had a high-contingency spelling pattern, the other was of low contingency. The words in each pair were matched for frequency and were as follows: *shoot–fruit*, *low–toe, zoos–shoes, spend–friend, ham–lamb, penny–many, start–heart, filled–build, good–could, store–door*. Ten monosyllabic words unrelated to the targets acted as neutral primes: *bread, bus, cup, arm, dog, book, fox, cat, pin, gran*, and 30 words with analogous rhyming nonwords were used as fillers.

When scoring the spellings, only the rime portion of the nonword was taken into account. Priming was considered to have occurred if the correct orthographic pattern for the rime was represented, for example *-ood* or *-ould* for [ud]. Spellings were classified according to whether they included a high-contingency (a common) or a low-contingency (an unusual) spelling following the high-contingency, low-contingency and unrelated primes.

In the unprimed condition, the 10-year-olds were more inclined to use high-contingency spelling patterns than the 8-year-olds. However, the incidence of the low-contingency spelling pattern was much smaller than that of the high-contingency alternative. Moreover, the spelling of both groups was significantly biased towards the low-contingency version by the presentation of low-contingency primes compared with high-contingency primes and neutral contexts.

The results of this experiment showed that, contrary to the views of Marsh and his colleagues (1980) and Campbell (1985), children who have attained a spelling age of only 8 years can use lexical information when spelling nonwords. The spellings of both the younger and the older spelling age groups were biased by the prior presentation of high-contingency and low-contingency primes. Moreover, the strong preference shown for high-contingency spelling patterns at an early stage seems to be gradually replaced by the more sophisticated choice of spelling pattern, depending upon available lexical information in the more advanced speller. Very similar results were obtained in a second experiment that used words with ambiguous spellings as primes, for example *queen–clean, hope–soap, box–rocks, bed–head*. In the unprimed condition, the children showed a preference for the more common ambiguous spelling pattern, and yet the different primes had distinct influences. Once again, the older spellers were subject to greater priming effects than the younger spellers.

Thus, we would argue that, from an early stage in their development, children are building up knowledge not only of simple sound–spelling correspondences but also about the probability of occurrence of different spelling–sound relations in the orthography. Indeed, it is striking that children who have reached a spelling age of as little as 8 years have considerable knowledge of sound-to-spelling contingency. Their knowledge of this subtle aspect of written language is evident in their selection of the more probable of two ambiguous spelling patterns when spelling an unfamiliar word. Thus, children's early spelling attempts are not simply limited to phoneme–grapheme conversion but rather, they make use of lexical knowledge. Of course, younger children use analogy much less frequently than more proficient spellers, who have a more significant knowledge base.

TAKING STOCK OF THE EVIDENCE

Our discussion of children's use of lexical and phonological strategies in spelling has focused upon the development of these two component skills. Necessarily, we have treated the two skills as though they were separable, but our underlying assumption has been that they interact throughout development. We suggest that a young child's imperfect phonetic rendering of a spelling provides a framework for the acquisition of orthographic knowledge. This framework is fundamental to the child's awareness of the diversity of ways in which sounds are represented in English spelling.

To take a simple example, a child may initially produce a semiphonetic spelling, for example *bak* for *bank*. The child will consider this as adequate until, after sufficient exposure to words ending in the nasal cluster *-nk* during reading, their lexical knowledge expands. Once the child has such lexical knowledge "active" in the input system (i.e. for reading), we propose that they will map their semiphonetic spelling *bak* (which can be considered to be an output code) onto the standard version. This mapping process should highlight any differences that exist between inputs and outputs. As a consequence, the child will modify the strategies available for producing this word and, more gradually, others that are similar to it. In our example, the child would learn that nasals have to be represented in spelling (as *n*, *m* or *ng*)—and that they should not just be treated as features of the vowel. It is not too difficult to imagine that the same basic mechanism could account for the way in which a child learns about ambiguous spelling patterns, such as *-ee* and *-ea*, and in the extreme, how they note exceptional spellings, for example *yacht*. In a similar way, a child's phonological strategies should direct their attention to silent letters in words (*lamb*, *catch*) and enhance their ability to learn them (Ehri & Wilce, 1982).

The foregoing discussion should make plain that stage models of spelling development, portraying the gradual replacement of phonological strategies by orthographic competence, do not adequately capture the intricacies of the learner's task. Models of the process of spelling development need to take account of the fact that neither the lexical nor the phonological strategies that children use are all-or-none processes. Nor do they work in isolation, as dual-route conceptualizations of the spelling process perhaps imply (cf. Beauvois & Dérouesné, 1981; Shallice, 1981). We propose instead that it is the interplay of these developing abilities that is critical to the acquisition of spelling. Our ideas are possibly best articulated within a framework in which mappings between orthography and phonology established during reading are used by the child to test hypotheses as to how these words are written. The hypotheses themselves are actively created by the child in the form of semiphonetic or phonetic spelling attempts. When a mismatch between their attempt and their stored knowledge is identified, future attempts at the word will be modified to reflect this newly acquired knowledge.

PREREQUISITES FOR THE DEVELOPMENT OF SPELLING: EVIDENCE FROM DYSLEXIA

Our deliberations upon the development of spelling in normal children beg the important question of the prerequisites for satisfactory acquisition. One of the important determinants of spelling, like reading, is phonological awareness (Bradley & Bryant, 1983). However, according to our argument, reading itself also contributes to the development of spelling (cf. Cataldo & Ellis, 1988). Since we have proposed that lexical knowledge fuels spelling acquisition, children with specific reading difficulties will inevitably experience spelling problems. In addition, more specific processing deficits, such as phonological difficulties or subtle visual defects, may hinder the process in particular ways.

The first implication of this hypothesis is that reading skill places an upper limit on spelling ability. This is almost always the case, and only in exceptional circumstances does a child's spelling proficiency exceed their reading skill. The second implication is that phonological deficits will have specific effects over and above those of poor reading. It is widely acknowledged that many dyslexic children have specific phonological deficits (Hulme & Snowling, 1992; Snowling, 1987). In some of our own work, we have focused on phonological processing at the level of output phonology (speech production) as an important feature in the explanation of dyslexic failure (Snowling et al., 1986; Hulme & Snowling, 1991). We believe that these deficits have important implications for the spelling development of dyslexic children. In essence, they exert an effect because abstract, speech-based codes provide inputs to the spelling system. Empirical observations have ruled out the possibility that spelling errors are the direct consequences of errors in speech production. Thus, many children misarticulate words that they can spell correctly (Dodd, 1980) and, of course, many correctly articulated words are misspelt. Nonetheless, it seems likely that the same malfunctioning processes that cause deficits in speech production compromise the use of phonological spelling strategies (Stackhouse & Snowling, 1992). The deficient processes may include segmentation at the phonemic level. It follows that dyslexics with phonological deficits should have difficulty in spelling phonetically. Such difficulties might be expected to have a serious impact more generally on the ability of dyslexics to learn to spell if, as we suggested, the generation of a phonological "framework" is fundamental to the acquisition of orthographic knowledge.

In a simple study designed to assess whether dyslexics do indeed have difficulties with phonological spelling strategies, we asked a group of such children, reading at the 7-year level, to spell a series of 30 words of one, two and three syllables. Their errors were then classified as phonetic (e.g. *kiton* for *kitten*, *coler* for *collar*) or dysphonetic (e.g. *sigregt* for *cigarette*, *tetr* for *tent*) and compared with the errors made by a normal group of 7-year-old readers. Although the dyslexics spelled as many words correctly as their reading age matched controls, there were significant group differences in the subjects' attempts to spell the one-and-two syllable words. While the dyslexics made a preponderance of dysphonetic errors, the normal readers made similar numbers of phonetic and dysphonetic errors (see Figure 6.2). Both groups made a majority of non-phonetic errors when spelling the three-syllable words, which were very difficult for them at this stage in their development.

These data suggest then that dyslexic children have more difficulty with the use of phonological spelling strategies than would be expected given their reading experience. The difficulties are attributable to problems with segmentation and perhaps other aspects of speech processing too. Indeed, some preliminary evidence from a single case study suggests that there may be continuities between underlying speech problems and spelling difficulties (Snowling *et al.*, 1991).

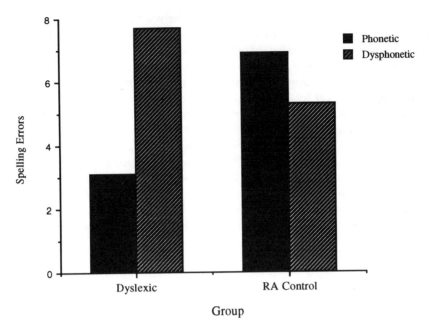

FIGURE 6.2   Histogram showing the distribution of phonetically acceptable and non-phonetic errors made by dyslexic readers and reading age matched controls.

Continuities Between Speech and Spelling

Our case study focused upon a dyslexic boy, aged 15, whom we had studied for some 7 years and whose case is documented extensively elsewhere (e.g. Snowling & Hulme, 1989). JM presents a clear example of a child whose reading and spelling difficulties are the consequence of underlying phonological deficits. In addition, he has subtle difficulties with speech production. In spite of his weaknesses, JM has learned to read and spell with remarkable proficiency, albeit given persistent difficulties with nonword reading and phonological spelling (Hulme & Snowling, 1992).

In one of the studies that we carried out, JM spelled a set of words designed to examine the effects of word frequency, syllable length and syllable stress on performance. JM's spelling was much poorer than that of reading age matched controls. However, just like the normal spellers, his performance was affected by the word frequency, word length and the stress pattern of the word he was attempting to spell. Moreover, although JM's spelling of two-syllable words fell within the normal range, his spelling of three-syllable words was clearly impaired. Interestingly, this finding tied in well with our observations that he also had difficulty in pronouncing polysyllabic words.

To carry out a more detailed analysis of JM's spelling errors, recognizing that JM's difficulties with speech were to an extent idiosyncratic, they were compared with those of six dyslexic children from the same class who spelled as many words correctly as he did. In this study, the spelling errors were classified into three categories: phonetic errors that portrayed the sound sequence of the words correctly, for example *blankit/blanket*, semiphonetic errors in which there were minor errors of phoneme–grapheme correspondence with the overall phonetic sequence being represented accurately, for example *banket/blanket*, *membship/membership*, and dysphonetic errors containing multiple errors involving phoneme–grapheme correspondence, omission and/or sequencing which did not portray the sound sequence correctly, for example *bagid/blanket* (cf. Snowling, Stackhouse & Rack, 1986).

JM made 16% phonetic, 18% semiphonetic errors and 66% dysphonetic errors. His performance was qualitatively different from that of the other dyslexics, who made between 36 and 97% phonetic errors (mean = 59.4%) and between 2 and 57% dysphonetic errors. Furthermore, at least some of his errors were plausibly related to problems with output phonology. These included errors in which the voicing feature of at least one consonant was misrepresented (*contanker* for *conductor*, *megcanit* for *mechanic*), those in which the sequence of sounds was misordered (*derege* for *degree*, *shapoon* for *shampoo*) and those in which segments were omitted (*hoile* for *hotel*, *dierant* for *direction*).

It is important to make clear at this point that JM had experienced some difficulties in producing the voiced/voiceless distinction in his speech throughout his development. This particular problem led us to make a strong hypothesis. We predicted that JM would have more difficulty than children of similar spelling age in transcribing consonants that differed according to a single voice feature within the context of words. Specifically, his atypical use of phonetic voicing would cause him confusion when spelling words containing /k/, /g/, /t/ or /d/.

We selected a set of words of two to four syllables in length, containing the consonants /k/, /g/, /t/, /d/. The list included items such as *maggot*, *trader*, *crocodile*, *caterpillar*, *helicopter* and *medallion*. We first made sure that JM could read the words, and then we asked him to spell those that we were confident he knew. We compared his performance with that of a much younger group of spellers whose spelling age was similar to his. These children were spelling at the 9-year level, and arguably the normal spellers were less familiar with the spoken forms of the target words than JM.

In spite of JM's greater familiarity with the words, the normal readers' spelling attempts were considerably more plausible phonologically than his. The majority were either phonetic, for example *crocodile* → *crocadile*, *mackintosh* → *macintosh*, or semiphonetic, for example *conductor* → *conduter* and *indian* → *indin*. In contrast, the majority of JM's errors were dysphonetic, for example *gardener* → *grander*, *helicopter* spelled as *hiolicoper*.

Of central interest was the way in which JM transcribed the voiced and voiceless consonants in his spellings. Altogether five of his errors (28%) resulted in a substitution of *k/g* or *t/d*, for example *crocodile* → *cocktell*, *conductor* → *contert*, *mackintosh* → *matindoss*. Six of the spelling age controls made voicing errors. However, these were infrequent; in four cases there was only one example, and two children, who both spelled fewer of the sample words correctly than JM, had more difficulty. They both made three voicing errors (fewer than 20%).

Clearly a few voicing errors are to be expected in the spelling of young children. This is particularly probable when they are asked to spell words with which they are relatively unfamiliar in spoken form. Given that JM was older than the comparison group employed here, it is likely that he was more familiar with the words in the sample. Yet, in spite of this advantage, he experienced more difficulty with the transcription of consonants with which he showed uncertainty in his speech. Two further types of error deserve comment. There were two instances of his omitting target consonants: he spelled *comedian* as *common* and *helicopter* as *hiolicoper*. In his speech he also showed some tendency to reduce consonant clusters. Finally, there was one example of an error in which he appeared to anticipate the /g/ and to write it twice, the first time with devoicing, i.e. *calligater* for *alligator*. Again, he did this to some extent in his speech, most notably in nonword repetition.

So, having set ourselves the difficult task of demonstrating continuities between JM's speech-processing difficulties and his spelling problems, we argued that his subtle difficulties with the voice/voiceless opposition were recapitulated in his spelling. It was not that JM pronounced a word wrongly and then went on to spell it in this incorrect way, but rather the tendency to have problems with particular phonological features that characterized his phonological (speech) system also affected his spelling from time to time. In short, JM had more difficulty with the spelling of voiced and voiceless consonants than to be expected, and there was a much greater tendency for him to spell polysyllabic words dysphonetically even than other dyslexic children of similar spelling age. JM's progress in spelling has been exceedingly slow, despite excellent remedial provision. We would argue that his inability to generate phonetically plausible versions of spoken words has left him without a framework on which to "hang" orthographic information. The spellings that he knows are likely to have been learned by "rote" during his remedial programme.

Visual Processing and Orthographic Knowledge

The idea that visual memory is used in order to learn spellings is by no means new. However, to date there are few empirical data that support this view and generally, there has been widespread rejection of the role of visual factors in reading and spelling development and difficulty (Vellutino, 1979). Returning to the way in which we have conceptualized the process of spelling acquisition, there must exist procedures for identifying the particular letter strings within a word that represent particular phonemes. Once these have been abstracted, they will be stored to develop the lexical knowledge-base. Conceivably, these procedures will draw upon visual processing and visual memory skills. It follows that individuals who have deficits in these areas may fail to develop lexical knowledge and to recognize how it influences and constrains spelling strategies.

Research in the field of visual processing and written language is not well developed (but see Lovegrove, 1991 and Stein, 1991 for reviews). It is highly likely that, as yet, the particular measures that will get at the crucial variables have not been identified. However, two single case studies are worthy of note. First, Rayner *et al.* (1989) reported the case of a university professor with dyslexic difficulties of developmental origin. A series of experiments suggested that this man was subject to a selective attentional deficit such that, when shown letter strings and required to identify a target letter in the centre of these, he was unable to do so. Letters in peripheral vision evidently masked his perception of letters at fixation. His reading performance was enhanced when words were presented one by one in a window that blocked out other visual information on the page. Although Rayner and his colleagues do not discuss this man's spelling in detail, it seems likely that he would be a phonetic speller, being unable to abstract and use higher-order spelling patterns extending over multi-letter strings.

We have ourselves reported the case of a young woman, JAS, with a history of dyslexic difficulties and a fairly serious spelling problem (Goulandris & Snowling, 1991). JAS, unlike the case we described earlier, JM, had normal phonological skills but her visual memory was seriously impaired. On a number of standardized and experimental tests of visual memory she performed like a 7-year-old and even her ability to copy letter sequences was deficient. The point we wish to make here is that JAS was a phonetic speller. She had no difficulty whatsoever in generating a phonologically acceptable version of a word. But, although she could read sufficiently for academic purposes, her orthographic knowledge was rudimentary. Thus, JAS's spelling errors included *major* → *mayjour*, *sensitive* → *censitive*, *image* → *immage* and *research* → *resurch*. Our hypothesis was that JAS was unable to retain knowledge of orthographic sequences because of her visual memory impairment. Unlike normal spellers, her use of phonological spelling strategies was not influenced by lexical knowledge.

CONCLUSIONS

The early part of this chapter focused upon the development of phonological spelling strategies and the acquisition of lexical knowledge. We characterized the development of spelling as an interactive process and pointed to the reciprocal relationships between phonological processing, lexical knowledge and spelling. More importantly, we have stressed that a variety of sources of knowledge are used by the novice in the early stages of spelling. Although phonological processing skills are not well developed, the young child will attempt to segment spoken words into sounds and to translate these sounds into letters. The extent to which he or she will be successful will depend at least in part upon the phonetic structure of the word to be processed including the number and the structure of its syllables. At the same time, the child will draw on his or her visual experience of words as acquired through reading; such orthographic knowledge will consist of information about words, word fragments and spelling patterns.

We have suggested that young children use phonological strategies to generate a framework upon which to organize orthographic information. We view the phonological framework as a critical foundation for the acquisition of orthographic knowledge (cf. Seymour, Bunce & Evans, 1992; Seymour, 1993). Thus, the framework serves to direct children's attention to the ways in which phonemes and other phonological units, such as rimes, are represented in the orthography, and ultimately the frequency with which different spelling patterns represent particular phonemes (sound-to-spelling contingency). Surprisingly, children show evidence of this knowledge even before they have fully mastered phonological spelling strategies.

Our discussion of dyslexia has indicated that selective difficulties affecting particular underlying skills can cause specific difficulties for the acquisition of component processes. Our experience leads us to suggest that deficits in phonological processing, such as those experienced by JM, have a more devastating effect upon spelling development than other sorts of cognitive difficulty, including low intelligence. We hypothesize that this is because children with such difficulties lack the ability to generate the phonological framework that directs their attention to orthography. In addition, subtle visual difficulties may also hinder the development of spelling proficiency in an orthography such as English where sound-to-spelling correspondences vary in consistency. Such difficulties seem to have impeded development in the case of JAS described by Goulandris and Snowling (1991).

The remedial teaching requirements of children who differ in the underlying reasons for their spelling problems are quite different. The description of spelling difficulties in terms of a processing model such as the one outlined here should be the first step towards the design of rational teaching programmes for these children. In turn, the evaluation of individualized teaching interventions should clarify aspects of models of the acquisition of spelling.

ACKNOWLEDGEMENTS

This chapter was prepared with the support of grant (G8801538) from the Medical Research Council.

REFERENCES

Barry, C. & Seymour, P. H. K. (1988). Lexical priming and sound-to-spelling contingency effects in nonword spelling. *Quarterly Journal of Experimental Psychology*, **40A**(1), 5–40.
Beauvois, M-F. & Désrousné, J. (1981). Lexical or orthographic dysgraphia. *Brain*, **104**, 21–50.
Bissex, G. L. (1980). *GNYS at Work: A Child Learns to Write and Read*. Cambridge, MA: Harvard University Press.
Bradley, L. & Bryant, P. (1983). Categorising sounds and learning to read: a causal connection. *Nature*, **301**, 419.
Burden, V. (1989). A comparison of priming effects on the nonword spelling performance of good and poor readers. *Cognitive Neuropsychology*, **6**, 43–66.
Campbell, R. (1983). Writing nonwords to dictation. *Brain and Language*, **19**, 153–178.
Campbell, R. (1985). When children write nonwords to dictation. *Journal of Experimental Child Psychology*, **40**, 130–151.
Cataldo, S. & Ellis, N. (1988). Interactions in the development of spelling, reading and phonological skills. *Reading Research Quarterly*, **11**, 86–109.
Dodd, B. (1980). The spelling abilities of profoundly prelingually deaf children. In U. Frith (Ed.) *Cognitive Processes in Spelling*. London: Academic Press.
Ehri, L. C. (1991). The development of reading and spelling in children: an overview. In M. Snowling & M. Thomson (Eds), *Dyslexia: Integrating Theory and Practice*. London: Whurr.
Ehri, L. C. & Wilce, L. S. (1982). The salience of silent letters in children's memory for word spellings. *Memory & Cognition*, **10**, 155–166.
Ellis, A. W. & Young, A. W. (1988). *Human Cognitive Neuropsychology*. Hove: LEA.
Frith, U. (1980). Unexpected spelling problems. In U. Frith (Ed.), *Cognitive Processes in Spelling*. London: Academic Press.
Frith, U. (1985). Beneath the surface of developmental dyslexia. In K. E. Patterson, J. C. Marshall & M. Coltheart (Eds), *Surface Dyslexia*. London: Routledge & Kegan-Paul.

Goswami, U. (1988). Children's use of analogy in learning to spell. *British Journal of Developmental Psychology*, **6**, 21–33.

Goswami, U. & Bryant, P. (1990). *Phonological Skills and Learning to Read*. London: LEA.

Goulandris, N. & Snowling, M. (1991). Visual memory deficits: a possible cause of developmental dyslexia? *Cognitive Neuropsychology*, **8**, 127–154.

Hulme, C. & Snowling, M. (1991). Deficits in output phonology cause developmental phonological dyslexia. *Mind and Language*, **6**, 130–134.

Hulme, C. & Snowling, M. (1992). Phonological deficits in dyslexia: a "sound" reappraisal of the verbal deficit hypothesis. In N. Singh & I. Beale (Eds), *Current Perspectives in Learning Disabilities*. New York: Springer-Verlag.

Lovegrove, W. (1991). Spatial frequency processing in dyslexic and normal readers. In J. Stein (Ed.), *Vision and Visual Dyslexia*. London: Wiley, pp. 148–154.

Marcel, T. (1980). Phonological awareness and phonological representations: investigation of a specific spelling problem. In U. Frith (Ed.), *Cognitive Processes in Spelling*. London: Academic Press.

Marsh, G., Friedman, M., Welch, V. & Desberg, P. (1980). The development of strategies in spelling. In U. Frith (Ed.), *Cognitive Processes in Spelling*. London: Academic Press.

Rayner, K., Murphy, L. A., Henderson, J. M. & Pollatsek, A. (1989). Selective attentional dyslexia. *Cognitive Neuropsychology*, **6**, 357–378.

Read, C. (1971). Preschool children's knowledge of English phonology. *Harvard Educational Review*, **41**, 1–34.

Read, C. (1973). Children's judgements of phonetic similarities in relation to English spelling. *Language Learning*, **23**, 17–38.

Read, C. (1975). Lessons to be learned from the pre-school orthographer. In E. H. Lennenberg & E. Lennenberg (Eds), *Foundations of Language Development, 2*. London: Academic Press.

Seymour, P. H. K. (1993). Un modele du developpement orthographique a double fondation. In J.-P. Jaffre, L. Sprenger-Charolles & M. Fayol (Eds), *Les Actes de la Villette: Lecture–Ecriture Acquisition*. Paris: Nathan Pedagogie.

Seymour, P. H. K., Bunce, F. & Evans, H. M. (1992). A framework for orthographic assessment and remediation. In C. Robson & C. Sterling (Eds), *Psychology, Spelling and Education*. Clevedon: Multilingual Matters.

Shallice T. (1981). Phonological agraphia and the lexical route in writing. *Brain*, **104**, 413–429.

Snowling, M. (1982). The spelling of nasal clusters by dyslexic and normal children. *Spelling Progress Bulletin*, **12**, 13–17.

Snowling, M. (1987). *Dyslexia: A Cognitive Developmental Perspective*. Oxford: Blackwell.

Snowling, M., Goulandris, N., Bowlby, M. & Howell, P. (1986). Segmentation and speech perception in relation to reading skill. *Journal of Experimental Child Psychology*, **41**, 489–507.

Snowling, M. & Hulme, C. (1989). A longitudinal case study of developmental phonological dyslexia. *Cognitive Neuropsychology*, **6**, 379–401.

Snowling, M. J., Stackhouse, J. & Rack, J. P. (1986). Phonological dyslexia and dysgraphia: a developmental analysis. *Cognitive Neuropsychology*, **3**, 309–339.

Snowling, M., Wells, B., Hulme, C. & Goulandris, N. (1991). Continuities between speech and spelling. *Reading and Writing*, **4**, 19–31.

Stackhouse, J. & Snowling, M. (1992). Barriers to literacy development in two children with developmental verbal dyspraxia. *Cognitive Neuropsychology*, **9**, 273–299.

Stein, J. F. (1991). Vision and language. In M. Snowling & M. Thomson (Eds), *Dyslexia: Integrating Theory and Practice*. London: Whurr.

Treiman, R. (1985). Phonemic analysis, spelling, and reading. In T. Carr (Ed.), *New Directions for Child Development: The Development of Reading Skills*. San Francisco: Jossey Bass, pp. 5–18.

Treiman, R. (1991). Children's spelling errors on syllable initial consonant clusters. *Journal of Educational Psychology*, **83**, 346–360.

Vellutino, F. R. (1979). *Dyslexia: Theory and Research*. Cambridge: MIT Press.

7

Sources of Constraint and Individual Variations in Normal and Impaired Spelling

PHILIP H. K. SEYMOUR AND HENRYKA M. EVANS
University of Dundee

Spelling data are embarrassingly easy to obtain. We, in common with many other investigators, have filing cabinets which are crammed with the pencilled records of attempts by normally developing and dyslexic children of differing ages. When considered in the absence of an appropriate theoretical framework these data are little more than curiosities—for example, demonstrations of the extraordinary diversity of spellings of words like *presbyterian* or *psychology* or *saucer*. Accordingly, this chapter will begin with a discussion of theories of the spelling process and its development. One conclusion will be that a complex system involving a number of different forms of linguistic constraint may be implicated. Another is that the question of individual variation—whether or not different patterns of spelling difficulty can be identified—is critical. Some data bearing on these issues will be presented.

SPELLING THEORY

Reviews of cognitive approaches to spelling were provided by Sterling (1992) and Seymour (1992) in a recent compilation. The reviews indicate that a "standard" position in British cognitive neuropsychology has been that English orthography, viewed as a "morphophonemic" script (Henderson, 1982), forces the formation of a dual-process architecture containing distinct lexical and non-lexical functions

Handbook of Spelling: Theory, Process and Intervention. Edited by G. D. A. Brown and N. C. Ellis.
©1994 John Wiley & Sons Ltd.

(Seymour & Porpodas, 1980; Morton, 1980; Ellis, 1982, 1984; Patterson & Shewell, 1987; Ellis & Young, 1988). This view has been questioned, partly in the light of demonstrations of lexical/semantic priming of letter choice in nonword spelling (Campbell, 1983; Barry & Seymour, 1988; Seymour & Dargie, 1990) and partly because current work on "connectionist" models of spelling suggests that a single learning mechanism may be capable of encoding both word-specific information and non-lexical generalizations (Seidenberg & McClelland, 1989; Loosemore, Brown & Watson, 1991).

Standard (Two-Process) Model

The psycholinguistic method used in evaluation of the standard theory has typically relied on a contrast between: (i) spelling-dictated nonwords (a test of the non-lexical process; and (ii) spelling-dictated words of varying frequency and regularity (a test of the lexical process). The method has been applied to neurological cases of "acquired dysgraphia". The apparent dissociation of word and nonword spelling appears to offer strong support for the two-process architecture (Ellis & Young, 1988; Shallice, 1988; McCarthy & Warrington, 1990) and has led to the identification of the contrasting patterns of:

- Phonological dysgraphia, defined as a selective loss of the non-lexical process required for nonword spelling, and
- Lexical dysgraphia, defined as a loss of the lexical or word-specific information needed for conventionally correct spelling of words

Theories of spelling development have tended to follow a broadly similar multi-process approach. Frith (1985) proposed that there were three strategies in children's spelling, which she referred to by the terms "logographic", "alphabetic" and "orthographic". The definition of the strategies appears to echo the classification of writing systems, with "logographic" spelling referring to whole-word knowledge unsupported by sound–letter knowledge, "alphabetic" relating to a transparent phoneme–grapheme spelling system, and "orthographic" to a morphophonemic system requiring the combination of morphemic units. Frith supposed that the strategies necessarily emerge in sequence, thus implicitly supporting Gleitman and Rozin's (1977) equation between the order of evolution of scripts and the developmental progression of the child.

Morton (1989) translated Frith's scheme into information-processing terminology, presenting a sequence of cognitive architectures each referring to a step in the developmental process. The diagrams indicate belief in the existence of an early logographic word memory, called the "lographemic store", which is allowed to lapse when alphabetic writing, using phoneme–grapheme relations, is established. The phoneme–grapheme process survives as a non-lexical translation system during a later orthographic phase when a "graphemic lexicon system" is being established "in which each word is noted with proper acknowledgement of the morphological structure" (Morton, 1989, p. 60).

These theories clearly open the possibility of distinctively different patterns of "developmental dysgraphia", depending on whether the impairment has its primary effect on the lexical (orthographic) process or on the non-lexical (alphabetic) process. This was acknowledged by Frith (1985), who distinguished between: (i) an "arrest" occurring during the alphabetic phase, which would produce a "classic" developmental dyslexia in which the capacity to generate phonologically plausible spellings would be lacking; and (ii) a "developmental dysgraphia" which resulted from a failure to transfer orthographic information from reading to spelling, resulting in "alphabetic" (phonetically plausible but lexically uninformed) output. A similar proposal was made by Boder (1973), who distinguished between "dysphonetic dyslexia", referring to children who were unable to spell by sound–letter associations but who could "revisualize" a proportion of words known for reading, and "dyseidetic dyslexia", in which word-specific knowledge was lacking and spelling tended to be phonetic.

Connectionist (Single-Process) Model

The objections to the standard model have depended in part on the evidence for "lexical" influences on the non-lexical process (Campbell, 1983; Barry & Seymour, 1988) and in part on more general considerations of parsimony, particularly the proposal that a single network might be capable of encoding both sound–letter associations and lexical specifics. Seidenberg and McClelland (1989) described a system which contained sets of orthographic units connected via sets of hidden units to sets of phonemic units. The system learned to read a vocabulary of words via a process of adjustment of weightings on connections which reduced the mismatch between actual output and target output. The critical point was that the system learned to read words of varying frequency and regularity and that this knowledge then generalized to the reading of unfamiliar nonwords. Seidenberg and McClelland treated this as a demonstration that a single-process system could succeed in both word and nonword reading. This claim has been questioned on empirical grounds, notably the view that the performance of the model with nonwords is substantially less impressive than that of human readers (Besner *et al.*, 1990). Nonetheless, the model stands as an exemplar of a single-process scheme.

In various papers Brown and his colleagues at Bangor (Loosemore, Brown & Watson, 1991; Brown & Loosemore, in press) have outlined and demonstrated an analogous model for sound-to-print association in spelling. The Bangor group assumed an account of regularity effects which is based on consistency of spelling in rhyme-defined word families. The performance of the model was affected by regularity in a manner which paralleled the results obtained from children at differing spelling levels. Brown & Loosemore (in press) have additionally reported results for nonwords constructed by replacing the onsets of the words falling into the regular and irregular sets. Their simulation indicated that generalization to nonwords occurred although error rates were higher than for words.

Brown proposed that the connectionist simulations supported the conclusion that learning spelling was primarily a matter of internalization of a statistical structure. He argued in addition that dyslexia resulted from a reduction in available processing resources (number of "hidden units" or connections). Simulations using under-resourced "dyslexic" models indicated that acquisition of the word types was delayed and that generalization to nonword spelling was specially affected.

Multi-Source Literagraphic Lexicon Model

The connectionist model suffers from certain limitations, some practical, such as the inability to specify output as a sequence of letters, others more fundamental. There is a theoretical commitment to a single process in which the capacity to abstract and generalize is central. It is assumed that non-lexical capabilities must be abstracted from lexical input rather than existing as a set of discrete sound–letter associations acquired by some other route (formal instruction, for example). In order to achieve this, the number of "hidden units" is restricted. Too many hidden units would allow the system to form one-to-one connections, so that it would, in effect, become a specialized lexical process of the kind postulated in the standard model.

From the present standpoint, the important consequence of this decision to accommodate both lexical and non-lexical aspects within a single system is that the model necessarily has difficulty in accounting for the contrasting patterns of dysgraphia. It is difficult to see how the introduction of "lesions" can reproduce the extreme dissociation represented by "phonological" and "lexical dysgraphia", or indeed any analogous developmental variations which may exist.

In the light of these objections there may be a case for introducing an alternative formulation. The proposed scheme, referred to as the "literagraphic lexicon" model, was previously outlined by Seymour and Evans (1988) and in the review by Seymour (1992). A diagrammatic representation is provided in Figure 7.1. The essence of the proposal is that the spelling system consists of a "letter sequence generator" which normally operates under the control of a number of external sources of constraint. The sequence generator contains a set of "letter identities". Input to the generator consists of a Go signal and a sequence length index. Given a signal (i.e. an instruction or an intention to spell or write), the generator will output a stream of letter identities

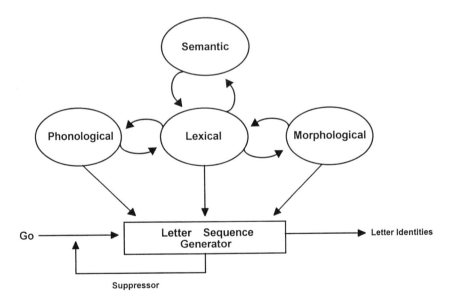

FIGURE 7.1   Schematic representation of multi-source literagraphic lexicon model of spelling.

of the specified length. The model also includes provision for a suppressor signal which can prevent or check output.

In the diagram, the generator is represented as operating under at least three sources of constraint. These correspond to abstract linguistic levels which represent: (i) phonological (possibly phonemic) structure, (ii) lexical identities and associated semantic structures, and (iii) morphological structure. It is supposed that activity within one or more of these components will constrain the output from the generator by sequential modifications to the availability of specific letter identities. It is claimed that this model represents the three sources of constraint which appear necessarily to be involved in the written production of morphophonemic alphabetic script, such as English.

The advantages of the system over the prior formulations appear to be the following:

1. Lexical/semantic priming effect. Nonword spelling will normally be based primarily on a phonological (phonemic) constraint on letter sequence generation. However, the presence of an alternative source of lexical constraint will provide an additional effect on output. The joint influence of these two sources is held to produce the additive effects of sound–spelling contingency and lexical or semantic priming on letter choice in nonword spelling (Barry & Seymour, 1988; Seymour & Dargie, 1990; Barry, 1992).
2. Patterns of acquired dysgraphia. In a normally functioning and fully established system, nonword spelling will depend mainly on phonological constraint whereas word spelling will depend on lexical and morphological constraints. Damage affecting input from the phonological source will give rise to a phonological dysgraphia in which nonwords cannot be written although word spelling is preserved. Damage affecting input from the lexical source will affect word spelling while leaving nonword spelling and phonologically motivated attempts at word spelling functional, yielding the pattern of "lexical" or "surface" dysgraphia. The postulation of a third, morphological source indicates that it would, in principle, be possible to preserve writing of morphologically complex nonwords, or to observe a condition of "morphological dysgraphia" affecting especially the formation of complex forms.
3. Patterns of developmental dysgraphia. It is assumed that, in normal development, the phonological and lexical sources of constraint probably emerge together (implying parallel rather than successive development of logographic and alphabetic aspects of spelling), although the morphological source, relating to Frith's (1985) "orthographic" stage of spelling, may appear somewhat later. The resources available to either of the two primary sources of constraint might vary as a consequence of underlying neuronal structure. If so, it would be possible to observe individuals who differed with regard to the relative contributions of the two sources. This would be observable in standard tasks, such as the writing to dictation of real words and nonwords. Hence, one might expect to find that, even in a normal population, there were variations in the relative degrees of success in word and nonword writing. Extreme impoverishment of resources, resulting in dyslexia, could affect one source more than the other, leading to developmental forms of "phonological" or "lexical dsysgraphia. Again, an implication of the model is that a special developmental difficulty, affecting morphological aspects of spelling, might, in principle, be observable.

SOURCES OF CONSTRAINT

According to the developmental scheme outlined by Frith (1985), progress in spelling can be viewed as a sequence of stages, each defined by a predominant "strategy". Four strategies were identified by Frith, referred to as symbolic, logographic, alphabetic and orthographic. In terms of the "literagraphic lexicon" model, these correspond to the following situations:

1. Output from the generator is unconstrained by the linguistic levels, yielding seemingly random letter sequences (symbolic spelling)
2. Output is constrained by the lexical source for individual items from a restricted spelling vocabulary but not for other items (logographic spelling)
3. Output is constrained by the phonological source, especially a phonemically segmented structure (alphabetic spelling)
4. Output takes account of conventions regarding representation and combination of free and bound morphemes (orthographic spelling)

Random letter sequence generation will not normally be observed in school-age children, possibly because output is inhibited when absence of effective constraint is detected. Thus, when instructed to spell an item, the child will refuse because he knows that he does not know. This is the function of the suppressor pathway in Figure 7.1.

In order to observe unconstrained output, it is necessary to consider special cases where the suppression function is not operating. One example was provided by Seymour and Evans (1988). This was an account of the literacy functions of a boy, AT, who suffered a genetic anomaly (XXXY syndrome) which was apparently associated with almost total blockage of development of alphabetic processes in both reading and writing. The alphabetic impairment was indexed by a complete inability to produce acceptable forms for dictated nonwords. AT nonetheless willingly produced written output when presented with words or nonwords. Much of this output had the appearance of random letter sequence generation. Examples of the responses are given in Table A1.1 of Appendix 1. The items were presented on two occasions separated by about 8 weeks. The responses have been grouped into three sets, such that set A contains mainly responses which appear generally unrelated to their targets, while set B includes examples where a minimal phonetic constraint appears to be operating, usually on the choice of the initial letter, and set C includes examples of spelling which show evidence of a lexical (logographic) constraint, resulting in more or less complete approximations to the spelling of target words or associates.

In order to examine the characteristics of normal spelling development, we will consider data collected from a class of children at a school in the East of Scotland during their first 3 primary years (Seymour & Evans, 1992). A fortuitous aspect concerned the children's responses to the names of their classmates. Names were written on work books and trays used to hold the children's work. The capacity to read one another's names was acquired spontaneously by all members of the class during the first school term. It appeared that this reading was achieved by a "logographic" process of direct, unmediated recognition of the names on the basis of critical letter features and other properties (Seymour & Elder, 1986). Capacity to write the names was monitored at intervals, generally twice in each term during years 1 and 2 and occasionally in year 3. As an illustration, Table A1.2 of Appendix 1 provides a record of the responses of one representative child, Richard, to his own and the other names over the period of the study. Richard was able to write his own name in term 1 prior to the acquisition of sound–letter knowledge (an instance of "logographic" spelling). Responses to the other names included refusals, single capital letters (possibly the features by which the names were discriminated) and some more elaborate responses (*Farran* → *Farrn*, *Daniel* → *Da*). The response *Ross* → *Rooz* suggests the possibility of a "doubling feature" which has been misplaced from the *s* to the *o*.

The progression towards conventionally correct name spelling illustrates the development of a dual (lexical and phonetic) constraint on output. A preliminary analysis was presented by Seymour and Evans (1991) in which a distinction was proposed between: (i) initial letters; (ii) simple or complex letters which were predictable on the basis of a knowledge of the dominant phoneme–grapheme associations; (iii) components which were phonetically ambiguous because they were unstressed in pronunciation; and (iv) unpredictable elements, having low contingency in the sound–letter association hierarchies. Phonetic constraint is evident in a progressive rise in correct spellings for predictable elements and, more significantly, in the introduction of sound-motivated spellings, using letters which do not occur in the names (e.g. the *-is* in *Maurice* → *Maris*; the *y* and *oo* in *Stuart* → *Styooert*; the *y* in *Daniel* → *Danyo*; the *o* in *Paula* → *Polu* or in *Laurie* → *Loe*). Lexical constraint is apparent when unstressed elements, such as the *on* of *Gordon*, are correctly written and, more obviously, when phonetically unpredictable elements are included (e.g. *Janine* → *Jnin*, *Maurice* → *Marics*, *Daniel* → *Danile*, *Paula* → *Pula*, *Laurie* → *Larues*).

The preliminary analysis reported by Seymour and Evans (1991) suggested that these two sources of constraint were built up progressively from the second term onwards. There was no clear evidence of stages of development, for example an "alphabetic" period of commitment to phonetic spelling followed by the introduction of word-specific elements in a later "orthographic" stage (Frith, 1985; Morton, 1989). This conclusion is somewhat in line with the proposals in favour of a "dual foundation" model of reading development (Seymour, 1990; Seymour & Evans, 1992), where it is suggested that logographic and alphabetic processing may be concurrent or parallel developments which jointly contribute to the formation of an orthographic system.

According to Frith (1985) and Morton (1989), a key aspect of the "orthographic" stage in spelling is the mastery of principles of word formation and morphology. The children taking part in Seymour and Evans's (1992) longitudinal study were asked to write some morphologically complex items during their primary 3 year. Two lists were used, one containing inflected forms (*-s*, *-ed*, *-ing* endings) and the other complex words in which a stem was combined with a prefix and suffix (e.g. *re + mark + able*). The first list yielded examples of phonetically motivated misspellings of *-ed* (*liked* → *likt*, *lackt*; *baked* → *beact*, *bakct*, *backet*; *amazed* → *amasd*; *washed* → *washt*), *-s* (*roses* → *rozez*; *kites* → *kitse*; *games* → *gamse*) and *-ing* (*rising* → *risen*; *finding* → *fiden*, *findeng*; *coming* → *cumin*). The second list proved well beyond the capabilities of the children at this age level. This is illustrated in Table A1.3 of Appendix 1, which shows examples of the responses to 20 complex words. There are numerous instances in which prefix and suffix structures were not known and phonetically or lexically motivated substitutions were provided (e.g. *ex + asper + ate → eggs + aspr + ayt*; *remarkable → ree + mark + ibl*).

These illustrative data appear consistent with a "literagraphic lexicon" model in which spelling output is subject to progressively developing constraint from at least three distinct sources. They suggest that random output is normally suppressed when a situation involving absence of effective constraint is detected, and that the three sources are probably established in parallel, with priority being given to the lexical and phonological sources and the fuller development of the morphological source occurring somewhat later.

INDIVIDUAL VARIATION

The literagraphic lexicon model allows that there could be variations in spelling patterns resulting from an imbalance in the resourcing of the phonological and lexical sources of constraint. The primary index of any such variation is expected to be the size and direction of the lexicality effect (the difference in error rate between nonwords and real words). Relative under-resourcing of the phonological influence should produce higher rates of error for nonwords than for words (a lexicality effect). Under-resourcing of the lexical influence will produce a contrasting pattern of higher rates of error for words than for nonwords (a reversed lexicality effect). An individual variation of this kind could be expressed as a scatter of cases on a two-dimensional surface defined by: (i) error rates for word spelling; and (ii) error rates for nonword spelling, as proposed by Ellis (1985) in his discussion of developmental dyslexia.

In order to explore these predictions further we will report data for normal and dysgraphic children of primary school age who participated in a study of word and nonword spelling. This was part of a larger investigation in which word and nonword reading, semantic decision and visual comparison were analysed by cognitive methods. There already exists, therefore, a discussion of individual variation in reading for this particular dyslexic sample (Seymour & Evans, 1993). This means that it should be possible to consider both: (i) whether there is evidence of heterogeneity of spelling disability; and (ii) if so, whether this corresponds to the heterogeneity observed in reading.

In the original study, we recruited a sample of primary school "dyslexic" cases from the Tayside area in Scotland. The referrals were from various sources (medical, educational, voluntary organizations). No exclusionary criteria were applied. For purposes of data analysis the cases were treated as individuals. We also tested children from the primary 3, 4 and 5 levels at schools in Fife and Dundee. Spelling age was determined by administration of the Schonell graded word list. Individuals were assigned to the "dysgraphic" category if there was a discrepancy of 1 year or more between actual age and spelling age. Information about the members of the sample can be found in Tables A2.I1 and A2.II1 of Appendix 2.

Items were sampled from Edwards and Gibbon's (1973) lists of words used by 5–7-year-old children. The vocabulary was submitted to a psycholinguistic analysis and stratified according to dimensions such as part of speech, concreteness of meaning, word frequency, word length, orthographic regularity and complexity. The latter variation was expressed as a three-category scheme, distinguishing between: (i) regular words, in which pronunciation was derivable by considering the dominant correspondence for each letter taken individually; (ii) rule-based words, in which pronunciation depended on dominant correspondences for letter groups; and (iii) irregular words, which contained low-frequency or unique correspondences. This variation was initially constructed from the standpoint of reading. Accordingly, it is not directly based on the "friends" vs "enemies" definition of regularity proposed by Loosemore, Brown and Watson (1991) or on the alternative "contingency" analysis of Barry and Seymour (1988). Nonetheless, the regular and irregular sets differed with regard to the amount of word-specific (lexical) knowledge which was required for conventionally correct spelling. It was considered, therefore, that the error difference between the irregular and regular words could serve as a rough index of a regularity effect in spelling.

The main set of materials consisted of three word lists, one for each level of regularity, each containing an internal variation in word frequency (high or low) and word length (3–6 letters). There were three corresponding nonwords lists. Examples of the materials appear in Seymour, Bunce and Evans (1992, Appendix 1). Several other lists were developed, some including an internal regularity variation, which were administered to some but not all of the subjects.

The lists were presented by dictation, generally in groups for the control subjects and individually for the dysgraphic cases. A disambiguating sentence was provided with the words. Each item was spoken twice by the experimenter. The data consisted of the responses written by the children which were classified as correct or incorrect for purposes of analysis.

The main interest attaches to the lexicality effect (word/nonword difference) in the control and dysgraphic samples. This is represented in Figure 7.2 in the form of a two-dimensional scattergraph on which individuals have been located in terms of: (i) error rate (per cent) on the lower-frequency items from the word lists; and (ii) error rate (per cent) for the items from the nonword lists. The procedure of plotting nonword errors against lower-frequency word errors was followed in order to maintain comparability with the results for reading reported by Seymour and Evans (1993). Use of the complete word set would lower the distribution of data slightly (i.e. would reduce the error rate for words) but would not alter the general appearance of the data. This is because the entire vocabulary was within the range of the children and because the frequency variation was consequently not a strong influence on error rate.

The results of the normal spellers have been represented as a series of polygons drawn to surround the scatter of data points produced by the members of each spelling age defined sample. The 7- and 8-year-old samples consisted mainly of children who were "at age" in spelling. At the higher levels the groups included increasing proportions of "advanced" spellers who were 1–2 years or more ahead of their ages. It seems clear that, at spelling ages of 7+ and 8+ years, the scatter of points fell on *both* sides of the diagonal representing equality of error on words and nonwords. In each age group slightly over 50% of the sample was located above the diagonal—a

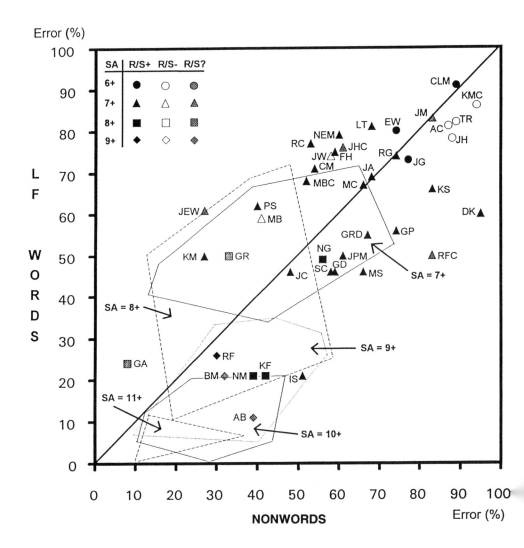

FIGURE 7.2   Scatter of dysgraphic cases on a surface defined by: (i) error rate (per cent) for spelling lower-frequency words; and (ii) error rate (per cent) for spelling nonwords. The symbols distinguish between cases of reading/spelling correspondence (R/S +), non-correspondence (R/S −) and good reader/poor speller cases (R/S?). Regions occupied by the spelling age control groups have been enclosed by polygons.

reversed lexicality effect. This was not true of the higher age levels, where almost all subjects were located below the diagonal.

These data indicate that the prediction (derived from the Bangor simulation) that error rates should in general be higher for nonwords than for words may require modification. For a given set of materials and developmental age, it seems that the generalization is true for some subjects but not for others. It is also apparent from Figure 7.2 that "normal" spelling is compatible with very wide variations in success for both words and nonwords (roughly in a range of 20–70% error for the younger ages). The outcome is compatible with the literagraphic lexicon model, since resourcing could favour the phonological influence and nonword spelling in some instances and the lexical influence and word spelling in others.

The figure also shows the locations of the individual dysgraphic cases. Like the controls, the cases can be divided into a group who fell on or above the main diagonal ("reversed lexicality") and a group who fell below the diagonal ("positive lexicality"). The division between the two was close to 50 : 50 for the sample as a whole. This outcome is contrary to the prediction (from the Bangor simulation) that dysgraphia should be characterized by a special impairment of nonword spelling. If this was correct, we would have expected to find that the cases were within the range of their spelling age controls for word spelling but outside the range for nonword spelling, i.e. the cases should have clustered in the empty lower right region of the graph. The outcome is consistent with the literagraphic lexicon model, since the under-resourcing could affect one influence more significantly than the other.

Appendix 2, Tables A2.I2 and A2.II2, gives a listing of scores for nonwords and words of high and low frequency plus values for the lexicality and frequency effects and their significance as assessed by chi-square tests. In the "above diagonal" series the reversed lexicality effect ranged from 0 to -34 and was significant at $p < 0.05$ or better in 12/20 cases. For the "below diagonal" series the positive lexicality effect varied between $+4$ and $+35\%$ and was significant in 9/22 cases. The tables indicate that frequency effects were generally small and not significant.

The data also allow us to consider whether the dysgraphia should be represented as "delay" rather than "deviance". An interpretation in terms of "delay" would be favoured if the dysgraphic cases fell within the range of their spelling age controls. We examined this possibility by considering the locations of the members of the 7-yr dysgraphic sample in relation to the region occupied by the 7-yr control group. There were 10 cases who fell within the control area. Of the remainder, six lay outside the range for word spelling, four lay outside for nonword spelling and two were outside for both. This indicates that no general conclusion regarding delay vs deviance can be supported. Further, a pattern in which cases are expected to fall within range for words but outside the range for nonwords, as predicted by the Bangor simulation, is not found. The outcome is consistent with the dual-source literagraphic lexicon model in which extreme under-resourcing of the lexical component will push word spelling beyond the control range while extreme under-resourcing of the phonological component will have a corresponding effect on nonword spelling.

CORRESPONDENCE WITH READING

The preliminary consideration of the scatter of cases in Figure 7.2 is encouraging for the view that there may be individual variations in the dysgraphic sample which are related to the lexical/non-lexical (word/nonword) contrast. However, in order to support this conclusion, we need to show that the "above diagonal" (reversed lexicality) cases differ from the "below diagonal" (positive lexicality) cases in ways which are consistent with the attribution of a "lexical" ("surface", "morphemic") or "phonological" dysgraphia.

One possibility is that a "dysgraphic" pattern in spelling will have features in common with a "dyslexic" pattern in reading. Indeed, Boder (1973) maintained that the "dyseidetic" and "dysphonetic" patterns applied to both reading and spelling. Frith's (1985) theory, by contrast, states that alphabetic "arrest" will affect spelling and reading (producing similar "phonological" patterns of dyslexia and dysgraphia), but that "lexical dysgraphia" (phonetic spelling) will usually co-occur with normally efficient reading (the type B good reader/poor speller described by Frith (1980)). The correspondence suggested by Boder would be expected according to a modification of Frith's theory in which orthographic development is seen as being jointly dependent on logographic and alphabetic processes, for example the "dual foundation" model of Seymour (1990) and Seymour and Evans (1992). The extension to the present situation would involve the claim that there are two sets of resources, associated respectively with logographic and alphabetic development, which contribute to reading and to spelling.

Seymour and Evans (1993) located their dyslexic cases on a surface defined by error rates for reading lower-frequency words and nonwords. The sample included 34 of the 42 dysgraphic cases whose locations are plotted in Figure 7.2. All but one of the cases fell *below* the diagonal representing equality of word and nonword reading. This indicates that reading, unlike spelling, is generally characterized by a positive lexicality effect. The cases were nonetheless, scattered fairly continuously within the lower triangle of the graph. On the basis of results obtained from an earlier investigation of older dyslexic cases (Seymour, 1986, 1990), it was anticipated that the cases lying close to the diagonal of the graph (i.e. having similar error rates for words and nonwords) would exhibit the features of "morphemic" (otherwise "surface" or "dyseidetic") dyslexia, whereas those lying considerably below the diagonal (i.e having substantially higher rates of error for nonwords than for words) would exhibit the features of "phonological dyslexia". This possibility was examined by bisecting the lower triangle of the graph into an "upper quadrant" and a "lower quadrant" and by then treating the cases falling in each region as separate series.

The cases were examined individually according to various indicators, including: (i) error rates for nonwords and high- and low-frequency words of varying regularity; (ii) reaction time levels and distribution shapes for words and nonwords; (iii) effects of word length on reaction time; (iv) incidence of "regularized" error responses and error response patterns. The results listed in the Appendix of Seymour and Evans's (1993) chapter support the following conclusions:

1. Cases falling in the upper quadrant were divisible into two subsets: (i) a group of "very impaired" cases who read very few words or nonwords; and (ii) a remaining group, designated as cases of "morphemic dyslexia", who read words and nonwords with similar error levels and dispersed reaction time profiles. These subjects were influenced by word frequency and spelling–sound regularity and produced some regularized error responses. Reading reaction time was strongly affected by word length. A primary impairment of a global word recognition process was inferred in these cases. It should be noted that superior performance with nonwords was *not* a feature of this group. Nonword reading appeared to be impaired to a degree which was dependent on the impairment of word reading.

2. The cases falling in the lower quadrant displayed a large discrepancy between word and nonword reading as the primary feature. It was proposed that these cases might also be subdivided into two groups, such that: (i) the cases of the first subset, referred to as "fast nonword readers", made rapid reactions to both words and nonwords as though relying on a fast global recognition process which was inappropriate for translation of unfamiliar forms; while (ii) members of the second subset appeared to use a very slow, laborious procedure when attempting nonwords which generated a widely dispersed reaction time distribution of quite different appearance from the fast distribution obtained for words. The lower quadrant cases may be viewed as instances of "phonological dyslexia", therefore, although there is a clear possibility that, in some instances at least, the difficulty with nonwords is attributable to poorly adapted visual processing rather than to a phonological difficulty as such.

For present purposes, the important implication is that the individual variation in reading was captured by the "upper quadrant" vs "lower quadrant" distinction. It follows that, in looking for a correspondence between reading and spelling, it will be appropriate to consider whether there is a match between "upper" vs "lower" quadrant location in reading and "above" vs "below" diagonal location in spelling. The results of this comparison are shown in Table 7.1. This identifies all of the dysgraphic cases in terms of their regional locations in reading and in spelling. The eight extra cases are children who occurred in the dysgraphic sample but not in the dyslexic sample (i.e. they were normal readers but poor spellers).

The results show a striking correspondence between the two classification schemes. A chi-square test on the 2×2 table (upper/lower quadrant $\times$ above/below diagonal) gave $\chi^2(1) = 14.44$, $p < 0.001$. The main exceptions were from the group who were "very impaired" in both reading and spelling. These cases fell at the outer extreme on both graphs where the regional distinctions may be of limited relevance. Aside from these exceptions, there was close agreement between the "morphemic" (upper quadrant) classification in reading and "reversed lexicality" in spelling. Similarly, there were only two instances of disagreement between a "phonological" classification in reading and a "positive lexicality" (below diagonal) classification in spelling.

According to Frith's (1980) data, the extra cases (dysgraphia without dyslexia) might be expected to show a "morphemic" pattern (alphabetic spelling) and should therefore be located above the diagonal. This was true of five of the eight cases. Of the three counter-examples, one case, AB, was dyslexic, but was not included in the reading

TABLE 7.1 Location of individual dysgraphic cases in a contingency table relating regional location in spelling ("above" vs "below" diagonal) to regional location in reading ("upper" vs "lower" quadrant).

Reading	Spelling		Total
	Above diagonal (reversed lexicality)	Below diagonal (positive lexicality)	
Upper quadrant			
Very impaired	EW CLM LT FH RG	AC KMC TR JH	9
Morphemic	CM NEM KM PS MB JA RC MC		8
Total	13	4	17
Lower quadrant			
Fast nonword		JG JC IS MS GP KS DK NM KF NG	10
Slow nonword	MBD JW	JPM GD SC GRD RF	7
Total	2	15	17
Extra cases			
Good reading/ poor spelling	JM JEW JHC GA GR	RFC AB BM	8
Total	5	3	8
Total	20	22	42

study because her age (11.6 years) was well outside the range covered by the remaining subjects. The dyslexia was strongly "phonological", with 60% errors on nonwords as against 3% on low-frequency words.

Tables A2.I3 and A2.II3 of Appendix 2 contain the individual scores for the regular, rule-based and irregular word lists together with the regularity effect (irregular–regular error percentage) and its significance according to a chi-square test. There was a positive regularity effect in all subjects. The effect was significant, often at $p < 0.001$, in all "above diagonal" cases and in 17/22 "below diagonal" cases. A Mann–Whitney test indicated that the effects were larger for the "above" cases (range $= 17–42$, median $= 33\%$) than for the "below" cases (range $= 6–51$, median $= 22\%$), with $W = 550.5$, $N = 20$ and 22, $p < 0.0025$. We can therefore conclude that regularity was an important factor in general and that the effect was enhanced among the "morphemic" (above diagonal) cases. Brown, Loosemore and Watson (1993) commented that regularity effects were equivalent in their control and dysgraphic samples. This point was checked for the present sample by comparing regularity effects for the 7-year-old control and dysgraphic groups. The control range (13–51, median $= 35$) did not differ significantly from the "above" or "below" 7-year dysgraphic results.

The tables also show the numbers of error responses to words produced by each subject and the percentage of these which could be classified as "phonetically plausible". A low value of this index is expected in cases of "phonological dysgraphia" (below the diagonal). There was some evidence of this ("above" median $= 41.5$, range = 12–69; "below" median = 35.5, range = 0–72) but the difference was not significant (Mann–Whitney $W = 480.5$, with $N = 20$ and 22).

CONCLUSIONS

Our objective in this chapter has been to present some ideas regarding the appropriate format for a developmental model of spelling. A starting point for this endeavour was the view that English orthography is a complex system in which a single symbol system (the letters of the alphabet) is used to represent a number of differing linguistic functions. These include: (i) the representation of sound structure; (ii) the indication of lexical identity; and (iii) the representation of morphological structure. It is our view that these constraints make conceptually distinct demands during the acquisition of the orthography and that it is important that they are adequately represented in a theory of the process. Thus, while we agree that there may be dangers in reifying the linguistic distinctions as processing pathways or strategies, as has occurred in the standard model, we also question the advisability of an overemphasis on the merging of the aspects in a single network, which appears to be the current programme of the connectionist modellers.

The literagraphic lexicon model (Figure 7.1) has the advantage of representing the important linguistic constraints while leaving open questions regarding their order of emergence during development and their placement in a single or multi-process architecture. In practice, the illustrative data we have presented suggest that the phonological and lexical constraints are built up side by side during the early stages but that the morphological constraint may be a somewhat later development. The strong effects of regularity observed in our study indicate a dominant role for the phonological influence.

We have taken the view that *individual variation* in liability to error in word and nonword spelling is critical for evaluation of the relative merits of single network and multi-source models. A complex system can handle individual variations because neurological trauma or developmental under-resourcing could affect different components in different individuals. The standard multi-process architecture (Ellis & Young, 1988) has enjoyed considerable success in adult neuropsychology simply because the hypothesis that particular components or pathways (e.g. the lexical and non-lexical processes) may be degraded or eliminated provides a ready account of the patterns of dissociation observed in the cases of acquired dysgraphia. Single system connectionist models appear inherently less comfortable with these data.

A main argument of this chapter has been that analogous developmental variations exist. We sought to represent the variation in "dimensional" terms as a scatter of cases on a surface defined by error rates for real words and error rates for nonwords (Figure 7.2). The dissociations appear less extreme than in acquired dysgraphia but nonetheless suggest that the phonological and lexical sources may be at least partially independent. The supporting observations were: (i) the wide variations in word and nonword error rates in the normal 7- and 8-year groups and the occurrence of both positive and negative lexicality effects; and (ii) the comparable variation in the size and direction of the lexicality effect in the dysgraphic sample, including the significant positive and reversed effects and the cases who lay outside the control range either for words or for nonwords. In our view, this evidence of individual variation strengthens the arguments in favour of multi-source models of the literagraphic lexicon type.

Our second main finding was that the dimensional variation in spelling corresponded closely to the variation we had found for reading (Seymour & Evans, 1993) in the analysis of dyslexic difficulties in the sample. This outcome supports Boder's (1973) identification of dysphonetic and dyseidetic reading/spelling patterns and is important for theories of literacy development. In the standard architecture (Morton, 1989) no necessary correspondence is anticipated since the reading and spelling processes are represented as being functionally distinct. The developmental model of Frith (1985) predicts a "phonological" pattern affecting both reading and spelling and a "lexical dysgraphia" which occurs in spelling but not reading (the type B good reader/poor speller). Our results are incompatible with this account because they suggest: (i) that there is a "morphemic" (lexical) pattern of disability in addition to the "phonological" difficulty; and (ii) because they show that the correspondence between reading and spelling occurs for the morphemic pattern as well as for the phonological pattern. It is also true that there is a group of type B cases (good readers/poor spellers) and that they tend to display the morphemic pattern predicted by Frith.

The match between reading and spelling suggests that the theoretical accounts of both domains will need to take account of lexical and phonological influences which derive from a common source. We suggest that this might be approached by merging the current literagraphic lexicon model of spelling with the comparable "dual foundation" model of reading (Seymour, 1990; Seymour & Evans, 1992). The assumptions underlying such a merger might be: (i) that a phonological source is a common basis for alphabetic reading and spelling which assists the formation of phonologically structured orthographic frameworks in both domains; and (ii) that the logographic process in reading is the source of the lexical/semantic constraint in spelling and, hence, of the "morphemic" pattern of dyslexia and dysgraphia.

In this chapter it has not been possible to give proper consideration to the possibility that there is a further source of constraint, concerned with morphological structure, which could be the basis for a third dimension of individual variation in spelling and possibly reading. This is an issue which might profitably be pursued in future research. However, it is perhaps worth noting that each of the three sources identified in the model (Figure 7.1) might be associated with the emergence of an appropriate form of linguistic awareness. A link between spelling and "phonological awareness" of the phonemic structure of speech is already well established (Goswami & Bryant, 1990; Ellis & Cataldo, 1992). It is possible that emerging awareness of the special (i.e. unpredictable) orthographic features of words might accompany development of the lexical source, and that a "syntactic awareness" of morphological structure may be needed for the spelling of complex forms.

ACKNOWLEDGEMENTS

The research reported in this chapter was carried out with the support of a grant from the Medical Research Council of the UK. The cooperation of our subjects and their parents and teachers is gratefully acknowledged.

REFERENCES

Barry, C. (1992). Interactions between lexical and assembled spelling (in English, Italian and Welsh). In C. M. Sterling & C. Robson (Eds), *Psychology, Spelling and Education*. Clevedon: Multilingual Matters.

Barry, C. & Seymour, P. H. K. (1988). Lexical priming and sound-to-spelling contingency effects in non-word spelling. *Quarterly Journal of Experimental Psychology*, **40A**, 5–40.

Besner, D., Twilley, L., McCann, R. S. & Seergobin, K. (1990). On the association between connectionism and data: are a few words necessary? *Psychological Review*, 97, 432–446.

Boder, E. (1973). Developmental dyslexia: a diagnostic approach based on three atypical reading–spelling patterns. *Developmental Medicine and Child Neurology*, **15**, 663–687.

Brown, G. D. A. & Loosemore, R. P. W. (in press). A computational approach to dyslexic reading and spelling. In M. Joshi & C. K. Leong (Eds), *Developmental and Acquired Dyslexia: Neuropsychological and Neurolinguistic Perspectives*. Dordrecht: Kluwer.

Brown, G. D. A., Loosemore, R. P. W. & Watson, F. L. (1993). Normal and dyslexic spelling: a connectionist approach. Manuscript in submission.

Campbell, R. (1983). Writing non-words to dictation. *Brain and Language*, **19**, 153–178.

Edwards, R. P. A. & Gibbon, V. (1973). *Words Your Children Use*. London: Burke Books.

Ellis, A. W. (1982). Spelling and writing (and reading and speaking). In A. W. Ellis (Ed.), *Normality and Pathology in Cognitive Functions*. London: Academic Press.

Ellis, A. W. (1984). *Reading, Writing and Dyslexia: A Cognitive Analysis*. London: LEA.

Ellis, A. W. (1985). The cognitive neuropsychology of developmental (and acquired) dyslexia. *Cognitive Neuropsychology*, **2**, 169–205.

Ellis, A. W. & Young, A. W. (1988). *Human Cognitive Neuropsychology*. London: LEA.

Ellis, N. C. & Cataldo, S. (1992). Spelling is integral to learning to read. In C. M. Sterling & C. Robson (Eds), *Psychology, Spelling and Education*. Clevedon: Multilingual Matters.

Frith, U. (1980). Unexpected spelling problems. In U. Frith (Ed.), *Cognitive Processes in Spelling*. London: Academic Press.

Frith, U. (1985). Beneath the surface of developmental dyslexia. In K. E. Patterson, J. C. Marshall & M. Coltheart (Eds), *Surface Dyslexia: Neuropsychological and Cognitive Analyses of Phonological Reading*. London: LEA.

Gleitman, L. R. & Rozin, P. (1977). The structure and acquisition of reading, I: Relations between orthographies and the structure of language. In A. S. Reber & D. Scarborough (Eds), *Toward a Psychology of Reading*. Hillsdale, N. J.: LEA.

Goswami, U. & Bryant, P. (1990). *Phonological Skills and Learning to Read*. London: LEA.

Henderson, L. (1982). *Orthography and Word Recognition in Reading*. London: Academic Press.

Loosemore, R. P. W., Brown, G. D. A. & Watson, F. L. (1991). A connectionist model of alphabetic spelling development and developmental and acquired dysgraphia. *Proceedings of the Thirteenth Annual Conference of the Cognitive Science Society*. Hillsdale, NJ: LEA.

McCarthy, R. A. & Warrington, E. K. (1990). *Cognitive Neuropsychology: A Clinical Introduction*. London: Academic Press.

Morton, J. (1980). The logogen model and orthographic structure. In U. Frith (Ed.), *Cognitive Processes in Spelling*. London: Academic Press.

Morton, J. (1989). An information processing account of reading acquisition. In A. M. Galaburda (Ed.), *From Reading to Neurons*. Cambridge, Mass.: MIT Press.

Patterson, K. E. & Shewell, C. (1987). Speak and spell: dissociations and word class effects. In M. Coltheart, G. Sartori & R. Job (Eds), *The Cognitive Neuropsychology of Language*. London: LEA.

Seidenberg, M. S. & McClelland, J. L. (1989). A distributed, developmental model of word recognition and naming. *Psychological Review*, **96**, 523–568.

Seymour, P. H. K. (1986). *Cognitive Analysis of Dyslexia*. London: Routledge & Kegan Paul.

Seymour, P. H. K. (1990). Developmental dyslexia. In M. W. Eysenck (Ed.), *Cognitive Psychology: An International Review*. Chichester: Wiley.

Seymour, P. H. K. (1992) Cognitive theories of spelling and implications for education. In C. M. Sterling & C. Robson (Eds), *Psychology, Spelling and Education*. Clevedon: Multilingual Matters.

Seymour, P. H. K., Bunce, F. & Evans, H. M. (1992). A framework for orthographic assessment and remediation. In C. Sterling & C. Robson (Eds), *Psychology, Spelling and Education*. Clevedon: Multilingual Matters.

Seymour, P. H. K. & Dargie, A. (1990). Associative priming and orthographic choice in non-word spelling. *European Journal of Cognitive Psychology*, **2**, 395–410.

Seymour, P. H. K. & Elder, L. (1986). Beginning reading without phonology. *Cognitive Neuropsychology*, **3**, 1–36.

Seymour, P. H. K. & Evans, H. M. (1988). Developmental arrest at the logographic stage: impaired literacy functions in Klinefelter's XXXY syndrome. *Journal of Research in Reading*, **11**, 133–151.

Seymour, P. H. K. & Evans, H. M. (1991). Learning to read and write the names of classmates. Paper presented at a meeting of the British Psychological Society, Bournemouth, April 1991.

Seymour, P. H. K. & Evans, H. M. (1992). Beginning reading without semantics: a cognitive study of hyperlexia. *Cognitive Neuropsychology*, **9**, 89–122.

Seymour, P. H. K. & Evans, H. M. (1993). The visual (orthographic) processor and developmental dyslexia. In D. M. Willows, R. S. Kruk & E. Corcos (Eds), *Visual Processes in Reading and Reading Disabilities*. Hillsdale, NJ: LEA.

Seymour, P. H. K. & Porpodas, C. D. (1980). Lexical and non-lexical processing of spelling in dyslexia. In U. Frith (Ed.), *Cognitive Processes in Spelling*. London: Academic Press.

Shallice, T. (1988). *From Neuropsychology to Mental Structure*. Cambridge: Cambridge University Press.

Sterling, C. M. (1992). Introduction to the psychology of spelling. In C. M. Sterling (Ed.), *Psychology, Spelling and Education*. Clevedon: Multilingual Matters.

APPENDIX 1—ILLUSTRATIVE DATA

TABLE A1.1   Examples of responses to word and nonword targets produced by AT (Seymour & Evans, 1988).

A.   Random (unconstrained) responses

kept	poegle	neetatng
yard	kcorss	gneetaeeaug
special	t68deet	pwnor
follow	rrrumu	rorheera
pie	akoorc	argmp
sep	ideffook	tpth
swaund	etakfed	gis
bracial	wroecheet	teey
shomb	fmrn	gmy
swamble	wllerdy	rfyrrfyfy

B.   Phonetically constrained responses

rock	roke	rokose
hand	hwce	heand
hello	hlod	hiloy
comic	kint	cooolrd
animal	aleupb	aloomald
cackom	crooottedffFFed	clmar
clise	corefddf	tety
squing	stewfed	geey
powth	bethfed	pleep
vind	rfrdd	veruy

C.   Lexically constrained responses

blue	bule	blue
door	door	droo
sun	sunf	sun
queen	queen	nqqueenej
ran	run	run
glad	ldcould	cpytr
swan	sook	snow
eight	cher	eigth
warsh	wooch	chlovef
trut	frog	ntnt

TABLE A1.2 One child's responses to the task of spelling classmates' names during the first 3 school years, illustrating the emergence of phonological and lexical constraint (Seymour & Evans, 1991).

							Terms					
	1	2a	2b	3a	3b	4a	4b	5a	5b	6a	6b	7	8
Richard	*	*	*	*	*	*	*	*	*	*	*	*	*
Emma	—	*	Emm	*	*	*	*	*	*	*	*	*	*
Farran	Farrn	Farrn	Farrn	*	*	*	*	*	*	*	*	*	*
Ross	Rooz	Roos	Rooz	Roos	*	*	*	*	*	*	*	*	*
Gordon	—	Gobn	godn	gordn	*	gorden	*	gorden	*	*	*	*	*
Ashley	A	Az	Azhle	Ashle	Ashalee	*	Ashely	*	*	*	*	*	*
Janine	J	Jen	Jnin	Janen	Janen	Janen	*	*	*	*	*	*	*
Maurice	—	Mars	Maris	Maris	Marics	Marics	Marice	*	*	*	*	*	*
Stuart	S	Sot	Stoout	Stevn	Styooert	St	Stoort	*	*	*	*	*	*
Amanda	M	Ama	Amadu	Amandur	*	Amana	—	*	Amnda	*	*	*	*
Daniel	Da	Dano	Danyo	Danyol	Danyal	Dainle	Daicele	Danile	*	Daiel	*	*	*
Nicola	N	Niu	Niclua	Niclu	Nichla	Nichola	Nichola	Nicala	*	*	*	*	*
Paula	Po	Polo	Polu	Polu	Polu	Pali	Pula	Palae	Palae	*	*	*	*
Eleanor	E	Eu	Elunr	Elenar	Elener	Elener	Elenar	Elenor	Elanoir	*	*	*	Elanor
Laurie	L	Loe	Loe	Laue	Larea	Larues	Laure	Larure	laure	Laure	Laurey	*	*
Gillian	G	—	Jill	Jillaein	Jillan	Jillen	gillein	gillean	Gilline	Jillen	Jillyan	*	*
Jennifer	J	Je	Jeif	Jenefer	Jenefer	Jenefer	Jenefer	Jenefer	Jenefer	Jenefer	Jenifer	Jenifer	Jenifer

*Correct response.

TABLE A1.3 Examples of responses to complex words by children in their third school year, illustrating an absence of morphological constraint (Seymour & Evans, 1992).

Target	Example 1	Example 2	Example 3
unusual	unusayel	unyoserl	unyooshyl
admiration	addmrishn	addmurashon	admerasoin
impossible	imqasipl	inposple	imposeble
instrument	instrmit	instomint	iestromet
remarkable	remarkle	remarkabul	reemarkibl
exasperate	eggsasprayt	eggzasperate	egsasperet
behaviour	beehavyour	behaveure	behaveor
discourage	discurig	discarige	discuridge
completely	komplatlay	comepletle	compleatly
delightful	delitefull	delighphl	delitphel
accuracy	acyarsy	akuresy	acursy
embroider	ebroyber	embrouder	embroyder
misfortune	misfortshin	missforchon	misfortoin
suspension	susbenshone	suspenchune	suspensen
secretive	seecktriv	seektrev	seckritive
ignorant	igarant	ignornt	igrant
centenary	sentry	sentinire	senteenery
abrasive	abrazev	abrazive	abraseve
connection	conecshon	konekshen	conecshone
perplexity	peliksty	perpecxetay	peplexity

APPENDIX 2—DYSGRAPHIC DATA

Appendix 2 provides information about the individual members of the dysgraphic sample. The cases have been grouped into two series. Series I contains individuals located on or above the diagonal in Figure 7.2 (zero or reversed lexicality effect). Series II contains the cases who were located below the diagonal (positive lexicality effect). Within each series the cases have been grouped according to spelling age. Cases with a spelling age below 7 years whose word and nonword error rates fell outside the range of the 7-year controls were classed as "very impaired". Cases whose spelling age was below 7 years but who fell within the 7-year control range for word spelling and/or nonword spelling were grouped with the other 7-year cases.

SERIES I—ABOVE DIAGONAL CASES

TABLE A2.I1 Details of "above diagonal" cases, showing sex, age at initial testing, Schonell spelling age (in years) and Wechsler verbal and performance IQ.

Subject	Sex	Chronological age	Schonell spelling age	Wechsler	
				VIQ	PIQ
EW	F	8.1	6.3	87	81
CLM	M	11.6	6.8	109	105
NEM	M	8.2	6.1	117	98
CM	F	7.6	6.3	107	108
MC	M	7.7	6.5	87	106
LT	F	8.8	6.7	75	92

(continued)

Table A2.I1 (*continued*)

Subject	Sex	Chronological age	Schonell spelling age	Wechsler VIQ	PIQ
FH	M	8.7	6.7	92	101
JM	F	7.4	6.7	67	76
RC	M	8.4	7.0	94	102
JA	M	8.6	7.1	114	109
JHC	M	8.4	7.1	103	95
JW	F	9.0	7.2	87	115
JEW	F	8.2	7.2	107	101
RG	M	10.5	7.3	74	70
MB	M	8.5	7.5	94	104
KM	F	10.9	7.5	98	98
MBC	F	9.2	7.6	81	73
PS	M	8.7	7.7	84	117
GA	M	9.6	8.1	118	126
GR	M	9.0	8.1	108	111

TABLE A2.I2   Error scores (per cent) for high- and low-frequency words and nonwords, frequency effects and lexicality effects for "above diagonal" cases, together with ranges of scores for 7- and 8-year spelling age normal controls.

Subject	Words High	Low	Frequency effect	Nonwords	Lexicality effect
Very impaired					
EW	72	80	8	74	−6
CLM	90	91	1	89	−2
7-yr range	25–67	35–72		16–71	
NEM	78	79	1	60	−19**
CM	62	71	9	54	−17*
MC	65	67	2	66	−1
LT	70	81	11	68	−13
FH	83	75	−8	59	−16*
JM	85	83	−2	83	0
RC	78	77	−1	53	−24**
JA	69	69	0	68	−1
JHC	67	76	9	61	−15
JW	67	74	7	58	−16*
JEW	43	61	18*	27	−34***
RG	58	74	16	74	0
MB	43	59	16	41	−18*
KM	43	50	7	27	−23**
MBC	57	68	11	52	−16*
PS	59	62	3	40	−22*
8-yr range	12–64	11–70		14–60	
GA	13	24	11	8	−16**
GR	43	50	7	33	−17*

Effect significant by chi-square test, *p<0.05, **p<0.01, ***p<0.001.

TABLE A2.I3 Error scores (per cent) for regular, rule-based and irregular words and regularity effects for the "above diagonal" cases. The table also shows the incidence of "phonetically plausible" (P+) errors.

| Subject | Word list | | | Regularity effect | | Errors | |
	Regular	Rule	Irregular		N	P+	Per cent
EW	57	80	91	34***	132	24	18
CLM	79	92	100	21***	155	19	12
NEM	54	87	92	38***	133	39	29
CM	54	72	77	23**	115	52	45
MC	48	66	90	42***	84	29	34
LT	63	75	96	33**	49	12	24
FH	54	88	94	40***	135	58	43
JM	63	92	98	35***	119	18	15
RC	52	87	92	40***	131	65	50
JA	52	81	85	33***	124	50	40
JHC	57	64	88	31**	114	32	28
JW	61	62	85	24**	118	37	31
JEW	39	43	68	29**	86	57	66
RG	51	63	89	38***	91	30	33
MB	32	47	73	41***	88	47	53
KM	30	47	61	31***	80	51	64
MBC	53	53	76	23**	105	51	49
PS	40	78	77	37**	64	34	53
GA	9	15	26	17*	29	20	69
GR	34	43	63	29**	81	51	63

Effect significant by chi-square test, *p<0.05, **p<0.01, ***p<0.001.

SERIES II—BELOW DIAGONAL CASES

TABLE A2.II1 Details of "below diagonal" cases, showing sex, age at initial testing, Schonell spelling age (in years) and Wechsler verbal and performance IQ.

| Subject | Sex | Chronological age | Schonell spelling age | Wechsler | |
				VIQ	PIQ
AC	F	8.8	6.2	108	100
KMC	M	8.8	6.4	75	80
TR	F	8.5	6.6	66	70
JH	M	9.1	6.8	94	117
JG	M	9.3	6.8	84	90
JPM	M	8.1	6.8	113	106
IS	M	9.2	7.1	95	115
DK	M	8.7	7.2	96	149
RFC	M	8.8	7.3	97	149
JC	F	9.8	7.4	98	113
GP	M	9.4	7.5	66	82
GD	M	8.8	7.5	115	118
SC	M	9.7	7.5	88	105
MS	M	10.1	7.8	82	90
GRD	M	11.8	7.8	67	96

(continued)

Table A2.II1 (*continued*)

Subject	Sex	Chronological age	Schonell spelling age	Wechsler VIQ	PIQ
KS	F	8.7	7.9	94	88
NG	M	10.0	8.3	87	90
NM	M	9.6	8.4	95	91
KF	F	9.4	8.5	103	95
BM	M	10.0	9.0	90	88
RF	F	11.3	9.4	79	86
AB	F	11.6	9.4	–	–

TABLE A2.II.2   Error scores (per cent) for high- and low-frequency words and nonwords, frequency effects and lexicality effects for "below diagonal" cases, together with ranges of scores for 7- and 8-year spelling age normal controls.

Subject	Words High	Low	Frequency effect	Nonwords	Lexicality effect
Very impaired					
AC	61	81	20*	87	6
KMC	90	86	− 4	94	8
TR	82	82	0	89	7
JH	70	78	8	88	10
JG	72	73	1	77	4
7-yr range	25–67	35–72		16–71	
JPM	46	50	4	61	11
IS	16	21	5	51	30***
DK	54	60	6	95	35***
RFC	49	50	1	83	33***
JC	48	46	− 2	48	2
GP	41	56	15	74	18*
GD	41	46	5	59	13
SC	34	46	12	58	12
MS	32	46	14	66	20**
GRD	43	55	12	67	12
KS	51	66	15	83	17**
8-yr range	12–64	11–70		14–60	
NG	49	49	0	56	7
NM	10	21	11	39	18*
KF	16	21	5	42	21**
9-yr range	0–22	3–36		10–58	
BM	13	21	8	32	11
RF	15	26	11	30	4
AB	10	11	1	39	28***

Effect significant by chi-square test, $*p < 0.05$, $**p < 0.01$, $***p < 0.001$.

TABLE A2.II3   Error scores (per cent) for regular, rule-based and irregular words and regularity effects for the "below diagonal" cases. The table also shows the incidence of "phonetically plausible" (P+) errors.

| Subject | Word list | | | Regularity effect | | Errors | |
	Regular	Rule	Irregular		N	P+	Per cent
AC	72	63	81	9	89	17	19
KMC	71	96	98	27***	154	19	12
TR	70	87	95	25***	144	29	20
JH	74	65	91	17	48	0	0
JG	66	68	84	18*	126	23	18
JPM	46	40	71	25***	91	26	29
IS	11	11	35	24**	34	15	44
DK	52	55	69	17	101	4	4
RFC	51	49	66	15*	90	33	37
JC	27	43	71	44***	82	46	56
GP	36	46	65	29**	91	19	21
GD	38	32	56	18*	73	31	43
SC	25	26	61	36***	68	29	43
MS	23	34	55	32***	65	15	23
GRD	30	37	81	51***	68	32	47
KS	52	45	74	22*	99	18	18
NG	39	43	61	22*	83	28	34
NM	16	6	23	7	21	12	51
KF	9	21	26	17*	20	10	50
BM	18	11	24	6	32	23	72
RF	11	8	35	24**	36	20	56
AB	7	4	19	12	18	7	39

Effect significant by chi-square test, $*p<0.05$, $**p<0.01$, $***p<0.001$.

8

Longitudinal Studies of Spelling Development

NICK C. ELLIS

University of Wales, Bangor

A number of models of the development of spelling have been progressively refined over the last 15 years (Ehri, 1986; Gentry, 1978, 1982; Henderson & Beers, 1980; Morris, 1983). These share the following commonalities: (i) they are based on analyses of spelling errors when children attempt to spell novel words (invented spellings), (ii) they are stage theories, proposing that qualitatively different cognitive processes are involved in children's spelling at different points in development and that there is a characteristic progression from stage to stage, (iii) they emphasize that phonological awareness plays a crucial role in children's early spelling but also that children eventually acquire orthographic descriptions of words. These models have been developed in parallel with cognitive developmental stage theories of reading acquisition (e.g. those of Marsh and his colleagues, 1980, 1981) which are also based on error analysis, which also hold that there are very different strategies of information processing used in reading at different stages of its development and which also emphasize the links between phonological awareness and reading development. Although synchronous, paradoxically these theoretical developments concerning reading and spelling were essentially independent until Ehri (1979, 1984) showed that the improvements in phonological awareness on which the acquisition of alphabetic reading is based are themselves a consequence of learning how sound segments in words are spelled conventionally, and hence Frith (1985) and Ehri (1986) proposed models of literacy development where reading and writing mutually influence and grow from each other.

The purpose of the current review chapter is to summarize briefly the modal aspects of stage theories of spelling development, reading development and Frith's integrative

Handbook of Spelling: Theory, Process and Intervention. Edited by G. D. A. Brown and N. C. Ellis.
©1994 John Wiley & Sons Ltd.

model and then to see how well these theories have fared in empirical tests from several longitudinal studies of development which have been prosecuted in recent years.

STAGES OF SPELLING DEVELOPMENT

The idea that children's misspellings reflect a developing sense of phonetic properties in words was pioneered by Read (1971, 1975, 1986), who found evidence that young inventive spellers used a system of grouping sounds together according to shared phonetic features. Thus they might represent a particular vowel sound in their spelling by substituting a letter whose *name* shared a salient phonetic feature with the sound. Read's exhaustive studies of invented spellings demonstrated that children use processes of both speech production and perception to group sounds together and that these categorizations may not coincide with the classification system used by adults:

> We now value spellings for what they can tell us about psycholinguistic processes. Standard spellings are of less interest, not because they represent successful instruction, but because they do not indicate how a child arrived at them. . . . Some non-standard spellings represent a more advanced conception of the task or the language than others. (Read, 1986, p. 47.)

This idea that spelling errors provide an index of children's metalinguistic understanding of language has allowed subsequent researchers to categorize developmental strategies in spelling. Henderson and Beers (1980) analysed samples of children's creative writing and assigned each error to a category according to the completeness of phonetic information mapped by the misspelling. On the basis of their work and that of Bissex (1980) and of Gentry (1978, 1982), it is now generally agreed that children move through five distinct stages of spelling, viz: "precommunicative", "semiphonetic", "phonetic", "transitional" and "correct" spelling. "Precommunicative" spellings are characterized by the strategy of randomly selecting letter strings to represent words (e.g. spelling *monster* as BTRSS, or *chirp* as 1MMPMPH). Throughout this chapter, children's spellings are in upper-case letters. Although at this stage children can produce letters in writing, their spellings reflect a complete lack of letter-sound or letter-name knowledge. "Semiphonetic" spellings contain a partial mapping of phonetic content. At this stage, (i) the speller begins to conceptualize that letters have sounds that are used to represent the sounds in words, (ii) the letters used to represent words provide a partial but not total mapping of the phonetic representation of the word being spelled, and (iii) a letter-name strategy is very much in evidence—where possible the speller represents words, sounds or syllables with letters that match their letter names (e.g. R for *are*; U for *you*; LEFT for *elephant*). At the "phonetic" stage, (i) phonological segmentation of spoken words is usually evident and, as a result, (ii) spellings contain a complete description of the sequence of sounds in pronunciations, (iii) all of the surface sound features of the words are represented in the spelling, (iv) children systematically show particular spellings for certain details of phonetic form such as tense vowels, lax vowels, preconsonantal nasals, syllabic sonorants, *-ed* endings, etc., but (v) letters are assigned strictly on the basis of sound without regard for acceptable letter sequence or other conventions of English orthography (e.g. IFU LEV AT THRD STRET IWEL KOM TO YOR HAWS THE ED for *If you live at Third Street I will come to your house. The End* (Bissex, 1980, p. 13). In the "transitional" stage, the child begins to adhere to more basic conventions of English orthography: vowels appear in every syllable (e.g. EGUL instead of the phonetic EGL for *eagle*); nasals are represented before consonants (e.g. BANGK instead of the phonetic BAK for *bank*); both vowels and consonants are employed instead of a letter-name strategy (e.g. EL rather than L for the first syllable of ELEFANT for *elephant*); common English letter sequences are used in spelling (e.g. YOUNITED for *united*), especially liberal use of vowel digraphs like *ai, ea, ay, ee*; silent *e* pattern becomes fixed as an alternative for spelling long vowels sounds (e.g. TIPE in place of the phonetic TIP for *type*), etc. Transitional spellers present the first evidence of a new orthographic strategy, moving from phonological to morphological and orthographic spelling (e.g. EIGHTEE instead of the phonetic ATE for *eighty*), but they have not fully developed knowledge of environmental factors such as the graphemic environment of the unit, position in the word, stress, morpheme boundaries and phonological influences. Acquisition of this knowledge, along with extended knowledge of word structure (e.g. prefixes, suffixes, contractions and compound words), an increased accuracy in using silent consonants and in doubling consonants, and simply in knowing when words "just don't look right" (i.e. in having a complete visual orthographic description of them) are elements which allow the mastery of "correct" spelling.

These descriptive categories for this developmental sequence are quite fine-grained. They can be more coarsely summarized as a shift from stage I of early attempts (which may be precommunicative or be based on visual copying of whole-word or symbol patterns (symbolic or logographic), or very rudimentary prephonetic attempts representing perhaps just the first sound of a word), through stage II reflecting varying degrees of mastery of the alphabetic principle, to stage III of correct orthographic or morphemic spelling (Ehri, 1986; Frith, 1985; Gentry, 1982).

STAGES OF READING DEVELOPMENT

Analyses of children's early reading errors (Biemiller, 1970; Torrey, 1979; Weber, 1970) led Marsh *et al.* (1981) to propose that the first stage of reading could be characterized as one of "linguistic substitution", where the child uses a strategy of rote association between a simple unsynthesized visual stimulus and an unanalysed oral response. "The child typically centres on one aspect of the visual stimulus such as the first letter and associates that with the oral response. . . . Their natural strategy is congruent with the 'whole word' approach to teaching reading" (pp. 201–202). Frith (1985) calls this the "logographic" stage. If the child does not know the word, she may guess on the basis of contextual cues.

Marsh *et al.* suggest that the child next progresses to "discrimination net substitution", where "the number of graphemic features a young child can process is limited initially to the first letter, and it is only later that additional features such as word length, final letter, etc. are added. The child at this stage appears to be operating according to a 'discrimination net' mechanism in which graphemic cues are processed only to the extent necessary to discriminate one printed word from another" (p. 203).

Marsh *et al.* call the next stage that of "sequential decoding", Frith terms it "alphabetic", Gough and Hillinger (1980) "deciphering", Harris and Coltheart (1986) "phonological-recoding". In all of these models this is characterized by the use of individual graphemes and phonemes and their correspondences. "It is an analytic skill involving a systematic approach, namely decoding grapheme by grapheme. Letter and phonological factors play a crucial role. This strategy enables the reader to pronounce novel and nonsense words" (Frith, 1985, p. 308).

Both models hold that the final stages of skilled reading take place by the use of "orthographic" strategies. Marsh *et al.* characterize this as being an extension to the simple decoding strategy (which was based on one-to-one correspondence) where the child now learns more complex rules of orthographic structure—the units are letter groups, and higher-order condition rules (like the magic *e* rule) are used. Frith, however, suggests that skilled reading involves orthographic strategies where the words are instantly analysed into orthographic units without phonological conversion: "The orthographic units ideally coincide with morphemes. They are internally represented as abstract letter-by-letter strings. These units make up a limited set that—in loose analogy to a syllabary—can be used to create by recombination an almost unlimited number of words" (Frith, 1985, p. 308). Both the models of Frith and Marsh *et al.* emphasize analysis of multiple letter orthographic units, but Frith is implying that practice at the analysis of orthographic sequences will eventually allow non-phonological whole-morpheme direct lexical access, with post-lexical phonological retrieval.

INTERACTIONS IN THE DEVELOPMENT OF READING AND SPELLING

The importance of Frith's (1985) model is that it provides a theoretical framework within which spelling and reading interact to advance the learner towards increased proficiency in each ability. It is a developmental model where reading and spelling both progress through stages of logographic, then alphabetic, and finally orthographic strategies. But her model does more than this in that it suggests reasons for the move from one stage to the next. The crux of her argument is that normal reading and spelling development proceed out of step, and that the adoption and use of a strategy in one domain may serve as a pacemaker for development of that strategy in the other. This is illustrated in Figure 8.1, which shows the points at which the domains are misaligned and the cross-domain influences that are suggested to occur.

Claim 1

Frith suggests that the beginnings of literacy lie in logographic reading whereby the child has a finite whole-word reading vocabulary and that the development of this means of reading results in its adoption as a strategy for spelling. Thus claim 1 is that "logographic reading is the pacemaker for the use of a logographic strategy in spelling". Evidence for a logographic stage of reading comes from Seymour and Elder (1986), who showed that 5-year-old beginning readers who were taught by a

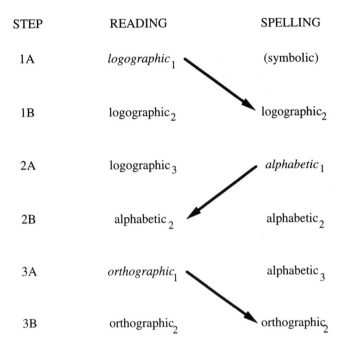

STEP	READING	SPELLING
1A	*logographic*₁	(symbolic)
1B	logographic₂	logographic₂
2A	logographic₃	*alphabetic*₁
2B	alphabetic₂	alphabetic₂
3A	*orthographic*₁	alphabetic₃
3B	orthographic₂	orthographic₂

FIGURE 8.1 Frith's model of reading and spelling acquisition; strategies acting as "pacemakers" at each step are italicized. Adapted from Frith (1985) by permission.

predominantly "look and say" method were able to read aloud words that they had been taught but nevertheless possessed no usable procedures for pronouncing new words. However, evidence for this driving the development of a logographic strategy of spelling is more hard to come by. There is little doubt that children are first brought to the importance of written words by seeing them, but several investigators, most notably Goswami and Bryant (1990, Chapter 3), seriously question the existence of a logographic stage of spelling.

Claim 2

At some points of development, reading and spelling are paradoxically out of synchronization. As Goswami and Bryant (1990, p. 148) put it: "It is still not clear why children are so willing to break up words into phonemes when they write, and yet are so reluctant to think in terms of phonemes when they read. But there can be little doubt that at first children's reading and spelling are different and separate. The most dramatic demonstration of this separation is the fact that young children often cannot read some words which they know how to spell and also fail to spell some words which they can read." Perhaps the major tenet of Frith's model, like that of Ehri (1986), is that children first gain explicit insight into the alphabetic code through practice at spelling and that it is this which causes a shift from a logographic reading strategy to an alphabetic approach. Claim 2 is therefore that "alphabetic spelling is the pacemaker for the use of an alphabetic strategy in reading". This can be broken down into two components: claim 2a is that "phonological awareness is much more related to early spelling than it is to early reading", claim 2b is that "this mutually supportive growth of phonological awareness and spelling acts as a pacemaker for the adoption of an alphabetic strategy of reading".

The flesh of the argument of claim 2 is as follows. It assumes that phonological awareness is important in the development of alphabetic reading (Bradley & Bryant, 1983; Ellis & Large, 1987, 1988) but it is when attempting to spell rather than to read that the child first realizes that a phonological strategy is useful in breaking up print–speech correspondences (Smith, 1978; Bryant & Bradley, 1980; Frith, 1981; Snowling & Perin, 1983). Early spelling practice typically involves dividing spoken words into phonemes and representing these phonemes with letters. In this way experience in spelling words affords the opportunity for making comparisons between the phonetic information in individual letters and sounds as they are embedded in the spoken word. Spelling practice helps to establish this abstract concept through two very concrete means—articulatory and kinaesthetic rehearsal—and by cross-modal correspondences so that orthographic units guide parsing breaks and provide labels for the sound chunks produced by the novice segmenter (indeed, when considering phonology, we cannot ignore our knowledge of orthography once acquired, as is evidenced by fourth-graders and above thinking that *pitch* has four phonemes but *rich* only three, whereas in both of these words a phonetic element corresponding to the extra letter *t* is present in articulation, Ehri & Wilce, 1985). Through repeated practice in spelling, the child may come to appreciate the subtle relationship between a symbol in the written word and its corresponding sound in the context of the spoken word. The discovery of this relationship is the key to alphabetic insight. The crux of the problem is "knowing how to combine the letters into units appropriate for speech" (Liberman & Shankweiler, 1979, p. 141). As children struggle to decompose words into individual phonemic units, they commonly experiment with various articulatory rehearsals of word parts and they search for distinguishable articulatory units that correspond to letter–sound units. This process of separating sounds in a word through consciously monitoring their own articulations may serve a dual purpose: it may both help the development of phonological awareness and enhance knowledge of the alphabetic principle. As children refine their ability to detect and isolate the sound content of spoken words through repeated practice in spelling, so they build a store of knowledge about the relationships among sounds, letters and pronunciations that can be applied to the task of reading (Chomsky, 1977; Ehri, 1986).

Claim 3

Finally, both Frith (1985) and Ehri (1986) suppose that considerable practice at reading by means of an alphabetic strategy encourages sufficient analysis of letter sequences in words to allow the reader to develop internal representations that are well specified in terms of letter-by-letter detail. These orthographic representations acquired through reading would then be exact enough to be transferred to spelling and to there constitute the knowledge that allows the shift from phonetic through transitional to correct spelling described above. Thus claim 3 is that "reading is the pacemaker for the development of orthographic spelling".

Frith's model is also important in that it explains different disorders of developmental literacy in terms of arrest at different stages of development. Since the present purpose is to assess it as an explanation of normal literacy development, these other claims will not be addressed further here.

If we want to study development then we must do so directly. Only when the same persons are tested repeatedly over time does it become possible to identify developmental changes and processes of organization within the individual. Cross-sectional studies which compare different groups of people at different points of acquisition must always come a poor second when small but reliable changes with age are to be detected, where teaching methods and teachers change with time, and where we do not wish to make the artificial assumption that the abilities of a younger cross-section were present in the older cross-section at a previous time (Ellis & Large, 1987). For these reasons we will only weigh the model against the two types of research paradigm which allow some degree of causal interpretation: longitudinal studies and experimental investigations of the effects of training.

TESTS FROM LONGITUDINAL STUDIES OF DEVELOPMENT

Phonological awareness and alphabetic reading

There have now been a number of longitudinal demonstrations that early phonological awareness (PA) predicts later reading achievement even when prior IQ is controlled (Bradley & Bryant, 1985; Ellis & Large, 1987; Lunberg, Olofsson & Wall, 1980; Mann, 1984; Stanovich, Cunningham & Cramer, 1984; see Wagner & Torgesen, 1987 and Goswami & Bryant, 1990 for reviews). It is clear, therefore, that there is a causal developmental sequence whereby alphabetic reading capitalizes on prior phonological abilities.

Reciprocal influences are also evident whereby, as metaphonological skills are made relevant and are practised in alphabetic reading, so they themselves are enriched (see Morais, Alegria & Content, 1987 for review). For example: (1) Portuguese adult illiterates who had never attended school for social reasons scored only 19% correct on tests of phoneme addition and deletion whereas matched subjects who had been taught to read and write in special classes in adulthood scored at over 70% levels. Thus Morais *et al.* (1979) concluded that the ability to deal explicitly with the segmental units of speech is not acquired spontaneously in the course of cognitive growth, but demands some specific training, which, for most persons, is provided by learning to read and write. (2) Alegria, Pignot and Morais (1982) showed that 6-year-old children trained to read using phonic methods were much better (58%) at phonemic segmentation than whole-word trained readers (15%). (3) Chinese literates who were taught to read *pinyin*, an alphabetic script, scored 83% on a test of segmental analysis, whereas non-alphabetic literates who could read logographs only scored 21% (Read *et al.*, 1986). Thus phonological segmentation is to some considerable extent a consequence of *alphabetic* literacy. (4) In a longitudinal investigation of 40 children learning to read English (Ellis & Large, 1988), reading ability at 5 and 6 years old better predicted phoneme segmentation skill 1 year later than phoneme segmentation predicted later reading. (5) Perfetti *et al.* (1987) used time-lag partial correlation analyses of first-grade children's development to demonstrate that whereas phoneme blending predicted later reading ability, this in turn predicted later proficiency at phoneme segmentation. They suggested that young children come to possess a basic, primitive awareness of the sounds of language on which alphabetic reading capitalizes. However, learning to read fosters attention to constituent principles of words and this results in the development of sophisticated segment analysis ability. As this is acquired, so there are further gains in reading itself.

Ellis and Cataldo (1990) put a similar case concerning different aspects of phonological awareness and the differential interactions of these with developing reading. Whereas early research into the relationship between reading and phonological awareness did not discriminate between different types of phonemic awareness tasks (Lewkowicz, 1980; Bradley & Bryant, 1985), more recent work suggests that the level of phonemic awareness demanded by the phonological tasks influences the strength of the relationship between reading and phoneme awareness (Backman, 1983). Stanovich, Cunningham and Cramer (1984) asked children to perform tasks involving the analysis of words for explicit sound content (non-rhyming tasks) and for the perception of overall similarity of sound content (rhyming tasks). They found that the non-rhyming, or analytic, and productive phonological tasks formed a cluster of related skills and that the rhyming tasks did not correlate strongly with the non-rhyming tasks. Snowling and Perin (1983) found that children's ability to perform a segmentation task was not significantly different from their ability in spelling, the close connection between these skills indicating the necessity of explicit PA in spelling. Thus there seem to be two, developmentally different, measurable levels of PA. Children's first awareness of the sound properties of speech is implicit and perceptual. Spontaneous play with rhyming and nonsense words is thought to reflect an overall sensitivity to the sound content of words (Chukovsky, 1968; Clark, 1978; Slobin, 1978). At this point they are not yet able to consciously reflect on language (Andresen, in Valtin, 1984; Shankweiler, Liberman & Savin, 1972). Valtin (1984) describes a three-stage model for the development of phonological awareness. Initially the child is not aware of the sound value of speech, s/he senses when, but not why, speech acts fail to be communicative. During the next stage, "children become increasingly able to abstract the language from the action and the meaning context and to think about some of the properties of the form of language. Their knowledge of language units is still implicit, however, and related to psycholinguistic units of speech" (Valtin, 1984, p. 214). Once the child achieves conscious awareness, s/he demonstrates explicit phonological awareness and can reflect upon, produce and manipulate phonemic units within spoken words. MacLean, Bryant and Bradley (1987) demonstrated in a longitudinal study that children's early experience of nursery rhymes results in their gaining initial implicit phonological awareness, Bradley and Bryant (1983) and Ellis and Large (1987) that very early reading capitalizes on this implicit phonological awareness, and the above studies, particularly Perfetti *et al.* (1987), that experience in alphabetical reading promotes more analytic and explicit phonological awareness at sub-syllabic levels.

Stanovich and his colleagues present a body of evidence which appears interestingly to contradict the above conclusions. They use tests of recognition of famous authors and titles to assess the amount to which individuals have been exposed to print and, by inference, the amount of reading that they have done. Although, as will be described below, print exposure is highly predictive of orthographic knowledge and vocabulary even when intelligence is controlled, it does not reliably predict phonological processing abilities (e.g. phoneme deletion or transposition) either in children (Cunningham & Stanovich, 1993) or in adults (Stanovich & West, 1989). These disparate results do not seem attributable to measurement instruments since they used similar sorts of phoneme segmentation tasks to those in the above studies. Cunningham and Stanovich (1993) invoke the twin studies of Olson *et al.* (1989), which demonstrated that the variance in word recognition associated with orthographic processing had much less heritability than did variance in word recognition associated with phonological processing and thus they suggested that phonological awareness of this type is less affected by experience afforded by print exposure. Another possibility is that amount of exposure to the written language *per se* is not the relevant variable—rather, in normal (as opposed to dyslexic) children, refined explicit phonological awareness at the level of the phoneme is acquired as a result of alphabetic literacy skill, which in turn is engendered by an introduction to grapheme–phoneme correspondences in spelling.

This leads us to the particular question of claim 2—what is the role of spelling in the coming together of phonological skills and reading?

Alphabetic Spelling, Phonological Awareness and Reading

There is now a useful collection of longitudinal studies which address the development of phonological awareness, reading and spelling. Unfortunately, while they are all informative, they also all have their problems. This section will briefly describe some representative studies and weigh claim 2 against their evidence.

L1. Lundberg, Olofsson and Wall (1980) presented the first longitudinal study where phoneme segmentation and synthesis skills measured during kindergarten in 143 Swedish children were used as predictors of reading and spelling development at the end of grade 1 and the beginning of grade 2. There were highly significant correlations between the PA measures and later reading and spelling, demonstrating the extreme importance of PA in literacy acquisition. Unfortunately, the study was marred by too easy a spelling test at grade 1, resulting in ceiling effects on this variable and lack of discrimination. It is difficult, therefore, to assess whether PA is more involved in early spelling than in reading (claim 2a) and impossible to look at causal interactions between early spelling and later reading (claim 2b).

L2. Tornéus (1984) investigated the causal relationships between intelligence (IQ), general language development (L), phonological awareness (PA: sound blending and segmentation), reading (R) and spelling (S) in 46 dyslexic and 44 control Swedish children at the end of grade 1 (IQ1, L1, PA1, R1, S1) and at the beginning (IQ2, R2, S2) and middle of grade 2 (S3). A number of causal models of interactions in their development were tested using LISREL. There was a very strong causal path from PA1 to spelling, but only a slight influence of general linguistic and cognitive development on spelling. The causal model for reading was similar, with the exception that it also included a direct causal path from cognitive development. Moreover, it was clear that the correlations between various aspects of PA and spelling at all grades measured (0.51–0.73) were considerably higher than those between PA and reading (0.33–0.53), a set of findings consistent with Frith's claim 2a that phonological awareness is initially much more involved in spelling than in reading. Unfortunately, there were no models which looked for interactions in effect from reading to spelling and vice versa, so it is difficult to assess Frith's claim 2b about pacemakers from this study (the failure to obtain an R3 measure also limits these possibilities here). Tornéus does provide tests of reciprocal models whereby PA could affect S (or R) and S (R) could in turn affect PA. These suggested much more of a causal role in development from PA to reading and spelling than the reverse. However, there are grave problems with these analyses: (i) solutions to such reciprocal path models are notoriously unstable in causal path analysis, (ii) PA was measured at time 1 only, the composite S variable was measured at times 1, 2 and 3, the composite R variable at times 1 and 2, and therefore the models fitted were looking for causal affects of, for example, spelling mid grade 2 on grade 1 PA. Since neither time nor development runs backwards, it is not surprising that there were low beta-weights on these paths. Contra Tornéus' claims, therefore, these models are not fair tests of, for example, Ehri's (1979) claim that phonological awareness arises from acquaintance with orthography gained from practice in spelling.

L3. Juel, Griffith and Gough (1986) assessed a well-motivated range of variables including IQ, listening comprehension, PA (phoneme segmentation and phoneme substitution), exposure to print, nonword reading, spelling recognition and production, reading comprehension and writing in over 100 children over the first two grades of their schooling in Texas. Unfortunately, they analysed the data with a series of cross-sectional rather than time-lag models and reanalysis is impossible as they do not provide time-lag correlations. Their cross-sectional data do replicate high correlations between PA and both reading and spelling. However, these correlations were of similar magnitude in both grades (their Table 3) and there is thus no evidence from their study that explicit PA is more related to grade 1 spelling than to reading (claim 2a). The lack of cross-lagged correlations precludes a test of claim 2b.

L4. Mommers (Mommers, 1987; Mommers *et al.*, 1986) describes a longitudinal investigation of the first 3 years of development of PA, reading and spelling in approximately 500 Dutch children. The study is admirable in that (i) word identification, spelling and reading comprehension were measured in parallel at, at least, five points in development and (ii) the investigators analysed the results with proper longitudinal causal path models. Unfortunately, (i) PA was only measured at the first point and so reciprocal effects of reading and spelling on PA growth cannot be assessed, (ii) as in many of the above studies, the reading and spelling tests included words both regular and irregular in terms of grapheme–phoneme correspondence and so we cannot disentangle alphabetic and orthographic strategies, (iii) such a complex data set limits the authors to reporting only the final models resulting from many iterative stages of model refinement. Even so, there is some tentative support for aspects of Frith's model. In the first place, there were strong effects of initial PA on immediately subsequent single word reading and spelling abilities, although there was no evidence of a greater contribution on spelling (claim 2a). In the course of model refinement, the investigators found it necessary to fit a path at the second point of measurement (4 months after the start of formal reading instructions) between spelling ability and word reading (SPo to DSo in their Figure 5), "a much stronger one than in the reverse direction" (Mommers, 1987, p. 136). In that this influence of spelling on reading is unique to this early stage of literacy development, this finding is highly supportive of Frith's suggestion of the influence of spelling on alphabetic reading (claim 2b). At all subsequent stages the best-fitting causal models had significant, although not large, influences in the reverse direction, i.e. from word reading to spelling: "There also exists an influence of decoding skill on spelling. In both decoding skill and spelling, orthographic representations stored in the lexicon play a part. . . . The repeated reading of words can only to some extent improve the quality of the orthographic representations" (Mommers, 1987, p. 140). These paths, although small, are supportive of claim 3.

L5. Cataldo and Ellis (Cataldo & Ellis, 1988; Ellis & Cataldo, 1990) charted the development of reading, spelling and phonological awareness in a group of 28 children during their first 3 years in school. During this time the children were tested at four intervals in reading and spelling real and nonsense words, phoneme segmentation and auditory categorization. The Wechsler Preschool Primary Scale of Intelligence was included in the set of initial assessments. A test of phoneme segmentation was given as a measure of explicit phonemic awareness and a test of auditory categorization was taken as a measure of implicit phonological awareness. The majority of the sample had only begun to attend school when the initial assessments were taken at the beginning of the school year, when their mean age was 4 years, 6 months. The children were retested at the end of their first school year, at the beginning of the second year and finally at the beginning of the third school year. Exploratory (LISREL) causal path analyses were used to investigate the contribution of each ability to the subsequent growth of skill in word recognition, spelling and phonological awareness over three measured phases of development. Phase 1 spanned the children's first year in school. Phase 2 charted the development from spring of the first school year to autumn of the second year. Phase 3 looked at development from the beginning of the second year in school to the beginning of the third year. The phase 1 pathweights from spelling to reading real words (0.31) and nonsense words (0.23) identified spelling as an important contributor to the early formation of reading. This pattern of influence was repeated in the second phase (spelling to reading real words 0.64 and nonsense words 0.60). The pronounced influence of spelling on reading contrasted with the meagre contributions of reading to spelling (phase 1: 0.10 real words, 0.06 nonsense; phase 2: 0.14 real, 0.00 nonsense) thus confirming claim 2b. Implicit PA initially predicted early attempts to read (0.36, 0.41) as well as to spell (0.38, 0.31) but lost its influence on both reading and spelling in the following two phases. In contrast to the diminishing predictive power of implicit PA, explicit PA consistently predicted spelling in all three phases (confirming claim 2a), this influence increasing with phase. Explicit PA only emerged as a strong predictor of reading in phase 3. To summarize the Ellis and Cataldo results, the early flow of information between reading and spelling appeared to be asymmetrical: knowledge gleaned from spelling contributed to reading. Similarly, both implicit and explicit PA affected spelling development, with explicit PA increasing its influence as the contribution of implicit PA diminished. Only later in the developmental sequence did explicit PA begin to contribute directly to reading.

L6. Berninger, Abbott and Shurtleff (1990) tracked visual language processes (1 s delayed visual recognition memory for a word or for a letter in a word), oral language processes (vocabulary and phoneme segmentation and deletion), reading (word naming and lexical decision) and spelling (written reproduction subsequent to seeing the word) in 42 children during their first grade of school in the US. Written and oral language abilities at the end of kindergarten predicted reading and spelling at the beginning of first grade. PA skills at this first measurement interval correlated 0.63 with whole-word presentation (WW) reading (lexical decision) but somewhat more so with WW spelling (0.74) and WW reading for naming (0.77). At the end of first grade the concurrent correlations with PA followed the same patterns, with lexical decision reading (0.47) lower than spelling (0.57), lower than reading for naming (0.74). It seems therefore that PA is initially more involved in spelling than in lexical access for reading (although it is involved in reading for naming). This accords with but qualifies claim 2a. Visual word recognition memory abilities at end of kindergarten correlated 0.55 with WW lexical decision reading, 0.63 with WW spelling and 0.63 with WW naming reading but these dropped dramatically in the concurrent correlations at the end of first grade to 0.26, 0.04 and 0.28 respectively. The fact that there are these visual correlates of both reading and spelling at the start of grade 1 but not at the end does lend some support to claim 1 that early reading and spelling are visual or logographic in nature and that there is then a shift from this to alphabetic processing.

L7. Goulandris (1991) reports a small longitudinal study of 27 British children to assess claim 2b. Verbal intelligence (vocabulary), nonword spelling, reading and spelling were used to predict reading and spelling 1 year later. Even when verbal intelligence, reading age and spelling age were partialled out, nonword spelling still predicted reading and spelling 1 year later, clearly demonstrating that a child's ability to generate phonetic spellings is the precursor of the eventual acquisition of alphabetic reading (claim 2b).

L8. Finally and most recently, there are the studies of Wimmer *et al.* (1991). The importance of these studies is that the initial testing was done on children within 1 month of joining school in Salzburg before any reading instruction had taken place. In the first study of 50 children, vowel substitution (their measure of PA) was a significant predictor of end of first-grade spelling ($r = 0.49$) and reading ($r = 0.45$), and these effects were significant even after IQ, initial letter knowledge and initial nonword reading abilities were partialled out. Study 2 investigated 42 children and the degree to which initial PA and rudimentary logographic (identification of ubiquitous logos such as "Coca Cola", "Milky Way") and alphabetic (the reading of logos printed in upper case to distort their original distinctive whole-word shape) reading skills predicted later reading of familiar words and nonwords and alphabetic and orthographic spelling. PA predicted later alphabetic spelling (0.31), reading accuracy (0.30), but not orthographic spelling (0.15). Logographic reading did not predict later reading (0.08), but alphabetic reading did more so (0.19), suggesting a change of reading strategy over this first year from logographic to alphabetic. Logographic reading did, however, predict later orthographic spelling (0.42). Most striking was the finding that PA skill at the end of the year was only moderately predicted by prior PA skill (0.31), but was highly correlated with reading accuracy at that time (0.53) and even more so with nonword spelling (0.66). In other words, over the course of the children's first year of entry into literacy, PA and spelling became strongly enmeshed abilities as a result of a symbiotic developmental relationship. Wimmer *et al.* summarize their article in the title "The relationship of phonemic awareness to reading acquisition: More consequence than cause but still important", and conclude that in most children quite limited exposure to reading and spelling instruction is sufficient to induce explicit awareness of phonemic segments of words.

These findings will be compared and brought together with the findings of training studies in the conclusions of this chapter.

Orthographic Reading and Orthographic Spelling

We have already described Mommers' (1987) finding of causal paths from word reading skill to spelling at later stages of development. Stanovich and his co-workers have produced a number of group studies that give further confirmation to claim 3. Stanovich and Cunningham (1992) argue that when reading, "whatever cognitive processes are engaged over word or word-group units (phonological coding, semantic activation, parsing, induction of new vocabulary items) are being exercised hundreds of times a day. It is surely to be expected that this amount of cognitive muscle-flexing will have some specific effects". They demonstrate in multiple regresson analyses that adults who read a lot (who have "high print exposure" as measured on Author and Magazine Recognition Tests) are better spellers even when non-verbal intelligence is controlled. The same is true for third- and fourth-grade children—Cunningham and Stanovich (1990) found that even after partialling out IQ, memory ability and phonological processing abilities, print exposure (the amount of reading the child did) accounted for significant variance in orthographic knowledge. This result is clear confirmation of claim 3—that the move to an orthographic strategy of spelling was driven by reading at later stages of development. However, Cunningham and Stanovich (1993) also show that it is true in the case of first-grade children. They demonstrate that 6–7-year-old children's ability to spell phonologically irregular words like *red*, *talk*, *mouse*, *rough*, which require consultation of an orthographic lexicon for conventional rather than phonetic spelling, was a separable component of variance in word recognition from phonological awareness. Furthermore, even at these young ages significant variance in the ability to perform correct orthographic spelling was accounted for by print exposure after phonological processing skill had been partialled out.

Thus there does seem to be clear evidence for claim 3—that exposure to the letter sequences of words in reading allows the child to develop orthographic representations that can then be used in spelling. However, these results qualify the claim in one important aspect—it seems that in normal children this is happening from quite early on in the development of literacy (grade 1) rather than being solely an aspect of a later third stage of reading and spelling development.

TESTS FROM TRAINING STUDIES

Studies involving training children in PA are fairly consistent in supporting claim 2a of Frith's model whereby phonological awareness is more involved in early spelling than in early reading—training in PA has its first effect on children's spelling:

T1. Bradley and Bryant (1983) taught metaphonological skills to 4- and 5-year-old children who could not read and who were at least two standard deviations below average in sound categorization ability. Some children were trained in categorizing common beginning (_hen_, _hat_), middle (_hen_, _pet_) and end _hen_, _man_) sounds, others received this training and, with the help of plastic letters, how each common sound was represented by a letter of the alphabet. The training had a positive effect on both reading and spelling measured over the next 4 years, and Bradley and Bryant concluded that "although others have suggested a link between phonological awareness and reading, our study is the first adequate empirical evidence that the link is causal". But there is more in their study than this. In the first place, there was much greater benefit from training sound categorization in conjunction with plastic letters which labelled the sounds, confirming the emphases of Ehri and Frith that phonological awareness is more readily acquired when it is related to orthography. In the second place, this training had more effect on later spelling (17 months' gain) than it did on later reading (8.5 months' gain).

T2. Tornéus (1984) reports a training intervention whereby 38 first-graders were assigned to either phonological awareness training or a general language activity control for 8 weeks. They were pre- and posttested on reading, spelling, sound blending and segmentation. Training of phonological skills was effective and among the children with the lowest phonological awareness pretest performance, specific phonological training improved spelling performance more than general language activities did. Phonological training did not, however, directly affect reading.

T3. Experimental evidence for claim 2b is provided by Ehri and Wilce (1987a), who taught kindergarten children to spell words by attending to constituent letter–sound sequences, and, when necessary, to phonetic, phonemic and articulatory cues. These children learned to read words better than children who were taught isolated letter–sound relationships. Thus children trained in _spelling_ were superior to the controls in their ability to use phonetic cues and letter–sound constituents when learning to _read_.

T4. Lundberg, Frost and Petersen (1988) trained over 200 Danish preschool children who had as yet no reading instruction in phonetic awareness and assessed the later effects on reading and spelling in first and second grades. Training had a small effect on rhyming and syllable manipulation abilities, and a dramatic effect on phoneme segmentation abilities. These improvements in turn had a large facilitative effect on grade 1 spelling ($p < 0.001$) but only a marginal immediate effect on grade 1 reading ($p < 0.10$). By the end of grade 2, however, the effect of training on spelling persisted ($p < 0.001$) and by now had a knock-on effect on reading ($p < 0.01$).

T5. Lie (1991) assessed the effects on later reading and spelling of the training of metaphonological skills in approximately 100 first-grade Norwegian children. Both training in phoneme identification and in phoneme segmentation and blending had a facilitative effect on later grade 1 and 2 reading and spelling, but again the initial effect on spelling was somewhat greater than that on reading. At the end of grade 1, students who had been trained in sequential phoneme segmentation scored significantly higher in spelling than students who had received positional (phoneme isolation) training, a result which stresses that it is important to phonologically analyse a word sequentially in order to spell it.

The results of T1, T2, T4 and T5 are all consistent with claim 2a that phonological awareness is much more involved in early spelling than in early reading. The findings of T3 and T4 moreover support pacemaker claim 2b that the acquisition of phonological awareness in spelling drives the development of alphabetic reading.

LONGITUDINAL STUDIES OF SINGLE CASES

No chapter on longitudinal tests of developmental models would be complete without describing one other essential source of evidence, that of detailed longitudinal clinical investigations of single cases. Unfortunately, there simply is not the space to do justice to this body of research and so while this small section may allow an assertion of formal completeness, it is readily acknowledged that this chapter is far from satisfactory in this respect.

Just one study will be used to illustrate the power of this approach, particularly with respect to Frith's claims about developmental arrest. The reader is referred to chapters in this volume by Seymour and Evans (Chapter 7), Campbell (Chapter 13), Kay and Hanley (Chapter 15), and Siegel (Chapter 12) for other examples and to exemplary studies by Temple (1988), Seymour and Elder (1985), Seymour and Evans (1992) and Snowling et al. (1992).

SC1. Seymour and Evans' (1988) study is relevant to claim 1. They analysed reading and spelling processes in a case (AT) of developmental disability associated with Klinefelter XXXY syndrome. Between the ages of 7 and 11 years old this boy's reading was almost entirely logographic—he had a sight vocabulary of perhaps over 500 words that he had been taught but was unable to do any sounding and blending, with error rates on nonwords between 95 and 99%. He could spell around 170 words but only managed 1/200 nonwords correctly. Thus AT showed an almost complete absence of alphabetic functions, i.e. his development was arrested at a logographic stage.

CONCLUSIONS

Frith's Model

The longitudinal studies reviewed above give considerable support for several of the claims of Frith's model. There is some evidence of a logographic first stage of reading (L6 and SC1), although no study can be found which provides corroboration for this driving a logographic stage of spelling (claim 1). Phonological awareness does seem more related in early development to spelling than to reading (L2 and L8, but compare L3 and L4), and training in PA first affects the development of spelling rather than reading (T1, T2, T4, T5), (claim 2a). The acquisition of PA through spelling engenders development of an alphabetic strategy of reading (L4, L5, L7, T3, T4) (claim 2b—see Ellis & Cataldo, 1990 for the pedagogical implications of this). The acquisition of orthographic knowledge through reading promotes orthographic spelling (L4 and Stanovich & Cunningham, 1992) (claim 3).

But these data also suggest some additions and qualifications. In the first place, they very clearly show that there are different facets of PA, and early implicit awareness of syllables and rhyme and a later sophisticated explicit ability at segmentation at the level of phonemes. Even very early reading seems to capitalize on this implicit phonological awareness which plays a role in the logographic reading otherwise characterized as being primarily visual in nature. The above studies also demonstrate that experience in alphabetic spelling and reading promotes the more analytic and explicit phonological awareness at sub-syllabic levels. In normal children this is acquired very quickly, and, although it remains to be determined by just how much, it seems likely that this comes more from alphabetic spelling instruction than from practice in alphabetic reading. Finally, although experience with reading allows the child to abstract knowledge of orthographic sequences which can then be applied in spelling, it seems that this is happening not just with mature readers who are solidly at an orthographic stage of reading, but also even with first-grade children at the beginnings of literacy. Frith's model, literally interpreted, is a strong stage model suggesting three very different strategies of reading and spelling at three discrete stages of development. Although this is probably true as a broad characterization, it seems that there are mutual influences between the alphabetic and orthographic aspects of reading and spelling at all stages of development.

A new skill invariably initially builds on whatever relevant abilities are already present, then, as it is used, it may well legitimatize and make more relevant (Istomina, 1975) those prior skills and so in turn cause their further development. Stanovich has persuasively argued the case for reciprocal relationships and bootstrapping effects: "In short, many things that facilitate further growth in reading comprehension ability—general knowledge, vocabularly, syntactic knowledge—are developed by reading itself" (Stanovich, 1986, p. 364); "interrelationships between the various subskills of reading and intelligence increase with age, *probably due to mutual facilitation*" (Stanovich, Cunningham & Feeman, 1984, p. 278, my emphasis). What is true of reading and intelligence also applies to the symbiotic development of spelling, reading and PA: they interact reciprocally over time. Finer-grained studies are now needed to further determine the contributions from one to the other, the representations of the mutual exchanges (visual, phonological, orthographic) and their particular content at each point in the acquisition of literacy. That being said, as a general description of literacy development, Frith's model holds many truths.

Suggestions for Further Research

The longitudinal studies that are available to date are informative but all have their flaws. We have now reached a position of sufficient theoretical and methodological development to design a longitudinal investigation that will properly inform us of the detailed cognitive interactions in the development of literacy and which will help us answer some of the remaining questions concerning reciprocal skill interactions: continuities or critical stages, the identity of the partners and the gifts they exchange. Future studies would benefit from adopting the following recommendations, some of which are illustrated in Figure 8.2.

Models of literacy development emphasize interactions between reading and spelling—one moment spelling is the pacemaker, the next reading. But they say more than this: spelling is the pacemaker of *alphabetic* reading, reading the pacemaker of *orthographic* spelling, etc. Therefore future studies should ensure that they assess the three different strategies of reading and spelling separately. For example, logographic reading strategies can be measured by comparing the reading of logos or known children's names in their normal whole-word form with that under mixed font or other visually distorted presentations as in the work of Wimmer, Zwicker and Gugg (1991) and Seymour; alphabetic reading can be hygienically assessed by nonword reading as in Ellis and Cataldo (1990); orthographic reading by the reading of words which are irregular or unusual in their grapheme–phoneme correspondences. Similar steps must be taken for the assessment of different aspects of spelling so that not two but six different aspects of literacy are assessed at each time-point as illustrated in Figure 8.2. Only when this is done can we identify if there are concurrent influences whereby, for example, orthographic spelling ability might be growing as a result of the acquisition of orthographic representations from reading *at the same time as* alphabetic reading is developing as a result of the acquisition of phonological segmentation ability and letter–sound correspondences from spelling practice.

It is now clear that there are different levels of phonological awareness and that rhyming or implicit PA seem more involved in facilitating early reading acquisition, whereas explicit phoneme-level PA seems to be more involved in, and more a consequence of, the acquisition of alphabetic spelling. At least these different aspects of PA need to be assessed, and the study could also usefully investigate the child's abilities of interim levels of PA at the onset-rime level (Goswami & Bryant, 1990). We also need to consider potential early precursors of PA, for example in early rhyming experience (MacLean, Bryant & Bradley, 1987; Bryant *et al.*, 1989, 1990).

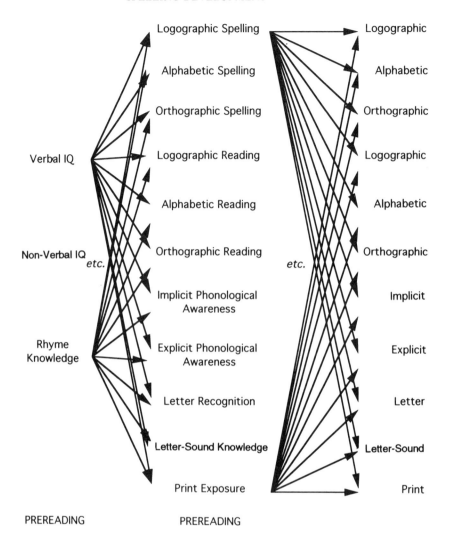

FIGURE 8.2   The awaited longitudinal study.

Given the ubiquitous influence of general ability, it is essential to control for relevant aspects of environmental and genetic advantage using different aspects of IQ as index variables (Ellis & Large, 1987).

These measures need to be taken early. There are persuasive reasons to believe that in normal children there are massive developments in PA as a consequence of the very beginnings of introduction to print. Thus the whole range of tests must be administered before this. They should also be closely spaced thereafter since developments move quickly, especially during the first 2 years, and otherwise influences are going to be missed.

The data should be analysed with a proper longitudinal causal path model. It is not enough to generate composite variables over several time periods as was common

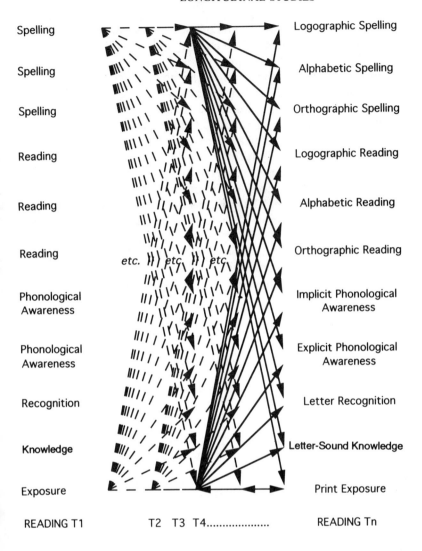

Spelling	Logographic Spelling
Spelling	Alphabetic Spelling
Spelling	Orthographic Spelling
Reading	Logographic Reading
Reading	Alphabetic Reading
Reading	Orthographic Reading

etc.

Phonological Awareness	Implicit Phonological Awareness
Phonological Awareness	Explicit Phonological Awareness
Recognition	Letter Recognition
Knowledge	Letter-Sound Knowledge
Exposure	Print Exposure

READING T1   T2 T3 T4....................   READING Tn

in early studies, nor simply to report best-fitting models within each cross-section. Furthermore, with so many variables, "tuned" models where a subset of paths are freed rest too much on the iterative steps of model building. It is therefore better to use causal path analysis in a descriptive fashion akin to factor analysis, employing low-constraint time series models as in Cataldo and Ellis (1988) and Ellis (1990). In these models *any* ability at the prior testing point is free to affect *any* ability at the subsequent time, thus allowing the determination of causal paths while controlling for indirect effects and common causes. It is also advisable to free all possible covariation within each time period, thus allowing for unexplained covariation resultant from unknown causes operating between time periods and avoiding overestimation/inflation of the specified between-time-period effects in this model. To avoid clutter in Figure 2.8 we show only some of these paths; however, it must be stressed that a proper statistical analysis of such a longitudinal study will involve all paths from each ability at a prior testing point to each ability at the next.

Our concern is literacy development rather than chronological development. Thus, although the data are more easily analysed in terms of chronological time slices (and they should so be analysed), so also it would be advantageous to reorganize the children, putting them into waves of comparable literacy development rather than chronological age. Then we would really have a chance to assess a stage rather than age model of reading and spelling acquisition.

Unlike spoken language, literacy rarely comes naturally. Its acquisition is heavily determined by instruction and we need to define how much of the course of development is a result of instruction. The most basic comparison would entail two groups of children, one exposed to more "whole-word" methods and the other to more "phonic" approaches.

Finally, for reliable estimation of these causal interactions the sample sizes need to be large, at least in units of hundreds rather than tens.

It is no small enterprise, but nonetheless it is a necessary one.

REFERENCES

Alegria, J., Pignot, E. & Morais, J. (1982). Phonetic analysis of speech and memory codes in beginning readers. *Memory & Cognition*, **10**, 451–456.

Backman, J. (1983). The role of psycholinguistic skills in reading acquisition: a look at early readers. *Reading Research Quarterly*, **18**, 466–479.

Berninger, V. W. (1986). Normal variation in reading acquisition. *Perceptual and Motor Skills*, **62**(3), 691–716.

Berninger, V. W., Abbott, R. D. & Shurtleff, H. A. (1990). Developmental changes in interrelationships of visible language codes, oral language codes, and reading or spelling. *Learning and Individual Differences*, **21**(1), 45–66.

Biemiller, A. (1970). The development of the use of graphic contextual information as children learn to read. *Reading Research Quarterly*, **6**, 75–96.

Bissex, G. L. (1980). *GNYS AT WRK: A Child Learns to Read and Write*. Cambridge, Mass: Harvard University Press.

Bradley, L. & Bryant, P. E. (1983). Categorizing sounds and learning to read—a causal connection. *Nature*, **301**, 419–421.

Bradley, L. & Bryant, P. (1985). *Rhyme and Reason in Reading and Spelling* (International Academy for Research in Learning Disabilities, No. 1). Ann Arbor: The University of Michigan Press.

Bryant, P. E. & Bradley, L. (1980). Why children sometimes write words which they do not read. In U. Frith (Ed.), *Cognitive Processes in Spelling*. London: Academic Press.

Bryant, P. E. & Bradley, L. (1985). *Children's Reading Problems*. Oxford: Blackwell.

Bryant, P. E., Bradley, L., MacLean, M. & Crossland, J. (1989). Nursery rhymes, phonological skills and reading. *Journal of Child Language*, **16**(2), 407–428.

Bryant, P. E., MacLean, M., Bradley, L. L. & Crossland, J. (1990). Rhyme and alliteration, phoneme detection, and learning to read. *Developmental Psychology*, **26**(3), 429–438.

Cataldo, S. & Ellis, N. (1988). Interactions in the development of spelling, reading and phonological skills. *Journal of Research in Reading*, **11**(2), 86–109.

Cataldo, S. & Ellis, N. C. (1990). Learning to spell, learning to read. In P. D. Pumphrey & C. D. Elliott (Eds), *Children's Difficulties in Reading, Writing and Spelling: Challenges and Responses*. Basingstoke: Falmer Press.

Chomsky, C. (1977). Approaching reading through invented spelling. In L. B. Resnick & P. A. Weaver (Eds), *The Theory and Practice of Early Reading*, Vol. 2. Hillsdale, NJ: LEA.

Chukovsky, K. (1968). *From Two to Five*. Berkeley: University of California Press.

Clark, E. V. (1978). Awareness of language: some evidence from what children say and do. In A. Sinclair, R. J. Jarvella & W. J. M. Levelt (Eds), *The Child's Conception of Language*. New York: Springer-Verlag.

Crain-Thoreson, C. & Dale, P. S. (1992). Do early talkers become early readers? Linguistic precocity, preschool language, and emergent literacy. *Developmental Psychology*, **28**(3), 421–429.

Cunningham, A. E. & Stanovich, K. E. (1990). Tracking the unique effects of print exposure in children: associations with vocabulary, general knowledge and spelling. *Journal of Educational Psychology*, **83**, 264–274.

Cunningham, A. E. & Stanovich, K. E. (1993). Children's literacy environments and early word recognition subskills. *Reading and Writing*, **5**, 193–204.

Ehri, L. C. (1979). Linguistic insight: threshold of reading acquisition. In T. G. Waller & G. E. MacKinnon (Eds), *Reading Research: Advances in Theory and Practice*, Vol. 1. New York: Academic Press.

Ehri, L. C. (1984). How orthography alters spoken language competencies in children learning to read and spell. In J. Downing & R. Valtin (Eds), *Language Awareness and Learning to Read*. New York: Springer Verlag.

Ehri, L. C. (1986). Sources of difficulty in learning to spell and read. *Advances in Developmental and Behavioural Paediatrics*, **7**, 121–195.

Ehri, L. C. & Wilce, L. S. (1985). Movement into reading: is the first stage of printed word learning visual or phonetic? *Reading Research Quarterly*, **20**, 163–179.

Ehri, L. C. & Wilce, L. S. (1987a). Does learning to spell help beginners learn to read words? *Reading Research Quarterly*, **22**, 47–65.

Ehri, L. C. & Wilce, L. S. (1987b). Cipher versus cue reading: an experiment in decoding acquisition. *Journal of Educational Psychology*, **79**, 3–13.

Ellis, N. C. & Cataldo, S. (1990). The role of spelling in learning to read. *Language and Education*, **4**, 1–28.

Ellis, N. & Large, B. (1987). The development of reading: as you seek so shall you find. *British Journal of Psychology*, **78**, 1–28.

Ellis, N. & Large, B. (1988). The early stages of reading: a longitudinal study. *Applied Cognitive Psychology*, **2**, 47–76.

Ellis, N. C. (1990). Reading, phonological processing and STM: interactive tributaries of development. *Journal of Research in Reading*, **13**, 107–122.

Frith, U. (1981). Experimental approaches to developmental dyslexia: an introduction. *Psychological Research*, **43**, 97–110.

Frith, U. (1985). Beneath the surface of developmental dyslexia. In K. Patterson, M. Coltheart & J. Marshall (Eds), *Surface Dyslexia*. London: LEA.

Gentry, J. R. (1978). Early spelling strategies. *The Elementary School Journal*, **79**, 88–92.

Gentry, J. R. (1982). Analysis of developmental spelling in GNYS AT WORK. *The Reading Teacher*, **36**, 192–200.

Goswami, U. & Bryant, P. (1990). *Phonological Skills and Learning to Read*. Hove: LEA.

Gough, P. B. & Hillinger, M. L. (1980). Learning to read: an unnatural act. *Bulletin of the Orton Society*, **30**, 171–176.

Goulandris, N. K. (1991). Alphabetic spelling: predicting eventual literacy attainment. In C. M. Sterling & C. Robson (Eds), *Psychology, Spelling and Education*. Clevedon: Multilingual Matters.

Harris, M. & Coltheart, M. (1986). *Language Processing in Children and Adults*. London: Routledge & Kegan Paul.

Henderson, E. H. & Beers, J. W. (Eds) (1980). *Developmental and Cognitive Aspects of Learning to Spell: A Reflection of Word Knowledge*. Newark, Del.: International Reading Association.

Istomina, Z. M. (1975). The development of involuntary memory in preschool age children. *Soviet Psychology*, **13**, 5–64.

Juel, C., Griffiths, P. L. & Gough, P. B. (1986). Acquisition of literacy: a longitudinal study of children in first and second grade. *Journal of Educational Psychology*, **78**(4), 243–255.

Lewkowicz, N. K. (1980). Phonemic awareness training: what it is and how to teach it. *Journal of Educational Psychology*, **72**, 686–700.

Liberman, I. Y. & Shankweiler, D. (1979). Speech, the alphabet, and teaching to read. In L. B. Resnick & P. A. Weaver (Eds), *Theory and Practice of Early Reading*. Hillsdale, NJ: LEA.

Lie, A. (1991). Effects of a training program for stimulating skills in word analysis in first-grade children. *Reading Research Quarterly*, **26**, 234–250.

Lundberg, I., Frost, J. & Petersen, O-P. (1988). Effects of an extensive program for stimulating phonological awareness in preschool children. *Reading Research Quarterly*, **23**, 263–284.

Lundberg, I., Olofsson, A. & Wall, S. (1980). Reading and spelling skills in the first school years predicted from phonemic awareness skills in kindergarten. *Scandinavian Journal of Psychology*, **21**, 159–173.

MacLean, M., Bryant, P. & Bradley, L. (1987). Rhymes, nursery rhymes and reading in early childhood. *Merrill-Palmer Quarterly*, **33**, 255–281.

Mann, V. A. (1984). Longitudinal prediction and prevention of early reading difficulty. *Annals of Dyslexia*, **34**, 117–136.

Marsh, G., Friedman, M. P., Welch, V. & Desberg, P. (1980). The development of strategies in spelling. In U. Frith (Ed.), *Cognitive Process in Spelling*. London: Academic Press.

Marsh, G., Friedman, M. P., Welch, V. & Desberg, P. (1981). A cognitive-developmental theory of reading acquisition. In T. G. Waller & G. E. MacKinnon (Eds), *Reading Research: Advances in Theory and Practice*, Vol. 3. New York: Academic Press.

Mommers, M. J. C. (1987). An investigation into the relationship between word recognition, reading comprehension and spelling skills in the first two years of primary school. *Journal of Reading Research*, **10**, 122–143.

Mommers, M. J., Van Leeuwe, J. F., Oud, J. H. & Janssens, J. M. (1986). Decoding skills, reading comprehension and spelling: a longitudinal investigation. *Tijdschrift voor Onderwijsresearch*, **11**(2), 97–113.

Morais, J., Alegria, J. & Content, A. (1987). The relationships between segmental analysis and alphabetic literacy: an interactive view. *Cahiers de Psychologie Cognitive*, **7**, 415–438.

Morais, J., Cary, I. L., Alegria, J. & Bertelson, P. (1979). Does awareness of speech as a sequence of phones arise spontaneously? *Cognition*, **7**, 323–331.

Morris, D. (1983). Concept of word and phoneme awareness in the beginning reader. *Research in the Teaching of English*, **17**(4), 359–373.

Morris, D. & Perney, J. (1984). Developmental spelling as a predictor of first-grade reading achievement. *The Elementary School Journal*, **84**(4), 441–457.

Olson, R. K., Wise, B., Conners, F., Rack, J. & Fulker, D. (1989). Specific deficits in component reading and language skills: genetic and environmental influences. *Journal of Learning Disabilities*, **22**, 339–348.

Perfetti, C. A., Beck, I., Bell, L. C. & Hughes, C. (1987). Phonemic knowledge and learning to read are reciprocal: a longitudinal study of first grade children. *Merrill-Palmer Quarterly*, **33**, 283–319.

Read, C. (1971). Preschool children's knowledge of English phonology. *Harvard Educational Review*, **41**, 1–34.

Read, C. (1975). *Children's Categorizations of Speech Sounds in English*. Urbana, Ill.: National Council of Teachers of English.

Read, C. (1986). *Children's Creative Spelling*. London: Routledge & Kegan Paul.

Read, C., Zhang, Nie, H. & Ding, B. (1986). The ability to manipulate speech sounds depends on knowing alphabetic reading. *Cognition*, **24**, 31–44.

Seymour, P. H. K. & Elder, L. (1986). Beginning reading without phonology. *Cognitive Neuropsychology*, **1**, 43–82.

Seymour, P. H. K. & Evans, H. M. (1988). Developmental arrest at the logographic stage: impaired literacy functions in Klinefelter's XXXY syndrome. *Journal of Research in Reading*, **11**, 133–151.

Seymour, P. H. K. & Evans, H. M. (1992). Beginning reading without semantics: a cognitive study of hyperlexia. *Cognitive Neuropsychology*, **9**, 89–122.

Shankweiler, D., Liberman, I. Y. & Savin, H. B. (1972). General discussion of papers. In J. F. Kavanagh & I. Mattingly (Eds) *Language by Ear and by Eye*. Cambridge, Mass: MIT Press.

Slobin, D. J. (1978). A case study of early language awareness. In A. Sinclair, J. Jarvella & W. J. M. Levelt (Eds), *The Child's Conception of Language*. New York: Springer-Verlag.

Smith, F. (1978). *Understanding Reading: A Psycholinguistic Analysis of Reading and Learning to Read*, 2nd edition. New York: Holt, Rinehart and Winston.

Snowling, M., Hulme, C., Wells, B. & Goulandris, N. (1992). Continuities between speech and spelling in a case of developmental dyslexia. *Reading and Writing*, **4**, 19–31.

Snowling, M. & Perin, D. (1983). The development of phoneme segmentation skills in young children. In J. Sloboda (Ed.), *The Acquisition of Symbolic Skills*. London: Plenum Press.

Stanovich, K. E. (1986). Matthew effects in reading: some consequences of individual differences in the acquisition of literacy. *Reading Research Quarterly*, **XXI**, 360–407.

Stanovich, K. E. & Cunningham, A. E. (1992). Studying the consequences of literacy within a literate society: the cognitive correlates of print exposure. *Memory & Cognition*, **20**, 51–68.

Stanovich, K. E. & West, R. F. (1989). Exposure to print and orthographic processing. *Reading Research Quarterly*, **24**, 402–433.

Stanovich, K. E., Cunningham, A. E. & Cramer, B. B. (1984). Assessing phonological awareness in kindergarten children: issues of task comparability. *Journal of Experimental Child Psychology*, **38**, 175–190.

Stanovich, K. E., Cunningham, A. E. & Feeman, D. J. (1984). Intelligence, cognitive skills, and early reading progress. *Reading Research Quarterly*, **XIX**, 278–303.

Temple, C. M. (1988). Red is read but eye is blue: a case study of developmental dyslexia and follow-up report. *Brain and Language*, **34**, 13–37.

Tornéus, M. (1984). Phonological awareness and reading: a chicken and egg problem? *Journal of Educational Psychology*, **76**(6), 1346–1358.

Torrey, J. W. (1979). Reading that comes naturally: the early reader. In T. G. Waller & G. E. MacKinnon (Eds), *Reading Research: Advances in Theory and Practice*, Vol. 1. New York: Academic Press.

Valtin, R. (1984). The development of metalinguistic abilities in children learning to read and write. In J. Downing & R. Valtin (Eds), *Language Awareness and Learning to Read*. New York: Springer-Verlag.

Wagner, R. K. & Torgesen, J. K. (1987). The nature of phonological processing and its causal role in the acquisition of reading skills. *Psychological Bulletin*, **101**, 192–212.

Weber, R. M. (1970). A linguistic analysis of first-grade reading errors. *Reading Research Quarterly*, **5**, 427–451.

Wimmer, H., Landerl, K., Linortner, R. & Hummer, P. (1991). The relationship of phonemic awareness to reading acquisition: more consequence than precondition, but still important. *Cognition*, **40**, 219–249.

Wimmer, H., Zwicker, T. & Gugg, D. (1991). Schwierigkeiten beim Lesen und Schreiben in den ersten Schuljahren: Befunde zur Persistenz und Verursachung (Problems in reading and writing during the early years of school: findings concerning the persistence and causes of these problems). *Zeitschrift fur Entwicklungspsychologie und Padagogische Psychologie*, **23**(4), 280–298.

9

Measuring Spelling Production Times: Methodology and Tests of a Model

PIPPA J. GLOVER AND GORDON D. A. BROWN

University of Wales, Bangor

In this chapter we describe a new methodology that we have developed to measure spelling production times, and we describe the results of some experiments we have conducted that use the methodology to constrain models of adult spelling. We argue that the examination of spelling production times as well as spelling error rates is necessary if we are to decide amongst even currently available models of spelling. We show that the spelling production time methodology can be used to examine the question of whether (and how) skilled error-free adult spelling is influenced by the sound-to-spelling characteristics of the items to be spelled, and also to test predictions of a particular connectionist model of spelling (see Chapter 16 of the present volume). More specifically, we find that skilled adult spelling production time is influenced by the number of sound-to-spelling "friends" and "enemies" that a word has.

As noted in Chapter 1 of this volume, the last decade has seen considerably more research published on reading than on spelling, and this had led to a correspondingly greater sophistication in the resulting models of the relevant processes. Some reasons for this were discussed in Chapter 1 (see also Chapter 2 by Barry). Foremost amongst these was the relative difficulty in assessing spelling production time as compared with the study of single-word reading. Indeed, there have been rather few published studies of spelling speed that we are aware of.

Handbook of Spelling: Theory, Process and Intervention. Edited by G. D. A. Brown and N. C. Ellis.
©1994 John Wiley & Sons Ltd.

METHODOLOGICAL ISSUES

There are obvious difficulties in measuring spelling production time accurately. Written spelling can be measured using keyboard responses, although this leads to additional sources of error (e.g. incorrect key-pressing) and also suffers from the problem that there will be high between-individual variation in typing expertise. These individual differences may mask any experimental effects under investigation. Alternative methods employing written output make use of pressure-sensitive graphics tablets, but such approaches are inevitably cumbersome and do not lend themselves to the speedy collection of experimental data to compare with, for example, the data that have been produced using the lexical decision paradigm for single-word reading. Studies that have used digitizer pads to examine writing/spelling have generally been concerned primarily with investigating writing processes in normal and dyslexic (e.g. Martlew, 1992) or dysgraphic (e.g. Sovik, Arntzen & Thygessen, 1987a, b) populations, rather than being concerned with the lexical or other variables that may influence the ease of deriving correct spellings.

A further problem with using written output is that processes involved in written spelling may not be the same as those involved in oral spelling, and indeed Lesser (1990) and others have argued, on the basis of neuropsychological evidence, that separable mechanisms are involved in oral and written spelling.

We now turn to a brief review of previous research on spelling production times. Sloboda (1980) conducted an experiment in which adults were presented with printed pairs of items representing possible alternative spellings of words, only one of which was the correct spelling. Although this methodology proved successful insofar as phonologically alike misspellings were more likely to give rise to incorrect responses, such a test cannot, of course, be used as a "pure" measure of spelling production time, because reading processes are also involved. For a further experiment Sloboda devised a task in which subjects were required to listen to words and then press a key according to how many letters were in the word. Reaction times on this task proved highly sensitive to the lengths of the words to be spelled. As Sloboda himself points out, however, production of a correct response on this task does not entail that a correct spelling has been derived, for often the most plausible misspelling of the word would have the same number of letters as the correct spelling. As Sloboda also points out, a problem with any technique that requires auditory presentation of a stimulus followed by a response is that response preparation may overlap temporally with stimulus processing.

Seymour and Porpodas (1980) describe their use of a task in which subjects were required to make decisions about the shape or the sound of a letter (indicated by a probe digit) in an auditorily presented word. Response times increased with the sequential position of the letter in the word, although there was a "recency" effect in that relatively fast responses were obtained when the last letter of the word was probed. It is, of course, possible that subjects could perform accurately on this task without deriving the entire spelling of a word.

It would be desirable if spelling production times could be assessed more directly using a methodology where the subjects' overt task is to spell words. Kreiner (1992) used a spelling probe task in which a single probe letter is presented and the subject is required to respond on the basis of whether or not that letter appears in the stimulus word. He used this task to examine effects of frequency and polygraphy, as well as correlations with measures of working memory capacity. However, as Kreiner himself points out, there are some difficulties associated with the use of this methodology. For example, it is possible that abnormal strategies are employed in a task of this type. He therefore also used a different methodology in which a voice-key was used to determine, in an oral spelling task with auditory presentation of the word to be spelled, the onset of the experimenter's reading of the word to be spelled and the beginning of the subject's spelling of the presented word. The end of the spelling of the word was signalled by a bar-press. It is unclear from Kreiner's description of his methodology how the offset of the presented word was determined. Also, the fact that subjects were required to press a space-bar "as quickly as possible after completing each spelling" (p. 773) is potentially problematic, because subjects might anticipate their completion of the spelling of a word to an extent that is not constant for different word types. Although the combination of two diverging methodologies, as used by Kreiner, undoubtedly represents an advance over previously employed methodology, we felt it desirable to explore techniques which would enable both the onset and offset of stimulus presentation and the onset of the subjects' response to be directly and accurately obtained.

DEVELOPING A NEW METHODOLOGY

In oral spelling the required response points may be schematized as shown in Figure 9.1. In this figure the first soundwave represents the experimenter's articulation of the word to be spelled and the second series of shorter waves is an idealized representation

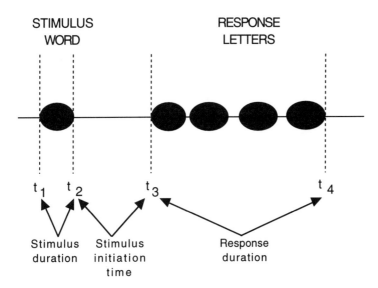

FIGURE 9.1 Idealized sound waveform of presented word and subject's response, to illustrate desired spelling production time measurements.

of the subjects' pronunciation of the individual letters of the word. The figure also shows the response time measurements that it would be desirable to obtain.

We have run a series of experiments using a computer to record both the spoken stimulus and the spoken response directly. Suitable software can then be used to display the waveform and read off the required times directly from the display. This can now be done using relatively cheap and widely available hardware and software; we used a Macintosh SE 30 computer in conjunction with Farallon's MacRecorder system for A-to-D conversion and SoundEdit software to record and display the soundwave. This system is both inexpensive and easy to use. The system works best with a computer which has sufficient memory to record several presented words and associated responses in one recording session; we found that 8 megabytes of memory allowed about 80 words and responses to be collected at a sufficient sound quality.

The main technical difficulty that is encountered concerns the need to obtain a good-quality recording with sufficiently low levels of background noise to enable the beginning and end points of speech input to be distinguished from background noise. Furthermore, it is desirable to present the stimuli to be spelled on a tape recorder, to ensure consistency of presentation across subjects. After considerable experimentation with different configurations, we found that the experimental arrangement depicted in Figure 9.2 worked best.

To use this system, the words to be spelled are first recorded on a high-quality cassette tape recorder. During an experimental session, the subjects hear words over headphones while the taped input is simultaneously fed into a mixer, the output of which is sent to the A-to-D converter linked directly to the computer. The subject spells

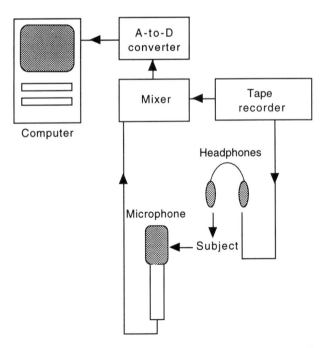

FIGURE 9.2   Schematic illustration of the experimental arrangement used.

the word letter by letter into a microphone and the microphone output is also directed to the mixer and thence to the computer via the converter. The computer therefore records both the stimuli and the responses in the same file. Using this configuration it is not difficult to obtain recordings of good enough quality to enable the required measurements to be obtained. An example soundwave is provided in Figure 9.3, which shows presentation of the word FALSE followed by the subject's (correct) spelling of the word.

Using this methodology it is easy to calculate the response initiation time measured from the offset of stimulus presentation ($t_3 - t_2$; see Figure 9.1 and Figure 9.3) or the onset of stimulus presentation ($t_3 - t_1$). We preferred the former measure, as stimulus presentation time ($t_2 - t_1$) will not be constant, although the use of the former measure carries with it the concomitant disadvantage that response preparation time may overlap with stimulus presentation. It is also possible to measure response duration ($t_4 - t_3$), as this will permit meaningful comparisons of responses to stimuli that are matched for length in letters. Below, we report the results of experiments that use these measures.

USING THE SPELLING PRODUCTION TIME METHODOLOGY TO TEST MODELS OF SPELLING

It is clear that a number of experimental manipulations could be employed using this general methodology. In the remainder of this chapter we use the method to test some predictions of the connectionist model of children's and adults' spelling that is described in Chapter 16. First, we discuss whether the spelling production time methodology can be used to shed any light on the debate, highlighted in Chapter 1, between dual-route and connectionist or "neural network" models of spelling in children and adults.

The present series of experiments is directed to the effects of sound-to-spelling regularity on spelling production time. What predictions does the dual-route model

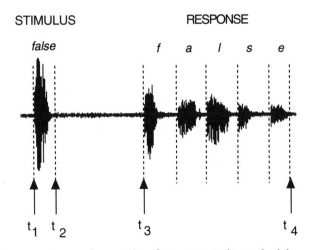

FIGURE 9.3 An example soundwave taken from an experimental trial.

make in this regard? The modal dual-route model of spelling clearly predicts that there should be effects of sound-to-spelling regularity on spelling error rates for children in the "alphabetic" phase of spelling development, for if children are reliant partly or solely on a sound-to-spelling translation routine of some kind then they will be unable to derive correct spellings for items containing irregular sound-to-spelling correspondences. The question of reaction times to irregular items is therefore irrelevant, for such words cannot be spelled correctly at all. A dual-route model may predict that some regular words will be spelled more quickly than others—perhaps those containing more common sound–spelling correspondences, or higher "contingency" correspondences (Barry & Seymour, 1988). However, most verbal descriptions of the dual-route framework are not sufficiently explicit to enable detailed predictions to be made.

The connectionist architecture described in Chapter 16 does, however, make clear predictions about which regular words will be most quickly spelled. Specifically, it predicts that words with many sound-to-spelling "friends" such as *pill* (with friends *kill*, *till*, *fill*, etc.) will be spelled more quickly than words with no friends, such as *bulb* (which has no rhyming friends or enemies). (Note that these word types will both generally be classified as "regular", and that there is no reason why both types could not be spelled successfully using a sound-to-spelling translation routine which incorporated low-frequency sound-to-spelling translation rules.) The prediction is made because the "error score" produced by the model to words with many friends is always lower than the error score to no-friends words (see Chapter 16), and it is assumed that the error score of the model will be monotonically related to spelling production time (we discuss this assumption in more detail below).

A similar situation obtains with regard to the different models' predictions regarding adult spelling production times. The connectionist model predicts that there will be independent effects of a word's sound-to-spelling friends (so the many-friends *pill* should be faster than the no-friends *bulb*) and sound-to-spelling enemies (a word like *soap*, with enemies *hope*, *rope*, *cope*, etc., will be slower than words with no enemies such as either *pill* or *bulb*). Again, the predictions made by the dual-route model about processing times when spellers have entered an advanced orthographic stage are less clear. Dual-route models of skilled adult *reading* are often assumed to give rise to regularity effects due to possible conflicts between the outputs of the two different systems for deriving pronunciations (e.g. Norris & Brown, 1985). However, this prediction cannot be generalized to dual-route models of spelling, for current models are not sufficiently explicit on this point. Indeed, it could be argued, on computational efficiency grounds, that the orthographic or lexical spelling route would develop to enable correct spelling of all words, and that there would be no advantage to the continued use of an (often unreliable) non-lexical sound-to-spelling translation route for the spelling of known words. This would apply to spelling more than to reading, given the greater ambiguity of the former mapping system. The evidence from acquired disorders of spelling suggests that both routines are available to skilled adult spellers, although this evidence does not force the conclusion that both routines are used in fluent spelling (although see Kreiner & Gough, 1990, for evidence that they are).

Thus, a critical question that can be addressed by examining spelling production times is whether or not errorless adult spelling is sensitive to the sound-to-spelling characteristics of the to-be-spelled items.

PREDICTIONS OF THE CONNECTIONIST MODEL
FOR SPELLING PRODUCTION TIMES

We now turn to a more detailed discussion of the derivation of predictions for spelling reaction times from the connectionist model. In Chapter 16 it is shown that, at all stages in learning, the model showed the greatest error score to items with no friends and many enemies (e.g. *soap*). The model showed the lowest error score to words with many friends and no enemies (e.g. *pill*) and an intermediate error score to words with neither friends nor enemies (e.g. *bulb*).

The error score is interpreted simply as a measure of the difficulty of mastering the sound-to-spelling correspondences of the relevant item. It is assumed that there are additional output processes that provide another source of potential error (see Chapter 18, by Houghton *et al.*, for a model of processes more akin to spelling output mechanisms). In testing the predictions of the model, it was assumed that a high error score in the model should be reflected in a higher error rate by children to the same words. This prediction was tested on normal children from four different age groups, and also on dyslexic children (Brown, Loosemore & Watson, 1993), and the results paralleled the behaviour of the model very closely.

However, as discussed above, it is possible that the effects of sound-to-spelling characteristics on skilled adult spelling will be different. One possibility is that adults will not be sensitive to the sound–spelling characteristics of words they spell quickly and correctly. A further possibility is that they will have automatized spelling to the point that they will be sensitive to facilitative effects of the frequency of sound-to-spelling correspondences (reflected in a "friends" effect) while not being slowed by inconsistent spellings (and hence exhibiting no "enemies" effect). It is not easy to test these possibilities by examining error rates, as it is unlikely that adults will produce sufficient errors on the words to allow rigorous evaluation of the predictions.

At this point, we should note a potential ambiguity that arises when deriving predictions from connectionist models (including our own). Connectionist models of lexical-level processing often do not specify the peripheral output processes that are necessary to produce an overt response. Rather, as described in Chapter 16, the measure of network performance is calculated over the "output units" of the network and these units typically encode some relatively abstract representation of (for example) the pronunciation or spelling of the relevant item. It is typically assumed that the error score for a particular word, which is a measure of the difference between the output that the network actually produces of that item and the pattern of activity that would represent the correct output perfectly, will be monotonically related to either a reaction time measure (e.g. Seidenberg & McClelland, 1989) or error rate (e.g. Brown, Loosemore & Watson, 1993). This seems reasonable, for the quality of the code that is provided to output processes is likely to be related to the time taken for such output processes to produce an overt response. It is also possible to "cascade" information gradually through a network so that the final pattern of activity on the output units is only reached gradually, and in this case the time taken to reach the output will be related to the error score in a non-cascading network (Cohen, Dunbar & McClelland, 1990). Use of the cascade approach can allow the examination of speed–error trade-offs, because error scores can be examined after a fixed amount of time. However, it is difficult to envisage how different item types, all encoded within the same set of weights, could produce responses at different points on a speed–accuracy trade-off function. Furthermore, there is no way for a connectionist model to predict that the ordering of conditions with respect to error rates could ever be different from the ordering of condition difficulty as assessed by reaction times.

New models such as that of Houghton (this volume, Chapter 18) may enable these problems to be addressed. In the meantime, however, we simply note that the fact that the predictions of a connectionist model are borne out when human error rates are examined does not mean that the same predictions would be upheld when reaction times to the same set of materials are measured.

One of the functions of the experiments described here was to test the predictions of a connectionist model of spelling as applied to spelling production times, rather than error rates, which have already been examined extensively in normal and dyslexic children (Brown, Loosemore & Watson, 1993).

THE EXPERIMENTS

We now describe the results of some experiments we have conducted using the spelling production time methodology described earlier. In the most general terms, these experiments can be seen as a test of the idea that sound-to-spelling information is used in skilled, correct adult spelling. More specifically, they look for effects of sound-to-spelling "friends" and "enemies" on spelling production times for skilled adult spelling. Here we simply summarize the basic results from two experiments; further experiments and more detailed analysis can be found in Brown, Glover and Holt (1993).

Experiment 1

Our first experiment was designed to test the hypothesis that there are separate effects of both sound-to-spelling friends and sound-to-spelling enemies on word spelling time. (These separate effects are predicted by the connectionist model described in Chapter 16).

To investigate the effects of sound-to-spelling friends on reaction times, we compared items which had friends but no enemies (e.g. *pill*) with those which had neither friends nor enemies (e.g. *bulb*). In a second comparison enemies' effects were examined, and friends' effects controlled for, by comparing those items which had enemies but not friends (e.g. *soap*) with those which had neither friends nor enemies (e.g. *bulb*).

The stimuli for the experiment consisted of 19 word triplets, each containing one item with friends and no enemies, one item with neither friends nor enemies, and one item which had enemies but no friends. In this and the other experiments described in this chapter, items were matched for word length, positional bigram frequency and written word frequency. The experimental equipment used was that described in the earlier part of this chapter. This enabled the measurement of response initiation time (the time from the end of presentation of the item to be spelled to the beginning of the subject's response; t_3-t_2 on Figure 9.1 and Figure 9.3) and total response duration ($t_4 - t_3$).

The stimuli were presented orally by the experimenter. Subjects were required to spell every item, and were requested to speak into a microphone, as clearly as possible. It was emphasized that when words which contained double letters (such as *teeth*) were presented, each letter should be spoken individually (i.e. *T-E-E-T-H*, not *t*-double-*e-t-h*).

We turn now to a description of the results of the experiment. Both reaction times and error rates were examined. All effects referred to here were significant at the 0.05 level in both by-subjects and by-items analyses.

Analysis of response initiation time revealed a clearly significant effect of spelling-to-sound "friends": the spellings of words with many friends were initiated faster than words with neither friends nor enemies (450 ms vs 520 ms). Responses to words with enemies were no slower than responses to words with no enemies or friends (530 ms). However, there were no effects of sound-to-spelling friends or enemies on response duration (the time from beginning to completion of the subjects' spelling of the item).

Finally, analysis of error rates to the three word types revealed a small effect of enemies: words with enemies were less likely to be spelled correctly at the first attempt.

These results provide support for the utility of the spelling production time methodology we have described. In particular, effects emerged in the reaction times analysis that would have been missed if only error rates had been analysed. The results clearly demonstrate that the spelling-to-sound characteristics of words can affect the speed with which oral spellings of them can be initiated.

How do the findings of this first experiment relate to the predictions of the connectionist model? We stated above that the model predicted independent sound-to-spelling effects of both friends and enemies. We also pointed out that there was no basis, intrinsic to the model as it stands, for claiming that the effects should occur on error rates, reaction times or both. Thus the results we obtained were consistent with the model, in that there were effects of both sound-to-spelling friends and sound-to-spelling enemies, although the former effect was evident in response initiation times and the latter on error rate. It should be noted that all the words that were used in this experiment would normally be spelled correctly by the undergraduates we used as subjects; the fact that some errors were produced is likely to be a result of the speed-emphasizing instructions that we gave our subjects.

In general, the clear effect of sound-to-spelling "friends" on spelling preparation time fits well with the connectionist model, which attaches importance to the spelling of rhyming neighbours when these support the correct spelling of the target word as well as to inconsistently spelled endings. Rule-based models, in contrast, tend to focus more on whether or not word spellings fit with the rules (i.e. whether or not they are irregular). However, we do not wish to claim that the results are necessarily inconsistent with dual-route models of adult models of spelling, although such models would need to be modified and made more specific to accommodate the precise pattern of results. In particular, a dual-route model would need to assume that the sound-to-spelling rules that make up the phonological spelling route are frequency-sensitive in some way, in order to account for the friends effect.

In summary, our first experiment demonstrated a clear effect of sound-to-spelling friends on spelling production time, and this fits well with the predictions of the connectionist model described in Chapter 16. A further experiment was undertaken in order to explore possible reasons for the lack of an enemies affect on reaction time.

Experiment 2

A possible reason for the effect of friends but not enemies on spelling production time is suggested by recent experiments on reading. In experiments that have measured single-word reading time, Brown (1987) found an effect of friends but not of enemies on naming latency. However, Jared, McRae and Seidenberg (1990) argued that Brown's failure to obtain an enemies effect reflected the fact that the enemies of the items they used were not high enough in frequency to cause reliable inhibition. They confirmed this experimentally, finding that if the enemies of a word are sufficiently high in frequency, then naming latencies to that item are increased.

Thus it is possible that the failure of experiment 1 to find an effect of enemies on spelling time was due to the fact that the enemies of our *soap*-type words (those with enemies and no friends) were not sufficiently high in frequency.

We tested this possibility directly in our second experiment by manipulating the frequency of the enemies of the items to be spelled. In this experiment, we compared spelling latencies to three matched triplets of items. Each triplet contained one item which had no friends and no enemies (e.g. *bulb*), one item which had no friends, but which had a high summed frequency of enemies (e.g. *bowl*), and one item which also had no friends, but which had a low summed frequency of enemies (e.g. *fund*). Thus the items varied only in whether or not they had enemies and in how frequent those enemies were. The items in each triplet were matched for word length, positional bigram frequency and word frequency per million.

Thus, if there is an effect of sound-to-spelling enemies that only emerges when the enemies are sufficiently high in frequency, spelling production times for the items with high-frequency enemies should be elevated relative to the times for the other two sets of items.

As before, we examined both response initiation time and response duration as well as error rate.

In this experiment, we found no differences between the three word types on response initiation time. However, analysis of response duration revealed that both words with high-frequency enemies (mean response duration: 1.5 s) and words with low-frequency enemies (1.51 s) had longer response durations than words with neither friends nor enemies (1.41 s). In the analyses of error rates, the only significant effect was an increased error rate to words with high-frequency enemies compared with neither friends nor enemies.

Thus, this experiment has indeed found an effect of sound-to-spelling enemies on spelling production time. In contrast to the results of the first experiment, however, the effect was evident on response duration rather than on response initiation time. Why is this? It is likely that subjects can exert some strategic control over their responding in this type of experiment and this may account for the different locus of the reaction time effect. In experiment 1, the majority of the words, (around 70%, including the practice items) had no enemies. This, in combination with the instructions to subjects requesting them to respond as quickly as possible, may have led subjects to adopt a strategy whereby they commence output of the first letter of the word as soon as sufficient graphemic information has been activated by the heard input. This would occur most quickly for the words with sound-to-spelling friends, leading to fast response initiation time, but less quickly for the words with neither friends nor enemies (because these words contain only unusual sound–spelling correspondences) or the words with enemies (because inconsistent sound–spelling correspondences are present, and so consistent grapheme-level activation will arise more slowly). Thus a fast-initiation strategy could explain the response initiation effects in experiment 1, and can also explain why higher error rates occur for the words with enemies, because of a speed–error trade-off. In experiment 2, in contrast, most of the words had enemies, and would have been spelled incorrectly if a response was initiated too fast. This may have induced a more conservative strategy in subjects, in which they wait longer before initiating a response for any item. Effects may therefore be "pushed back" and appear as increased response durations for items with enemies.

Although this explanation of the fine-grained pattern of results must remain tentative, the experiment does clearly show that the presence of sound-to-spelling enemies can inflate spelling production times. Furthermore, there is tentative evidence that the effect of enemies depends on their combined frequency. Although the response duration increase was evident whether the words had high- or low-frequency enemies, only words with high-frequency enemies showed elevated error rates compared with words with neither friends nor enemies. Although the comparison between high-frequency enemy and low-frequency enemy words was not statistically significant, the results do provide suggestive evidence that frequency of enemies may influence spelling production processes.

DISCUSSION

We argued at the beginning of this chapter that there is a need for experiments examining spelling production time as well as error rates. We described the methodology we have developed for examining the oral spelling of auditorily presented words. This is particularly useful for examining skilled, accurate, adult spelling. The results of the two experiments we have described provide clear evidence that skilled adult spelling does make use of sound-to-spelling constraints, for they demonstrated effects of the sound–spelling characteristics of words on both response initiation time and response duration.

More specifically, we found separate effects of sound-to-spelling friends and sound-to-spelling enemies. These effects are generally consistent with the predictions of the connectionist model of spelling that we describe in Chapter 16, although the data are underdetermined by the model in that the model does not specify the expected locus of effects (i.e. on error rates or reaction times). We conclude with the suggestion that the examination of spelling production times is necessary if we are to gain a greater understanding of cognitive processes involved in normal and abnormal spelling.

REFERENCES

Barry, C. & Seymour, P. H. K. (1988). Lexical priming and sound-to-spelling contingency effects in nonword spelling. *Quarterly Journal of Experimental Psychology*, **40**(A), 5–40.

Brown, G. D. A. (1987). Resolving inconsistency: a computational model of word naming. *Journal of Memory and Language*, **23**, 1–23.

Brown, G. D. A., Glover, P. J. & Holt, L. (1993). *Investigating skilled adult spelling using production time measures*. Unpublished manuscript.

Brown, G. D. A., Loosemore, R. P. W. & Watson, F. L. (1993). Normal and dyslexic spelling: a connectionist approach. Manuscript in submission.

Cohen, J. D., Dunbar, K. & McClelland, J. L. (1990). On the control of automatic processes: a parallel distributed processing account of the Stroop effect. *Psychological Review*, **97**(3), 332–361.

Jared, D., McRae, K. & Seidenberg, M. S. (1990). The basis of consistency effects in word naming. *Journal of Memory and Language*, **29**, 687–715.

Kreiner, D. (1992). Reaction time measures of spelling: testing a two-strategy model of skilled spelling. *Journal of Experimental Psychology: Learning, Memory and Cognition*, **18**(4), 765–776.

Kreiner, D. & Gough, P. B. (1990). Two ideas about spelling: rules and word-specific memory. *Journal of Memory and Language*, **29**, 103–118.

Lesser, R. (1990) Superior oral to written spelling: evidence for separate buffers? *Cognitive Neuropsychology*, **7**(4), 347–366.

Martlew, M. (1992). Handwriting and spelling: dyslexic children's abilities compared with children of the same chronological age and young children at the same spelling level. *British Journal of Educational Psychology*, **62**, 375–390.

Norris, D. & Brown, G. D. A. (1985). Race models and analogy theories: a dead heat? Reply to Seidenberg. *Cognition*, **20**, 155–168.

Seidenberg, M. S. & McClelland, J. L. (1989). A distributed, developmental model of word recognition and naming. *Psychological Review*, **96**, 523–568.

Seidenberg, M. S., Waters, G. S., Barnes, M. A. & Tanenhaus, M. K. (1984). When does irregular spelling or pronunciation influence word recognition? *Journal of Verbal Learning and Verbal Behavior*, **23**, 383–404.

Seymour, P. H. K. & Porpodas, C. (1980). Lexical and non-lexical processing of spelling in dyslexia. In U. Frith (Ed.), *Cognitive Processes in Spelling*. London: Academic Press.

Sloboda, J. A. (1980). Visual imagery and individual differences in spelling. In U. Frith (Ed.), *Cognitive Processes in Spelling*. London: Academic Press.

Sovic, N., Arntzen, O. & Thygessen, R. (1987a). Writing characteristics of "normal", dyslexic and dysgraphic children. *Journal of Human Movement Studies*, **13**, 171–187.

Sovic, N., Arntzen, O. & Thygessen, R. (1987b). Relation of spelling and writing in learning disabilities. *Perceptual and Motor Skills*, **64**, 219–236.

Part III

Abnormal Spelling

10

Spelling Processes of the Reading Disabled

DALE M. WILLOWS

Ontario Institute for Studies in Education, Toronto

RUTH SCOTT

Brock University, Ontario

Although reading disabilities have been of interest to researchers for nearly 80 years and have been the subject of dozens of books and hundreds of articles, the spelling processes of the reading disabled have been relatively little documented and studied in the same period. This lesser attention to spelling disabilities dates back to the time of Orton. In an article titled "Special disability in spelling", Orton (1931) commented that, "Usually an inability to spell is treated as of more or less minor importance, in sharp contrast to a reading disability" (p. 169). Confirming that little has changed in this regard, Frith, in more recent years—in her article on "The similarities and differences between reading and spelling problems"—pointed out that "children who have problems with both reading and writing are called 'dyslexic', not 'dysgraphic', even though, as a group, dyslexic children have consistently lower spelling achievement than reading achievement" (1983, p. 453).

Despite this past neglect, there has been an upsurge of interest in the spelling processes of disabled readers over the past 10–15 years. The purpose of the present chapter is to review prevalent perspectives on the spelling processes of the reading disabled in order to determine potentially productive directions for future research. The chapter is organized into five main sections. The first—based on an examination of the writings of Hinshelwood and Orton—provides some early history of beliefs about the relation between reading and spelling disabilities, and points to some

Handbook of Spelling: Theory, Process and Intervention. Edited by G. D. A. Brown and N. C. Ellis.
©1994 John Wiley & Sons Ltd.

important insights and unanswered questions raised by this early work. The second considers measurement issues in the study of the spelling processes of disabled readers and examines some key findings generated by different kinds of measures. The third surveys current theories concerning the spelling processes of the reading disabled. The fourth discusses the literature on the phenomenon of "unexpectedly poor spellers" that has been popularized by the work of Frith. The final section summarizes methodological and conceptual limitations of past attempts at understanding the spelling processes of the reading disabled and suggests some directions for future investigation.

EARLY PERSPECTIVES ON THE SPELLING PROCESSES OF THE READING DISABLED

Pioneers in the field of reading disability included observations on spelling in their clinical reports. In this section reflections by Hinshelwood and Orton on disabled readers' spelling processes are discussed, pointing to some interesting insights and to some potentially important issues that have not as yet been adequately explored by researchers.

Hinshelwood's Observations

Poor readers/good spellers

Almost since developmental reading disability was first described in the literature as "word-blindness", researchers and clinicians have acknowledged the pervasiveness of spelling difficulties among the reading disabled. Thus, one of Hinshelwood's (1917) observations, in his fascinating and insightful little monograph *Congenital Word-Blindness*, is surprising. In that book, Hinshelwood, an ophthalmologist, presented case studies of a dozen individuals who would, by their descriptions, be designated as disabled readers in current terminology. The unexpected observation was that all but one of the 12 congenitally word-blind children were, according to Hinshelwood, "able to spell well" (p. 56). One's first reaction to such a statement is that something must be amiss: perhaps Hinshelwood was not as good a clinician as he seemed to have been, or perhaps his standards for good spelling were not high, or perhaps his cases were not the same types of individuals that current reading clinicians see on a daily basis. There is, however, another possibility that has interesting implications for both theory and practice.

Old-fashioned and modern reading methods

Hinshelwood pointed out that different approaches to teaching reading had been used with the good and poor spellers. The 11 good spellers were taught to read by "the old-fashioned method" (p. 105), while the one poor speller was taught by the "modern look-and-say method". Understanding the distinction between these methodologies is crucial. The old-fashioned approach at that time was the ABC method, in which children were taught to read by spelling each word aloud before it was pronounced

(Huey, 1908). Thus spelling was learned through oral repetition, but, as Huey pointed out, "Just how naming the letters was supposed to assist in pronouncing the word (i.e. reading) it is difficult to see" (p. 266). Moreover, Huey attested to the effectiveness of oral repetition as a teaching method for spelling when he added that: "The value of the practice in learning to spell doubtless had much to do with blinding centuries of teachers to its uselessness for the reading of words and sentences" (p. 266). In contrast, as Hinshelwood explained, in the modern look-and-say approach, "the child is taught at once to recognize printed words as a whole, as a series of pictures just like Chinese symbols or Egyptian hieroglyphics, and not to recognize the words first by a process of analysis and spelling them out letter by letter" (1917, p. 104). It thus appears that what Hinshelwood meant by "spelling" was oral spelling and that word-blind children who were taught to read by spelling each word before pronouncing it were successful oral spellers, while those who were taught to read by a sight method were not. In view of Hinshelwood's speculation, it is interesting to note that two recent articles have presented data to support the value of simultaneous oral spelling as an effective technique for reading disabled children (Kearney & Drabman, 1993; Thomson, 1991).

There are at least two lessons that can be gleaned from the observations of Hinshelwood. One is that what is meant by terms such as "spelling" or "spelling ability" may require more careful definition than is immediately apparent. A second is that teaching practices may have some role in determining the patterns of difficulty experienced in learning to spell (and read) and thus should probably be taken into account in studies of spelling (and reading) processes.

Orton's Insights

Framed in the terminology of the time and embedded in the context of his neurological theory, Orton's observations concerning the relation of reading and spelling disabilities have been little discussed in recent literature. This omission is unfortunate because, although the theoretical framework that he espoused may no longer be supportable,[1] his clinical reflections on the nature of spelling disabilities were very perceptive and few recent discussions of the characteristics of dyslexics' spelling are more insightful. Moreover, some of Orton's observations seem to provide alternative accounts of aspects of the relation between reading and spelling disabilities discussed in the current literature. Several of the points raised by Orton that have particular relevance to issues addressed in our review of current literature are presented in the following subsections on: oral and written spelling, spelling in and out of context, phonetic spellings, good readers who are poor spellers, and the use of spelling error analysis as an approach to understanding written language disabilities.

Oral and written spelling

In his thoughtful paper 14 years after Hinshelwood's (1917) book on word-blindness, Orton (1931) elaborated on the nature of spelling disabilities, making a clear distinction

---

[1]Orton's original theory may not be consistent with present conceptualizations, but a neo-Ortonian view of reading disabilities has recently been presented in the neuropsychological literature (Corballis & Beale, 1993).

between oral and written spelling. This distinction, which might well be a very important one, is little considered in present-day research literature. In describing the association between spelling and reading problems, Orton wrote that "children with a marked reading disability are almost always bad spellers" (p. 167). He went on to point out that the problem might sometimes be in written but not in oral spelling, stating that "occasionally a poor reader will learn to spell fairly readily by rote auditory memory and when examined upon recently acquired lists of words will show a fair degree of skill" (p. 167). He elaborated further that "These implants . . . if not reinforced by the visual recall are evanescent and if such a child be examined upon a list of words one or two years below his current efforts he will generally be found to have lost many of the words which he knew at an earlier period" (p. 167). Although this explanation may not be entirely satisfactory, Orton's attention to differences in the demands inherent in oral and written spelling tasks should be heeded by current researchers.

Orton's comment raises an additional point that researchers have not adequately addressed. He indicated that although some disabled readers may be able to learn to spell using auditory rote memory, they often do not retain what they have learned that way over an extended time. Although this suggestion is consistent with clinical observations, empirical studies of spelling acquisition involving long-term retention measures are rare (Dreyer, Shankweiler & Luke, 1992).

Spelling in and out of context

Orton also pointed out that "A similar discrepancy may often be seen between a child's ability to pass spelling tests in school and his ability to make use of the same words in propositional writing" (p. 167). This point is also consistent with clinical observations and may be pertinent to understanding written language disabilities as well. Researchers investigating the spelling of the reading disabled have, however, virtually ignored spelling in written compositions, focusing predominantly on spelling in lists using either recognition or production tasks. Given that some reading and/or spelling disabled individuals may be able to learn to spell words in dictated lists that have been memorized by rote but may have difficulty spelling the same words in written compositions (where the cognitive demands are greater), there is a clear need to examine the relation between disabled readers' spelling in lists and in compositions and to investigate the processing factors involved in these two types of spelling situation.

Phonetic spellings

Within the context of his neurological model of reading disability, Orton had a special interest in letter and word "reversals" as potentially reflecting underlying differences in brain functioning of disabled and normal readers. In particular, he suggested that disabled readers manifested a hemispheric imbalance that limited the reliability of the visual image and forced them to depend on auditory information. He argued that a lack of constancy in the recall of mirror reflection visual engrams from the left and right hemisphere resulted in a failure to establish "a quick association between the visual engrams of the letters of a word and their sounds", further contending that "When this failure is severe it serves as an obstacle to the acquisition of both reading and spelling" (p. 175), adding also that "Apparently it may exist . . . in a lesser grade which does not prevent the establishment of engrams sufficiently clear and constant for recognition and hence for reading. Such engrams however may not be adequate for accurate recall of the 'look' of a word necessary for spelling non-phonetic words or for the easy recognition of errors after they have been made" (p. 175). Orton also commented that "Not infrequently such a child will say of his own product, 'That doesn't look right but I can't see what's wrong with it'. Naturally this failure to incorporate the visual element into the association throws most of the burden of spelling upon the auditory memory with consequent attempts at phonetic spellings" (p. 175).

In essence, Orton (1931) contended that although disabled readers might have adequate cues available to recognize words in the context of reading, they over-rely on auditory/phonological cues in spelling, thus producing phonetic spellings of non-phonetic words. As will be discussed in a later section, some current views of spelling disabilities attribute the problem to "partial cue" reading. Although based on a different theoretical account, the partial cue hypothesis is surprisingly similar to Orton's view and also reflects the observation that disabled spellers often produce spellings that are accurate phonetically but that lack the appropriate orthographic patterns (especially the more complex ones) required to make the spellings "look right".

Good readers/poor spellers

Orton (1931) made another significant observation when he noted two categories of individuals with spelling disabilities, "some with reading disability and some without it" (p. 170). His recognition of a group of good readers who are poor spellers pointed to a phenomenon that has received considerable attention in the recent literature and which will be discussed in more detail in a later section. He explained the phenomenon in terms of his theoretical position, stating that "Reading . . . requires a much less accurate degree of visual representation in the association process than does spelling, and it is therefore not surprising to find individuals whose visual engrams are adequate for the recognition associations required in reading but quite inadequate for recall and hence are not serviceable for spelling" (p. 167).

An additional remark by Orton deserves special attention in that it may well explain some of the inconsistencies in present-day findings concerning good readers who are poor spellers. He commented that "the special disability in spelling may stand out as an isolated defect although not infrequently the history of the child's progress in school gives evidence of an earlier reading disability" (p. 167). This suggestion of earlier reading problems among individuals who later become good readers but poor spellers is consistent with clinical observations and will be discussed further in the section on recent research on good readers/poor spellers.

Spelling error analysis

A final topic concerning spelling disabilities suggested by the writing of Orton (1931) and remaining current today is the potential value of spelling error analysis as a reflection of processing deficits underlying reading disabilities. Given the extent of the spelling error analyses in Orton's writings, we cannot do justice here to the breadth of his insights. Throughout his article on spelling disability Orton illustrated various kinds of processing problems reflected in disabled spellers' errors. While some of his examples—such as those involving static and kinetic reversals in children's writing—were offered as evidence in support of his neurological theory of variations in the establishment of unilateral cerebral dominance, others were presented to illustrate problems in the processing of phonology. For example, he pointed out that "the vowels are a particularly fertile source of errors in spelling as they are in a reading disability" (p. 175). He also indicated that "confusions are more frequent between two letters representing somewhat similar sounds" (p. 177), presenting examples of confusions between the voiced and voiceless consonants, among others. In other words, Orton pointed to spelling errors that he interpreted as evidence of both visual and phonological deficits underlying reading and spelling disabilities. These anticipated the dyseidetic/dysphonetic error distinction (Boder, 1971) discussed in the next section on problems inherent in the analysis of spelling error patterns.

MEASUREMENT ISSUES IN ASSESSING SPELLING PATTERNS

In the early investigations of disabled readers' spelling processes—discussed in the previous sections—inferences seem to have been based entirely on subjective qualitative analysis of spelling errors. Since that time much effort has been made to develop more objective quantitative approaches. Recent findings—reviewed in the later sections on current research—have been based largely on objective quantitative measures involving a right/wrong criterion or multiple-choice spelling recognition. Although this movement towards quantitative analysis is generally a very positive one, it has not eliminated measurement problems associated with the study of spelling. In the present section, several prevalent approaches to spelling analysis will be discussed as they relate to the spelling problems of the reading disabled. These include classification of spelling errors according to standard schemes, analyses of children's inventive spellings as reflections of stages of spelling development, examinations of spelling-error patterns to determine subtypes of reading disabilities, and experimental quantitative measures of spelling.

Standard Scoring Schemes

Although the majority of standardized spelling tests simply employ a right/wrong criterion, some have attempted to examine children's use of various knowledge sources by structuring spelling lists to assess specific patterns systematically. Some measures such as the Diagnostic Spelling Test (Kottmeyer, 1959) and the Spelling Errors Test (Spache, 1976) have focused on phoneme–grapheme correspondence knowledge. Other tests have attempted to differentiate between the child's "phonic spelling abilities" and "memory for orthographic spellings" by comparing accuracy on predictable (i.e. phonetic) and unpredictable (i.e. non-phonetic) words, as in the Test of Written Spelling—2 (Larsen & Hammill, 1986).

Few standardized spelling tests have attempted to undertake more detailed analysis of spelling errors in order to reflect the complexity of spelling processes. Moreover, although standardized measures may be an improvement over the very subjective non-standardized approaches that preceded them, even the standardized ones are fraught with problems. This is particularly true when they are used to compare the spelling patterns of good spellers and disabled spellers. For one thing, as Nelson (1980) pointed out, such schemes are often unreliable because the error types are not uniquely defined and mutually exclusive, the individual elements in multiple-error words being impossible to distinguish objectively and reliably. In addition, because of the limited numbers of errors in each of the relatively large number of categories in scoring schemes (usually 10–20 categories or subcategories), quantitative analysis of results is usually not feasible. Furthermore, if good and poor spellers attempt to spell the same list of words then the good spellers will make few errors, and the poor spellers' errors must be judged within a context of very inaccurate spellings that are largely guesses. Finally, the use of age-based norms is probably inappropriate in assessing the quality of spelling errors, which should be judged against those of younger children within the context of level of spelling achievement. That is, spelling errors should not be considered "abnormal" unless they deviate from the "normal" patterns of spelling development. As a result of the various concerns listed here, Nelson (1980) developed a "word equated spelling test" and compared the quality of errors made by groups of dyslexics and normal controls. She interpreted her results as evidence that "the quality of dyslexic children's spelling is essentially normal" (p. 485).

Linguistic Analyses and Spelling Stages

A very significant advance in our understanding of children's spelling processes came out of developmental analyses of spelling patterns. In examining the spontaneous writing of precocious preschool children, Read (1971) discovered that, prior to formal instruction, children's "invented spellings" reflected amazingly perceptive phonological analysis (in part reflecting reliance on articulatory cues). Additional studies of children's invented spellings (e.g. Beers, 1980; Chomsky, 1979; Gentry, 1978) led to descriptive accounts of young children's progression through a series of "stages of spelling development" reflecting the knowledge sources used by children in their spellings. These demonstrated a gradual shift in children's hypotheses about the nature of the English spelling system, from very simplistic to quite complex. For example, Gentry's (1978) stages included deviant (*PAHIe* for *giant*), pre-phonetic (*MSR* for *monster*), phonetic (*PPL* for *people*), transitional (*highcked* for *hiked*) and standard spelling. The stages ranged from early ones in which children base their spellings largely on the assumption of a simple phonetic representation of speech to later interactive stages reflecting children's phonological, orthographic and morphological knowledge (Schwartz & Doehring, 1977).

A few researchers have used linguistic analyses and developmental stage frameworks to investigate the spelling processes of disabled readers. Schwartz (1983) conducted a systematic developmental comparison of spelling patterns of good spellers, poor spellers and learning/reading disabled spellers (ages 8–10) to examine their ability to abstract spelling patterns. Her findings indicated that the abstraction of spelling patterns by the learning disabled was considerably delayed compared to both the good and the poor spellers. In a task where subjects were required to spell nonsense syllables, she found that non-standard spelling patterns (e.g. *gabe* was spelled *gab* and *juffle* was spelled *jufl*) persisted in 10-year-old disabled spellers (44%) after they had decreased or dropped out for the good (5%) and poor spellers (20%), reflecting performance patterns more characteristic of the preschoolers and beginning spellers described by Read (1971). Schwartz (1983) pointed out two significant problem areas in the spelling development of the learning disabled: weakness in the ability to segment words into phonemes and use sound–symbol correspondences, and difficulty in moving from reliance on phonology to the morphological and visual/orthographic representation necessary for correct spelling.

Ehri (1992) also applied a spelling-stages approach to examine the spelling development of "fast growing readers", "slow growing readers" and disabled readers, tested at three points during grades one and two. Using increasingly challenging spelling lists that retained some of the same words across all six testing points, she assessed how spelling productions changed across the testing points and how the groups differed in their development. The percentage of children in each group whose spellings fit into four stages (non-phonetic, semiphonetic, phonetic and correct) was examined. Ehri concluded that although the disabled readers' spellings became more phonetically accurate over time, they still retained a "non-phonetic" quality, in contrast with those generated by more successful readers. She pointed out that medial vowel sounds seemed to represent a particular source of difficulty for the disabled readers. Ehri also observed specific difficulties among the reading disabled with morphological endings and with patterns such as silent letters that depend on visual familiarity with orthographic patterns.

The findings of both Schwartz (1983) and Ehri (1992) are consistent with those from a variety of other studies examining progression through stages of spelling development by the reading disabled. A reasonable conclusion from all of these studies is that learning/reading disabled individuals progress through the same spelling stages as normally achieving individuals, but at a slower pace (Gerber, 1984; Gerber & Hall, 1987).

Despite the fact that linguistic analyses and spelling-stages frameworks have provided insights into the complexity of the factors underlying the spelling of both normal and disabled spellers, they too have some limitations. These approaches normally judge words as falling into one stage/category or another when in reality different processes may be operative in different parts of the same word. In addition, by coming up with a percentage of words that fit into each stage, they come up with a developmental stage for a given child, without consideration for whether a child's spelling stage may reflect the relative difficulty of the words the child is attempting to spell. In most cases subjective judgements are involved in determining spelling stages, and yet there is little evidence concerning interrater or test–retest reliability for the judgements in most studies. Lastly, the concept of "good phonetic equivalence" that sometimes underlies judgements of the extent to which spellers have relied on phonetic representation in their spelling productions has been criticized on both logical and empirical grounds in the literature (Gerber & Hall, 1987).

Boder's Reading–Spelling Test

The notion that reading disabled individuals might differ in terms of the nature of their processing weaknesses—some learners being "audiles" and others "visiles"— has long been appealing to clinicians and educators. Thus Boder's (1971) concept that the spelling patterns of reading disabled individuals might provide a window into the nature of their "subtype" of reading difficulties achieved almost immediate popularity. Using measures of their word recognition and spelling of known and unknown words, she developed a method for classifying reading disabled individuals based on their apparent relative deficits in phonological and visual processes. Her work eventuated in the Boder Test of Reading–Spelling Patterns (Boder & Jarrico, 1982), which provides a standardized approach for subtyping reading disabled children as "dysphonetic", "dyseidetic" and "mixed dysphonetic–dyseidetic". Although this test, both in its unpublished and standardized versions, has enjoyed considerable popularity, especially in the neuropsychological literature, it has serious psychometric weaknesses. A key feature of the test involves scoring disabled readers' spellings of words they can and cannot read in terms of whether there is "good phonetic equivalence" between the words attempted and the spellings of them. Not surprisingly, the problem of determining good phonetic equivalence, especially for the disabled readers, represents a serious impediment to scoring the spelling reliably. As discussed by Willows and Jackson (1992), the complex methodology and subtyping scheme produce results that are lacking in both reliability and validity. Moreover, a comparison of findings from studies using Boder's subtyping approach seriously challenges the test's usefulness. However, these findings do not rule out the possibility that some other more reliable and valid method of examining the spelling patterns of the reading disabled might provide important insights into the role of different areas of processing weakness in reading disabilities.

Experimental Measures of Spelling

Because of the difficulties associated with qualitative analyses of spelling patterns, many basic researchers examining the spelling processes of the reading disabled have employed objective quantitative measures such as multiple-choice tasks that pit one theory of spelling processes against another. In cases where spelling production tasks have been used, the spelling lists often involve nonsense words to avoid the possibility that the disabled group might have had less experience reading and/or spelling the words on the test list. Although these approaches render the measures "cleaner", they fail to address some of the complexities reflected in more qualitative measures. In addition, because most of the basic experimental literature has examined spelling out of context, the theoretical perspectives generated by such research may say little about spelling processes in the context of written composition, where the processing load is much greater. Indeed, if the clinical observations of Orton (1931) and others (e.g. Willows, in press b) are corroborated by controlled research, the spelling of the reading disabled in their own creative writing may be even less accurate relative to that of good spellers than it is out of context, and it might reflect a different combination of processing factors than it does in cleaner experimental situations.

CURRENT VIEWS ON THE SPELLING PROCESSES
OF THE READING DISABLED

Between the time of Orton's work in the 1920s and 30s until the early 1970s the spelling processes of the reading disabled were almost entirely ignored by theoreticians. Over the past two decades, however, there has been considerable speculation concerning the nature of the interrelationships between reading and spelling. Studies have investigated whether the skills required to be a competent reader are substantially different from those needed to be a good speller. Researchers have asked, "Are reading disabilities inherently different from spelling disabilities?".

Some theorists have argued for a disconnection between reading and spelling. Bryant and Bradley (1980) suggested that in the beginning stages of reading and spelling children use quite different strategies. Young children tend to rely on visual chunks for beginning reading rather than graphophonemic relationships. Beginning spellers, however, rely quite quickly on graphophonemic cues. Bryant and Bradley hypothesized that poor readers fail to transfer the phonological strategy they use in spelling to the demands of decoding in reading. Similarly, such children specialize too strongly in the phonological strategy for spelling and do not utilize the visual skills which they apply in reading.

Frith (1980) supported the strategy selectivity theory of Bryant and Bradley, suggesting that readers tend to read either "by eye" or by "ear". Those who read "by eye" rely on partial cues to determine meaning and do not consult graphophonemic patterns. On the other hand, individuals who read "by ear" utilize a full cueing strategy, since decoding requires attention to all parts of the word. A partial cueing strategy may supply sufficient information for most normal reading tasks, but provides less opportunity for acquiring knowledge of the underlying spelling system. Frith interpreted her study as indicating that most poor spellers read "by eye", thereby depriving themselves of potentially useful orthographic information.

The positions taken by Bryant and Bradley and by Frith, however, have been disputed by other researchers. Waters, Bruck and Seidenberg (1985) contradicted Bryant and Bradley concerning strategy selectivity as well as Frith's theory of reading "by eye" and spelling "by ear". They argued that poor spellers may only use spelling–sound correspondences for unfamiliar words, since only misspellings were examined in Frith's study. They also questioned the conclusion that the children in these studies were using different cognitive processes in reading and spelling, because there was little attempt to evaluate their single-word recognition skills.

Waters et al. (1985) addressed these concerns in their study of third-grade children by having the children read and spell nonwords and five types of real words that differed in terms of their regularity for reading and spelling. The results were interpreted as showing that poor readers and poor spellers did not exhibit strategy selectivity. Students used similar processes for reading and spelling; they used spelling–sound information for both. The study suggested that use of spelling–sound correspondences underlies both good reading and good spelling skills at this age level. Although poor readers and poor spellers had inferior knowledge of spelling–sound information, they attempted to use this information in reading and spelling nonetheless.

Bruck and Waters (1988) extended the previous study to older children (mean age 10.7) who met the exclusionary criteria for developmental dyslexia. The subjects were administered tasks to assess (a) their use of phonological and visual information for word recognition, (b) their knowledge of spelling–sound correspondences for word recognition and (c) their use and knowledge of phonological and visual information for spelling. The dyslexic children's performance was compared with that of normal children of the same reading and spelling levels (mean age 7.6). The results indicated that dyslexic children did not use qualitatively different processes to read and spell words. Bruck and Waters concluded that the same essential processes underlie reading and spelling and that poor knowledge of spelling–sound correspondences is a major impediment in the acquisition of both reading and spelling skills.

Several other studies have analyzed the reading and spelling strategies of children who are poor readers and poor spellers to determine whether they use qualitatively different strategies from normal readers and spellers. Gerber (1984, 1985), in studying learning disabled students between second and sixth grade, found that subjects were able to produce spelling attempts which, in qualitative terms, resembled those expected from younger, normally achieving peers. The learning disabled students appeared to be developmentally delayed in critical cognitive processes which contribute to successively more skilled spelling. These processes include the ability to organize and rapidly access previously learned information, routines and knowledge. Spelling errors were shown to represent limited information and/or ability to formulate strategies for how to apply information in order to solve spelling problems. Gerber suggested the need for supplementary instruction in general problem-solving skills as they relate to the acquisition of basic academic skills such as reading and spelling.

Anderson (1985), in studying college students who were poor readers and poor spellers, also found evidence of limited orthographic knowledge and poor problem-solving strategies. These students exhibited strategies and errors which reflected a delay in the developmental sequence. They had not made the qualitative shift to visual strategies to supplement graphophonemic strategies and often used strategies similar to those of primary-aged children. These students failed to utilize visual information about the letter-by-letter structure of words or to attend to the morphological relationships between words. Therefore, they displayed limited ability to spell new words through the use of analogy with known words stored in their personal lexicon. The reliance on the non-lexical rather than lexical channels resulted in their having difficulty spelling irregular words and polysyllabic words with unstressed and silent letters as well as words derived from the same lexical base.

Oliver (1985), in an unpublished doctoral thesis, examined everyday writing and dictated lists of a group of adolescent poor readers and poor spellers. Although the subjects conformed closely to the normal stages of spelling development, more primitive spelling characteristics seemed to be present longer than would be expected in normally developing children. The sample appeared to hold rigidly to phonetic, or non-lexical spelling strategies and, consequently, seemed not to have developed normally in the acquisition of visual, meaning, derivational and analogy spelling strategies.

From the preceding studies it would appear that there are complex interrelationships between the acquisition of reading and spelling skills. Both at the knowledge and the concept level, deficiencies in one skill area could reasonably have an impact on the other skill. Englert, Hiebert and Stewart (1985) cautioned, however, that progress in one aspect of spelling or reading does not necessarily guarantee transfer of this strategy to the other skill area. When learning disabled students were trained in using an analogy strategy for spelling, their use of this strategy in spelling non-instructed words increased. No comparable gains were detected, however, in the use of analogies for reading unfamiliar words. Conversely, mildly disabled children trained to read sight words did not necessarily generalize that knowledge to spell new words. Englert *et al.* hypothesized that these results may reflect a slower rate of development of production skills (e.g. spelling) than recognition skills (e.g. reading). They suggested that if further research confirms this lag, stimulation of spelling skills without attention to the student's developmental reading level might have little effect on reading performance.

INVESTIGATIONS OF GOOD READERS WHO ARE POOR SPELLERS

If reading and spelling are so closely related, as indicated above, good readers should also be good spellers and poor readers could be expected to be poor spellers. A group of students which achieves normally in reading tasks but poorly in spelling should not, logically, exist. As Orton (1931) had noted, however, comparisons of achievement in reading and spelling uncover students who display a marked discrepancy between reading and spelling performance.

If it can be shown that the good reader/poor speller represents a distinct subtype of learner, some basic theoretical questions underlying current views of reading and spelling may have to be reexamined. Are reading and spelling actually separate processes which simply share many features, so that progress in one area may not be marked by growth in the other? Does the good reader/poor speller represent a point on a developmental continuum between good readers/good spellers and poor readers/poor spellers or does such a group possess a distinct learning profile?

Frith (1980) compared the performance of a group of adolescent good readers/good spellers (Good), good readers/poor spellers (Mixed) and poor readers/poor spellers (Poor) on a variety of component reading and spelling skills. When spelling error patterns were classified as phonetic or non-phonetic, the Good and Mixed groups were found to have a high proportion of phonetic errors, suggesting a basic knowledge of graphophonemic principles. Subjects in the Poor group, however, produced a high proportion of non-phonetic spellings. Frith concluded that the Mixed group could use sound-to-letter correspondence rules, but did not seem to know the precise letter-by-letter structure of a word. She hypothesized that in languages with strictly phonetic orthographies, the Mixed group would not exist.

Frith (1980) explained the existence of good readers/poor spellers by Bryant and Bradley's (1980) strategy specialization theory, and suggested that such individuals read "by eye" but spell "by ear". In a subsequent discussion of the good reader/poor speller phenomenon (1986), Frith suggested that these students have mastered the orthographic strategy in reading, but have failed to transfer it to spelling. As a result, they are able to spell regular words (presumably by using the alphabetic principle), but have persistent spelling problems with irregular words.

Jorm (1981, 1983) supported Frith's findings that the Mixed group made more phonetically accurate errors than their poor reader/poor speller counterparts, and resembled more closely the error patterns of good spellers, indicating an ability to utilize sound-to-print conversion rules. Jorm found, however, that while the Mixed group was similar to the Good in reading comprehension, when single-word recognition was tested the Mixed group resembled more closely the Poor subjects.

The studies of Frith and Jorm have been reviewed by Waters, Bruck and Seidenberg (1985) and Bruck and Waters (1988, 1989). As mentioned earlier, contrary to Frith's findings that good readers/poor spellers have adequate knowledge of the basic spelling–sound correspondences for reading and spelling, their findings suggested that this group does not possess good knowledge of graphophonemic relationships for either reading or spelling. Waters *et al.* (1985) found in their study of third-grade children that both the Mixed and Poor groups produced a smaller proportion of phonetically accurate errors than did the Good in tasks which included nonwords and five types of words that differed in terms of their regularity. Furthermore, even though the children in the Mixed group had been matched with children in the Good group on reading comprehension, the number and type of errors made by the Mixed subjects on both the reading and spelling tasks were more similar to those of the Poor subjects than to those of the Good subjects.

These contradictory findings are critical, since they call into question the designation of the good reader/poor speller as a distinct subtype of speller. Bruck and Waters (1989) tried to determine to what degree these discrepant results reflected differences in methods of subject selection and of error analysis. Two different sets of criteria were used to identify the Mixed group. Subjects were selected on the basis of standardized reading comprehension and spelling test scores or on the basis of standardized single-word recognition and spelling test scores. The phonetic accuracy of the spelling errors was assessed using two different scoring systems—one that took positional constraints into account and one that did not. In addition, children were identified at two different age levels, allowing for developmental comparisons. Regardless of age or reading ability, Poor and Mixed spellers had difficulty converting sounds into positionally appropriate graphemes.

Scott (1991) studied a number of component reading and spelling skills of seventh-grade Good, Mixed and Poor subjects. Tests were administered to assess spelling achievement, reading comprehension, reading rate, single-word recognition skills, the use of analogies in reading and spelling, and morphological knowledge in both oral and written forms. Errors on a dictated spelling test were analyzed and classified according to the Qualitative Inventory of Word Knowledge (Schlagel, 1982). A structured interview was also held with each subject to investigate a number of areas related to school experiences, general interests and attitudes towards reading and writing.

The results of this study were consistent with those of Bruck and Waters (1988, 1989). Not only did the Mixed group perform more poorly than the Good on graphophonemic tasks, the pattern was sustained on all measures of word recognition, morphological knowledge, and in three major categories of spelling error features. Mixed and Poor groups were similar on 22 of 30 variables. They differed only on reading comprehension tasks (due to selection procedures) and on a single test of oral morphological knowlege. The good readers/poor spellers, therefore, did not seem to represent a distinct subtype of poor spellers. They did not make qualitatively better spelling errors than the Poor group, nor did they appear to use different processes than other poor spellers. A discriminant function analysis confirmed that the relationship between reading and spelling skills is multi-dimensional. Based on the variables entered into the analysis, membership in the good reader/good speller group was likely to involve strong word recognition skills, the ability to move from derived to base forms in an oral context and rapid reading rate.

The results of the studies by Bruck and Waters (1988, 1989) and Scott (1991) would seem to indicate that reading and spelling skills are highly interdependent. Skilled reading and spelling depend on some of the same skills, and deficiencies in component reading skills would seem to be related to poor spelling performance.

The fact that good readers/good spellers, good readers/poor spellers and poor readers/poor spellers seem to differ from each other in degree rather than in kind of difficulty is quite consistent with emerging "normal variation" views about the nature of written language disabilities (e.g. Perfetti, 1986; Shaywitz et al., 1992). One such framework (Willows, 1991, in press a) conceptualizes difficulties in reading and writing as reflecting processing weaknesses in the areas inherent in the processing demands of the task. Moreover, the fact that poor spellers who are good readers seem to be quite similar in their areas of processing deficit to poor spellers who are poor readers may also indicate that the two groups are not discrete at all, but rather represent an artifact of the older age ranges included in nearly all of the studies. With the exception of the study by Waters et al. (1985) involving third-graders, the research comparing good readers/poor spellers with poor readers/poor spellers has involved subjects who were relatively old (e.g. few of the studies involved subjects below 12 years of age), and none of the published studies has examined the early reading processes of good readers/poor spellers. Blaszczykiewicz and Willows (1991), in an unpublished study, attempted to select groups of good readers/poor spellers to compare them with poor readers/poor spellers at each of grades 2, 4 and 6 from a large sample of children (nearly 400) involved in a study of the development of orthographic processes. These researchers abandoned this attempt as a result of their being unable to find enough good readers/poor spellers at grades 2 and 4 to make statistically meaningful comparisons. As Orton (1931) implied, school histories might indicate that older good readers/poor spellers had difficulty in the early stages of reading acquisition but that they overcame these early reading problems. Within a normal variation framework the individuals who are able to become successful readers eventually might have had less severe processing weaknesses that allowed them to compensate in word recognition (i.e. in reading), although spelling—a more demanding recall task—persisted as a source of problems.

CONCLUSIONS AND FUTURE DIRECTIONS

In sum, although much progress has been made since the time when Orton (1931) pointed to the interrelationship between reading and spelling disabilities, a number of potentially important issues have been largely ignored in the literature. Some of these were first raised by Orton and have not been addressed adequately since his time. For example, he clearly distinguished between oral and written spelling, but few studies of spelling processes consider that different mechanisms might be involved in these two types of spelling. Although oral spelling is rare in current educational contexts, list spelling of studied words might essentially reflect oral spelling processes "gone underground", relying on auditory rote memory. Another neglected distinction in the literature is between spelling recognition and spelling production. Although measures of both types have been widely used in the literature, they have not often been compared to determine the extent of common variance. Ignoring potential differences between these types of measures has led to a degree of circularity in the literature examining interrelationships between reading and spelling processes. For example, in some investigations a multiple-choice "spelling recognition" task has been used as a measure of spelling, while in other studies a virtually identical multiple-choice "word recognition" task has been used as a measure of reading. Finally, Orton also made a distinction between the processing demands of spelling in lists and in context, and yet the vast majority of studies of disabled readers' spelling processes have involved spelling in lists and very few studies have explored the relation between disabled readers' spelling in and out of context (e.g. Oliver, 1985). Although developmental studies of spelling stages have often involved examining children's invented spellings in their creative writing, rarely have these studies related their findings to the development of reading skill (e.g. Clark, 1988; Ehri, 1992). In view of the fact that it is contextual spelling that is of ultimate interest, there is a clear need for much more research on the contextual spellings of the reading/spelling disabled.

Another area of deficiency in the literature that has important implications for both theory and practice is the widespread failure to take classroom teaching/learning issues into account. It may well be, as Hinshelwood (1917) implied, that classroom teaching practices in reading and spelling influence the spelling patterns that are observed, and that, as Orton (1929) argued, these practices may have differential effects on disabled and normal readers. There is a need for more teaching studies and observational studies in the classroom to determine how various teaching practices (e.g. inventive spelling, direct instruction in phonics, formal spelling) influence reading and spelling acquisition (e.g. Bradley & Bryant, 1985; Cataldo & Ellis, 1988; Juel, 1988), especially for the children who are at risk for having learning difficulties. As well, teaching studies need to examine the effectiveness of various approaches to spelling instruction on the retention of spellings over both short and longer terms (Dreyer, Shankweiler & Luke, 1992).

ACKNOWLEDGEMENT

The authors wish to express their thanks to Karen Sumbler for her helpful comments in the preparation of this chapter.

REFERENCES

Anderson, K. (1985). Spelling errors and strategies of college students who are good readers/good spellers and poor readers/poor spellers on four complex word patterns. (Doctoral dissertation, Georgia State University, 1982) *Dissertation Abstracts International.*

Beers, J. (1980). Developmental stages of spelling competence in primary school children. In E. Henderson & J. Beers (Eds), *Development and Cognitive Aspects of Learning to Spell: A Reflection of Word Knowledge.* Newark, DE: International Reading Association.

Blaszczykiewicz, L. & Willows, D. M. (1991). *A developmental study of cognitive variables influencing the relation between reading and spelling as children progress through grades 2, 4 and 6.* Unpublished manuscript. Ontario Institute for Studies in Education.

Boder, E. (1971). Developmental dyslexia: prevailing diagnostic concepts and a new diagnostic approach. In H. R. Myklebust (Ed.), *Progress in Learning Disabilities*, Vol. 2. New York: Grune and Stratton, pp. 293–321.

Boder, E. & Jarrico, S. (1982). *The Boder Test of Reading–Spelling Patterns.* New York: Grune and Stratton.

Bradley, L. & Bryant, P. (1985). *Rhyme and Reason in Reading and Spelling* (International Academy for Research in Learning Disabilities, Monograph Series, Number 1). Ann Arbor, MI: University of Michigan Press.

Bruck, M. & Waters, G. (1988). An analysis of the spelling errors of children who differ in their reading and spelling skills. *Applied Psycholinguistics*, **9**, 77–92.

Bruck, M. & Waters, G. (1989). An analysis of the component reading and spelling skills of good readers–good spellers, good readers–poor spellers, and poor readers–poor spellers. In T. Carr & B. A. Levy (Eds), *Reading and its Development: Component Skills Approaches.* New York: Academic Press, pp. 161–206.

Bryant, P. & Bradley, L. (1980). Children write words they do not read. In U. Frith (Ed.), *Cognitive Processes in Spelling.* London: Academic Press, pp. 355–370.

Cataldo, S. & Ellis, N. (1988). Interactions in the development of spelling, reading and phonological skills. *Journal of Research in Reading*, **11**, 86–109.

Chomsky, C. (1979). Approaching reading through invented spelling. In L. B. Resnick & P. A. Weaver (Eds), *Theory and Practice of Early Reading*, Vol. 2. Hillsdale, NJ: LEA, pp. 43–65.

Clark, L. K. (1988). Invented spelling versus traditional spelling in first graders' writing: effects on learning to read and spell. *Research in the Teaching of English*, **22**(3), 281–309.

Corballis, M. C. & Beale, I. L. (1993). Orton revisited: dyslexia, laterality, and left–right confusion. In D. M. Willows, R. Kruk & E. Corcos (Eds), *Visual Processes in Reading and Reading Disabilities.* Hillsdale, NJ: LEA.

Dreyer, L. G., Shankweiler, D. & Luke, S. D. (1992). Children's retention of word spellings in relation to reading ability. Paper presented in the symposium "Developmental Perspectives on the Reading–Spelling Connection in Monolingual and Bilingual Children" at the annual meeting of the National Reading Conference, San Antonio, Texas.

Ehri, L. C. (1992). Spelling development in developing readers and disabled readers. Paper presented in the symposium "Developmental Perspectives on the Reading–Spelling Connection in Monolingual and Bilingual Children" at the annual meeting of the National Reading Conference, San Antonio, Texas.

Englert, C., Hiebert, E. & Stewart, S. (1985). Spelling unfamiliar words by an analogy strategy. *Journal of Special Education*, **19**(3), 291–306.

Frith, U. (1980). Unexpected spelling problems. In U. Frith (Ed.), *Cognitive Processes in Spelling.* London: Academic Press, pp. 496–515.

Frith, U. (1983). The similarities and differences between reading and spelling problems. In M. Rutter (Ed.), *Developmental Neuropsychiatry.* New York: Guilford Press, pp. 453–472.

Frith, U. (1986). A developmental framework for developmental dyslexia. *Annals of Dyslexia*, **36**, 69–81.

Gentry, J. (1978). Early spelling strategies. *The Elementary School Journal*, **79**, 88–92.

Gerber, M. M. (1984). Orthographic problem-solving of learning disabled and normally achieving students. *Learning Disability Quarterly*, **7**, 157–164.

Gerber, M. M. (1985). Spelling as concept-governed problem solving: learning disabled and normally achieving students. In B. Hutson (Ed.), *Advances in Reading/Language Research*, Vol. 3. Greenwich, CT: JAI Press, pp. 39–75.

Gerber, M. M. & Hall, R. J. (1987). Information processing approaches to studying spelling deficiencies. *Journal of Learning Disabilities*, **20**, 34–42.

Hinshelwood, J. (1917). *Congenital Word-Blindness*. London: H. K. Lewis.

Huey, E. B. (1908/1968). *The Psychology and Pedagogy of Reading*. Cambridge, MA: MIT Press. (Originally published by The MacMillan Company in 1908).

Jorm, A. F. (1981). Children with reading and spelling retardation: functioning of whole-word and correspondence-rule mechanisms. *Journal of Child Psychology and Psychiatry*, **22**, 171–178.

Jorm, A. F. (1983). Specific reading retardation and working memory: a review. *British Journal of Psychology*, **74**, 311–342.

Juel, C. (1988). Learning to read and write: a longitudinal study of 54 children from first through fourth grade. *Journal of Educational Psychology*, **80**, 437–447.

Kearney, C. A. & Drabman, R. S. (1993). The write–say method of improving spelling accuracy in children with learning disabilities. *Journal of Learning Disabilities*, **26**, 52–56.

Kottmeyer, W. (1959). *Teacher's Guide for Remedial Reading*. St Louis, MO: Webster Division, McGraw-Hill.

Larsen, S. C. & Hammill, D. D. (1986). *Test of Written Spelling—2*. Austin, TX: Pro-Ed.

Nelson, H. E. (1980). Analysis of spelling errors in normal and dyslexic children. In U. Frith (Ed.), *Cognitive Processes in Spelling*. New York: Academic Press, pp. 475–493.

Oliver, K. (1985). The spelling characteristics of an adolescent poor reader/poor speller group. *Dissertation Abstracts International*, **46**(12), 4237B. (University Microfilms No. 85-26, 907).

Orton, S. T. (1929). The "sight reading" method of teaching reading as a source of reading disability. *Journal of Educational Psychology*, 135–142.

Orton, S. T. (1931). Special disability in spelling. *Bulletin of the Neurological Institute of New York*, **1**(2), 159–192.

Perfetti, C. A. (1986). Continuities in reading acquisition, reading skill, and reading disability. *Remedial and Special Education*, **7**, 11–21.

Read, C. (1971). Pre-school children's knowledge of English phonology. *Harvard Educational Review*, **41**, 1–34.

Schlagel, R. (1982). A qualitative inventory of word knowledge: a developmental study of spelling, grades one through six. *Dissertation Abstracts International*, **47**(03), 915A. (University Microfilms No. 86-11, 798)

Schwartz, S. (1983). Spelling disability: a developmental linguistic analysis of pattern abstraction. *Applied Psycholinguistics*, **4**, 303–316.

Schwartz, S. & Doehring, D. G. (1977). A developmental study of children's ability to acquire knowledge of spelling patterns. *Developmental Psychology*, **13**, 419–420.

Scott, R. (1991). *Spelling and reading strategies of seventh grade good readers/good spellers, good readers/poor spellers, and poor readers/poor spellers*. Unpublished doctoral dissertation. Ontario Institute for Studies in Education, University of Toronto.

Shaywitz, S. E., Escobar, M. D., Shaywitz, B. A., Fletcher, J. M. & Makuch, R. (1992). Evidence that dyslexia may represent the lower tail of a normal distribution of reading ability. *New England Journal of Medicine*, **326**, 145–150.

Spache, G. D. (1976). *Diagnosing and Correcting Reading Disabilities*. Boston, MA: Allyn and Bacon.

Thomson, M. (1991). The teaching of spelling using techniques of simultaneous oral spelling and visual inspection. In M. Snowling & M. Thomson (Eds), *Dyslexia: Integrating Theory and Practice*. London: Whurr.

Waters, G., Bruck, M. & Seidenberg, M. (1985). Do children use similar processes to read and spell words? *Journal of Experimental Child Psychology*, **39**, 511–530.

Willows, D. M. (1991). A "normal variation" view of written language difficulties and disabilities: implications for whole language programs. *Exceptionality Education Canada*, **1**(3), 73–103.

Willows, D. M. (in press a). A framework for understanding learning difficulties and disabilities. In R. P. Garzia (Ed.), *Vision and Reading*. St. Louis, MO: Mosby.

Willows, D. M. (in press b). Assessment and programming for reading and writing difficulties. In R. P. Garzia (Ed.), *Vision and Reading*. St. Louis, MO: Mosby.

Willows, D. M. & Jackson, G. (1992). *Differential diagnosis of reading disability subtypes based on the Boder Test of Reading–Spelling Patterns: issues of reliability and validity*. Paper presented as part of the symposium "Spelling Processes of the Reading Disabled" at the annual meeting of the American Educational Research Association, San Francisco.

11

On the Development of Lexical and Non-Lexical Spelling Procedures of French-Speaking Normal and Disabled Children

JESUS ALEGRIA AND PHILIPPE MOUSTY

Université libre de Bruxelles

The French orthography, despite some peculiarities, belongs to the family of deep orthographic systems (Gak, 1976; Catach, 1980), as opposed to shallow or superficial ones. Shallow systems represent language at the phonological level. Deep systems partially represent language at the phonological level too, but simultaneously include aspects of morphology and syntax (Klima, 1972; Gleitman & Rozin, 1977). This often creates conflicting situations. For example, to represent the morphology of French verbs, unpronounced letters are added. As a result, different spellings are associated to some homophonous members of the same morphosyntactic paradigm:

il change/ʃɑ̃ʒə/   (he changes)
ils changent/ʃɑ̃ʒə/   (they change)

changer/ʃɑ̃ʒe/   *er* infinitive (to change)
changé/ʃɑ̃ʒe/   *é* past participle (changed)

These examples show that morphological and syntactic aspects of language that are not marked at the phonological level are, nevertheless, orthographically represented. French orthography also presents complexities at the phonological level, as shown in the following examples:

Handbook of Spelling: Theory, Process and Intervention. Edited by G. D. A. Brown and N. C. Ellis.
©1994 John Wiley & Sons Ltd.

/ʃ/ → *ch* is consistent
/ã/ → *an* is inconsistent, *en* is a frequent alternative
/ʒ/ → *g* is inconsistent, *j* is a plausible alternative

In the first case, phonological knowledge is sufficient to spell correctly the/ʃ/ phoneme. In the two others, lexical knowledge is necessary: *change* contains *an* (not *en*) and *g* (not *j*). Furthermore, in both examples of inconsistency, the intra-word context comes into play to constrain spelling:

/ã/ → *an* is more frequent than /ã/ → *en* within words
/ã/ → *en* is more frequent than /ã/ → *an* at the beginning of words
/ʒ/ → *g* or *j* before *e* and *i*. Before *a*, *o* and *u*, the letter *g* cannot be used

Véronis (1988) conducted a computer simulation study aimed at evaluating the productivity of sound-to-spelling transcription rules (SSTRs). The corpus contained 3724 current words (function words were excluded) including 19 072 phonemes. The results show that about 50 SSTRs allow 88% of the phonemes to be transcribed correctly but only about 50% of the words. An increase in the number of rules did not improve the spelling performance of the model. So an SSTR-based strategy permits not more than half of the French words to be spelled correctly. The other words contain spelling irregularities that cannot be derived from the phonology. It is clear that in order to spell French correctly, the child must possess and use a number of linguistic abilities that go far beyond the SSTRs.

One case that illustrates particularly clearly the different linguistic dimensions involved in French orthography concerns the relationships between the phoneme /s/ and the grapheme *s*, which is its most obvious transcription. The first point to be underlined is that /s/ is one of the most frequent phonemes in French. In the Véronis (1986) quantitative evaluation, /s/ occupies sixth place in a ranking containing 36 phonemes and represents 5.25% of the total number of occurrences. At the same time, it is one of the most inconsistent phonemes since it can be spelled as *s*, *c*, *ss*, *ç*, *t* and *x*. In the Véronis (1988) study, the author calculates the "phoneme transcribability" by SSTR and finds that /s/ occupies the fourth poorest place with 72.82% correct transcriptions. Only the phonemes /o/, /ã/ and /ɛ/ presented poorer scores. Finally, the grapheme *s*, which is the dominant transcription for /s/, stands in a rather complex relation to its pronunciation. At the end of words it serves as a morphosyntactic marker (for nominal plural and as a personal ending of verbal forms) or is simply part of the lexical definition (for example *mais* (but) and *mai* (the month of May)). In both cases, the final *s* is silent except when it is followed by a word beginning with a vowel (provided certain syntactic conditions are met). Word internally, *s* stands for /z/ or /s/ depending on the context (/z/ when between two orthographic vowels, otherwise /s/).

The acquisition of the whole system implies the use of complex skills: phonological, morphological, lexical and syntactic. An adequate experimental design could potentially allow us to follow the development of each of them, their interrelations and their failure in the disabled child. The present report is, however, limited to the role played by the two basic procedures intervening in spelling: lexical and SSTR non-lexical.

The theoretical framework adopted here retains the most generally agreed aspects of the spelling models developed during the last 20 years. Most of the models discussed in the influential book on cognitive processes in spelling edited by U. Frith in 1980 more or less explicitly refer to the two above-mentioned procedures.

It is necessary to add that calling upon these two procedures is not sufficient to solve the problem of spelling. What is missing from the model is an explicit statement about the way both procedures interact at different levels. A first level concerns the development of the whole system. It has been proposed that the orthographic lexicon develops as a result of the phonological activity (see, e.g. Ehri, 1980, 1991; Gough & Walsh, 1992; Perfetti, 1991). According to this view, the phonological component is necessary for the whole system to develop. A second level concerns the contribution of each process in real-time spelling. For example, as said before, spelling can reflect morphosyntactic constraints (Carlisle, 1988; Rubin, 1984, 1987; Templeton & Scarborough-Franks, 1985). The question arises of how these constraints are combined with the phonological and the lexical procedures, each one sometimes contradicting the other in the process of spelling words in context.

Another important source of interaction between the lexical and the non-lexical processes in spelling concerns the involvement of analogies. It has been shown that, at least in normal spellers, analogical processes intervene in word and in pseudoword spelling (Campbell, 1983; Barry & Seymour, 1988; Seymour & Dargie, 1990). Analogical spelling is lexically derived. Therefore, its presence can cast doubt on the existence of a non-lexical pathway. However, it may be that analogical processes participate in spelling through the phonological system. This procedure can, indeed, easily integrate an SSTR system including lexically determined rules (for example, the rule /-ɑ̃ʒə/ → -ange can develop under the lexical influence of words like change, mange, . . .). This account for the effects of analogy assumes that the rules in the phonological pathway can be lexically activated (e.g. a word like venger will activate the → -enge instead of the → -ange rule). The mere existence of analogical effects in spelling implies an interaction between the lexical and non-lexical procedures which needs elaboration.

Finally, one problem that a strict dual-process model cannot easily deal with concerns the spelling of words involving lexical activity without understanding. Evidence in ordinary spelling comes from what has been called "slips of the pen" (e.g. there instead of their) (Ellis, 1979; Hotopf, 1980). According to the classical dual-process view, the lexical representations of words are activated through their meaning. In the example above, the item there has been activated in the lexical store without any semantic contribution. This may lead to the addition of a third pathway which allows lexical spelling without meaning. The strongest evidence in favour of this pathway comes from acquired disorders of spelling (Patterson, 1986).

The literature about acquired spelling disorders has produced strong evidence of the reality of the two basic spelling procedures discussed so far (see Barry, this volume, Chapter 2). Many of the "surface" and "phonological" dysgraphics have rather severe problems with both spelling and reading. More intriguing are the cases of adults presenting developmental syndromes similar to the acquired syndromes, but having reached good literacy levels. Campbell and Butterworth (1985) have reported the case of an undergraduate student with a disorder analogous to the acquired phonological syndrome (see also Funnell & Davison, 1989, for a similar case). More recently, Goulandris and Snowling (1991) have described the case of another undergraduate student presenting a developmental surface dyslexia and dysgraphia syndrome. Those cases roughly correspond to the taxonomy proposed by Boder (1971): the "dysphonetic" subjects present similarities with the phonological syndrome and the "dyseidetic" subjects with the surface syndrome. However, the subjects described by Boder were less extreme cases than those referred to above.

An important question is whether each of the two basic reading and spelling procedures can develop independently and afford normal literacy. Bryant and Impey (1986) have shown that, in a population of normal young readers and spellers, it is possible to find subjects who are strongly biased towards the use of the phonological procedure and others who are biased towards the lexical procedure. These subjects presented a pattern of reading and spelling abilities as extreme as those described in the literature as being pathological (see, e.g. Temple & Marshall, 1983, for a developmental phonological case, and Coltheart et al., 1983, for a surface one). They conclude that each procedure alone can support normal development. This is not in itself a new idea. The undergraduate students examined by Campbell and Butterworth and by Goulandris and Snowling demonstrate that it is possible to compensate a functional deficit in one procedure by an exceptionally good performance in the other. What is controversial in the Bryant and Impey point of view is that a substantial proportion of the ordinary school population possess strongly biased reading and spelling procedures which remain extreme, suggesting that these procedures develop independently.

A different model of reading and spelling development supposes that the elaboration of lexical representations results from the activity of the phonological procedure. The shift from an alphabetic–phonological reading and spelling procedure to an orthographic–lexical procedure is a good example of the manner in which the two basic procedures can be articulated in developmental models. An efficient phonological procedure is a necessary condition for the development of the lexical procedure. Gough and Walsh (1992), Freebody and Bryne (1988) and Byrne, Freebody and Gates (1992) have convincingly argued against the notion that the lexical and the non-lexical procedures may develop independently to reach levels roughly beyond the third grade of normal reading and spelling. Exceptional cases (like the subject reported by Campbell and Butterworth) may be explained by exceptional compensatory mechanisms.

THE PRESENT STUDY

In order to investigate some of these issues further, we carried out a study to examine the development of the two basic spelling procedures, the phonological and the lexical procedures, as well as their relationships in the developmental process, in normal and disabled children. The study was mainly descriptive and contrasted "consistent" and "inconsistent" SSTRs. The consistent rules were either contextually independent (/ʃ/ → ch independently of contextual factors) or contextually dependent (/g/ followed by e → gu). In the inconsistent conditions, the target phoneme presented a "dominant" transcription (/s/ → s) and a "non-dominant" one (/s/ → c) depending on the frequency of the "graphoneme".[1] For the reasons explained above, the phoneme /s/ and the grapheme s will be under special focus in the inconsistent condition of this study (see Alegria & Mousty, in preparation, for further analyses of the /s/–s association).

The consistency manipulations were aimed at revealing the way in which phonologically based processes develop. Two extreme conditions were considered. First, we examined the consistent–context-independent cases, which include SSTRs that are almost 100% productive. These rules are hypothesized to be adopted earlier than the inconsistent but dominant rules, which are less productive. Second, we looked at the inconsistent–non-dominant cases, which inevitably require the use of lexical procedures. These were assumed to reveal the development of orthographic representations. In addition, the case of the consistent–context-dependent graphonemes was worth considering, because rules are as productive as in the consistent–context-independent condition but involve more or less complex conditions of application. It is plausible that the spelling of those items is not independent of lexical procedures.

Two groups of subjects were examined: normal and disabled children. The normal children were second, third and fifth graders of an ordinary school which used a phonic method of reading instruction. There were 22 subjects in grade 2, 24 in grade 3 and 18 in grade 5. Their mean ages were 7;7, 8;9 and 10;10 years, respectively. The second graders were tested during the second part of the school year so that all of them had reached a spelling level beyond the first steps in phoneme transcription. First graders were not considered because their spelling and reading performances seemed to depend very much on the particular classroom in which they happened to be (Leybaert et al., 1994).

The disabled group came from a special school for children with a specific delay in literacy acquisition. As is routine procedure in Belgium, these children have been detected as presenting reading and spelling problems but not intellectual ones (they must have an IQ of at least 85) by an official institution that decided to send them to the special school. The school integrated each child in a class corresponding to his/her reading and spelling level. The subjects came from four consecutive classes that we shall call A, B, C and D. The number of children per class was 12, 14, 10 and 12, respectively, and their mean ages were 11;3 (10;0–12;6), 11;7 (10;6–12;7), 12;5 (10;5–13;7) and 12;11 (11;5–14;5) years, respectively. These children, even in class A, had no problems for reading and spelling simple phonological structures. It is not impossible, then, that a pure phonological dyslexic child would never reach the classes of disabled children where we began to work.

Subjects were tested collectively in their classroom. They were presented with series of written sentences with one or more missing words. The experimenter read aloud the whole sentence and repeated the missing word(s) in turn. The subject's task was to write down each word at its correct place in the written sentence. The

---

[1]According to Véronis (1986), a "graphoneme" is the couple of a grapheme and its phonematic counterpart. The concept of grapheme corresponds to the "functional spelling units" of Venezky (1970). So, /s/ → s (serpent), /s/ → c (cigarette) and /s/ → sc (science) are examples of French graphonemes.

words included critical graphonemes that were either consistent or inconsistent. The consistent items could be context independent or dependent. The inconsistent items presented a dominant or a non-dominant spelling.

In the consistent–context-independent condition, the following SSTRs were considered: /v/ → v; /p/ → p; /ʃ/ → ch; /i/ → i; /a/ → a; /u/ → ou; and /ø/ → eu. These items allowed comparison of vowel and consonant spelling (/i/, /ø/, /a/, /u/ vs /v/, /p/, /ʃ/) on the one hand, and simple and complex graphemes (i, a, v, p vs ou, eu, ch) on the other hand. In addition, the graphonemes (/R/ → r, /l/ → l) were examined in two different positions: they were either included in a consonantic cluster (e.g. C/R/V) or constituted an isolated consonant at the beginning or end of a syllable (e.g. /R/V or V/R/). This was designed to evaluate the subject's ability to mentally isolate phonemes before applying SSTRs.

In the consistent–context-dependent condition, the items were: /g/e-i → gu (/g/e-i stands for /g/ followed by the letters e or i); /k/e-i → qu;[2] and /N/b-p → m (/N/ stands for nasal vowels like /ɔ̃/, /ɑ̃/ or /ɛ̃/ that are spelled with the letter m before the letters p or b (no<u>m</u>bre, cha<u>m</u>bre, ti<u>m</u>bre, . . .) and otherwise with the letter n).

In the inconsistent condition, three cases were considered: (1) #,C/s/e-i (/s/ at the beginning of a word or preceded by a consonant) → s in the dominant version and c in the non-dominant one; (2) G/z/V (/z/ preceded by an orthographic vowel noted G) → s in the dominant case and z in the non-dominant one; and (3) G/s/e-i → ss in the dominant case and c in the non-dominant one.

In the analysis of the data, only the critical graphonemes were considered (i.e. if the word cigarette /sigaRɛt/ was used to test the /s/ → c rule, only the letter(s) corresponding to the initial phoneme was taken into account.

Figure 11.1 represents the mean percentage of correct responses for the consistent items, per condition and per class, in the control and disabled children. The results strongly depended on the context (see the top graphs). In the context-independent case, the scores exceeded 90% correct in both groups from the very beginning. In the context-dependent condition, however, scores were rather poor. Two ANOVAs, one per group, carried out with context and class as factors showed that both these effects were highly significant in each group, as well as their interaction. Further analyses showed that the context effect was significant for second and third graders but not for fifth graders in the control group. This effect remained significant, however, even in the most skilled class of disabled children.

The graphonemes used in the consistent–context-independent condition included two independent factors: vowel vs consonant and simple (one phoneme → one letter) vs complex (one phoneme → several letters) cases. The scores as a function of these variables are presented in the middle graphs. Only the simple vs complex factor was relevant in the poorest class of the disabled children; performance was better for simple than for complex items. In all of the other cases, the performance was too high to show any difference between the conditions.

---

[2]This rule is not entirely consistent: there are some French words with the /k/e-i → k graphoneme (e.g. kilogramme, kilomètre, kératine, . . .).

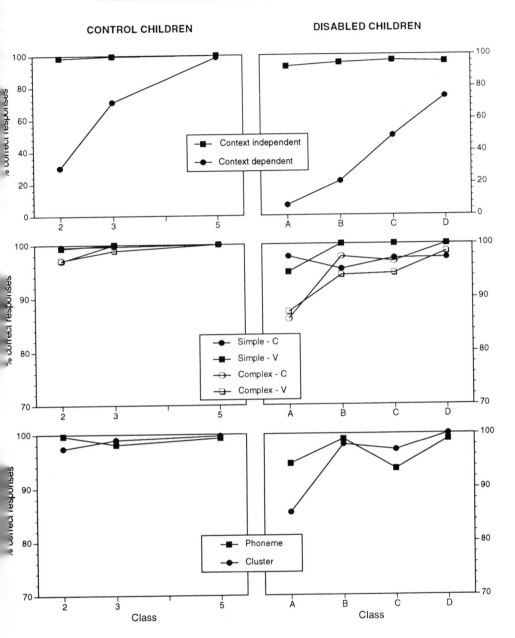

FIGURE 11.1   Percentage of correct responses on consistent items for each class of control and disabled children.

The bottom graphs show the results for the spelling of the phonemes /R/ and /l/ (which are among the most consistent French phonemes) when they are included in a consonantic cluster (e.g. /kR/V) as opposed to when they are not (e.g. /R/V or V/R/). The scores were almost perfect in all groups, except in the less advanced

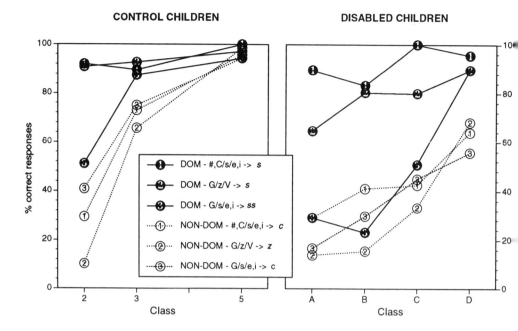

FIGURE 11.2   Percentage of correct responses on inconsistent items for each class of control and disabled children.

group of disabled children where the cluster condition was slightly, but significantly, weaker than in the other condition.

The results obtained in the inconsistent condition present a complex pattern (see Figure 11.2). In two out of the three graphonemes examined, graphoneme 1 (# ,C/s/e,i → s/c) and graphoneme 2 (G/z/V → s/z), the expected dominance effect clearly appeared, showing that the dominant versions were spelled at a level almost as good as if they were consistent. The non-dominant version was extremely poor at the beginning and improved with schooling. The results in the third case (graphoneme 3: G/s/e,i → ss/c) were rather poor in both the dominant and the non-dominant versions from the beginning onwards. Two ANOVAs, one per group, were performed considering graphoneme (1, 2 and 3), dominance (dominant vs non-dominant) and class as factors. The critical triple (graphoneme by dominance by class) interaction was significant in both the control and the disabled group. In the control group, local analyses revealed a highly significant interaction between class and dominance for the graphonemes 1 and 2 but not for the graphoneme 3. In the disabled group, this interaction was significant for the graphonemes 2 and 3 but not for the graphoneme 1. Finally, it is important to note that in the control group, dominance was highly significant until the third grade but no longer in the fifth grade. In the disabled group, however, it remained significant even in the most skilled class. As can be observed in Figure 11.2, this class of disabled children and the third graders reached equivalent levels of performance. Note that a similar outcome characterized the results of the consistent conditions (see Figure 11.1).

This suggests that the spelling level of third graders is reached by the disabled children with a delay of about 4 years on average.

SUMMARY AND CONCLUSIONS

The present study was confined to the spelling processes that are generally considered as being the most basic: phonological and lexical. The former are based on a corpus of rules that allow speech sounds to be translated into graphemes and the latter consist in a set of word representations containing orthographic specifications that can be accessed for spelling. Our research has been aimed at examining the way in which these two systems develop in normal and in disabled French-speaking children. Let us first consider the conclusions that can be drawn from the results concerning the first steps into spelling. Afterwards, we shall examine the question of the evolution of the system.

The First Steps into Spelling Acquisition

The study began with children attending second-grade classes. They had all been taught to read and spell with an alphabetic method for more than 1 year. They were all able to spell almost perfectly words using consistent–context-independent SSTRs. This was also the case even for the less advanced subjects of the disabled group. These subjects still showed some residual difficulties at spelling the phonemes /R/ and /l/ when they were included in consonantic clusters. This might reflect slight phonemic awareness troubles. The results, however, were rather good (about 90% correct), so they do not force the conclusion that the less advanced subjects do not possess metaphonological abilities at a sufficient level. Similarly, it is interesting, in this context, to recall that the disabled children did not show any difference between vowel and consonant spelling. Difficulties in the conscious manipulation of phonemes would probably produce better results for vowels than consonants. It has been shown that the former are easier to isolate than the latter; this was particularly clear in young dyslexic children (Morais, Cluytens & Alegria, 1984). Thus, all our subjects possessed the basic metaphonological abilities that enabled them to analyse utterances into their segmental constituents and to translate them into graphemes.

Concerning the spelling procedures demonstrated by the less advanced subjects, the factors examined (consistency, dominance and context) determine the performance in a complex way but the general pattern of results is rather similar in both groups of children. A simple account of these results is to suppose that the first steps into spelling are based on simplified rules. The data reported allow us to make some statements about the characteristics as well as the possible origin of these rules.

Rules are productivity independent. The evidence comes from two sources. First, the *consistent*–context-dependent items produced extremely poor results. Second, some *inconsistent*–dominant items (/s/ → s and /z/ → s) were almost perfect. At the same time, the corresponding non-dominant cases (/s/ → c and /z/ → z) were almost totally ignored. An interesting exception is the spelling of the intervocalic /s/, whose dominant version is *ss*. This item reached about 50% correct responses in the control group and 30% in the disabled one, far less than the results obtained with the two other dominant cases, /s/ → s and /z/ → s. The typical error was to spell the intervocalic /s/ with s (then pronounced /z/) instead of ss. These results are difficult to reconcile with an interpretation of the dominance effects in terms of rule frequency *per se*: dominant cases are more frequent than non-dominant cases, hence they are acquired first. It seems more likely that subjects have a default rule like "spell /s/ and /z/ as s everywhere". The other spellings, c and z, which are indeed non-dominant, but also ss, which is dominant, can be considered as marked cases, rarely used at the earlier spelling stages we investigated, probably because they have not yet been taught at school (see below). Then, the default rules involving inconsistent graphonemes, despite their relatively modest productivity values, are used as if they were as systematic as the consistent rules, which are almost 100% productive.

Beside the productivity-independent characteristics of the rules, the present study shows that these rules are also context-independent. The scores on consistent items were practically perfect with context-independent items (e.g. /i/ → i everywhere) and almost null if contextual constraints were to be taken into account (i.e. /g/ before e or i → gu). In these cases, children spelled the items as if it were contextually independent (i.e. /gi/ → gi, which is pronounced /ʒi/).

The notion that young children do use exclusively context-independent SSTRs was further examined in a pseudoword spelling task including the phonemes /s/ and /z/ placed in different contexts (Alegria & Mousty, in preparation). The results for the disabled children were clear-cut: /s/ and /z/ were almost always spelled as s, the default grapheme, whatever the context in which they were included. A control group of second graders spelled /z/ with s, like the disabled ones, but adopted the grapheme ss to spell /s/ in 50% of the cases. More importantly, this score showed some context sensitivity: ss was slightly preferred to s in pseudoword internal position while the opposite occurred at the beginning of the pseudowords. Therefore the tendency to spell /s/ with the grapheme ss, which is marked in a contextually bound manner, was already present in some particular cases in the less advanced group of normal subjects.

If it is assumed that the first steps into spelling acquisition discussed so far involve relying on a set of simplified rules, the question of their origin arises. The notion that they have evolved through reading and spelling experience seems unlikely. We have found numerous examples of rules that do not reflect the statistical properties of French orthography. For example, the less skilled among our subjects systematically used the rule /ʃ/ → ch, which is almost always correct, but also /s/ → s, which is not at all. The most plausible origin of the initial rules is explicit classroom instruction. Those rules could basically be something like: one phoneme → one grapheme (e.g. /s/ → s, /ʃ/ → ch, . . .). They are taught following a programme that reflects the frequency of both the phonemes and the SSTRs. Finally, initial instruction does not include contextual constraints. This can easily account for the fact that consistent and inconsistent but dominant cases produced similar results in spite of their differences in frequency. Teachers seem to follow a programme that presents the dominant cases as if they were consistent. As a result, subjects succeeded in spelling the dominant cases at more than 90% correct but failed almost completely with the non-dominant cases. Moreover, at the beginning, the teaching programme does not consider relatively infrequent segments ($/z/$ for example), nor contextual constraints, although they are totally consistent and concern frequent segments. For example, the *n* in the grapheme corresponding to all nasal vowels *an, en, in, on, ain*, etc., changes into *m* before *b* and *p*, but this regularity is totally ignored at the beginning. Similarly, children overgeneralize primitive rules like $/g/ \rightarrow g$ and $/k/ \rightarrow c$ to contexts where they are not correct any longer (i.e. $/g/e,i \rightarrow ge$-gi), probably because these restrictions have not yet been taught them. A minor point that could be added concerns the rules including double graphemes like *ch* and *eu*. This factor had no effect on the performance of second graders but double graphemes still produced slight difficulties in the disabled group, suggesting that teachers begin with "one segment → one letter" rules. Finally, some of the teachers' remarks addressed to us concerning our tests (e.g. "You can't put this word into the test because it contains something that I have not yet taught in class") corroborate the existence of a programme.

Referring to a taught system of rules as a psychological explanation of empirical data can seem rather unsatisfactory. Indeed, it could be purely *ad hoc* because programmes are more or less arbitrary, and differ from one another, so that they could explain the data whatever they are. A less problematic situation has been investigated by Read (1986) with his young creative spellers, and by Treiman (1993) with older children attending classes that allow and promote personal involvement in the discovery of spelling processes. The general conclusion, however, seems to be that whatever the path the child adopts or undergoes, spontaneous or imposed from above, it will initially incorporate an important variability in its detailed composition. The final product, however, will be a set of rules sufficiently powerful to allow individual reading and spelling. The elaboration of the mature reading and spelling system will depend on the personal involvement in those activities. As a consequence, the teacher's role will rapidly decrease and perhaps disappear. It may be expected then that the spelling performance reflects the properties of the orthographic system on the one hand and their interactions with the properties of the cognitive system on the other. This will be our main concern in the next section. What is perhaps surprising is that the spelling mechanisms of normal children after more than 1 year of school seem to reflect nothing more than an explicitly learned set of rules.

Beside the notion that during the first steps into spelling acquisition children do use naïve productivity- and context-independent SSTRs learned at school, we have not found any evidence of lexically driven spelling procedures. The results observed with inconsistent–non-dominant items are clear-cut. The performance on these cases, which need the use of lexical orthographic representations, was indeed extremely poor in both groups. Further evidence on this matter has been collected in another experiment in which inconsistent–non-dominant graphonemes were included in words of high or low frequency (Alegria & Mousty, in preparation). In agreement with the present interpretation, frequency effects were absent at the lowest reading levels in the normal as well as in the disabled groups of children.

Subsequent Development of Spelling Procedures

The conditions that were poor at the earlier stages of spelling improved with schooling in a radically different way in the control and in the disabled groups.

The performance with the inconsistent–non-dominant items increased rather rapidly between second and third grade in the control group. This "acceleration" was totally absent in the disabled group. The same difference appeared with the consistent but contextually determined items. It is important to keep in mind that the present data are not longitudinal, so that we must be cautious when interpreting the slopes, especially that of the disabled group. However, the great majority of the disabled children remained in the special school until the end of primary education, and they moved from class to class each year with a probability that is, as indicated by the mean ages of the successive classes, inferior to the control group. So, the slopes translated into individual developmental tendencies are even smoother than suggested by the figure.

The acceleration in the development of inconsistent–non-dominant items in the normal group suggests that it is during this period of time that the orthographic lexicon incorporates a large number of relatively infrequent words. If we assume that the lexical representations develop as a result of reading activity, the results suggest that the reading processes have reached a degree of efficiency that allows the control children to read more extensively.

The mechanism underlying this process is probably self-learning (whose basic features have been proposed by several authors: Ehri, 1980; Frith, 1980; Gough & Walsh, 1992; Jorm & Share, 1983; Perfetti, 1991; Stanovich, 1986, among others). According to this account, phonological processes are the dynamic element in the elaboration of lexical representations and, finally, in the development of the whole spelling system. All the abilities involved in the elaboration of the system underlying phonological reading and spelling are necessary for the lexical system to develop, but they are not sufficient. The disabled children examined in the present study possessed reasonably good phonological abilities but remained poor at the lexical level. This suggests that their word identification processes allow them to read but not to develop an orthographic lexicon efficiently.

A tentative account can be proposed to explain this difference. Studies comparing reading and spelling abilities in the same children have revealed the existence of a group of children who are good readers but poor spellers (Bruck & Waters, 1990; Frith, 1980; Waters, Bruck & Seidenberg, 1985). It has been demonstrated that they reach high reading levels by using compensatory reading procedures based on linguistic redundancy (Bruck & Waters, 1990; Waters, Bruck & Seidenberg, 1985). Frith has argued that these "mixed" subjects identify words using partial instead of full orthographic cues. The basic feature that characterizes good spellers could be their word-processing mechanisms, which are based on full cues, in Frith's terms. The present data are compatible with the notion that word processing based on full cues is a necessary condition for the elaboration of an orthographic lexicon which is useful for word spelling. In a subsequent study (Alegria & Mousty, in preparation) designed to evaluate the lexical spelling procedures more directly, the effect of word frequency on the spelling of inconsistent–non-dominant graphonemes was examined. The critical feature of this experiment was that normal and disabled children were matched on the basis of a reading comprehension test. The results showed stronger frequency effects in the former than in the latter group. In agreement with the present speculations, frequency effects which reflect lexically based spelling processes emerge beyond the abilities that are assessed by a reading comprehension test.

An account of the difficulties encountered by the disabled group in developing an orthographic lexicon that can be articulated easily with the previous one has been recently proposed by Goulandris and Snowling (1991). According to these authors, surface dyslexia may be due to a non-specific visual memory deficit. The case they describe is that of a successful reader presenting a developmental surface syndrome with severe difficulties in tasks requiring the visual recognition of geometric shapes and the reproduction of Greek letters or abstract letter-like sequences. The authors assume that this impairment has prevented the subject from developing detailed orthographic representations of words. This account may in principle explain the use of partial cues in reading. It simply results from the subject's inability to store full cues as a consequence of a general visual memory deficit.

To conclude on this point, the disabled subjects examined in the present study have a profile globally similar to the surface dyslexics. They suffer, as a group, a strong delay in lexical spelling while their phonological processes are relatively good.

A final point that deserves attention concerns the development of the ability to spell consistent graphonemes that are contextually constrained. It is striking that these entirely consistent items showed such a poor performance. The explanation of the failure at the earlier stages considered was that the corresponding rules had not yet been taught. Afterwards, the performance may develop as a result of lexical or of phonological procedures, these now including contextual constraints, or of both. Consistent–context-dependent items show developmental curves that are almost exactly the same as those of inconsistent–non-dominant items. This happened in the normal as well as in the disabled children, even though the evolution of performance differs from one group to the other. The most economical explanation is that performance depends exclusively on lexical procedures in both conditions. The lexical involvement in word spelling when lexical information exists is identical in both conditions. So, if a second source of information (i.e. the rule-based source) was involved in the consistent–context-dependent condition, performance should exceed that observed in the inconsistent–non-dominant condition (where rules are not involved). The absence of a clear advantage of the former relative to the latter condition argues in favour of a pure lexical explanation of the results in both conditions.

This rather surprising conclusion needs some qualification for at least two reasons. First, this explanation supposes that the frequencies of the words used in both conditions are equivalent, and this was indeed the case.[3] The second reason involves the way in which the two basic procedures are combined in order to produce spelling. The explanation just proposed implicitly supposes that the lexical and the rule-based procedures are hierarchically organized, with the latter intervening solely when the former does not provide any response. For example, to spell the word *guerre* (war) the orthographic lexicon is first consulted. The rule-based procedure will be used only if an orthographic representation is not found. The response will be correct if the (correct) orthographic representation is found or if the contextual rule is available

---

[3]The mean logarithmic values of the word frequencies taken from *Trésor de la Langue Française* (1971) were 3.17 in the inconsistent–non-dominant condition and 3.62 in the consistent–context-dependent condition. The difference was non-significant.

($/g/e \rightarrow gu$). In the other cases, the response will be an error (produced, for example, by the use of the primitive context-independent rule $/g/ \rightarrow g$). According to this model, the effects of rules are simply added to those of the lexical activity. The tentative conclusion concerning the consistent–context-dependent condition, stating that "nothing is added", depends on the adhesion to the notion that the orthographic lexicon is consulted first, before the rules, which are applied in turn, from the more constrained to the less constrained.

More complex modes of interaction between the lexical and non-lexical procedures can be conceived that are likely as the one just discussed. For example, the availability of rules as well as of orthographic representations may depend on their respective frequency, so that some rules could "overtake" the orthographic representation and impose their spelling. In the case of the word *guerre*, the naïve $/g/ \rightarrow g$ rule could be so strong that it eventually hinders the activation of both the orthographic word representation and the contextual rule. The results obtained in the consistent–context-dependent condition may be exceptionally poor because the rules examined have more primitive competitors that are especially strong. The evolution of spelling could depend on the inhibition of these rules. The questions raised are important because they concern one of the less understood problems: that of the interactions between the two basic spelling procedures. The experiments currently undertaken are aimed at collecting data to constrain speculation on this matter.

ACKNOWLEDGEMENTS

The study reported in this chapter was supported by the National Fund for Scientific Research ("Loterie Nationale", convention 8.4505.92) and by the Ministry of Education of the Belgian French-speaking Community (Concerted Research Action, convention 91/96-148). We are grateful to the staff and children from the schools "Etablissement d'Enseignement Primaire Spécial" (Court-St-Etienne) and "Ecole de la Sainte Famille" (Braine-Lalleud).

REFERENCES

Alegria, J. & Mousty, P. (in preparation). The development of spelling procedures in French-speaking, normal and disabled children: effects of frequency and lexicality.

Barry, C. & Seymour, P. H. K. (1988). Lexical priming and sound-to-spelling contingency effects in nonword spelling. *Quarterly Journal of Experimental Psychology*, **40A**, 5–40.

Boder, E. (1971). Developmental dyslexia: a diagnostic screening procedure based on three characteristic patterns of reading and spelling. In B. Bateman (Ed.), *Learning Disorders*, Vol. 4. Seattle: Special Child Publications.

Bruck, M. & Waters, G. S. (1990). An analysis of the component spelling and reading skills of good readers–good spellers, good readers–poor spellers, and poor readers–poor spellers. In T. H. Carr & B. A. Levy (Eds), *Reading and its Development*. San Diego, CA: Academic Press, pp. 161–206.

Bryant, P. & Impey, L. (1986). The similarities between normal readers and developmental and acquired dyslexics. *Cognition*, **24**, 121–137.

Byrne, B., Freebody, P. & Gates, A. (1992). Longitudinal data on the relations of word-reading strategies to comprehension, reading time, and phonemic awareness. *Reading Research Quarterly*, **27**, 141–151.

Campbell, R. (1983). Writing nonwords to dictation. *Brain and Language*, 19, 153–178.

Campbell, R. & Butterworth, B. (1985). Phonological dyslexia and dysgraphia in a highly literate subject; a developmental case with associated deficits of phonemic awareness and processing. *Quarterly Journal of Experimental Psychology*, 37A, 435–475.

Carlisle, J. F. (1988). Knowledge of derivational morphology and spelling ability in fourth, sixth, and eighth graders. *Applied Psycholinguistics*, 9, 247–266.

Catach, N. (1980). *L'orthographe Française: Traité Théorique et Pratique*. Paris: Nathan.

Coltheart, M., Masterson, J., Byng, S., Prior, M. & Riddoch, J. (1983). Surface dyslexia. *Quarterly Journal of Experimental Psychology*, 35A, 469–495.

Ehri, L. C. (1980). The development of orthographic images. In U. Frith (Ed.), *Cognitive Processes in Spelling*. London: Academic Press.

Ehri, L. C. (1991). Learning to read and spell words. In L. Rieben & C. A. Perfetti (Eds), *Learning to Read*. Hillsdale NJ: LEA, pp. 57–63.

Ellis, A. W. (1979). Slips of the pen. *Visible Language*, 13, 265–282.

Freebody, P. & Byrne, B. (1988). Word-reading strategies in elementary school children: relations to comprehension, reading time, and phonemic awareness. *Reading Research Quarterly*, 23, 441–453.

Frith, U. (1980). Unexpected spelling problems. In U. Frith (Ed.), *Cognitive Processes in Spelling*. London: Academic Press.

Funnell, E. & Davison, M. (1989). Lexical capture: a developmental disorder of reading and spelling. *Quarterly Journal of Experimental Psychology*, 41A, 471–487.

Gak, V. G. (1976). *L'orthographe du Français, Essai de Description Théorique et Pratique*. Paris: Selaf.

Gleitman, L. R. & Rozin, P. (1977). The structure and acquisition of reading I: relations between orthographies and the structure of language. In A. S. Reber & D. L. Scarborough (Eds), *Toward a Psychology of Reading: The Proceedings of the CUNY Conference*. Hillsdale, NJ: LEA.

Gough, P. B. & Walsh, M. A. (1992). Chinese, Phoenicians and the orthographic cipher of English. In S. Brady & D. Shankweiler (Eds), *Phonological Processes in Literacy*. Hillsdale, NJ: LEA, pp. 199–210.

Goulandris, N. K. & Snowling, M. (1991). Visual memory deficits: a plausible cause of developmental dyslexia? Evidence from a single case study. *Cognitive Neuropsychology*, 8, 127–154.

Hotopf, W. H. N. (1980). Slips of the pen. In U. Frith (Ed.), *Cognitive Processes in Spelling*. London: Academic Press.

Jorm, A. F. & Share, D. L. (1983). Phonological recording and reading acquisition. *Applied Psycholinguistics*, 4, 103–147.

Klima, E. S. (1972). How alphabets might reflect language. In J. F. Kananagh & I. G. Mattingly (Eds), *Language by Ear and by Eye*. Cambridge, Mass: MIT Press.

Leybaert, J., Alegria, J., Deltour, J. J. & Skinkel, R. (1994). Apprendre à lire. Rôle du langage, de la conscience métaphonologique et de l'école. In J. Grégoire & B. Piérart (Eds), *Évaluer les troubles de la lecture: Les nouveaux modèles théoriques et leurs implications diagnostiques*. Bruxelles: De Boeck.

Morais, J., Cluytens, M. & Alegria, J. (1984). Segmentation abilities of dyslexics and normal readers. *Perceptual and Motor Skills*, 58, 221–222.

Patterson, K. (1986). Lexical but nonsemantic spelling? *Cognitive Neuropsychology*, 3, 341–367.

Perfetti, C. A. (1991). Representations and awareness in the acquisition of reading competence. In L. Rieben & C. A. Perfetti (Eds), *Learning to Read*. Hillsdale, NJ: LEA, pp. 33–44.

Read, C. (1971). Pre-school children's knowledge of English phonology. *Harvard Educational Review*, 41, 1–34.

Read, C. (1986). *Children's Creative Spelling*. London: Routledge & Kegan Paul.

Rubin, H. (1984). *An investigation of the development of morphological knowledge and its relationship to early spelling ability*. Unpublished doctoral dissertation, University of Connecticut, Storrs, CT.

Rubin, H. (1987). The development of morphological knowledge in relation to early spelling ability. *Haskins Laboratories Status Report on Speech Research*, SR-89/90, 121–131.

Seymour, P. H. K. & Dargie, A. (1990). Associative priming and orthographic choice in nonword spelling. *The European Journal of Cognitive Psychology*, **2**, 395–410.

Stanovich, K. E. (1986). Matthew effects in reading: some consequences of individual differences in the acquisition of literacy. *Reading Research Quarterly*, **21**, 360–407.

Temple, C. M. & Marshall, J. C. (1983). A case study of phonological dyslexia. *British Journal of Psychology*, **74**, 517–535.

Templeton, S. & Scarborough-Franks, L. (1985). The spelling's the thing: knowledge of derivational morphology in orthography and phonology among older students. *Applied Psycholinguistics*, **6**, 371–390.

Treiman, R. (1993). *Beginning to Spell: A Study of First-Grade Children*. New York: Oxford University Press.

Trésor de la Langue Française (1971). Paris: Klincksieck.

Venezky, R. L. (1970). *The Structure of English Orthography*. The Hague: Mouton.

Véronis, J. (1986). Etude quantitative sur le système graphique et phono-graphique du français. *Cahiers de Psychologie Cognitive*, **6**, 501–531.

Véronis, J. (1988). From sound to spelling in French: simulation on a computer. *Cahiers de Psychologie Cognitive*, **8**, 315–334.

Waters, G. S., Bruck, M. & Seidenberg, M. (1985). Do children use similar processes to read and spell words? *Journal of Experimental Child Psychology*, **39**, 511–430.

12

The Modularity of Reading and Spelling: Evidence from Hyperlexia

LINDA S. SIEGEL

Ontario Institute for Studies in Education, Toronto

Spelling is assumed by most theorists to be a cognitive process involving the use of higher-level syntactic, semantic, phonemic and graphemic information, in addition to visual memory and phonological processes (e.g. Cohen, 1980; Seymour & Porpodas, 1980; Smith, 1980). However, in this chapter I will argue that the ability to spell words correctly is a cognitive process that may exist independently of other language and cognitive skills. I will report a case of a child with very advanced spelling and reading skills whose performance in all other cognitive areas was significantly below average. The extraordinary spelling and reading skills of this child, in spite of severe difficulties in other cognitive areas, suggests that reading and spelling may be modular processes that are not necessarily dependent on these higher-level semantic and syntactic processes. I will discuss these cases in relation to the concept of hyperlexia, a term first used by Silberberg and Silberberg (1967, 1968) to refer to children who recognize written words well beyond what would be expected according to their level of intellectual functioning. The majority of the reports of cases of hyperlexia have concentrated on the superior reading skills of these hyperlexic children, but there have been some intriguing reports of superior spelling skills in children with very low levels of cognitive and language functioning.

In this chapter, I will review the concept of hyperlexia in relationship to reading and spelling and speculate about the meaning of these cases for the analysis of the processes involved in reading and spelling. I will argue that reading and spelling are

Handbook of Spelling: Theory, Process and Intervention. Edited by G. D. A. Brown and N. C. Ellis.
©1994 John Wiley & Sons Ltd.

modular processes that exist independently of general cognitive and linguistic skills. I will present evidence that these children have phonological skills that are superior to their semantic, syntactic and orthographic skills.

CHARACTERISTICS OF HYPERLEXIA

Hyperlexia is an extremely rare condition in which a child has advanced reading skills in spite of severe language and cognitive deficits (e.g. Aram & Healy, 1988; Burd & Kerbeshian, 1988; Cain, 1969; Cobrinik, 1974, 1982; Elliot & Needleman, 1976; Frith & Snowling, 1983; Healy, 1982; Healy et al., 1982; Huttenlocher & Huttenlocher, 1973; Kistner, Robbins & Haskett, 1988; Mehegan & Dreifuss, 1972; Siegel, 1984). Although there is no definitive definition of hyperlexia, there are certain critical features of this syndrome. The child must read words at a level far superior to that of most children of the same chronological age, in spite of the fact that the child has low overall levels of intellectual functioning. Typically, precocious word recognition skills are observed early in the child's development, prior to the introduction of formal reading instruction. Speech development is often severely delayed and conversational speech may be totally absent or at least very poorly developed. Expressive language may exhibit a variety of abnormalities, such as dysarthria, echolalia and perseveration. Attention deficits are often reported in these children with or without associated hyperactivity. In addition, relatively better developed rote memory skills than comprehension and syntactic knowledge are consistently reported. Hyperlexia appears particularly frequent in high-functioning autistic children (e.g. Whitehouse & Harris, 1984), but it is important to stress that most of the cases of hyperlexic children that have been reported are *not* of autistic children although these children may have autistic features. Both hyperlexia and autism appear to exist on a continuum, with varying degrees of impairment and overlap between the conditions.

Less agreement has been noted in the degree to which comprehension is present in these children. Varying levels of comprehension have been reported in the literature, from a total absence, to single word and even simple sentence comprehension. Further, the extent of general cognitive delay has varied between reports. These children typically have intelligence scores in the moderate to severely retarded range on standardized intelligence tests. However, several investigators have included children in the average range of intelligence in the hyperlexic samples (Goldberg & Rothermel, 1984; Richman & Kitchell, 1981; Welsh, Pennington & Rogers, 1987), but I do not believe that these cases constitute true hyperlexia.

There are some very early reports of hyperlexia. Phillips (1930) and Parker (1917) describe the case of Gordon, who "has a talent for words". At the age of 10, he was at "the zero point in the scale of social efficiency" and "he could not be taught to dress himself or do anything efficient". His IQ on the Stanford–Binet was 65, he had very poor language and vocabulary skills but excellent visual spatial and mechanical skills. He demonstrated echolalia and some of the other signs of autism, although that term did not exist at the time the article was written. He could, however, repeat stories that he had heard even months before verbatim; he did seem to understand the meaning of some words. Phillips and Parker report that Gordon loved books but do not provide any details of his reading skills, except that he appears to have read very well. Phillips also reports that Gordon could spell but "cannot recognize the words he has learned to spell when he sees them in print" (p. 250). He was able to remember entire books, even months after he had read them, but he could not remember numbers, diconnected monosyllables or pictures. When shown books he was only interested in the words, not the pictures. He was able to write compositions that were age-appropriate in terms of ideas. Here is an example of a composition that he wrote at age 10:

> The Earth is round like a ball. We live on the Earth. We can see the sun shineing [sic] up in the sky. We can see the moon at night. We can say our prars [sic] to God at Night. We get up in the morning and dress ourselfs [sic]. We see the people all around us. We see the flowers growing on the bushes. We can see the trees blowing in the wind. We can feel the wind blowing hard. It makes us cold. We can see the horses stamping their feet on the ground.

This story contains three spelling errors that indicate good phonological but poorer orthographic skills. All of these errors are equivalents to the correct spelling but indicate a poor knowledge of orthography, for example in the case of *shineing e* does not precede the suffix *-ing* in English and *f* is not followed by *s* in plural forms. Obviously, his reading and spelling skills were far superior to his cognitive and language skills.

TOWARDS A DEFINITION OF HYPERLEXIA

The difficulty of diagnosis was recognized as early as Phillips (1930) before the term "hyperlexia" even existed. As Phillips (p. 246) has noted, "The differential diagnosis of the type of feeblemindedness known as imbecility is by no means an artisan's job. No foot rule, scale, or point system has been devised or will ever be devised that will relieve the clinician of long, patient, and discriminating analysis in arriving at a diagnosis". Definitions employed to identify hyperlexic children have, for the most part, been idiosyncratic to each specific study. For example, Goldberg and Rothermel (1984) adopted two criteria to define their sample: advanced word recognition was observed before the onset of formal instruction and was accompanied by "language arrest and/or behavioural fragmentation". One of the eight subjects in this study (case 6) had a full scale IQ of 100 and primary behavioral/social problems (for example distractibility and problems relating to peers). Given this child's cognitive ability, good word recognition ability was not unexpected. Thus, a label of hyperlexia appears inappropriate for children of average intelligence.

Investigators have attempted to employ a discrepancy definition in the identification of hyperlexic children. Richman and Kitchell (1981) identified children as hyperlexic if their word recognition (Wide Range Achievement Test—WRAT) was 2 years above what would be expected from their Wechsler Intelligence Scale for Children Full Scale IQs (WISC-FS). Nine out of 10 of their subjects had WISC-FS scores in the low average to average range. Welsh, Pennington and Rogers (1987) attempted to establish an operational definition based on such a discrepancy criterion for identifying hyperlexic children. These investigations identified a reading quotient (RQ) equal to a reading age measure (PIAT Reading Recognition age equivalent) divided by a mental age estimate (WISC-R FS age equivalent). An RQ of 1.2 was identified as a cut-off for hyperlexia. The investigators suggest that this is equal to the discrepancy in the opposite direction often required to identify reading disabled children. However, the difficulties with using a discrepancy definition to identify reading disabled children are many, as has been previously outlined (see Siegel, 1988, 1989, 1992; Siegel & Metsala, 1992). In Welsh et al.'s sample, FS IQ scores ranged from 52 to 119 and verbal IQ scores ranged from 57 to 125.

It does not appear useful to identify children of average cognitive ability as hyperlexic. Although these children may be of interest in the study of individual differences in reading achievement (for example see Jackson & Biemiller, 1985 and Pennington, Johnson & Welsh, 1987), they do not form a homogeneous group with children functioning in the moderate to severely developmentally deficient range of cognitive ability. In this chapter, I will define hyperlexia as single-word reading precocity in children with general cognitive and language deficiencies. Operationally, this definition limits hyperlexia to individuals with moderate to severe deficits in cognitive functioning on a standardized intellectual test and, most importantly, advanced word recognition skills. These cases of children with low levels of general cognitive functioning but advanced word recognition are, of course, of great importance for the study of reading because of the paradox that they pose for assumptions about the importance of cognitive and language skills for reading.

A small percentage of reported cases of hyperlexia have been found to have extraordinary spelling skills. The presence of these superior skills creates problems for assumptions about the importance of cognitive and linguistic factors in spelling. It is particularly paradoxical that children with low levels of cognitive and language skills can be good spellers. The complexity of English orthography and the multiple ways to represent these pronunciations would seem to necessitate the presence of reasonable cognitive and language skills.

Most of the studies of hyperlexic children have concentrated on their reading skills but there have been reports of some children with advanced spelling skills. In this chapter I will discuss these cases of children with excellent spelling skills but significantly below-average language and cognitive skills. I will first present a detailed case study of a child who was first seen at age 7 years, 7 months and then again at age 11 years, 1 month. This child had very advanced reading and spelling skills but below-average cognitive and language functioning as indicated by standardized and experimental intelligence and language tests.

A CASE STUDY OF HYPERLEXIC READING AND SPELLING

TP was 7 years, 7 months when he was first seen. He displayed extraordinary reading and spelling skills but below-average cognitive and language skills. He was seen again at age 11 years, 1 month. A detailed account of his cognitive, language and reading skills and spelling is presented in detail below.

TABLE 12.1   Performance of TP
on the WISC-R.

Age	7/7	11/1
Verbal scales		
Vocabulary	6	4
Similarities	6	6
Comprehension	5	7
Arithmetic	7	9
Information	9	9
Digit Span	13	13
Performance scales		
Block Design	11	7
Object Assembly	7	11
Picture Arrangement	9	11
Picture Completion	9	6
Coding	5	6
IQ		
Verbal	78	81
Performance	87	87
Full scale	81	83

General Cognitive Functioning

TP's scores on the WISC-R at 7 years, 7 months and 11 years, 1 month are shown in Table 12.1. As can be seen in Table 12.1, TP, at both ages, had low scores on the three subscales that were most related to expressive language skills—Vocabulary, Similarities and Comprehension. At the younger age, his language typically indicated an inability to use abstract terms. For example, when asked about the similarity between a candle and a lamp, he said "Like a light in your house", and when asked about the similarity between a cat and a mouse, he said, "The cat is chasing the mouse". Even at 11 years, he was rarely able to use abstract items. For example, when asked about the similarity between a piano and a guitar, he said that they "can be played with your fingers" and when asked about the similarity between an apple and a banana, he said that they both "can be eaten". Most children of 11 would use the term "food" to refer to both of them. At 11, he could *not* verbalize the similarity between a cat and a mouse. He was, however, able to use the term "feelings" to refer to the similarities of anger and joy.

His definitions of words showed the same concrete level of language. At 7 years, when asked to define a clock, he said, "Tick tock, it rings in the morning" and to define a hat, he said, "You wear it in the summer". At 11/1, his answers showed a slightly higher level of abstraction abilities. He said of a clock, "People use it to tell time" and of a hat, "People wear it on their heads". However, even at 11/1 he still was significantly below the level expected for his age in the ability to use abstractions. He defined a *donkey* by saying that it "has long ears and kicks" instead of saying it was an animal as most children his age would do. For *prevent* he said, "Preventing for fires" and for *gamble*, "Trying to win money" and when queried, said, "Rolls dice". Notice the awkward syntax of his responses to the last two items.

His language also displayed a feature that is not characteristic of normal speech at the ages at which he was tested. His answers to questions were sometimes syntagmatic associations. For example, at 11/1, when asked a question, "In which direction does the sun set?", he said, "Sun down" and, at 7/7, when asked about the meaning of join, he said, "Join in the circle of love" (this phrase is from a song that he had learned in school). At 7/7, when asked to define a clock, he merely said, "Tick-tock" and when asked to define a knife, he merely said, "Cut".

These responses indicate very poor abstraction abilities and a lack of vocabulary and syntactic knowledge. As we will see, his reading and spelling skills seem paradoxical in light of these significantly below-average language and cognitive skills.

Listening Comprehension

At 11/1, his listening comprehension scores were very poor. He was administered the Durrell Listening Comprehension Test, which involved responding to questions based on stories read aloud to him. His score was more than two grade levels below his current grade level. He could answer some of the questions that required a verbatim answer but seemed incapable of answering questions based on inferences.

Reading

Early precocity

His mother reported that he was fascinated by books and liked to read before he entered school. He could read fluently as early as the age of 3. According to reports from his kindergarten teacher, TP could read fluently at age 5 before he had any formal reading instruction. At 5 years, 9 months, he achieved a score at the grade 3 level on the Woodcock Word Attack subtest, a measure of pseudoword reading, and at a similar level on the Word Identification Subtest. He performed at the grade 1.9 level on the Word Comprehension and Passage Comprehension subtests, but these subtests have picture cues to the meaning of the words and sentences.

Age 7/7

In spite of his below-average cognitive functioning, TP's reading skills were extraordinary. His score on the Wide Range Achievement Test—Revised (WRAT-R) was at the percentile 87 (standard score 117). This score was more than two deviations *above* his IQ score. At 7/7, most of the reading errors that he made were omissions of very difficult words that were clearly not in his vocabulary, such as *aeronautic*, *quarantine* and *rescinded*. He did make some vowel and consonant errors, for example *abuse* read as *aboose* and *recession* read as *rezession*, but as noted earlier, he read many words significantly above the level expected for his age.

On a task involving the reading of 40 high-frequency regular (e.g. *came, five, feet*) and exception (e.g. *have, said, give*) words, he read them all correctly. The mean score for 7-year-old children with normal reading skills on this task was 37.04; the standard deviation was 3.46. TP's score is indicative of excellent reading skills but is not atypical for good readers of his age.

At age 7/7, he was administered the Gilmore Oral Reading Test (Gilmore & Gilmore, 1968), which requires the child to read passages aloud and answer questions on those passages. His score for accuracy was above the 95 percentile and his score for comprehension was in the average range. He was able to read fluently and with expression. He could answer factual questions but could not answer any question that was not directly in the text. For example, one passage contained the following sentences (among others): "Bob is eleven years old. His sister, Jane, is nine". He could answer questions for which the verbatim answers appeared in the text, for example, "How old is Jane?", "What color is the house?", but could not answer any question that required an inference such as "Who is the older child?" or "What part of the day is it?". (The answer could only be inferred from activities, for example, eating breakfast, leaving for school, mentioned in the story that typically take place in the morning but the time of day was not directly indicated in the text.) Another indication of the verbatim, but not conceptual, nature of his responses was his answer to the question, "What kind of garden does Mother have?" when the sentence in the story was "Mother goes out to her lovely flower garden". He said "lovely" and when asked what that meant and what was in the garden he did not know. Thus, he could remember the specific language of the passage but did not have the cognitive skills to interpret it.

He could read many words of which he did not know the meaning. At age 7/7, he was administered the Peabody Picture Vocabulary Test—Revised (PPVT-R) in the traditional way, that is, a word was read aloud to him and he was required to point to the one picture among four that represented the word. Approximately 2 weeks later he was given the same list of the words and asked to read these words. There were many words, even common object ones, that he could read but not point to the correct picture, for example *sail, disappointment, pitcher, human, vine, casserole, scalp, weasel, balcony, locket, amazed, tubular*. This pattern indicates a severe semantic deficit.

His phonological skills were outstanding. On a standardized test of pseudoword reading, the Woodcock Reading Mastery Tests Word Attack subtest, his score was at the 98 percentile. He made the following errors on vowel pronunciations—*chad* was pronounced as *chod, nan* as *nen, ap* as *ape, straced* as *stacid* (with a short vowel) and *gouch* as *gotch*. The remainder of his errors were difficulties with unpredictable consonants, for example *cigbet* was pronounced as *kigbet* and low-frequency consonant clusters, for example the silent *g* in *grouthe*, the silent *k* in *knonk* and the silent *p* in *pnomocher* were pronounced. A few of the pseudowords were read as words—*ap* as *ape, haff* as *raft, whie* as *white*—but the latter error was corrected immediately. The reading of pseudowords as real words is a somewhat unusual pattern for a good reader of this age. Most of the time, the good readers show an incomplete application of grapheme–phoneme correspondence rules but do not read pseudowords as real words.

He was administered a task that required the pronunciation of four-letter pseudowords, some of which could be pronounced with the analogy to a regular or to an exception word (e.g. *mive* like *give* or *hive*, *gead* like *bead* or *head*). His score on this was 81.25%. The mean of normal readers of his age was 91.69% correct so that his score was somewhat lower than normal readers. His errors were all vowel mispronunciations, for example *mive* was read as *meeve*, *hant* was read as *haint*. For the pseudowords in which there was a choice of two pronunciations, *bave* as *bav* (like *have*) or *bave* (like *gave*), he usually selected the rule-based response with the exception of *gove*, which was read as *gov* like *love* instead of like *cove*, and *woth*, which was read to rhyme with *both* as opposed to *cloth*. Most normal readers of his age performed in a similar manner with the exception of *gove*, which was typically read to rhyme with *cove*.

TP was administered a task in which he was presented with 18 pseudowords, each of which could be read in two ways, by analogy to a real word or by the grapheme–phoneme correspondence conversion rules of English, for example *dastle* by analogy to *castle* or with the *t* by GPC rules, or *sinth* by analogy to *ninth* or with a short vowel *i*. TP's performance on the task was 89% correct. The mean for good readers of this age was 80% correct. His two errors were on the item *sinth*, in which he pronounced the *th* as *ch*, and *lagon*, in which he pronounced the *g* as *j*. These errors are somewhat unusual for a child his age. Most of the time he used a pattern typical of good readers of his age, that is, he used the rule-based, rather than the analogy pronunciations.

In summary, his reading skills were very good; his pattern of errors was not markedly deviant from that of other good readers of his age.

Visual and orthographic processing

Phonological recoding is one route in reading; direct lexical (visual) access can also occur. TP was administered two tasks that were designed as measures of visual and phonological processing. Olson *et al.* (1985) have developed two tasks that provide a direct contrast between the visual and phonological processing routes. In the phonological task, the child has to specify which of two pseudowords, presented visually, sounds like a real word (e.g. *kake–dake*, *joap–joak*). In the visual task, the child is presented with a real word and a pseudoword (e.g. *rain–rane*, *boal–bowl*) and has to select the correct spelling. These tasks are designed so that only one process can operate in each task. That is, in the visual task both choices sound exactly the same, so that visual memory for the orthography of a word must be used; phonological processes are not helpful in this case because sounding out the words would produce the identical responses to each word. For the phonological task, recall of the visual pattern would not be useful because neither alternative is a correct visual pattern in the English lexicon. However, one of the alternatives, when sounded out, does produce an English word, although it is obviously not the correct orthographic form.

In the visual task, he achieved a score of 100% correct; the average score for good readers of his age is 84%. On the phonological task, he achieved a score of 65% correct; the mean for good readers of his age is 72%. His performance was clearly superior on the visual and somewhat below the level that would be expected on the phonological task. The pseudoword reading skills of TP were quite advanced; therefore, his relatively poorer performance on this phonological task may seem paradoxical. In fact, this phonological task required *lexical* access. As his vocabulary was impoverished, he may have been able to decode the pseudowords but not been able to recognize which of the two alternatives was correct. Some examples of items that he missed were *blug–bloe*, *klass–cliss* and *hote–hoap*.

He was administered an orthographic task, designed to measure his awareness of certain orthographic features of the English language (Siegel, in press). This task measured the ability to recognize legal and illegal orthographic combinations of English letters. The task was a two-choice one in which the children were presented with 17 pairs of pronounceable pseudowords, one of which contained a bigram that never occurs in an English word in a particular position and the other of which contained an orthographic string that occurs in English. Examples are *filv–filk*, *moke–moje*, *vism–visn* and *powl–lowp*. His score on this task was 82%. The mean score for the normal readers of his age was 70% and his score was almost one standard deviation above the mean. This pattern would seem to indicate excellent orthographic skills, somewhat better than most good readers of his age, and the predominance of reading by the visual route but with good phonological skills, except for the inability to use the latter in lexical access. This dissociation between phonological and semantic skills illustrates modularity of phonological processing as outlined by Stanovich (1988).

Age 11/1

At the age of 11/1, his reading scores were excellent. On the WRAT Reading Test, his word recognition skills indicated a standard score of 110, that is, on a percentile score of 75. His errors in reading were almost entirely a result of his poor vocabulary in that he read the letters properly but did not arrive at the correct pronunciation because he did not know the word. Typically, these errors involved placing the stress on the wrong syllable, for example *horizon*, *intrigue* and *emphasis* were decoded correctly but the stress was incorrect. He did make some errors on vowel sounds, for example *threshold* was pronounced with a long *e*, the *ei* in *seismograph* was pronounced with a short *e*, the *ea* in *endeavor* was pronounced with a long *e* sound. These vowel errors represent correct pronunciations of these vowels in other orthographic contexts.

He was also administered the Word Identification subtest of the Woodcock Reading Mastery Test—Revised. His score was at the 89th percentile. Most of the words that he missed were clearly not in his vocabulary, such as *zymolysis*, *inordinate* and *artesian*, but again he decoded them correctly. He made some errors that indicated that he was using GPC rules, for example *miser* was read with a short *i* instead of a long one and *naive* was pronounced as *nave*. In addition, he read the list of 40 high-frequency regular and irregular words (discussed previously) correctly, which is typical of good readers of his age.

On the Word Attack subtest of the Woodcock Reading Mastery Test—Revised, his score was at the 65th percentile. He had some difficulty with vowels: *ift* was read as *eeft*, *whie* was read as *wee*, *gaked* was read as *gacked* (with a short vowel) and *cyr* was read as *sair*. He missed some of the low-frequency consonants, for example *adjex* was read as *adject* and the silent *k* on *knoink*, the silent *g* in *grouthe* and the silent *p* in *pnomocher* were read. In spite of these errors, his knowledge of GPC rules was excellent.

His score on the task that involved the reading of pseudowords (e.g. *dastle, sinth*) by analogy or rules was 100% and he read 67% by rules and 33% by analogy. This pattern was very typical for good readers of his age but his overall score was slightly above the average of 93% for good readers of the same age. His performance on this task at age 7/7 had also been above the average of that of good readers of the same age.

His score on the task that involved the reading of pseudowords such as *mive, gead*, some of which could be read by GPC rules or analogy to an irregular word, was 94% and he read most by GPC rules. This performance was very typical for good readers of his age. There were two items for which he chose the analogy *vone* like *done* instead of *tone* and *kear* like *bear* instead of *hear*. These choices were also common and were made by approximately 30% of the good readers of his age.

At age 11/1, his score on the visual task, described earlier, which involved discriminating between a word and a pseudohomophone, was 100% as it had been at age 7/7. On the phonological task, which involved discriminating between a pseudoword and a pseudohomophone, his score was 58% (chance level). The mean score for good readers at age 11 was 82% and his score was almost three standard deviations below the mean for normal readers and approximately half a standard deviation *below* the score for reading disabled 11-year-olds. As was noted earlier, this task measures phonological decoding and lexical awareness and the latter was obviously a problem because of his impoverished vocabulary, although the particular pseudohomophones used were high-frequency words. It should be noted that he was not required to pronounce the pseudohomophone, just to discriminate between it and a pseudoword. He made errors on pairs such as the following: *carn–kard, fite–fipe, neach–teech, hoap–hote, bair–beal*. Obviously, these pseudohomophones represent high-frequency words that are clearly within the vocabulary of a typical 11-year-old.

On the orthographic awareness task, his score was 70%, which was almost one standard deviation below the poor readers and one half a standard deviation below that of the reading disabled. It should be noted that his performance on this task was very good at age 7/7 and very poor at age 11/1. This task requires abstraction skills. It could be that at 7/7 he was using these skills but at 11/1 some semantic and syntactic skills were more developed, but not sufficiently developed. However, if he relied on these poorly developed semantic and syntactic skills, rather than visual memory skills, his performance on the orthographic task would have been inadequate because this task requires good visual memory skills.

He appears to be using a phonological as opposed to a visual route for the recognition of correct spellings. I base this conclusion on a task that was administered to him in which he was shown two pronounceable pseudowords with identical pronunciations and required to select which one could be a word. One of the choices had a bigram or trigram that never occurs in English in that position. Some examples of items include *dayk, dake, wibz–wibs* and *laip–lape*. His score on this task was 33% correct, which is significantly below the level expected for his age and below chance levels. He was administered a task that involved choosing between two pronunciations of a pseudoword, and that involved an analogy to a real word and a pronunciation using CPC rules, for example *risten*, pronounced to rhyme with *listen*

or with the pronunciation of the *t*, or *fody* to rhyme with *body* or with a long *o*.
Most of the time he selected the rule-based, as opposed to the analogy pronunciation.
On a task that involved the pronunciation of pseudowords that would be pronounced
with the analogy to a regular or to the exception word (e.g. *mive* like *give* or *hive*,
gead like *bead* or *head*), he chose the pronunciation that indicated the use of GPC
rules rather than analogies to the exception words.

Reading comprehension

At age 11/1, his reading comprehension skills, as measured by standardized tests,
appeared to be average for his age and grade level. He achieved a score at the 40th
percentile on the Stanford Reading Test, a test that involves reading passages silently
and answering questions on the material in the passages. He was not able to answer
correctly any questions that involved making an inference but he was able to find
verbatim information in the text. As most of the questions do not involve inferences
(see Tal, Siegel & Maraun, in press for an extended discussion of this issue), he
achieved a reasonable score. He achieved a score at the 66th percentile on the
Woodcock Johnson Passage Comprehension Test, which is a cloze reading test that
involves filling in the missing words in passages but does have pictures to accompany
the text. However, his errors indicated a lack of awareness of syntax. For example,
in a passage about snapping turtles, he filled in the blank in this sentence, "Snapping
____ are sold commercially in large numbers", with the word *them*.

On one of the word reading tasks that involved the reading of some fairly low-
frequency words such as *shepherd*, *leopard*, *muscle*, he would look at each word and
formulate a sentence and then read the word. He seemed to be incapable of reading
the words if they were not in a sentence, although he was able to read isolated words
on other tasks.

Spelling

When tested by a psychologist with the WRAT Spelling Test at 5 years, 9 months,
TP's performance was extraordinary. It was equivalent to the average child at the
beginning of grade 3, standard score >154, percentile greater than 99.9. He printed
the first 10 words and then got tired of the task and spelled the remainder orally.

Age 7/7

TP's spelling performance at 7/7 was extraordinary for his chronological age. Table
12.2 shows the words that he was able to spell correctly and the errors he made on
the WRAT-R, a spelling dictation test, when he was age 7/7. His spelling performance
was at the 98th percentile for his age. He spelled many difficult words correctly. His
errors appear to be reasonable phonological equivalents to the target word but contain
unusual orthographic strings, for example *aes* in his incorrect spelling of *purchase*,
ff at the end of *brief* and the *aic* in *character*. It should be noted that his fine-motor
coordination, and consequently his writing, was significantly below the level expected
for his chronological age. Samples of his spelling are shown in Figure 12.1.

TABLE 12.2   Spelling performance of TP
on the WRAT-R at age 7/7.

Spelling errors		
Dictated word		TP's response
purchase		purchaes
brief		breaff
success		sixses
reasonable		resinble
occupy		ocupie
character		charaicter
Words spelled correctly		
go	cut	grown
cat	cook	nature
in	light	explain
boy	must	edge
and	dress	kitchen
will	reach	surprise
make	order	result
him	watch	advise
say	enter	imaginary

At age 7/7, he was administered a list of pseudowords to spell, the Spelling of Sounds subtest from the GFW Sound Symbol Tests. His score was at the 81st percentile. The only difficulties he had were with vowels (e.g. *stabe* was spelled as *stab*) and unpredictable consonants (e.g. *shif* was spelled as *chif*). Some samples of his spelling of pseudowords are shown in Figure 12.2. In spite of severe fine-motor coordination problems, he was able to spell most of the pseudowords with which he was presented.

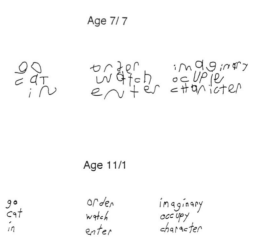

FIGURE 12.1   Examples of TP's spelling at age 7/7 and 11/1.

FIGURE 12.2   Examples of TP's spelling of the pseudowords *bab, tash, chid, nen, unhip* and *hes*.

He was administered the Sound–Symbol Association subtest of the GFW Sound–Symbol Tests in which he was required to associate geometric symbols with pseudowords and remember increasingly long lists of these symbol–pseudoword associations. His performance on this task was well above average, at the 75th percentile. This high level of performance is another illustration of his excellent rote memory skills and suggests that at least one route that he has learned to read and spell is by rote association between words as visual, rather than linguistic, symbols and their sounds.

At age 11/1, his spelling was also extraordinary. His standard score on the WRAT spelling test was 120 and his score was at the 91st percentile. Samples of his spelling are shown in Table 12.3. At 11/1, the only error that indicated a lack of understanding of English orthography was *result* spelled as *resuht*. It is as if he has not mastered the orthographic conventions of the language but understands the sounds represented by letters. His phonology appears to be in advance of his knowledge of orthograpy. Spelling has a visual memory component and a phonological component and TP's performance indicates strengths in both areas. His fine-motor coordination had improved significantly, as shown by samples of his spelling in Figure 12.1.

Table 12.4 shows TP's spelling errors at age 7 and 11 and errors on the same words made by good spellers of the same age and spelling level. In general, the errors of TP seem to be a better phonological than visual match to the target (e.g. *breaff* for *brief, prijudis* for *prejudice*) but, for the most part, do not seem markedly different from those of good spellers at the same age and spelling level.

Arithmetic

TP's standard score on the WRAT Arithmetic subtest was 92, percentile 30. He was able to solve some sample mental arithmetic problems and seemed to have some conceptual skills in that he could correctly answer questions concerning which of two

TABLE 12.3   Spelling performance of TP on the WRAT-R at age 11/1.

	Spelling errors
Target	Response of TP
result	resuht
success	sucsess
commission	comission
appropriation	apropriatian
enthusiasm	inpusiasm
criticize	critisize
prejudice	prijudis
belligerent	beligerant
occurrence	ocurance

Words spelled correctly

go	cut	grown	reasonable
cat	cook	nature	imaginary
in	light	explain	occupy
boy	must	edge	character
and	dress	kitchen	society
will	reach	surprise	official
make	order	advice	recognize
him	watch	purchase	familiar
say	enter	brief	beneficial

TABLE 12.4   Spelling errors of TP compared with non-hyperlexic children.

7-year-olds	
TP	JR, JN, DV, BP
purchaes	perches, purches, priches
breaff	breefh, brefe, breef, prave
sixses	succsess, sexces, sucses, sixses
resinble	resinable, reanabul, resinabull
ocupie	oqupie (2)
charicter	charactor

11-year-olds	
TP	GB, SM, YS, SB
resuht	
sucsess	succsess
comission	commision (2), comation
apropriation	appriatoin, appropration
inpusiasm	enthusiasim, entusiasuim
critisize	critizise, critisize, critise
prijudis	predgidist, predunize
beligerant	bedigerant, bligerant, biligerant (2)
ocurance	ocurrance, occurance (3)

numbers is bigger, 28 or 42. He had great difficulty writing the numbers and the numbers that he produced were very primitively drawn, similar to his writing of the letters that are shown in Figure 12.1.

Memory

On a test of rote memory for numbers, the Digit Span subtest of the WISC-R, TP had scaled scores of 13 at both ages; in each case these scores represent performance one standard deviation above the mean expected for his chronological age.

TP was administered a working memory task (Siegel & Ryan, 1989) that involved the simultaneous processing of linguistic information and remembering the information. He was presented aurally with sentences with a word missing at the end and was required to specify the word that was missing, for example, "On my hands, I have 10 ____ ". He was then required to remember the words from two, three, four or five sentences. At age 7/7, his score was more than two standard deviations below the mean for normal readers of his age and approximately one standard deviation below the mean of disabled readers of his age. Although his rote memory skills were above average (e.g. Digit Span), memory that required conceptual skills and more sophisticated linguistic processing was below average.

At age 11/1, the rote memory skills were well above average as indicated by his performance on the Digit Span task, which was one standard deviation *above* the level expected for his age level. On the working memory task described earlier, his performance was one and a half standard deviations below the level expected for his age.

At age 11/1, he was administered a short-term memory task. The short-term memory task was similar to those used by Shankweiler *et al.* (1979) but with some minor procedural differences. For this task the individuals were shown cards with five letters on them. Half of the sets had rhyming letters, *b, c, d, g, p, t, v* (the *z* had to be eliminated from the rhyming sets because it is pronounced zed in the Canadian dialect), and half of the sets were composed of non-rhyming letters, for example *h, k, l, q, r, s, w* (*y* was included in the Shankweiler *et al.* study but eliminated from the non-rhyming sets in this study). There were seven trials of each type, and the order was intermixed and determined randomly. The stimuli were presented for 3 s and then the cards were removed. The individual was required to write down the letters that had been on the card. The maximum scores were 35 for the rhyming and non-rhyming sets. Only letters recalled in the correct serial position of each trial were scored as correct. His score on this task was 89% correct, which was significantly above the level expected for normal readers of his age.

Language

When TP spoke spontaneously, his language had an artificial, mechanical quality. He did not appear to be interested in communicating with the listener and often did not make eye contact. During one of the sessions, when he was 11/1, he suddenly leapt out of his chair and ran to the blackboard in the room and started telling a story based on a violent encounter of aliens in space and drew some pictures of "spacemen". He did not make eye contact with the examiner and the story was not very coherent. He seemed totally uninterested in talking to the examiner and in eliciting any response from the examiner. At 7/7, he was administered an oral cloze task to measure syntactic awareness skills (Siegel & Ryan, 1989). In the oral cloze task, a sentence is read aloud to the child and the child is required to fill in a missing word. Examples of sentences include: "Jane ____ her sister ran up the hill"; " Betty ____ dug a hole with her shovel"; "The girl ____ is tall plays basketball". Sentences were read aloud to TP and he was required to fill in the missing word in the sentence. This task measures awareness of various syntactic features, including, for example, subject–verb agreement, prepositions and irregular verb inflections. TP's score on this task was 50% correct, which was significantly lower than that of children of the same age with normal reading skills. He had difficulty with irregular verbs, and when he was given the sentence "Betty ____ a hole with her shovel" he said "digged"; with conjunctions, and for the sentence "Jane ____ her sister ran up the hill" he said "catched"; and with relative pronouns, for example for "I want to play with a toy ____ is fun" he said "is". The quality of his responses was significantly lower than normal readers of his age.

At age 11/1, he was administered the same task. He achieved a score of 60% correct, almost two standard deviations below that of normal readers of his age and average for reading disabled children of his age. He still had difficulty with conjunctions and relative pronouns; some examples of his responses were "Jane ____ her sister ran up the hill" ("raced"), "Paul's mother picked up the toys ____ and books" ("big") and "I want to play with a toy ____ is fun" ("because"). Obviously, these answers indicate poor syntactic skills.

Behaviour

TP was referred for psychiatric assessment at 4 years of age, because of severe behavior problems. His behavior was "out of control" and he "seemed unaware of expected behavior". He was diagnosed as having a severe language deficit with "pervasive intellectual and behavioral consequences". He was referred to a program to help with his language and behavioral difficulties. In kindergarten, at age 5, he was reported as "fairly cooperative" but "isolated from his peers" and not involved in class discussions. He was very interested in calendars. During a class discussion of birds, he did not participate but sat in a corner and read a book about birds. He was interested in mechanical devices and enjoyed operating the record player and reading the record jackets.

At age 7/7, TP attempted to bite one of the blocks when the Block Design subtest was being administered. He put his head down and attempted to put his mouth to the block. This type of behavior has been reported with autistic children. When TP was 7/7, his mother completed the Connors Parent Questionnaire (Goyette, Connors & Ulrich, 1978). She rated his behavior as being more than two standard deviations above the mean on the Psychosomatic Scale, two standard deviations above the mean on the Learning Problems and the Anxiety Scales and almost two standard deviations above the mean on the Hyperactivity and Conduct Problem Scales.

At 11/1, his mother completed the Connors Parent Questionnaire. His mother's ratings of his behavior indicated that on the Hyperactive, Anxiety, and Learning Problems Scale he was at least two standard deviations above the mean for his age on the Psychosomatic Scale his score was more than one standard deviation above the mean for his age.

Fine-Motor Skills

In spite of excellent spelling skills, TP's handwriting indicated a very poor level of fine-motor coordination at age 7/7. Samples of his writing on the spelling dictation test are shown in Figure 12.1. On a standardized test of fine-motor coordination, the Beery Test of Visual–Motor Integration (VMI), his score was age equivalent 5 years, 4 months, with a percentile score of 4. Examples of his performance on the Beery VMI are shown in Figure 12.3.

At age 11/1, his printing showed a great improvement but there was still some awkwardness in making the letters, as shown in the bottom part of Figure 12.1. On the Beery VMI, his score at 11/1 was at age level 6 years, 5 months, percentile 8, indicating very serious difficulties in this area. Examples of his performance on the Beery at age 11/1 are shown in Figure 12.3.

The poor quality of his fine-motor coordination is shown in Figures 12.1, 12.2 and 12.3. His manner of constructing letters was awkward and unusual. For example, when writing the *p* and the *h*, he made the loop part first and then the stem.

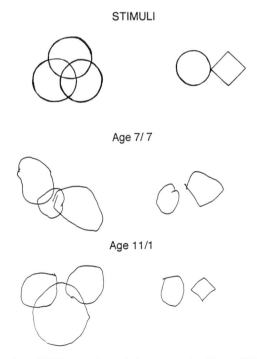

STIMULI

Age 7/7

Age 11/1

FIGURE 12.3   Examples of TP's copying of shapes on the Beery VMI at 7/7 and 11/1.

SUMMARY

TP clearly had a dissociation between comprehension and reading skills. On questions that required abstraction and/or inference abilities, either in spoken or written form, his performance was clearly below average. His semantic processing skills, syntactic awareness and vocabulary were also below average. However, his phonological skills were above average, as was his rote memory for information presented aurally or visually, which was well above average. He was able to use this combination of phonological and visual memory skills and to read words, pseudowords, sentences and paragraphs fluently. This pattern suggests that reading and spelling are modular processes.

OTHER REPORTS OF HYPERLEXIC SPELLING

TP is not the only case of a hyperlexic with advanced spelling skills although these skills are very rare. Burd *et al.* (1987) report the case of a child, R, who was very delayed at 4 years of age but who could read very well at 7½. His IQ was 91 (Verbal 101, Performance 84) with excellent word recognition and spelling recognition skills. In fact this child was not technically hyperlexic at the time that the advanced spelling was reported.

Seymour and Evans (1992) report above-average spelling in the case that they reported; MP could write letters in response to sounds in advance of his classmates. Spelling was advanced but not as much as reading. The same was true for the spelling of pseudowords. The "phonetic plausibility" of MP's spelling errors was in the range of his classmates. In addition, there were errors that suggested "partial lexical retrieval", for example *skhool* and *geues*.

On a test of spelling of unusual prefixes (e.g. *abhor*), unusual suffixes (e.g. *rheumatism*) and complex words (*accuracy*, *secretive*), MP's performance was above average but not outstanding. Thus, Seymour and Evans (1992) conclude, "There is a suggestion here, therefore, that a level of spelling that implies a grasp of morphological structure may be slightly less easily acquired by MP than the more fundamental aspects of the orthographic system. However, the results gave no indication of an impairment in this area" (pp. 113–114). Seymour and Evans appear to be suggesting two routes to correct spelling, a phonological route and a lexical (visual, orthographic) route. For the phonological route in spelling, the individual translates each sound into a letter or combination of letters. In the orthographic route, the individual uses visual memory skills, rather than phonological rules, to recall the spelling of a word. Obviously, it is often difficult to discriminate between these two alternatives.

Goldberg and Rothermel (1984) report some hyperlexic subjects with high levels of spelling recognition on the PIAT, in which the child has to select the correct spelling from among three foils for a word read aloud. The scores of some of their subjects, however, appear to be quite low but there is insufficient detail reported.

Goodman (1972) identified a child with a severe language deficit who had reasonably high levels of reading and spelling and superior rote memory skills. There was some indication of relatively good visual discrimination and on spatial tasks (e.g. object assembly) but very poor ability to navigate and function in space and difficulties with fine-motor coordination. Cain (1969) has also reported that one of his three cases of high-functioning autistic children could spell as well as read quite well. Silberberg and Silberberg (1967) report advanced spelling skills in two hyperlexic children but these children had IQ scores well in the normal range (112, 113). Whitehouse and Harris (1984) reported several of the children in their study showed "hypergraphia", that is, unusual spontaneous writing ability, but there was no indication of their spelling ability.

PROGNOSIS OF HYPERLEXIA

Some children with hyperlexia have been reported to show improvement and to benefit from attempts at remediation with time (e.g. Burd et al., 1987; Burd & Kerbeshian, 1988; Fisher, Burd & Kerbeshian, 1988; Huttenlocher & Huttenlocher, 1973; Mehegan & Dreifuss, 1972). Burd et al. (1987) report one case similar to TP. The child, A, was a fluent reader and like TP had an IQ of 78 at age 7 (Verbal 73, Performance 87). By the age of 11, her IQ was 97. Burd et al. have reported that all of the subjects in their study showed improvements in IQ after the onset of reading skills. It should be noted that they used very strict criteria for the diagnosis of hyperlexia. Burd also noted that all of their subjects improved in social relatedness skills but some peculiarities have persisted. In addition, although there were improvements in speech, some abnormalities in speech are still apparent.

Burd et al. offer two possible explanations for the improvement of children with hyperlexia. One of these is the possibility that although the language and instruction that they receive is "poorly organized with regard to syntactical structures and the sequencing of content" (p. 411), printed material is "more organized (e.g. topic sentences in paragraphs, and so forth) and contains more organized syntactical structures" (p. 412). They also note that it is possible that "hyperlexia simply serves as a marker for a sequence of cognitive growth that begins with the ability to recognize words" (p. 412).

CONCLUSIONS

TP had very poor abstraction skills in that he did not appear to know or be able to use terminology indicating abstract or general concepts. His development of language abilities was significantly below that expected for his age and grade. However, his reading and spelling abilities were outstanding at age 7 years, 7 months and very good at age 11/1. How can this paradox be explained?

His phonological decoding skills were better than his orthographic skills, at least in some cases. His score on the orthographic task that involved memory for letter sequences in words was very low. His spelling errors were better phonological than visual matches. The acquisition of orthographic representations at the lexical level may be facilitated by other forms of word knowledge (e.g. semantic knowledge and phonological or spoken word knowledge). Or conversely, it is possible that cognitive and language deficits in hyperlexics impede the development of these other sources of lexical knowledge, which facilitate acquisition of higher-level orthographic representations in normal readers. Shallice, Warrington & McCarthy (1983) note that "An orthographic unit could only be present in word form if the letter-group which it detected actually existed as an English word. Indeed, it is plausible that the (lexical level) units might well be restricted to the subset of such letter groups that had some functional phonology or semantic correspondence" (p. 128). For hyperlexic children, the number of meaningful, functional units is necessarily limited by their pervasive language and cognitive deficits. Therefore, the development of lexical orthographic representations may be influenced by semantic and phonological lexical knowledge. The semantic and phonological store would thus be implicated in the functioning of word recognition in hyperlexic children, albeit indirectly. Rather, what may differentiate hyperlexics from other low-functioning children appears to be their unimpaired ability to acquire orthographic-to-phonological correspondences at each level of analysis; hyperlexics' oral language comprehension appears comparable to that of children with similar cognitive profiles. These children appear to read much as skilled word decoders but lexical-level representations may be constrained by comprehension or word knowledge limitations. The phenomena of hyperlexic reading and spelling would appear to support a relatively modular view of word recognition skills. That is, decoding skills appear able to develop quite independently of other types of lexical knowledge. Lacking this lexical knowledge, TP's orthographic skills did not develop.

In the early stages of normal reading acquisition, a child's semantic system appears to be more developed than his/her word decoding skills. This is seen in more frequent semantic than phonological substitutions in early text reading (Stanovich, 1981). It appears that for hyperlexic children the opposite is true. The errors that TP made in oral language and reading indicated that his semantic and syntactic skills were significantly below normal.

These cases of hyperlexia illustrate that phonological processing and rote memory skills are sufficient for gaining some information from text, but in the presence of severe deficits in semantic and syntactic skills, reading and spelling can be adequate but higher-level language and cognitive skills are required for true comprehension and the ability to make inferences from text.

ACKNOWLEDGEMENTS

The research reported in this chapter was supported by a grant from the Natural Sciences and Engineering Research Council of Canada. This chapter was written while the author held a Senior Research Fellowship from the Ontario Mental Health Foundation. The author wishes to thank Suzanne Rossini for her help and Letty Guirnela for secretarial assistance.

REFERENCES

Aram, D. M. & Healy, J. M. (1988). Hyperlexia: a review of extraordinary word recognition. In L. K. Obler & D. Fein (Eds), *The Exceptional Brain: Neuropsychology of Talent and Special Abilities*. New York: Guilford Press, pp. 70–102.

Aram, D. M., Rose, D. F. & Horowitz, S. J. (1984). Developmental reading without meaning. In R. N. Malatesha & H. A. Whitaker (Eds), *Dyslexia: A Global Issue*. NATO ASI Series.

Burd, L., Fisher, W., Knowlton, D. & Kerbeshian, J. (1987). Hyperlexia: a marker for improvement in children with pervasive developmental disorder? *Journal of the American Academy of Child and Adolescent Psychiatry*, **26**, 407–412.

Burd, L. & Kerbeshian, J. (1988). Familial pervasive development disorder, Tourette disorder and hyperlexia. *Neuroscience & Behavioral Reviews*, **12**, 233–234.

Cain, A. C. (1969). Special "isolated" abilities in severely psychotic young children. *Psychiatry*, **32**, 137–149.

Cobrinik, L. (1974). Unusual reading ability in severely disturbed children. *Journal of Autism and Childhood Schizophrenia*, **4**, 163–175.

Cobrinik, L. (1982). The performance of hyperlexic children on an "incomplete words" task. *Neuropsychologia*, **20**, 569–577.

Cohen, G. (1980). Reading and searching for spelling errors. In U. Frith (Ed.), *Cognitive Processes in Spelling*. London: Academic Press, pp. 135–158.

Elliot, D. E. & Needleman, R. M. (1976). The syndrome of hyperlexia of hyperlexia. *Brain and Language*, **3**, 339–349.

Fisher, W., Burd, L. & Kerbeshian, J. (1988). Markers for improvement in children with pervasive developmental disorders. *Journal of Mental Deficiency Research*, **32**, 357–369.

Frith, U. & Snowling, M. (1983). Reading for meaning and reading for sound in autistic and dyslexic children. *British Journal of Developmental Psychology*, **1**, 329–342.

Gilmore, J. V. & Gilmore, E. C. (1968). *Gilmore Oral Reading Test*. New York: Harcourt Brace, Jovanovich.

Goldberg, T. E. (1987). On hermetic reading abilities. *Journal of Autism and Developmental Disorders*, **17**, 29–44.

Goldberg, T. E. & Rothermel, R. D. (1984). Hyperlexic children reading. *Brain*, **107**, 759–785.

Goodman, J. (1972). A case study of an "autistic savant": mental function in the psychotic child with markedly discrepant abilities. *Journal of Child Psychology and Psychiatry*, **13**, 267–278.

Goyette, G. H., Connors, C. K. & Ulrich, R. F. (1978). Normative data on the revised Connors Parent and Teacher Rating Scales. *Journal of Abnormal Child Psychology*, **6**, 221–236.

Healy, J. M. (1982). The enigma of hyperlexia. *Reading Research Quarterly*, **17**, 319–338.

Healy, J. M., Aram, D. M., Horowitz, S. J. & Kessler, J. W. (1982). A study of hyperlexia. *Brain and Language*, **17**, 1–23.

Huttenlocher, P. R. & Huttenlocher, J. (1973). A study of children with hyperlexia. *Neurology*, **23**, 1107–1116.

Jackson, N. E. & Biemiller, A. J. (1985). Letter, word, and text reading times of precocious and average readers. *Child Development*, **56**, 196–206.

Kistner, J., Robbins, R. & Haskett, M. (1988). Assessment and skill remediation of hyperlexic children. *Journal of Autism and Developmental Disorders*, **18**, 191–205.

Mehegan, C. C. & Dreifuss, F. E. (1972). Hyperlexia: exceptional reading ability in brain damaged children. *Neurology*, **22**, 1105–1111.

Olson, R., Kliegl, R., Davidson, B. J. & Foltz, G. (1985). Individual and developmental differences in reading disability. In T. G. Waller (Ed.), *Reading Research: Advances in Theory and Practice*, Vol. 4. New York: Academic Press, pp. 1–64.

Parker, S. W. (1917). A pseudo-talent for words—the teacher's report to Dr. Witmer. *The Psychological Clinic*, **11**, 1–17.

Pennington, B. F., Johnson, C. & Welsh, M. C. (1987). Unexpected reading precocity in a normal preschooler: implications for hyperlexia. *Brain and Language*, **30**, 165–180.

Phillips, A. (1930). Talented imbeciles. *The Psychological Clinic*, **18**, 246–255.

Richman, L. C. & Kitchell, M. M. (1981). Hyperlexia as a variant of developmental language disorder. *Brain and Language*, **12**, 203–212.

Seymour, P. H. & Evans, H. M. (1992). Beginning reading without semantics: a cognitive study of hyperlexia. *Cognitive Neuropsychology*, **9**, 89–122.

Seymour, P. H. K. & Porpodas, C. D. (1980). Lexical and non-lexical processing of spelling in dyslexia. In U. Frith (Ed.), *Cognitive Processes in Spelling*. London: Academic Press, pp. 443–474.

Shallice, T., Warrington, E. K. & McCarthy, R. (1983). Reading without semantics. *Quarterly Journal of Experimental Psychology*, **35A**, 111–138.

Shankweiler, D., Liberman, I. Y., Mark, L. S., Fowler, C. A. & Fischer, F. W. (1979). The speech code and learning to read. *Journal of Experimental Psychology: Human Learning and Memory*, **5**, 531–545.

Siegel, L. S. (1984). A longitudinal study of a hyperlexic child: hyperlexia as a language disorder. *Neuropsychologia*, **22**, 577–585.

Siegel, L. S. (1988). Evidence that IQ scores are irrelevant to the definition and analysis of reading disability. *Canadian Journal of Psychology*, **42**, 201–215.

Siegel, L. S. (1989). IQ is irrelevant to the definition of learning disabilities. *Journal of Learning Disabilities*, **22**, 469–478.

Siegel, L. S. (1992). An evaluation of the discrepancy definition of dyslexia. *Journal of Learning Disabilities*, **25**, 618–629.

Siegel, L. S. (in press). Psychological processing deficits as the basis of developmental dyslexia. In J. Riddoch & G. Humphries (Eds), *Cognitive Neuropsychology and Cognitive Rehabilitation*. Hillsdale, NJ: LEA.

Siegel, L. S. & Metsala, J. (1992). An alternative to the food processor approach to subtypes of learning disabilities. In N. N. Singh & I. Beale (Eds), *Perspectives in Learning Disabilities: Nature, Theory and Treatment*. New York: Springer-Verlag.

Siegel, L. S. & Ryan, E. B. (1989). The development of working memory in normally achieving and subtypes of learning disabled children. *Child Development*, **60**, 973–980.

Silberberg, N. & Silberberg, M. C. (1967). Hyperlexia: specific word recognition skills in young children. *Exceptional Children*, **34**, 41–42.

Silberberg, N. E. & Silberberg, M. C. (1968). Case histories in hyperlexia. *Journal of School Psychology*, **7**, 3–7.

Smith, P. T. (1980). Linguistic information in spelling. In U. Frith (Ed.), *Cognitive Processes in Spelling*. London: Academic Press, pp. 33–50.

Stanovich, K. E. (1981). Attentional and automatic context effects in reading. In A. M. Lesgold & C. A. Perfetti (Eds), *Interactive Processes in Reading*. Hillsdale, NJ: LEA.

Stanovich, K. E. (1988). Explaining the differences between the dyslexic and garden variety poor reader: the phonological–core variance-difference model. *Journal of Learning Disabilities*, **21**, 590–604, 612.

Tal, N. F., Siegel, L. S. & Maraun, M. (in press). Reading comprehension: the role of question type and reading ability. *Reading and Writing: An Interdisciplinary Journal*.

Welsh, M. C., Pennington, B. F. & Rogers, S. (1987). Word recognition and comprehension skills in hyperlexic children. Brain and Language, 32, 76–96.

Whitehouse, D. & Harris, J. C. (1984). Hyperlexia in infantile autism. *Journal of Autism and Developmental Disorders*, **14**, 281–289

13

Spelling in Prelingual Deafness

RUTH CAMPBELL

Goldsmiths College, University of London

For most of us, spelling requires that we map words already known by ear to a written form. Because of this, the spelling skills of people without normal spoken language are of interest. In principle, they might show us the extent to which effective spelling requires a fully specified, firmly established basis in normally acquired spoken phonological structures.

In the precursor to the present volume, Frith's *Cognitive Processes in Spelling* (1980), Dodd explored the extent to which born deaf people had access to the phonological structure of English which could be used to support spelling. Her results pointed in two apparently contradictory directions. On the one hand, the deaf in her study—English youngsters, schooled in an oral tradition where lipreading is the major communicative system—were able to use speech-sound-to-letter mappings quite effectively since they were able to spell nonsense words which were spoken to them and could only be perceived by lipreading. But, on the other hand, the deaf in her studies were less likely than hearing controls to show sensitivity to letter-sound regularities in spelling known words (see also Dodd & Cockerill, 1985). In general, while the hearing control group tended to misspell irregular words (*sword, ocean*) rather than regular ones (*rent, strong*), this pattern did not characterize the deaf. This general picture—of some awareness of letter-sound mappings, together with suggestions of an ability to "decouple" speech-sound regularity and spelling pattern in a manner not available to hearing youngsters—characterizes several studies of deaf spelling. However, the interpretation of this pattern has varied, depending on the particular viewpoint of the investigator and the theoretical constructs that

Handbook of Spelling: Theory, Process and Intervention. Edited by G. D. A. Brown and N. C. Ellis.
©1994 John Wiley & Sons Ltd.

informed the study. One of the achievements of explorations of deaf cognition in the last 12 years has been to gain a firmer understanding of some apparently inconsistent patterns observed in populations who are born deaf and who learn to spell in an alphabetic language.

Among the earliest modern-day proposals concerning spelling and deafness was that of Gates and Chase (1926), who predicted that the deaf would not be as "misled" as normal hearing youngsters in spelling words with unique and unpredictable sound–spelling patterns (words like *yacht*). Their supposition was that, unlike hearing youngsters, the deaf would not be so predisposed to use simple letter-to-sound mappings in their spellings: they would be less dependent on assembled (sub-lexical) routines (Patterson, 1982). Their deaf subjects, like Dodd's (1980), confirmed this prediction, showing no regularity effect in their spelling. Hearing controls showed a regularity effect.

Gibson, Shurcliff and Yonas (1970) required their deaf and hearing control college subjects to copy short letter strings presented visually. They predicted that the advantage in copying pronounceable compared with non-pronounceable letter strings, reliably achieved in hearing populations, would be absent in the deaf. Their rationale was that of Gates and Chase: that is, the deaf would not be able to use the letter-sound pattern of English in order to remember and write the strings. However, to their surprise, these investigators found that the slope of the accuracy function for pronounceable strings (e.g. *zif*) compared with non-pronounceable ones (*rch*) was identical for their deaf and hearing subjects. Both groups were more accurate at copying, that is spelling, pronounceable strings. Moreover, in both groups, regression analysis showed that pronounceability was the most salient predictor of accuracy, and not positional frequency ratings of the letters, string length or any other possible confound with pronounceability. The deaf group in this study were students at Gallaudet College, the foremost higher education institution for the deaf in the USA. Students at that time may have included those whose first language was Sign (ASL) as well as orally trained youngsters. This unexpected finding caused the authors to turn their theoretical position completely around. Now, rather than the deaf being deficient at phonological skills, it was proposed that, for hearing people and for the deaf, learning to read and write could be *solely* an orthographic matter, depending entirely on the statistical distributions of written letters in words, and that pronounceability was a statistical red herring; really, it was just an index of orthographic regularity.

> . . . pronounceability ratings are measuring orthographic regularity (rules governing the internal structure of English words) . . . . Writing is a surrogate for speech; but orthographic rules are rules in their own right and apparently can be learned as such, quite aside from the fact that any word they produce maps predictably to speech sounds. Sound would seem thus to be not necessarily a part of the individual's processing in forming higher units of reading, although historically it formed them in the spelling patterns of the written language. An intelligent deaf child does master and use the regular spelling patterns of the language in processing graphic material and is facilitated by their presence. The redundancy contributed by invariant mapping to speech sounds may well make it easier for the hearing child to pick up the common spelling patterns and regularities as he learns to read, but clearly it can be done without this. (Gibson, Shurcliff & Yonas, 1970, p. 71)

It is interesting to note the resonance between Gibson et al.'s approach and that of modern associationists using PDP systems to model the acquisition of linguistic regularities (e.g. Rumelhart, McClelland & the PDP Research Group, 1986). However, such an overarching orthographic view fails to provide any purchase on some of the most robust phenomena of spelling, which all point to speech-related processes at work in people with normal hearing. Misspellings homophonous with target words outnumber all other types of misspelling and people are notoriously poor at discriminating homophonous misspellings from the correct ones (see e.g. Campbell & Coltheart, 1984). The thrust of work on the development of literacy in alphabetic languages in the last decade reiterates a close connection between the development of specific speech skills and learning to read and write. There is a close interactive relationship between phonemic awareness and learning to spell and read (Bertelson, 1986; Goswami & Bryant, 1990). At the very least there appears more to effective English spelling than the mastery of orthographic regularities on the basis of exposure to written forms.

Moreover, despite the claims of Gibson et al., it is possible to separate orthographic and phonological processes in word spelling and reading. Words and letter strings can be generated which are orthographically regular but map onto an unexpected phonology (e.g. steak) , and the opposite is also true (e.g. gnu). Many studies in the last decade have attempted to disconfound statistical orthographic regularity from phonological regularity in the examination of word processing in all modalities and in different subject groups.

In spelling, words in which the sound-to-spelling pattern is regular and predictable (phonologically regular words for spelling) are generally spelled more accurately than other words. This is particularly true in younger and less literate groups and for words that are rarer rather than common (Burden, 1992; Bruck, 1988; Bruck & Waters, 1990; Juel, Griffith & Gough, 1986; Seymour, 1992; Stanovich, Nathan & Vala-Rossi, 1986; Waters, Bruck & Malus-Abramowitz, 1988; Waters, Bruck & Seidenberg, 1985; Waters, Seidenberg & Bruck, 1984). This pattern in turn suggests that strong reliance on phonological mappings can be a circumscribed phase in the acquisition of literacy; it tends to appear as the learner starts to master a vocabulary of words and may fade somewhat as word spellings become more familiar. Frith (1985) suggests that spelling depends on these mappings for a longer period than does reading, with an alphabetic phase (reliant on simple sound-to-letter mapping rules) in spelling preceding and outlasting alphabetic reading in most children learning English.

Since so much work suggests that phonological as well as orthographic processes are strongly implicated in spelling in normal populations (despite a good deal of individual variation and despite our relative ignorance of spelling in languages other than English), perhaps we should question Gibson et al.'s conclusion. Is it possible that both hearing and deaf youngsters, far from being sensitive solely to orthographic regularities in spelling, are also sensitive to phonological structures, and that is why they performed so similarly in the copying task? That, after all, would be in line with Dodd's demonstration that the deaf can spell words nonsense words that they lipread. If, as Gibson et al. claim, spelling in the deaf merely reflected orthographic skills, how could these be used to map speech events onto letters?

There is strong evidence from a variety of sources that the deaf can be sensitive to phonological regularities in written material, even when orthographic regularities are taken into account.

Leybaert and Alegria (1993) show that born deaf people (Belgian students) are susceptible to Stroop effects in colour naming that follow the same gradient of interference as that for hearing children (from unpronounceable to pronounceable nonwords, to non-related words to colour words) whether manual or spoken responses were required. Furthermore, both groups showed marked interference in naming the colour carrier when it was a homophone of a colour word, suggesting that it was the speech representation of the colour word that caused specific interference. Hanson and Fowler (1987) reported that deaf Gallaudet college students, like hearing controls, were sensitive to rhyme struture in a paired lexical decision task. Thus they were faster at deciding that two words were displayed when those words rhymed (*hare, pair*) than when they did not (*are, pair*). Care was taken to control for orthographic similarity in this study. To date, these are the only studies that I know which suggest a *covert* sensitivity to the speech-sound structure of the written word in the deaf: that is, a sensitivity that is not under voluntary strategic control by the subject. As far as voluntary use of phonological strategies is concerned, there is plenty of evidence that the deaf can and often do use "inner speech". The deaf may use phonological working memory. Thus, as Conrad (1970) first demonstrated, they can show effects due to sound similarity in remembering lists of written letter names like *b*, *g*, *t*, *d*, *v*, where recall is poorer than for lists of letter names that do not rhyme, such as *h*, *n*, *r*, *s*, *l*. Nevertheless, the pattern of dependence on speech sounds in the deaf can show less consistency than in hearing youngsters, appearing in some but not other tasks. For example, deaf children tend not to use rhyme as a paired associate cue in picture recall when it is reliably used by reading-age matched children (see Campbell & Wright, 1990; Campbell, 1992), and individual differences in the use of phonological strategies can be more marked in deaf groups than in hearing ones and tend to correlate with speaking skill (Conrad, 1979; Hanson, Liberman & Shankweiler, 1984; Leybaert, 1993).

With all this in mind, it is worth re-examining claims about the "purely" orthographic skills of the young deaf speller suggested by Dodd's work. Experimental work should control carefully for phonological and orthographic regularity in sound-to-letter patterns. The developmental context should be carefully delineated. Most hearing children are (over)reliant on alphabetic spelling between the reading ages of 8 and around 11; is their "hyper-regularity" to be the yardstick for measuring the spelling skill of deaf youngsters of similar reading age?

Hanson, Shankweiler and Fischer (1983) examined spelling in Gallaudet College students of varied instructional and linguistic background. Several had Sign as a first language, others had an oral upbringing. They read at tenth-grade level (reading age 15–16 years). The researchers used a sentence-frame procedure to test spelling, in which students had to complete a written sentence with the missing word. The deaf group were as sensitive to regularity in spelling as were chronological controls. We (Campbell & Burden, in press) have recently completed a study with less accomplished English deaf students. They were school leavers and from oral backgrounds. Their reading age was around 10 years (fifth-grade level), a literacy stage at which reading age matched controls might be expected to show strong regularity effects in their spelling. Ours was a picture spelling task for simple concrete words. Target words varied systematically in frequency and regularity. Three levels of regularity were examined: "regular" words, where the sound-to-letter mapping was predictable and consistent; "exception" words, consisting of mildly irregular and more obviously irregular words, including members of word-ending families like *glove* (*stove*); "strange" words, with unique sound–letter spelling patterns (*soap*, *choir*). For all word groups, statistical word likeness (orthographic regularity in Gibson *et al.*'s terms) was similar. Words were either high or low frequency by published norms (Carroll & White, 1973). In order to spell regular words correctly, one needed to know simple letter-to-sound mapping rules to generate the correct (and only the correct) spelling. To spell exception words correctly, one needed to know rules about word endings and letter combinations and the exceptions to those rules. To spell strange words correctly, the idiosyncratic spelling and its pronunciation needed to be known. Under these conditions our deaf subjects were *more* accurate than their reading age peers at spelling but not as good as their real age matched controls. That is, for these deaf youngsters, spelling skill was in advance of their reading age tested by comprehension studies. These two aspects of deaf literacy, first that the deaf are generally poorer at reading and writing than their IQ predicts, and secondly that their spelling tends to be better than their reading, are facts which are almost universally noted and to which I shall return. More interestingly for the moment, there were no differences between the deaf and the younger hearing group in their pattern of sensitivity to regularity. All were significantly worse at spelling "strange" than "exception" or "regular" words, and for both groups word frequency moderated the effect (low-frequency words showed a more marked effect at each level). Qualitative patterns of error indicated further similarities. Whatever their hearing status, spellers made mistakes that respected the phonological structure of the target word. For example, *sqwrl* was a misspelling for *squirrel* and occurred in the deaf and the hearing children's writings. Admittedly, our criterion for phonological misspellings was a broad one: we included misspellings that, when lipread, could be confused with the target. On the stricter criterion, where misspellings had to sound like the target when pronounced aloud, Hanson *et al.*'s deaf subjects generated fewer phonologically plausible misspellings than did the subjects in our studies.

Both these studies, where statistical features of written English (orthographic regularity) were controlled, suggest that deaf youngsters' spellings, both for rather poor reader–spellers and for good ones, are sensitive to the phonological structure of the written language; in this, they resemble hearing youngsters of similar reading ability. Studies which fail to show such effects—from Gates and Chase through to Dodd and Cockerill (1985)—have, of course, also been reported. The discussion so far has suggested that at least some of the differences in outcome and interpretation may reflect different criteria for word selection (separating orthographic and phonological variables), different levels of word-spelling skill generally (better reader–spellers are less reliant on alphabetic skills) and varying comparisons with hearing groups of different ages and skill. Failure to find "phonological effects" could reflect all or any of these factors. Furthermore, I am not claiming that the deaf show *identical* patterns to hearing controls in terms of their use of phonological structures, only that evidence for the use of such representations can be found, and that it can appear *similar* to processes used by hearing youngsters.

But behind the claim that deaf spelling is phonology-sensitive lies a problem. How can any deaf child "know" the full phonological specification of the spoken language represented in writing? While some phonology may be available from lipreading, it is extremely underspecified; lipreading alone cannot, for example, discriminate the spoken words *loan* and *donor*. If such underspecification characterizes the deaf child's phonology acquired from vision alone, how can "unseen" phonological structures inform his/her spelling? There are a number of possibilities; all, however, converge on the linguistic, and hence abstract and amodal, nature of phonology. A phoneme is the minimal meaning unit of the language; its definition is not in terms of speech structures, but of linguistic ones. In principle, *anything* could comprise a phonetic feature contributing to phonemic distinctiveness. Written letters, for instance, may have such a role. Hanson, Shankweiler and Fischer (1983) point out that, just as hearing readers can come to know "silent" morphophonological linguistic facts through reading, for example the "hidden" relationship between *sign* and *signature*, where the *g* is spoken in one case but not the other, "so might deaf readers similarly induce these structural facts" (p. 340).

Furthermore, for many deaf people, phonological structures in the spoken language might be available in communication by means other than lipreading. Fingerspelling, for instance, though it tends to be used only for proper names, nevertheless can carry otherwise underspecified phonological contrasts. Fingerspelling was a means invented by hearing people for communicating with the deaf by spelling words letter by letter. Each letter is represented by a specific hand-and-finger pattern. Both Sign users and orally trained deaf people use fingerspelling. There is some evidence that preliterate young deaf children spontaneously use it if it is in their language environment (Padden & LeMaster, 1985). It is not yet at all clear, though, that fingerspelling necessarily delivers awareness of the segmental structure of speech to the deaf, though it may convey some sense of individual letters (see Leybaert, 1993). It does not seem to be used spontaneously in learning to read. However, when directed to its significance in mapping letters to speech sounds, the deaf child can make use of this (Hirsh-Pasek & Treiman, 1982; Krakow & Hanson, 1985; Treiman & Hirsh-Pasek, 1983). A possible analogy here is with the hearing child who becomes aware that acronyms in her speech vocabulary represent letter names (OK, BBC, USA). In English the analogy is weak because letter names and their sounds are different. Yet it is a feature of preliterate hearing children's spontaneous spellings that they make use of English letter names as speech segments (*RT* for arty). Fingerspelling, having similar status in the developing deaf child's language scheme to letter names for the child with normal hearing, may then have a place in developing phonological knowledge—but it is still an obscure place because of the fragmentary and unsystematic way in which fingerspelling is used in Sign and other deaf languages.

There is, however, a system which does deliver phonemic contrasts systematically to the observer. This is the sign system called cued speech (Cornett, 1967). Cued speech comprises speech (lipreading for the observer) with accompanying handshapes that disambiguate the phonemic structure according to predetermined rules. Deaf children raised in a cued speech environment can show short-term memory and rhyme-judgement skills indistinguishable from those of age-matched peers; both show clear evidence of a strong grasp of phonology, with identical strategic control of phonological resources (Alegria *et al.*, 1992). Deaf children who are taught cued speech at school are not so advantaged, but nevertheless can show useful effects of such specific training. It is too early to know whether cued speech as a first language enables deaf youngsters' literacy to proceed along lines indistinguishable from those of hearing youngsters, but the prognosis suggests such development (see e.g. Perier, 1987). It is very likely that their spelling will show every sign of completely normal dependence on phonological structures. Preliminary studies by Alegria and his group (see Alegria & Charlier, 1992) further show that the cued hand positions that perform this phonological work function just as phonetic features do. That is, in isolation they have no role and it is only when they function with lipshape as phonological forms that speech comprehension and perception is achieved.

Many deaf communication systems offer other "aids" to phonological specification, including visual spectrograph readings and tactile information gained by placing the fingers on the speaker's vocal cords. Both deliver the phonetic feature of voicing, by visual or haptic means, to the interpreter. These, too may perform a similar function to the handshapes of cued speech, though it is not clear that their linguistic status is as well formed.

No "indigenous"[1] Sign languages for the deaf capture the phonological distinctions of the spoken language community. They are not designed to. Nevertheless, minimal meaning distinctions are captured in Sign that correspond to phonemic differences in speech. Differences in hand position or speed of action can have the same functional status as phonemic contrasts in distinguishing two signed "words" (Klima & Bellugi, 1979; Kyle & Woll, 1983). This may give the language learner a metatheoretic insight into the structure of language that is itself useful in learning to spell. There is no published evidence that children raised with Sign as a first language are poor at spelling. If anything, literacy may be achieved more readily by Sign-raised than oral-raised children (see Rodda & Grove, 1987), possibly because many oral-raised children are simply not getting sufficiently detailed specifications of words in phrases to acquire competence in language analysis.

So far, then, I have shown that the deaf can make use of phonological structures in spelling and I have indicated some ways in which speech phonology may be available to them through cues from other modalities than seen speech. With the exception of cued speech, which appears to be well placed to provide a full and systematic phonological structure for the effective comprehension of speech, the deaf appear to do this with a very underspecified phonological base. How do they do this? One possibility is that orthographic skills enhance and inform phonological ones in an interactive and dynamic way. Essentially, the deaf may use a developing knowledge

---

[1]A number of languages have been designed by hearing people which transcribe morpho-phonological regularities of the spoken tongue onto a signed form. The aim of these systems seems to be essentially prescriptive: they are used to induce "grammatically correct" speech in the deaf when using the spoken tongue. Paget-Gorman Signed English is an example of one such system. These systems very rarely form the native language experience for a deaf child and are rarely learned as a second language by the deaf. They can be used successfully by some deaf people with training. I classify them as non-indigenous deaf language systems.

of letter-to-sound mappings to improve their own knowledge of the sounds in the language, much as Hanson *et al.* suggested. One mechanism for achieving this may be through connectionist architectures.

Seidenberg and McClelland (1989) have described a parallel distributed processing model for learning the relationships between written and spoken words. The model specifies mappings, through a hidden unit layer, between orthography (letters) and phonology (from speech sounds). It does not include a lexical level of representation, though words are the form of input to the system—spoken words for phonological representations and written words for orthographic ones. It does not instantiate, directly, any particular set of rules concerning which letters map to which sounds. Such regularity emerges from the model by virtue of feedback (from the hidden units) on specific weighting patterns. Because the mappings are distributed across the net of correspondences, such learning becomes sensitive to regularities in the system as a whole. Phonological regularity does not, in this type of model, constitute a set of specific letter-to-sound rules, but rather the emergence of the most systematic mappings between orthography and phonology within a multiply interconnected network. Among the many ways in which the model fits the experimental data, it shows "normal" patterns of sensitivity to regularity in lexical decision for (low-frequency) written words that vary in their degree of regularity. The model has not yet been used to simulate spelling, nor the interaction of spelling and reading in normal development, although this would be a fairly obvious and natural development.

While (somewhat unsuccessful) attempts have been made to simulate acquired reading problems of lesioning the model (Patterson, Seidenberg & McClelland, 1989), the effects of deafness have not been simulated. To do this, it would be necessary to train the model on a systematically restricted set of phonological inputs; only those that could safely deliver phonological information from seen speech could be used (e.g. bilabial contrasts, point vowels). This would be equivalent to part-lesioning the model between the speech input and the phonological unit layer. Given the parallel, interconnected nature of the model, the interesting questions are whether such a lesion need impair the acquisition of regularity sensitivity in reading and writing and whether phonological specifications could be further "educated" by exposure to orthographic material. The data from the deaf studies reported here suggest a reasonably positive answer to the first question. If all other components of the model are functional (in particular, if the hidden layer unit is functioning effectively), then, since orthographic learning will occur, phonological and orthographic regularity effects may also emerge. It may be sufficient that distinctive *orthographic* representations map from a single phonological event onto different meanings (as for homophones in hearing people) for more detailed phonological representations to emerge. This, however, is a hypothetical prediction; only a simulation will generate an answer. As for the second question, it is possible that, as a result of exposure to written words, regularities might emerge which could in turn "educate" the phonological level of representation into more detailed ones. That is, literacy may provide a valuable "bootstrap" to increase phonological skills in the deaf. The claim here is not that improving spelling will make the deaf student like a hearing one, but that the deaf reader–speller could, through exposure to written forms, refine and extend the necessary knowledge of letters in words through the use of abstract, amodal, phonological processes. These may, phenomenologically, be unlike the "speech in the head" that characterizes so many hearing people's reports of how they segment and generate letters in words that they spell. For example, the deaf may be more susceptible to strategic switching, and a phonological event may leave an idiosyncratic trace in memory (see Campbell, 1992). These processes are nevertheless phonological, for they serve to distinguish and delineate meanings effectively in the spoken/written language.

Dodd's (1980) demonstration of two aspects of phonological skills in deaf youngsters' spelling was timely and useful. This review has taken the position that, at least as far as spelling is concerned, deaf youngsters—whatever their background—do not show particularly paradoxical features in their spellings. They make use of phonological structures in the spoken language, though these might be missed in some tests, and it is likely that exposure and training to an alphabetic orthography can train residual phonological capabilities to a level where they contribute effectively to the deaf person's ability to communicate in written (and even spoken) language.

ACKNOWLEDGEMENTS

Very large portions of this chapter were based on collaborative work with Vivian Burden, financed by a project grant from the MRC of Great Britain.

REFERENCES

Alegria, J. & Charlier, B. (1992). The role of lipreading and cued speech in the development of phonological representation in deaf children. Symposium on Lipreading: XXV International Congress of Psychology, Brussels, 1992.

Alegria, J., Leybaert, J., Charlier, B. & Hage, C. (1992). On the origin of phonological representations in the deaf: hearing lips and hands. In J. Alegria, D. Holender, J. J. de Morais & M Radeau (Eds), *Analytic Approaches to Human Cognition: In Honour of Professor Paul Bertelson*. Amsterdam: Elsevier.

Backman, J., Bruck, M., Herbert, M. & Seidenberg, M. (1984). Acquisition and use of spelling–sound correspondence in reading. *Journal of Experimental Child Psychology*, **38**, 114–133.

Bertelson, P. (1986). The onset of literacy. *Cognition*, **24**, 1–30.

Bruck, M. (1988). The word recognition and spelling of dyslexic children. *Reading Research Quarterly*, **23**, 51–69.

Bruck, M. & Waters, G. S. (1988). An analysis of the spelling errors of children who differ in their reading and spelling skills. *Applied Psycholinguistics*, **9**, 77–92.

Bruck, M. & Waters, G. S. (1990). An analysis of the component reading and spelling skills of goodreaders–goodspellers, goodreaders–poorspellers and poorreadeers–poorspellers. In T. Carr & B. A. Levy (Eds), *Reading and its Development: Component Skills Approaches*. New York: Academic Press.

Burden, V. (1992). Why are some "normal" readers such poor spellers? In C. Sterling & C. Robson (Eds), *Psychology, Spelling and Education*. London: Multilingual Matters.

Campbell, R. (1992). Speech in the head? In D. Reisberg (Ed.), *Auditory Imagery*. Hillsdale, NJ: LEA, pp. 73–94.

Campbell, R. & Burden, V. (in press). Phonological awareness, reading and spelling in the profoundly deaf. In B. de Gelder & J. Morais (Eds), *Phonological Awareness and Literacy: Comparative Approaches*. New York: Academic Press.

Campbell, R. & Coltheart, M. (1984). Gandhi: the nonviolent route to spelling reform? *Cognition*, **17**, 185–192.

Campbell, R. & Wright, H. (1990). Deafness and immediate memory for pictures: dissociations between inner speech and the inner ear? *Journal of Experimental Child Psychology*, **50**, 259–286.

Carroll, J. B. & White, M. N. (1973). Word frequency and age of acquisition as determiners of picture-naming latency. *Quarterly Journal of Experimental Psychology*, **25**, 85–95.

Conrad, R. (1970). Short-term memory processes in the deaf. *British Journal of Psychology*, **81**, 179–185.

Conrad, R. (1972). Short term memory in the deaf: a test for speech coding. *British Journal of Psychology*, **67**, 173–180.

Conrad, R. (1979). *The Deaf School Child*. London: Harper, Row.

Cornett, O. (1967). Cued speech. *American Annals of the Deaf*, **112**, 3–13.

Dodd, B. (1980). The spelling abilities of profoundly prelingually deaf children. In U. Frith (Ed.), *Cognitive Processes in Spelling*. London: Academic Press.

Dodd, B. & Cockerill, H. (1985). Phonological coding deficit: a comparison of spelling errors made by deaf, speech disordered and normal children. *Beitraege zur Phonetik und Linguistik*, **48**, 405–415.

Frith, U. (1985). Beneath the surface of surface dyslexia. In K. Patterson, J. C. Marshall & M. Coltheart, (Eds), *Surface Dyslexia*. London: LEA.

Gates, A. I. & Chase, E. H. (1926). Methods and theories of learning to spell tested by studies of deaf children. *Journal of Educational Psychology*, **17**, 289–300.

Gibson, E. J., Shurcliff, A. & Yonas, A. (1970). Utilization of spelling patterns by deaf and hearing subjects. In *Basic Studies in Reading* (H. Levin & J. P. Williams, Eds), New York: Basic Books.

Goswami, U. & Bryant, P. E. (1990). *Phonological Skills and Learning to Read*. Hove: LEA.

Hanson, V. L. & Fowler, C. (1987). Phonological coding in word reading: evidence from hearing and deaf readers. *Memory & Cognition*, **15**, 199–207.

Hanson, V. L., Liberman, I. Y. & Shankweiler, D. (1984). Linguistic coding by deaf children in relation to beginning reading success. *Journal of Experimental Child Psychology*, **37**, 378–393.

Hanson, V. L., Shankweiler, D. & Fischer, F. W. (1983). Determinants of spelling ability in deaf and hearing adults: access to linguistic structure. *Cognition*, **14**, 323–344.

Hirsh-Pasek, K. & Treiman, R. (1982). Recoding in silent reading: can the deaf child translate print into a more manageable form. *Volta Review*, **84**, 71–82.

Juel, C., Griffith, P. & Gough, P. (1986). Acquisition of literacy: a longitudinal study of children in first and second grade. *Journal of Educational Psychology*, **78**, 243–255.

Klima, E. S. & Bellugi, U. (1979). *The Signs of Language*. Cambridge, MA: Harvard University Press.

Krakow, R. A. & Hanson, V. (1985). Deaf signers and serial recall in the visual modality: memory for signs, fingerspelling and print. *Memory & Cognition*, **13**, 265–272.

Kyle, J. & Woll, B. (Eds) (1983). *Language in Sign: An International Perspective*. London: Croom Helm.

Leybaert, J. (1993). Determinants of reading ability in deaf individuals: the roles of phonological codes. In M. Marschark & D. Clark (Eds), *Psychological Perspectives on Deafness*. Hillsdale, NJ: LEA, 269–310.

Leybaert, J. & Alegria, J. (1993). The development of written word processing: the case of deaf children. *British Journal of Developmental Psychology*, **11**, 1–29.

Padden, C. & LeMaster, B. (1985). An alphabet on hand: the acquisition of fingerspelling in deaf children. *Sign Language Studies*, **47**, 161–171.

Patterson, K. E. (1982). The relation between reading and phonological coding. In A. W. Ellis (Ed.), *Normality and Pathology in Cognitive Function*. London: Academic Press, pp. 77–112.

Patterson, K. E., Seidenberg, M. S. & McClelland, J. L. (1989). Connections and disconnections: acquired alexia in a computational model of reading processes. In R. G. M. Morris (Ed.), *Parallel Distributed Processing: Implications for Psychology and Neurobiology*. Oxford: Oxford University Press.

Perier, O. (1987). L'enfant a l'audition deficiente. Aspects medicaux, educatifs, sociologiques et psychologiques. *Acta Otorhinolaryngologica Belgica*, **41**, 129–420.

Rodda, M. & Grove, C. (1987). *Language, Cognition and Deafness*. Hillsdale, NJ: LEA.

Rumelhart, D., McCelland, J. L. & the PDP Research Group (1986). *Parallel Distributed Processing: Explorations in the Microstructure of Cognition, Vol. 1, Foundations*, Cambridge, Mass: MIT.

Seidenberg, M. S. & McClelland, J. L. (1989). A distributed, developmental model of word recognition and naming. *Psychological Review*, **96**, 523–568.

Seymour, P. H. K. (1992). The psychology of spelling: a cognitive approach. In C. Sterling & C. Robson (Eds), *Psychology, Spelling and Education*. London: Multilingual Matters.

Stanovich, K. E., Nathan, R. G. & Vala-Rossi, M. (1986). Developmental changes in the cognitive co-ordinates of reading ability and the developmental lag hypothesis. *Reading Research Quarterly*, **21**, 199–202.

Treiman, R. & Hirsh-Pasek, K. (1983). Silent reading: insights from congenitally deaf readers. *Cognitive Psychology*, **15**, 392–365.

Waters, G. S., Bruck, M. & Malus-Abramowitz, M. (1988). The role of linguistic and visual information in spelling: a developmental study. *Journal of Experimental Child Psychology*, **45**, 400–421.

Waters, G. S., Bruck, M. & Seidenberg, M. S. (1985). Do children use the same processes to read and spell words. *Journal of Experimental Child Psychology*, **39**, 511–530.

Waters, G., Seidenberg, M. S. & Bruck, M. (1984). Children's and adults' use of spelling sound information in three reading tasks. *Memory & Cognition*, **12**, 293–305.

14

Orthographic Structure and the Spelling Process: A Comparison of Different Codes

KATHRYN LINK AND ALFONSO CARAMAZZA

Dartmouth College, Hanover

What is the relationship between orthographic structure and the spelling process? For example, when expressing the notion BOOK in writing, is the process different for the person who writes *book* versus one who writes *libro* or كتاب or 書 ?[1] These diverse orthographic outcomes are solutions to the same computational problem; each writer converts semantic information into orthographic output. Can we say that they solve this problem in fundamentally the same manner, regardless of the shape of the orthographic output? In other words, is it possible to make general claims about how we spell without acknowledging the idiosyncratic structure of different orthographies?

If we create a model that only speaks to the shared features of different orthographies and fails to acknowledge their idiosyncratic properties, will we have said anything meaningful about the spelling process? After all, the four examples of written words presented above appear to be very different in terms of how they

---

[1] In this chapter stimuli and responses will be reported using the following conventions: spoken words will be in quotes—"dog"; spoken pseudowords will be in IPA—/feyf/; written words will be italicized—*dog*; graphemic representations, i.e. the abstract letter identities that comprise the spelling of a word, will be in brackets—⟨dog⟩; semantic representations will be in capital letters—DOG; and glosses for foreign words will be in parentheses—"cane" (dog).

Handbook of Spelling: Theory, Process and Intervention. Edited by G. D. A. Brown and N. C. Ellis.
©1994 John Wiley & Sons Ltd.

are spatially organized. Upon closer examination we will also discover that the way in which these written words relate to the organization of sound and meaning in the spoken language is very different, one from the other. Can we create a model of the spelling process which, at a general descriptive level, captures the fundamental equivalence of the spelling process across orthographic systems, but also accommodates the specific features of various orthographic structures?

In this chapter we will examine the adequacy of a proposed universal model of the spelling process to accommodate diverse orthographic codes. The examination will proceed as follows. First, we will describe a model of the spelling process and discuss the empirical evidence, particularly the spelling performance of English and Italian brain-damaged patients, that supports not only hypotheses about the general structure of the model, but also specific hypotheses about the nature of representations and operations at each stage of processing of the model. Second, we will ask whether a model of the spelling process based on evidence from alphabetic codes such as English and Italian is suitable for explaining the spelling process in other codes. To do this we will present a brief description of the orthographic structure of Arabic and Mandarin Chinese and a discussion of the possible implications of their structural features for our model of spelling. Finally, we will argue that although the proposed model of the spelling process provides a plausible framework for describing the fundamental procedures by which alphabetic codes are processed, the model requires further elaboration in order to accommodate all of the important features of Arabic. The adequacy of the proposed model for Mandarin Chinese is seriously questioned.

THE GENERAL ARCHITECTURE OF THE SPELLING PROCESS

Researchers have developed models of the spelling process that include a number of relatively autonomous processing subcomponents (e.g. Caramazza *et al.*, 1987; Ellis, 1987), see Figure 14.1. The model makes several basic assumptions. The most important is that spelling normally involves directly activating stored lexical–orthographic representations from semantic input. This assumption is schematically represented in the model by the line from the box labeled ''semantic lexicon'' to the box named ''orthographic output lexicon''. It is assumed that this process is common to diverse tasks such as spontaneous writing, written naming and writing to dictation. Lexical–orthographic representations are assumed to specify the identity and order of the graphemes that comprise the spelling of a word. Spelling of aurally presented *unfamiliar* words is assumed to involve a fundamentally different process: a plausible spelling is assembled by converting the phonological input into a graphemic representation by the application of sub-lexical, phonology-to-orthography conversion procedures. Other important assumptions include the postulation of a graphemic output buffer where graphemic information is temporarily held in preparation for conversion into specific forms for output, and the claim that the output of the phonology-to-orthography conversion process can activate representations in the orthographic output lexicon. Finally, in this model, we do *not* assume that lexical–orthographic representations can be activated directly from the phonological input lexicon, bypassing the semantic system (the so-called third route).

Support for this model principally rests on evidence from neuropsychological studies of the impaired spelling performance of brain-damaged subjects. The differential disruption of spelling for different types of stimuli or tasks (e.g. impaired performance in spelling familiar words in the face of spared ability to spell pseudowords, or impaired performance in written but not oral spelling, and so forth) has been interpreted as support for the hypothesized functional architecture of the spelling process. That evidence can be summarized as follows:

1. The independence of the lexical and the sub-lexical (phonology-to-orthography) procedures has been proposed in order to account for two complementary patterns of spelling performance in brain-damaged patients. In spelling to dictation tasks, some patients present a preserved ability to spell pseudowards but impaired ability to spell words. These patients produce phonologically plausible errors, such as "chair" → *chare*, when they are asked to spell words with ambiguous sound-to-spelling mappings (see, e.g. Baxter & Warrington, 1987; Beauvois & Dérouesné, 1981; Goodman & Caramazza, 1986a; Patterson, 1987). This pattern of performance is hypothesized to result from a functional impairment to the lexical spelling procedures, i.e. damage to the processes by which lexical–semantic representations activate stored graphemic representations in a store of orthographic lexical entries, the orthographic output lexicon.

   Conversely, other patients have been reported who are unable to spell pseudowords (e.g. /feyf/) but are able to spell words, including irregular words such as *yacht* (e.g. Bub & Kertesz, 1982; Roeltgen, Sevuch & Heilman, 1983; Shallice, 1981). This pattern of performance is hypothesized to result from a functional impairment to the sub-lexical spelling procedures, i.e. damage to the processes by which orthographic output is produced in the *absence* of stored (lexical) graphemic representations. This set of procedures is schematically represented in Figure 14.1 by the phonology-to-orthography conversion mechanism.

2. The model of the spelling process in Figure 14.1 schematically represents the hypothesis that lexical–orthographic knowledge is represented independently of lexical–phonological knowledge, in the orthographic output lexicon and the phonological output lexicon, respectively. Each output lexicon receives direct activation from the semantic lexicon. This stands in contrast to the view that orthographic processing is necessarily mediated by phonology (e.g. Luria). Support for the hypothesized independence of the orthographic and phonological output lexicons comes from the case studies of patients who demonstrate normal comprehension of single words (presumably indicating intact semantics) yet produce semantic errors in only *one* modality of output, either spoken or written.

   Patients have been reported who make semantic errors (e.g. they might produce the response *table* instead of *chair*) in *spelling* tasks, but make no semantic errors in corresponding *oral* production tasks. Conversely, other patients produce semantic errors in oral reading and naming tasks, but not in spelling (Caramazza & Hillis, 1991). The dissociation in the production of semantic errors in oral versus written output in these patients restricts the locus of damage to independent components of processing in which lexical forms (either phonological or graphemic)

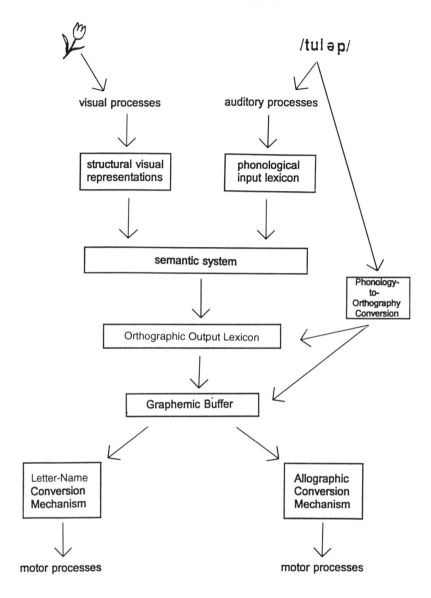

FIGURE 14.1   Schematic representation of a model of the spelling process.

are activated for output. That is, the observed dissociation in performance can only be accounted for by a model of the spelling process in which the orthographic output lexicon and the phonological output lexicon are independent.

3. The performance of several well-studied dysgraphic patients has been used to support the existence of a graphemic buffer in the spelling process (e.g. Caramazza *et al.*, 1987; Hillis & Caramazza, 1989; Posteraro, Zinelli & Mazzuchi, 1988). The pattern of spelling performance produced by these patients is characterized by

qualitatively and quantitatively similar errors in all spelling tasks, regardless of the type of stimulus (words or pseudowords), modality of input (written naming to pictures or writing to dictation) or modality of output (written or oral spelling). In addition, spelling performance is only affected by graphemic factors such as stimulus letter length, and all errors can be described in wholly graphemic terms without appeal to factors such as lexical status or phonological or semantic properties. It is difficult to account for this pattern of spelling performance without postulating a deficit to a common level of processing, such as the graphemic buffer, which is implicated in processing all types of stimuli in all spelling tasks.

4. Processes for written versus oral spelling diverge beyond the graphemic output buffer. The allographic conversion mechanism is responsible for selecting the specific visuo-spatial form of each grapheme, for example selecting ⟨b⟩ → *B* versus ⟨b⟩ → *b*. The letter-name conversion mechanism is responsible for selecting the name associated with each abstract grapheme, for example ⟨b⟩ → "be"; ⟨k⟩ → "kay". The independence of the allographic conversion mechanism and the letter-name conversion mechanism has been proposed to account for the dissociation of written and oral spelling performance in brain-damaged patients (Goodman & Caramazza, 1986b; Kinsbourne & Rosenfield, 1965; Kinsbourne & Warrington, 1965). Whereas some patients produce spelling errors such as "grief" → *griel*; "borrow" → *gorrow* on tasks of written spelling (written naming of pictures and writing to dictation) but no errors on oral spelling tasks, other patients produce the complementary pattern of errors, for example they might orally spell "G""R""I""E""L" for "grief", but show no difficulty whatever in writing the very same words. This dissociation can only be accounted for by a model of spelling in which independent, peripheral components of processing are responsible for oral versus written spelling output.[2]

THE NATURE OF REPRESENTATIONS AND OPERATIONS INVOLVED IN THE SPELLING PROCESS

Thus far we have briefly reviewed some of the evidence in support of the general architecture of the spelling process. That is, the focus has been on the major components of processing which are assumed to comprise the spelling system. Although these claims are not trivial—they do make substantive, controversial claims (e.g. the assumption of independent processes in spelling familiar and unfamiliar words)—they are nonetheless fairly general and relatively unconstrained (e.g. the nature of the content of the orthographic output lexicon is left unspecified). The tendency of most work in cognitive psychology and neuropsychology to remain at this general level of analysis has rightly been criticized (e.g. Rapp & Caramazza, 1992; Seidenberg, 1988). Can we say anything more detailed about the representations and the operations implicated in the spelling process? A more complete understanding of the spelling process requires answers to at least, but not only, the following questions:

---

[2]For a discussion of more peripheral mechanisms in spelling, see Margolin (1984) and Ellis (1987).

1. What is the nature of the knowledge represented in the orthographic output lexicon?
2. How is this information activated and processed?
3. How does the phonology-to-orthography conversion mechanism work?

In this section of the chapter we will present several hypotheses, and the evidence used to support them, which have been offered as partial answers to these questions. Because of space limitations we will focus on issues of graphemic representation. However, we will begin with a brief summary of our assumptions regarding the manner of activation of these graphemic representations.

Semantic input to the orthographic output lexicon necessarily activates, in parallel, multiple orthographic entries in a set defined by their semantic relatedness. The performance of dysgraphic patients who produce semantic errors such as "dollar" → *money*, despite demonstrated preservation of lexical–semantic representations, has been offered to support this assumption (Caramazza & Hillis, 1991). The production of semantically (as opposed to formally) related errors by these patients is hypothesized to result from the inappropriate, supra-threshold activation of a particular orthographic lexical representation (in the example, ⟨money⟩) from among a set of semantically related exemplars activated by the lexical–semantic representation (DOLLAR, in the above example).

What sort of information is encoded in an orthographic lexical representation? Minimally this information must include the identity and order of graphemes in the sequence that comprises the lexical entry. In the past it has been argued that other information in addition to this strictly graphemic knowledge is also part of the orthographic representation. Although it is not the focus of the current chapter, there is compelling evidence for the representation of grammatical class membership and morphological structure within orthographic lexical representations (for a discussion of the evidence for the representation of knowledge regarding grammatical class, see Caramazza & Hillis, 1991; for a discussion of the representation of morphological knowledge, see Badecker, Hillis & Caramazza, 1990). We now turn to hypotheses regarding the nature of graphemic representations.

Hypothesis 1: Graphemic Representations are Multi-Dimensional Objects

We have presented evidence that there is a level of processing in writing which involves computing a graphemic representation that specifies, at least, the identity and order of the abstract letter identities that comprise a word. Is this the only information represented at this level of processing? Evidence from the performance of a dysgraphic subject, LB, suggests that we must assume a considerably richer structure for graphemic representations (Caramazza & Miceli, 1989, 1990; see also Cubelli, 1991; McCloskey *et al.*, in press; Tainturier & Caramazza, in press, for similar conclusions with other patients).

LB's errors consisted of substitutions, deletions, additions and transpositions of letters. Thus, for example, he spelled "colore" as *conore*, "aperto" as *apeto*, "taglio" as *tatglio*, and "camera" as *carema*. He made qualitatively similar errors in oral and written spelling in both dictation and naming tasks. He also made the same types of errors in delayed but not immediate copy, and he made qualitatively similar errors to words and pseudowords. Because error performance was unaffected by type of task or by type of stimulus (word vs pseudoword), the most probable locus of damage was considered to be the graphemic buffer—the level at which grapheme representations are computed in all types of tasks involving oral or written spelling. If we assume that these errors are the product of LB's reliance on an impaired graphemic buffer, then an analysis of the characteristics of these errors ought to reveal properties of the graphemic representations processed in the buffer.

If the only structure represented at this level of the spelling process were to consist of information about letter identities and their order (say, the ordered string of graphemes ⟨C⟩⟨H⟩⟨A⟩⟨I⟩⟨R⟩ for the word "chair"), then errors should be explicable by appeal to these two factors alone. However, LB's performance was subject to constraints that are not explicable in terms of only these two features of graphemic representations.

One constraint on LB's spelling errors concerned the pattern of substitution errors: these errors virtually always involved substituting a consonant for a consonant or a vowel for a vowel, as can be seen in Table 14.1. Furthermore, LB's transposition errors always occurred either between consonants or between vowels (e.g. "stadio" → sdatio), but not between a consonant and a vowel (e.g. "strano" −/→ sartno). If the only information in graphemic representations consisted of letter identities, then we would have expected substitution and transposition errors to be unaffected by the consonant/vowel (CV) value of the letter identities (e.g. we would have expected, everything else being equal, the probability of substituting a consonant for a vowel to be the same as the probability of substituting a consonant for a consonant). However, as noted, the CV value of grapheme completely determined the type of substitution and transposition errors produced by LB. This pattern of performance suggests that the patient had access to information about the consonant/vowel status of the specific graphemes he was unable to produce correctly. In other words, information about the identity of graphemes is independent of their CV value (for additional evidence to support this conclusion see Cubelli, 1991).

Another constraint on LB's performance concerned deletion errors. Errors virtually only occurred for consonant or vowel clusters; singleton consonants or singleton vowels were not deleted, as can be seen in Table 14.2.

Thus, for example, LB produces many errors such as "nostro" → nosro, but no errors such as "denaro" → denro. This constraint on deletion errors did not result from the fact that the latter type of error might more frequently violate phonotactic constraints (i.e. constraints on pronounceability). LB produced many errors that violated phonotactic constraints of Italian (e.g. "crollo" → rcollo, where the

TABLE 14.1 LB's distribution of substitution errors in spelling six-letter words.

Stimulus	Response	
	Consonant	Vowel
Consonant	299	0
Vowel	2	219

TABLE 14.2   LB's deletion errors for letters in consonant and vowel clusters and for consonant and vowel singletons.

	Stimulus type	
	CC or VV cluster	C or V singleton
No. of deletion errors		
Consonant	288	1
Vowel	21	1

sequence *rc* is not a legal syllable–initial cluster in Italian). Instead, it would seem that the constraint of LB's performance concerned whether the resulting letter string respected possible CV structures of Italian, independent of their phonological value (pronounceability). Once again, if the only information represented at the grapheme level were to consist of the identity and order of letter identities, then we would have expected the probability of deletion errors to be independent of the CV structure of the target response. However, this was not the case—the probability of a deletion error was determined by the CV structure of the target response. Thus, a plausible implication of this result is that graphemic representations specify graphosyllabic information—information about possible grapheme sequences in the language.

Finally, LB's performance with geminates (double consonants) was also subject to strict constraints. Substitutions almost invariably involved both members of a geminate cluster (e.g. "sorella" → *soretta*); transpositions always involved both members of a geminate cluster ("sorella" → *solerra*, and not "sorella"-/ → *solerla*); geminate duplications only occurred in the context of another geminate in the word (e.g. "fritto" → *frritto*); and gemination could be shifted to another consonant in the word ("sorella" → *sorrela*). If geminate consonants were to be represented as two independent letter identities, then we would have expected, for example, that individual graphemes could enter in exchange errors (e.g. "sorella" → *solerla*) or that the probability of substituting one of the two letters in a geminate cluster would be independent of the probability of substituting the other letter in the cluster, as would be the case for any other consonant cluster (e.g. *tr*). As indicated, however, the results clearly disconfirmed the latter hypothesis—errors on geminates behaved differently from errors on other types of consonant clusters. A plausible inference about the nature of graphemic structure that is supported by the reported results is that geminates are represented by a single grapheme with independent information about their number. This assumption allows us to explain the existence of gemination shift errors ("sorella" → *sorrela*), the production of geminate errors only in words already containing a geminate ("fritto" → *frritto*), the double substitution errors in geminate clusters ("sorella" → *soretta*) and the transposition of geminate clusters ("sorella" → *solerra*). The existence of these errors would remain unexplained on the assumption that geminates are represented as two independent letter identities.

The strong constraints on the distribution of spelling errors observed for LB suggest that graphemic representations specify considerably more structure than just information about the identity and order of graphemes. Specifically, the results reviewed here allow the conclusion that graphemic representations constitute

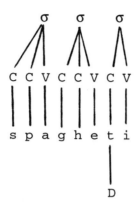

FIGURE 14.2   Schematic representation of the orthographic structure of the word *spaghetti*.

multi-dimensional objects specifying indepenent types of orthographic information. Thus, (1) the constraints on errors with geminate consonants suggest that the identity of graphemes is specified independently of information about their quantity; (2) the constraints on substitution errors suggest that information about the consonant/vowel status of graphemes is specified independently of their identity; and (3) the constraints on deletion errors suggest that graphemic representations specify graphosyllabic structure. These hypotheses are shown schematically in Figure 14.2. In this figure the identity/quantity distinction is captured by the independent specification of the number (D) from the identity of a grapheme (t); the independence of the CV status of a grapheme is captured by representing the two types of information on separate tiers; and the orthographic structure is captured also by representing this information on a separate level.

Hypothesis 2: Orthographic Representations are Spatially Organized Abstract Graphemic Entities

How is the order of graphemes represented in a given lexical entry in the orthographic output lexicon? Evidence from neglect patients (Baxter & Warrington, 1983; Caramazza & Hillis, 1990; Hillis & Caramazza, 1989) supports the claim that order information in orthographic representations is "spatial" rather than ordinal. The spelling performance of NG will serve to illustrate the sort of evidence used to support this claim (Caramazza & Hillis, 1990).

NG originally presented with unilateral neglect, i.e. she had a striking perceptual disorder that disproportionately affected a spatially defined part of visually presented objects. Although she demonstrated normal spoken language, eye movements and visual fields, she had difficulty processing the right side of objects and written words. Her spelling performance was characterized by errors on the right end of words, for example "floor" → *floore*; "unit" → *unite*; "sneeze" → *sneed*; "cloud" → *clou*. This right neglect effect is quite dramatic, as can be seen in Table 14.3(a); NG did not

TABLE 14.3(a)   Rate of spelling errors at each position of left aligned words for NG.

Length in letters	Position in word						
	1	2	3	4	5	6	7
				Left aligned			
4	0	2	13	25			
5	0	0	6	20	29		
6	0	0	5	15	26	39	
7	0	0	3	5	15	28	51

TABLE 14.3(b)   Rate of spelling errors at each position of centered words for NG.

Length in letters	Position in word						
	1	2	3	4	5	6	7
				Word center			
				X			
4			0	2	13	25	
5		0	0	6	20	29	
6		0	0	5	15	26	39
7	0	0	3	5	15	28	51

produce errors in the initial (leftmost) letters of words. When NG's spelling performance for individual positions in a word is shown as a function of their distance from the center of the word, as in Table 14.3(b), it becomes apparent that NG produced very few errors on the *left half* of words, regardless of the length of the word. The implication of this finding is that the level of orthographic representation that is damaged in patient NG is one at which the representation is word (or grapheme string) centered.

Further evidence in support of the conclusion that the impairment in NG concerned a word-centered, graphemic representation was provided by the fact that NG produced errors on the right end of words in tasks of written and oral spelling, delayed copying, and in backwards spelling, for example when asked to spell "church" backwards NG produced "R"'"U"'"H"'"C" (*chur*). Table 14.4 presents the distribution of errors in various spelling tasks as a function of letter position. As can be seen in this table, NG made spelling errors only at the end of the word, irrespective of the type of output (spoken or written) or the order of orthographic presentation (forward or backward).

TABLE 14.4   Distribution of errors as a function of letter position for NG, given in % of total errors.

Task	Letter position in six-letter words					
	1	2	3	4	5	6
Written spelling	0	0	6	19	31	46
Oral spelling	0	1	2	7	29	60
Backward spelling	0	0	1	12	34	53
Delayed copying	0	1	1	13	28	57

These results require that we assume that in the course of spelling a word there is a level of processing at which word-centered graphemic representations are computed. These representations must be independent of the perceived visuo-spatial format of the target response since spelling performance was the same in written and oral spelling. The sequential order of the component graphemes of this representation must be essentially spatial rather than ordinal since performance was the same for forward and backward spelling (see Caramazza & Hillis, 1990; Hillis & Caramazza, 1989, for discussion of this issue).

Hypothesis 3: The Mechanism for Conversion of Phonology to Orthography Operates over Units Larger than the Single Letter

Thus far evidence has been presented to support hypotheses regarding the nature of the representations and operations involved in spelling familiar words. What can be said about the sub-lexical procedures, i.e. the procedures by which unfamiliar words are spelled? Specifically, what is the nature of the phonology-to-orthography conversion mechanism? A review of the evidence from a dysgraphic patient, JG, who presented with disproportionate difficulty in spelling words versus pseudowords, will serve to illuminate several characteristics of this mechanism (Goodman & Caramazza, 1986a).

JG's spelling performance was characterized by the production of phonologically plausible errors. When unable to retrieve lexical–orthographic representations for spelling, JG produced a pronounceable, but unattested, orthographic form (e.g. "coarse" → *korse*; "jealous" → *jellis*; "senate" → *cenit*). If we assume that these errors are the product of JG's reliance on the phonology-to-orthography conversion mechanism, then an analysis of the characteristics of these errors ought to reveal properties of the process that produced them.

An analysis of the error "senate" → *cenit* will serve as an example. What are the characteristics of the response *cenit* that make it a plausible, albeit incorrect, spelling of the word "senate"? Simply put, the letters C, E, N, I, T combine to make the sound /sɛnɪt/, just as do the letters S, E, N, A, T, E in the word *senate*. Thus, the letter C in the response was selected because it can make the sound /s/. But the letter S also makes the sound /s/; how did JG select to convert the sound /s/ into C rather than S?

Goodman and Caramazza observed that JG's selection of one grapheme option from among a set of options was sensitive to the frequency of occurrence of that phoneme-to-grapheme mapping in the language. Table 14.5 illustrates this fact by presenting a comparison of the distribution of grapheme-to-phoneme correspondences in JG's responses compared to the distribution of these correspondences in the language, as documented by Hanna *et al.* (1966). The table is divided into intial, medial and final syllable position. Within each of these three positions one can compare the second column (% JG), the percentage of times JG selected a particular letter to refer to a given sound (in a word she misspelled), to the third column (% NM), the number of times that letter is used in the written language to refer to that given sound, according to Hanna *et al.*'s frequency count. The percentages for columns 2 and 3 are strikingly similar. The implication of this is that JG does not always

TABLE 14.5   Distributions for the phoneme /s/; JG versus the norms.

	Initial			Syllable position Medial			Final		
	#times* JG	%† JG	% NM‡	#times JG	% JG	% NM	#times JG	% JG	% NM
S	90	77.6	77.8	25	100.00	96.9	64	61.0	62.3
C	23	19.8	15.9		0.0	2.6	36	34.3	20.3
SS	2	1.7	2.1		0.0	0.5	5	4.8	14.5
SC	1	0.1	1.1					0.0	1.5
X		0.0	2.3						
ST								0.0	0.3
PS		0.0	0.6						
Z		0.0	0.1					0.0	0.2
SW		0.0	0.1						
SCH		0.0	0.1						

*Raw scores for the selection of particular graphemic options.
†Percentage that each graphemic option was chosen relative to all other possible mapping options with the respective within-syllable position (column percentages thus add up to 100%).
‡NM, norms, taken from Hanna *et al.* (1966, p. 79).

produce the most frequent phoneme-to-grapheme mapping in the language, but rather she produces responses in proportion to their attested occurrence in the language.

In addition, the table demonstrates that the probability with which a phoneme–grapheme correspondence is produced is not independent of its position in a word. For example, JG produced the letter S for the sound /s/ in syllable initial position 77.6% of the time, whereas she produced S for /s/ in syllable medial position 100% of the time. JG's selection of the /s/ → S correspondence reflects the frequency of occurrence of that particular phonology-to-orthography correspondence in syllable initial versus syllable medial position in the language. The implication of these results is that JG's spelling production was sensitive to orthographic context within the syllable. Further confirmation of the context-sensitive nature of the conversion procedure is given in Table 14.6. This table shows the distribution of the use of letters C and S for /s/ before vowels. JG respected the value of the sound of C when followed by various vowels; for example, when asked to write the word "senate" to dictation she wrote *cenate*, because C before E can sound like /s/, but would not write *curf* for "surf" because C before U does not have the sound /s/. Only

TABLE 14.6   Distribution of the use of the letters C and S for /s/ before vowels by JG.

	C $N = 23$	S $N = 56$
A	0	18
E	18	20
I	2	8
O	0	5
U	1	3
Y	2	2

once did JG select an illegal "C + vowel" combination, producing C in front of U ("circle" → *curcle*).

The implication of these results is that either the conversion procedure is relying on a unit larger than one grapheme (perhaps a syllable) or it is a context-sensitive system.

Thus far we have reviewed the neuropsychological evidence that supports the hypothesized general architecture of the spelling process as it is schematically represented in Figure 14.1. In addition, hypotheses about the orthographic representations and the operations computed within the processing subcomponents of this model have been presented. The evidence reviewed thus far has drawn from the performance of brain-damaged patients who premorbidly spoke/read/wrote an alphabetic language, either English or Italian. If the proposed model of the spelling process is in fact a universal model of the spelling process, rather than simply a model of the spelling process in English and Italian, then it should account for the production of written output in a variety of orthographic codes.

In the following sections we will briefly present features of two disparate orthographic codes, Arabic and Mandarin Chinese, and assess the possible implications of their orthographic features for the model of the spelling process presented in the preceding pages.

ARABIC

Background Information

Modern Standard Arabic, the written form of the principal language spoken in the Arab world, is a Semitic language written in connected, alphabetic script from right to left on a horizontal axis (see Ferguson, 1972, for a discussion of the relationship between spoken and written language in Arabic). Space limitations preclude us from discussing in detail interesting features of the orthographic structure of Arabic that are not strictly graphemic, for example, the morphological composition of Arabic words. One should note, however, the fact that Arabic word formation is accomplished through complex derivational and inflectional affixation. A consequence of these morphological processes is that there is a high correlation between semantic and formal (orthographic and phonological) similarity among words in the Arabic lexicon. Table 14.7(a) provides examples of words derived from the root كتب [KTB] WRITING.[3] The root of an Arabic word pertains to some semantic concept, such as WRITING; all words derived from that root will be semantically and formally related to the root, and hence to each other. Note that the derivational and inflectional affixes in Tables 14.7(a) and 14.7(b) include prefixes, infixes and suffixes of both consonants and vowels.

---

[3]Phonology-to-orthography is unambiguous in Modern Standard Arabic. However, some phonemic contrasts in Modern Standard Arabic have disappeared in colloquial dialects of Arabic. Speakers of colloquial Arabic may be influenced by their spoken language when asked to write Modern Standard Arabic words. For example, the phonemic contrast between /ẓ/ and /z/ has disappeared in Egyptian colloquial Arabic. Therefore the Standard word منظر [MNẒR] /manẓar/ (view) is pronounced as /manzar/—as if it were writen as منزر [MNZR]—by Egyptians. The loss of this phonemic contrast may influence Egyptian writers of Arabic to confuse the letters ظ /ẓ/ and ز /z/ in spelling tasks.

TABLE 14.7(a)   Examples of words derived from the root كتب [KTB] WRITING.

	Arabic	Roman transcription	IPA transcription	Gloss
1	كتب	KTB	/kataba/	he wrote
2	يكتب	YKTB	/yiktub/	he writes
3	مكتوب	MKTWB	/maktuub/	written
4	كتابة	KTAB "bound T"	/kitaabah/	writing
5	مكتب	MKTB	/maktab/	office
6	كتاب	KTAB	/kitaab/	book
7	مكتبة	MKTB "bound T"	/maktabah/	library
8	كتاب	KTAB	/kuttaab/	Qura'anic School
9	كاتب	KATB	/kaatib/	writer

TABLE 14.7(b)   Examples of words from the root كتب [KTB] WRITING with various inflectional affixes.

10	تكتب	TKTB	/taktub/	she writes
11	تكتبي	TKTBY	/taktubiy/	you (feminine, singular) write
12	اكتب	AKTB	/ʔaktubu/	I write
13	يكتبون	YKTBWN	/taktubunna/	they (masculine, plural) write
14	نكتب	NKTB	/naktubu/	we write
15	كتبت	KTBT	/katabat/	she wrote

Our consideration of the strictly graphemic features of orthographic representations will focus on two characteristics of this code: (1) Arabic script is composed of two sorts of graphemes—letters and diacritics; (2) each letter of Arabic has several context-determined allographic forms. These features are described in more detail below.

1. *Arabic script is composed of two sorts of graphemes—letters and diacritics.* A word in Arabic is typically written as a sequence of letters. The 28 letters of the Arabic alphabet represent the 28 phonemic consonants of Modern Standard Arabic. Three of these letters, ي , و and ا (Y, W and A, respectively) are also used to represent the three long vowels of Arabic, /ii/, /uu/ and /aa/. The other three phonemic vowels, /i/, /u/ and /a/, are not written in typical texts (newspapers, novels, textbooks). They may be marked with optional diacritics in special texts such as children's books and the *Koran*. Table 14.8 presents pairs of words written in marked (with diacritics) and unmarked (without diacritics) form.

TABLE 14.8   Arabic words with and without diacritics.

Phonology	Gloss	With diacritics	Without diacritics
maghuud	effort	مَجْهُودٌ	مجهود
tawfiiq	success	تَوْفِيقٌ	توفيق
kuttaab	Qura'anic school	كُتَّابٌ	كتاب

The examples of marked words in Table 14.8 contain a variety of diacritics: the fatha, ´ , above a letter indicates that the vowel /a/ follows it; the kasra, ﹼ , indicates the vowel /i/; the dumma, ﹾ , indicates the vowel /u/. Diacritics can also indicate morphological and phonological features in addition to short vowels. For example, item number 3 in Table 14.8 contains a shadda with fatha, ﹽ , which indicates that the letter below this mark (the letter ﺕ [T] should be geminated and followed by the vowel /a/. The sukuun ﹾ indicates silence—no vowel follows the marked consonant. Note that the long vowels /uu/, /ii/ and /aa/ are written as letters preceded by a diacritic, whereas the short vowels /u/, /i/ and /a/ are indicated simply by diacritics.

Although the dual grapheme nature of Arabic script is often presented as a contrast between consonants and vowels, it is more accurate to describe the contrast as one between letters and diacritics. As the examples in Table 14.8 demonstrate, letters may refer to consonants and vowels and diacritics may refer to vowels and to phenomena such as consonant gemination and "silence".

2. *Each letter of Arabic has several context-determined allographic forms.* Modern Standard Arabic is written in connected script on a horizontal axis from right to left. Breaks in the script indicate either (a) interword boundaries or (b) spaces caused by particular "non-connecting letters" that lack ligatures to following letters. This second sort of break in the script is smaller than the interword break. These "non-connecting letters" (ا د ذ ر ز ظ ط and و) have only one allographic form, i.e. they are always written in the same manner regardless of their position in a word or of their immediate orthographic context. When they are preceded by another letter they are connected to it by a small ligature. However, they never connect to following letters. See for example, the letter ر in the word شرح [ʃRḤ] /ʃaḥra/ (he explained).

The other 20 letters of the alphabet have two to four allographic forms. These allographs are referred to as having initial, medial, final or isolated form. The letter ه [H] also has a special final form to indicate feminine words: ة called "bound t". Table 14.9 presents several examples of allographs.

TABLE 14.9   Allographic forms of the letters [R], [X], [S] and [H].

	Roman	Isolated	Final	Medial	Initial
All allographs equivalent	[R]	ر	ر	ر	ر
Two distinct allographs	[X]	ح	ح	ح	ح
Four distinct allographs	[H]	ه	ه / ة	ﻬ	ﻫ

TABLE 14.10 Allographs of the letter ه [H] /h/.

Arabic word	Roman transliteration	Gloss	Description of allograph
هنا	HNA	here	Initial form because it is word initial
مشهد	MʃHD	scene	Medial form because it is word medial and preceded by a connecting letter
طاهر	ṬAHR	visible	Initial form because although it is word medial, it is preceded by a "non-connecting letter"
منه	MNH	with him	Final form because it is word final
رحلة	RḤA "bound T"	journey	Final form, "bound T" because it is word final and a feminine word
دعوة	DʕW "bound T"	invitation	Isolated form, "bound T" because it is in word final position and is preceded by a "non-connecting" letter

The appropriate allograph is determined by the letter's position in a word and by the letter that immediately precedes the target letter. Consider the words in Table 14.10, where the letter ه [H] is written in various allographic forms.

Implications for the General Architecture of the Spelling Process

It is necessary to examine the adequacy of the proposed model of the spelling process for Arabic at two levels. First, one must assess whether the general architecture of the model is consistent with the computational requirements for processing Arabic orthography. Second, one must assess whether the specific hypotheses regarding the nature of orthographic representations and operations implicated in the various subcomponents of the spelling process can account for the features of Arabic orthography. This assessment will necessarily focus on computational adequacy because we are not familiar with experimental evidence that is relevant to the claims offered here.

The model of the spelling process presented thus far is not obviously inadequate to describe the manner in which orthographic output is generated in Arabic. Arabic words, like words in English and Italian, contain sub-lexical and lexical information that could plausibly be processed by two relatively independent sets of procedures.

The lexical procedures in Arabic would include the activation of semantic knowledge (in the semantic lexicon) which then activates in parallel a set of orthographic representations held in a store of graphemic, lexical entries (the orthographic output lexicon). Arabic, like English and Italian, is an alphabetic language and therefore each graphemic entry in the lexicon comprises a set of graphemes. Given that an Arabic word must be spelled in individual grapheme units, it appears computationally necessary that the orthographic entry with the most activation be held in a short-term memory store (the graphemic output buffer) while each grapheme is processed serially. Because Arabic graphemes can be written in a variety of styles or can be named aloud in oral spelling, it seems plausible that a model of the spelling process diverges after the graphemic buffer to accommodate the processing of these output formats (the allographic conversion mechanism and the letter-name conversion mechanism).

The existence of sub-lexical procedures for the processing of spelling in Arabic seems plausible. Arabic writers are able to produce orthographic output for any given phonological input, regardless of its word or pseudoword status. The correspondence of phonology-to-orthography in Arabic is relatively transparent; a given sound in Arabic can be written only one way. The fact that there are many homographs in unmarked Arabic, i.e. words that have different pronunciations and meanings but are spelled in the same way in unmarked texts, does not present a particular challenge to the sub-lexical procedures of the spelling process at this level of analysis.[4]

The model of the spelling process schematically represented in Figure 14.1 appears to be adequate, at least at the level of the general architecture, to accommodate the general computational requirements of producing Arabic orthographic output. This could, of course, be because of the superficial nature of the claims made by this model, rather than the aptness of these claims for Arabic. For the moment we will put these general claims aside and assess the adequacy of the hypotheses regarding specific claims about representations and operations within the processing subcomponents that comprise the model in light of the features of Arabic reviewed in the above section.

The Structure of Orthographic Representations in Arabic

The claim has been made that orthographic representations are complex, multi-dimensional entities consisting of information regarding graphemic identity, graphemic quantity, consonant/vowel status and graphosyllabic structure. Arabic orthography includes each of these features. However, the representation of each of these features may not be identical to the representation of these features in English and Italian. We will consider the distinction between grapheme identity and consonant/vowel status, and the distinction between grapheme quantity and identity.

The grapheme identity tier

Consider the example given in Table 14.11 of the words كتاب [KTAB] /kitaab/ (book) and كتب [KTB] /kataba/ (he wrote), written in marked and unmarked form.[5] In the column labeled "Marked", the diacritics are transliterated into lower-case Roman letters to clarify their position in the orthographic sequence of

---

[4]Homography has obvious implications for the reading process in a given written word with multiple readings. Note that these multiple readings generally do not arise from ambiguity in the orthography-to-phonology correspondence, but rather from the ambiguity of Arabic. How is it that Arabic readers arrive at a particular reading for *unwritten* elements when the word is written in unmarked form? For a discussion of these issues in reading another semitic language, Hebrew, see Bentin, Bargai and Katz (1984) and Frost and Bentin (1992).

[5]For ease of exposition a Roman transliteration of the Arabic word will be used; capital letters will represent graphemes written as letters in orthographic output, lower-case letters will represent graphemes that may or may not be written as diacritics in orthographic output.

TABLE 14.11   Specification of grapheme identities in marked and unmarked words.

	Marked	Unmarked
Arabic letters = consonants and vowels; diacritics = vowels and sukuun	كِتَابْ	كتاب
Roman transliteration	KiTaAB #	KTAB
Abstract representation	KiTaAB # or KTAB	
Arabic letters = consonants; diacritics = vowels	كَتَبَ	كتب
Roman transliteration	KaTaBa	KTB
Abstract representation	KaTaBa or KTB	

a, fatha; i, kasra; #, sukuun.

a marked word; letters are transliterated as capital Roman letters. In the column labeled "Unmarked", only the letters have been transliterated into capital Roman letters. The important question for understanding the spelling process in Arabic is, how are these letters and diacritics specified on the grapheme identity level of orthographic representations? Are the identities of letters ⟨K⟩, ⟨T⟩, ⟨B⟩ and ⟨A⟩, as well as the identities of diacritics ⟨a⟩, ⟨i⟩ and ⟨#⟩, represented at this level? One might suggest that since diacritics are only optionally produced as orthographic output, they do not have the same status on the grapheme identity tier of the orthographic representation as do "real" letters. But it is precisely because these diacritics *can* be produced in orthographic output that they must be accounted for at *some* level of representation within the spelling process.

There are a number of possible accounts:

Hypothesis 1. The orthographic lexicon represents each word redundantly, once with diacritics and once without, for example /kataba/ → ⟨KTB⟩ and ⟨KaTaBa⟩.

Hypothesis 2. Stored orthographic representations only encode information about graphemes that correspond to written letters. Diacritics may, if desired, be added to the letter sequences at a separate, later stage of the spelling process and this set of procedures is *independent* of the lexical procedures, for example /kataba/ → ⟨KTB⟩ + ⟨a⟩, ⟨a⟩, ⟨a⟩.

Hypothesis 3. The full representation—letters and diacritics—is specified in an equivalent manner, regardless of whether they refer to letters or diacritics, for example /kataba/ → ⟨KaTaBa⟩. Such a formulation of the story would require that a later stage in the spelling process decides which parts of the representation are to be encoded into a visuo-spatial (or naming) pattern for output. We will discuss this more fully below when considering the role of the allographic conversion mechanism.

At present we have no empirical evidence to favor any of these three hypotheses, in part because the computational problem encountered in Arabic is different from any problem thus far encountered in the study of the spelling process in English and Italian. In English and Italian the investigation of orthographic structure focused on the interaction between the grapheme identity tier and other tiers such as quantity and consonant/vowel tiers, proceeding on the most obvious assumptions regarding the representation of grapheme identity. In Arabic it is not obvious which graphemes are specified on the grapheme identity tier of orthographic representations. If the first hypothesis is correct and Arabic is stored in two lexicons, a marked and an unmarked one, much in the same way perhaps as a bilingual speaker might have an English and an Italian lexicon, then the processing implications are not unique to Arabic. If either hypothesis 2 or 3 is correct, then we will have to solve unique computational problems: for the second hypothesis we will have to determine how a secondary procedure for adding diacritics is accomplished; for the third hypothesis we must determine how disparate abstract graphemes are parsed and converted into different formats for output.

The hypotheses offered in response to these computational problems will have consequences for the other levels of representation. For example, an account which selects either the first or third hypothesis, in which diacritics are specified in orthographic representations, has processing implications for the proposed quantity tier of representation which are different from the processing implications of hypothesis 2. We will examine these implications in more detail below.

The quantity tier

A level of representation is proposed where information regarding the quantity of grapheme identities in a given orthographic representation is encoded. Thus far the hypothesis has been offered to account only for adjacent repeated letters in Italian (e.g. *fatto, donna*) and English (e.g. *little, tunnel*) (Caramazza & Miceli, 1990; McCloskey *et al.*, in press; Tainturier & Caramazza, in press). The claim has not extended to account for non-adjacent repeated letters (e.g. the Ts in *tent*).

If one accepts the preceding analysis of the representation of grapheme identity in Arabic, in which letters and diacritics are specified in the orthographic representation (hypotheses 1 and 3), then Arabic *never* has adjacent identical abstract grapheme identities. A diacritic always intervenes between identical letters. The written output, however, does include double and triple identical letter sequences. The examples in Table 14.12 illustrate this point. The unmarked word تبّع is written with three adjacent [T]s; this can be transcribed as [TTTBʕ]; the three adjacent and identical [T]s appear to be like adjacent identical letters in English and Italian. However,

TABLE 14.12   Examples of single, double and triple identical letter sequences.

	1	2	3
IPA	tabaʕa	tatabaʕa	tatatabaʕa
Arabic, marked	تَبَّع	تَتَبَّع	تَتَتَبَّع
Arabic, unmarked	تبّع	تتبّع	تتتبّع
Abstract representation, hypotheses 1 and 3	TaBaʕa	TaTaBaʕa	TaTaTaBaʕa
Abstract representation, hypothesis 2	TBʕ	TBʕ	TBʕ

TABLE 14.13   The abstract representation of Shadda and Sukuun.

Gloss	Qura'anic school
IPA	k u t t a a b
Arabic (marked)	كُتَّاب
Abstract representation	C V C ? V V C ?
	K u T * a A B #

*shadda, indicates gemination.
#sukuun, indicates silence.

if we follow the dictates of hypothesis 1 or 3, the abstract representation of this orthographic string is ⟨TaTaTaBaʕa⟩, in which the three graphemes ⟨T⟩ are not adjacent, and therefore are not accounted for by the hypothesis of the quantity tier as it is currently formulated. If, instead, one prefers hypothesis 2, in which the diacritics are not specified in the orthographic representation in the orthographic output lexicon, then multiple, identical grapheme identities *are* adjacent, and may be represented in a manner similar to the proposed representation of such grapheme sequences in English and Italian. This point is also illustrated in Table 14.12 in the cells labeled "Abstract representation, hypothesis 2".

Neuropsychological evidence supports the hypothesis of the representation of quantity information independently of grapheme information for adjacent identical letters in English and Italian words. The adequacy of this hypothesis for Arabic orthography depends on our claims about the nature of the representation of grapheme (letter and diacritic) identities, and the determination of the level of representation at which the notion of adjacency is relevant, at the level of the abstract orthographic representation or at the level of actual orthographic output.[6]

The consonant/vowel tier

The claim that consonant/vowel status is represented independently of grapheme identity is not obviously inadequate to describe Arabic. This representational tier is added schematically in Table 14.13.

The original hypothesis claims that each grapheme identity is designated as either a consonant or a vowel. However, if one accepts the notion that all graphemes, regardless of their physical instantiation as letters or diacritics, are part of the orthographic representation, then a challenge is posed by the diacritics sukuun ° and shadda ّ . Remember that sukuun signifies silence—a letter marked with this

---

[6]The representation of morphological information in Arabic will have important consequences for the determination of which level of representation is relevant for the notion of adjacency. Many multiple, adjacent identical letters, such as the example تَتَبَّع [TTTBʕ], are composed of polymorphemic affixes. To the extent that morphology is represented in a decomposed form in the lexicon or individual morphemes comprising a polymorphemic word are represented on independent tiers, graphemes that are ultimately adjacent in orthographic output may be non-adjacent at the level of abstract representation. For a discussion of a multi-dimensional representation of morphology in spoken Arabic see McCarthy (1981).

TABLE 14.14   The role of the ACM in Arabic.

	Marked	Unmarked
Arabic	كَتَبَ	كتب
Roman transliteration	KaTaBa	KTB
Abstract representation, hypothesis 3	KaTaBa	KaTaBa
Allographic conversion mechanism	كَ ᵗ بـ	كَ ᵗ بـ

diacritic has no vowel following it—and shadda indicates consonant gemination. How would one designate consonant or vowel for these graphemes, since they are neither?[7] It may be the case that in Arabic the relevant specification will be letter/diacritic rather than consonant/vowel at this level of orthographic representation.

However the issues regarding the specification of quantity and letter/diacritic versus consonant/vowel status are resolved, there will be processing implications for the allographic conversion mechanism.

The allographic conversion mechanism

The context-sensitive allographs of Arabic present computational problems which must be resolved in order to develop an explicit account of the representation of graphemes in the allographic conversion mechanism (ACM). These problems are of two kinds. First, what is the role of the ACM in selecting to write or not to write optional diacritics? And second, what is the role of the ACM in selecting the appropriate allograph of each of the 20 letters of the alphabet which have two to four different visual spatial forms?

First, consider the role of the allographic conversion mechanism in selecting optional diacritics. Each of the hypotheses regarding the specification of letters versus diacritics in orthographic representations has different consequences for the operations of the ACM. Remember that in the account of the structure of orthographic representations in which abstract graphemes are fully specified whether they refer to letters or diacritics, and there is no redundant representation of entries, one marked and the other unmarked, we left the process of selecting the appropriate physical instantiation of each grapheme for the allographic conversion mechanism. On this account (hypothesis 3), the marked and unmarked versions of the written word *"he writes"* /kataba/, represented in Table 14.14, stem from a common underlying graphemic representation. In the unmarked version, the allographic conversion mechanism selects "null script" (nothing) as the output for the ⟨a⟩ grapheme (diacritic). In the marked version, the allographic conversion mechanism selects the diacritic fatha as the output for the grapheme ⟨a⟩.

---

[7]The problem of how to represent diacritics that lack apparent consonant/vowel status is not special to Arabic. Italian and English employ apostrophes to "stand in" for various graphemes, e.g. ci e → c'e (there is), in Italian; cannot → can't, in English. No hypotheses have yet been formulated to account for the production of the grapheme "apostrophe' in either of these codes. Nor has an account been offered of how accents are processed in Italian.

On the account of hypothesis 2, the diacritics would be added to the letter sequence by an independent set of procedures. At what level in the spelling process would this set of procedures intersect with the lexical procedures, prior to the allographic conversion mechanism or later? Only on the account of hypothesis 1, in which there is a lexical representation for every marked and unmarked version of a word, is extra work for the ACM avoided.

Now consider the selection of allographs for the 20 letters of the Arabic alphabet that have two to four context-sensitive forms. Our account, based on evidence from English and Italian, thus far states that allographs of a particular letter are thought to share common underlying orthographic representations. The appropriate allograph to be produced is selected at the level of the ACM. Remember that unlike case or font in English and Italian, Arabic allographs have non-optional physical instantiations which are determined by the immediate orthographic context. How does the ACM interact with the graphemic buffer to maintain letter sequence and to transfer letter context information which pertains to appropriate allograph selection in Arabic? In other words, are features such as initial, medial and final indicated at the level of graphemic buffer and then slotted for prodution by the ACM, which must then decide, for example, that ﻊ [H] in the sequence مشهد [MSHD] /maʃhad/ (scene) is written differently from ﺡ [H] in the sequence طاهر [ṬAHR] /ṭa:hir/ (visible), even though they are both marked "medial"? Or does the graphemic buffer indicate "put the ⟨H⟩ in 'visible' in initial rather than medial form because it is preceded by ⟨A⟩"?

Summary

The features of Arabic orthography presented here pose serious questions about the adequacy of current hypotheses regarding the nature of orthographic representations and operations computed within the model of the spelling process that we optimistically described as a preliminary *universal* model.

The central question concerns what exactly is specified in the orthographic representation of Arabic words, i.e. are letters and diacritics specified on a shared level of representation? The answer we give to this question has implications for processing. We have attempted to briefly present some of these implications in this chapter. To summarize, if we hypothesize that diacritics are in fact represented in the orthographic output lexicon, just as letters are, then we must hypothesize some mechanism by which the representations of diacritics are eliminated from actual orthographic output in unmarked text. If instead we hypothesize that diacritics are not represented in the orthographic output lexicon, then we must hypothesize some mechanism by which they are added to actual orthographic output in marked text.

Either scenario would have implications for hypotheses regarding operations of the allographic conversion mechanism. The addition or deletion of abstract graphemes must be accomplished prior to the execution of motor commands for written or oral spelling. The presence of diacritics and letters, as well as the context-sensitive nature of allographs in Arabic, compel us to articulate more detailed hypotheses regarding the operations of the allographic conversion mechanism.

The nature of the operations of the phonology-to-orthography conversion mechanism is also affected by our hypotheses regarding orthographic structure. The problem of determining the status of diacritics and letters exists here, too. For example, is incoming phonology culled of extraneous sounds such as short vowels and gemination, leaving only certain sounds (consonants and long vowels) to be converted into letters when a subject is asked to write an unfamiliar word to dictation? How would this culling take place? Or instead, are all parts of the incoming signal converted into abstract graphemes and a later stage of processing selects whether to spell the graphemes as letters, diacritics or "null script"?

MANDARIN CHINESE

Background

It is estimated that one billion people speak some form of Chinese; within the broad category Chinese there are at least five dialectal groupings, of which Mandarin is but one (Li & Thompson, 1990, in *The World's Major Languages*, p. 811). For the purpose of presenting a brief summary of the "Chinese" writing system we will focus on contemporary Mandarin orthographic and linguistic facts.

Mandarin has traditionally been characterized as morphosyllabic, i.e. the characters of the orthographic code refer to sound at the level of the syllable rather than the phoneme, and they refer to meaning at the level of the morpheme rather than the word (De Francis, 1989). However, two-thirds of contemporary Mandarin words are compounds (Li & Thompson, 1990), and the interpretation of the interaction among the multiple morphemes, characters and syllables which comprise these compound words may lead to a reappraisal of this traditional characterization (Law & Caramazza, in press). Space limitations preclude us from discussing many interesting features of Mandarin orthography, including issues pertaining to compounding. We have decided to focus on graphemic characteristics of single characters. This focus is not completely arbitrary. Although many words in modern Mandarin are compounds, high-frequency words are predominantly single characters (Li & Thompson, 1981). Also, morphological affixation, which is so important to languages such as Arabic, English and Italian, is not prevalent in Mandarin, and to the extent that morphemes are bound together in Mandarin, the orthography does not indicate this; characters are not grouped by interword spaces. Mandarin text is typified by the equidimensional presentation of characters, i.e. every character occupies the same amount of space and is equally spaced one from another. This is true regardless of the morphological relationships (such as affixation and compounding) that may exist between characters. The following sentences may serve to illustrate this point:

1. 你　說　說　那　件　事
　 ni　shou　shou　nei　jian　shi
　 you speak a little that—classifier matter
　 "Speak a little about that matter!"

2. 我　吃　了　三　碗　飯
   wo　chi　le　san　wan　fan
   I eat—perf. three bowl rice
   "I ate three bowls of rice"

A model of the spelling process must, at the very least, explain the manner in which single characters are processed. Our consideration of the graphemic features of orthographic representations will focus on two characteristics of single characters. (1) Individual Mandarin characters may be simple or complex. Complex characters are composed of subcomponents which may contain information about the sound and meaning of the character as a whole. (2) Mandarin characters have a non-linear spatial organization. These features are described in greater detail below:

1. *Individual Mandarin characters may be simple or complex. Complex characters are composed of subcomponents which may contain information about the sound and meaning of the character as a whole.* A given character in Mandarin refers to a given syllable in the spoken language. Unlike alphabetic codes like English and Italian, the individual phonemes that comprise each syllable are not independently represented, nor is the tone, a phonemic contrast in Mandarin but not in English and Italian, independently represented. This essential difference between Mandarin orthography and alphabetic languages can be illustrated by comparing the way in which similar syllables are rendered in Mandarin, English and Italian (see Table 14.15). Note that in the English and Italian examples there is a grapheme that specifically refers to the onset of the syllable l → /l/; a separate grapheme (in the case of Italian) or graphemes (in the case of English) refers to the syllable rhyme: i → /i/ and ee → /i/, respectively. In the Mandarin example there is no part of the character that specifically refers to the onset or rhyme of the syllable /li/, nor does any portion of the character 利 independently specify which of the four tones this particular syllable of Mandarin has. The character as a whole refers to this sound. This is not to say that the sound /li/ in Mandarin is always and only written as 利. In fact, the 10 characters presented in Table 14.16 all have the pronunciation /li/ with a falling tone.

Each character in Mandarin does have internal structure. It is composed of one to roughly 30 strokes. Characters composed of multiple strokes that can be parsed into subcharacter units are called "complex characters"; characters that cannot be parsed into subcharacter units are called "simple characters". Examples of these character types are offered in Table 14.17.

TABLE 14.15 Orthography corresponding to the syllable /li/ in Chinese, English and Italian.

Chinese	English	Italian
利	lee	li

TABLE 14.16   Characters having the pronunciation /li/. (Examples are adapted from the *Soothill Syllabary*, cited in De Francis, 1989.)

	Character	IPA
1	俐	li
2	浰	li
3	唎	li
4	痢	li
5	箌	li
6	莉	li
7	鬁	li
8	鼻	li
9	悧	li
10	梨	li

TABLE 14.17   Examples of simple and complex characters.

Simple characters			Complex characters		
手	so	hand	兒	er	child
月	yue	month	抱	bao	to embrace
人	ren	person	這	zhe	this

Subcharacter components of complex characters are called "phonetics" and "significs". Phonetics offer some phonological information about the character as a whole. This information is not about specific features of the syllable to which the character refers, such as phonemes or tone (as discussed above), nor is it completely reliable. For example, all of the complex characters in Table 14.16 have the pronunciation /li/ with a falling tone. Each of these characters contains the phonetic 利 , which has the sound /li/, on the right-hand side of the character. However, the characters in Table 14.18 also contain the phonetic 利 /li/ but numbers 1, 2 and 3 have a rising tone, number 4 has a mid tone, and numbers 5–9 have even less in common with the sound /li/.

Phonetics vary in how reliably they predict the sound of the syllable to which a character refers. This inconsistency in the correspondence between a particular phonetic and a given sound in Mandarin may appear to be like the "inconsistent" mapping of particular graphemes to phonemes in Italian or English. For example, in Italian, the letter C may sound like /tʃ/ or /k/. Orthographic context is needed to determine which of these two sounds the C refers to in a given word. The I following the CC in *cinema* tells us C → /tʃ/, whereas the A following C in *canta* (he sings) tells us C → /k/. In fact, this mapping is very consistent: there is a rule that says

TABLE 14.18 Complex characters containing the phonetic 利 /li/ having various pronunciations. (Examples are adapted from the *Soothill Syllabary*, cited in De Francis, 1989.)

	Complex character	IPA
1	蜊	li
2	犁	li
3	猁	li
4	莉	li
5	矲	le
6	麳	le
7	厤	le
8	詞	lian
9	鉫	qian

C → /tʃ/ before I and E, and C → /k/ before A, O and U. In the examples of Mandarin characters in Table 14.18, the subcharacter component to the right of the phonetic 利 /li/ determines that number 4 refers to the sound /li/ whereas 9 refers to /qian/. But we cannot write a rule that neatly predicts which graphemic combinations render /li/ versus which render /qian/.

The phonetics presented thus far all appear on the right-hand side of complex characters, and although this is the most common position for a phonetic, it is not always the case. Table 14.19 presents 10 characters, all of which contain the phonetic 黃 /huang/. Note that the phonetic may appear to the right (numbers 1–4, 6 and 10), on the left (number 7) or on the bottom (numbers 5, 8 and 9), as well as on the top (not shown) of a complex character. The placement of the phonetic in any of these positions does not seem to affect the reliability of the grapheme-to-sound correspondence or the phonological structure of the syllable referred to. This is not to say that the placement of the phonetic is capricious; each character is spatially organized in a particular, albeit non-linear, way.

Complex characters may also contain a signific, a graphemic element that offers some information about the meaning of the character as a whole. Like phonetics, the predictive value of particular significs varies greatly. Significs usually occur on the left of complex characters, but this is not mandatory. Table 14.20 offers a number of examples of characters containing the signific 目 "eye". Note that the signific appears in a number of positions in the character, and that the meaning of the character is not always transparently related to the concept "eyes".

In summary, characters do not explicitly refer to the phonemes which comprise a syllable. Instead, they refer to the phonological shape of the syllable as a whole. Subcharacter units called significs and phonetics may provide some information about the sound and meaning to which the character refers, but this information is not reliable in the same way that alphabetic information is.

TABLE 14.19 Complex characters containing the phonetic 黃 /huang/ in different positions in the character and having various pronunciations. (Examples are adapted from the *Soothill Syllabary*, cited in De Francis, 1989.)

	Complex character	IPA
1	潢	huang
2	璜	huang
3	磺	huang
4	蟥	huang
5	簧	huang
6	鷬	huang
7	鐄	huang
8	癀	huang
9	廣	guang
10	横	heng

TABLE 14.20 Complex characters containing the signific 目 "Eye".

Character	IPA	Gloss
眉	mei	eyebrows
睹	du	to witness
看	kan	to look
眩	xuan	dizzy
盾	dun	shield

2. *Mandarin characters have a non-linear spatial organization.* Strokes and character subcomponents which comprise a single character are not arranged in a linear order within each character frame. Instead, a character frame may contain elements on the right, left, top or bottom. Written strokes are executed in a conventional order (as learned in school) that is generally left to right and top to bottom. (Tzeng *et al.*, 1986). Figure 14.3 illustrates the order in which strokes are executed in order to write the character "same" or "together".

In alphabetic codes such as Arabic, English and Italian, the spatial sequence of graphemes corresponds to the temporal sequence of phonemes to which they refer; the linear format reflects this. Because a Mandarin character refers to an unanalyzed syllable rather than to the phonemes that comprise the syllable, the code need not reflect spatial/temporal correspondence within subcharacter/sub-syllabic units; the organizational structure of individual characters is freed from the linear format because

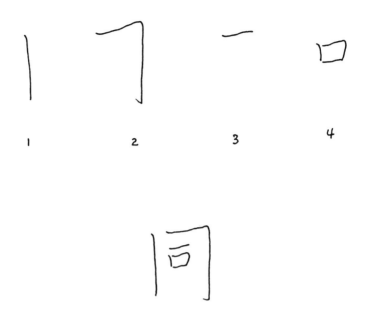

FIGURE 14.3   The sequence of four strokes that comprise the character "Same" or "Together".

it need not encode this spatial/temporal correspondence at the subcharacter/sub-syllabic level.

Implications for the General Architecture of the Spelling Process

As with our consideration of Arabic, it is necessary to examine the adequacy of the proposed model of the spelling process for Mandarin at two levels. First, one must assess whether the general architecture of the model is consistent with the computational requirements for processing Mandarin orthography. Second, one must assess the adequacy of the specific hypotheses regarding the nature of orthographic representations and operations computed within the various subcomponents of the spelling process for the features of Mandarin orthography.

It is not clear that the distinction between lexical and sub-lexical processing is computationally motivated for Mandarin. To be sure, there is internal structure to characters, but this structure is organized (possibly) with regard to significs and phonetics, not with regard to the designation of individual sounds—*either phonemes or syllables*. Significs and phonetics may be exploited when a subject writes (or reads), but the manner in which this knowledge is used to accomplish the task of spelling appears to be fundamentally different from the use of sub-lexical phonology-to-orthography correspondence knowledge in alphabetic languages. We wish to emphasize that the fundamental problem should *not* be construed to be that Mandarin orthography refers to sound at the syllable rather than phoneme level, and, therefore, the sub-lexical/lexical distinction is unmotivated. Rather, it is because the relationship between a character or subcharacter unit and the sound of a syllable is not systematic, and therefore the phonology-to-orthography conversion procedure is not productive, as it is in alphabetic languages, that we must question the assumption of a sub-lexical/lexical processing distinction. A walk through these hypothesized procedures may clarify this point.

The lexical procedure in Mandarin is not obviously different from that proposed for alphabetic languages, at least at the level of the general architecture of the spelling process. In a writing to dictation task, familiar, lexical, phonological input would activate knowledge stored in the phonological input lexicon, which in turn would activate knowledge in the semantic lexicon, which in turn would activate knowledge in the orthographic output lexicon. The nature of the representation and operations computed in these lexicons is not straightforward, and requires considerably more analysis, but at a general level one can accept this description of the lexical procedure for Mandarin.

Now consider the putative sub-lexical procedure. The sub-lexical procedure of the model schematically represented in Figure 14.1 is hypothesized to process the spelling of novel words. How might a Mandarin speaker spell a novel word? It has already been noted that the subject cannot convert individual phonemes into corresponding graphemes. Instead, the input unit of processing must be a syllable and the conversion procedure depends in part on the nature of that syllable. There are two logical possibilities: (a) the syllable could be familiar, its novelty arising from the syntactic or semantic context; and (b) the syllable could be unfamiliar but phonemically legal, i.e. it is a member of the set of theoretically available syllables in Mandarin phonology, but it is not a syllable that is actually used in the spoken language. How would each of these novel syllable types be spelled?

1. If the phonological input is a familiar syllable, rendered novel only by the syntactic or semantic context (e.g. if one were to hear the sound of the word "cat", in the sentence "She cat the book and walked away", the first syllable "cat" is familiar, but it is in a novel context), then the Mandarin subjects might write the familiar syllable through a lexical procedure, selecting the most frequent character that has this sound, even though it might be contextually inappropriate. Alternatively, he might represent the sound using a subcharacter unit—a phonetic. Of course, this phonetic would have to be one which has no lexical value when standing alone, i.e. it cannot be *both* a phonetic and a simple character, otherwise this "sub-lexical" account is not meaningfully different from the lexical account. The determination of which account is correct is an empirical issue, which, to our knowledge, has not been examined thus far.

2. If the syllable were unfamiliar but phonemically legal, then it would seem that a "best fit" lexical procedure might be possible. The subject could select a stored orthographic representation that corresponds to a stored phonological input representation that most nearly approximates the phonological input. For example, if a subject were asked to write a character for a novel sound, say (for expository purposes) /li/ with a falling tone, he might opt to write the character that refers to the sound /li/ with a rising tone, because it best approximates the phonological

input. Alternatively, the relevant unit of processing for this rather sketchy "best fit" procedure could be the phonetic rather than the character; the subject would write the phonetic which most closely approximates the unfamiliar syllable.

Either account involves a procedure for arriving at a phonology-to-orthography correspondence that is not "principled" or productive in the way that the hypothesized procedure is presumed to work in alphabetic languages. In the example above of writing the unfamiliar sound /li/ with a falling tone, a Mandarin subject can have little confidence that the character (whether it be a phonetic or a complex character) he writes can be read by another subject as /li/ with a falling tone. In contrast, an English subject asked to write the unfamiliar sound /feyf/ may write it as *fafe*, *phafe* or *faif*. He may be very confident that another reader of English will read any of these orthographic products as /feyf/. This is because phonology-to-orthography correspondence is principled and productive in alphabetic languages.

The point of discussing these alternative accounts of novel syllable writing in Mandarin is not to offer serious and well-formed hypotheses about the spelling procedure in Mandarin. Rather, the point is to question the assumption of adequacy of a sub-lexical/lexical processing distinction in Mandarin, given that the nature of phonology-to-orthography correspondence in Mandarin is fundamentally different from alphabetic languages, and to suggest that this assumption requires computational and empirical evidence to support it.

Other aspects of the general architecture of the spelling process are seriously challenged by the facts of Mandarin. The computational necessity of a graphemic output buffer for Mandarin is not obvious. Unlike alphabetic languages, in which each graphemic entry in the lexicon is composed of a set of graphemes which must be rendered individually in one of several allographic forms, hence motivating the existence of a short-term memory store (the graphemic output buffer), lexical entries in Mandarin are not obviously composed of a comparable set of graphemes. Although Mandarin characters have internal structure and appear to have subcharacter parts, we do not know which of these parts is in fact the relevant unit of *graphemic* processing. It is not obvious whether the set of 'graphemes' that comprise the lexical entry is the set of (a) strokes, (b) phonetic and signific, (c) some unit intermediate between strokes and phonetics/significs or (d) the character as an atomic whole. The determination of the relevant unit of graphemic processing in the orthographic output lexicon has implications for the general architecture of the spelling process presented schematically in Figure 14.1. If the character is an unanalyzable whole in the orthographic lexicon then the graphemic output buffer, as an entity distinct from a response buffer for visual forms in general, lacks theoretical motivation.[8]

The computational roles of other processing subcomponents in the proposed model, such as the allographic conversion mechanism and the letter-name conversion mechanism, are also unclear. Whereas the spelling process is computationally required to diverge after the graphemic output buffer in alphabetic languages in order to account for the production of oral and written spelling, Mandarin has no such

---

[8]Of course, these characters are complex objects that would need to be stored temporarily for sequential output of strokes.

computational requirement (because there is no oral spelling and no allographs as currently defined), and therefore no theoretical motivation for processing components such as the allographic conversion mechanism and the letter-name conversion mechanism.

It is not obvious that the proposed general architecture of the spelling process is adequate to accommodate the facts of Mandarin. The existence and independence of sub-lexical and lexical procedures and the role of the graphemic buffer within the general architecture of the spelling process must be supported by theoretical argument and empirical evidence before we can claim that our model of the spelling process encompasses the facts of Mandarin.

Setting aside these reservations about the adequacy of the model at a general processing level, we turn now to an examination of the adequacy of the specific hypotheses regarding the nature of orthographic representations and operations computed in the spelling process. The claims regarding the orthographic structure of alphabetic languages are fairly detailed. What is the comparable level of representation for Mandarin?

The most important problem is in determining the relevant units of orthographic representation in Mandarin. In alphabetic languages we speak of letters, words and morphological units, and although the contribution and definition of these units can be controversial, we have some sense that they are relevant units. Although there is internal structure in characters such as strokes, phonetics and significs, it is not clear that these are the relevant units for the spelling process. Are these structures encoded in the orthographic lexicon, or, instead, are characters stored as unanalyzed wholes?

By analogy to the structure of orthographic representations in alphabetic codes, one could hypothesize that characters are stored in analyzed form in the lexicon. What sort of knowledge would need to be encoded in a multi-dimensional representation of Mandarin characters? One hypothesis is that significs and phonetics are stored as independent units within the lexicon along with information designating the possible "alliances" that each signific and phonetic could enter into. Information would also need to be encoded regarding the possible position within the character frame that a particular signific or phonetic could assume. This hypothesis would appear to obviate the highly redundant representation of those significs and phonetics that occur in many complex characters, by representing them only once along with the pertinent information about the combinations which they may form. However, given that there are no obvious rules that capture the nature of all possible combinations which significs and phonetics may form, the representation of this information would be a list. This list does not appear to be significantly different from a simple list of all characters without appeal to subcharacter components, i.e. a lexicon of unanalyzable character units.

Summary

The facts of Mandarin present serious challenges to the proposed model of the spelling process, both at the level of the general architecture and at the level of hypotheses regarding the nature of orthographic representations and operations computed within processing subcomponents. The assumption of a dual-route model of the spelling process in which sub-lexical and lexical procedures constitute two independent means of producing orthographic output is not computationally motivated for Mandarin. Neither is the assumption of a processing role for a graphemic output buffer, an allographic conversion mechanism or a letter-name conversion mechanism. In short, it is not clear that the investigation of the writing process in Mandarin is well served by working within the framework of the general architecture of the spelling process as presented in this chapter. Rather, cognitive psychologists must provide theoretical arguments and empirical evidence that supports the use of this framework; the burden of proof is on those investigators who claim that it is reasonable to assume the appropriateness of this general framework.

The most basic question about the nature of orthographic representations in Mandarin remains to be seriously investigated. What is the relevant unit (or units) of graphemic processing in Mandarin? No serious discussion of the spelling process can proceed without a well-formed hypothesis in answer to this question. Experimental investigations which have sought to implicate "sub-lexical" knowledge in the process of reading Chinese have merely demonstrated that the system is opportunistic—any available information about the sound or meaning of a character in Mandarin may affect reading performance. But this does not describe, let alone explain, the process by which this occurs. More evidence, specifically about writing, needs to be marshalled in order to make serious claims about the spelling process in Mandarin.

GENERAL CONCLUSION

The optimistic introduction to this chapter suggested that the model of the spelling process that is schematically represented in Figure 14.1 is a preliminary universal model. An assessment of the adequacy of this model to accommodate the orthographic facts of two different codes, Arabic and Mandarin, has met with mixed results. The proposed general architecture of the model appears to be appropriate for the production of spelling in Arabic. The hypotheses regarding the nature of orthographic representations and operations computed within this architecture, although based on the orthographic facts of English and Italian, also appear to be generally adequate to account for the orthographic facts of Arabic. On a more detailed level of analysis, however, these hypotheses are insufficiently articulated to speak to the complex processing issues posed by Arabic orthography. The final determination of the adequacy of the proposed model of the spelling process for Arabic must await a finer and more thorough investigation of normal and impaired spelling in Arabic. However, we remain optimistic that further investigations of Arabic can be properly guided by asking questions about the structure of Arabic orthography within the framework of the proposed model. We encourage further theoretical and empirical analyses of the writing process in Arabic because we think the insights gained there will contribute to a more detailed model of the spelling process for all alphabetic codes.

We are less optimistic about the adequacy of the proposed model for accommodating the facts of Mandarin. There are serious challenges to the general architecture of the processing model as well as to hypotheses about the nature of orthographic representations. It is not clear that the investigation of the writing process in Mandarin is well served by working within the framework of the general architecture of the spelling process as presented in this chaper. The adequacy of this model of the spelling process for Mandarin cannot be assumed. We should be cautious in insisting that a model of the spelling process predicated on computational issues specific to alphabetic codes is in fact universal. Non-alphabetic codes such as Mandarin may be processed in a radically different manner from that in which alphabetic codes are processed.

ACKNOWLEDGEMENTS

The work reported in this chapter was supported by a grant from the Human Frontiers Science Program and NIH grant NS22201 to Dartmouth College. KL is now at Vermont Law School.

REFERENCES

Badecker, W., Hillis, A. & Caramazza, A. (1990). Lexical morphology and its role in the writing process: evidence from a case of acquired dysgraphia. *Cognition*, **35**, 205–243.

Baxter, D. M. & Warrington, E. K. (1983). Neglect dysgraphia. *Journal of Neurology, Neurosurgery and Psychiatry*, **45**, 1073–1078.

Baxter, D. M. & Warrington, E. K. (1987). Transcoding sound to spelling: single or multiple sound unit correspondence? *Cortex*, **23**, 11–28.

Beauvois, M. F. & Dérouesné, J. (1981). Lexical or orthographic agraphia. *Brain*, **104**, 21–49.

Bentin, S., Bargai, N. & Katz, L. (1984). Orthographic and phonemic coding for lexical access: evidence from Hebrew. *Journal of Experimental Psychology: Learning, Memory and Cognition*, **10**(3), 353–368.

Bub, D. N. & Kertesz, A. (1982). Deep agraphia. *Brain and Language*, **17**, 47–166.

Caramazza, A. (1992). Is cognitive neuropsychology possible? *Journal of Cognitive Neuropsychology*, **4**(1), 80–95.

Caramazza, A. & Hillis, A. (1990). Spatial representation of words in the brain implied by studies of a unilateral neglect patient. *Nature*, **346**(6281), 267–269.

Caramazza, A. & Hillis, A. (1991). Lexical organization of nouns and verbs in the brain. *Nature*, **349**(6312), 788–790.

Caramazza, A. & Miceli, G. (1989). Orthographic structure, the graphemic buffer and the spelling process. In C. Von Euler, I. Lundberg & G. Lennerstrand (Eds), *Brain and Reading*. Macmillan/Wenner-Gren International Symposium Series.

Caramazza, A. & Miceli, G. (1990). The structure of graphemic representations. *Cognition*, **37**, 243–297.

Caramazza, A., Miceli, G., Villa, G. & Romani, C. (1987). The role of the graphemic buffer in spelling: evidence from a case of acquired dysgraphia. *Cognition*, **26**, 59–85.

Cubelli, R. (1991). A selective deficit for writing vowels in acquired dysgraphia. *Nature*, **35**, 258–260.

De Francis, J. (1989). *Visible Speech: The Diverse Oneness of Writing Systems*. Honolulu: University of Hawaii Press.

Ellis, A. W. (1982). Spelling and writing (reading and speaking). In A. W. Ellis (Ed.), *Normality and Pathology in Cognitive Functions*. London: Academic Press.

Ellis, A. W. (1987). Modelling the writing process. In G. Denes, C. Semenza, P. Bisiacchi & E. Andreewksy (Eds), *Perspectives in Cognitive Neuropsychology*. London: LEA.

Ferguson, C. (1972). Diglossia. In P. P. Giglioli (Ed.), *Language and Social Context*. Harmondsworth: Penguin.

Frost, R. & Bentin, S. (1992). Reading consonants and guessing vowels: visual word recognition in Hebrew orthography. In R. Frost & L. Katz (Eds), *Orthography, Phenology, Morphology and Meaning*. Advances in Psychology Series, Volume 94. New York: Elsevier, North-Holland, pp. 27–44.

Frost, R., Katz, L. & Bentin, S. (1987). Strategies for visual word recognition and orthographic depth: a multilingual comparison. *Journal of Experimental Psychology: Human Perception and Performance*, **13**(1), 104–115.

Goodman, R. A. & Caramazza, A. (1986a). Aspects of the spelling process: evidence from a case of acquired dysgraphia. In *Language and Cognitive Processes*, Vol. 1. VNU Science Press, pp. 263–296.

Goodman, R. A. & Caramazza, A. (1986b). Dissociation of spelling errors in written and oral spelling: the role of allographic conversion in writing. *Cognitive Neuropsychology*, **3**, 179–206.

Hanna, R. R., Hanna, J. S., Hodges, R. E. & Rudorf, E. H. (1966). *Phoneme–Grapheme Correspondences as Cues to Spelling Improvement*. US Department of Health, Education and Welfare, Office of Education, Washington, DC: US Government Printing Office.

Hillis, A. & Caramazza, A. (1989). The graphemic buffer and attentional mechanisms. *Brain and Language*, **36**, 208–235.

Kinsbourne, M. & Rosenfield, D. B. (1974). Agraphia selective for written spelling: an experimental case study. *Brain and Language*, **1**, 215–225.

Kinsbourne, M. & Warrington, E. K. (1965). A case showing selectively impaired oral spelling. *Journal of Neurology, Neurosurgery and Psychiatry*, **28**, 59–64.

Law, S. & Caramazza, A. (in press). Cognitive processes in writing Chinese characters: basic issues and some preliminary data. In B. de Gelder & J. Morais (Eds), *Speech and Reading: Comparative Approaches*. Hove: LEA.

Li, C. N. & Thompson, S. A. (1981). *Mandarin Chinese: A Functional Reference Grammar*. Berkeley: University of California Press.

Li, C. N. & Thompson, S. A. (1990). Chinese. In B. Comrie (Ed.), *The World's Major Languages*. New York: Oxford University Press.

Margolin, D. I. (1984). The neuropsychology of writing and spelling: semantic, phonological, motor, and perceptual processes. *Quarterly Journal of Experimental Psychology*, **36A**, 459–489.

McCarthy, J. (1981). A prosodic theory of nonconcatenative morphology. *Linguistic Inquiry*, **12**(3).

McCloskey, M., Badecker, W., Goodman-Shulman, R. & Aliminosa, D. (in press). The structure of graphemic representations in spelling: evidence from a case of acquired dysgraphia. *Cognitive Neuropsychology*.

Patterson, K. E. (1987). Acquired disorders of spelling. In G. Denes, C. Semenza, P. Bisiacchi & E. Andreewsky (Eds), *Perspectives in Cognitive Neuropsychology*. London: LEA.

Posteraro, L., Zinelli, P. & Mazzucchi, A. (1988). Selective impairment of the graphemic buffer in acquired dysgraphia: a case study. *Brain and Language*, **35**, 274–286.

Rapp, B. & Caramazza, A. (1992). Cognitive neuropsychology: from impaired performance to normal cognitive structure. In R. Lister & H. Weingartner (Eds), *Perspectives on Cognitive Neuroscience*. Oxford: Oxford University Press.

Roeltgen, D. P., Sevush, S. & Heilman, K. H. (1983). Phonological agraphia: writing by the lexical–semantic route. *Neurology*, **33**, 755–765.

Seidenberg, M. (1988). Cognitive neuropsychology: the state of the art. *Journal of Cognitive Neuropsychology*, **5**(4), 403–426.

Shallice, T. (1981). Phonological agraphia and the lexical route in writing. *Brain*, **104**, 413–429.

Tainturier, M. J. & Caramazza, A. (in press). The status of double letters in graphemic representations. *Journal of Memory and Language*.

Tzeng, O. J. L., Hung, D. L., Chen, S., Wu, J. & Hsi, M. S. (1986). Processing Chinese logographs by Chinese brain damaged patients. In H. Kao, G. P. Van Galen & R. Hossain (Eds), *Graphonomics: Contemporary Research in Handwriting*. Amsterdam: Elsevier Science.

15

Peripheral Disorders of Spelling: The Role of the Graphemic Buffer

JANICE KAY

University of Exeter

RICHARD HANLEY

University of Liverpool

John has just retired as a teacher in a senior post at a large and busy secondary school. Reading and writing are the tools of his trade, but he also reads and writes for pleasure and is a learned and articulate man. However, after a mild stroke in 1990, something happened to affect his writing ability, though we can find little evidence that other aspects of his language are impaired. Here is an illustration of how John writes now; it is his discription of the Cookie Theft picture (Goodglass & Kaplan, 1983), a widely used means of eliciting both written and spoken output in dysphasia assessment (see Figure 15.1).

Before his stroke, John made very few errors—confident in knowing how words are spelled, susceptible merely, like all of us, to occasional and inadvertent "slips of the pen". Now, he still writes fluently and fast, but makes more errors. There is a characteristic pattern to his spelling and one can get something of a flavour of it from studying Figure 15.1. The majority of words are written correctly, including uncommon words like *deluge* and words which are low in imageability and frequency like *contents* and *melodious*. He corrects most of his errors immediately, and given that he sometimes writes the correct form of the error elsewhere in the text (e.g. *offerings* is written correctly before he misspells it as *offerrerings*), these observations

---

Handbook of Spelling: Theory, Process and Intervention. Edited by G. D. A. Brown and N. C. Ellis.
©1994 John Wiley & Sons Ltd.

An overworked and somewhat slakkerbrange woman is trying to cope with the wor ies of bringing up two wawward childreen and ~~cope with~~ grappel with the daily round. Her two children, a girl of about ten and a boy of about eleven are in the ~~me n~~ meantime amusing themselves as well they might by emptying the contents of the ~~caek~~ ~~cakepin~~ lin. Mother, meanwhile, is somewhere between the melodious offerings of the Jimmy ~~Jought~~ Young Show and Radio 1's late t offerrerings.

The fact that she is carried along in the melodies of yesteryear, merging with the latest pop ~~recorg~~ record, results in a deluge of water that ~~cassc~~ ~~caseakes~~ ~~cascatles~~ cascades onto the ~~flow~~ floor.

The scene contrasts with that of the carefully trimmed garden and lawn outside; a homely background of ~~ordiliness~~ orderliness.

FIGURE 15.1   John's written description of the Cookie Theft Picture. Note that his spoken description is normal. Crossed out words are John's own corrections.

suggest that his knowledge of how words are spelled remains intact. Some of his spellings, such as *grappel* and *elevern*, appear to be phonological in nature, spelled how they sound rather than how they look, but as we will shortly see, this does not seem to be the appropriate way of describing them. We have looked formally at linguistic variables that are known to affect spelling success by giving John single words to spell to dictation (see Table 15.1). The most important factor that influences the probability that a word will be spelled correctly is the number of letters that it has: the longer the word, the more likely errors are to occur. The effect of letter length remains even when the probability of an error on a word is scaled by the number of letters in the word (Caramazza *et al.*, 1987). John is sometimes affected by how frequently a word occurs in written English. However, this is not a particularly robust effect: he produced fewer errors in spelling more common than less common words on two out of our three tests. Imageability does not affect spelling success and neither does grammatical class nor spelling regularity. The last finding is important, since it demonstrates that John does not rely on sound to spell—if he did, then irregular words like *castle* and *mortgage* would be misspelled, perhaps like *cassul* and *moregige*—and this suggests that errors like *elevern* for *eleven* may not be true "phonological" errors.

John's spelling errors are always structurally similar to the word he intends to write. They involve particular difficulties with individual letters and letter clusters, even though the letters themselves are well formed and fluently executed. As study of Figure 15.1 shows, letters substitute for other letters or letter groups (e.g. *record* → *recorg*), and letters are inserted (e.g. *eleven* → *elevern*), deleted (e.g. *latest* → *latet*) or transposed (e.g. *grapple* → *grappel*). By convention, errors falling into just one of these categories are classified as "single error types". When they occur as combinations of these categories (e.g. *Joughl* for *Young* may consist of substitution of *J* for *Y*, transposition

TABLE 15.1   Summary of JH's spelling performance.

	N	% correct
Written spelling to dictation		
Words		
Letter length		
3-letter	20	90.0
5-letter	20	95.0
7-letter	20	70.0
9-letter	20	70.0
Imageability		
High imageability	40	95.0
Low imageability	40	90.0
Frequency (test 1)		
High frequency	40	92.5
Low frequency	40	92.5
Frequency (test 2)		
High frequency	32	100.0
Medium frequency	32	81.3
Low frequency	32	65.6
Frequency (test 3)		
High frequency	80	95.0
Low frequency	80	82.5
Regularity		
Regular words	40	72.5
Exception words	40	75.0
Nonwords		
Letter length		
3-letter	6	83.3
4-letter	6	66.6
5-letter	6	50.0
6-letter	6	16.6
Spelling aloud to dictation		
Words		
Letter length		
7-letter	25	92.0
8-letter	25	88.0
9-letter	25	100.0
10-letter	25	72.0
11-letter	25	72.0
12-letter	25	76.0

(and substitution) of *g* and *n/h* and insertion of *l*), they are classified as "mixed error types".

Similar errors occur whatever the task, and whether words are handwritten, typed or spelled aloud. Spelling nonwords to dictation is affected in just the same way as spelling words (see Table 15.1).

THE ROLE OF THE GRAPHEMIC BUFFER

For purposes of discussion, we can view the process of spelling as made up of two distinct stages. During the first stage an abstract graphemic representation is constructed for the item to be spelled. Ellis (1982) has characterized this procedure by claiming—at least for "phonologically deep" languages like English—that spellings for familiar words are addressed by consulting a spelling, or graphemic, lexicon. Unfamiliar words—new words like new product names or street names—will not be represented and so their spellings must be constructed by using stored knowledge about sound and spelling correspondences. While some theorists have proposed that these two procedures are independent (e.g. Ellis, 1982; Margolin, 1984), others have argued for an integrated, non-independent, system (e.g. Campbell, 1983).

The second stage consists of the steps that must be undertaken to transform an abstract representation of the intended spelling into a concrete realization—one that will be compatible with the required mode of output (that is, writing down the spelling, or typing it or spelling it aloud). As a minimal requirement, an abstract representation must signal what letters are in the word and their position. At least initially, however, information about the actual form that the output will take, such as which letters are to be written in capitals and which in lower case, is not specified. This takes place in subsequent stages. Mediating the transformation of material from abstract information about letter identities to actual letter shapes (for written spelling) or letter names (for spelling aloud) is a "graphemic buffer". This system holds the information temporarily while it is currently being worked on. It is important that while an abstract representation is held temporarily information about letter identities and their order is maintained. Disruption of this system—either momentarily, as in inadvertent "slips of the pen", or more long term, as in acquired brain damage—may result in loss or corruption of information about letter identity and position.

According to this way of characterizing the spelling system, then, damage to different components should have readily identifiable consequences. Some people with acquired spelling disorders appear to have difficulties in deriving abstract lexical representations for words (e.g. Hatfield & Patterson, 1983), while others seem to be impaired in constructing new spellings for unfamiliar words (e.g. Shallice, 1981). These disorders implicate impairments to central spelling processes—at the level of the graphemic spelling lexicon, for example, or at the level of sound–spelling conversion procedures. Damage to a graphemic buffer, on the other hand, might be expected to affect equally the spelling of familiar words and unfamiliar nonwords, because spelling knowledge will already have been formulated (from either or both lexical and sub-lexical sources). For the same reason, semantic and morpho-syntactic factors such as imageability and word class should not affect spelling success. And because the graphemic buffer is a way-stage in transforming abstract spelling knowledge into the desired output form, then deficits should be apparent regardless of the way spelling is elicited (e.g. spontaneous writing, writing to dictation) and mode of output (e.g. writing, typing or spelling aloud). Some of these criteria derive from assumptions about the ways in which a hypothesized graphemic buffer is believed to operate, while others result directly from observations of day-to-day slips of the pen and from psycholinguistic descriptions of neurological patients.

TEMPORARY DISRUPTION OF PERIPHERAL SPELLING PROCESSES—SLIPS OF THE PEN

On occasion in writing, as in speech, we are prone to lapses which result in inadvertent slips. Such errors of performance are to be distinguished from errors of knowledge in which a word is written incorrectly because we are unsure of the spelling. Several authors have investigated unintentional "slips of the pen" in the hope that such errors will shed light on the processes underlying the written production of language (e.g. Chedru & Geschwind, 1962; Ellis, 1979; Hotopf, 1980; Wing & Baddeley, 1980). The difficulties in collecting a large sample of slips of the pen from which to draw reliable generalizations are not to be underestimated. Different authors have used different methodologies. Wing and Baddeley (1980), for example, collected and collated errors derived from a number of individuals writing under time pressure (under exam conditions). Others (e.g. Ellis, 1979; Hotopf, 1980) have relied on cataloguing their own errors, collected over several months.

For the purposes of this discussion, we will not describe slips of the pen which appear to arise at levels above that of the letter (e.g. slips at the lexical level). Instead, we will focus on the nature of letter-level errors and concomitant position effects. Ellis (1979) distinguishes a number of letter-error types, among them transpositions, deletions (omissions) and substitutions. (Note that Ellis does not include a separate category of insertions, though the notion of adding an extraneous letter is incorporated in categories of letter transposition, as in "immediate repetition of one letter or more than one letter".)

Ellis suggests that transposition errors can be described as arising at a *graphemic* level: that is, at a stage—after an appropriate lexical form has been looked up, and prior to a more concrete realization of the stimulus—at which abstract letter identities are represented. We are treating this stage as the domain of the graphemic buffer. Ellis' reasoning is that transposition errors are accommodated to the appropriate case (e.g. *J. Neurol. Neurosurg.* → *J. $\underline{S}$euro*; *Pye Cambridge* → *Py$\underline{ce}$*), which means that they are unlikely to be occurring at a stage at which case has already been assigned. Deletions, on the other hand, are attributed to a later *allographic* level, a level at which abstract graphemic identities are realized in an appropriate physical form (e.g. the abstract letter <a>, for example, has allographs {a} and {A}). This is because deletions involved masking of identical allographic variants (e.g. *than, wen*—the {h} in *than* masking the {h} in *when*); errors indicating graphemic masking (e.g. *None* → *Noe*, *Geography* → *Georaphy* did not occur).

Ellis (1979) also claims that substitution errors occur at an allographic stage, during a "process of translation from an allographic code to a graphic product" (p. 276). This is primarily because of an observed physical similarity between the intruding letter and the replaced letter. Indeed, Ellis notes a similarity of *motoric* movements involved in forming each of the letters. This is a slightly different account from that offered by Ellis (1982), in which letter substitutions are attributed to errors in selecting allographs themselves.

Wing and Baddeley (1980) focus on the nature of a buffer impairment in contributing to normal slips of the pen. Analyses of which letter positions were most vulnerable to error revealed that errors occurred more often on middle letters than on either beginning or end letters (which did not differ significantly). This finding is hard to explain in terms of decay of the memory trace (since one would expect end-letter positions to be most vulnerable). On the other hand, it can be accounted for in terms of interference from neighbouring letters, an effect which is limited, the authors claim, to only a very few adjacent letters in the memory buffer. The authors identified four types of slip: deletions of letters; transpositions, in which two adjacent letters are reversed; substitutions of an incorrect letter; and insertions of an additional letter. They also looked at the distribution of each error type across each letter position (errors were "normalized" across five letter positions). Differing patterns of distributions for the error types led the authors to conclude that separate processes are responsible for the production of insertions and transpositions, though they suggested that deletions and substitutions may have a common origin.

SELECTIVE IMPAIRMENT OF THE GRAPHEMIC BUFFER—ACQUIRED SPELLING DISORDERS

Reports of selective damage to the graphemic buffer have been few, although several have been described in considerable detail. Initial attempts to characterize a graphemic buffer deficit were made by Nolan and Caramazza (1983). Interpretation of this case is complicated by the patient's additional dysphasic deficits, however, and we will not consider it further. More recently, five patients with acquired spelling disorders have been documented who appear to present with a graphemic buffer deficit (FV—Miceli, Silveri & Caramazza, 1985; LB—Caramazza *et al.*, 1987; Caramazza & Miceli, 1990; SE—Posteraro, Zinelli & Mazzucchi, 1988; CW and CF—Cubelli, 1991). As it turns out, all five of these patients are native Italian speakers.

Ironically, patient FV (Miceli, Silveri & Caramazza, 1985), who according to the criteria discussed above has a clear graphemic buffer impairment, was described by the authors as having a more central spelling difficulty within a sub-lexical writing route. Let us go into the patient's case in greater depth. FV made a rapid recovery from mild aphasia (characterized by "the presence of phonemic substitutions in speech production, naming and repetition") following a mild stroke. Syntactic and semantic aspects of comprehension, auditory comprehension, spoken naming and reading (both words and nonwords) were all within normal limits when his spelling was investigated. Indeed, he still continued to practise as a lawyer. Writing difficulties persisted, however, and remained highly stable during testing over a 2-month period. In formal testing of writing to dictation, he made errors on 22.3% of words and 30.8% of nonwords. Both in spontaneous writing and writing to dictation, FV's errors tended to occur on longer words and this was confirmed in formal testing (while no other significant effects of word variables were observed). His errors all involved single letters or combinations of letters and consisted of substitutions (e.g. *portafoglio → portofoglio*), insertions (e.g. *elica → eclica*), deletions (e.g. *unicorno → unico no*) and transpositions (e.g. *fanale → falane*), or combinations of two of these types (e.g. *peloso → perolo*). The largest category of error was substitution of one letter for another (46%), followed by insertions (16%), deletions (7%) and transpositions (3%). As one might expect from these types of errors, the misspellings that FV produced were generally nonwords, and could even occasionally result in orthotactic violations (e.g. *splivo → sfivo*). More typically, though, letter errors respected orthographic structure; interestingly, the authors note that vowels tended to substitute for vowels and consonants for consonants. Error patterns and percentages of each type of error were closely similar when FV was asked to write nonwords to dictation. Thus far FV's spelling performance closely parallels what one might expect from a graphemic buffer deficit.

There were a number of inconsistencies in the pattern, however. First, as we have seen, FV made slightly (but significantly) fewer errors in writing words than nonwords. One might argue, as the authors do, that this finding poses no especial problems for a graphemic buffer deficit hypothesis; better performance with words might simply reflect the greater success of a monitoring strategy when only partial information is available in the buffer. Second, no effect of letter order was observed; errors occurred with the same frequency in initial, middle and final positions of the string. This again may not be particularly problematic for the hypothesis; because the operation of the buffer is theoretically underspecified, there are no motivated predictions concerning whether damage will inevitably result in differential position effects. There is a precedent from another language domain, however. Ellis, Flude and Young (1987) describe a case of acquired *reading* disorder in which information about letter identity is impaired while knowledge of letter position appears to remain intact.

What the authors themselves feel is hard for a graphemic buffer deficit account to explain is FV's excellent performance in a copying-from-memory task. In this task, FV performed "essentially flawlessly", even when a 10-second delay was interposed between seeing a printed letter string (both words and nonwords were presented as stimuli) and reproducing it in his own handwriting. Models of spelling assume that this task, which clearly requires the stimulus word to be held temporarily, demands the operation of the graphemic buffer (e.g. Ellis, 1982), and thus one would anticipate that FV's ability to copy after a delay would be impaired in just the same way as his spelling under normal conditions. The authors themselves consider—and reject— the possibility that FV uses in delayed copying not a graphemic pattern but a graphic pattern. In other words, the stimulus is treated as a complex line drawing and held in a non-linguistic visual memory system. This is highly unlikely, however, since FV was required to transform what he saw initially (a printed word) into cursive script, implicating a more abstract graphemic code.

However, there may be an alternative means of explaining FV's good performance. Ellis (1982), for example, suggests that the ability to copy "graphemically" (that is, to transform the input as happens when printed letters are written as cursive script) in patients who have difficulty in writing spontaneously implies a link between the visual analysis system (part of the *reading* system) and the graphemic buffer. This in itself would not necessarily account for FV's preserved ability to copy, and to copy after a delay, since *any* refreshing of the buffer—whether from spelling systems or from visual analysis—would encounter the same difficulty. As Shallice (1988) points out, however, it is possible that FV makes use of a strategy that allows visual information from the reading system to be fed into the graphemic buffer grapheme by grapheme, with the aid of visual attention processes, thereby bypassing difficulties in maintaining multi-letter strings.

Not all patients with a putative graphemic buffer deficit behave in the same way on this task. If FV's preserved ability to copy depends on the adoption of a particular strategy, then it is one that is either unavailable to patient LB (Caramazza *et al.*, 1987; Caramazza & Miceli, 1990) or that he fails to use. LB had just as much difficulty in copying after a delay as in writing spontaneously or to dictation. He copied correctly only 64% of words and 38% of nonwords, making more errors with longer letter strings and producing substitute letters, deletions, insertions and transpositions of letters. As the authors note, spelling errors on this task were qualitatively identical to those produced in dictation and other writing tasks.

Apart from differences on the copy-from-memory task, LB behaves very like FV. Word spelling is affected by stimulus length (even after correcting for the number of letters in the string), but not by other variables. Spelling errors primarily involved difficulties in deriving the correct letter structure, resulting in substitutions, insertions, additions and transpositions. As one might expect, effects of stimulus length and error type are paralleled in LB's nonword spelling. Moreover, they occur in all ways of testing written spelling and in oral spelling of words and nonwords. All in all, then, LB presents with a "typical" profile of what one would expect of selective damage to the graphemic buffer.

The one discordant note is that, like FV, he makes substantially more errors in spelling nonwords than familiar words; in writing to dictation, for example, he made 41% word errors compared with 57.9% nonword errors, and this was observed across all spelling tasks. To find out the reason for the discrepancy, the authors attempted to test systematically centrally located mechanisms assumed to contribute to nonword spelling. LB also had an acquired reading disorder that affected his ability to *read* nonwords but not words (Caramazza *et al.*, 1985). This problem is attributed to a phonological output buffer deficit. However, Caramazza *et al.* (1987) reject this as an account of his greater difficulty in *spelling* nonwords because of his relatively well-preserved ability to repeat nonwords (between four and 12 phonemes in length). Nonetheless, when a delay was interposed between hearing a nonword and repeating it (filled by asking LB to write down the nonword), ability to repeat the nonwords declined substantially compared with word repetition, which remained flawless. Caramazza *et al.* (1987) conclude that LB has a "subtle phonological processing deficit that affects his performance in processing nonwords", though they do not commit themselves to an account of what the deficit might be.

While FV did not show any especial effect of letter position in the distribution of his spelling errors, analysis of LB's spelling performance (with both words and nonwords) revealed that letters in medial positions were more vunerable to error than flanking letters (initial and final). This finding supports Wing and Baddeley's contention (based on "normal" slips of the pen) that medial graphemes are "read out" less efficiently than flanking graphemes.

A similar analysis of the spelling errors of patient SE, reported by Posteraro, Zinelli and Mazzucchi (1988), also demonstrated that errors were predominantly made in medial positions. In terms of the criteria for a graphemic buffer deficit, SE's spelling performance arguably provides a better fit as a case of selective damage to the graphemic buffer than either FV or LB. Arguable, perhaps, because of the small number of words and nonwords on which testing and error analyses were actually based. The authors found no evidence of effects of word variables other than word length. Spelling was affected in similar ways irrespective of task and whether written or oral output was elicited. Like LB, and unlike FV, SE's copying from memory was also affected; she was able to copy 12/12 four-letter words after an imposed delay, but only 4/12 seven-letter words.

Errors produced in spelling both words and nonwords consisted primarily of deletions (e.g. *simbolo* → *sibolo*; *insetto* → *intto*), while for FV and SB, substitutions constituted the largest error category. There may be a number of reasons for this difference, however. One might simply be the result of the small number of errors on which analyses were performed for SE (29 written spelling errors for words, compared with 138 errors for FV and 178 for LB). Another reason is more interesting. SE was tested with four-letter and seven-letter words and nonwords. In writing to dictation, written naming and delayed copying she made no errors in writing four-letter words; errors occurred in response to the longer materials (and a similar pattern can be seen for the nonword stimuli). As Posteraro *et al.* note, for patient LB as well, deletions became the more numerous error type, both for words and nonwords, as stimulus length increased (Caramazza et al., 1987, Table 8).

The final patient we will discuss in this section is CW, recently reported by Cubelli (1991). CW fulfils all the criteria indicative of a selective graphemic buffer deficit. In addition, delayed copying was impaired in the same way and to the same degree as other spelling tasks. Unlike the previous case, SE, patient CW produced a large number of letter substitutions, as well as deletions, additions and transpositions. Cubelli analyses a large number of error responses made by CW, in which 409 letters were produced incorrectly. The author does not break down error categories by stimulus length, though it is pertinent to note that, unlike SE, patient CW did not show error-free performance on four-letter items. No information is given about the distribution of errors across letter position.

So far in this section we have discussed in detail the cases of four Italian patients who appear to present with a selective graphemic buffer deficit. We have set out similarities between the cases and attempted to highlight elements of each case that do not automatically fall out of a simple account of the ways in which impairment can affect the operation of a graphemic buffer. Our patient John, like the other patients, can be described as showing a graphemic buffer impairment (see Table 15.1). However, the usefulness of such observations about John and the other patients is in what they can tell us about the ways in which graphemic representations are structured and processed.

THE STRUCTURE OF GRAPHEMIC REPRESENTATIONS

Cubelli (1991) noted that CW's letter errors primarily involved vowels. Significantly more errors were made in writing vowels than consonants in all tasks and regardless of whether the patient wrote in cursive script or in capital letters. No difference was found in writing stressed and unstressed vowels. CW systematically substituted vowels for vowels, and when he did produce errors involving consonants, substituted consonants for consonants. Cubelli also reports a second patient, CF, who showed a brief, transient, deficit in writing. When asked to write his name, the name of the place where he lived and those of five objects, he omitted all vowels, leaving a blank space between correctly written consonants. Cubelli suggests that while there are reports of patients who leave blank spaces for letters they are unable to retrieve (e.g. Katz, 1991; Morton, 1980), a deficit confined to vowels has not been reported before. He claims that evidence from his two cases, CW and CF, which appears to demonstrate a clear consonant/vowel opposition, reveals a functional reality in the way that abstract graphemes are represented in the spelling system and within the graphemic buffer.

We can make a case that for patients FV, LB, CW and CF there is clear evidence that the consonant/vowel status of graphemes is differentially specified in spelling (relevant data are not available for SE). Both FV and LB (Caramazza *et al.*, 1987; Caramazza & Miceli, 1990; Miceli, Silveri & Caramazza, 1985) tended to produce errors in which vowels substituted for vowels and consonants for consonants (according to Miceli et al., 1987, this occurred on 97% of FV's errors and 99% of LB's errors (Caramazza & Miceli, 1990)). We have seen that Cubelli's patient CW did the same (on 99% of instances of substitution error), and we will show that it is also the case for our patient John. Graphemic representations, then, have more structure than would be supposed by the hypothesis that they consist of linearly ordered strings of graphemes.

Caramazza and Miceli (1990) went on to carry out further detailed analyses of LB's spellings, and, on the basis of this work, they claim that graphemic representations have a "multi-dimensional structure". According to their hypothesis, graphemic representations are organized in "tiers" or dimensions of information. The first dimension in this multi-dimensional structure is a grapheme identity tier, which conveys information about which graphemes are actually part of the spelling. The second dimension, the CV tier, specifies the way in which grapheme identities are organized into a consonant–vowel structure. This, in turn, is governed by a third dimension, the graphosyllable tier, which represents the graphosyllable boundaries in the word. Therefore, to use one of Caramazza and Miceli's examples, the Italian word *sconto* would be represented as: $\{\langle s\text{-}C\text{-}\sigma_1\rangle, c\text{-}C\text{-}\sigma_1\rangle, \langle o\text{-}V\text{-}\sigma_1\rangle, \langle n\text{-}C\text{-}\sigma_1\rangle, \langle t\text{-}C\text{-}\sigma_2\rangle, \langle o\text{-}V\text{-}\sigma_2\rangle\}$, where C and V indicate consonant and vowel and σ indicates syllable (subscript shows position in word). There is also a separate tier concerning quantity, which indicates the number of graphemes in the string. Thus, again to take an example from Italian, in the case of words like *stella*, which have doubled or "geminate" consonants, a single grapheme will be associated with two positions in the CV frame, and this will be marked accordingly (D-x-C standing for doubled consonant):

$\{\langle$s-C-$\sigma_1\rangle$, $\langle$t-C-$\sigma_1\rangle$, $\langle$e-V-$\sigma_1\rangle$, $\langle$D-l-C-$\sigma_2\rangle$, $\langle$a-V-$\sigma_2\rangle\}$. On the other hand, graphemes that simply occur twice in the same word but are not geminates, such as $\langle$t$\rangle$ in *atleta*, are specified twice in the quantity dimension.

It is important to realize that although the concept of the graphosyllable is a theoretical notion clearly derived from phonology, Caramazza and Miceli (1990) assume that observed "syllabic" effects stem from the way *spellings* are represented, rather than deriving from underlying *phonological* factors. Therefore, they propose that "whatever similarities there may be between the processing principles that embody phonotactic constraints and those that embody graphotactic constraints, these are fairly abstract: the relationship is one of similarity of principle and not similarity of content" (p. 294).

We shall consider carefully the nature of the evidence which provokes Caramazza and Miceli to assume a highly complex structure for graphemic representations. The authors suggest that there are five major facts about LB's spelling which prompt their conclusions. Before we go into these findings, we need to clarify a distinction drawn by Caramazza and Miceli between simple and complex words. The terms are intended to capture a difference between words in Italian that have a simple alternating CV pattern and more complex CV words that deviate from this pattern. Thus, in the six-letter materials used by the authors, simple CV words have a CVCVCV structure like *tavolo*; complex CV words are those like *nastro*, which has a CVCCCV structure, and *albino*, which has a VCCVCV structure. Note that far more Italian words have a regular, simple, CVCVCV structure than corresponding English words.

1. *Substitution and transposition errors virtually always respected consonant or vowel status.* Both for simple and complex CV words, consonants almost always substituted for, or were transposed with, other consonants; similarly, vowels almost always substituted for, or were transposed with, other vowels. This occurred for 736/741 (99%) substitution errors, for example. Note that there were no clear phonological or visual relationships between target and error letters.

   Why exactly is this finding, replicated in other patients we have described, incompatible with the view that spelling representations encode simply *grapheme* identity? Because, on this view, there is no motivated reason to expect that incorrectly produced letters should respect the CV status of the target response. According to the multi-dimensional hypothesis, on the other hand, the systematicity of these errors falls out of the view that CV tier information will force selection of graphemes which respect the CV status of the target response.

2. *Simple CV words were more often correctly spelled than complex CV words.* The finding that simple CV words are more resistant to error is taken by the authors to reflect the important part played by graphosyllables in the processing and transmission of graphemic information. That is, it is assumed that CV sequences are more robust than all other consonant and vowel graphosyllables, such as CVC and CCV clusters, so that fewer errors will occur in producing alternating CV sequences (CVCVCV) than more complex sequences. Further evidence to support this view comes from the particular patterns of error produced in response to simple and complex CV words, which brings us to the next finding.

3. *There was an essentially non-overlapping distribution of error types for simple CV and complex CV words.* For simple CV words, error types were almost always

letter substitutions and non-adjacent letter exchanges/transpositions. Deletions and insertions were rare. In contrast, for complex CV words, letter deletions, insertions and shifts were produced frequently, and as frequently as substitutions and exchanges. We can put this another way: in the case of a single consonant, deletion, insertion, shift and adjacent letter transposition errors did not tend to occur when the consonant was flanked by vowels, and, in the case of a single vowel, when it was flanked by consonants—in other words, these errors almost invariably involved consonant clusters and vowel clusters, rather than CV sequences. Let us look at the pattern of deletion errors, for example. Ninety-nine per cent of LB's single-letter deletions occurred in VV and CC (non-geminate) clusters, and while 92% of these errors involved the deletion of one of two consonants in a cluster (e.g. *urlare → ulare, sfondo → sondo*), only one error involved the deletion of a singleton consonant (e.g. *tregua → treua*). These error patterns are accounted for by invoking a minimum complexity principle (MCP), such that, *in response to a damaged representation, the least complex graphosyllabic sequence consistent with the available information will be produced.* Since, in abstract, the simplest graphosyllable consists of a consonant and vowel, this will have two consequences when we consider the nature of errors which have been observed to occur. First, CV sequences will be more resistant to damage than other sequences, but when impairment does occur, it will take predictable forms. Thus, according to the MCP, one might expect that errors to CV sequences will not be deletions but substitutions and non-adjacent exchanges which still preserve CV structure. For example, one would predict that errors like *fanale → farale* (substitution) or *vagone → gavone* (non-adjacent exchange) would occur (and these are, indeed, real examples), but not *fanale → faale* or *vagone → oagvne*. Deletion of *n* in *fanale* results in a more complex graphosyllable than is the case when a consonant is substituted. The same is true if vowel exchanges with consonant in *vagone*, rather than consonant with consonant.

Second, the MCP predicts that there will be an observable tendency for errors concerning complex graphosyllables to result in simplified CV sequences. Thus, errors to consonant clusters and vowel clusters might well result in deletions, such as *grembo → gembo*, in which the CCV graphosyllable simplifies to a CV graphosyllable. Deletions were the major error category produced in response to complex CV words.

4. *Geminate clusters were highly resistant to error.* Although, as we have seen, CC clusters were vulnerable to error, geminate clusters did not follow this pattern and were not susceptible to error types found with other CC clusters. Thus, for geminate clusters (in fourth and fifth letter position) in words like *crollo*, LB makes very few errors (only 1.4% across both positions), while for (non-geminate) consonant clusters in the same letter positions, he produced significantly more errors (13% in position 4 and 3% in position 5). Examination of the distribution of errors involving geminate consonants (69 errors in total) reveals that while some of them fall into existing categories (e.g. substitution errors), there are also new types of error specifically affecting geminates. There are, for example, 25/69 instances of shift of the geminate feature (e.g. *sorella → sorrela*), which appear to indicate that information that there is consonant doubling in the word is independent of the

actual identity of the doubled consonants. Furthermore, exchange errors involving the geminate cluster (10/69) never involved just one of the consonants (e.g. *sorella → solerra*, but not *sorella → solerla*), which suggests that geminate consonants behave as a single unit.

5. *Graphemic and not phonological structure determined the distribution of errors.* Caramazza and Miceli propose that the constraints operating on LB's spelling are strictly graphological in nature. In other words, they note, "the basic elements, 'consonant' and 'vowel' in a graphemic representation do not have phonological content" (p. 276). Their case is supported by the demonstration that LB's spelling errors did not appear to be sensitive to the phonological characteristics of the words he was attempting to spell. Thus, a substantial number of his errors (76) violated phonotactic constraints of Italian (e.g. *sfondo → fsondo, scalda → slcada*). Note that the graphemic sequence *slc* is well formed according to hypothesized graphotactic constraints, because it is specified in terms of *number* of *graphemic* consonant or vowel sequences, and not in terms of the corresponding phonological content of these sequences.

As an additional line of evidence, the authors discovered that CC and VV clusters corresponding to single phonemes behaved as two graphemes rather than as a single phonological unit (e.g. *gn* is pronounced as the single phoneme /ñ/ in *carogna* and *ignoro*, but was treated as two graphemes in the errors *carocna* and *igroro*).

DOES JOHN'S SPELLING SUPPORT THE CONJECTURE THAT GRAPHEMIC REPRESENTATIONS HAVE A MULTI-DIMENSIONAL STRUCTURE?

We have suggested that John's written spelling profile is most appropriately characterized as a graphemic buffer impairment, according to criteria set out above. Do detailed analyses like those carried out by Caramazza and Miceli support their proposal that graphemic representations have a multi-dimensional structure? We set out to examine this conjecture by looking at John's written spelling performance in detail.

Even since his stroke, John is a better speller than LB. Out of 6295 words that we have analysed so far, only 525 (or 8.3%) were misspelled. The total includes words written in connected text as well as individual words presented for dictation. Tables 15.2 and 15.3 set out the distribution of error types and their incidence according to stimulus length.

TABLE 15.2 Distribution of single-type errors in written word spelling to dictation.

	No. of incorrect responses (%)	No. of incorrect letters (%)
Substitution	218 (58.1)	253 (57.3)
Insertion	66 (17.6)	66 (14.9)
Deletion	79 (21.0)	111 (25.1)
Transposition: exchanges	9 (2.4)	9 (2.0)
Transposition: shifts	3 (0.8)	3 (0.7)

TABLE 15.3   Incidence of error types as a function of stimulus length (percentages in brackets).

	Substitution	Insertion	Deletion	Transposition	Mixed	Total
4-letter	38 (65.5)	5 (8.6)	8 (13.8)	1 (1.7)	6 (10.3)	58
5-letter	38 (56.7)	10 (14.9)	5 (14.9)	4 (6.0)	10 (14.9)	67
6-letter	37 (44.5)	10 (12.0)	17 (20.5)	2 (2.4)	17 (20.5)	83
7-letter	41 (45.6)	12 (13.3)	15 (16.7)	3 (3.3)	19 (21.1)	90
8-letter	20 (40.8)	12 (24.4)	10 (20.4)	1 (2.0)	6 (12.2)	49
9/12-letter	27 (36.0)	10 (13.3)	21 (28.0)	1 (1.3)	16 (21.3)	75
Total	201	59	76	12	74	

We must stress, however, that even this small number represents a substantial impairment compared with John's premorbid ability. It makes it less easy, though, to carry out analyses on large data sets: LB, in contrast, produced errors on approximately one third (1079/3300, or 33.6%) of the words he was asked to spell. Despite this practical difficulty, we believe that we have enough information to examine in depth the specific claims made by Caramazza and Miceli.

What we wanted to know, first of all, was whether John's spelling is affected by the CV complexity of words. There are good reasons why one might *not* expect this to be the case for a graphemic system operating within the currency of written English. Modern Italian spelling employs the regular Latin alphabet. Italian orthography is almost phonetic; once the regular equivalences of sound and spelling are mastered, Italian can be read and written correctly. There are no exceptions (except in some dialects). Italian has substantially more words with simple alternating CV sequences than English. Geminate consonants have a highly predictable function. Thus, the opposition of "long" and "short" consonants, for example, is a highly regular feature indicated by single versus double consonant: *sera* (evening), *serra* (he tightens); *fato* (fate), *fatto* (done); *casa* (house), *cassa* (box); *capello* (hair), *cappello* (hat). English orthography, in contrast, has a far more complex structure, which has arisen through a variety of interesting historical reasons (e.g. Scragg, 1976). There are less obvious regularities in terms of CV structure and consonant doubling. The benefits, therefore, of a system in which information about graphosyllabic structure is incorporated into the processing of graphemic representations are less easy to identify.

Effects of Simple Versus Complex CV Structure

We combed through all the spellings which John had done for us (both in single-word spelling tasks and connected written prose) to find words of five, six and seven letters which had either a simple or a complex CV structure. We found 179 simple CV words (e.g. *tiger*, *colonel*) and 1218 complex CV words (e.g. *sheet*, *weekend*) of these letter lengths. Turning to John's ability to spell these words, we discovered that he spelled 149/179 (83.2%) of simple CV words correctly, compared with 1017/1218 (83.5%) of complex CV words. We can find no indication, therefore, that John was better able to spell words with an alternating, simple, consonant–vowel structure.

Another question we can ask of these data is whether there is any suggestion of a difference in the distribution of error types for simple CV and complex CV words. Recall that Caramazza and Miceli report that LB produced almost exclusively substitutions and (non-adjacent) letter exchanges in misspelling simple CV words— accounting for 98.8% (420/425) of the errors. Letter deletions and insertions occurred only rarely (5/425); shift errors never occurred. In contrast, for complex CV words, letter deletions, insertions and shifts were as frequent as substitutions and exchanges. As we have stressed before, in examining John's responses to simple CV words we are dealing with small numbers of errors. Even so, there is little sign of a non-overlapping distribution of single error types in comparing simple and complex CV words (see Table 15.4).

While two-thirds of John's errors to simple CV words are substitutions (63.6%), the remaining third are insertions (27.3%) and deletions (9.1%). None was a letter exchange. The pattern in response to complex CV words is similar: he also tends to produce substitutions (58.7%), followed by insertions (15.7%) and deletions (18.6%). LB, on the other hand, made fewer substitutions (31.1%) and rather more deletions (38.7%). One explanation for LB's profile is that consonant clusters in complex CV words tended to be simplified into single consonants—following the minimum complexity principle—as in *strada* → *stada*, *spiare* → *piare*. We can find no evidence, then, that John's spelling is subject to a similar constraint.

Interestingly, while statistically more of LB's errors affected CC clusters than CV clusters in the same letter positions, John made significantly *fewer* CC than CV errors in the same letter positions across the six-letter words in our sample.

Do Substitution and Transposition Errors Primarily Respect Consonant/Vowel Status?

The answer to this question is a resounding yes for substitution errors. John made 253 letter substitutions. Of these 201 (79.4%) involved consonants, while 52 (20.6%) involved vowels. In the majority of cases, consonants substituted for consonants (189/201; 94%) and vowels substituted for vowels (46/52; 88.5%). Transposition errors constituted only a small percentage of single error types (3.2%). The majority were adjacent letter exchanges, involving, in the main, vowel/consonant switches (e.g. *Portugal* → *Portgual*).

TABLE 15.4 Distribution of single-type errors for simple CV and complex CV words (percentages in brackets).

	Simple		Complex	
Substitution	14	(63.6)	101	(58.7)
Insertion	2	(9.1)	32	(18.6)
Deletion	6	(27.3)	27	(15.7)
Transposition: non-adjacent letter exchange	0		0	
Transposition: adjacent letter exchange	0		9	(5.2)
Transposition: shifts	0		3	(1.7)

Are Geminate Clusters Highly Resistant to Error?

Analyses of six-letter words which either had a geminate consonant in positions 3 and 4 (e.g. *butter, funnel*) or a non-geminate consonant cluster (e.g. *jacket, pencil*) revealed no significant difference between the two word types ($\chi^2 = 1.05$; $p = 0.305$). Qualitative analyses also indicated that, in a substantial number of instances, the geminate cluster did not appear to behave like a single unit. Thus, 13% of errors involved substitutions of one of the consonants in the cluster (e.g. *kettle → catley, wedding → weeding*)—for LB, this figure was only 0.7%. Furthermore, the production of a new geminate in a word that did not contain a geminate (e.g. *tavolo → tavvolo*) was extremely rare in LB's corpus of errors (10/4400, 0.2%). Although it did not happen frequently in John's spelling errors, it happened sufficiently often for it to be noticeable (25/525, 4.8%), as in *salad → sallad, children → childreen, necklace → necllace*.

Is it Graphemic or Phonological Structure which Determines the Structure of Errors?

Examination of LB's errors suggests that it is graphemic structure and not phonology that determines the distribution of errors in his performance. In particular, Caramazza and Miceli show that LB's errors violated phonotactic constraints, and that phonological segments corresponding to two consonants (e.g. *sc → /ʃ/, gn → /ñ/*) behaved like any other CC cluster (except geminate clusters).

John's spelling errors are generally graphologically *and* phonotactically acceptable (perhaps this is because CC sequences are not so vulnerable to error as they were in LB's corpus). Howevever, even adopting a conservative criterion for what we will take as phonotactically illegal, we can find a small percentage of cases which are unacceptable phonologically but are legitimate graphemic sequences (in terms of number) (e.g. *clerk → clrek, precept → precedt, qualms → quatms, skirt → skirwt*).

It is clear that John's spellings do not always respect single sounds corresponding to two consonants. We can find 25 instances (out of 525, 4.8%) in which CC and VV clusters corresponding to single phonemes (e.g. /θ/, /f/, /ʃ/), are not treated as single units (e.g. *bath → balh, nephews → nefhews, fishing → fissing*).

FURTHER GRAPHOLOGICAL CONSTRAINTS ON JOHN'S SPELLING

There is little evidence that we can gather from analyses of John's spellings to support the notion of a graphosyllable tier incorporated within the structure of graphemic representations. On the other hand, there is clear evidence that his spelling is affected by the consonant and vowel structure of words he attempts to spell. Indeed, our findings suggest that consonants may be more vulnerable to error than vowels. While consonants seem to be more error-prone than vowels in LB's spelling, the difference is not marked: for substitution errors, for example, he makes errors with 437/741 consonants (59%) and 304/741 vowels (41%). For John, on the other hand, the difference is substantial: for substitution errors, 201/253 (79.4%) involved consonants while only 52/253 (20.6%) involved vowels. This difference is comparable in magnitude to that observed by Cubelli for his patient CW. In this case, though, the difference was in the opposite direction, with vowels more vulnerable to error: errors were made on 82.9% of vowels but only on 17.1% of consonants.

We have also noted other interesting aspects of John's spelling. For LB, the majority of substitution errors consisted of duplication of letters occurring elsewhere in the stimulus (e.g. *tesoro → teroro*). Thus, out of 741 letter substitutions that LB makes, 506 (68.3%) were duplications while only 235 (31.7%) were letters that did not appear in the intended target. In contrast, John's letter substitutions do *not* primarily involve letters in the stimulus word (195/253, 77.1%). Only 58/253 (22.9%) were duplications of letters occurring elsewhere in the stimulus.

We were keen to find out whether we could identify any relationship between the correct letter and its substitute which could explain why John produces so many "new" letters, rather than duplications. First of all, we looked at phonetic similarity between the letter that was substituted and the intended letter. A distinctive feature analysis which examined differences in manner, voice and place (three distinctive features) showed that in 25% (48/189) of cases the two letters differed by only one distinctive feature (e.g. in *bomb → bomp*, /b/ → /p/ differ in voicing), in 23% of cases they differed by two distinctive features (e.g. in *bank → band*, /k/ → /d/ differ in voicing and place of articulation) and in 5% of cases they differed by three distinctive features (e.g. in *wish → wist →* , /h/ → /t/ differ in voicing and place and manner of articulation). The remaining instances (47% of consonantal substitutions) showed little phonetic similarity.

More strikingly, perhaps, the intended letter and its substitute often share a close *visual* structural similarity. We used an ordering of visual similarity employed by Patterson and Kay (1982) and based on that devised by Bouma (1971) for confusion matrices in letter recognition by non-brain-damaged subjects. The ordering is primarily meant to reflect clusters within which the similarity is clear, such as ascenders, descenders, letters composed of a "loop on a stick" (*b, d, p, g, q*), the "little roundish letters" (*a, o, c, e*). *X* and *z*, which do not occur very often, were eliminated, resulting in a 24 × 24 matrix (see Figure 15.2).

The implication from Figure 15.2 is that visual similarity appears to play a prominent role in John's letter substitutions. Although there are exceptions, the majority of substitutions lie near the diagonal, suggesting that visual features of letters may be a major factor in producing substitute letters.

DISCUSSION

Let us summarize the argument we have put forward in this chapter. We have conjectured on the basis of John's spelling performance, not only in written spelling but also in typing and spelling aloud, that he has a "graphemic buffer deficit", in the way that it is characterized by Caramazza *et al.* (1987), Ellis (1982), Margolin (1984) and Miceli, Silveri and Caramazza (1985).

We have compared in detail the spelling profile of John with another similar patient, LB, described by Caramazza and Miceli (1990). Caramazza and Miceli use evidence from LB's written spelling to construct a complex theory of the way in which graphemic

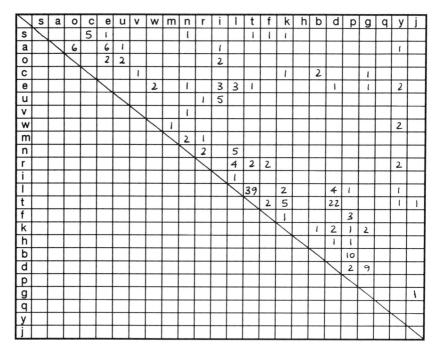

	s	a	o	c	e	u	v	w	m	n	r	i	l	t	f	k	h	b	d	p	g	q	y	j
s		5		1							1			1	1	1								
a			6	6	1						1												1	
o				2	2						2													
c						1								1				2		1				
e								2		1		3	3	1				1		1			2	
u												1	5											
v								1																
w									1														2	
m										2	1													
n											2		5											
r														4	2	2							2	
i													1											
l														39	2			4	1				1	
t															2	5		22					1	1
f																1			3					
k																	1	2	1	2				
h																		1	1					
b																			10					
d																				2	9			
p																								
g																								1
q																								
y																								
j																								

FIGURE 15.2   A confusion matrix for lower-case letters with letters sharing visual features placed close together in the ordering. Clear instances of letter misidentifications are shown in the matrix, which if folded for direction (thus, confusion between *a* and *o* may mean *a → o* or *o → a*.

representations are structured. The theory elaborates a multi-dimensional structure for such representations, so that four separate tiers of information are linked in each unit of graphemic analysis. Although early work (e.g. Ellis, 1982; Wing & Baddeley, 1980) claimed that graphemic representations simply conveyed information about graphemic identities and their position, Caramazza and Miceli suggest that information about consonant–vowel status and graphosyllable structure is also fundamental to the structure of such representations. Cubelli (1991) independently provides evidence to support the reality of a consonant–vowel distinction.

   Our analyses of John's written spelling errors also support the view that consonant–vowel status is marked in graphemic representations. However, we can find little evidence to back up the claim that graphosyllabic structure is marked in graphemic representations, at least in the way set out by Caramazza and Miceli. The authors argue that the "default" graphosyllable, the least complex in terms of consonant–vowel structure, is the CV sequence—all other patterns being more complex. In Italian, with its highly regular orthographic and phonological structure, the CV sequence is indeed common, and considerably more common than in corresponding English words (at least in alternating CV sequences). We could find little evidence in John's spelling that such sequences were less vulnerable to error. Indeed, John made more errors on CV sequences (whether the words had a simple or a complex structure) than CC sequences in corresponding letter positions. We conjecture that it is hard to see, in an orthography such as written English, how such a processing system for spelling (depending on the CV syllable as the "basic" level in the graphosyllabic tier) could arise—at least in the way envisaged by Caramazza and Miceli, which incorporates the notion of a minimum complexity principle, as well as a particular hierarchy of graphemic complexity. At the same time, we acknowledge that their view may be a perfectly adequate processing account of the structure of written Italian.

However, there is one major difficulty with the evidence we have adduced to challenge the details of the Caramazza and Miceli theory as a "universal" account of the structure of graphemic representations. Like LB, John makes more substitution errors than any other type of error. Unlike LB, though, we have revealed that the majority of substituting letters do not occur elsewhere in the word, and that they often bear a distinct visual similarity to the target. As we noted above, Ellis (1979, 1988) suggests that such errors actually arise not at a graphemic level, but at a more peripheral stage at which stroke selections are made. Thus, Ellis (1988) states that, "I propose that letter substitutions based on physical similarity indicate problems in activating appropriate graphic motor patterns in response to input from the allographic level" (p. 111). In support of this view, Ellis summarizes the neurological case reported by Zangwill (1954) of a patient, apparently with a relatively peripheral writing impairment, in whom visual similarity played a determining part in producing letter substitutions (e.g. *H* for *K*, *u* for *y*, *k* for *b*). Perhaps it is the case, then, that the majority of John's spelling errors do not arise at a graphemic level, and therefore do not constitute appropriate evidence with which to address Caramazza and Miceli's hypothesis?

A search through relevant literature reveals that substitution errors have been attributed to difficulties at a number of different levels: at the level of the graphemic buffer (e.g. Caramazza *et al.*, 1987; Caramazza & Miceli, 1990; Miceli, Silveri & Caramazza, 1985), at the level of selecting allographs (e.g. Ellis, 1982) and at the level of selecting graphic motor patterns in response to input from the allographic level (e.g. Ellis, 1979, 1988). Shallice (1988) suggests that substitution errors arising from difficulties in selection from the graphemic buffer will not necessarily be visually similar to replaced letters, and may also be duplications of letters elsewhere in the word—which neatly describes the substitution errors produced by LB and FV (Miceli *et al.*, 1987). As we have discussed, physical similarity in letter substitution errors is held to arise at the level of selecting graphic motor patterns. We do not, however, subscribe to the view that at least some of John's spelling difficulty arises at this level. Unlike Zangwill's (1954) patient, John does not present as a person with difficulty in monitoring which programmed letter strokes have already been executed (Margolin, 1984). He does not show general signs of apraxic agraphia: writing is fluently and rapidly executed, with no ill-formed letters or stroke errors. More pertinently, perhaps, John not only produces substitution, insertion, deletion and transposition errors in writing, but also in spelling aloud and typing. As we have noted, this pattern would appear to indicate that difficulties arise at a level *prior* to the operation of processes specialized for different types of output. Rather, we suggest that John's pattern of impairment reflects one particular way in which abstract graphemic representations can be impaired. For John, consonants are considerably more susceptible to damage than vowels. We suggest that the observed physical similarity between intended letter and substituting letter arises from this fact—that is, that partial information from abstract representations activates more concrete realizations (whether for written, spoken or typed output), resulting in a physical similarity that is not *purely* visual, phonological or motoric in nature.

ACKNOWLEDGEMENTS

We gratefully acknowledge the help of both JH and Anne Whateley, speech and language therapist, in preparing this chapter. The first author is supported by a Wellcome Trust University Award.

REFERENCES

Bouma, H. (1971). Visual recognition of isolated lower-case letters. *Vision Research*, **11**, 459–474.

Campbell, R. (1983). Writing nonwords to dictation. *Brain & Language*, **19**, 153–178.

Caramazza, A. & Miceli, G. (1990). The structure of graphemic representations. *Cognition*, **37**, 243–297.

Caramazza, A., Miceli, G., Silveri, M. C. & Laudanna, A. (1985). Reading mechanisms and the organisation of the lexicon: evidence from acquired dysgraphia. *Cognitive Neuropsychology*, **2**, 81–114.

Caramazza, A., Miceli, G., Villa, G. & Romani, C. (1987). The role of the graphemic buffer in spelling: evidence from a case of acquired dysgraphia. *Cognition*, **26**, 59–85.

Chedru, F. & Geschwind, N. (1962). Writing disturbances in acute confusional states. *Neuropsychologia*, **10**, 343–353.

Cubelli, R. (1991). A selective deficit for writing vowels in acquired dysgraphia. *Nature*, **353**, 258–260.

Ellis, A. W. (1979). Slips of the pen. *Visible Language*, **13**, 265–282.

Ellis, A. W. (1982). Spelling and writing (and reading and speaking). In A. W. Ellis (Ed.), *Normality and Pathology in Cognitive Function*. London: Academic Press.

Ellis, A. W. (1988). Normal writing processes and peripheral acquired dysgraphias. *Language and Cognitive Processes*, **3**, 99–127.

Ellis, A. W., Flude, B. & Young, A. W. (1987). "Neglect dyslexia" and the early visual processing of letters in words. *Cognitive Neuropsychology*, **4**, 465–486.

Goodglass, H. & Kaplan, E. (1983). *Assessment of Aphasia and Related Disorders*. Philadelphia: Lea & Febiger.

Hatfield, F. M. & Patterson, K. E. (1983). Phonological spelling. *Quarterly Journal of Experimental Psychology*, **35A**, 451–468.

Hotopf, N. (1980). Slips of the pen. In U. Frith (Ed.), *Cognitive Processes in Spelling*. London: Academic Press.

Katz, R. (1991). Limited retention of information in the graphemic buffer. *Cortex*, **27**, 111–119.

Margolin, D. I. (1984). The neuropsychology of writing and spelling: semantic, phonological, motor and perceptual processes. *Quarterly Journal of Experimental Psychology*, **34A**, 459–489.

Miceli, G., Silveri, M. C. & Caramazza, A. (1985). Cognitive analysis of a case of pure dysgraphia. *Brain & Language*, **25**, 187–196.

Miceli, G., Silveri, M. C. & Caramazza, A. (1987). The role of the phoneme-to-grapheme conversion system and of the graphemic output buffer in writing: evidence from an Italian case of pure dysgraphia. In M. Coltheart, G. Sartori & R. Job (Eds), *Cognitive Neuropsychology of Language*. London: LEA.

Morton, J. (1980). The logogen model and orthographic structure. In U. Frith (Ed.), *Cognitive Processes in Spelling*. London: Academic Press.

Nolan, K. E. & Caramazza, A. (1983). An analysis of writing in a case of deep dyslexia. *Brain & Language*, **20**, 305–328.

Patterson, K. E. & Kay, J. M. (1982). Letter-by-letter reading: phonological descriptions of a neurological syndrome. *Quarterly Journal of Experimental Psychology*, **34A**, 411–441.

Posteraro, L., Zinelli, P. & Mazzucchi, A. (1988). Selective impairment of the graphemic buffer in acquired dysgraphia: a case study. *Brain & Language*, **35**, 274–286.

Scragg, D. G. (1976). *A History of English Spelling*. Manchester: Manchester University Press.

Shallice, T. (1981). Phonological agraphia and the lexical route in writing. *Brain*, **104**, 413–429.

Shallice, T. (1988). *From Neuropsychology to Mental Structure*. Cambridge: Cambridge University Press.

Wing, A. M. & Baddeley, A. D. (1980). Spelling errors in handwriting: a corpus and distributional analysis. In U. Frith (Ed.), *Cognitive Processes in Spelling*. London: Academic Press.

Zangwill, O. L. (1954). Agraphia due to a left parietal glioma in a left-handed man. *Brain*, **77**, 510–520.

Part IV

Computational Models

16

Computational Approaches to Normal and Impaired Spelling

GORDON D. A. BROWN

University of Wales, Bangor

RICHARD P. W. LOOSEMORE

University of Warwick, Coventry

The three chapters in this section of the book all describe "connectionist" or "neural network" models of spelling. In this chapter we give a brief introduction to connectionist modelling, and argue that adopting a computational approach can help us to develop better models of spelling and gain a different kind of understanding of the processes involved in normal spelling and the kinds of problems that could lead to impaired spelling development.

The rest of the chapter is devoted to a description of our own connectionist model of normal and dyslexic spelling development. We use the connectionist approach to investigate the difficulty, in computational terms, of learning to spell different types of words; types that differ in their sound-to-spelling characteristics. This leads to a new classification of word types, and to the realization that it is insufficient simply to classify words as "regular" or "irregular" in their sound-to-spelling correspondence. We show that a simple connectionist model can learn to spell both regular and irregular words (as traditionally defined) with a reasonable degree of accuracy. We then describe the results of some experiments we have conducted which show that children, when asked to spell the same words that the model has learned to spell, exhibit the same type of difficulty on the same word type as does the model.

Handbook of spelling: Theory, Process and Intervention. Edited by G. D. A. Brown and N. C. Ellis.
©1994 John Wiley & Sons Ltd.

In particular, words which contain sound-to-spelling correspondences which are either unusual (i.e. low-frequency) or irregular (i.e. with exceptions) cause particular difficulty both for children at various stages of development and for the model.

The fact that the level of difficulty experienced by the model on different word types so closely mirrors the pattern of difficulty found in children is taken as evidence that the process of learning to spell can usefully be viewed as one of mastering a set of statistical associations between representations of the phonological forms of words and representations of their orthographies. This kind of approach stands in contrast to "cognitive" or "information-processing" approaches which refer to the "rules" or "strategies" that children use at different stages in learning to spell.

We also use the model to examine the question of whether developmentally dyslexic spelling problems can be characterized in terms of the amount of computational resource that dyslexics bring to the task of learning to spell. We show that reducing the computational capacity of the spelling learning network leads to slower and less accurate learning of both regular and irregular words. We briefly describe the results of an experiment on dyslexic spellers which demonstrates that the pattern of difficulty experienced by "dyslexic" versions of the model is very similar to that experienced by dyslexic children. In the final section, we use our own model and those reported in the subsequent two chapters (by Olson and Caramazza and by Houghton *et al.*) to draw out some general conclusions about the utility of computational modelling in general, and connectionist modelling in particular, to our understanding of normal and disturbed spelling development.

THE NEED FOR COMPUTATIONAL MODELS

Many of the chapters in this book refer to some version of the "dual-route" model of spelling, in which there are two separate routines available by which the correct spelling of a word may be derived. Such models are generally verbally described, often with an accompanying diagram (see, e.g., Barry, this volume, Chapter 2). This kind of approach has proved useful in improving our understanding of both normal and impaired spelling development, as well as the acquired disorders of spelling sometimes observed in patients with acquired brain injuries. However, models may be more rigorous if they are expressed *formally* in some way. A formal specification of a model will usually mean either a mathematical description of the model and the way it works, or the implementation of the model in the form of a computer program.

In the present section we focus on computational implementation of models of spelling. There are several advantages to expressing models in the form of computer programs. First of all, such expression can provide a guarantee that the relevant model is workable, i.e. that it includes all the knowledge and mechanisms necessary for the system to perform the task that it is designed for. It is easy to be misled by an elegant verbal description of a psychological model into the belief that the model is *explanatory* in that it has specified the relevant causal mechanisms, can exhibit the relevant behaviour and also give rise to novel predictions. However (as we ourselves have found to our cost in a number of areas of psychology), when one tries to write a computer program to implement even an apparently simple psychological model, it is common to find that many crucial details as to how the model is supposed to work are left unspecified. Thus if a verbally specified model is incomplete, it can be very difficult to detect the incompleteness without actually going through the discipline of attempting to write a computer program to express the model.

A second, and related, reason to implement models computationally concerns the derivation of predictions from the model. Implementing a model in the form of a computer program provides an effective guarantee that the behaviour of the model can be examined under any simulated conditions. Thus predictions can be systematically derived from the model. These can then be tested and possibly disconfirmed experimentally, thus ensuring that the model has true explanatory content rather than being nothing more than a redescription of data that already exist. In contrast, when a model is incompletely specified, as is frequently the case with purely verbally described models, it is not always possible to determine unambiguously what the predictions of the model in particular circumstances will be. This can lead to problems in deciding whether or not to accept the results of a specific experiment as evidence for or against the model concerned.

Thirdly, a related consideration concerns the explanatory constructs that are used in the model. This applies to cognitive models in particular. For example, information-processing models frequently refer to "strategies", "mental stages", "rules", "representations", and so on. Unfortunately it may not always be clear exactly what these constructs are, how they are supposed to work, and whether different researchers mean the same thing when they talk about them. Because these psychological constructs are internal, they cannot be observed directly. Many people have pointed to the dangers in postulating internal mechanisms which have arbitrary complexity in an attempt to explain some aspect of behaviour, for there is a danger that the unobservable mechanisms that are proposed may not be explanatory at all and indeed may not be anything more than a redescription of the relevant data. If the relevant rules and processes form part of a computer program, however, then there can be no disputes about what is meant by them, because it is possible for anyone to examine or recreate the program and see exactly how the postulating mechanisms are supposed to work.

A further reason for implementing models in the form of computer programs confirms the complexity and predictability of the relevant underlying processes. In the case of weather forecasting or the modelling of traffic flows, for example, the systems under study are so complex that it is impossible to predict their behaviour without simulating the system in some way. We believe it is likely that this will also turn out to be the case in psychology for models of spelling.

A further advantage of computational modelling is the increased insight given to the modeller as the nature of the problems is revealed. Parts of some process which intuitively seemed extremely easy to solve may turn out to be unexpectedly problematic when one is required to have a sub-routine in one's program to cope with them. Thus, for example, the true complexity of tasks like visual object recognition or auditory speech perception, which seem effortless to us, has been dramatically underlined by the failure of decades of attempts to build computer programs to carry out the same tasks as fast and accurately as humans. In many cases it is only by trying to imitate how the brain carries out a task that we have come to realize just how hard the task is to solve, and we suspect that the same may turn out to be true for models of spelling.

The three chapters in this section each demonstrate new insights as a direct result of the attempt to build computational models of spelling, and we do not discuss their conclusions further here. First we return to a brief description of the connectionist approach to the computational modelling of psychological processes.

CONNECTIONISM

Over the past decade or two there has been a great interest in building computational models of psychological processes that are based, more or less loosely, on the known structure of the brain. In computational terms, the brain can be viewed as being made up of a vast number of processing components (neurons or synapses) which are, in comparison with the central processing unit of modern digital computers, both relatively simple and relatively slow. Thus the computational power of the brain appears to come from its possession of a vast number of computing elements which are heavily interconnected (each unit being connected to around 10 000 other ones on the average in the brain). Attempts to simulate brain-like architectures by building interconnected networks of simple artificial neurons (neural networks) have shown that such networks exhibit many psychologically plausible characteristics such as learning capability, the ability to generalize and respond to novel input, graceful degradation of performance under damage, flexible pattern perception and completion, and many others (see, e.g., papers in Rumelhart & McClelland, 1986a and in McClelland & Rumelhart, 1986). The units in such models are generally simpler by far than real neurons in the brain, but the use of such models has nevertheless led to greater understanding of many psychological processes.

How does a simulated neural network operate? Artificial neurons in connectionist models usually have an "activation value" associated with them, often between 0 and 1. This is sometimes thought of as being analogous to the firing rate of a real neuron. Sometimes binary-valued artificial neurons are used, and these must take on the value of either 0 or 1. Psychologically meaningful objects (such as the pronunciation of words) can then be represented as patterns of this activity, i.e. the presence of 0s and 1s across sets of artificial neurons. For example the word *soap* might be represented by the pattern 101100011, while the word *pill* is represented as the pattern 001011100. In our model of spelling development, to be described below, one sub-population of the units in the network is used to represent the pronunciations of words and another sub-population is used to represent the orthographic forms of words.

The units in the artificial network are typically multiply interconnected by connections with variable strengths or weights. These connections permit the level of activity in any one unit to influence the level of activity in all the units that it is connected to. The connection strengths can be adjusted by a suitable learning algorithm, in such a way that when a particular pattern of activation appears across one population it can lead to a desired pattern of activity arising on another set of units. Thus, for example, when a pattern of activity is imposed on the subset of units in the spelling model that are used to represent the pronunciation of words, this can lead to the formation within the artificial network of a pattern of activity on the separate, but connected, sub-population of units that are designated to represent the spelled form of words. If the connection strengths have been set appropriately by the learning rule, then it may be possible for units representing the pronunciation of a particular word to cause the units that represent the correct spelling of that word to become activated. This means that the network could be said to have learned how to spell a word with that pronunciation.

Finally, these networks have the capacity to store many different associations within the same artificial network. These properties of the networks have been extensively described and explored elsewhere (e.g. McClelland & Rumelhart, 1986; Rumelhart & McClelland, 1986a).

We now attempt to explain the principles behind our own connectionist model of spelling, which in general terms works in the same way as the generic connectionist network described above. The architecture of the model, and the form of representations it uses, are in many respects similar to the connectionist model of reading developed by Seidenberg and McClelland (1989a).

The form of the model is illustrated in Figure 16.1. The population of artificial neurons that are used to represent the pronunciations of words are at the bottom of the figure, and are labelled "input units". The units that represent the spelled form of words are at the top of the figure, labelled "output units". These two populations of units are totally interconnected via an intermediate layer of units called "hidden units" (so called because they are hidden from direct contact with the input or the output). The presence of these hidden units enables more difficuly input/output

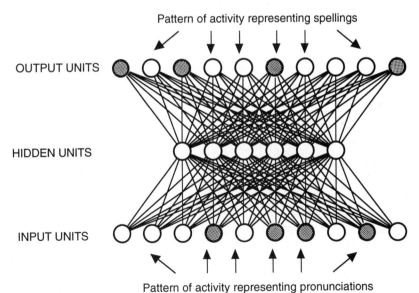

FIGURE 16.1 The architecture of the connectionist model. Only some units and connections are illustrated.

mappings to be learned than would be possible if the input units were directly connected to the output units. Each input (pronunciation) unit was constrained to take on the value either 0 or 1. We wanted the model to learn to spell a vocabulary of 225 words. Thus we needed to be able to represent the pronunciation of each of those words as a pattern of 0s and 1s on the input units of network, and have a network learn the right strengths of connection between units such that a pattern of activation would appear on the output units that corresponded to the correct spelling of that word. There were 50 input units to represent the pronunciations of words and 50 output units to represent the spelling of words. Thus a distinctive pattern of 50 0s and 1s is used to represent the spelling and pronunciation of each one of the 225 words. For each pronunciation or spelling representation, an average of 12 units were switched on and the rest were switched off. Thus "distributed representations" were employed, in that the representation of each word's pronunciation and spelling was distributed over all the input units. The input representations were chosen in such a way that words of similar pronunciation (e.g. *soap*, *hope*) had similar representations. The spellings of words were represented in a similar way on the output units. We do not go into the full details of the representations here (see Brown, Loosemore & Watson, 1993 for more details). However, the basic idea (following Rumelhart & McClelland, 1986b) is that each word can be seen as being composed of a series of phoneme or letter "triples". Thus, using _ as a symbol for the space before or after a word, *soap* can be seen as composed of the four triples _*so*, *soa*, *oap* and *ap*_. If a connectionist network was given one artificial neuron for each possible triple of letters that occurs in the vocabulary to be represented, then it would be possible to represent *soap* by giving the value 1 to all the neurons that stood for one of the four triples (listed above) contained in *soap*, with every other neuron being given the value 0. This would then allow every word to be represented as a unique pattern of 0s and 1s over the set of artificial neurons.

This idea formed the basis of the representational scheme originally employed by Rumelhart and McClelland (1986b) and we adopted a similar scheme in the present model although it differed in detail.[1]

Vocabulary of the Model

We were particularly interested in the model's ability to learn to spell three different types of word (see Table 16.1). The 225-word vocabulary included 19 words which were spelled in an entirely consistent way, i.e. they only had sound-to-spelling friends, where "friends" are defined as words which share the rime segment of the item (see Treiman, this volume, Chapter 4) and are spelled in the same way. An example of such an item is the word *kill*, which has only friends (*hill*, *will*, *till*). In standard terminology these would be considered regular words. A second set of 19 words had only sound-to spelling "enemies", such as *soap*, which has enemies *hope*, *cope*, *rope*, etc. (Enemies are defined as words which share a rime pronunciation but are spelled in a different way.) Such words may be considered irregular. A third category of words, like *bulb*, was included (*bulb* has no phonological neighbours spelled either

TABLE 16.1 Classification of word types.

Word	Friends	Enemies	Classification
soap	*None*	*hope, rope*, etc.	Irregular
kill	*hill, will*, etc.	None	Regular
bulb	None	None	?

the same or differently). We were particularly interested in the model's relative ability to learn to spell these different types of words with consistent or inconsistent sound-to spelling correspondences. The remaining words in the model's 225-item vocabulary were chosen to provide friends and enemies for the words just described.

Learning in the Model

We were interested, then, in whether the model could learn to spell words of the type we described above and, if so, which it would learn most quickly and accurately. In this section we briefly describe how the learning process works. Again only the general principles involved will be given (for details, see Brown, Loosemore & Watson, 1993).

Successful spelling in the model depends upon the network having the right strengths of connections between the units used to represent the pronunciation of words and the units used to represent the spelling of words. This is because the patterns of activation over the pronunciation units can only give rise to the appropriate patterns of activation on the spelling units if the weights on the connections between them are set appropriately. Prior to any learning, these connection strengths (weights) are set to small random values. Therefore, when a pattern of activation is imposed upon the pronunciation representing units, to represent the pronunciation of a particular word, the resulting pattern of activation that is produced on the spelling units will be random before any learning has taken place. The learning process works by imposing the pronunciation representations of each of the 225 words on the network one by one, and examining the pattern of spelling unit activation which is produced in response to each word. This, as just stated, will be random originally. For each word, the learning algorithm calculates the difference between the level of activity that is produced on each spelling unit and the level of activity that would be necessary for the correct spelling of the word to be represented. A small adjustment is made to the connectionist strength to that unit in such a way that when the same process occurs again a closer approximation to the correct pattern of spelling activation will be produced. Small incremental changes to every connection strength are made in this way so that the performance of the network gradually improves. As only incremental changes are made, it is necessary for many trials of learning to take place before any words are spelled correctly. Each "epoch" of learning consists of a presentation of all the 225 words and an adjustment of all the connection strengths such that the spelling representations corresponding to each word's pronunciation become closer to the desired (correct) spelling pattern.

The performance of each word during learning can be characterized as the difference between the pattern of activity that is actually produced on the spelling units of the network when that word is presented and the pattern of activation that would represent the correct spelling of that word. This is known as the "error score". Thus the lower the error score for a particular word at any point in learning, the better the model is doing on that word. Thus learning in the network will be reflected by a reducing error score. (There are alternative ways of assessing the performance of the network which can be interpreted more directly as a percentage of words that are spelled correctly. For a discussion of the model's performance in these terms, see Brown, Loosemore & Watson, 1993.)

Results

Figure 16.2(a) shows the average error scores during learning for 19 of each of the three word types described above. It can be seen that performance on all three word types improves over time during learning, reflected in reducing error scores. It can also be seen that words with friends and no enemies, for example *pill*, are at all stages in learning spelled most accurately by the model, words with sound-to-spelling enemies but no friends, for example *soap*, are spelled least accurately, and words with neither friends nor enemies come somewhere in between. An alternative way of looking at these results is to say that a given level of accuracy is achieved on consistently spelled words (those with only friends) at an earlier stage in learning than for words with sound-to-spelling enemies.

Comparison with Human Data

In order to test the predictions of the model regarding the level of difficulty of the various word types, we gave four groups of children, at different stages of development, the same three sets of 19 words as had been learned by the model. To ensure that the words were in the children's vocabulary, we conducted comprehension tests on individual subjects and looked only at the error rate of the words that were known by the children. The results can be seen in Figure 16.2(b), which shows the error proportions for the three different word types for the four groups of children of different ages. It can be seen that the pattern of performance is very similar for the children and for the model. The children, like the model, improve in spelling accuracy over time but at all stages in development they have particular difficulty with the words with sound-to-spelling enemies (e.g. *soap*) and least difficulty with the friends-only words (e.g. *pill*).

How should we interpret these results? It is important to emphasize that the good fit between model and data is achieved even though the model contains within it nothing that appears to correspond to explicit sound-to-spelling translation rules of any type. All the information in the model is included in the representations of the words and the strength of connections between representing units. Furthermore, the mechanism of the model contains nothing which corresponds to the distinction between two different spelling routines in the standard dual-route model. Thus it is possible to spell both regular and irregular items with just one mechanism.

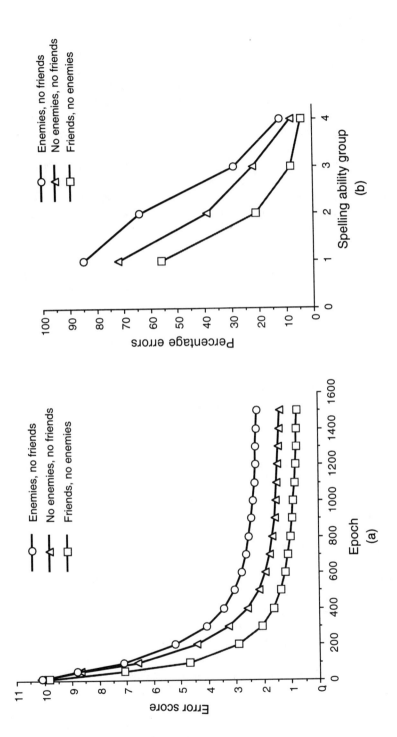

FIGURE 16.2 (a) Error score to the three different word types in the model during learning. (b) Percentage errors for the three different word types for normal subjects in four spelling ability/age groups.

DEVELOPMENTAL DYSLEXIA IN THE MODEL

We wished to examine the possibility that developmentally dyslexic spelling could be characterized in terms of limited computational resources being used during learning to spell. Such an account, if it could be sustained, would contrast with traditional information-processing stage accounts, which refer to the absence of a particular spelling-processing strategy in dyslexic populations. Seidenberg and McClelland (1989a,b; Seidenberg, 1989) have already proposed a similar account of dyslexic reading.

To investigate this hypothesis in the context of the model described above, we varied the computational capacity or resources of the network by altering the number of hidden units in the network and examining its learning performance (it will be recalled that the hidden units intervene between the input units (used to represent the pronunciation of words in the network) and the output units (used to represent the spelling of words in the network)). The larger the number of hidden units, the larger the number of connections in the network, and the greater its capacity to learn new associations. In the simulations described above, which we regard as a simulation of aspects of normal spelling development, the model was given 35 hidden units. We repeated the simulation with two further models which were identical in all respects except that one was given only 20 hidden units and the other was given only 15. These can be thought of as attempts to create a "mildly dyslexic" model and a "severely dyslexic" model.

Figure 16.3 shows the reducing error scores for the three types of words for all three versions for the model side by side. It can be seen that the "dyslexic" versions of the model learned more slowly, and reached a lower level of performance after any given amounts of learning. However, all three versions of the model showed the same qualitative pattern of differences between the three different types of words throughout learning.

This is of particular interest because it has sometimes been suggested that dyslexic children will show reduced effects of spelling-to-sound or sound-to-spelling regularity. (e.g. Frith, 1985). This is because one account of developmental dyslexia suggests that dyslexics have been unable to make the transition to alphabetic reading and/or spelling strategies. If this is so, they should be less liable to show effects of spelling-to-sound or sound-to-spelling regularity. Thus the presence of a regularity effect can be used as a marker for the use of alphabetic processing. If dyslexics suffer a selective problem with alphabetic processing, they should show a reduced regularity effect. In experiments designed to test this issue it is traditional to use a spelling-age match design. This involves comparing performance of dyslexic children with that of younger non-dyslexic children who are spelling at the same level. Because the two groups are matched for spelling level, it can be assumed that if any differences between the group are found this will not be simply a consequence (rather than a possible cause) of their spelling problems. We therefore carried out an analogue of the spelling-age match design on the dyslexic and non-dyslexic versions of the connectionist model. To do this, we took the three different models at the different stages in learning at which they were performing equally well on "regular" words (those with only friends). The point we chose was reached after 130 epochs of learning for the "non-dyslexic" model

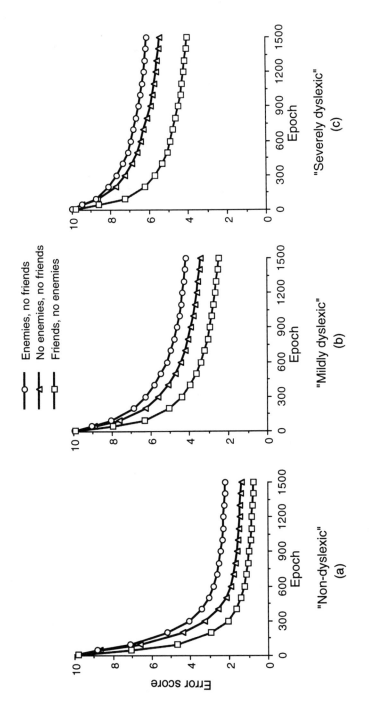

FIGURE 16.3   Error score to the three different word types in "normal" and "dyslexic" versions of the model.

(with 35 hidden units), after 390 epochs for the "mildly dyslexic" model (with 20 hidden units) and after 1580 epochs for the "severely dyslexic" model (with just 15 hidden units). We then examined the error score of the models to irregular words (those with only sound-to-spelling enemies) at that point in learning. The results are shown in Figure 16.4(a). The error score for the three different models on regular words was the same, because the models were chosen to be the same. However, the model also showed approximately equal error scores for the irregular words. We interpret this as demonstrating that the dyslexic and non-dyslexic models show equivalent effects of sound-to-spelling regularity.

Does the same apply to real dyslexic children? We carried out an experiment to test the predictions of the model as applied to dyslexia. We gave the same three sets of words as used in the previous experiment and simulations to two groups of dyslexic children. All the children were at a special school for children with reading problems, and on average had a reading age more than 2½ years behind their chronological ages. In addition, all children had been independently assessed as dyslexic. (For further details of the subject groups see Brown, Loosemore & Watson, 1993.)

The results can be seen in Figure 16.4(b). This clearly shows that both groups of dyslexic subjects showed equal-sized effect of words' sound-to-spelling characteristics when compared with the non-dyslexic subjects. This is consistent with an account of dyslexia in which dyslexics eventually have the same processing strategies available to them as normal subjects, but are delayed in their acquisition of these strategies—in other words, their processing is "delayed" rather than "deviant". Work on reading in dyslexia has found similar results, in that most studies of dyslexic reading have found equivalent-sized regularity effects in dyslexic and non-dyslexic populations (Brown & Watson, 1991). However, studies of reading have also shown that dyslexics tend to have particular trouble in nonword reading when compared with non-dyslexic reading at the same level (Rack, Snowling & Olson, 1992), and this has been taken as evidence for the use of qualitatively different reading strategies in the dyslexic population. Furthermore, there is some evidence that a similar picture pertains in spelling, and there is evidence that dyslexics will show particular problems in spelling nonwords when compared with non-dyslexics (e.g. Martlew, 1992). We therefore compared the ability of the different (dyslexic and non-dyslexic) versions of the model, again matched on spelling ability for regular words, on error score to nonwords. The results are shown in Figure 16.5, where it is clear that the dyslexic versions of the model do show impaired nonword spelling performance, even though they have shown equal-sized effects of sound-to-spelling regularity. This would generally be taken, if found in an experiment, as evidence for qualitatively different processing in the dyslexic population. It should therefore be noted that there are no qualitatively different mechanisms in the dyslexic version of the model. Rather the models differ only quantitatively, that is, in the extent of their computational resources. Further research will be needed to confirm the nonword processing deficit in dyslexic spelling more thoroughly than has been done to date. However, it does seem that the paradoxical pattern of findings observed in dyslexic children (equal-sized regularity effects combined with a selective nonword spelling deficit when compared with appropriate controls) is reproduced in the model.

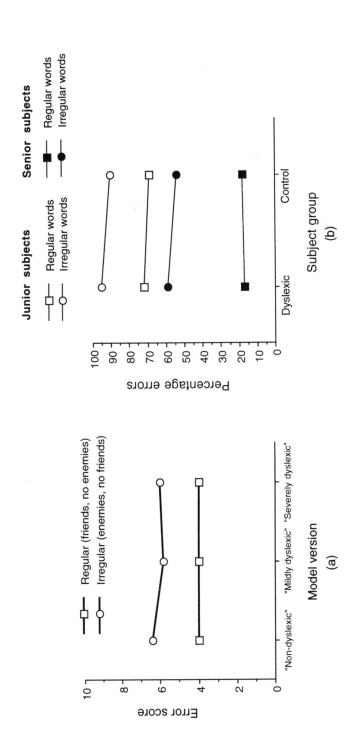

FIGURE 16.4 (a) Error score to regular and irregular words in the three different word types for dyslexic and control subjects. (b) Percentage errors for the three different word types for dyslexic and control subjects.

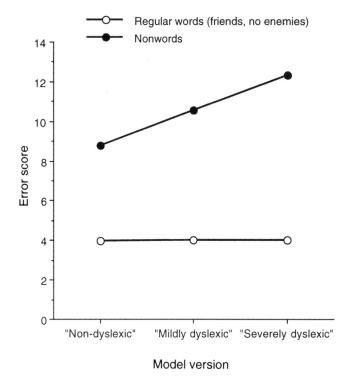

FIGURE 16.5   Error score to nonwords and regular words in the "normal" and "dyslexic" versions of the model.

To conclude this section, we suggest that much of the progression of difficulty in normal spelling, and the pattern of spelling performance exhibited by developmentally dyslexic children, can be well characterized in connectionist terms. Specifically, developmentally dyslexic spelling can be explained as reduced computational resources being available to the model.

DISCUSSION

In this final section we review the findings and discuss them with reference to the issues raised in the introduction to the present chapter: are computational models useful in helping us to understand spelling processes?

First of all, we focus on the ability of connectionist models to account, using very basic learning mechanisms, for data previously assumed to require the postulation of more complex cognitive mechanisms. In the most general terms, connectionist models such as the one described here operate using very simple principles of basic associative learning, of the type known to exist in animals. It is important, we suggest, to explore the ability of simple associative learning to account for so-called cognitive phenomena, for we should not invoke complex cognitive constructs such as "rules" or "strategies" in our explanations of psychological processing if we do not need to. Indeed, we see this as one of the primary roles of connectionism. Even though it may be neccessary to postulate richly structured internal mechanisms to account for some aspects of language performance, it is important to account for as much data as we can in more epistemologically conservative terms. Only when we encounter data that we cannot explain in terms of simple learning principles should we be prepared to assume the existence of more complex mechanisms.

Thus we view the success of the model in accounting for much of the variance in children's error rates, as described above, not as evidence that we have developed a complete model of spelling, but rather as evidence that some proportion of spelling error data from children can indeed be accounted for "non-cognitively".

The approach is also of interest because it suggests a different way of viewing both normal and dyslexic spelling development—as a task of mastering the statistical associations between a set of patterns representing the phonological forms of words and a set of patterns representing the orthographic forms. Under this characterization, the computational difficulty of the mapping will determine how rapidly it is learned, and this is what we found in the model and in children.

Furthermore, developmental dyslexia can be viewed as a lack of computational resources being made available in the task of learning to spell. Indeed, such an explanation can provide an account of why dyslexic children can exhibit equal-sized sound-to-spelling regularity effects to non-dyslexic children at the same time as a selective deficit in nonword processing. It is likely that degrading the quality of the phonological representations available to the model would have much the same effect, and we are currently running simulations to assess this possibility. In the case of reading, there is already plentiful evidence that the nature of the representations made available to a connectionist model can dramatically influence the performance of nonwords relative to word reading. Thus the original Seidenberg and McClelland (1989a) connectionist model of reading was criticized for its poor non-reading performance (Besner et al., 1990), but providing a similar connectionist architecture with different representations can dramatically improve reading performance (Bullinaria, 1993; Phillips & Hay, 1992; Plaut, McClelland & Seidenberg, 1992).

We suggested in the introduction that the attempt to build computational models of psychological processes can lead to the development of novel hypotheses. This was indeed the case with the model we have described briefly in this chapter: the prediction of separate "friends" and "enemies" effects, which has been confirmed experimentally led to the suggestion that the development of fluent and automatic application of sound-to-spelling knowledge (however that knowledge is characterized) might proceed independently of knowledge of exceptional sound-to-spelling correspondences (see Brown, Loosemore & Watson, 1993, for further details).

In conclusion, there is a long way to go before a computationally explicit model of spelling can account for all currently available spelling data. However, it could be argued that current, verbally specified models of normal and impaired spelling development are not sufficiently explicit or even truly explanatory, for they do not specify the mechanisms underlying developmental change in enough detail to enable the models to be expressed formally. We would argue that the discipline of attempting to build working models is not only useful but essential if spelling is to be fully understood, and that the three chapters in this section of the book have all led to insights that would have been unlikely to emerge except within a computational approach.

NOTE

1. We used a distributed Wickeltriple representation. A complete (50-bit) pattern was created for every triple that occurred in the vocabulary. Word patterns were then made by superimposing the relevant triple patterns and assigning the ON value to any unit for which one or more of the triples had an ON value. The same method was used to construct patterns for both phoneme triples and letter triples. Each of the output units is assigned a unique set of similar triples (from the set of all possible triples, not just those that occur) for which it will tend to be in the "on" state. To make each set, three groups of 15 letters are chosen, each group being associated with a particular position in the triple. The response set then comprises all those triples that can be made by selecting one letter from each of the three groups (a total of 3375). Rather than simply allow an output unit to be in the "on" state if the triple occurred in that unit's response set, we ensured that all triples had exactly the same number of units in the "on" state (the four whose response sets most closely matched the triple). The net effect of this encoding scheme is that, to the extent that two triples overlap, they tend to be represented by patterns with "on" bits in similar positions. Although there are well-known limitations to this type of representation (Prince & Pinker, 1988), it suffices for the vocabulary of the present model.

REFERENCES

Besner, D., Twilley, L., McCann, R. S. & Seergobin, K. (1990). On the association between connectionism and data: are a few words necessary? *Psychological Review*, **97**, 432–446.

Bullinaria, J. (1993). Neural network models of reading without Wickelfeatures. Unpublished manuscript. University of Edinburgh.

Brown, G. D. A., Loosemore, R. & Watson, F. L. (1993). Normal and dyslexic spelling: a connectionist approach. Manuscript in submission.

Brown, G. D. A. & Watson, F. L. (1991). Reading in developmental dyslexia: a connectionist approach. In M. Snowling & M. Thomson (Eds), *Dyslexia: Integrating Theory and Practice*. Oxford: Whurr.

Frith, U. (1985). Beneath the surface of developmental dyslexia. In K. E. Patterson, J. C. Marshall & M. Coltheart (Eds), *Surface Dyslexia*. Hillsdale, NJ: LEA.

Martlew, M. (1992). Handwriting and spelling: dyslexic children's abilities compared with children of the same chronological age and young children at the same spelling level. *British Journal of Educational Psychology*, **62**, 375–390.

McClelland, J. L. & Rumelhart, D. E. (Eds) (1986). *Parallel Distributed Processing: Explorations in the Microstructure of Cognition*, Vol. 2. Cambridge, MA: MIT Press/Bradford Books.

Norris, D. (1993). A quantitative model of reading aloud. Unpublished manuscript. MRC Applied Psychology Unit Cambridge.

Phillips, W. A. & Hay, I. M. (1992). Computational theories of reading aloud: multi-level neural net approaches. Technical report CCCN-13, Stirling University, December 1992.

Plaut, D. C., McClelland, J. L. & Seidenberg, M. S. (1992). Reading exception words and pseudowords: are two routes really necessary? Paper presented at the Annual Meeting of the Psychonomic Society, St Louis, MO, November 1992.

Prince, A. & Pinker, S. (1988). Wickelphone ambiguity. *Cognition*, **30**, 189–190.

Rack, J. P., Snowling, M. J. & Olson, R. K. (1992). The nonword reading deficit in developmental dyslexia: a review. *Reading Research Quarterly*, **27**(1), 29–51.

Rumelhart, D. E. & McClelland, J. L. (Eds) (1986a). *Parallel Distributed Processing: Explorations in the Microstructure of Cognition*, Vol. 1. Cambridge, MA: Bradford Books/MIT Press.

Rumelhart, D. E. & McClelland, J. L. (1986b). On learning the past tenses of English verbs. In J. L. McClelland & D. E. Rumelhart (Eds), *Parallel Distributed Processing: Explorations in the Microstructure of Cognition*, Vol. 2. Cambridge, MA: MIT Press/Bradford Books.

Seidenberg, M. S. (1989). Visual word recognition and pronunciation: a computational model and its implications. In W. Marslen-Wilson (Ed.), *Lexical Representation and Process*. Cambridge, MA: MIT Press/Bradford Books.

Seidenberg, M. S. & McClelland, J. L. (1989a). A distributed, developmental model of word recognition and naming. *Psychological Review*, **96**, 523–568.

Seidenberg, M. S. & McClelland, J. L. (1989b). Visual word recognition and pronunciation: a computational model of acquired skilled performance and dyslexia. In A. Galaburda (Ed.), *From Reading to Neurons*. Cambridge MA: MIT Press/Bradford Books.

17

Representation and Connectionist Models: The NETspell Experience

ANDREW OLSON

University of Birmingham

ALFONSO CARAMAZZA

Dartmouth College, Hanover

"Neural" network models of cognitive processes have often been accompanied by a series of theoretical claims that put them in competition with modular and symbolic theories (Rumelhart *et al.*, 1986; Rumelhart and McClelland, 1986; Seidenberg & McClelland, 1989). Models based on symbolic operations have been said to provide only an approximate account of phenomena that are more accurately described by connectionist models. To buttress this claim, neural network models have been reported to account for significant amounts of data while doing without components of traditional symbolic models (Hinton & Shallice, 1991; Rumelhart & McClelland, 1986; Seidenberg & McClelland, 1989; Sejnowski & Rosenberg, 1987). At the same time, there is often a more or less forcefully stated assumption that the particulars of the network implementation are relatively unimportant. The exact representation for input and output, learning procedure and the model parameters do not matter (within some broad limits) as long as sufficiently powerful learning procedures map the chosen level of input to the chosen level of output (see Seidenberg & McClelland, 1989; but see also McCloskey, 1991).

Handbook of Spelling: Theory, Process and Intervention. Edited by G. D. A. Brown and N. C. Ellis.
©1994 John Wiley & Sons Ltd.

Such an account makes little of aspects central to symbol-processing theory. Both the elimination of components and the implication that the exact form of representation is unimportant challenge the arguments that relate data and theory in the symbolic account. Symbolic theories have connected the *nature* of representation to what tasks can be accomplished with that representation, the speed and manner in which the tasks are carried out, the errors that will be made and their likelihood, and the way a damaged system will behave. Psychologists and neuropsychologists have assumed that different representations will make learning more or less difficult, take different amounts of time to compute, make different errors more likely, or break down in different ways. With sufficiently clever and detailed tests it has been thought that different representations and the processes operating on them can be distinguished. A theory of a cognitive system specifies the nature of the representations it utilizes and the processes that operate on these representations as they are manipulated within or across domains during a task. In theories of spelling (e.g. spelling to dictation), one would describe how processing passes from initial representation of speech sounds to the motor sequences necessary to produce letters in speech or writing.

If the choice of representation is relatively unimportant, and the data used to argue for various levels of representation can be shown to result, instead, from a powerful learning rule, the characteristics of the input/output corpus shaping a network and the number of "units" it is allowed, then the relationship between data and theory established in symbolic/modular accounts is called into question. The focus shifts from specifying the nature of representations to characterizing statistical regularities in the environment and judging proper network size. Questioning the symbolic account, however, does not provide a new form of explanation. If symbolic accounts are not adequate, the logic of a new form of explanation must be provided, one that does not rely on the terms of symbolic accounts, so that a dialogue between connectionist theory and data can take place using the new vocabulary. If, on the other hand, the performance of a connectionist model follows directly from the choice of representations it uses and the architecture it embodies, then questions of representation remain central to theorizing and model building.

We will explore these general issues by examining a particular connectionist model that learns to spell. We will evaluate the model in the light of symbolic accounts of spelling and, in particular, we will focus on levels of representation that have traditionally been part of many theories of language processing, but have been targeted for elimination in several recent connectionist accounts (Hinton & Shallice, 1991; Rumelhart & McClelland, 1986; Seidenberg & McClelland, 1989): supra-segmental and lexical representations. In order to do this, we will examine how the representations the model uses influence its performance. We will also consider what sort of theorizing our model allows, and what guidance it gives us when we have to go beyond initial performance and modify the model to improve it.

This will not be an evaluation of connectionism in the abstract, for, as Minsky and Papert (1988) have pointed out, trying to decide issues at that level of generality, divorced from particulars, is likely to be either impossible or meaningless. There is no logical necessity for symbolic and connectionist accounts (broadly defined) to be mutually exclusive, despite the fact that discussions of connectionist models and symbolic and modular theories have often been cast in such terms (e.g. Touretzky & Hinton, 1985). Particular models may have formal capacities that can be shown to be sufficient or insufficient for particular tasks, and some computational models may be more useful than others in helping us to *understand* how a cognitive system works. Instead of considering the capabilities of connectionism at a very general level, we will examine the kind of theorizing a particular connectionist model allows in the domain of spelling.

NETspell is a backpropagation network that converts phonemes to graphemes, spelling regular and irregular, familiar and unfamiliar words by the same network. It does not apparently have supra-segmental (e.g. abstract consonants and vowels, syllables or feet) or lexical representations. In this sense it is similar to models proposed by Rumelhart and McClelland (1986), Sejnowski and Rosenberg (1987), Seidenberg and McClelland (1989) and Hinton and Shallice (1991). NETspell is among several recent connectionist models that have mapped representations of letters or sounds directly onto semantic or onto output representations, without making use of more abstract intermediate units. Supra-segmental units including the syllable are eliminated as epiphenomenal; data used to justify these units are said instead to reflect statistical patterns in the corpus (e.g. Seidenberg, 1987). Grammatical categories become part of the semantic system and are distinguished in semantic terms, not because they are formal categories in the syntax. Properties thought to be listed in the lexicon (e.g. whether a verb is "irregular" in its past tense form) are handled by the learning rule.

Before describing the architecture and training of NETspell, it will be useful to briefly mention arguments from the larger context of linguistic systems that have been used to suggest that lexical and supra-segmental levels of representation are required. Evidence for lexical and supra-segmental representations has come from language change, from the way children's language develops and from the distribution of language types throughout the world. Other evidence comes from people's judgements of acceptable or unacceptable linguistic forms, from the distribution of forms within a language or from the units required to state linguistic generalizations most efficiently. An adequate theory of language capacities must have the potential to account for data from all of these areas, though at any one time a theory may not attempt to capture the full range. Accounting for data in a limited domain is not sufficient, however, if the model cannot, in principle, be extended to become part of the more comprehensive language system that must contain it.

A lexicon, one of the candidates for elimination, has been thought to provide the locus where the different levels of linguistic representation—phonological, morphological, syntactic, semantic—are linked for individual roots. As such, it is also the place where exceptional items can be marked. Kim *et al.* (1991) note that verbs made from nouns always take a regular past tense ending, even if they are the homophone of another verb that has an irregular past tense:

- *brake* (noun)/*break* (homophone irregular verb)
  He braked the car suddenly
  But not, He broke the car suddenly (to mean that he stopped it)

- *ring* (make a circle around)/*ring* (as in "ring a bell")
  He ringed the city with artillery
  But not, He rang the city with artillery
- *sleigh/slay*
  He sleighed down the hill
  But not, He slew down the hill
- *right/write*
  He righted the boat after capsizing
  But not, He wrote the boat after capsizing

A lexicon has been critical in accounting for these facts. If we note that exceptions can only be marked for items listed in the lexicon, the pattern follows. Only lexically listed *verbs* can be marked for an irregular past tense. Properties of derived verbs cannot be listed since nouns cannot be marked for *verb* inflection. A denominal verb, therefore, must be given the regular ending even if its sound is identical to an existing irregular verb. The word's grammatical/morphological status, and not its phonological neighborhood, governs how it is inflected. Models that aim to dispense with lexical representation must be able to account for this evidence without resorting to a lexicon or its functional equivalent.

Another level of representation that has been eliminated in recent connectionist models of language processing (more or less explicitly—see Seidenberg, 1987, for an explicit example) is abstract structure built above the individual segments of words: namely syllabic structure. Linguists have, at times, considered whether syllables capture useful generalizations, and some prominent accounts of phonology have tried to do without them (notably, Chomsky & Halle, 1968). Recent linguistic theory, however, has rejected these attempts and recognizes syllables as an important level of representation. Some of the arguments in this area are worth reviewing to avoid rediscovering the same reasons through modeling.

Syllables are necessary to state linguistic generalizations. Certain American and British dialects of English, for example, have a rule that governs when /r/ is pronounced. An /r/ is deleted in two contexts: before another consonant and at the end of words (e.g. *barter* is pronounced *bawta*). The context "before another consonant or at the end of a word" also often appears in phonological rules of other languages. The concept "syllable" allows these two contexts to be unified. An /r/ before another consonant will be part of the syllable centered on the preceding vowel. An /r/ at the end of a word will also be part of the syllable that includes the previous vowel. Using syllables we can express the generalization with a single context: /r/ is deleted when it is in the coda of a syllable. Syllables are necessary to express the full generality of a pattern, explaining why otherwise arbitrary contexts repeatedly appear together in phonological rules (Kaye cited in Romani, 1992).

Syllables are also required to describe the distribution of medial consonant clusters in languages that allow complex consonant clusters. The set of possible word–medial consonant clusters can loosely be described as the set of legal word–final consonant clusters followed by a syllable boundary, followed by the set of legal word–initial clusters (see Haugen, 1956a,b). The set of consonants that can occur in one of the medial positions will change depending on where the syllable boundary dividing the consonants falls. Three-consonant medial clusters, for example, can have two syllabic divisions: C_1C_2/C_3 and C_1/C_2C_3 (where / marks the syllable boundary).The possible consonants that can appear in C_1 and C_3 change depending on where the syllable boundary occurs. C_1, for example is either a syllable-final segment or the first segment of a coda cluster. When C_1 is syllable final, a wide range of segments can occur there, including /n/, /m/, /r/, /l/, plus (at least) /k/, /b/, /p/ and /t/. Liquids (/r/ and /l/) and nasals (/n/ and /m/), however, are the only possibilities when C_1 is the first segment of a coda cluster. Depending on where the syllable boundary is, then, possibilities for C_1 are either wider or more restricted. Always allowing the full set of consonants in position one or three would admit the possibility of illegal clusters like *kbt*. The abstract unit "syllable" allows one to compactly state the conditions that determine when a consonant position allows a restricted set of phonemes. (Using syllables is not the only way of producing legal sequences if we confine the evidence to a sufficiently restricted context. If we evaluate only what a model *produces*, for example, it would be possible to produce only legal phonological sequences by listing all occurring sequences in a table and only producing entries from the table. Crucially, however, this procedure cannot explain why certain entries are in the table and not others. Attempts to formulate medial consonant cluster constraints in terms of "triphones" would have the same difficulty. In sum, knowing *how* a model produces its results is relevant to evaluating the model's performance).

These examples give a feel for the arguments that lexical and supra-segmental levels of representation are required in the larger context of linguistic systems. If evidence from reading and spelling also converges on these levels of representation, our confidence in the overall theory is increased by the convergence. If the evidence does not converge, we must seek ways in which contradictory aspects can be explained or resolved.

There is a certain amount of evidence that lexical and supra-segmental representations are important in spelling and reading. Two kinds will be especially relevant in the discussion to follow: distributional evidence and evidence from brain-damaged patients. If we consider the distribution of spellings in English the influence of word position is clear. Several spellings occur only in word-initial or word-final position, and others are much more common in one word position than another. The diphthong /aɪ/ (as in *by*), for example, is only spelled *y* when the vowel is the final segment of the word (e.g. *dry*). This spelling does not ever occur in word-initial position, where the most common spelling is *i* (as in *idea*). Double consonants are also prohibited in word-initial position. The *gue* of *morgue* only appears word-finally as a spelling of /g/. /dʒ/ is usually spelled *j* in word-initial position (as in *jeans*), but *g* (or *ge*) is the most common spelling word-finally, where the *j* spelling does not occur (e.g. *stage*). The *ck* spelling of /k/ (as in *back*) does not occur in word-initial position. Even in this brief survey, it is clear that a spelling system without word-position information will have great difficulty capturing these facts as generalizations. When a network cannot generalize, it is forced to learn mappings in less efficient ways (e.g. to store several/many occurrences), resulting in a larger load on its computational resources. As Minsky and Papert (1988) pointed out in their exploration of network properties, what a network cannot represent, it cannot learn. The same point could be restated in the present context: what a model cannot represent, it cannot generalize over.

Patterns of data from brain-damaged patients who have difficulties in reading or spelling have been instrumental in developing models of these tasks. Such patterns also suggest that lexical and supra-segmental representations are involved in orthographic processing. If there are lexical and non-lexical processes involved in spelling, for example, it should be possible to damage one while leaving the other intact, and vice versa. If supra-segmental structure is represented, the range of deletion, insertion, substitution and transposition errors that occur may be governed by this structure.

Shallice (1981) reported a patient who showed one half of a double dissociation between lexical and non-lexical processes. The patient had difficulty spelling novel words (nonwords for experimental purposes, spelled correctly 18% of the time) but preserved ability to spell both regular and exceptional words that were familiar (spelled correctly 94% of the time). Shallice concluded that the patient had experienced damage to the non-lexical spelling processes responsible for constructing spellings of novel words. Lexical representations of familiar words were preserved.

Beauvois and Dérouesné (1981) reported the opposite pattern. They described a patient who could spell novel words in plausible ways, but who had difficulty spelling existing words in proportion to how irregular their spellings were. Irregular words were spelled poorly, words that had ambiguous possible spellings were spelled better, and words with only one possible spelling were most often spelled correctly. They interpreted the patient's capacity to spell existing words in inverse proportion to the number of phonologically plausible spellings and his ability to generate plausible spellings of novel words as evidence that non-lexical processes for constructing spellings were preserved. Lexical processes responsible for specifying the precise spelling of irregular or ambiguous words had been damaged. (Analogous patients have been reported in the literature on acquired reading difficulties. See Beauvois & Dérouesné, 1979; Bub, Cancelliere & Kertesz, 1985; Funnell, 1983; Marshall & Newcombe, 1973; Patterson, 1982; Shallice & Warrington, 1980; see also discussion of these patients in Coltheart, 1985 and Coltheart, 1981.) In models that do not make use of lexical representations it must be possible to produce both of these patterns under damage, and, in particular, it must be possible for damage to result in the Shallice pattern, which is more closely associated with preserved lexical representations.

Neuropsychological evidence has also suggested that supra-segmental representations are involved in spelling. Caramazza and Miceli (1990) reported a patient who had spelling difficulties following a stroke. He deleted letters, substituted one for another, transposed them, or inserted letters when spelling familiar and unfamiliar words. These letters were not, however, substituted, deleted or transposed at random. In nearly all cases, substitutions were vowel for vowel and consonant for consonant (99.3%). Non-adjacent letter exchanges also only transposed consonants with other consonants and vowels with other vowels (100%). In addition, consonants from clusters were deleted more often than simple consonants. Caramazza and Miceli interpreted this pattern as evidence that spelling representations involve abstract consonant and vowel representations linked to individual letter identities. Differing rates of deletion for consonants in clusters and simple consonants imply that the syllabic or cluster position of the consonant is represented, since cluster consonants and non-cluster consonants must be distinguished in order for them to be treated differently. Models without supra-segmental representations must be able to produce these patterns when damaged. In particular, within-category transposition errors must be possible. Transposition errors are particularly diagnostic because they cannot result from substitution of one segment by a similar one (where consonants might be called more similar to other consonants and vowels to other vowels).

NETSPELL: A MODEL OF THE SPELLING SYSTEM

To evaluate the performance of a connectionist model that does not have lexical or supra-segmental representations we developed a model of spelling that converts sound symbols to letters. Its form is similar to that of NETtalk, and draws heavily on the work of Sejnowski and Rosenberg (1987). We have called the model NETspell. It consists of three layers of units. One layer codes input to the network, one layer codes output, and there is an intermediate layer to aid in the mapping from input to output. Input consists of a seven-phoneme window, three phonemes of context on either side of a central phoneme. Fifty or 51 (depending on the simulation) units code each phoneme position, with each unit coding a single phoneme (local coding), resulting in either 350 or 357 input units in all. Output consists of 292 or 246 units, one for each of the graphemes in the dictionary (also local coding). The network is trained to produce only the grapheme that corresponds to the phoneme in the central position. Other phonemes provide the context necessary to distinguish phoneme-to-grapheme mappings that occur in different words.

A word is presented to the network by putting the first phoneme in the center window and the following phonemes in the three slots to the right. On successive iterations the phonemes of the word are moved from right to left, so that each phoneme occupies the central position in the window. Units in the input layer are either on or off according to phoneme codes. Input units are connected to units in the middle layer by weighted connections that determine how strongly a unit in the input layer will turn on a unit the next layer up. A final set of weighted connections connect middle-layer units ("hidden units") to units in the output layer, and determine which output units are turned on. The output unit that is turned on most strongly is considered the network's guess. Guesses are corrected using the backpropagation algorithm (Rumelhart, Hinton & Williams, 1986). If the network guesses the wrong spelling for an item, the weights on connections are changed in proportion to the amount each weight contributes to the incorrect guess, so that the network will be more likely to produce the correct answer the next time it sees the same input/output pair. In this way, items presented over and over eventually lead to connection weights that result in more accurate responses.

NETspell was trained on corpora of 1000 and 1628 words in which phonemes had been put into one-to-one correspondence with graphemes. These corpora were generated by taking larger dictionaries, sorting them by Kucera and Francis (1967) surface frequency and sampling them to get a set of words representative of the frequency distribution in the language. Regular and irregular words appeared in both training sets. Networks trained on the different dictionaries will be labeled "network 1000" and "network 1628". The phoneme codes for network 1000 were taken from the NETtalk corpus. Network 1628 was trained on a dictionary sampled from the Hanna *et al.* corpus (1966).

Forcing a one-to-one correspondence between phonemes and graphemes makes certain arbitrary choices necessary. Normally, for example, final *e* is coded with the vowel whose pronunciation it affects, and thus *bite* has the graphemes *b*, *i-e* and *t*. In a word like *range*, however, the proper grapheme for the final *e* is not as clear. If the final *e* is taken away, both the pronunciation of the vowel and the pronunciation of the *g* are affected, but the *e* only appears with one of the letters whose pronunciation it affects (*a-e* and not *ge*). A one -to-one coding also means that two phonemes cannot be mapped to one grapheme, and so when /ks/ is spelled *x*, a new phoneme standing for /ks/ is used. The "*x*" case artificially simplifies what the network has to learn, the "range" case probably complicates the network's task.

Network 1000 was trained on 60 passes through the 1000-word corpus, for a total training exposure of 60 000 words. The network's level of performance for phoneme-to-grapheme mapping was nearly identical to the performance reported for NETtalk. Percentage correct for graphemes rose quickly and leveled off near 94% correct. As mentioned above, the grapheme corresponding to the output unit that was on the most was considered the network's guess, but only as long as some unit was above a 0.3 threshold level (where activation values can range from 0 when a unit is off to 1 when the unit is fully on). If all units were below 0.3, the network was considered not to have been able to select a grapheme. We will discuss these responses in more detail below.

The learning curve for words was less steep and had reached 70% correct at the end of training but was still rising. A word was counted as correct only when all graphemes in the word were guessed correctly. Since phoneme–grapheme pairs that were not learned occurred in more than one word, performance on words was worse than on graphemes.

Network 1628 reached a similar level of performance. Per cent correct for phoneme-to-grapheme mapping rose quickly to above 90% and then leveled out. After training on 100 times through the corpus (162 800 words), per cent correct for phoneme-to-grapheme matches was 96%. Words reached a final per cent correct of 83% (Figure 17.1).

In all, 319 of network 1000's words were not spelled correctly. Three hundred and sixty-two phoneme-to-grapheme errors were made on these words. Of the 362 errors, 18% were errors in which a response was made but it was incorrect. The remaining 82% of the time, the network did not activate any unit above the 0.3 threshold. Of the errors in which a response was made, most were phonologically plausible regularization errors (e.g. *syntax* → *sintax*, *deficient* → *dificient*, *labyrinth* → *laborinth* and *endorse* → *indorse*).

In network 1628, the same pattern was observed, i.e. responses above the threshold level most often resulted in phonologically plausible regularization errors. Two hundred and seventy-four words from the corpus were not spelled correctly at the end of training. Three hundred and five phoneme-to-grapheme conversion errors were made while spelling the 274 words. For 266 of the phoneme-to-grapheme errors the

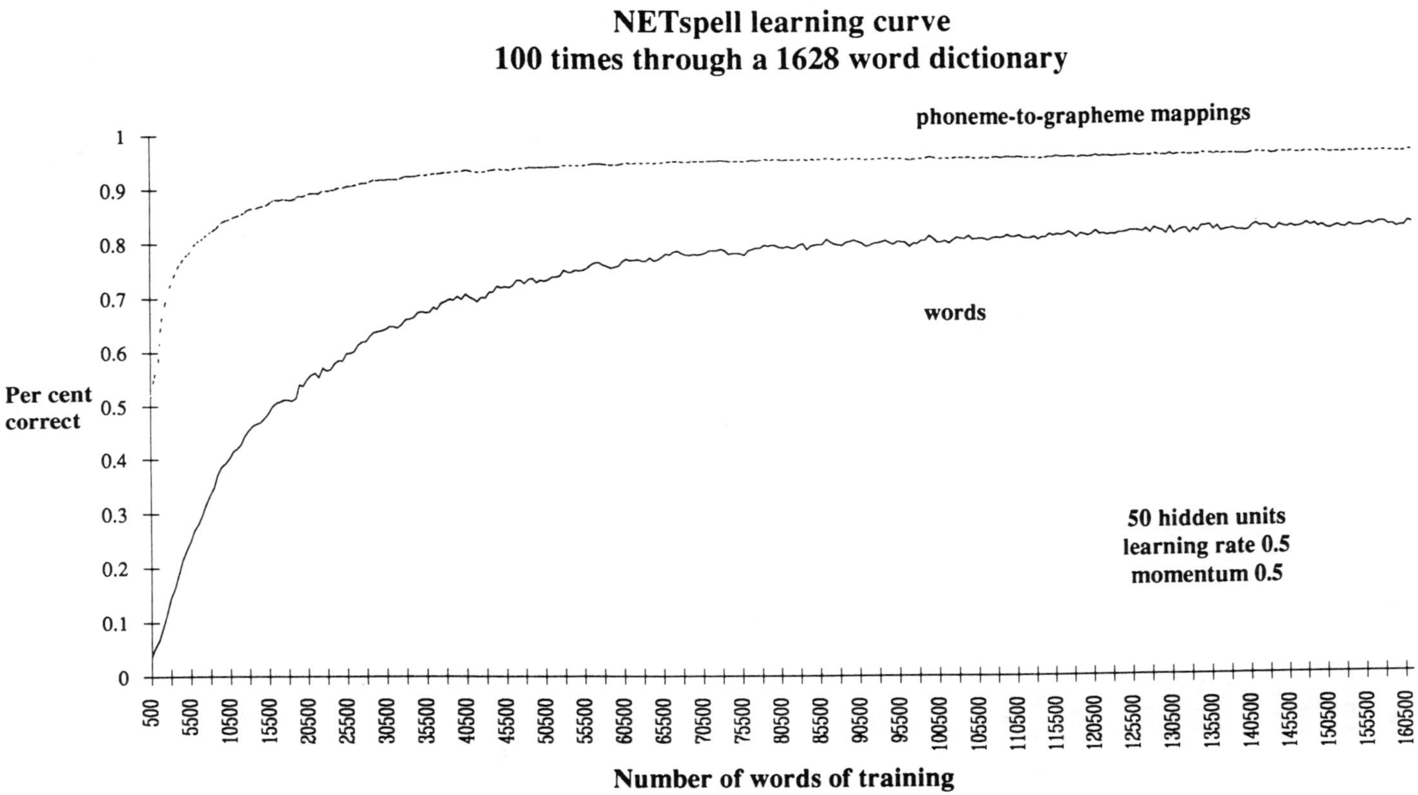

NETspell learning curve
100 times through a 1628 word dictionary

phoneme-to-grapheme mappings

words

50 hidden units
learning rate 0.5
momentum 0.5

Per cent correct

Number of words of training

FIGURE 17.1 NETspell learning curves.

TABLE 17.1 Spellings of untrained words produced by
network 1000.

Untrained Word	NETspell spelling
time	time
over	over
must	must
major	majer
report	reporte
inside	incide
floor	floar
nation	nation

network failed to choose a grapheme (all output units less than 0.3). Thirty-eight of the 39 phoneme-to-grapheme errors for which the network did select a response were phonologically plausible errors. One error was implausible (*Tsar → sar*. Initial /z/ is never spelled *s*).

That the spellings are regularizations can be seen in Figure 17.2, which plots correct graphemes against graphemes the network picked in error. Graphemes are plotted according to how often, in the dictionary, they spell the phoneme the network was choosing a spelling for. Except for the initial two points on the graph, the graphemes the network picked in error were clearly more common spellings than the graphemes it should have chosen. (The initial two points came from the words *gentian* and *esoteric*. In *esoteric*, the final /k/ was spelled *ck*, a spelling which occurs 7.79% of the time as a spelling of /k/. The correct spelling *c* occurs 63.06% of the time. The schwa in *gentian* was spelled *o*, which occurs 30.45% of the time as a spelling of schwa, while the proper spelling (*a*) occurs an almost equivalent 28.61% of the time. We will have more to say about these errors later.)

To test whether the NETspell network could generalize its knowledge to spell unfamiliar items, we gave it words it had not been trained on. If successful, we would expect NETspell to generate phonologically plausible spellings for the words it had not seen (that is, the spellings should be pronounced in the same way as the word being attempted). It is, perhaps, appropriate to note here that judging what is phonologically plausible is not possible independent of a theory specifying the context phoneme-to-grapheme mapping is sensitive to. The phoneme /i/ (long *e*), for example, is most commonly spelled *y* in word-final position (83.91% of the time), but almost never spells /i/ in word-initial position (1.79% of the time—one exception word: *yclept*). If phoneme-to-grapheme mapping is sensitive to word position, *yther* is not a plausible spelling of *ether*. If phoneme-to-grapheme mapping is not sensitive to word position, it may be a plausible spelling. Similar issues arise in the treatment of final *e* (e.g. *a* can sometimes spell long *a*—e.g. *baby, acorn*—does this mean that *fat* is a plausible spelling of *fate*?) and letter contexts (e.g. *c* is pronounced /s/ in front of the letters *i, e* and *y*, but /k/ in front of other vowels. Is *cricit* a plausible spelling of *cricket*?). In the absence of a theory, errors are scored less systematically. In Table 17.2, clearly implausible errors are labeled "implausible". Errors that are implausible given the context, but which could be plausible if mappings are not sensitive to some contexts, are labeled "context violations". In other counts, benefit of the doubt is

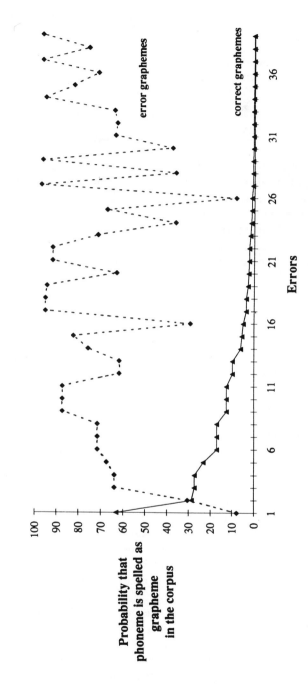

FIGURE 17.2 NETspell's interpretable errors are nearly all regularization errors. Error graphemes are more probable spellings than their correct counterparts.

TABLE 17.2 Spellings of untrained words produced by network 1628.

	Number	Per cent
Plausible	27	(87.09)
Implausible	2	(6.45)
zipper → sipper		
harpsichord → harplocurd		
Context violations	2	(6.45)
commentary → comentere		
bare → bar		

usually given, so that if spellings occur some other place in the language the spelling is called plausible (though there is clearly some room for interpretation of context effects here). Unfamiliar items were, for the most part, either spelled correctly or spelled in phonologically plausible ways (Tables 17.1 and 17.2).

To test NETspell further, we "lesioned" the network in several ways to see whether it would produce the patterns of error that have been attributed to damaged lexical and non-lexical processes in brain-damaged patients. "Lesions" to network 1000 were carried out by either removing random weights from the network or adding a random amount of noise to each of the weights. Network 1628 was damaged by adding a random amount of noise to each of the weights. Since we do not know how brain damage can transform a neural system, or, in fact, how different forms of "damage" can effect neural network models, these lesion types were selected arbitrarily to sample the performance of a system damaged in some way. They are similar to other "lesions" reported in the literature (e.g. Patterson, Seidenberg & McClelland, 1989).

When a random number between ±0.45 was added to each weight in network 1000, overall performance on words dropped 6% to 64% correct on words. Of the errors, 18% were errors in which a response was generated. Eighty-two per cent were errors in which no response was above the 0.3 threshold. There were 26 new errors in which a response was made. Of these, 24 were phonologically plausible errors and two were phonologically implausible errors (*myopia* spelled *meropia*, and *practical* spelled *practibal*).

Zeroing weights in the network produced similar results. Zeroing a random 2% of the weights also dropped network performance on words to 64% correct. Eighteen per cent of the errors were actual responses. Eighty-two per cent of the time no response was above threshold. Of the new error responses, 15 were phonologically plausible and one was phonologically implausible (*juicy* spelled *jisie*).

Zeroing 5% of the weights led to a larger performance drop. Forty-five per cent of words were spelled correctly after the "lesion". Of the errors, 34% were responses above the threshold and 66% were responses in which no unit was active above 0.3. Of the responses above threshold, 4% were phonologically implausible (e.g. *conjecture* spelled *conjedure*, *will* spelled *wle* and *forethought* spelled *foreuought*).

"Lesions" to network 1628 were made by adding or subtracting a random amount between 0 and 0.45 or between 0 and 0.9 to all the weights in the network. Each of these lesion types was done twice, resulting in two moderate lesions and two severe lesions. The two lesions in which a random amount up to ±0.45 was added resulted in

TABLE 17.3 Percentage phonologically plausible and implausible errors made by NETspell after ±0.45 noise lesion. Percentages for brain-damaged patients thought to spell non-lexically are also shown for comparison.

Error type	Number	Per cent
NETspell ±0.45 lesion 1		
Plausible	23	(72)
Implausible	9	(28)
NETspell ±0.45 lesion 2		
Plausible	24	(63)
Implausible	14	(37)
Patient TP (Hatfield & Patterson, 1983)		
Plausible	210	(58)
Implausible	152	(42)
Patient JG (Goodman & Caramazza, 1986)		
Plausible	99	(87)
Implausible	15	(13)

performance similar to that found with network 1000. Overall spelling performance decreased from 83% correct before the lesion to 82% correct after lesion 1, and to 79% correct after lesion 2. New errors in which a response was identifiable were primarily phonologically plausible, although there were some that were implausible (new errors were of two types: high activation responses that the network had not produced before, and responses that had been below threshold before the lesion but that resulted in above threshold responses after the lesion). This pattern of performance is similar to that reported for patients who are hypothesized to have damaged lexical processes, and who, as a result, spell by using non-lexical procedures (Table 17.3).

New errors made by the network were primarily on irregular words. One measure of irregularity involves tabulating the phoneme-to-grapheme mapping in each word that has the lowest probability of occurring. Words that have one or more low-probability phoneme-to-grapheme mappings are irregular. Those with only high-probability phoneme-to-grapheme mappings are regular. Following Goodman and Caramazza (1986), we will call words with at least one phoneme-to-grapheme mapping that occurs in less than 10% of the spellings in the corpus low-probability words. Other words will be classified as high probability. Table 17.4 shows that most of NETspell's errors after a ±0.45 lesion occur on low-probability words. This is less true for lesion 1 than lesion 2, but lesion 2 still has slightly more errors on irregular than regular words (all errors, both those resulting in above threshold responses and those resulting in below threshold responses, are counted here). Lesion 1 and, to a lesser extent, lesion 2 demonstrate, again, that it is possible to damage NETspell and produce a pattern of errors that is similar to the pattern reported for brain-damaged patients who have been said to spell non-lexically.

Whether errors are genuinely concentrated on irregular items depends on the number of irregular items in the corpus. If there are more irregular items and the probability of making an error is constant, more irregular than regular items will be spelled incorrectly. A comparison of the distribution of regular and irregular items in the corpus (columns 2 and 3 of Table 17.5) and the number of regular and irregular items

TABLE 17.4 Performance on words with high and low probability phoneme-to-grapheme correspondences (regular and irregular words) for both NETspell after a ± 0.45 noise lesion and brain-damaged patients thought to be spelling non-lexically.

	High-probability words (regular words)		Low probability words (irregular words)	
	Number	Per cent	Number	Per cent
NETspell ± 0.45 lesion 1	15	(27)	41	(73)
NETspell ± 0.45 lesion 2	47	(47)	54	(53)
Patient TP (Hatfield & Patterson, 1983)				
July 1979	19	(37)	33	(63)
April 1980	9	(27)	24	(73)
Patient JG (Goodman & Caramazza, 1986)	3	(11)	24	(89)
Patient RG (Beauvois & Dérouesné, 1981)				
Degree 0 words vs degree 2 & 3 words	7	(25)	21	(75)

TABLE 17.5 Distribution of words based on their lowest probability phoneme-to-grapheme mapping for words in the corpus, and errors produced by two ± 0.45 lesions. Irregular words fall in the low end of the distribution (Categories 0–5 and 5–10).

Lowest p → g probability in	Corpus Number of words	Per cent	Lesion 1 Number of new errors	Per cent	Lesion 2 Number of new errors	Per cent
0–5	498	(31)	31	(55)	42	(42)
5–10	193	(12)	7	(12)	8	(8)
10–15	109	(7)	3	(5)	4	(4)
15–20	211	(13)	5	(9)	12	(12)
20–25	59	(4)	2	(4)	8	(8)
25–30	110	(7)	1	(2)	3	(3)
30–35	65	(4)	0	(0)	5	(5)
35–40	121	(7)	5	(9)	5	(5)
40–45	34	(2)	0	(0)	1	(1)
45–50	36	(2)	0	(0)	3	(3)
50–55	2	(0.1)	0	(0)	0	(0)
55–60	25	(2)	0	(0)	0	(0)
60–65	77	(5)	1	(2)	6	(6)
65–100	88	(5)	0	(0)	3	(3)

on which new errors were made (columns 4 and 5 and 6 and 7 of table 17.5) confirms that although there are indeed more irregular items in the corpus, errors occur on them out of proportion to their numbers. The percentage of items in category 0–5 or 5–10 is greater for words on which errors were made than for words in the corpus. If only errors in which NETspell was able to give a response are considered, the trend is even stronger (lesion 1: 72% of errors in the 0–5 category; lesion 2: 67% of errors in the 0–5 category). After lesioning, NETspell does find irregular words harder to spell than regular words.

Patients who are assumed to spell non-lexically are able to give plausible spellings to nonwords. We gave NETspell 39 words that it had not been trained on to test how well it generalized its knowledge of phoneme–grapheme correspondences to

TABLE 17.6   Spellings of untrained words after ±0.45 noise lesion. Unfamiliar items are still largely spelled in phonologically plausible ways. Nonword spelling by patients thought to spell non-lexically is included for comparison.

	Number	Per cent
Lesion 1		
Plausible	28	(72)
Implausible	1	(3)
zipper → sitter		
Context violations	2	(5)
commentary → comentere		
bare → bar		
Unscoreable errors (below threshold responses)	8	(20)
Lesion 2		
Plausible	27	(69)
Implausible	3	(8)
zipper → sisser		
burgher → berga		
dairy → drrhre		
Context violations	0	(0)
Unscoreable errors (below threshold responses)	9	(23)
Patient JG (Goodman & Caramazza, 1986)		
Plausible	34	(100)
Implausible	0	(0)
Patient RG (Beauvois & Dérouesné, 1981)		
Plausible	109	(99)
Implausible	1	(1)

unfamiliar items. When those items in which all graphemes were above threshold are cored, unfamiliar items are largely spelled in phonologically plausible ways (Table 17.6).

Although the percentage of phonologically plausible errors is not quite as high as for the patients, some nonwords that were given implausible spellings were the same words that were spelled implausibly by the undamaged network. Thus, the lesions did not significantly affect the network's ability to spell unfamiliar items.

When the lesion was more severe (±0.9), the network's performance was worse. Overall performance dropped from 83% correct to 54% for lesion 1, and to 47% correct for lesion 2. Since there are more errors as a result of these lesions, we can

TABLE 17.7   Percentage of phonologically plausible and implausible new errors resulting from a ±0.9 noise lesion. This more severe lesion causes mostly phonologically implausible errors.

Error Type	New high activation errors	
	Number	Per cent
Lesion 1		
Plausible	294	(39)
Implausible	454	(61)
Lesion 2		
Plausible	250	(29)
Implausible	604	(71)

TABLE 17.8 Percentage correct for words with high and low-probability phoneme-to-grapheme correspondences (regular and irregular words) after a ±0.9 noise lesion.

	High-probability words (regular words)		Low-probability words (irregular words)	
	Number	Per cent	Number	Per cent
NETspell ±0.9 Lesion 1	278	(39)	441	(61)
NETspell ±0.9 lesion 2	380	(43)	505	(57)

adopt a more conservative standard for judging phonologically implausible errors. We will count errors as phonologically implausible only if there are no examples in the dictionary of the input phoneme being mapped to the grapheme picked by the network. Even with a more conservative criterion, however, most of the new high activation errors are phonologically implausible (Table 17.7).

A more severe lesion still affects irregular words more than regular words (Table 17.8), although the tendency for errors to occur on words that have low-probability grapheme options is not as strong as before (Table 17.9). The difference between the percentage of error words in the 0–5 category (columns 4 and 5 and 6 and 7 in Table 17.9) and the percentage of words from the corpus in the same category (columns 2 and 3 in Table 17.9) is not as great as in the case of the more moderate lesions.

Consistent with NETspell's increased number of implausible errors when spelling familiar words, ±0.9 noise lesions also resulted in more implausible errors when the network was spelling unfamiliar words (Table 17.10).

TABLE 17.9 Distribution of words based on their lowest probability phoneme-to-grapheme mapping for words in the corpus, and for errors produced by two ±0.9 lesions. Irregular words fall in the low end of the distribution (Categories 0–5 and 5–10).

Lowest p → g probability in	Corpus Number of words	Per cent	Lesion 1 Number of new errors	Per cent	Lesion 2 Number of new errors	Per cent
0–5	498	(31)	306	(43)	373	(42)
5–10	193	(12)	81	(11)	89	(10)
10–15	109	(7)	54	(8)	43	(5)
15–20	211	(13)	93	(13)	120	(14)
20–25	59	(4)	25	(3)	31	(3)
25–30	110	(7)	56	(8)	59	(7)
30–35	65	(4)	26	(4)	30	(3)
35–40	121	(7)	28	(4)	58	(7)
40–45	34	(2)	6	(1)	5	(0.6)
45–50	36	(2)	8	(1)	17	(2)
50–55	2	(0.1)	1	(0.1)	2	(0.2)
55–60	25	(2)	1	(0.1)	6	(0.7)
60–65	77	(5)	20	(3)	32	(4)
65–100	88	(5)	12	(2)	20	(2)

TABLE 17.10   Percentage of phonologically plausible and implausible spellings of untrained words after ±0.9 noise lesion.

	Number	Per cent
Lesion 1		
Plausible	21	(54)
Implausible	9	(23)
Context violations	1	(3)
Unscoreable errors (below threshold responses)	8	(21)
Lesion 2		
Plausible	19	(49)
Implausible	11	(28)
Context Violations	2	(5)
Unscoreable errors (below threshold responses)	7	(18)

NETspell's performance is encouraging. To the usual standards, it could be argued that NETspell is a successful model of the spelling system. A single network learns to spell both regular and irregular words without a lexicon. The errors it makes are like those people most commonly produce: phonologically plausible spellings of the intended word (Masters, 1927; Watson, 1935). After damage, the network produces phonologically plausible errors, the pattern reported by Beauvois and Dérouesné (1981), Hatfield and Patterson (1983) and Goodman and Caramazza (1986). More severe lesions start to degrade performance past the point reported for these patients, but less severe lesions produce a relatively good match. It is possible to damage NETspell and produce the pattern of brain damage that has been associated with preserved non-lexical spelling in the face of impaired access to lexical information.Thus, a major body of spelling results have been simulated. Perhaps spelling is not an ability that relies crucially on lexical and supra-segmental representations, even if they are required by other linguistic systems. Other modelers have had similar success using different representations (e.g. Brown & Loosemore, this volume, Chapter 16), and so it seems that spelling is mainly a statistical problem of matching some input to some output representation in order to capture the basic distribution of sounds and letters in the language. As long as the patterns in the environmentally provided data are not obscured by the representation, a wide range of representations will be successful and the particular kind chosen is not crucial. The learning rule will capitalize on statistical redundancies that exist in the environment. Statistical redundancies from the environment, not the form of representation, may be the most important factor in determining behavior.

A FURTHER CRITIQUE

When one looks in detail, however, NETspell is not without problems. Some of these are specific, related to the form of the implementation we have selected. Others are more general, concerning the type of theorizing that is possible within this framework. All, however, point in the same direction. Network performance is intimately connected to the representations we have chosen for spelling. Both positive and negative features of network performance reflect this choice, and nothing, in the end, comes "for free". We turn, first, to some specific problems in NETspell's performance.

One difficulty is how, exactly, to interpret network responses. In both its damaged and its undamaged condition, NETspell makes a significant number of responses in which no unit is active above the 0.3 threshold. We have decided to say arbitrarily that the network is unable to generate a response in these cases, but what does this mean? Do we count these errors as deletions? If so, the number of phonologically implausible errors will rise. Or do we take the most active unit, no matter how low its activation is? Again, the number of implausible errors will rise because choices will be governed as much by random low-level activation in the output units as by information about how a phoneme should be spelled. If we discount these errors, we ignore an important aspect of NETspell performance because it does not have ready interpretation. In all of these cases NETspell comes off more poorly. All models, though, may have some aspects of performance that are difficult to evaluate. The difficulties should be noted, however, so their importance can be evaluated. Since a significant number of NETspell's responses fall into this category, they cannot be ignored.

NETspell's absolute level of performance is more problematic. How well does the network spell after all? When trained on the 1000-word corpus (network 1000), it reached 70% correct on words after 60 exposures to each word, or 60 epochs. Spelling 1000 words correctly, however, is well within the capacities of many spellers. Why did NETspell not reach 100%? After 100 epochs of training on a 1628-word dictionary (network 1628), performance was at 83% on words and was climbing very slowly, if at all (see Figure 17.1). Again, 1628 words are well within the range of many vocabularies. Perhaps NETspell was not spelling so well after all. If some of the network parameters were not set correctly, this might prevent us from spelling all the words correctly. Since connectionist principles do not, as yet, provide guidance for how to change a network to improve performance, changes were made more or less arbitrarily. As the results in Table 17.11 show, changes did not improve network performance.

Even with 200 hidden units, the network did not improve above 83% correct, so the level of performance reached was not a function of limited network size. This experiment with "tinkering" reveals a more general aspect of working with networks

TABLE 17.11   Percentage correct on words after changes to NETspell network parameters.

Learning rate	Momentum	Number of hidden units	Per cent correct after 100 epochs
0.5	0.5	50	83
0.75	0.5	50	83
0.75	0.1	50	83
0.25	0.9	50	79
0.5	0.5	30	78
0.5	0.5	40	82
0.5	0.5	200	77

TABLE 17.12 Errors violating the context governing the pronunciation of *c* from a larger corpus of unfamiliar words given to network 1628.

Unfamiliar word	Context error response
kitchen	citchon
kite	cit
kitty	cite
links	linkc
lists	listc
coyote	ciote
aerospace	erospac
social	coshle

to which we return later. When things go wrong, what principles are available to guide attempts to improve performance?

Looking more closely at the mappings the network has to learn and the representations it uses gives some indication of why our tinkering was not more successful. One set of problems have to do with the orthographic context available to the network. As we noted in our discussion of the distributions of spellings in English, the pronunciation of *c* depends on the following vowel letters. A *c* preceding *i*, *e* and *y* is pronounced /s/. Preceding other vowels it is pronounced /k/. For a spelling to be plausible when *c* is used, the vowel letter must not change the intended pronunciation. Network 1000, however, made several errors in which the vowel changed the pronunciation of the preceding letter, making the error implausible. *Current*, for example, was spelled *cerent*, *khaki* was pronounced *cacy* and *provoke* was pronounced *provoce*. Another way of testing whether a network has learned this generalization is to look at how the network spells unfamiliar words and see if context violations occur. On a larger list of unfamiliar words, network 1628 made several errors which violate the context governing how *c* is pronounced (Table 17.12).

These mistakes were made because, although the network is provided with a *phonemic* context on input, it has no graphemic context to limit the choice of vowels once a *c* letter has been picked. The errors can be traced to inadequate representations which lack sufficient graphemic context. This, however, suggests that an account of the representations necessary for a task is crucial.

It is worth noting that Goodman and Caramazza (1986) have reported a patient (JG) who, following a closed head injury, had a spelling difficulty that was characterized by phonologically plausible errors. Despite her errors, however, she almost never made mistakes of the sort made by the network. Instead, she selected vowels following *c* that were appropriate for the phoneme she was spelling. Their result suggests that the processes people use to construct phonologically plausible spellings can be sensitive to the context the network failed to represent. Patient TP, reported by Hatfield and Patterson (1983), *did* make errors which involved violations of graphemic context (e.g. *biscuit → biscit*, *parcel → parcle*). The question for the network, however, is whether it is *possible* to capture the generalization that would allow it to produce the pattern of performance reported for JG. Since an undamaged network appears unable to learn this generalization, there is little reason for optimism.

TABLE 17.13 Percentage correct on words. Networks with recirculation of hidden unit values vs networks with no recirculation. Recirculation of hidden unit values did not improve overall performance on words.

Learning rate	Momentum	Number of hidden units	Per cent correct no recirculation	Per cent correct recirculation
0.5	0.5	50	83	77
0.5	0.5	40	82	77
0.5	0.5	30	78	75

A larger window providing some graphemic context would solve this problem, but how large a window is required? Connectionist principles, by themselves, give no guidance. The necessary size might be decided by looking at spelling distributions to gauge the distance over which letters interact to influence each other, but this is a traditional question of representational adequacy and suggests that connectionist models cannot dispense with these concerns.

We did try one general approach to problems of arbitrary context that has been proposed in the connectionist literature (Elman, 1990). This approach requires that hidden unit activation values from iteration N be "recirculated" to become part of the input at iteration $N+1$. Using this method, recirculated information is likely to have decreasing strength over time. The "fed back" hidden unit values that are part of the input on iteration $N+1$ will include the influence of iteration N, but the values at iteration $N+2$ will include influences from iteration N *and* iteration $N+1$, and so on. If on each iteration the importance of a context is reaffirmed (i.e. it influences hidden unit values), its presence in the input may not diminish greatly, but if several intervening items do not use the context to change hidden unit values, its influence will decrease. Whether across only one or several items, the presence of an important context in the recirculated values may be overwhelmed by other information. These speculations aside, either contextual problems were not a large factor in NETspell's overall level of performance or recirculation did not provide the relevant information because recirculation of hidden unit values did not improve the network's overall percentage correct on words (Table 17.13).

The nature of the representation and the problem the network must solve can explain some other failures to learn. NETspell has no way of distinguishing homophones because identical phoneme patterns cannot be mapped to different spellings. This did not affect the percentage correct for 1000- or 1628-word dictionaries because homophones were removed before training, but some other words reduce to the homophone case given the seven-phoneme window for input. To spell *gentian*, for example, the network must learn that the reduced vowel is spelled *a*. Other words, however, have the same set of phonemes in the window when spelling the reduced vowel, and they pick a different spelling. *Pension* and *detention* have the phonemes /enʃən/ in the input window when the *o* spelling is being selected; the phonemes that distinguish these words fall outside the three-slot context. Since two words pick the *o* spelling and only one is spelled with *a* and since the *o* spelling is more common in the /ʃən/ context, the *a* spelling cannot be learned (both of the errors that were not regularization errors in the undamaged network were examples of this type:

esoteric and *gentian*). Again, this difficulty could be solved by extending the input window, but the same comments concerning size noted above would be relevant.

There is another, more subtle, form of this difficulty that may also be causing problems. *Aisle* is a word the network failed to learn. The *ai-e* spelling of the diphthong /aɪ/ was not mastered. The phonemes of *aisle*, /aɪᵊl/, are also in the window for *mile*, *while* and *smile*, except that these words also have some phonemes to the left of the /aɪ/. Since the network cannot use a lack of information (e.g. the *lack* of anything to the left of the phoneme /aɪ/ to change its responses, a network that spells *aisle* correctly must use the /aɪᵊl/ context to choose the spelling *ai-e* for /aɪ/. In a sense *ai-e* must become the default spelling of /aɪ/ when it precedes /ᵊl/. *Smile*, *while* and *mile* must use their initial segments to overrule the *ai-e* spelling and pick *i-e*. This means, however, that each word must store its overruling context separately. In our networks, the other occurrences of /-aɪᵊl/ are too powerful. Correction towards *i-e* overpowers the single occurrence of *ai-e*. This preserves the intuition that *-ile* is the regular spelling of /aɪᵊl/, but makes *aisle* impossible to spell.

If this style of network were successful at spelling *aisle*, it might reverse the intuitive regularity of the spellings. *Ai-e* might, in some sense, be the default, and *i-e* could be chosen when contexts overrule the *ai-e* spelling. This is not, in principle, wrong, but it suggests some predictions. If such a network was, in fact, possible to train, and it was given an unfamiliar word that did not share leftward phoneme context with some other *-ile* word, it might pick the *ai-e* spelling. Whether people would choose such a spelling for unfamiliar words is an empirical question.

Many of the items that NETspell fails to learn may involve this problem. If a spelling is sufficiently rare, and the context available to distinguish the item sufficiently similar to other words, the other items may simply make it impossible to change weights enough to capture the rare spelling. The network does not have enough opportunity (the downside of frequency sensitivity) and it does not have the contextual tools necessary to solve this problem.

Words might be easier to distinguish if we enhanced the context, for example by including word boundary information so that boundaries could condition spellings, or by letting network values range from −1 (off) to +1 (on). In either case, however, the problem was identified by a traditional consideration of representational properties and a possible solution was suggested by the same.

We have seen in the introductory discussion that word position information could be useful in capturing many generalizations regarding spelling distributions. We implied that models that have such information should be able to capture the range of English spellings more efficiently than models without. Using the current example, we can see how the choice of representation might influence the computational load on the network. If there were symbols or structures identifying word position (boundary markers of the sort used in *The Sound Pattern of English* by Chomsky & Halle, 1968, are one example but not the only possibility), they could be used to capture the unique characteristic of *aisle*, the fact that it includes the phonemes /aɪl/, *and nothing more* (e.g. / # aɪᵊl # / can be distinguished from / # paɪᵊl # /, *pile*, because boundary markers, as opposed to blanks, *can* influence decisions in the network). With boundary information, the network can mark *aisle* as the odd context and let a default take care of other *i-e* items. In such a network, in line with our intuitions, *aisle* is an exceptional item and is stored as such and *i-e* could be stored once for the other items. The efficiency with which a network can solve a mapping problem depends on the representations it has available to do the mapping.

To confirm that NETspell had difficulty capturing constraints based on word position, we gave the network a large corpus of unfamiliar words to spell. If word-position constraints were somehow captured by NETspell, no violations of these constraints would be expected in spellings of unfamiliar words. The presence of violations, however, constitutes evidence that NETspell could not learn word-position restrictions (Table 17.14). It is not sufficient that patterns be present in the environment if representations cannot code the patterns in a generalizable form.

We have noted that our current network could not spell homophones, but that a successful model should be able to do so (at least as it would fit into a larger model, if not in its current form). What distinguish homophones are differences in grammatical category and/or meaning, so it seems natural to assume that semantic or grammatical category input, along with phonemes, would allow the necessary distinctions. Distinguishing homophones, then, lies outside the scope of what we have modeled. The difficulty is that NETspell has no knowledge of how to segment groups of phonemes into individual lexical items. What it knows about are phoneme–grapheme correspondences. How, then, will it be possible to have grammatical category or semantic information, which is relevant at the level of lexical items and not individual phoneme–grapheme pairs, present as the appropriate set of phonemes are moved through the window? And, if it is possible to do so, how will the combination of things that must be present together—grammatical information,

TABLE 17.14 Word-position constraints on spelling and violations of those constraints produced by NETspell when spelling unfamiliar words.

	Example Unfamiliar word	Constraint NETspell violation
Double-consonant spellings	*collapse*	Prohibited in word-initial position, some prohibited in word-final position (e.g. *cc*), some prohibited in all positions (e.g. *ii*) or after another vowel
	ledge	*lledge*
	fascism	*fassiism*
	inexperience	*inexperaeence*
	logistics	*logisticc*
Phoneme /ʃ/	*function*	*ti* spelling does not occur in word-initial position
	chagrin	*tiogrin*
Phoneme /dʒ/	*judge*	*dg* and *dj* spellings do not occur in word-initial position
	adjust	
	jet	*dget*
	judicial	*djudishle*
Phoneme /r/	*write*	*wr* only occurs in word-initial or syllable-initial position, not as the spelling of a consonant cluster
	groat	*gwroat*

TABLE 17.15   Consonant and vowel consistency in NETspell's substitution errors after lesions. Results from a patient who makes consonant-for-consonant and vowel-for-vowel substitutions are included for comparison.

	C → C errors V → V errors		C → V errors V → C errors	
	Number	Per cent	Number	Per cent
NETspell ±0.45 lesion 1	1/4	(25)	3/4	(75)
NETspell ±0.45 lesion 2	4/8	(50)	4/8	(50)
NETspell ±0.9 lesion 1	155/346	(45)	191/346	(55)
NETspell ±0.9 lesion 2	197/298	(66)	101/298	(34)
Patient LB (Caramazza & Miceli, 1990)	640/643	(99)	3/643	(0.5)

semantic information and phonemes that make up the item—differ from a lexical representation? Finally, if we do have such a network but say that it does not have lexical representations, what violence does this do to the conceptual divisions in the model?

One form of evidence we noted to suggest there are independent lexical and non-lexical processes was the different patterns of performance possible after brain-damage. We also summarized evidence that suggests that orthographic representations include a specification of abstract consonant or vowel status independent of letter identity. We have described the process of damaging our network. None of the "lesions" we tried resulted in a pattern of consonant-for-consonant and vowel-for-vowel substitutions or transpositions. To see if the network is consistently substituting consonants for consonants or vowels for vowels, it is necessary to look at the phonologically implausible errors the network makes. Since phonologically plausible errors are likely to be consonant for consonant or vowel for vowel based on their phonological relationship, evidence for abstract CV identity must come from errors that are not pronounced like the target. NETspell showed no tendency to preserve consonant or vowel identity when making phonologically implausible errors (Table 17.15).

Transpositions, in this network, only occur when two segments, by chance, participate in independent, reciprocal substitutions (i.e. *b* substitutes for *g* in one position, while *g* substitutes for *b* in another position). If substitutions were consonant for consonant and vowel for vowel, this might be possible. Since substitutions did not remain in category, transpositions would not remain in category either.

NETspell produced only one pattern of errors as a consequence of our "lesions": the pattern reported by Beauvois and Dérouesné (1981) and attributed to a lexical system rendered inoperative by damage. This is perhaps not surprising, since NETspell has only been taught phoneme–grapheme mappings. The pattern reported by Shallice (1981), preserved spelling of familiar items with impaired spelling of unfamiliar items, was not observed. This is crucial, however, because the Shallice pattern provides the main evidence that lexical knowledge can be preserved in the face of damage to non-lexical processes and is the part of the overall pattern that suggests that lexical processes exist. NETspell does not have a lexicon, but, to date, it cannot produce the data from brain damage that are associated with preserved lexical representations in the first place. Once again, what is represented by the network determines its performance:

in this case the patterns it will produce after damage. A powerful general learning rule and a rich data environment cannot make up for representational inadequacy. A similar reading model that claims success without a lexicon suffers from the same difficulty in producing only one pattern of dyslexia: that traditionally associated with a preserved *non*-lexical component (Patterson, Seidenberg & McClelland, 1989). The pattern associated with *preserved* lexical information (e.g. Beauvois & Dérouesné, 1979) was not observed.

It might have been evident in the preceding sections that conclusions about NETspell often had to be hedged. "It seems", "apparently" or "it is likely" need to be used to describe network performance. This points to another, more theoretical, difficulty with NETspell: how it makes its choices, how it operates, is difficult to understand. Since the way it goes about picking spellings is opaque, it is hard to draw firm conclusions about its organization. The range of performance that is possible cannot really be evaluated without dissecting the network after it has been trained to see what functional significance the pattern of weight values has (even then, see Lamberts & d'Ydewalle, 1990). We have tried, for example, only a very few of the possible types of "lesions" that could be used to disrupt network performance. It is possible that some lesion could produce the patterns the network has shown no capacity to display so far. Without understanding more about how the network accomplishes the spelling task, however, it is impossible to tell. Unless we dissect the network to see how it goes about spelling, the only apparent way to find out what range of "lesioned" performance is possible is to search the very large space of possible lesions (removing units, moving all weights towards zero, removing connections, disrupting only high or low weights, are examples that give some feel for the large number of possible disruptions). A trained network is the beginning, not the completion of an explanatory account (McCloskey, 1991; Olson & Caramazza, 1991).

The opacity of networks like NETspell has several consequences. The implications that data have for models is less clear. We have noted several patterns of data that NETspell has failed to simulate. Not knowing how it works, however, it is difficult to decide what should be changed to improve the model. Those insights that are possible come from traditional analyses of the representations used and their adequacy (e.g. noting that word-position information might improve performance). Connectionist principles, by themselves, rarely give direction (trying recirculation of hidden unit values might be considered an exception), and our experience with arbitrary changes in network parameters was disappointing.

Not knowing how NETspell solves the problem also makes it difficult to evaluate how interesting the solution is. Some solutions are more interesting than others. Some, for example, will plainly become unmanageable as the scale of a problem assumes the size encountered by human cognitive systems. Since networks are often trained on very limited sets of data, this characteristic could be especially problematic (see Minsky & Papert, 1988). This is not to say that network modeling should not be pursued or that tinkering might not yield some surprises. Instead, we suggest that demonstration models are no substitute for formal analysis, at some stage, that explores the sorts of solutions different kinds of networks allow or will learn. Artificial intelligence found similar lessons in its experience with "toy worlds".

The fact that NETspell succeeds in modeling certain results does not outweigh crucial failures, and giving weight to the number of successful modeling results distorts the way theories are traditionally evaluated. In addition to the question of crucial failures, we should be confident that the model solves the problem in a non-trivial fashion that can be extended when there are issues of scale. There is nothing in NETspell's performance to date that suggests we will not rediscover the need for lexical and/or supra-segmental representations. Our results, in fact, reaffirm the central position issues of representation have held in cognitive science, and show that network models are not immune from the consequences of these analyses.

One might be tempted to conclude that these results are only relevant to NETspell and do not apply more generally to other models in the literature. No model, however, can escape the consequences of the representations it uses. We may sometimes be surprised at what kinds of operations a particular representation will support, and networks can be a part of exploring the properties of representations. Networks cannot, however, learn generalizations their representations do not allow. Brute force methods (e.g. memorization) are often available for getting items correct and so how a model performs a task, not simply its rate of success or failure, is relevant to evaluating its performance. How NETspell does a task is often unclear because its operations are opaque. This is a property also, however, shared by many networks in the literature (e.g. Hinton & Shallice, 1991; Seidenberg & McClelland, 1989; Sejnowski & Rosenberg, 1987). NETspell's more specific problems accounting for data associated with supra-segmental or lexical representations are also shared by other networks, as we have seen in the case of the Seidenberg and McClelland (1989) model above (Patterson, Seidenberg & McClelland, 1989; see Besner *et al.*, 1990 for a critique, also Seidenberg & McClelland, 1990 for a reply). Our results are not confined to the particular implementation we have chosen.

Very little in this critique has not been present in other commentary on connectionist models (e.g. Fodor & Pylyshyn 1988; Lachter & Bever, 1988; Lamberts & d'Ydewalle, 1990; McCloskey, 1991; Minsky & Papert, 1988; Pinker & Prince, 1988). In the context of a particular model that resembles others in the literature, however, the points may receive the benefit of a concrete example. In the end, we agree with Minsky and Papert (1988) that the future of these models, broadly defined, is likely to be very bright indeed. There is no reason, for example, that network modelers cannot benefit from the insights developed by symbol processing theorists. The formal properties of networks can be explored and defined. The capacities of model types (not just network models) can be matched to characteristics required by cognitive tasks. How computational models operate can be explored so they participate more perspicuously in explanatory accounts. Clearly, there is much to be done, and no question that casting symbolic theories in computational form will be revealing for modelers, theorists and experimentalists alike.

ACKNOWLEDGEMENTS

We would like to thank Bill Bogstad and Suraj Surendrakumar for their help in the modeling work. We would like to thank Terry Sejnowski for his help and computer time. Thanks also to

Glyn Humphreys for computer time. Thanks go to Gary Dell for suggesting that we try a recirculation algorithm. The research reported here was supported in part by NIH grant NS22201 and by a grant from the Human Frontiers Science Program to Alfonso Caramazza.

REFERENCES

Beauvois, M. F. & Dérouesné, J. (1979). Phonological alexia: three dissociations. *Journal of Neurology, Neurosurgery & Psychiatry*, **42**, 1115–1124.

Beauvois, M.F. & Dérouesné, J. (1981). Lexical or orthographic agraphia. *Brain*, **104**: 21–49.

Besner, D., Twilley, L., McCann, R. S. & Seergobin, K. (1990). On the association between connectionism and data: are a few words necessary? *Psychological Review*, **97**, 432–446.

Bub, D., Cancelliere, A. & Kertesz, A. (1985). Whole-word and analytic translation of spelling to sound in a non-semantic reader. In K. Patterson, J. Marshall & M. Coltheart (Eds), *Surface Dyslexia: Neuropsychological and Cognitive Studies of Phonological Reading*. London: LEA.

Caramazza, A. & Miceli, G. (1990). The structure of graphemic representations. *Cognition*, **37**, 243–297.

Chomsky, N. & Halle, M. (1968)*The Sound Pattern of English*. New York: Harper & Row.

Coltheart, M. (1981). Disorders of reading and their implications for models of normal reading. *Visible Language*, **15**, 245–286.

Coltheart, M. (1985). Cognitive neuropsychology and the study of reading. In M. Posner & O. Marin (Eds), *Attention & Performance XI*. Hillsdale NJ: LEA.

Elman, J. L. (1990). Finding structure in time. *Cognitive Science*, **14**, 179–211.

Fodor, J. A. & Pylyshyn, Z. W. (1988). Connectionism and cognitive architecture: a critical analysis. *Cognition*, **28**, 3–71

Funnell, E. (1983). Phonological processes in reading: new evidence from acquired dyslexia. *British Journal of Psychology*, **74**, 159–180.

Goodman, R. A. & Caramazza, A. (1986). Aspects of the spelling process: evidence from a case of acquired dysgraphia. *Language and Cognitive Processes*, **1**, 263–296.

Hanna, R. R., Hanna, J. S., Hodges, R. E. & Rudorf, E. H. (1966). *Phoneme–Grapheme Correspondences as Cues to Spelling Improvement*. Washington, DC: US Department of Health, Education, and Welfare, Office of Education.

Hatfield, F. M. & Patterson, K. E. (1983). Phonological spelling. *Quarterly Journal of Experimental Psychology*, **35A**, 451–468.

Haugen, E. (1956a). Syllabification in Kutenai. *Language*, **22**, 196–201

Haugen, E. (1956b) The syllable in linguistic description. In M. Halle *et al*. (Eds), *For Roman Jakobson*. The Hague: Mouton.

Hinton, G. E. & Shallice, T. (1991). Lesioning an attractor network—investigations of acquired dyslexia. *Psychological Review*, **98**, 74–95.

Kim, J. J., Pinker, S., Prince, A. & Prasada, S. (1991). Why no mere mortal has ever flown out to center field. *Cognitive Science*, **15**(2), 173–218.

Kucera, H. & Francis, W. N. (1967) *Computational Analysis of Present -Day American English*. Providence, Rhode Island: Brown University Press.

Lachter, J. & Bever, T. G. (1988). The relations between linguistic structure and associative theories of language learning: a constructive critique of some connectionist learning models. *Cognition*, **20**, 195–247.

Lamberts, K. & d'Ydewalle, G. (1990). What can psychologists learn from hidden-unit nets? *Behavioral and Brain Sciences*, **13**, 499–500.

Marshall, J. C. & Newcombe, F. (1973). Patterns of paralexia: a psycholinguistic approach. *Journal of Psycholinguistic Research*, **2**, 175–199.

Masters, H. V. (1927). A study of spelling errors. *University of Iowa Studies in Education*, **4**, 1–80.

McCloskey, M. (1991). Networks and theories: the place of connectionism in cognitive science. *Psychological Science*, **2**, 387–395.

Minsky, M. & Papert, S. (1988). *Perceptrons*. Cambridge, Mass: MIT Press.

Olson, A. C. & Caramazza, A. (1991). The role of cognitive theory in neuropsychological research. In S. Corkin, J. Grafman & F. Boller (Eds), *Handbook of Neuropsychology*. Amsterdam: Elsevier.

Patterson K. E. (1982). The relation between reading and phonological coding: further neuropsychological observations. In A. Ellis (Ed.), *Normality and Pathology in Cognitive Functions*. San Diego, CA: Academic Press.

Patterson K. E., Seidenberg, M. & McClelland, J. L. (1989). Connections and disconnections: acquired dyslexia in a computational model of reading processes. In R. Morris (Ed.), *Parallel Distributed Processing: Implications for Psychology and Neurobiology*. Oxford: Oxford University Press.

Pinker, S. & Prince, A. (1988). On language and connectionism: analysis of a parallel distributed processing model of language acquisition. *Cognition*, **28**, 73–193.

Romani, C. (1992). The representation of prosodic and syllabic structure in speech production. Unpublished PhD dissertation. The Johns Hopkins University, Department of Psychology.

Rumelhart, D. E., Hinton, G. E. & McClelland, J. L. (1986). A general framework for parallel distributed processing. In D. Rumelhart & J. L. McClelland (Eds), *Parallel Distributed Processing: Explorations in the Microstructure of Cognition*, Vol. 1. Cambridge Mass: MIT Press.

Rumelhart, D. E., Hinton, G. E. & Williams, R. J. (1986). Learning internal representations by error propagation. In J. L. McClelland & D. Rumelhart (Eds), *Parallel Distributed Processing: Explorations in the Microstructure of Cognition*, Vol. 1. Cambridge Mass: MIT Press.

Rumelhart, D. E. & McClelland, J. L. (1986). On learning the past tenses of English verbs. In D. Rumelhart & J. L. McClelland (Eds), *Parallel Distributed Processing: Explorations in the Microstructure of Cognition*, Vol. 2. Cambridge, MA: MIT Press.

Seidenberg, M. S. (1987). Sublexical structures in visual word recognition: access units or orthographic redundancy? In M. Coltheart (Ed.), *Attention and Performance XII: Reading*. Hillsdale, NJ: LEA.

Seidenberg, M. S. & McClelland J. L. (1989). A distributed, developmental model of word recognition and naming. *Psychological Review*, **96**, 523–568.

Seidenberg, M. S. & McClelland, J. L. (1990). More words but still no lexicon: reply to Besner et al. (1990). *Psychological Review*, **97**, 447–452.

Sejnowski, T. J. & Rosenberg, C. R. (1987). Parallel networks that learn to pronounce English text. *Complex Systems*, **1**, 145–168.

Shallice, T. (1981). Phonological agraphia and the lexical route in writing. *Brain*, **104**, 413–429.

Shallice, T. & Warrington, E. K. (1980). Single and multiple component central dyslexic syndromes. In M. Coltheart, K. Patterson & J. Marshall (Eds), *Deep Dyslexia*. London: Routledge & Kegan Paul.

Touretzky, D. S. & Hinton, G. E. (1985). Symbols among the neurons: details of a connectionist inference architecture. *Proceedings of the Ninth International Joint Conference on Artificial Intelligence*, pp. 238–243.

Watson, A. (1935). *Experimental Studies in the Psychology and Pedagogy of Spelling*. New York: Bureau of Publications, Teachers College, Columbia University.

18

Spelling and Serial Recall: Insights from a Competitive Queueing Model

GEORGE HOUGHTON, DAVID W. GLASSPOOL AND TIM SHALLICE

University College London

The process of spelling a known word from memory requires not only the recall of the letters comprising the word but also their production in the correct order, whether the output medium be writing, typing or some other. Spelling can therefore be treated, at least in part, as a problem of serial recall (Wing & Baddeley, 1980). In this chapter we advance the argument that a proper understanding of spelling will require that the representations and processes enabling serial recall play a central role. To make this case we first consider certain aspects of spelling error data, from both normal and impaired subjects, which implicate serial order mechanisms. Current proposals for the kinds of serial order representations involved in spelling are evaluated in the light of these data and are found wanting. Following this, we describe some results from ongoing work using a neural network approach to serial order known as "competitive queueing" (Houghton, 1990, 1994; Rumelhart & Norman, 1982), which we show can account for a wide range of error data.

SERIAL ORDER ERRORS IN SPELLING

Error data have played a significant role in the development of models of serially ordered behaviour, for instance in typing (MacNeilage, 1964; Shaffer, 1975;

Handbook of Spelling: Theory, Process and Intervention. Edited by G. D. A. Brown and N. C. Ellis.
© 1994 John Wiley & Sons Ltd.

Rumelhart & Norman, 1982), language production (Dell, 1986; Mackay, 1970, 1972) and in the articulatory loop (Burgess & Hitch, 1992). The rationale behind the use of such data is that the observed regularities found in serial order errrors (e.g. length effects, serial position effects, types of error, etc.) are revealing with respect to underlying representations and mechanisms. This approach has been applied to the study of the spelling process, with, for instance, Hotopf (1980) and Wing and Baddeley (1980) analysing serial order errors found in written corpora produced by normal subjects. More recently, data from acquired dysgraphic patients (Caramazza *et al.*, 1987; Caramazza & Miceli, 1990; Jonsdottir, Shallice & Wise, submitted; Margolin, 1984) have been used to argue for the existence of some kind of "graphemic buffer", which temporarily stores, in parallel, the letters of a to-be-spelled word while they are being successively translated into appropriate actions. Damage to this buffer is proposed to result in errors such as substitutions, omissions, exchanges, etc. (Caramazza *et al.*, 1987). These data are considered in more detail below.

Errors may be defined as deviations in performance from some normative standard. It is important to distinguish between what might be termed "competence" and "performance" errors. Competence errors arise due to inaccurate or incomplete "knowledge", whereas performance errors (or "slips") are due to some failure in the process of translating (accurate) knowledge into action. Competence errors in spelling arise from inaccurate internal representations of the written form of words. In the strictest case, such errors will typically be associated with particular poorly learned words, and will be repeated each time the word is attempted. The error will not be noticed by the subject and cannot be corrected without external input. Performance errors arise as a result of the spelling process and as such may not be associated with individual words. Subjects making such errors might be expected to detect them, and be able to correct them. It is not inconceivable that there may also be errors which are partly due to both factors, i.e. some representations may be "in principle" adequate to support correct recall, but yet may be sufficiently "fragile", in some manner, that use of them is highly susceptible to disruption.

In this work, we are almost entirely concerned with performance errors or slips, though the model we describe later is able to show an interaction between the recall process and how "well learned" a particular word is. We here describe some of the dominant characteristics of what we conceive of as "serial order errors", both in normal and in impaired subjects.

Normal Subjects: Wing and Baddeley (1980)

Wing and Baddeley (1980) analysed spelling errors produced by 40 students taking entrance examinations to Cambridge Colleges in 1976. Study of the scripts yielded 1185 errors, of which 847 were classified as slips (i.e. the student knew the correct spelling but made a performance error). The authors classified slips into four types, described here in decreasing order of frequency:

1. Omissions: a letter is omitted from the target words, for example *likely → likly*. $N = 412$, $= 49\%$.

2. Substitutions: a letter in the target word is replaced by an incorrect letter, for example *desirable → desireble*. $N = 304$, $= 36\%$.
3. Insertions: an additional, incorrect, letter is added to the target word, for example *political → polictical*. $N = 108$, $= 13\%$.
4. Reversals: two adjacent letters occur in reverse order, for example *cannot → cannto*. $N = 23$, $= 2\%$.

Wing and Baddeley report clear serial position effects such that errors of all types are much more common at medial positions than at either end of words. The finding of few errors at the (right-hand) end of words was unexpected, as the authors supposed letters to be loaded in parallel into a serial buffer, and to be subject to "decay" during output. The longer the letter spent in the buffer, the more "decayed" it would become, thereby being prone to error.[1] Different error types showed some difference in sensitivity to serial position. Along with the observation of different numbers of each error type, this led the authors to conjecture that the various error types arose from different causes. Unfortunately, as well as predicting the wrong serial position curves, the "serial buffer" hypothesis is too computationally underspecified to shed any light on this issue. (Indeed, under any intuitive notion of what a serial buffer may be, it is hard to see why letters should change identity (substitutions) or swap positions (reversals), or how they can be pushed along to later positions by an insertion. We consider buffer theories in more detail in the following section.)

Acquired Dysgraphia—Graphemic Buffer Disorder

In this section we consider the pattern of spelling errors produced by two acquired dysgraphic patients, the Italian patient LB studied by Caramazza *et al.*, (1987) and Caramazza and Miceli (1990) and the English patient AS studied by Jonsdottir, Shallice and Wise (submitted). The spelling problems in these patients are characterized as involving a deficit to the "graphemic buffer", this being a putative store in which activated grapheme representations are held while a word is being written. Since many of the findings in these two studies are so similar, we will illustrate them largely by reference to the earlier Caramazza *et al.* study on LB. Discussion of AS will be confined to pointing out relevant similarities and differences.

Patient LB

Caramazza *et al.* (1987) and Caramazza and Miceli (1990) discuss at length error data generated by an Italian patient, LB, which they take to support the existence of a graphemic buffer. The errors produced by LB are taken to be due to damage

---

1 "[W]e will assume single successive words are registered in the buffer. Further we will suppose that normally individual letters, rather than letter groups, are represented in the buffer in a linear fashion that corresponds to the spatial order of the letters in the written word. . . [W]e assume that registration of the letters in the buffer is virtually simultaneous ...If there is a decay of the memory trace for each letter with time there will then be difficulty in retrieval of items occurring later in each word." (Wing & Baddeley, 1980, p. 253)

TABLE 18.1   Percentage of words showing errors as a function of length for subject LB. Adapted from Caramazza *et al.* (1987), Table 3.

Number of Graphemes	Per cent incorrect
4–5	15
6–7	34
8–9	67
10–12	90

to this structure. Many of the errors produced by LB are clearly indicative of some form of structural constraint on errors. For instance, LB produces exchange errors where two letters swap positions. It is observed, however, that in most cases consonant letters (i.e. letters which typically represent consonants) swap with consonant letters, and likewise for vowel letters. In the current work we ignore these constraints and focus on the errors simply as serial order errors and consider their occurrence as a function of such variables as word length and serial position.[2]

Caramazza *et al.* used a number of spelling tasks with LB, including spelling to dictation and written naming, where the subject is asked to write the name of a pictured object. The data we consider will be drawn from these latter two tasks.

Word length effects

Caramazza *et al.* (1987) report that word length has a major effect on the incidence of errors over all tasks. For instance, Table 18.1 shows per cent errors made at words of different lengths in the dictation task.

The same increasing pattern with roughly similar proportions at each length was found in the written naming task. The word sample used in spelling to dictation controlled for grammatical class, abstractness/concreteness and word frequency. There was no effect of these variables, leading to the hypothesis of a selective deficit of the "graphemic buffer" which stores letters while they are being serially produced, irrespective of their source.

Serial position effects

Caramazza *et al.* (1987) report serial position effects on total number of errors very similar to the Wing and Baddeley results discussed above, i.e. many more errors were produced medially than at the beginnings and ends of words. The results produced a nearly symmetric inverted-U shaped curve of number of errors against serial position. This result held over all word lengths.

---

[2]Caramazza and Miceli (1990) do not actually argue that these patterns reflect an online influence from the words' pronunciation during spelling. Rather, they propose that the "phonological" information is directly contained in the orthographic representation. Letters are separated into C (consonant) and V (vowel) types, and are chunked into graphemic "syllables" (see Fig 18.12 for an example). There are clearly important differences between this approach and the postulation of online phonological influence (Jonsdottir, Shallice & Wise, submitted). However, we here disregard these differences, treating both approaches as involving phonology-based structural constraints on spelling.

Error types

As in the Wing and Baddeley study, error types fall into classes of substitutions, omissions, exchanges and insertions. We consider these in turn in order of frequency. In addition, Caramazza et al. provide data regarding "geminate" errors, i.e. a special class of error invloving words containing a double letter.

1. Substitution errors. Substitution errors are the most frequent in the corpus (49.3% of single-type errors). Since only 10.9% of these errors resulted in real words, this suggests an absence of lexicality constraints. Very importantly, most substitutions (68.3%) were duplications of letters already in the target word. Of these, most were anticipations (75%). Thus just over half of all substitutions are caused by a to-be-produced letter displacing the current target letter.
2. Omission errors. Omission errors formed 27% of the corpus. It is important to mention that virtually all of these occurred for words with "complex" syllable structure—i.e. not of the form CVCV, etc. This suggests the patient's spelling was receiving strong support from the regular CV structure of Italian (Jonsdottir, Shallice & Wise, submitted). As with other errors, omissions were most frequent in medial positions and mostly involved one letter, occasionally two.
3. Exchange and shift errors. Exchange errors (called reversals in the Baddeley and Wing study) formed 24% of errors, shifts 3.8%. (Shift errors involve a letter in the target word moving to the wrong place.) Transpositions gave lexical results in only 3% of cases.
4. Insertion errors. Insertion errors are the least frequent in the corpus (6.4%). Very importantly, 80.2% of insertion errors were duplications of letters occurring elsewhere in the target word. In this they resemble substitution errors.
5. Geminate errors. LB produced errors on words containing a geminate (or doubled) letter which have a unique pattern of considerable interest. A high proportion of geminate errors involve the shift of the geminate feature to an incorrect grapheme (ABCCDE → ABBCDE). Geminate duplication occurs, but a new geminate is hardly ever placed in a word which does not already have a geminate. In exchange errors involving geminates, the geminate cluster behaves as a single entity and is never split. This leads the authors to the conclusion that the orthographic representation of a geminate consists of a single letter with a special "doubling" marker attached. We return to the issue of geminates later.

TABLE 18.2 Per cent errors made by LB on dictated nonwords as a function of word length. Adapted from Caramazza *et al.* (1987), Table 3.

Number of Graphemes	Per cent incorrect
4–5	27
6–7	51
8–9	73
10–12	100

Word–nonword comparisons

LB was also tested on his spelling of dictated nonwords. His per cent error rate as a function of word length for nonwords is shown in Table 18.2 (from Caramazza *et al.* (1987), Table 3).

The monotonic trend is clearly identical to the case for words shown above, with a 10–15% increase in errors for nonwords over words at all word lengths. Furthermore, the distribution of total errors (inverted-U) and the percentage of each error type for words and nonwords is very similar. This leads the author to the conclusion that "The striking similarity in distribution of error types for words and nonwords is consistent with the hypothesis that the patient's difficulties in spelling words and nonwords have a common source".

Caramazza *et al.* (1987) and Caramazza and Miceli (1990) argue that the data support the idea that spelling involves the operation of a graphemic buffer, into which letters are loaded before being serially output. This buffer is conceived to be some sort of serially structured short-term store, as postulated by Wing and Baddeley (1980), discussed above. We return to this point later.

Patient AS

Jonsdottir, Shallice and Wise (submitted) discuss data from an English patient, AS, showing spelling difficulties rather similar to those shown by LB. For instance, the number of errors produced by AS increases as a function of word length in a remarkably similar way to LB. A comparison of the two patients' data is shown in Figure 18.1, illustrating the almost linear decline in per cent correct as a function of length. It may be noted that LB is slightly better than AS at all word lengths. Jonsdottir *et al.* argue that this may be due to the highly regular phoneme → grapheme of Italian

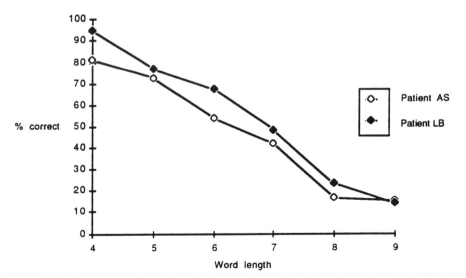

FIGURE 18.1   Percentage of words spelled correctly as a function of word length for subjects LB (Caramazza *et al.*, 1987) and AS (Jonsdottir *et al.*, submitted).

orthography, compared to English. The Italian patient may be better able to use phonological support in his spelling, since use of a regular phoneme → grapheme mapping is more likely to produce the correct output in Italian than in English.

Other aspects of the AS data are also highly consistent with LB, and with the Wing and Baddeley data for normal subjects. For instance, LB produces the familiar curve for number of errors against serial position, with the maximum in the medial positions and a monotonic decrease on either side towards the beginning and end. However, AS shows fewer errors in the initial portions of words than in the final portions, whereas LB shows better performance at the ends of words. This discrepancy might conceivably reflect the fact that the highly inflected nature of Italian makes the endings of many words rather similar. For "complex" words (i.e those not exhibiting simple CV structure) the proportion of errors of each type produced by AS strongly mirrors the proportions produced by LB on complex words. Finally, when the per cent of errors produced by AS as a function of serial position is broken down by error type, the individual curves remain very similar to the pattern for all errors, with a strong trend towards increasing errors as one moves towards the middle of the word.

This completes our review of the major types and distributions of serial position errors which spelling models must account for. In the following section we consider how well these data sit with the two approaches to serial order representation in spelling which we are familiar with from current models.

SERIAL ORDER REPRESENTATIONS IN SPELLING MODELS

It is clear that any viable theory of spelling must commit itself to claims regarding the representation and control of serial order information during the spelling process. We here consider two current approaches: spatial representations and serial buffers.

Spatial Representations

Much of the recent interest in connectionist models in cognitive psychology has focused on the perceptron architecture introduced by Rosenblatt (1962). Perceptron networks (with two or more layers of units) are simple feedforward devices which can learn to map points (vectors) in an input space to points in an output space. The mapping is computed for all dimensions of the input–output spaces in parallel, and is typically achieved in a single pass of activation from input to output (via any intermediate layers). The desire to use this architecture in the linguistic domain (MacWhinney & Leinbach, 1991; Rumelhart & McClelland, 1986; Seidenberg & McClelland, 1989) has led to the development of purely spatial encodings of the temporally or serially structured objects common in language (e.g. words, syllables, etc.). Full consideration of the consequences of this strategy is beyond the scope of the current work. However, we note here that the use of these representations is entirely technology driven, i.e. it arises from the desire to use a processing architecture which lacks any temporal dynamics and which therefore may be inherently unsuited to modelling serially organized behaviours. (To our knowledge, none of the linguistic representations used in such models has ever been given any psychological or empirical motivation.)

The model of Brown and Loosemore (this volume, Chapter 16) is an example of the use of this architecture in the spelling domain. The model takes as input some (spatial) representation of the sound of a monosyllable and maps it in parallel to a highly distributed orthographic representation. Thus Brown *et al.* dispense with the serial aspects of spelling altogether. Some later process must decode the spatial representation to generate a series of letters. Since there is nothing in Brown *et al.*'s trigram-based representation itself which would lead one to expect the kinds of error patterns discussed above, this ordering process must be the locus of such problems. However, it seems that no plausible letter ordering scheme could be based on the Brown *et al.* representation. This because the representation is (a) in terms of trigrams rather than letters, and (b) each trigram representation is distributed over four units by a rather convoluted coding scheme (see Brown and Loosemore, this volume, Chapter 16, for details). The serial output mechanism would have to be able not only to linearize this representation, but to do so in a manner which could lead to errors of the type discussed above. This does not seem a particularly likely prospect. As Brown *et al.* note, "the output pattern [produced by the model] does not directly indicate how the model is spelling the word". In the absence of any indication to the contrary, we conclude that this sort of approach to serial order will not yield insight into the data considered here.

Olson and Caramazza (this volume, Chapter 17) use a network with the same three-layer feedforward architecture as Brown *et al.*, mapping directly from sound to spelling. However, Olson and Caramazza induce some seriality into the model by having the phonological representation scanned serially by means of a moving window centred on particular phonemes. Unfortunately, the model requires one-to-one phoneme → grapheme mappings. This leads to a word such as *bite* (three phonemes, four letters) being represented as three "graphemes", *b*, *t* and *i-e*, the latter representing both the second and fourth letters of *bite*. Thus the model does not generate spellings as a series of letters and some later process is still needed. Olson and Caramazza report that 82% of the models's errors consist of it making no supra-threshold response at all. Most of the remaining 18% are phonologically plausible regularizations. There are no reports of errors of the type catalogued by Wing and Baddeley for normal subjects, nor of the characteristic serial position curve. When "lesioned", the model produced more regularization errors, but in no substantial degree approximated the error performance of the dysgraphic patients discussed above. Indeed, it seems unlikely that the model will produce such errors, given its serial, one-to-one mapping of phonemes to "graphemes". For instance, a transposition error of the type *solve → slove* (from the Wing & Baddeley, 1980 corpus) would require that the *l* node became inappropriately active ahead of time, somehow suppressing the grapheme *o*. Once produced, this grapheme must be deactivated and must not become active again when its usual phoneme /l/ is in the centre of the phonemic window, but must be supplanted by the *o* which it replaced. We see no way in which such a series of events could take place with this architecture.

Serial Buffers

The standard approach to the representation and control of serial order within the classical "information-processing" paradigm has been to postulate the existence of some kind of serial buffer. A buffer is thought of as a short-term store existing between two processes A and B, where process B acts on the output of process A. If B processes information more slowly than A, in particular if it operates serially on items which A generates in parallel, then a buffer is required between the two processes to hold the items generated by process A until process B is ready to act on them. If B must process the outputs of A in some particular order, then the buffer must represent this order in some fashion. The simplest assumption apears to be that the buffer has serial structure (equivalent to, say, an ordered set) so that the first item to be processed by B is in location 1, the second in location 2, and so on. Further assumptions must be added to specify how process B acts on the buffer. For instance, does it always take its input from position 1 or does it move along the buffer, consuming items at successive locations? In the first case, items in the buffer must shift along one location as earlier items are consumed (as occurs, for example, in retrieval from a push-down store). In the second case, process B must either remember where it is in the buffer as it successively consumes input or must repeatedly scan the buffer from "left" to "right" until it finds a filled location (with items dropping out of the buffer as they are consumed). Different assumption leads to different consequences.

Serial buffers have been invoked in models of spelling, both for handwriting and typing. For instance, in the typing domain, Shaffer (1975) proposes that in typing a word, all the letters composing it are first copied simultaneously into a buffer which preserves ordinal position. Letters in the buffer are sequentially translated into finger movements. The translation process selects which letter to type by virtue of a pointer to the current position. Shaffer proposes that errors can occur during loading of the buffer (ordinal position is not preserved) and during translation, due to pointer failure. According to Shaffer (p. 431), "Failures of pointers in [the] buffer to indicate correctly the current location of output lead to repetition or loss of material".

As noted earlier, Wing and Baddeley (1980) adopt a similar position with regard to handwriting. They add the assumption of decay of letter identities in the buffer over time, and note that this fails to predict the observed serial position curve, with errors concentrated at medial positions. Shaffer's model would appear to predict a flat curve.

Caramazza et al. (1987) discuss the impairment of their patient LB (described in detail above) in terms of damage to a graphemic output buffer.[3] However, the precise formal nature of the buffer is not specified, and no algorithm for converting its contents into serial behaviour is given. Thus no better account is given of the errors considered above than could be derived from either Shaffer (1975) or Wing and Baddeley (1980). These accounts offer no well-motivated explanation of most of the data considered above: for instance, the serial effects, word–nonword differences, geminate errors or differences in proportions of error types. On the reasonable

---

[3]In Caramazza and Miceli (1990) representations in this buffer are grouped into "graphosyllables" and vowel and consonant letters are distinguished. We ignore these complications here.

assumptions that (a) longer words take longer to write and that (b) within some time unit there is a finite probability of the occurrence of whatever it is that causes an error, then the probability of error should increase with word length. However, these models give no grounds for predicting the slopes of the per cent correct curves shown in Figure 18.1. All one can predict is that they should fall monotonically. (Incidentally, if time is the crucial variable, as proposed by Wing and Baddeley (1980), then words written quickly should show fewer errors than words written slowly. This strikes us as unlikely.) Proposals based on serial buffers thus suffer from being either computationally underspecified or, where specified, from being at odds with serial order data of the kind discussed above.

Conclusions

We conclude that, to date, there are no proposals within either the connectionist or information-processing paradigms, which give a satisfactory theoretical basis for the understanding of serial order errors in written spelling. In the remainder of the chapter we make a case for the application of the idea of "competitive queueing" to these issues.

COMPETITIVE QUEUEING MODELS OF SERIAL ORDER

Spelling a word is a form of serially ordered recall from memory, and as such might be considered akin to typing or saying the word (Margolin, 1984. See Figure 18.5). If the word is known, recall is from long-term memory (LTM). In spelling nonwords from dictation, short-term memory for the sound of the word is implicated. The data of Caramazza et al. (1987) and Jonsdottir et al. (submitted) discussed above suggest that, in both cases, letters comprising the to-be-spelt word become active in parallel, before being sequentially realized as motor output. The interaction between parallel and serial processes necessitates some form of buffer storage, and serial order slips occur in the translation from parallel to serial processing. In impaired subjects, brain damage may be considered to have made this translation process less reliable than usual, resulting in a large number of serial order errors.

In attempting to understand serial order errors in spelling, it is clearly desirable to make as few domain-specific assumptions as possible. Thus while we allow that specific mechanisms must exist to support the general ability to generate serial behaviour from memory, we would wish, as far as possible, to treat spelling in terms of these more general mechanisms. In order to do this, of course, we need a candidate mechanism for the general case. This mechanism should be psychologically motivated in at least one relevant area, having been used with some success to explain some range of data. In addition, we propose that the mechanism should not make use of ordered structures as primitives (e.g. serial buffers). As noted above, no well-defined example of such devices appears capable of explaining serial order phenomena in a plausible manner. In this work we therefore seek an approach which does not take serial order for granted, but rather has to explain it by building a serial order capacity out of the interactions of simple processing elements.

In such circumstances, an obvious approach is to examine neural network models. These models are constructed by linking up sets of simple processing elements to produce more complex behaviour. Networks operate naturally in parallel and no serially ordered primitives are provided. Thus the representation and control of serial order is a genuine problem in neural networks. As long as modelling efforts are guided by insights from empirical data, the attempt to generate serial behaviour from neural networks might be expected to yield models with more explanatory value than that provided by the ordered primitives of classical models. We thus take as our starting point the class of neural network models known as "competitive queueing" (CQ) models (Houghton, 1990). While individual examples of such models (discussed further below) show many architectural differences, they have in common that, for some behavioural "chunk" composed of an ordered set of elements, many (possibly all) of the elements are accessed in parallel, but with an "activation gradient" being established over the items (the "queue"). This activation gradient is used in such a way that the earlier an item is to be produced (or establish control over the next stage of processing), the more active it will be. The most active item at any time is suppressed once it has been output, allowing reset of the overall activation pattern and selection of the next item. Selection depends on activation level, and items in the queue compete to be selected, hence the name "competitive queueing" (Houghton, 1990).

The basic components of such an approach appear to have occurred to a number of authors independently. For instance, a mathematical model of this sort was sketched by Grossberg (1978) to account for serial position effects in list learning paradigms. The first computationally implemented model which fits the above characterization appears to be that of Rumelhart and Norman (1982). This model attempted to explain a variety of error types occurring in typing. Typing data are highly relevant to the issue at hand, and a number of authors have explicitly proposed that handwriting and typing access the same buffer representation (see e.g. Margolin, 1984). We therefore consider this model in more detail.

The Rumelhart and Norman (1982) Typing Model

Rumelhart and Norman (1982) (henceforth R&N) attempt to model a variety of data from skilled typing. Of particular interest in the current context is that they model serial order slips such as transposition errors, for example *which → whihc*, and doubling shift errors, for example *screen → scrren*, in which the wrong letter in a target word is doubled. In the R&N model, illustrated in Figure 18.2, when a word (or word fragment) is to be typed nodes representing the letters in the word are *equally* activated in parallel by word → letter connections (e.g. *e, r, y, v* are activated if the word is *very*). Letter nodes have inhibitory connections between them arranged such that a letter to appear at position p_i in the output inhibits all letters to appear at later positions. Thus the first letter to be output receives no inhibition and later letters receive successively more. The net excitation received by any letter therefore decreases the later it is to be produced. Given that the activation level achieved by a node increases with increasing net excitation, this sequence-specific lateral inhibition induces an activation gradient over the letter nodes. The most active letter node has the

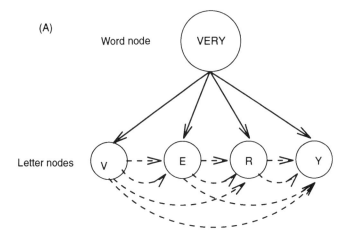

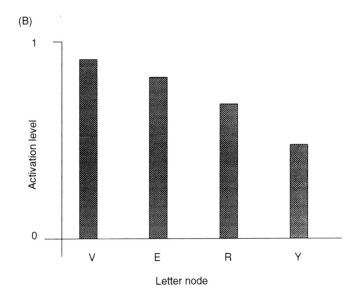

FIGURE 18.2   Competitive queueing in the Rumelhart and Norman (1982) model of serial order control in typing. (A) Nodes representing letters to be typed in some words are accessed in parallel by spread of activation for a word node (*very*). Letter nodes inhibit all nodes standing for letters which are to appear later in the word (Full Line, Excitatory Connection; Dashed Line, Inhibitory Connection). (B) The combination of top-down activation and sequence-specific lateral inhibition establishes an activation gradient over the letter nodes such that the earlier a letter is to be typed the more active it is. The activated letters may be thought of as forming an unstructured "queue". They compete for control of output on the basis of their activation level. The winning node is inhibited after generating a response.

greatest control of output and determines what letter is typed. The simultaneous activation of to-be typed letters allows R&N to model co-articulation effects, in which the hand position of the typist anticipates upcoming letters. (The prevalence of this anticipatory hand positioning is one of the strongest reasons for postulating parallel activation of a set of letter nodes.) Following production of a given letter, the node representing it is inhibited. This removes the inhibitory effect of that node on the other active nodes, and resets the activation gradient. What was previously the second most active node will now receive no inhibition and, being most active, will control the following response. This process is repeated until all letters in the sequence have been typed.

The model produces transposition errors when the wrong letter node has become the most active at the wrong time (say due to noise or some other form of interference). After being produced this node is inhibited, at which time the most active node is likely to be the one which represents the letter which should have been produced. Thus the two letters swap places. R&N propose a "type only" representation of letters, i.e. each letter identity is represented by a single node, and each time the letter is to be typed this node must be active. The model prohibits the use of "copies" or "tokens" of the type such as are commonly assumed in symbolic models. This means that, to cope with doubled letters (e.g. the *e* in *screen*), R&N propose the existence of a "doubling schema". Ideally, when a letter is to be doubled, the doubling schema will be active. After the first element of the doublet is typed, the schema acts, in some not altogether clear manner, to prevent the usual post-output suppression from taking place, allowing the action to be repeated. After the completion of the doublet, the doubling schema is deactivated by some means. Doubling shift errors (*screen → scrren*) occur when the schema is active at the wrong time. Thus the use of type-only representations, along with the idea of a post-output suppression process, leads to the need for a special device for handling doublings. This provides an explanation for the otherwise mysterious finding that doubling can shift.

Despite the empirical utility of its recall dynamics, the R&N model has serious limitations as a model of recall from LTM. In particular, the manner by which it establishes the required activation gradient over the queue necessitates the use of sequence-specific lateral inhibitory connections (Figure 18.2). Unfortunately, this prevents sequences containing shared elements in different orders (e.g. *silt, slit, list*) from being simultaneously represented in LTM, since their lateral connection patterns are incompatible and would interfere with each other. For instance, suppose a network that "knows" the words *silt, tills* and *list* is trying to produce the word *list*. Initially all letter nodes *s, i, t, l* are activated by equal top-down activation. In this case, though, the *l* node would be inhibited by all the other activated nodes (due to the connections needed to produce the other words), and hence could not achieve the dominant activation required to initiate recall. In fact, all four nodes would be equally inhibited by each other, and no activation gradient at all could be achieved. A further fatal problem involves words such as *prop* with a repeated letter. There is no connection pattern of the type proposed by R&N capable of supporting the production of this word, since the *p* would have to be both the least and most inhibited element, being both first and last in the sequence. To cope with this R&N have to "parse" such a word into two parts, *pro* and *p*, which do not contain a repeat. First the *pro* section is generated in the manner described above, followed by the *p* alone.

The R&N model provides intuitively satisfying explanations for a variety of data involving errors in serial recall. The errors are generated, as suggested above, at the interface between parallel and serial processes. Rather importantly, it is able to generate serial output *without recourse to a serial buffer*. Items in a word are activated in parallel but are not stored in some serial structure. It is indeed the lack of any such structure which makes the model error-prone. Unfortunately, the structures (connection patterns) needed to support this dynamics are internally inconsistent and lacking in generality. Furthermore they are coded by hand and cannot be learnt by the model. More recent work adopting this general approach has provided solutions to these problems (Houghton, 1990). This work forms the basis of the current model.

A General Architecture for Competitive Queueing

The development of this line of theory due to Houghton (1990) retains the desirable dynamics of the R&N model while solving the problems mentioned above. In this model (initially applied to speech production, in which, as in typing, co-articulation is a ubiquitous phenomenon), every word learnt has its own word-level representation (as in the R&N model). However, all sequence-specific information is located in the connections from the word to the letter level. In contrast to the R&N model, in which sequence information is in the pattern of lateral inhibitory links, these connections do not lead to interference. In addition, though, this model expands the dynamical foundations of the CQ class by reconceptualizing the role of the "word node". Instead of being a standard connectionist unit which serves as a steady source of activation, Houghton proposed that the word level (more generally, the "sequence" level) generates a time-varying "control signal", i.e. a pattern of activation which varies during the course of learning and recall. Crucially, this control signal may have more than one dimension (i.e. be generated by more than one node). In Houghton's model, the control signal has two dimensions, being generated by a pair of nodes labelled I and E nodes (for "initiator" and "end" nodes). During recall the activation pattern over these nodes changes with time, such that to begin with only the initiator node is active. As time passes the initiator node's activation decays and the activation of the end node increases. This changing pattern of activation from the "sequence" level allows different items in the sequence to become maximally active at different times. The architecture and dynamics of this model are described in more detail later on.

Houghton demonstrated that such a network can learn sequences using a simple Hebb-type learning rule, and can handle sequences with repeats, such as *prop* (these properties are discussed in more detail below). During recall, the task of selecting the most active item at any time and then suppressing it is achieved by a "competitive filter". The activation pattern at the item node level is copied to the filter by one-to-one excitatory connections (see Figure 18.3). Competitive interactions within the filter select out the most active filter node and inhibit the rest (see Houghton, 1994, for discussion). This node then feeds back in an inhibitory fashion to the item node which activated it, causing it to be suppressed. This allows reset of the item node activation

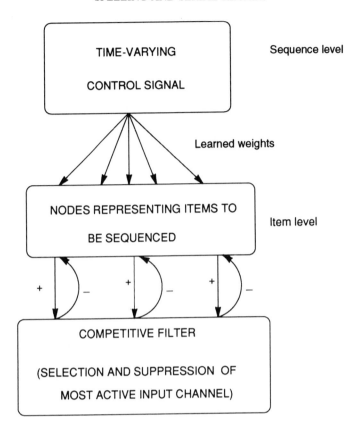

COMPETITIVE QUEUEING ARCHITECTURE

FIGURE 18.3 Organization of a competitive queueing model, following Houghton (1990). The "sequence level" generates a time-varying signal to the item level. Learned weights in the sequence → item pathways generate and maintain the desired activation gradient. Peak-picking and inhibition is effected by a "competitive filter".

pattern in the manner discussed above. A schematic diagram of this version of competitive queueing is shown in Figure 18.3.

The characteristic pattern of recall dynamics of CQ models is shown in Figure 18.4. This shows recall of the syllable /s t r i ng/ (represented as a string of phonemes) in the Houghton (1990) model. Each curve in the graph shows the activation level over time of a node representing one of the phonemes. Each curve is labelled by the phoneme it represents at the point it wins the competition and is subsequently suppressed.

The central novelty of this architecture, and the source of its improved functionality compared to the R&N model, is the replacement of the usual, one-dimensional, steady state signal generated by the sequence level with a time-varying signal of more

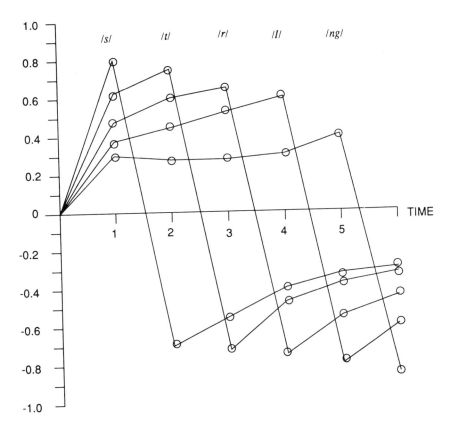

FIGURE 18.4 Serial recall in the Houghton (1990) competitive queueing model. The recalled item is the word (syllable) "string", here represented as a string of phonemes. Each curve is labelled by the phoneme it represents at the point at which the phoneme is the most active.

than one dimension. This signal is repeated in each recall event, and may be considered "endogenous" to the system. Time, or serial position, is represented in a continuous, distributed fashion by the state of the internal signal. Within recall of a learned "chunk" the signal does not repeat itself, and the state of the signal is more correlated with itself the closer two moments or positions are. Thus discrete serial positions are represented internally in a continuous manner, and without the need to allocate specific nodes to specific positions. By allowing the recall of unpredictable, environmentally supplied time series on the basis of an internally generated, predictable time series, the model reduces the unknown to the known.

In principle, this internal signal might be of arbitrary complexity and dimensionality. The use of complex signals, with low temporal correlation, increases the memory capacity of the architecture (by making successive positions more distinct), but at a cost. The more complex the signal becomes, the greater the need to explain how it is accurately generated (or recalled). Thus the increase in power is bought at the cost of pushing the central problem of serial recall back into the model—we are forced to ask, what controls the controller?—threatening an infinite regress. It seems wise, therefore, to try and constrain the use of this device in some way, in the absence of any direct empirical constraint. In the model described below, we use a variant of the simple 2-D control signal used by Houghton (1990). This has the advantages of (a) having the lowest dimensionality, i.e. two, that could conceivably work; (b) being monotonic in each dimension, i.e. each component of the signal has a simple time-course; and (c) being tied to the beginning and end of the sequence—i.e. the "temporal edges" which separate the sequence out from the continuous flow of events. Properties (a) and (b) help ensure that the problem of recalling the control signal is not more difficult than recalling the learned sequence. A model with a 2-D, monotonic signal can learn and recall non-monotonic sequences (i.e. ones with repeats) with up to around seven items (maximum seven dimensions). Thus the model effects "data reduction" in predicting a high-dimensional time series on the basis of a two-dimensional one. Property (c) relates the signal to important, identifiable structural points in the sequence.

In further work, this general form of CQ (with some additional factors) has been applied to the modelling of serial recall in the articulatory loop by Burgess and Hitch (1992) and Glasspool (1991). The Burgess and Hitch (1992) model, which can perform single-trial serial learning, accounts for a variety of data on serial recall including span, word length effects, primacy effects and a variety of error types including paired transpositions. In the Burgess and Hitch model, the control signal is referred to as the "context" and, compared to Houghton (1990), has high dimensionality. This increased complexity significantly improves the single-trial learning capacity of the model. Further work by Glasspool (1991) extends this model to handle nonwords, and provides an improved account of transposition data.

Thus CQ models have been productively applied to the control of serial order in the domains of typing, speech and short-term serial recall. Hence, in relation to modelling spelling, CQ models fulfill our requirement for an approach which, while geared to the problem of serial order generally, avoids making specific assumptions about spelling. Apart from this, it turns out that the CQ model of Houghton (1990) has a number of specific properties which establish a good initial fit to those aspects of the dysgraphic data which appear to implicate serial order problems. These basic properties and the results of our first efforts at exploiting them in the spelling domain are described below.

A CQ MODEL OF SERIAL ORDER REPRESENTATION IN SPELLING

The model presented here was developed as a first attempt at modelling the serial order errors discussed above within the competitive queueing (CQ) paradigm. As such, the basic architecture is largely that described by Houghton (1990). The main refinements are the addition of a mechanism for the production of double letters (geminates) and the addition of random noise to node activations during the recall process to model impaired performance of the system. In the interests of accessibility, the following description of the model is largely informal and emphasizes its functional properties. Nonetheless it is necessary to assume at least a basic knowledge of the components and operational characteristics of neural network models. A complete formal specification is provided in the appendix. References to equations made in the informal description are to equations specified in the Appendix.

Relation of the Model to Other Components of the Spelling Process

Before describing the model in detail, it will be useful to attempt to relate it to the traditional "box-and-arrow" models of the spelling process described by numerous authors, for example Morton (1980), Shallice (1981), Ellis (1982), Margolin (1984), Caramazza *et al.* (1987). Shallice (1988) considers a number of such models based on a survey of a wide range of relevant data. Figure 18.5 shows a simple model derived from Shallice's discussion.

In this model, abstract letter codes are temporarily stored in the graphemic output buffer, from which they are read out serially by whichever process is currently active (e.g. writing, typing, oral spelling). These codes may be loaded into the buffer by lexical routes (paths labelled I in Figure 18.5) or non-lexical routes (paths marked II). The graphemic output lexicon (GOL) is a store of learned spellings of individual words. Entries in the GOL can be accessed directly from semantics or possibly via an entry in the phonological lexicon. The learned spellings of the GOL, when activated,

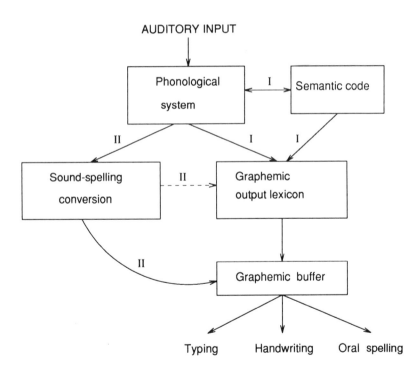

FIGURE 18.5 A box-and-arrow model of some components of the spelling process, derived from Shallice (1988). Pathways labelled I show the lexical route to spelling, those labelled II the non-lexical route. The current model is concerned with the properties of the graphemic output lexicon and the graphemic buffer.

are loaded into the graphemic buffer for serial output. The other "non-lexical route generates a series of graphemes via the sound → spelling mapping (see Olson & Caramazza, this volume, Chapter 17) which are stored serially in the graphemic buffer. An alternative possibility, shown in Figure 18.5 by the dotted arrow, is that the non-lexical route operates via a short-term memory adjunct to the GOL, setting up a novel lexical representation which then accesses the buffer in the usual fashion. Such a process would presumably be required in learning the spelling of new words (setting up new nodes in the GOL) from hearing them.

In relation to this scheme, the current model deals only with the route from the GOL. The model can learn letter strings and stores each one separately in the equivalent of the GOL. During recall the letter identities comprising the target string become activated via activation of particular nodes in the GOL. We are not concerned here with where activation of the GOL comes from and we have not implemented any form of phonological input to the spelling process. It is also not clear to what extent one would wish to consider the current model as implementing a graphemic buffer. To the extent that this construct is simply a place holder for the truism that spelling must involve the activation of letter identities, then the current model implements a buffer. However, it has little in common with more substantive interpretations of the buffer as a special serial storage device, complete with ordered slots (which exist whether occupied or not) and devices such as "pointers" (Shaffer, 1975). In our model, output letter codes are activated *in situ* (i.e. wherever they are stored), and are not copied or loaded into any independently existing structure.

Architecture

The model is an instantiation of the general CQ architecture shown in Figure 18.3 and discussed above. Its specific form is shown in Figure 18.6. The network consists essentially of three layers of nodes. Nodes in the model are able to take on real-valued positive or negative activation levels in the range $[-1,1]$, with a resting level activation of 0. In the absence of stimulation, a node's activation decays gradually to zero. Negative activation values represent suppressed states of activation and do not propagate. That is, "negative activation", though represented on the same scale, is qualitatively different from positive activation. One may consider the resting level, 0, as representing a threshold above which activations propagate along the connections. Negative activations thus represent sub-threshold states. In the absence of external input, nodes in the suppressed state will return spontaneously to the resting level activation at a rate determined by a free parameter of the model. Equations governing the response of nodes to external input are provided in the Appendix (Equations 18.1–18.4).

The first layer (the sequence, or word, layer) contains sets of pairs of nodes which provide a time-varying control signal for each word to be recalled. The second layer consists of individual letter nodes, activated by feedforward weights from sequence nodes (layer 1) in such a way that during recall a gradient of activation is set up across the graphemes of the to-be-recalled word, with the first grapheme to be recalled the most active. The third layer implements the "competitive filter", with nodes which initially mirror the pattern of activation at layer 2 via feedforward excitatory links.

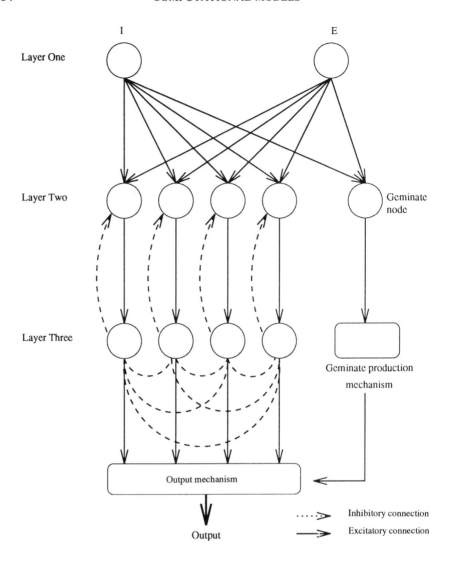

FIGURE 18.6   Outline of the model's architecture. See text for discussion.

These nodes are, however, fully interconnected with strong inhibitory links and perform "peak-picking", so that the node receiving the strongest input from the letter layer soon inhibits all others. This layer thus "chooses" at any moment the most active node in layer 2. Such a choice constitutes the output by the system of the corresponding grapheme.

The sequence layer consists of pairs of nodes, termed I (initiate) and E (end) nodes, as discussed earlier. Every word learned by the model is assigned to a separate pair of these nodes. Thus the spelling of words is represented as a string of letters (up to about eight items long) and each string is stored "orthogonally", in the sense that

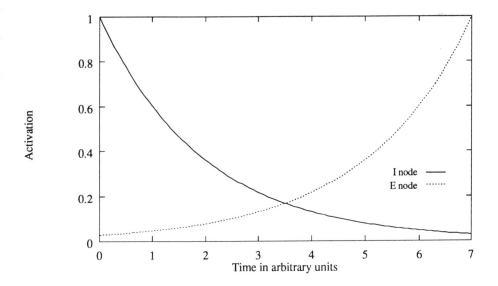

FIGURE 18.7   I and E node activation curves during recall for a seven-letter word. In the simulations discussed below we make the assumption that the rate of rise in activation of the E node is sensitive to the length of the target word, peaking at the point at which the last letter is to be produced.

its sequence level representation does not share nodes with any other sequence. Different sequences may, of course, be more or less correlated at the item level. The activation pattern over the I and E nodes provides the two-dimensional, time-varying control signal discussed in the previous section. The activation of these nodes during recall follows the pattern shown graphically in Figure 18.7 (the activation pattern is somewhat different during learning, as explained below). The curves in Figure 18.7 are generated by Equations 18.1–18.3 of the Appendix.

The I node and E node each connect via feedforward excitatory links to all nodes in the second layer. This layer consists of 26 grapheme identity nodes, one representing each letter of the alphabet, and a single "geminate" node. As well as receiving input from the sequence layer, the layer 2 nodes are interconnected by weakly inhibitory links, and each feeds back to itself via a weakly excitatory link, forming an "on-centre, off-surround" arrangement which tends to emphasize the most active node at any time. Each letter node receives a one-to-one inhibitory input from its corresponding competitive filter (layer 3) node. (See Appendix, Equation 18.5.)

A further node at layer 2, the "geminate marker", serves to double the currently output grapheme when its activation exceeds that of any other node, thus producing a geminate in the output stream. This works in an analogous fashion to the doubling schema of the R&N model discussed above. There are two motivations for the addition of a specific mechanism for the production of geminates. First and most important, such provision is required due to the basic architecture's inability to produce two (or more) occurrences of the same item consecutively although the system has no difficulty in producing two occurrences when separated by other items.

The basic system is thus, for example, able to produce the sequence "ABA", but is unable to produce "AAB". Secondly, looking at a variety of human data, it is clear that there is something special about the treatment of geminates. The fact that geminates can shift, both in typing (Rumelhart & Norman, 1980) and in writing (Caramazza *et al.*, 1987), strongly indicates that the representation underlying doubled letters does not contain two tokens of the same type in succession. If this were the case, geminates would be in no way special, and doubling shift errors would be inexplicable. Ideally, one wants a theory that explains *why* geminates should be special, apparently requiring a special device whose "timing" may occasionally go wrong. The CQ architecture, by being able to produce geminates unaided, provides just such a theory.

The third layer, the competitive filter, consists of 26 nodes, each of which receives input via a strongly excitatory link from a single grapheme node at layer 2. The nodes at layer 3 again form an on-centre, off-surround arrangement, but here with much stronger mutually inhibitory and self-excitatory connections (Appendix, Equation 18.6). This increased competition at layer 3 generates "winner-take-all" behaviour. Strong inhibitory links from the competitive filter back to the letter layer serve to inhibit the most active letter node at each step in recall, allowing the next most active to win at the competitive filter at the next step. In this way the gradient of activations over letter nodes is transformed into the sequential activation of corresponding nodes in layer 3. Rather than a stationary gradient of activations over layer 2 nodes, the time-varying control signal from layer 1 permits the gradient to change during recall, allowing the system to recall words containing repeated letters and preventing the decay of letters to be produced towards the end of the word.

The only modifiable weights in the network are those on the feedforward connections between layer 1 and layer 2. These are adjusted during the learning and practice phases (discussed below) so as to give correct sequential recall. In addition to the weights, the model has a number of free parameters, listed in the Appendix, which must be set by hand. Adjusting these parameters leads to variations in the detailed behaviour of the model. However, we are confident that the behaviour of the model discussed below is robust with respect to these parameters, in the sense that any parameter setting which permits the model to reliably learn and recall sequences will show the same general pattern of breakdown under noise.

Learning

The model learns the spelling of a word as a temporal sequence of letters. The aim of the learning process is to set the values of the weights on the layer 1 to layer 2 connections such that at recall the correct sequence of "winning" nodes is produced at layers 2 and 3. There are only two limits on the form of words which can be learned. First, there is a limit to the length of word which can be correctly learned, around eight letters being the current maximum. For short words of up to three or four letters the network is able to learn the spelling in a single presentation (see section "Initial exposure", below). For longer words a short period of supervised learning (typically between 10 and 30 trials) is required before recall is correct (section "Practice", below). Secondly, the network is unable to learn sequences in which a letter appears more than twice consecutively (e.g. "ABBBC"). These limits appear not to be serious, and may even be considered a virtue. We postulate that words exceding the span of the model must be chunked in some way, so that spelling of them is hierarchical (we have not so far attempted to deal with hierarchically strucured sequences). Indeed, the model may be taken as providing a rationale for why longer sequences should be stored hierarchically. Note that it does this without assuming some arbitrary, empirically derived "buffer length". It is simply an emergent property of the model that the longer the sequence, the more difficult it is for the model to store it. Regarding the "ABBBC" problem, words in which letters are repeated more than twice in succession simply appear not to exist. The model may be taken as providing grounds for why this is.

Initial Exposure

The learning procedure adopted is basically that of Houghton (1990). The word to be learned is presented as a sequence of graphemes. The sequence is preprocessed to identify any geminates, which are presented to the network as a single occurrence of the appropriate grapheme concurrently with a "geminate marker". If the word to be learned is new, an uncommitted pair of sequence nodes are assigned to it. (The model has no built-in "novelty detector" which would allow it to recognize a word as new by itself. This would require the addition of a reading (and lexical access) component to the model.) At the beginning of the learning procedure, the I node is given its maximum activation. Thereafter it suffers exponential decay (Appendix, Equation 18.2), with an asymptote of 0. During presentation of the sequence, the E node remains at its rest activation of zero. The word to be learned by the model is "fed-in" one grapheme at a time, assuming left-to-right processing of an input letter string. As each grapheme arrives, the layer 2 node representing it becomes maximally active and thereafter decays at a constant rate. The pattern of activation over the letter nodes during learning is thus that the most recently input letter is most active, with earlier letters being successively less active (Appendix, Equation 18.7). The weights on the layer 1 → layer 2 connections (sequence → item node connections) are updated at each timestep according to a simple "Hebbian" learning rule, i.e. the weights linking the I node with the letter nodes are incremented in proportion to their simultaneous activation levels (Appendix, Equation 18.8).

After all letters of the words have been presented in this manner, the weights from the I node to the relevant grapheme nodes will have assumed a profile (assuming that no letters were repeated) such that the weight to the first grapheme is largest and the weight to the last grapheme is smallest, due to the decay of the I node during presentation. The activation levels of the actual grapheme nodes will, however, have the opposite trend, since the first presented grapheme will have had more time to decay than the last presented grapheme. At this point, sequence offset, the E node is given its maximum activation level and a further weight learning stage takes place, according to the same simple rule (Equation 18.8). Weights are thus learned from the E node to letter nodes which tend to increase in magnitude towards the end of the word.

Practice

For short words, up to four graphemes in length, the network's recall is correct after a single presentation using the learning procedure outlined above. With longer words, correct recall requires a short period of supervised practice following the intitial presentation.[4] In the practice phase the word is recalled (by the normal recall procedure described below) and the correct version is presented concurrently, so that at each timestep the system has access to the correct response. If an incorrect grapheme is produced, the weights from the I and E nodes to the corresponding layer 2 node are reduced slightly, and the weights to the node corresponding to the correct response are slightly increased. If the node is not triggered when it should be, the weights to the I and E nodes are both increased, and if the node is triggered when it should not be, the weights to the I and E nodes are reduced. The equations governing practice are described in the Appendix (Equations 18.9 and 18.10). Equivalent equations govern the geminate feature node.

Overlearning

Using the learning and practice schemes described above, the network would be deemed to have correctly learned the spelling of a word as soon as the weights have been adjusted to the point that the correct spelling is recalled in the absence of noise. In order to investigate the relative robustness of words and nonwords, for which some human data exist, the network was given the ability to overlearn words. This has the effect of increasing the margin between the activation level of the most active grapheme (layer 2) node at any recall timestep and that of the next most active. This may be assumed to result from the continual reinforcement of the representation for familiar words or from a small degree of "momentum" in the weight change rules, such that the weight changes continue to occur in the same direction for some time after the initial learning experience. In the implemented model, the effect of overlearning during practice is simulated by setting a lower limit on the size of the margin between the "winning" letter node and "best loser". If the margin is smaller than this limit, the system behaves as though the best loser had in fact won and applies the appropriate weight change rules (see the Appendix), with the result that the margin is increased. This may be thought of as inducing fault tolerance into the model. A similar effect can be achieved by having the model learn under noise in activation levels, allowing the weights to change until the noise does not affect performance. However, this is a much more lengthy procedure, since recall will frequently be correct (leading to no change in the weights) and learning must continue until some criterion (e.g. no errors in 1000 trials) is reached. We thus prefer the much simpler and quicker method of setting margins.

---

[4] Limits on single-trial learning in the model are related to the simplicity and low dimensionality of the control signal (I and E node activation pattern). If signals of higher dimension are used (as, for instance, in Burgess & Hitch, 1992; Glasspool, 1991), then the single-trial learning capacity can be increased.

Recall

At the start of recall, the I node is given its maximum activation level. At each timestep during the recall process, the I and E nodes take activation levels as shown in Figure 18.7. This time-varying activation, filtered through the weights generated by the learning procedure, generates a time-varying activation pattern over the letter nodes which is successively sampled and reset by the competitive filter to generate serial output. The dynamics of recall are thus essentially identical to the Houghton (1990) model. An example is given above in Figure 18.4. Further examples, including strings with repeated items, can be found in Houghton (1990).

The production of geminates (doubled letters) requires the participation of the geminate marker (Figure 18.6). The geminate feature node is considered to be part of layer 2, but it does not connect to layer 3 and so does not compete for output with the other letter nodes. Rather, this node is intended to indicate the presence of a "geminate feature" in the spelling by "firing" or becoming operative at the appropriate time. There are a number of ways in which this could be arranged. This behaviour is currently implemented as follows. If at any timestep the geminate feature node is more active than any other layer 2 node, it is considered to be triggered, and the grapheme which is currently being output is doubled in the output representation. The geminate feature node is then strongly inhibited to prevent spurious reactivation. Without more precise and informative data regarding what is happening when people repeat an action as part of a sequence, any proposed scheme for geminates must at present be somewhat *ad hoc*. The proposed scheme fits reasonably well into the general framework of competitive queueing, allowing geminate features to be learned and activated in much the same way as letter nodes. Triggering the geminate at the point at which it is most active also has the virtue of eliminating the need for an explicit threshold. This means that activation levels throughout the model can be depressed or amplified across the board without leading to bizarre doubling errors.

Some mechanism must exist for stopping the recall process when all the letters of a word have been output. How this is achieved is an important theoretical question which has received little attention, presumably because of the dominance of the serial buffer metaphor (recall stops when the buffer is empty, or an empty "cell" is found). We have implemented a number of schemes in the model including:

- Stopping when the correct number of graphemes have been recalled. This assumes some separate representation of the number of letters in a word.
- Stopping when the overall activation level of the letter nodes falls below some threshold. This is the nearest equivalent to "emptying" the buffer in this model.
- Adding a special "end of sequence" grapheme to all words. Recall stops when this grapheme wins the competition. This has the effect of making all words one letter longer than they appear.

We are not entirely happy with any of these schemes, and would generally prefer one in which output was being compared to some internal template (or "efference copy") which was able to detect the end of the word. Unfortunately this requires a recognition scheme. Further work is needed in this area, preferably guided by empirical constraints.

SIMULATIONS OF ERROR DATA

In this section we report the results of our first attempts to simulate data of the sort considered above using the CQ architecture. In particular, we are interested to see to what extent we can replicate at least the gross features of errors which implicate the orthographic or graphemic "buffer" (Caramazza *et al.*, 1987; Margolin, 1984). To the extent that we can do this, we shed light on the basis of these errors and add some sorely needed theoretical substance to the notion "buffer".

Methodology

In attempting to model error data, decisions have to be made regarding the manipulations made to the basic model which under normal circumstances, must be capable of correct performance. It seems likely that different aspects of the error data considered here arise from different factors. For instance, on the basis of their different rates and distributions, Wing and Baddeley (1980) argue that reversal (transposition) and omission errors must arise from different underlying mechanisms. In a concrete example of this, Burgess and Hitch (1992) use the CQ mechanism to model both transposition and omission errors in serial recall. Transposition errors arise due to noise in the "queue" leading to selection of the wrong item at the wrong time. Omission errors arise if no output node in the competitive filter achieves a high enough activation to generate a response. One could similarly ask many specific questions about the current model based on disruption of its different components. For example, one might investigate what happens:

- If the top-down control signal becomes degenerate or incoherent during learning and/or recall?
- If word node → letter node (L1 → L2) communication is disrupted, say due to noise in the weights?
- If interactions between the letter level and the competitive filter are disrupted?

We are not at present in a position to answer such questions in any detail, though they form part of our ongoing investigations. In the simulations discussed below (which are the results of our first efforts in this domain), we have avoided making any highly specific commitments regarding architectural impairments. Instead we have simply taught the network words of varying length and composition, and then monitored errors produced when the network is subjected to random noise at the letter level (the "graphemic buffer") during recall. The addition of noise to letter node activations simply means that the queue is not as stable as it would normally be. The main justification for this manipulation is that, before one begins to investigate very specific hypotheses, it is advisable to discover what the consequences are of comparatively simple impairments. This provides a baseline against which the contributions of more specific impairments may be evaluated.

Results

Simulations were carried out to discover the effect of three variables on the model's performance in the presence of noise at the letter level. The variables were:

1. Word length
2. Presence or absence of geminates
3. Lexicality, i.e. word/nonword differences

In addition we investigated the proportions and serial position curves of various error types generated during recall.

To anticipate the results described in detail below, compared to the data from patients AS and LB discussed above, the model exhibits all the error types shown by these patients, and performs well with regard to the variables of word length, geminate behaviour and lexicality. With regard to the finer details of the dysgraphia data considered above (the relative proportions and serial position curves for different error types) performance is less good, but in most areas the results show the correct trends.

In the simulations described below, the magnitude of the random noise applied during recall was held constant at ± 0.05. Using higher levels of noise degrades performance across the board but does not significantly affect the pattern of results reported below. Other network parameters were set to the values given in the Appendix. As mentioned above, we are confident that the phenomena described below are robust properties of the model and will be found for any setting of these parameters under which the model is capable of functioning normally.

Word length

The network was taught words of length three to eight letters, with and without geminates. None of the test words contained repeated letters (apart from geminates), and the words with geminates contained a single geminate as near to the centre of the word as possible. With noise added, the network recalled the learned words 500 times each. The percentage of correct responses for each word length is shown in Figure 18.8.

With the exception of the anomalous result for geminated three-letter words, the relationship between word length and error rate appears to be roughly linear, as reported by Caramazza and Miceli (1990) for LB and Jonsdottir, Shallice and Wise

TABLE 18.3 Word length effects on proportion of errors for subjects LB, AS and the model.

Word length	% correct		
	LB	AS	Model
4	95	81	78
5	76	72	50
6	66	53	38
7	48	41	24
8	23	17	16

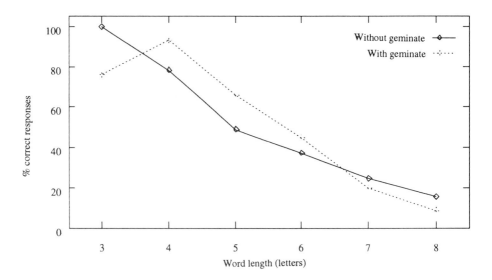

FIGURE 18.8   Word length vs percentage of correct responses.

(submitted) for AS (see Figure 18.1 for the equivalent data for AS and LB). At the level of noise used, the model's performance was worse at virtually all word lengths than either AS or LB. For ease of comparison, the per cent correct for LB, AS and the model at word lengths from four to eight letters is shown in Table 18.3. (The patient data are for spelling words to dictation.)

It is possible that, with modifications, the model's recall could be made more robust. However, at present we are more concerned with the fact that it shows roughly linear decline in performance with a slope comparable to that of the dysgraphic subjects. Indeed, in comparison to AS, the model's performance on words of length n is very close to that of AS on words of length $n + 1$. It should be borne in mind that, at present, the model has to recall wordforms without any assistance from phonological input. Jonsdottir et al. argue that LB's performance is assisted by the regular phoneme $\rightarrow$ grapheme mapping of Italian. Patient AS would likewise receive at least some support from knowing the sound of English words.

Over a range of word lengths, the model shows better recall on words with geminates than on those without, reflecting the fact that for an n-letter word with a geminate the network has only to activate and control $n - 1$ letter identities. This result is reported by Caramazza and Miceli (1990) for LB on words of six letters.

The fall-off in performance with increasing word length appears to be due to two factors. First, since random noise is applied as each letter is recalled, the probability that at least one error will occur obviously increases with the number of letters to be recalled. A second factor is the use of the same two-dimensional control signal (pattern of I and E node activation) at all word lengths. For longer words, more separable events must be "packed" into the same weight space. This results in nearby positions having more highly correlated representations, leading to letter nodes having more similar activation levels during recall and being more likely to be confused.

Increase in errors with word length is thus related to the model's natural "span". This result is highly robust and appears to hold for all settings of the model's parameters at which correct recall is possible. With respect to the distinction between competence and performance errors made at the beginning of the chapter, while these are clearly performance errors (being induced by noise during recall), the model's competence is less noise-tolerant, more prone to failure in performance, the longer the word is. Thus this pattern of data is actually due to an interaction between competence and performance.

Error types and proportions

From data obtained from the simulations described above, the erroneous responses made at each word length were classified into those containing a single error and those containing more than one. For those responses in which only one error could be identified, this error was classified as an insertion, a deletion, an exchange, a shift or a substitution, according to the criteria of Caramazza *et al.* (1987). Error classification and counting was carried out automatically by programs written for that purpose. All the basic error types (exchanges, shifts, substitutions, etc.) were observed.

The proportions of each error type at each word length are shown in Figure 18.9.

Caramazza and Miceli (1990) report comparable data for six-letter words. At first sight their reported error proportions (Figure 18.10) match very well with those from the model for six-letter words, the various error types appearing in the same relative proportions, although the absolute values are different.

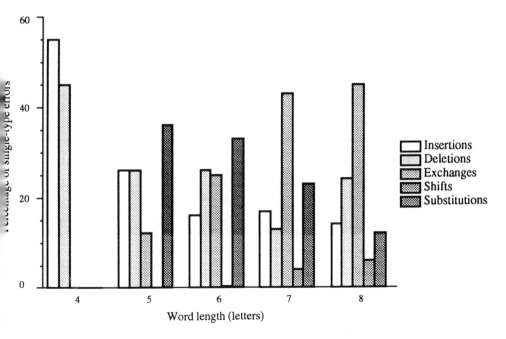

FIGURE 18.9   Proportions of error types at each word length produced by the model.

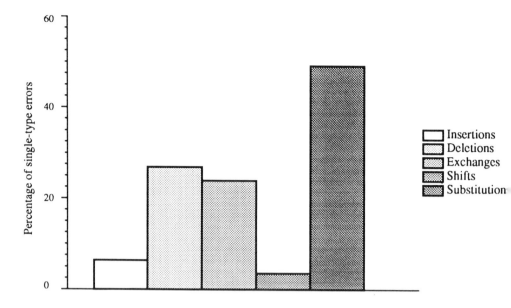

FIGURE 18.10   Proportions of error types for six letter words produced by LB. (Adapted from Caramazza & Miceli, 1990.)

We would not wish to make too much of this similarity, however. As discussed above, detailed understanding of the aetiology of different error types (e.g. omissions compared to insertions) must surely make reference to different aspects of the underlying mechanism. It would be remarkable if we were able to closely model this highly complex pattern of data simply as a consequence of the addition of noise to letter node activations. Therefore we merely note here that the model is susceptible to all the major error types, and can exhibit these errors in different proportions.

Serial position curves

As already discussed, studies of serial order errors by both normal and dysgraphic subjects (LB and AS) show that errors are more likely to occur in word-medial positions.

   The current model tends to show the correct form of serial position curve for errors, with fewer errors at the beginning and the end, but the curve tends to peak rather more towards the end of the word, particularly for substitution errors, than the human data would suggest. Figure 18.11 shows the serial error curves generated by the model with a six-letter word for the five different error types.

   This overall pattern of performance arises largely from the form of the two-dimensional control signal governing learning and recall. The detailed pattern of the model's performance in this regard appears to be an emergent property both of the learned representation of sequences and of the dynamics of recall (i.e. once again, this error pattern is explained as an interaction between competence and performance factors). Unfortunately this interaction is somewhat complex and we

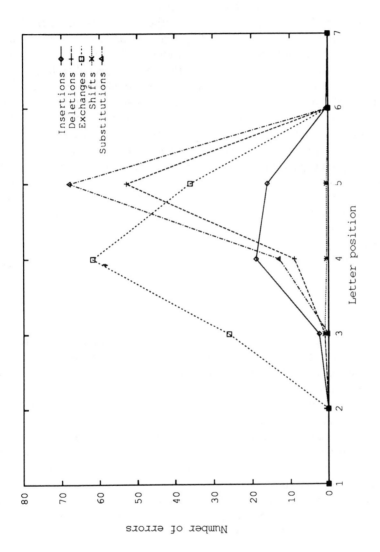

FIGURE 18.11 Serial positions of errors in six-letter words without geminates.

cannot claim to have developed a full, mathematical, understanding of what is happening.[5] Intuitively, the following factors appear to be important. First, during recall the control signal is changing most rapidly at the beginning and end of the words (see Figure 18.7). This means that successive states of the signal are more correlated during medial portions of recall. This is likely to lead to more confusions at medial positions, as the activation pattern being received by the letter nodes is not changing rapidly. However, the effect of the control signal on the letter nodes cannot be considered in isolation from the learned weights in the L1 → L2 pathways. It is possible that, in addition, medial positions are less well discriminated by the learned weights. Recall of initial portions of the word is especially robust in the model. Once again this appears to be an emergent interaction between the learned weights, which are highest overall for initial positions, with good positional discrimination, and the form of the control signal during recall. Although we cannot at present be more precise about the details, we would emphasize that the account the model gives of these data is *not* simply in terms of properties of the graphemic "buffer". Quite clearly, we could not possibly claim that certain buffer positions (beginning and end) are somehow more reliable or accessible for the simple reason that our model does not actually have any buffer postitions. But beyond this, we claim that these data cannot be understood by reference to any localized properties of buffer storage. The state of the buffer in this model is continuously modulated during recall by the control signal (and by feedback from the competitive filter). This modulation intimately involves the learned pathways connecting the control signal (sequence level) to the letter level.

Geminates

As in the typing data discussed by Rumelhart and Norman (1982), Caramazza and Miceli (1990) report that words with geminates lead to their subject LB producing specific types of errors (see above). The current model can learn and recall words with geminates if it is equipped (like the Rumelhart and Norman model) with a special device which, when triggered, causes the currently dominant letter to be doubled. When the model is run with noise, this naturally leads to geminate errors. To illustrate this, the model was run 300 times on six-letter words containing a single geminate. The types and percentage of geminate errors produced by the model are shown in Table 18.4 (the percentage figures are for the 300 runs, thus 10% represents 30 errors).

As is clear, the most common error with geminates is the movement of the geminate feature to the wrong grapheme. This is in accord with the data of Caramazza and Miceli (1990). Geminates do not appear spuriously in words which do not already contain a geminate and the geminate node never failed to trigger in a word containing

---

[5]Analysing the model is difficult because the dynamics of competitive queueing are highly non-linear, both during learning and recall. In addition, learning and recall interact in the practice phase of learning. Nevertheless, the problem is not intractable. In other work, Glasspool (1991) presents analyses predicting the likelihood of error at various serial positions in a variant of the Burgess and Hitch (1992) CQ model of the articulatory loop. Houghton (1994) analyses the dynamics of the inhibitory feedback loop governing interactions between letter nodes and the competitive filter.

TABLE 18.4 Numbers of geminate errors produced by the model from 300 runs with a six-letter word.

Number of shifts	
Forwards	10%
Backwards	15%
Overall	25%
Number of duplications	0.3%

a geminate. Thus we found no geminate deletions or "insertions". Caramazza and Miceli report some geminate deletions, but essentially no insertions. It seems to us likely that alternative parameter settings of the model (say, governing geminate triggering) would allow it to occasionally "miss" a geminate, thus allowing geminate deletions to occur. Very rarely, a second geminate may appear in a response already containing one. Caramazza and Miceli report somewhat more of these than we found.

The pattern of geminate errors in writing and typing is compelling evidence for the involvement of a special device in their production. Explaining why this device should exist provides an important constraint on theories of serial order. Caramazza and Miceli (1990) accept the need for such a device (on empirical grounds) but have no real need for it on theoretical grounds. That is, they represent the written form of a word as an ordered set of graphemic "syllables", each syllable being a two-layer tree with letter tokens as terminals. Geminates are represented by attaching a "geminate marker" to the letter token to be doubled (see Figure 18.12 (A)). However, as noted in Houghton (1994), this representational machinery could easily represent a doubled letter as simply two successive occurrences of the same letter token (Figure 18.12 (B)). As this would obviate the need for an otherwise useless device (the geminate marker), and the associated machinery needed to recognize and process it, it would appear to be the preferred representation. However, it would provide no basis for understanding the data considered above. This situation contrasts with that of the Rumelhart and Norman (1982) model, in which the model simply could not generate geminates without a special device. The same is true of the current model.

Novel vs familiar words

A recurrent theme in discussion so far has been that the pattern of the performance errors of the model cannot be understood without reference to its "competence", i.e. the way in which it represents sequence information in its pattern of weights. Sets of weights can be sufficient to generate correct recall, but can nevertheless be more or less noise tolerant, and be differentially so at different positions and for words of different lengths. By use of the notion of "overlearning" (see above), the robustness of representations can also be manipulated, up to some limit. We here hypothesize that when a subject is required to write a nonword to dictation, a process of sound → spelling conversion takes place which generates a serial pattern of activation over letter nodes, perhaps a number of times if the word is rehearsed. At the same time, serial learning of the grapheme sequence takes place, generating a motor plan

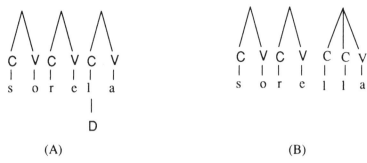

FIGURE 18.12   (A) Representation of the orthographic structure of the word *sorella* according to Caramazza and Miceli (1990). The symbol C stands for consonant letter, V for vowel letter. Words are divided into graphemic "syllables". Doubling of a letter is indicated by the attachment of a doubling marker, D, to the letter to be doubled. (B) The representational machinery assumed by Caramazza and Miceli (ordered sets of trees) could represent the word *sorella* as shown, without recourse to a doubling marker.

for the novel word which guides output. (This process corresponds to the dotted line linking the sound → spelling conversion mechanism to the graphemic output lexicon in Figure 18.5.) We can simulate this in the model by assuming the existence of a reliable sound → spelling conversion mechanism, which generates a sequence of letter node activations, and having the network learn a new word in the usual way. However, for novel words, the model gets less experience with the word than with familiar words. In the limit, we could give the model only a single trial of learning with the novel word. We know that, given the control signal we are using, the model will probably make errors after only a single learning trial if the word is longer than about four letters (remember that the model cannot at present use phonological information to support recall). It is thus obvious in this case that the model will show more errors on novel than on familiar words, because it does not have weights sufficient to correctly recall novel words, even in the absence of noise. In the present simulation we therefore decided to suppose that the network had, in fact, had sufficient opportunity (say by rehearsal, or by virtue of a better learning algorithm) to generate a set of weights sufficient in principle to generate correct recall. However, the kind of overlearning accompanying repeated practice and experience of the word had not taken place. We then compared the network's recall of novel and familiar words of lengths 3–8 letters under the noise conditions described above. The model was given 500 trials on novel words of each length and errors were counted automatically. Table 18.5 shows the results (per cent correct) compared with those for familiar words (without geminates) given above.

Thus even when the model is given the chance to learn a word to criterion, its performance still suffers compared to familiar words. In this simulation, this is due to the pattern of recall for novel words being less "robust" than for familiar words. The absence of overlearning in novel words means that successive positions are less well discriminated. In the presence of noise, this leads to more disruption of the queue. Compared to the LB data reported by Caramazza *et al.* (1987) (Table 18.2 of this chapter), the model shows the same overall decline, starting at words of 4–5 letters, with a difference in error rate for nonwords of the order of 10–12 percentage points

TABLE 18.5 Comparison of word length effects in the model between words and nonwords. Figures are per cent correct at each word length.

Word length	Words	Nonwords
3	100	100
4	78	77
5	50	33
6	38	23
7	24	14
8	16	5

at each word length from 5–8. As with familiar words, the model's performance on nonwords is worse overall than LB's.

Caramazza *et al.* report that, apart from this overall decline, LB's performance on words and nonwords is otherwise comparable. That is, LB shows the familiar serial position curve for both words and nonwords and makes similar errors in similar proportions for both classes of stimuli. This pattern is to be expected on the basis of the current model, as the representation underlying the generation of nonwords is much the same as that underlying words (being constructed by the same learning algorithm). Recall of nonwords exhibits precisely the same pattern as that for words, but is simply less robust across the board. Hence the model explains both the differences *and* the similarities between the two classes.

While the general pattern of results shown in this simulation is to be expected, given any understanding of the model, it is not a trivial property. It neatly illustrates the fact that in a model such as this learning and representation (even to criterion) is not "all or nothing". When the model "knows" a word it does not, as in classical information-processing (or "symbolic") models, store it away as an ordered set of copies of letter symbols. In such a model, either a veridical copy is stored or it is not. If it is, then it should always be properly recalled. Thus the representation of any word, whether old or new, is essentially the same and leads to the same pattern of recall. The current model differs radically from this kind of theory. By contrast, it does not store symbols and cannot represent objects such as ordered sets. Its "representation" of a sequence consists of its ability to reconstruct a time-varying activity pattern over units representing elements of the sequence. This ability is acquired through learning, but is not "all or nothing". In particular, two representations, both sufficient for correct recall, may not be equally robust.

Conclusions

We conclude from the above results that these preliminary investigations make plausible our hypothesis that many aspects of spelling difficulties can be seen as arising from the underlying problem of the representation and control of serial order. The model shows good agreement with data involving effects of word length, serial position, presence of geminates and lexicality (word/nonword contrasts). Error types found in human data are found in the model. Rather importantly, the pattern of data produced by the model can be understood, to a reasonable approximation, in terms of the model's structure and dynamics (this is not always the case for network models; see Olson and Caramazza, this volume, Chapter 17). Thus, as well as simulating these data, the model provides novel explanations for many of them. In particular, the model indicates that many patterns of performance cannot be understood without a detailed theory of "competence" (representation), and that competence cannot be considered "all or nothing".

On the negative side, since recall is entirely based on learned letter strings with no internal structure, and with no input from phonology, the model does not show putative constraints of orthographic structure (Caramazza & Miceli, 1990) and shows no tendency towards producing the phonologically plausible errors reported by, for instance, Beauvois and Dérouesné (1981) and which can also be found in the graphemic buffer syndrome (Jonsdottir, Shallice & Wise, submitted).

GENERAL CONCLUSIONS

In this chapter we have described some initial results obtained in an attempt to develop a detailed computational model of the representation and control of serial order in spelling. Our initial hypothesis was that if the spelling process was parasitic upon more basic serial recall mechanisms, then the application of an empirically motivated model of serial recall to spelling should yield insight into certain aspects of spelling data. On the basis of its previous application in a number of related domains, we chose the competitive queueing architecture as our starting point, refraining at this stage from adding in any substantive domain-specific assumptions. We believe that the results reported above provide ample support for our hypothesis and justify our choice of architecture. We are not aware of any other formally well-defined model capable of simulating the range of data considered above, with or without *ad hoc* design specifications.

Nevertheless, the work reported here is only a starting point, and no attempt has yet been made to incorporate such influences on the spelling process as sound → spelling mapping (Beauvois & Dérouesné, 1981; Hatfield & Patterson, 1983; Olson & Caramazza, this volume, Chapter 17) or sub-lexical orthographic structure (Caramazza & Miceli, 1990). At present we cannot say what problems the attempt to integrate such factors with the current model will bring, though the impact on the simple architecture described here may well be substantial. However, on the basis of the results obtained so far, we anticipate that the basic structural and dynamical features of competitive queueing will continue to play a central explanatory role.

REFERENCES

Beauvois, M. F. & Dérouesné, J. (1981). Lexical or orthographic agraphia. *Brain*, **104**, 21–49.
Burgess, N. & Hitch, G. (1992). Towards a network model of the articulatory loop. *Journal of Memory and Language*, **31**, 429–460.
Caramazza, A. & Miceli, G. (1990). The structure of graphemic representations. *Cognition*, **37**, 243–297

Caramazza, A., Miceli G., Villa, G. & Romani, C. (1987). The role of the graphemic buffer in spelling: evidence from a case of acquired dysgraphia. *Cognition*, **26**, 59–85.

Dell, G. S. (1986). A spreading activation theory of retrieval in sentence production. *Psychological Review*, **93**, 283–321.

Ellis, A. W. (1982). Spelling and writing (and reading and speaking). In A. W. Ellis (Ed.), *Normality and Pathology in Cognitive Functions*. London: Academic Press.

Glasspool, D. W. (1991). Competitive queueing and the articulatory loop: an extended network model. MSc thesis. University of Manchester.

Grossberg, S. (1978). Behavioral contrast in short-term memory: serial binary memory models or parallel continuous models? *Journal of Mathematical Psychology*, **3**, 199–219.

Hatfield, F. M. & Patterson, K. E. (1983). Phonological spelling. *Quarterly Journal of Experimantal Psychology*, **35A**, 451–468.

Hillis, A. E. & Caramazza A. (1990). The effects of attentional deficits on reading and spelling. in A. Caramazza (Ed.), *Cognitive Neuropsychology and Neurolinguistics: Advances in Models of Cognitive Function and Impairment*. Hillsdale, NJ: LEA.

Hotopf, W. H. N. (1980). Slips of the pen. In U. Frith (Ed.), *Cognitive Processes in Spelling*. London: Academic Press.

Houghton, G. (1990). The problem of serial order: a neural network model of sequence learning and recall. In R. Dale, C. Mellish & M. Zock (Eds), *Current Research in Natural Language Generation*. London: Academic Press.

Houghton, G. (1994). Inhibitory control of neurodynamics: opponent mechanisms in sequencing and selective attention. In M. Oaksford & G. D. A. Brown (Eds), *Neurodynamics and Psychology*. London: Academic Press.

Jonsdottir, M., Shallice, T. & Wise, B. W. (submitted). Language-specific differences in graphemic buffer disorder.

Keele, S. W., Cohen, A. & Ivry, R. (1990). Motor programs: concepts and issues. In M. Jeannerod (Ed.), *Attention & Performance, XIII: Motor Representation and Control*. Hillsdale, NJ: Erlbaum.

MacKay, D. G. (1970). Spoonerisms: the structure of errors in the serial order of speech. *Neuropsychologia*, **8**, 323–350.

MacKay, D. G. (1972). The structure of words and syllables: evidence from errors in speech. *Cognitive Psychology*, **3**, 210–227.

MacNeilage, P. F. (1964). Typing errors as clues to serial ordering mechanisms in language behaviour. *Language and Speech*, **7**, 144–159.

MacWhinney, B. & Leinbach, J. (1991). Implementations are not conceptualisations: revising the verb learing model. *Cognition*, **40**, 121–157.

Margolin, D. I. (1984). The neuropsychology of writing and spelling: semantic, phonological, motor and perceptual processes. *Quarterly Journal of Experimental Psychology*, **36A**, 459–489.

Morton, J. (1980). The logogen model and orthographic structure. In U. Frith (Ed.), *Cognitive Processes in Spelling*. London: Academic Press.

Rosenblatt, F. (1962). *Principles of Neurodynamics*. New York: Spartan.

Rumelhart, D. E. & McClelland, J. L. (1986). On learning the past tenses of English verbs. In D. E. Rumelhart & J. L. McClelland (Eds), *Parallel Distributed Processing, Vol. 1, Foundations*. Cambridge, Mass: MIT Press.

Rumelhart, D. E. & Norman, D. (1982). Simulating a skilled typist: a study of skilled motor performance. *Cognitive Science*, **6**, 1–36.

Seidenberg, M. & McClelland J. L. (1989). A distributed, developmental model of word recognition and naming. *Psychological Review*, **96**, 523–568.

Shaffer, L. H. (1975). Control processes in typing. *Quarterly Journal of Experimental Psychology*, **27**, 419–432.

Shallice, T. (1981). Phonological agraphia and the lexical route in writing. *Brain*, **104**, 413–429.

Shallice, T. (1988). *From Neuropsychology to Mental Structure*. Cambridge: Cambridge University Press.

Wing, A. M. & Baddeley, A. D. (1980). Spelling errors in handwriting: a corpus and a distributional analysis. In U. Frith (Ed.), *Cognitive Processes in Spelling*. London: Academic Press.

APPENDIX—FORMAL SPECIFICATION OF THE MODEL

ACTIVATION FUNCTIONS

Sequence Node (I and E Node) Activations

The I node starts with high activation which decays during recall, while the E node starts with a low activation which increases, reaching a maximum coincident with the production of the final letter in the learned word. With time modelled as a series of discrete steps, these activations follow the equations:

$$A_1(t_0) = A_{max_1} \tag{18.1}$$

$$A_1(t+1) = \delta_1 A_1(t) \tag{18.2}$$

$$A_E(t) = A_{max_E} \delta_1^{(l-t)} \tag{18.3}$$

Where $A_1(t)$ and $A_E(t)$ are the activations of the I and E nodes at timestep t, A_{max_1} and A_{max_E} are the maximum allowed activation levels for I and E nodes, t_0 is the first timestep, l is the word length and δ_1 is a fixed decay parameter, $0 \leqslant \delta_1 \leqslant 1$.

Item (Letter) Node Activations

At each timestep, each layer 2 (letter) node has its activation updated according to the equation:

$$A_i(t) = \delta_2 A_i(t-1) + Sf(net_i(t)) + \eta \tag{18.4}$$

where $A_i(t)$ is the activity of node i at timestep t, $net_i(t)$ is the net input to node i at time t and η is a random noise value symmetrical about 0.

The term S represents a variable "gain control" parameter which modulates the effect of the net input depending on the current state of activation of the unit. It is defined by:

$$S = \begin{cases} 1 - A_i(t-1) & \text{if } net_i(t) > 0 \\ 1 + A_i(t-1) & \text{otherwise} \end{cases}$$

The function f "squashes" the net input into the range $[-1, 1]$ and is defined by:

$$f(x) = \frac{2}{e^{-x\tau} + 1} - 1$$

τ is a "temperature" parameter, which sets the slope of the sigmoid function $f(x)$.

NET INPUTS

The net input to any node is the sum of all inhibitory and excitatory inputs to that node. For layer 2 (letter) nodes this comprises the sum of excitatory input from layer 1, self-excitatory input from the node itself, inhibitory input from other layer 2 nodes and inhibitory input from the layer 3 competitive filter nodes. For letter node i at any timestep:

$$\text{net}_i = A_I W_{Ii} + A_E W_{Ei} + e_2 [A2_i]^+ - \sum_{j=1, j \neq i}^{n} m_2 [A2_j]^+ - b_{3 \to 2} [A3_i]^+ \qquad (18.5)$$

where $A2_i$ and $A3_i$ are activations of node i in layers 2 and 3, A_I and A_E are the activations of the I and E nodes, W_{Ii} and W_{Ei} are the weights from the I and E nodes to node i, e_2, m_2 and $b_{3 \to 2}$ are the magnitudes of self-excitation, mutual inhibition and backinhibition from layer 3 respectively. The notation $[x]^+$ indicates that only positive activation values are propagated, i.e:

$$[x]^+ = \begin{cases} x & \text{if } x > 0 \\ 0 & \text{otherwise} \end{cases}$$

The activations of competitive filter layer (layer 3) nodes are updated according to Equation 18.4 (with a different decay rate δ_3 replacing δ_2). For the competitive filter, the net input to each node comprises the sum of excitation from the corresponding layer 2 node, inhibition from other filter nodes and self-excitation:

$$\text{net}_i = a_{2 \to 3} [A2_i]^+ + e_3 [A3_i]^+ - \sum_{j=1, j \neq i}^{n} m_3 [A3_j]^+ \qquad (18.6)$$

where $a_{2 \to 3}$ is the weight of the layer 2 to layer 3 connections, e_3 is the magnitude of the self-excitatory links and m_3 is the magnitude of mutual inhibition. This equation achieves "peak picking" amongst letter nodes using standard lateral inhibition. This process can be rather slow if initial activations are similar. For more efficient selection, the third term of the left-hand side of Equation (18.6) can be replaced by Equation (9) of Houghton (1994).

LEARNING

Initial Exposure

The procedure adopted is that of Houghton (1990). The word to be learned is presented as a sequence of graphemes. The sequence is preprocessed to identify any geminates, which are presented to the network as a single occurrence of the appropriate grapheme concurrently with a "geminate marker". If the word to be learned is new, a new pair of sequence nodes are assigned to it. At the beginning of the learning procedure, the I node is given its maximum activation (Equation 18.1). Thereafter it decays at each timestep according to Equation 18.2. During learning the E node remains at its rest activation of zero.

At each timestep, one grapheme and a geminate status are presented to the system. The corresponding grapheme identity node in layer 2 is given an activation of 1.0. If the grapheme represents a geminate, the geminate feature node in layer 2 is additionally set to 1.0. The activations of all layer 2 nodes *not* set to 1.0 in this manner decay according to the equation:

$$A_i(t) = \delta_2 A_i(t-1) \qquad (18.7)$$

Where $A_i(t)$ is the activation of letter node i at timestep t and δ_2 is a constant decay parameter, $0 \leqslant \delta_2 \leqslant 1$.

The weights on the layer 1 to layer 2 connections are updated at each timestep according to the Hebbian learning rule:

$$\Delta W_{ij} = \epsilon A_i A_j \qquad (18.8)$$

where W_{ij} is the weight on the connection from layer 1 node to layer 2 node j, A_i is the activation of layer 1 node i, A_j is the activation of letter node j and ϵ controls the rate of learning.

Practice

The learning procedure described above may not be sufficient to produce an adequate set of weights in a single trial. The practice procedure is based on that which Houghton (1990) showed to be equivalent to a gradient descent. The word is recalled, and the correct version is presented concurrently, so that at each timestep the system has access to the correct response. If an incorrect grapheme is produced, the weights from the I and E nodes to the corresponding layer 2 node are reduced slightly, and the weights to the node corresponding to the correct response are slightly increased. Note that random noise is *not* added to the node activations during practice (η in Equation 18.4 is set to 0).

The following equations are applied separately to the weights from both the I node and the E node to the letter node which should have "won" (Equation 18.9) and the node which actually did "win" (Equation 18.10).

To reinforce the correct response:

$$\Delta W_{correct} = \rho(W_{max} - W_{correct})A_{L1}A_{correct} \tag{18.9}$$

And to "punish" the incorrect response:

$$\Delta W_{actual} = -\rho W_{actual}A_{L1}A_{actual} \tag{18.10}$$

In Equations (18.9) and (18.10) the subscripts "correct" and "actual" refer to the letter node which should have won and that which actually did respectively, ρ is a small "learning rate" parameter $0 \leqslant \rho \leqslant 1$ and A_{L1} is the activation of the I or E node. The term W_{max} in Equation 18.9 represents a ceiling on weight values. As the actual value of a weight approaches the maximum, any positive changes become smaller and smaller.

Equivalent equations govern the geminate feature node. If the node is not triggered when it should be, the weights to the I and E nodes are both increased according to:

$$\Delta W_G = \rho(W_{max} - W_G)A_{L1}A_G \tag{18.11}$$

And if the node is triggered when it should not be, the weights to the I and E nodes are reduced:

$$\Delta W_G = -\rho W_G A_{L1}A_G \tag{18.12}$$

PARAMETER VALUES

The model contains a number of free parameters, typical values for which are given here.

Parameter	Meaning	Value
δ_1	I and E node decay rate	0.6
δ_2	Layer 2 activation decay rate	0.6
δ_3	Layer 3 activation decay rate	0.6
e_2	Layer 2 self-excitation magnitude	0.4
m_2	Layer 2 mutual inhibition magnitude	0.4
$b_{3 \to 2}$	Magnitude of inhibition from layer 3 to layer 2	4.0
$a_{2 \to 3}$	Magnitude of excitation from layer 2 to layer 3	0.6
e_3	Layer 3 self-excitation magnitude	0.4
m_3	Layer 3 mutual inhibition magnitude	1.0
ρ	Practice rate	0.1
W_{max}	Maximum weight	2.0
τ	Sigmoid "temperature"	1.2

Part V

Remediation

19

Teaching Spelling: Bridging Theory and Practice

NATA K. GOULANDRIS

National Hospitals College of Speech Sciences, London

The last two decades have generated extensive research on spelling with researchers stressing the cognitive complexity of a process which was once considered no more than trivial rote learning. So much consequential research has appeared that it has become virtually impossible for practising teachers to stay abreast of the numerous papers which have direct relevance to the classroom. The purpose of this chapter, therefore, is to consider selected empirical findings which have had a major impact on our current understanding of how children learn to spell and to examine their practical implications and possible repercussions on our view of current teaching practice.

SPELLING DEVELOPMENT

When we refer to a child's spelling ability, we normally refer to the number of words the child can spell correctly. Increasingly, however, we have realized that children are not only learning an assortment of correct spellings but are simultaneously extracting information about the rules which underlie their language's spelling system (Ehri, 1985). Therefore, it is important to distinguish between the words children have learned by heart and their understanding of the spelling system as revealed in their attempts to spell unfamiliar words.

Far from comprising mindless rote-learning, the acquisition of spelling, like other language skills, requires the construction of a rule-based system (Henderson, 1980). Hypotheses are generated on the basis of a child's current knowledge and experience

Handbook of Spelling: Theory, Process and Intervention. Edited by G. D. A. Brown and N. C. Ellis.
©1994 John Wiley & Sons Ltd.

of written language. For example, beginning spellers generally believe that spellings reflect pronunciation (Read, 1986) and many of their early spellings reproduce pronunciation surprisingly faithfully. Additional rules are revised in light of further evidence and exceptions are gradually taken into account. The complexity of the English language, which simultaneously represents various aspects of spoken language (Albrow, 1972), makes learning a protracted process and it consequently takes many years for a speller to master our written language system.

Spelling development can be broadly characterized as consisting of two overlapping periods. During the first, referred to by Frith (1985) as the alphabetic phase, the child concentrates primarily on how a word sounds and attempts to spell by transcribing all the speech sounds noted. Spelling by sound is gradually phased out, with spellings becoming increasingly sensitive to positional and lexical constraints until a high proportion of correct spellings have been learned (Ehri, 1985; Frith, 1985). Frith refers to this period as the orthographic phase because spellers gain increased awareness of recurring letter strings and begin to process these letter strings as orthographic patterns and as units of meaning.

EARLY SPELLING

Ask children from 5 upwards to spell an unfamiliar word and you will usually hear the children pronounce the word slowly, often more than once. Moreover, it is typically the poor speller who does not resort to these simple tactics, having not yet understood the invaluable spelling cues which can be extracted from a word's pronunciation. Children who have sufficient knowledge of letter names and letter sounds are usually able to produce creditable invented spellings by matching their letter knowledge to lexical pronunciations. For example, when asked to write a story depicted in a cartoon about a boy who persuades his mother to buy a puppy, these 6-year-old children wrote as follows (children's spellings are in upper-case letters):

1. WAST THAY WES A LUTL BAY HE THAUOD A DOG IN A SOR WEINDO.
   Once there was a little boy. He saw (sawed) a dog in a shop window.
2. WUN DAY JOHN WOCK UP AND TLD THAT HE WOTID TO BY A PUPY.
   . . . THAY LUCT AOT SID THE WINDO.
   One day John woke up and told that he wanted to buy a puppy. . . . They looked outside the window.
3. WUNST A PPON A TIM. A BOW AST HIS MOM IF HEY COOD BIY A DOG.
   Once upon a time. A boy asked his Mom if he could buy a dog.
4. ONSCE APNE A TIM KEVEN ASCD HES MOM.
   Once upon a time Kevin asked his Mom.

All these examples have common characteristics. First, they contain several words spelled conventionally, for example, DAY, JOHN, UP, TO, A, HE, DOG. Many words are spelled just as they sound, for example WUN, THAY, COOD, PUPY, BY and BIY (for buy), ASCD (asked), A PPON (upon). Anyone reading these words would have no difficulty recognizing them despite the unusual spellings. Other spellings contain correct consonants but incorrect vowels, for example LUTL (little), BAY (boy), WEINDO (window), LUCT (looked), AOT (out). But note how skilfully the child has identified that *ed* corresponds to the /t/ sound in the word *looked* and how close the spelling AOT is to the pronunciation of the word *out* when the word is said particularly slowly. Sometimes the children use the letter name to represent the long vowel as in WOCK (woke), SID (side), TIM (time) and WINDO (window) (Read, 1986). One error, THAUOD (saw), reflects a lisp and demonstrates how immature pronunciation influences spelling. Surprisingly few spellings are non-phonetic and would not be recognized if they appeared out of context, for example ONSC (once), APNE (upon). Although these spellings are still rudimentary, it is clear that young spellers can communicate quite effectively by basing their spellings primarily on their pronunciations of words.

Charles Read (1986) has also shown that beginning spellers are highly influenced by the phonetic characteristics of words which most skilled adult spellers no longer notice. For example, they spell words beginning with *tr* such as *train* or *trip* using the letters *chr* because they have noticed the phonetic similarity between words beginning with *tr* and those beginning with *ch*. Beginners also omit nasals, i.e. *n* and *m*, when they occur before consonants as in *plant*, *bumpy* or *went*, spelling the words as PLAT, BOPY, WET even though when spelling nasals which occur before vowels the nasals are rarely omitted, for example, NUBRS for *numbers* or NOO for *new*. Read suggests that children omit the nasal because they only perceive a change in the quality of the vowel—a phonetically accurate interpretation. Experience of standard orthography eventually teaches them to disregard these subtle phonetic distinctions and adopt standard spellings.

From this we have an important clue, namely, the extreme importance of three different but related abilities in the early stages of spelling acquisition: pronunciation, awareness and perception of speech sounds (usually referred to as phonological ability) and knowledge of sound–letter correspondences. If children model their spellings upon their pronunciation, any aberration from the correct pronunciation will result in an incorrect spelling. If they are unable to discern and distinguish between the speech sounds in their language, they will not be able to segment or split the word into component speech sounds or phonemes in order to construct a spelling. In addition, inability to segment words adequately will prevent them from understanding that a particular sound often maps on to a specific letter and so is likely to hinder their ability to appreciate the relationship between letters and sounds. Conversely, spellers may both perceive and segment the word correctly but still be unable to construct a spelling if their knowledge of letter–sound correspondences is inadequate.

As children learn to spell words they gradually begin to discover orthographic regularities enabling them to make generalizations about possible spellings. At the simplest level, they may begin to generalize that words which begin with a certain sound will also begin with the same letter. Once this conclusion has been reached, the new rule can be used as a basis for generating new spellings. Further generalizations involving other sound–spelling mappings, or the way in which the written language represents the past tense by adding the suffix *ed*, contribute to an expanding rule system.

More experienced spellers eventually realize that spelling by sound is unreliable since the same speech sounds can be represented using alternative spelling patterns of which only one will be correct. The short /e/ sound in the word *bed*, for example, can be spelled as *e* or as *ea* in the word *head*. In addition, many words have exceptional spellings which can never be correctly worked out when spelling by sound, as, for example, in the word *yacht*. However, all spoken words, no matter how unique the spelling, provide some hints about their spelling within their pronunciation, hence the underlying strength of an alphabetic system. As spelling improves, learners proceed from the assumption that written language is based exclusively on phonology to the gradual incorporation of morphemic, syntactic and orthographic information (Henderson, 1980; Read, 1975).

Word-Specific Knowledge

Concurrently, the speller is acquiring word-specific knowledge, often learning to spell a number of words which may contain complex and sometimes unusual spelling patterns, for example *dinosaur* and *Christopher*. These words may have been learned as a consequence of repeated encounters in their reading or in response to a conscious attempt to learn about them. In general, however, beginning spellers have a sparse spelling vocabulary when entering school. They are usually able to spell their own names, the names of their siblings and a few useful words such as *Mum*, *Dad* and *love* (Goulandris, unpublished data). The spurt in writing skills occurs when children realize that even if they do not know how to spell a word, they can still devise a spelling by transcribing the sounds in the words they are attempting to write.

IMPORTANT FINDINGS AND THEIR IMPLICATIONS FOR TEACHING

Role of Phonological Awareness

Speech is composed of a series of continuous speech sounds, often referred to as "the speech stream". A speech sound, or phoneme, is difficult to identify or extract from within a word because the phonemes in running speech overlap. Phonological awareness, the ability to perceive units of sound, phonological processing, the skill required to manipulate sound segments of spoken language, and phonemic segmentation, the capacity to divide spoken words into phonemes or speech sounds (e.g. /c/ /a/ /t/), are all crucial components and predictors of successful literacy acquisition. Evidence for this link is by now incontrovertible. Children who can discriminate and manipulate phonemes with ease learn to read and spell more successfully than peers who do not have these skills (Bradley & Bryant, 1983; Snowling, 1987; Stuart & Coltheart, 1988). Even knowledge of nursery rhymes at the age of 3 is highly predictive of future reading and spelling ability (Maclean, Bryant & Bradley, 1987).

One important debate has centred around whether phonological awareness is needed in order to read and spell or whether the very act of learning to read and spell initiates the development of phonological awareness. Studies which have demonstrated the predictive ability of preschool phonological awareness provide strong evidence that phonological ability facilitates the acquisition of literacy skills—the more developed the child's skills, the easier the transition from spoken to written language. Research on invented spelling (Gentry, 1978; Read, 1975) provides another source of evidence, since at the very least, a modicum of sound skills is required if a child is to analyse spoken output and transform it into a written version of the spoken word.

However, several studies have indicated that learning to read and spell an alphabetic language in which each speech sound (phoneme) is represented by one letter or groups of letters (grapheme) extends phonological awareness. Thus individuals who have not learned to read or spell an alphabetic language perform significantly worse on tasks which require manipulating phonemes than controls who are able to read an alphabetic language (Morais *et al.*, 1979; Read *et al.*, 1986).

There is increasing evidence that the relationship between phonological awareness and reading and spelling is reciprocal. If phonological awareness is developed in the preschool years, the child is able to understand the critical relationship between sounds and letters when literacy instruction commences. Moreover, since learning to read and spell requires the learner to divide words into smaller components and to link spelling patterns to each sound unit, the task of acquiring literacy leads to greater dexterity when dealing with phonemes and in turn to more competent phonological processing. This additional proficiency enhances literacy skills, with each small improvement producing further improvement in the other domain.

More specifically, beginners' efforts to identify the sounds in words when first learning to spell serve as a catalyst in the elaboration of phonological skills (Cataldo & Ellis, 1990). Their attempts to discern and isolate the component sounds in each word engender constant refinement of their phonological skills. Thus spelling becomes a highly important learning tool, not only leading a child to proficiency in spelling but augmenting competence in the type of sound skills known to be pivotal for the successful learning of reading. Phonological skills are vital when learning to spell because they enable children to understand the alphabetic link between the sounds heard in spoken words and the letters used to represent them in written language.

Conversely, individuals who have severe difficulties with phonological processing have persistent and intractable difficulties with spelling (Snowling, Stackhouse & Rack, 1986). For example, spellers who perform poorly on tasks which require them to divide words into their component sounds have more difficulty spelling nonwords and make fewer phonologically plausible errors (errors which sound like the word they are trying to spell) than controls (Rohl & Tunmer, 1988). The ability to segment words into their component parts remains important even in the later years. Perin (1983) reported that adolescents with spelling difficulties were less proficient at spoonerisms (a demanding phonological awareness task) than controls.

Practical implications

Fortunately, several training studies have contributed to our understanding of how phonological awareness should be developed within a preschool and early primary school environment. The main conclusions are as follows.

Fostering phonological skills in the preschool years will substantially improve children's literacy attainment in subsequent years. Olofsson and Lundberg (1985) reported that training children's sound skills in kindergarten not only improved their ability to blend words but also resulted in fewer childen failing to acquire literacy skills. Introducing rhyming activities and related sound skill training in the nursery and reception classes seems the obvious solution. The inclusion of nursery rhymes, jingles and amusing poems in the preschool curriculum will ensure that most children become proficient in these vitally important skills at an early age and that those who are having unusual difficulties can be provided with additional practice before they are introduced to reading. Group activities intended to refine sound skills such as "I spy", rhyme recognition, rhyme generation and deleting and adding either syllables or speech sounds to form new words are entertaining and valuable games.

Importance of Spelling in the Development of Literacy

Children first learn alphabetic skills through spelling and not, as previously assumed, through reading. In 1985 Frith proposed that children first use sound–letter mapping when attempting to spell and that the phonic knowledge obtained through spelling is eventually transferred to reading, consequently enabling the beginning reader to decode unfamiliar words and to recognize the importance of letter order. Since then several studies have confirmed this developmental sequence.

Bryant and Bradley (1980) demonstrated that children could read a number of words they could not spell and could spell a number of words they could not read. Visually distinctive words such as *school*, *light* and *train* were quickly recognized but were too orthographically complex to spell. In contrast, a number of words which could be sounded out such as *sit*, *bun* and *ran* were spelled correctly but were not read. The researchers concluded that beginners use different strategies for reading and spelling, basing their reading on rapid visual recognition of stimuli and their spelling on sound-based encoding procedures. Suspecting that children who could spell by sound could also decode words if encouraged to do so, the researchers asked the children to read some simple nonsense words, interspersing them with the words the children had previously been unable to read. The introduction of nonword reading obliged the children to adopt a phonic strategy for reading and enabled them to decode the words which had previously baffled them. This demonstrated that the children had latent decoding ability which they were not yet spontaneously applying to their reading.

Practical implications

These findings accentuate the value of developmental writing and a directed discovery approach to spelling in which children are encouraged to invent their own spellings but are provided with constant guidance and appropriate feedback to maintain their interest and enthusiasm.

Structured, multi-sensory teaching programmes designed to teach children with specific learning difficulties or dyslexia have consistently emphasized the value of teaching reading via spelling (Hornsby & Shear, 1975). By concentrating on spelling rather than reading, learners' attention is drawn to the orthographic and phonological characteristics of words, the inexperienced reader being steered away from an over-reliance on visual and predictive strategies. Excessive reliance on psycholinguistic clues accentuates non-orthographic features of written language in contrast to the spelling process, which draws the attention to orthographic characteristics.

Teaching Children to Link the Sound Pattern in a Word to a Spelling Pattern is a Highly Effective Method of Helping Backward Children Learn to Read and Spell

In a seminal training study, Bradley and Bryant (1983) tested 400 children between the ages of 4 and 5 and identified a group who had difficulty categorizing words according to the beginning, middle or final speech sounds. Predicting that these children would be "at risk", they divided them into four groups comprising two experimental groups and two control groups. One group was given sound categorization training in which they categorized pictures according to their common sounds, for example *cat*, *mat* and *hat*. The second group was given instruction in sound categorization using the same pictures but was also taught to relate similarities or differences in sound patterns to the spelling patterns of the words using plastic letters. The third group was taught to sort the pictures according to their semantic category. The fourth group, a second control group, received no teaching. While both the first and second groups showed gains in reading ability, only the group which had received instruction in the relationship between speech sounds and word spellings also showed improved spelling. In other words, teaching a child how spelling patterns represent sound patterns improves eventual reading and spelling ability more than teaching phonological skills in isolation. The results clearly suggest that teaching phonological skills must be explicitly linked to spelling patterns to effect improvement of literacy skills.

Hatcher, Hulme and Ellis (1994) reported an intervention study comprising 128 children aged 7–8 with reading problems. Children, allocated to one of four matched groups, received 40 hours of reading instruction, or 40 hours of instruction in sound skills, or 40 hours of both reading and sound skill training, or no intervention of any kind. Children who received phonological training alone developed better sound skills but did not make comparable progress in reading. In contrast, the children who had received both types of instruction concurrently showed the greatest improvement in reading and spelling. So, once again, we have further evidence that once children have begun school, remediating phonological skills in isolation does not automatically improve literacy skills. Remedial instruction needs to forge alphabetic links in which the sounds in words and the letters used to represent them in written language are explicitly taught.

Practical implications

Encouraging autonomous development of sound skills and sound–letter mapping through developmental writing can be extremely beneficial to most children. Teachers should help the learner pay attention to the sequence of speech sounds within a word and stress that the sequence of sounds needs to be retained in the written version. However, although many children are able to extrapolate sound–letter mappings with minimal instruction, some children are unable to do so and require systematic teaching before they can produce plausible invented spellings. It is this group of children who will benefit most from instruction which develops both phonological and literacy skills in tandem.

Learning Alphabetic Regularities is an Important Precursor of Conventional Spelling

Alphabetic spelling, the ability to construct spellings on the basis of speech sounds, is a fundamental step in the acquisition of spelling and appears to be a prerequisite for learning the more difficult spellings which do not conform to alphabetic regularities (Frith, 1985). Children who cannot spell simple regular words such as *pin* and *fun* will not have the necessary foundation to learn other more complex spelling patterns.

The crucial role of alphabetic spelling is to provide a basic structure against which new spellings can be examined and learned. Once a beginning speller has set up expectations about the spelling of an unfamiliar word using letter-sound knowledge, it becomes easier to recognize unusual spellings and to identify the parts of words which require particular attention. Spellers anticipate the spellings of novel words according to their current orthographic knowledge (Ehri, 1985). When they encounter the correct spelling they can appraise the accuracy of their expectations. For example, to the less experienced speller the word *philosophy* could be spelled as *filosefy* or *filosofie*. The use of *ph* to represent the /f/ in these instances needs to be noted and recalled. In contrast, the more experienced speller may be familiar with the spelling of the names *Phil* and *Sophie* and have expectations which are more in line with the correct spelling of *philosophy*.

Difficulty acquiring alphabetic spelling skills is an important diagnostic sign which should not be overlooked. Children whose spellings are almost impossible to recognize, because they do not sound in the least like the word the child is attempting to spell, invariably have weak sound skills and associated problems with deducing and learning sound–letter rules even when such rules have been expressly taught. Because invented spelling can be used as a measure of children's phonological skill, it has been shown to be a good predictor of reading ability (Mann, Tobin & Wilson, 1987).

Nonword spelling has also proved to be an effective predictor of spelling ability. In a longitudinal study (Goulandris, 1992), 27 children, aged 6 and 7, were asked to spell nonsense words such as *ind*, *rin*, *bep*, *sike*, *gittle* and *hamily*. Nonsense word spelling was considered a purer measure of alphabetic skills than real word spelling. Of particular interest was whether nonword spelling ability would predict the children's eventual spelling skills. When the influences of verbal intelligence and reading age at the time of testing were eliminated statistically, a child's ability to spell nonwords phonetically (so that they sounded like the words being spelled) predicted both reading and spelling scores on two standardized tests the following year. This result suggests that the skills necessary for nonword spelling, namely segmentation and application of sound–letter rules, are crucial steps in the acquisition of literacy.

Practical implications

Given the extensive converging evidence that at least a minimal level of phonological awareness is required before children are able to produce invented spellings, it is surprising that spelling is not yet used as the most transparent measure of applied phonology. Children who continue to have difficulties when the majority of their peers have begun to produce creditable invented spellings should receive explicit instruction in phonological awareness and spelling. Children whose sounds skills are immature or exceptionally weak require a variety of games designed to focus their attention on speech sounds, with explicit instruction in rhyming, sound segmentation, identifying sounds in different parts of the words, detecting identical speech sounds in a series of words and adding or subtracting speech sounds to words. In addition, they should be taught sound–letter rules with the express intention of applying this knowledge to spelling. Difficulties differentiating between phonetically similar speech sounds such as /k/ and /g/; /f/, /v/ and /th/ and excessive problems identifying vowels, especially short vowels, are particularly noticeable among children with serious spelling problems (Snowling *et al.*, 1991). Speech therapists and teachers who have had some training in phonetics will be able to provide spellers who make these types of errors with appropriate training.

It is vital to identify poor spellers at the outset and not allow them to become frustrated by their inability to produce invented spelling in line with their peers. Children who have excessive difficulties in the early school years are likely to have even more severe difficulties as they move up the school if appropriate intervention is not provided as soon as possible. In a longitudinal study of 32 children, the four children who were unable to spell simple words and nonwords in the second year of the infants school made little progress in the ensuing years and proceeded to secondary school with extremely low levels of reading and spelling despite having attended an excellent school and received remedial tuition (Goulandris, unpublished).

Role of Orthographic Regularities

Orthographic knowledge can be defined as the child's current understanding of how the writing system functions (Ehri, 1985). Children make generalizations about orthography (the spelling system) using their limited experience of written language as the data base. As they accumulate more experience of written language, generalizations are likely to become more sensitive to plausible alternatives and more accurate.

The English writing system is said to represent different aspects of spoken language: phonemic, morphemic and lexical. Phonemic information derived from the pronunciation of words, is represented by alphabetic regularities. Alphabetic regularities comprise invariant sound–letter mappings, discussed above, such as that the /b/ sound is always represented by the letter *b* but also include more elusive conditional regularities such as the use of *g* and *c* before the vowels *e*, *i* and *y* to represent the sounds /dʒ/ or /s/.

A morpheme is the smallest unit of meaning. Morphemes are represented in written language by a precise letter string such as *graph* meaning *to write*. Morphemes may also indicate the grammatical function of a word, i.e. *ing* in the word *laughing*. A morpheme retains its spelling whenever it appears in written language and so provides a rich source of orthographic predictability. Spellers learn to abstract these morphemic regularities over an extended time span because the large number of morphemic regularities require more orthographic knowledge than the learning of phonemic regularities. At the outset children may be confused by spellings which provide grammatical information but contravene alphabetic principles, such as the use of the *s* suffix to denote plurals with *s* producing a /z/ sound in the word *dogs* or of the past tense suffix *ed*. (Compare the sound of the *ed* in *slipped*, *danced*, *landed*). In the long run, however, spellers who are able to recognize that words which are composed of identical morphemes share both a common spelling pattern and a common meaning, for example *automobile, automatic, autograph, autobiography*, etc., can derive short cuts for learning and constructing new spellings.

Many relatively competent spellers have difficulty learning how to add endings or suffixes to root words. Fortunately, there are clear rules indicating how suffixes should be appended to words and these can be taught comparatively easily at the appropriate time.

Lexical consistency, the fact that words which have related meanings often share the same spelling pattern, such as *autumn* and *autumnal*, *sign* and *signal*, provides additional spelling information. These connections are often not fully appreciated by spellers and need to be explicitly taught by teachers.

Another type of orthographic regularity is language specific and is based on probability of occurrence, i.e. which letters are likely to appear together and in which position. In English, three important types of orthographic regularities are evident. First, certain letter patterns such as *ing*, *tion* and *ture* recur frequently, enabling the learner to predict the sequence and coexistence of certain letter patterns. Other letter strings are illegal and never appear in written English, for example *czr* or *hlw*. Secondly, a particular letter or letter string is more likely to be used when spelling a certain phoneme than others. In spelling the sound /k/, the most probable grapheme will be *c* as in *cat*, *could* and *cut* unless the /k/ sound is to be followed by *i*, *e* or *y*, in which case the letter *k* will be used as in *kind* or *kettle*. More unusual spellings of /k/ such as *ch* and *que* occur less frequently. Implicit knowledge about the probability of occurrence of letter patterns to represent phonemes is of considerable value, enabling spellers to generate unfamiliar spellings with a high degree of accuracy.

Positional constraints, the fact that certain letter patterns can only appear in specific portions of a word, are another type of orthographic regularity. For example, *ck* never appears at the beginning of words. Spellers who contravene positional constraints produce peculiar looking spellings.

Some learners fail to make valid generalizations regardless of how much exposure they have had to the printed word. Inability to perceive these different types of regularities may differentially affect spelling output, some spellers producing phonetic spellings without regard for orthographic and morphemic regularities (Goulandris & Snowling, 1991) with others failing to appreciate even basic sound–letter regularities (Snowling, Stackhouse & Rack, 1986). These individuals will need comprehensive and explicit instruction intended to help them discern the different types of orthographic regularities.

Practical implications

Word sorts as recommended by Henderson (1980) are an invaluable technique for encouraging children to perceive alternative types of regularities. The instructor selects an assortment of words which exemplify one or several types of regularities. The children are then asked to sort the words according to suggested criteria or are required to examine the words and select one or more characteristic which is common to a number of words. Needless to say, the regularities or similarities which teachers can draw upon are vast. Beginners can sort words according to initial, medial or final phonemes, by clusters (words beginning with *st*, ending with *mp*), by common letter strings, *ing*, *oa*, *ough*, by rimes, for example *ent* as in *bent*, *dent*, *sent*, *lent*, *went*, by prefixes, for example *anti*, *sub* and *pre*, or by suffixes, for example *-able*, *-ful* and *-ly*.

How does a teacher know which type of regularity needs clarification and further instruction? This information is usually remarkably apparent in children's free-writing. Spelling errors can be classified according to broad categories of error: alphabetic, morphemic, lexical or orthographic. Further investigation within the categories enables teachers to identify the exact rules which are still causing difficulties (Goulandris, 1990). Once learners have grasped the basic alphabetic regularities, the teacher can nurture the learners' awareness of other types of spelling information and so facilitate the learning process.

Spelling by Analogy to Familiar Words

When asked to spell unfamiliar words, children sometimes refer to their existing spelling vocabulary for orthographic information. Spontaneous remarks made while children were spelling nonwords (Goulandris, 1989) showed that children often prefer using a rhyming word to help them spell a novel word to sounding out a word phoneme by phoneme. For example, when asked to spell *sike* they remarked that it resembled the word *like* and that *hamily* was just like *family*. Similarly, a child wishing to spell the new word *mound* may perceive that it rhymes with the familiar word *found* and that the two words can be spelled in a similar way once the discrepant letter has been altered. This procedure is referred to as "spelling by analogy" (Marsh *et al.*, 1980).

There are several studies showing that young children are able to apply lexical information to produce new spellings. Goswami (1988) presented 7-year-old subjects with a visible clue word such as *beak* to see if this information would enable them to construct a spelling of an unfamiliar word such as *bean* or *peak*. She found that having a visible clue word available helped children considerably when they were asked to spell analogous words. In a further experiment intended to evaluate children's ability to use recently acquired spellings (Goswami, 1988), subjects were first taught pairs of words which could be used to form analogies in the later portion of the experiment, for example *rose*, *nose*, *seat*, *neat*. Subsequently the children were required to spell words which could be spelled by analogy to the words they had just learned, for example *chose*, *hose*; *beat*, *meat*. The children's spelling improved substantially after training, indicating that once they had learned to spell certain words, they were able to make use of the recently acquired orthographic knowledge to spell by analogy.

In order to investigate whether young spellers are able to draw upon stored lexical knowledge to help them generate novel words, we asked children to listen to a series of words and nonwords and spell only the words (Goulandris & Snowling, in preparation) (for a more detailed account of this experiment see Snowling, this volume,

Chapter 6). Barry and Seymour (1988) report that adults have acquired precise knowledge specifying which letter strings are more likely to represent particular phonemes than others. For example, /e/ is generally represented by the letter e and only occasionally represented by the letters ea. They refer to this knowledge as "contingency" and suggest that it predisposes spellers to use more common letter strings when writing new words or nonwords. Accordingly, we were interested in discovering whether young spellers have acquired any awareness of the frequency with which various alternative spelling patterns are likely to represent vowels and whether such knowledge would influence how they spelled nonwords. If young children proved to be sensitive to contingency, we wondered whether the two types of knowledge (word-specific knowledge and knowledge of probability of occurrence) would influence and interact with each other?

Forty children aged 8 and 10 years were asked to listen to a series of words and nonwords and write the nonwords only. The nonwords were preceded by an unrelated word (e.g. *bread* or *bus*), a rhyming nonword with a predictable or high-contingency vowel (e.g. *shoot* or *low*) or a rhyming word with a more unusual or low-contingency vowel which would not be spelled correctly without some word-specific knowledge (e.g. *fruit* or *toe*). Children proved to be influenced both by the lexical items which preceded the nonword they were spelling and by the degree of contingency of the preceding word. If the word contained a very unlikely spelling pattern, the children were less likely to adopt it and stuck to a more predictable spelling pattern.

This experiment suggests that even moderately skilled spellers have sufficient orthographic knowledge to predict with uncanny accuracy whether a spelling is probable or implausible. Despite their limited experience of written language, these children have extrapolated a complex network of information about the frequency of occurrence of letter strings. In addition, the same inexperienced spellers are able to retrieve spellings of words they have just heard and use the spelling patterns contained therein to help them generate a spelling of a nonword.

The finding that children are able to use lexical information when inventing spellings has important theoretical and practical implications. If children are able to use word-specific knowledge to generate new spellings, then we need to propose developmental models which emphasize the reciprocal nature of the learning process. It may be necessary to view early spelling acquisition as an interactive process in which the formation of rules is to a great extent derived from information provided by current word-specific knowledge. Children who have learned a number of words by rote may be inclined to use the lexical information to generate hypotheses about letters and their relationships to the sounds in the words.

Practical implications

Spelling new words using existing spelling information has several important advantages over using sound–letter rules. First, it requires considerably less phonological processing competence, since segmentation and application of sound–letter rules requirements are substantially reduced and only the initial phonemes need to be exchanged. Use of analogy will, therefore, be easier for children who have acquired some lexical knowledge but are as yet inept users of correspondence rules. For example, the spelling of the word *nook* could be derived from the familiar word *look* even though the speller might not know how the /ook/ portion of the word would be represented using spelling–sound rules. In addition, use of analogy often enables spellers to access the correct spelling patterns. For example, *louse* spelled by analogy to *mouse* will result in the conventional spelling whereas the alphabetic rendition of *lous* or *lows* will not.

Of course, it will not have escaped the reader's notice that analogy strategies will often lead to incorrect orthographic information being applied. If *head* is written using the lexical analogue *bed* the result will be *hed*, while the word *brought* written by analogy to *caught* will produce *braught*. Note, however, that such spellings are no less correct than an alphabetic rendition, indeed the first example was identical to the alphabetic rendition. Furthermore, correct analogous spellings are often more orthographically plausible than an alphabetic spelling. Therefore, serious consideration should be given to encouraging children to use analogy strategies when spelling in order to increase awareness of alternative orthographic patterns and prevent over-reliance on phoneme-by-phoneme encoding strategies.

Increasing evidence that learners naturally make use of the rimes of familiar words to construct novel spellings suggest that teaching word families, i.e. *hand, band, sand, stand, bland,* may be a more effective way of helping children acquire orthographic knowledge than has previously been acknowledged. Explicit instruction designed to heighten awareness that changing the onset and retaining the rime can generate rhyming words families has been shown to be particularly beneficial (Bradley & Bryant, 1983). Teaching is more effective if the learner already knows how to spell a word containing the rime in question, i.e. *ow* in *cow*, before the other words in the family are introduced.

REMEDIATION—A CASE STUDY

One important dilemma teachers and psychologists often face is identifying the most effective teaching methods for a particular child. The balance of cognitive strengths and weaknesses varies and accordingly individuals respond differently to alternative teaching methods. Wendy Clifton (1992) in collaboration with Maggie Snowling and myself undertook a single case study of a dyslexic boy in order to evaluate the efficacy of two alternative types of intervention, a multi-sensory approach and a visual approach.

EB, a boy of above average intelligence (Full Scale WISC-R IQ = 124), was 11 years, 7 months at the time this intervention study commenced. Despite having received specialist teaching once a week for 3 years, his reading and spelling difficulties persisted. His reading age was 9 years, 11 months (British Abilities Scale Reading Test) and his spelling age was 7 years, 10 months (Vernon Graded Word Spelling Test). Phonological processing skills, especially phoneme segmentation, remained weak and manipulation and knowledge of sound–letter rules was poor.

EB was still having difficulties with particular spelling patterns, such as *ink, ire, ture, stle,* and it was decided to target groups of words containing a number of these unfamiliar letter strings. Eight sets of 5 words were assembled and were further subdivided into matched pairs to ensure that the words were of equal difficulty in both teaching conditions. Pairs of words were matched for length, number of syllables, frequency of occurrence in the English language, length of letter string pattern and degree of complexity of consonant clusters.

A multiple baseline design was used to measure improvement over time. By systematically comparing the two types of intervention using matched sets of words, this design enables the experimenter to use the subject as his own control. The experiment was divided into two phases. Two matched sets of words were taught in each phase, one using multi-sensory teaching (A) and the other using visual methods (B). Each teaching phase lasted 6 weeks with a 2-week break in between the end of phase 1 and the beginning of phase 2.

EB was tested several times prior to the commencement of the intervention to provide a stable baseline and to ensure that improvement was not occurring spontaneously. The first period of intervention (multi-sensory teaching) lasted 3 weeks. At the completion of the first portion of phase 1 both taught and untaught words were tested and the extent of improvement recorded. If only the taught words had improved this would provide evidence that the teaching method was effective. The second set of words was then taught using the visual procedure. At the end of the second 3-week intervention period both taught and untaught words were tested again to determine any progress due to intervention. Spelling attainment was measured before teaching (baseline measure) and then again 4 days, 3 weeks and 6 weeks after the teaching of a particular group of words was discontinued. The entire procedure was repeated again in phase 2 but different sets of matched words were presented and the order of the teaching methods was reversed.

The multi-sensory procedure adopted was as follows. The pupil was asked to repeat the word being learned and to form the word using plastic letters. He was then required to examine the word and to divide it into phonological segments such as syllables, onset and rime units or phonemes, as applicable. If the word also contained shorter words these were noted. Consonant blends (i.e. *pr*, *st*), shared rimes (the vowel and subsequent consonants within the syllable, i.e. *out* in *shout*) and letter patterns were highlighted. The word was then finger-traced on different surfaces to provide kinaesthetic feedback and to form memory traces in motor memory. Finally, the pupil checked to see that the spelling was accurate and corrected his spellings as necessary.

The second set of words was then taught using the visual procedure. The visual whole-word teaching strategy differed from the multi-sensory procedure in that words were taught as one unit and no attempts were made to segment the word in any way or to identify component spelling patterns. Instead, the pupil was encouraged to recall the word as a sequence of letters. The pupil was first told to read the word and spell it using plastic letters. He was then asked to look at the word, close his eyes and create a mental image of it. He was encouraged to imagine projecting the word onto three different surfaces in the room and to change the colours of the writing and the background as desired. For example, the word could be visualized written in dripping paint or in brightly coloured chalk on boards of differently coloured surfaces. Once EB was satisfied that the word had been learned, he wrote the word, checked it and corrected it if necessary.

The results of the experiment showed that the multi-sensory intervention produced excellent results in both phases. In phase 1, EB attained 100% accuracy on the words taught using the multi-sensory procedure, both immediately after intervention and 6 weeks later. The visual intervention produced good results directly after the period of teaching but the outcome was disappointing 6 weeks later, when spelling accuracy dropped to the 50% level. In phase 2, EB recalled all the words which had been learned using the multi-sensory and the visual procedures at the end of the instructional period. The multi-sensory technique still produced superior learning and retention after 6 weeks but its superiority was not as marked in this phase because the visual learning resulted in an 80% accuracy rate compared to 100% accuracy rate for the multi-sensory intervention.

It is worth considering why the multi-sensory procedure resulted in better retention than the visual procedure. The process of analysing words into component segments, letter strings, clusters and onset–rime segments appears to draw the speller's attention to the precise orthographic structure of each word and encourages the speller to group words according to word families. Indeed, the crucial component of the multi-sensory procedure was its emphasis on a variety of phonological and orthographic segmentation procedures and on noting how other words contained similar segments. This type of segmentation was expressly omitted in the visual procedure, which emphasized a whole-word strategy. Hatcher, Hulme and Ellis (1994) have stressed the value of making explicit links between the phonology of spoken words and the letters used to represent them in written words, referring to this explicit type of teaching as "phonological linkage". This is precisely the type of teaching which forms the basis of the multi-sensory procedure used so successfully with EB. This study therefore lends further support to theories which emphasize that training in phonological skills must be deliberately linked to reading and spelling activities.

Interestingly, there were also significant increases in EB's scores on standardized tests following the period of intervention (14 weeks), with spelling age improving approximately 1½ years and reading accuracy and reading comprehension improving approximately 2 years. This suggests that EB was not just learning a few isolated word families but was learning more effective strategies for analysing and recalling unfamiliar words.

Whereas this study clearly demonstrates that multi-sensory teaching was particularly effective for EB, it should not be concluded that multi-sensory teaching will necessarily be equally effective for all pupils since individual differences are likely to play an important role in determining the success of alternative types of remediation. However, it should be stressed that there are now numerous studies attesting to the effectiveness of the multi-sensory approach (Stoner, 1991) and that it is an instructional technique which merits more empirical research. Moreover, the experimental method described above may have direct relevance to the classroom and a simple adaptation could prove useful for teachers who wish to identify the most effective teaching programme for individuals with severe difficulties.

The research findings outlined above emphasize the importance of helping children develop phonological awareness in the early years. This sensitivity to the sound patterns in language provides learners with the key to discovering the fundamental relationship between speech sounds and the letters used to represent them—crucial for understanding the mechanics of an alphabetic language. Moreover, alphabetic knowledge appears to serve as a framework for the learning of more complex orthographic patterns. However, children also use existing knowledge of word spellings to provide them with another source of information about orthography and teaching should encourage children to use this source of information. In conclusion, it should be stressed that spelling is not an isolated skill but is a vital constituent of emerging literacy. By teaching children to spell we also teach them about written language and encourage the development of more accurate decoding and word recognition skills.

ACKNOWLEDGEMENT

This chapter was prepared with the support of grant (G8801538) from the Medical Research Council.

REFERENCES

Albrow, K. H. (1972). *The English Writing System: Notes Towards a Description*. London: Longman.

Barry, C. & Seymour, P. H. K. (1988). Lexical priming and sound-to-spelling contingency effects in nonword spelling. *Quarterly Journal of Experimental Psychology*, **40A**(1), 5–40.

Bradley, L. & Bryant, P. E. (1983). Categorising sounds and learning to read—a causal connection. *Nature*, **301**, 419–421.

Bryant, P. E. & Bradley, L. (1980). Why children sometimes write words which they do not read. In U. Frith (Ed.), *Cognitive Processes in Spelling*. London: Academic Press, pp. 355–370.

Cataldo, S. & Ellis, N. (1990). Learning to spell, learning to read. In P. D. Pumphrey & C. D. Elliott (Eds), *Children's Difficulties in Reading, Writing and Spelling: Challenges and Responses*. Basingstoke: Falmer Press, pp. 101–125.

Clifton, W. (1992). Spelling intervention in developmental dyslexia: a single case study. Unpublished MSc Thesis. National Hospitals College of Speech Sciences.

Ehri, L. (1985). Sources of difficulty in learning to spell and read. In M. L. Wolraich & D. Routh (Eds), *Advances in Developmental and Behavioural Paediatrics*. Greenwich, Conn: Jai Press, pp. 121–195.

Frith, U. (1985). Beneath the surface of developmental dyslexia. In K. E. Patterson, J. C. Marshall & M. Coltheart, Eds), *Surface Dyslexia*. London: Routledge & Kegan-Paul.

Gentry, J. (1978). Early spelling strategies. *The Elementary School Journal*, **79**, 88–92.

Goswami, U. (1988). Children's use of analogy in learning to spell. *British Journal of Developmental Psychology* **6**, 21–34.

Goswami, U. & Bryant, P. (1990). *Phonological Skills and Learning to Read*. Hove: LEA.

Goulandris, A. M. (1989). Emergent spelling: the development of spelling strategies in young children. Unpublished PhD Thesis. University of London.

Goulandris, N. (1990). Children with spelling problems. In P. Pinsent (Ed.), *Children with Literacy Difficulties*. London: David Fulton.

Goulandris, N. (1992). Alphabetic spelling: predicting eventual literacy attainment. In C. M. Stirling & C. Robson (Eds), *Psychology Spelling and Education*. Clevedon, Avon: Multilingual Matters.

Goulandris, N. K. & Snowling, M. (1991). Visual memory deficits: a plausible cause of developmental dyslexia? Evidence from a single case study. *Cognitive Neuropsychology*, **8**, 127–154.

Hatcher, P., Hulme, C. & Ellis, A. W. (1994). Ameliorating early reading failure by integrating the teaching of reading and phonological skills: the phonological linkage hypothesis. *Child Development*, **65**, 41–57.

Henderson, E. H. (1980). Developmental concepts of word. In *Developmental and Cognitive Aspects of Learning to Spell: A Reflection of Word Knowledge* (E. H. Henderson & J. W. Beers, Eds), Newark, Delaware: International Reading Association.

Hornsby, B. & Shear, F. (1975). *Alpha to Omega*. London: Heinemann.

Maclean, M., Bryant, P. & Bradley, L. (1987). Rhymes, nursery rhymes and reading in early childhood. *Merrill-Palmer Quarterly*, **33**, 255–282.

Mann, V. A., Tobin, P. & Wilson, R. (1987). Measuring phonological awareness through invented spellings of kindergarten children. *Merrill-Palmer Quarterly*, **33**, 365–91.

Marsh, G., Freidman, M., Welch, V. & Desberg, P. (1980). The development of strategies in spelling. In U. Frith (Ed.), *Cognitive Processes in Spelling*. London: Academic Press, 339–354.

Morais, J., Cary, L., Alegria, J. & Bertelson, P. (1979). Does awareness of a sequence of phonemes arise spontaneously? *Cognition*, **7**, 323–331.

Olofsson, A. & Lundberg, I. (1985). Evaluation of long term effects of phonemic awareness training in kindergarten. *Scandinavian Journal of Psychology*, **26**, 21–34.

Perin, D. (1983). Phonemic segmentation and spelling. *British Journal of Psychology*, **74**, 129–144.

Read, C. (1975). Lessons to be learned from the pre-school orthographer. In E. H. Lennenberg & E. Lennenberg (Eds), *Foundations of Language Development, 2*. London: Academic Press.

Read, C. (1986). *Children's Creative Spelling*. London: Routledge & Kegan Paul.

Read, C., Zhang, Y., Nie, H. & Ding, B. (1986). The ability to manipulate speech sounds depends on knowing alphabetic spelling. *Cognition*, **24**, 31–34.

Rohl, M. & Tunmer, W. E. (1988). Phonemic segmentation and spelling acquisition. *Applied Psycholinguistics*, 335–350.

Snowling, M. J. (1987). *Dyslexia. A Cognitive Developmental Perspective*. Oxford: Basil Blackwell.

Snowling, M., Hulme, C., Wells, B. & Goulandris, N. (1991). Continuities between speech and spelling in a case of developmental dyslexia. *Reading and Writing*, **4**, 19–31.

Snowling, M. J., Stackhouse, J. & Rack, J. P. (1986). Phonological dyslexia and dysgraphia: a developmental analysis. *Cognitive Neuropsychology*, **3**, 309–339.

Stoner, J. C. (1991). Multi-sensory reading instruction. *Reading and Writing*, **3**, 19–30.

Stuart, M. & Coltheart, M. (1988). Does reading develop in a sequence of stages? *Cognition*, **30**, 139–181.

20

Organizing Sound and Letter Patterns for Spelling

LYNETTE BRADLEY

University of Oxford

LAURA HUXFORD

Cheltenham and Gloucester College of Higher Education

So much emphasis has been placed on learning to read in our educational system that it has always been difficult for those with spelling difficulties to find the help they need. When help is given, it rarely seems to be successful. One reason for this is that methods of teaching spelling have concentrated on the way in which spellings seem to be remembered by those who have no difficulty with them. Students are encouraged to look at a word and to remember what it looks like. But is this the best way to help children whose spelling skills are inadequate? Is this the way in which young children begin to spell? How do these skills develop?

Children begin to write by learning to spell the words of their language which they speak and hear. Evidence from observation and the study of early spellings (Read, 1971, 1975, 1986; Treiman, 1993), from longitudinal (Bradley & Bryant, 1983; Cataldo & Ellis, 1988; Lundberg, Olofsson & Wall, 1980) and training studies (Ball & Blachman, 1991; Bradley & Bryant, 1983; Lundberg, Frost & Petersen, 1988) all suggest that phonological cues, which capture the sound structure of our language, are probably most important in early spelling. Because our writing system is alphabetic, children also need to discover the relationship between phonemes and graphemes to be able to spell the words they want to write. When they can divide a word into

Handbook of Spelling: Theory, Process and Intervention. Edited by G. D. A. Brown and N. C. Ellis.
©1994 John Wiley & Sons Ltd.

phonemes (sounds), they use a letter (grapheme) or group of letters to reproduce each phoneme when they write a word. So to be able to transcribe the words they want to spell, some form of letter knowledge becomes essential (Bradley & Bryant, 1991; Read, 1986; Treiman, 1993).

Finally, we must ask how successful spellers develop a detailed visual memory for words so that they can reproduce them accurately. Even young children entering school for the first time quickly learn to remember the spelling of hundreds, and then thousands of different words. How do young children manage to remember all the different combinations of letters?

PHONOLOGICAL CUES AND SPELLING

When young children begin to spell, and have a limited experience of print, the sounds of their own language must be their richest resource. But the success of learners, whether they are children or adults, is related to the degree to which they are aware of the underlying phonological structure of words (Liberman & Shankweiler, 1985). The way in which young children develop an explicit awareness of phonemes has intrigued researchers for the last 20 years or more. Many different tasks have been devised to try to capture this development, and the tapping task developed by Liberman and her colleagues is probably one of the better known ones (Liberman *et al.*, 1977). They asked children to tap out the number of syllables and of phonemes in spoken words. Elkonin, on the other hand, asked children to move a counter for each phoneme in a word (Elkonin, 1975). Zhurova (1964) trained 3-year-old children to isolate the first sound of their own name, while Fox and Routh (1975) had some success when they asked 3-year-olds to say "just a little bit" of a phrase, a word, or a syllable. In the syllable task, the "little bit" which the children had to produce was a phoneme.

Children with spelling problems invariably find phonological tasks difficult. Bradley investigated the perceptual and cognitive difficulties experienced by a large group of British dyslexic children, and was intrigued to find that most of the children were insensitive to rhyme when compared with younger children reading normally and at the same level (Bradley, 1979). She found that a small group of the dyslexic children who were successful on rhyme and alliteration judgement tasks were also significantly better at spelling than those backward readers who found the phonological task difficult, though there were no significant differences between them in age, IQ or reading age (Bradley & Bryant, 1978). The relationship between children's phonemic awareness and spelling has been explored too in studies where groups of children have been matched on spelling ability. In the Rohl and Tunmer (1988) Australian study, young good spellers were better at a phonemic segmentation tapping task than older children matched for spelling age. Bruck and Treiman (1990) also found that a group of Canadian dyslexic children had more difficulty on auditory and visual deletion tasks than younger children who were matched for spelling age. In all of these studies, the investigators concluded that the phonological tasks differentiated between the good and the poor spellers.

LETTER KNOWLEDGE AND SPELLING

Both Read (1986) and Treiman (1993) show us that young children's ability to segment words into their constituent phonemes is an important part of learning to spell, and suggest that children use their knowledge of letter names to access the writing system. Read (1971), for example, showed that young children's first attempts at spelling were by writing the sounds they could hear in words. Their ability to hear sounds in words, coupled with their knowledge of letters, determined the form of the spellings they produced. As the earliest sound children generally represent in spelling a simple word is the initial phoneme, followed by focus on the initial and final phonemes (Clay, 1989; Gentry, 1981; Treiman, 1993), they might write a word such as car as cr because these are the sounds they perceive, or because the letter name r is pronounced as ar. Children can also demonstrate a heightened acuity for phonemes which most adults have lost, which can result in unexpected or too many letters in their early spellings, such as *mayul* for *mail*, *oolwias* for *always*, or *trap* spelled as *chrap* (Read, 1986; Treiman, 1993).

In a cross-sectional study with kindergarten children in the United States, Liberman *et al.* (1985) also looked at phonemic segmentation skill in relation to spelling, but they included a test of letter knowledge too. They found that while phonemic segmentation accounted for 67% of the variance in the children's spelling performance, a further 20% of the variance was accounted for by letter knowledge.

THE RELATIONSHIP BETWEEN PHONOLOGICAL AWARENESS, LETTER KNOWLEDGE AND SPELLING

Longitudinal Studies

Several longitudinal studies have been carried out to investigate the role that phonological cues and letter knowledge play in the development of young children's literacy skills, but not all of them have taken the relationship between these early skills and spelling into account in their analyses (Tizard *et al.*, 1988; Share *et al.*, 1984).

One of the earliest longitudinal studies to include both letter knowledge and a test of phonological sensitivity also looked at the relationship with both spelling and reading. This was the first of two longitudinal studies carried out in the United States by de Hirsch, Jansky and Langford (1966) and Jansky and de Hirsch (1972). They were looking for a battery of tests to identify high-risk children in kindergarten. In their first study they tested children on a battery of 37 tests which included both letter knowledge and rhyming. However, they found that 20 of the 37 tests they had included had predictive possibilities at the 5% confidence level when the children were given reading and spelling tests in the second grade. From these 20 tests they selected a more manageable index of only 10 tests for a larger study with 450–500 children in New York, and the rhyming test was one of the tests that was dropped.

Although Huxford (1993) was primarily interested in the way phonological skills develop in young children, and in how these developing skills relate to the earliest stages of spelling and reading, she did test letter knowledge as well. She realized that the children's ability to demonstrate phonemic segmentation skill when they wrote a word could depend on their letter knowledge. The youngest child in the study was almost 4 years old. She followed 46 young children from the time that they could identify only the first phoneme of a spoken word until they were able to spell simple three-letter words successfully. At four common assessment points in her longitudinal study she found significant correlations between the children's phonemic segmentation skill and their progress in spelling. Phonemic segmentation made a significant contribution to the children's scores on both real word and nonword spelling tests at each assessment point, even after differences in the children's age, receptive vocabulary and letter knowledge had been taken into account.

Like many other researchers (Maclean, Bryant & Bradley, 1987; Share *et al.*, 1984), Huxford accepted either the letter name or sound as letter knowledge, and we will use this term unless we need to specify one or the other. It is interesting to note that in her longitudinal study she confirmed the Liberman *et al.* (1985) cross-sectional finding, as the children's phonological skill accounted for a significant amount of the variance in their spelling scores after the variance in letter knowledge had been taken into account.

Rhymes and rimes

Rhyming tasks have proved to be one of the most successful ways of testing the very young child's sensitivity to the sounds in words. This is probably because many children use rhymes as part of their early language play (Chukovsky, 1963). It has been suggested that children have an implicit rather than an explicit phonological sensitivity in these early years which is captured on the rhyming tasks (Cunningham, 1990; Stanovich, 1992). On the other hand, tests of alliteration and rhyme do capture sensitivity to the intra-syllabic units onset and rime, which may coincide with phonemic units. They have been used as a phonological measure in several longitudinal studies which have looked at the acquisition of spelling skill. In other studies, investigators have asked children to produce words to rhyme with a stimulus word. Lundberg, Olofsson and Wall (1980) tested 200 children on a range of word synthesis and word analysis tasks, including rhyme production, in their longitudinal study. Using path analysis, they found a relationship between rhyme production and spelling in the group of 51 children who were 6-year-old non-readers at the start of the study 1 year earlier.

In another longitudinal study, the Oxford group suggested that children might develop an early sensitivity to the phonology of their language through their experience of linguistic routines such as nursery rhymes. Indeed, they found that 3-year-old children's knowledge of nursery rhymes enhanced their developing phonological sensitivity, which was measured on rhyme and alliteration judgement tasks a year later (Maclean, Bryant & Bradley, 1987) and on a more explicit phoneme detection task a year after that when the children were 5½ years old (Bryant *et al.*, 1988).

In the course of this study the children were tested repeatedly, and they were given many different tasks to test their developing phonological sensitivity. The children's letter knowledge was tested too, and the researchers found that the children's skill at rhyme judgements and letter knowledge at age 4½ years made significant and independent contributions to their progress in spelling 2 years later (Bradley & Bryant,

(1991). Indeed, a single combined score of the two measures accounted for 64% of the variance in spelling, and was a better predictor than either of the two measures on their own. The researchers also found that the children's knowledge of nursery rhymes at age 3 still accounted for variance in the spelling scores 3 years later after phonemic segmentation skill had been taken into account, and concluded that rhyme must play a special part in the connection between nursery rhymes and spelling.

Cataldo and Ellis (1988) also looked at these same factors in a longitudinal study, but they were particularly interested in the transition from implicit to explicit phonemic awareness and how these were related to learning to spell. They followed 28 children from the age of 4 and 5 years. The children were tested for their spelling, rhyming ability as a test of *implicit* phonemic awareness and phonemic segmentation as a test of *explicit* phonemic awareness at the beginning of the study and then again at the end of the first and second years. Letter knowledge was tested at the beginning and end of the study.

Using path analysis, these investigators found a strong relationship between implicit phonological awareness and the earliest form of spelling. Implicit phonological awareness also predicted explicit phonological awareness at this early stage in the children's development. The authors suggest that implicit phonological awareness, children's ability to recognize and manipulate rhyme, not only develops into an explicit phonological awareness but provides a contribution itself to early spelling, which seems to be in complete agreement with the Oxford findings. Cataldo and Ellis suggest that implicit phonological awareness becomes less important to spelling as children's explicit phonological awareness develops and becomes increasingly important for both real word and, not surprisingly, nonword spelling. The children's skill at real word spelling helped the development of their explicit phoneme awareness, possibly because it helped them to learn about the internal structure of words and the relationship between phonemes and letters or groups of letters. Interestingly, no relationship was found between letter–sound knowledge and spelling in this study. Nevertheless, taken together, the data reviewed above provide strong support for a relationship between phonological sensitivity, knowledge of letter names and the early stages of learning to spell.

Longitudinal studies are helpful for tracing the relationship between early skills, such as nursery rhymes or rhyming, and skills that develop later on, such as reading or spelling. But like correlations, they only serve to show that the relationship exists, and we cannot be sure that the first skill influences the second. The relationship could well be a reciprocal one (Bryant & Bradley, 1985). In fact, it is widely acknowledged that while early phonological sensitivity precedes learning to read, some of the more sophisticated phonological skills are developed through reading experience (Bertelson *et al.*, 1985; Ehri, 1985).

Training Studies

Properly controlled training studies, on the other hand, do help us to determine cause–effect relationships. If we can train a particular skill, such as rhyming, and show that spelling improves as a result, we can be reasonably confident that rhyming skill contributes to success in spelling later on.

Rhyming was just one of the variables included in an impressive Scandinavian study carried out by Lundberg, Frost and Petersen (1988). They tested almost 400 Danish children on their letter knowledge and rhyming skill and on a wide range of phonological awareness tests. They then trained 235 of these Danish preschool children in different aspects of phonological awareness. The training sessions, which were given daily for 8 months, included rhyming games and stories and nursery rhymes, rhythmic dancing and walking exercises, and games which involved dividing spoken words into smaller units. After the training these children did better on the same tests that they had been given earlier than the children who were not given this training, and subsequently made better progress in spelling. The training effect was specific, and did not have a significant effect on the children's vocabulary or their informal learning of letter names.

Another study which looked at letter knowledge, phonemic awareness and spelling was carried out in the United States with three groups of kindergarten children by Eileen Ball and Benita Blachman (1991). One group of children were trained in phonemic segmentation, rhyming and letter knowledge. A second group of children were given training in language activities, and also the letter-knowledge training, while a third group were tested but not trained. The training groups were seen for 20-minute sessions four times a week for 7 weeks. At the end of the study the children trained in phonemic awareness had made significantly more progress in spelling than the other two groups. There was no difference between the groups in letter-name knowledge, but the trained groups were better at letter sounds.

Bradley has carried out several training studies to try to discover how children's spelling skill develops. One of the earliest studies was an integral part of a longitudinal study which involved more than 400 young children who were recruited before they had learned to read (Bradley & Bryant, 1983, 1985). The children were given a wide range of tests, including the rhyme judgement tests (Bradley 1980, 1984, 1992). The 65 children who had most difficulty on this test, and could be matched with each other, were included in the training study.

For the training study children were divided into three groups, matched for their scores on the rhyme judgement task, age, sex, school class, vocabulary score and intelligence. The children in the first group were given phonological training, and half this group were shown how the phonemes in the words they categorized could be represented by graphemes, using plastic alphabetic letters. The second group were trained to categorize the same words semantically, while the third group were tested but not trained. The children who received training had 40 10-minute sessions (6 hours, 40 minutes altogether) over the next 2 years. The training had a remarkable effect on the children's spelling progress: 2 years later, when the children were 8–9 years old, the children given phonological training were 4 months ahead of the trained control group and 10 months ahead of the untrained control group. On the same spelling test the children who had received phonological training and had also been shown how the sound categories mapped on to letter strings were a further 13 months ahead of the children who had phonological training only, 17 months ahead of the trained control group and almost 24 months ahead of the untrained control group. Their mean spelling age was 3 months higher than the mean spelling age of the 300 children who had done well on the phonological sensitivity tasks initially.

Five years after the project had ended, when the children were 13 years old, they were tested again (Bradley, 1987, 1989, 1990). Although they had not been seen in the intervening years by the research team, more than half of the children from the control groups had received remedial help from special educational services. All the children had made progress, but the children who had received less than 7 hours' instruction categorizing sounds and letters when they were 6 and 7 years old were just as far ahead of all the other children on a spelling test as they had been when they were tested at the age of 8 years.

This study offers convincing evidence in support of a cause–effect relationship between phonological sensitivity and learning to spell. The particular advantage gained by the children taught to understand the connection between sound categories and orthographic spelling patterns suggests that the two together make a formidable contribution to children's early progress in spelling, as the data from other studies suggested. Bradley had developed the method in her work with learning disabled children at Park Hospital, Oxford, and maintains that early intervention is especially important for these children because it is this early organization of the sound categories which lays the foundation for organizing orthographic spelling patterns in memory. Later spelling instruction without this foundation gives children lots of spelling patterns but no way of organizing them in memory; then, like any disorganized storage system, it is difficult to catalogue new material and difficult to retrieve individual items efficiently and intact.

Bradley did run another training study for dyslexic children with very severe spelling problems (Bradley, 1981). In this study she attempted to validate the popularity of the many multi-sensory teaching techniques (Fernald, 1943; Gillingham & Stillman, 1977). She adapted Gillingham and Stillman's simultaneous oral spelling technique and compared it with other methods which controlled for different aspects of it, such as letter naming or writing the word to be learned. The children gained significantly from this particular multi-sensory approach, and Bradley maintained that this was because they learned to integrate the different strategies. However, she also cautioned that the technique only helped the student to learn one word at a time; such methods need to be combined with phonological and orthographic categorization, such as rhyming, if the student is to be able to generalize from this spelling to other words that sound and look alike.

CATEGORIZING SOUND PATTERNS FOR SPELLING

The foundations for spelling are laid down before the children come into contact with print at all, in their early language play and especially in their rhyming games (Bradley, 1988). Rhyming words have more sounds in common than any other words except identical ones, so the sound connection is an easy one to hear. *Humpty dumpty* and *diddle fiddle* may be introduced in the form of nursery rhymes, but there is ample evidence that this rhyming practice begins in the cradle (Snow, De Blauw & Van Roosmalen, 1979; Trevarthen, 1986, 1987; Vihman, 1981). Certainly, by the time most children come to school, and before they begin to read, they are well able to make judgements about rhyming words, as the data from more than 400 non-readers in the Bradley and Bryant (1983) study show. The pre-readers' scores on the rhyme judgement tests were well above chance level.

These children have a sound categorizing system already, then, before they learn to read, as a foundation for their spelling memory organization. All they need to do is to learn how to map the letter string categories on to the sound system that is already organized. Read, Treiman and Huxford each show that the children are experimenting in their attempts to discover these connections in their early creative spelling. In a further longitudinal and training study Bradley attempted to show how young children continue to bring the two together.

Bradley wanted to ensure that these kindergarten children were beginning to recognize word patterns so that she could get some measure of their developing memory for orthographic spelling patterns. So in the new study the children were non-readers by the Lundberg, Frost and Peterson (1988) definition, but in fact it was found that most of the children could read about five words and write about three words on specially devised tests of words most frequently found in the writing of young children. Almost 180 children were tested to find 60 children at this moment in their development. Their memory for orthographic spelling patterns (a term to denote letter string memory, visual memory for words or memory for spelling) was measured by a memory for visually presented words task. Each child was shown 10 words, one at a time. The word was presented for 5 seconds and then removed, and the child asked to write the word. The words featured on all most frequently used word lists, but could not be worked out by simple phoneme–grapheme correspondence rules.

As well as being given a range of reading and spelling tests and the usual rhyme judgement tests (Bradley, 1980, 1984, 1992), the children were given a novel rhyme test. This was a test of incongruent rhymes. In the usual congruent rhyme judgement tests the rhyming words both sound and look alike, for example *need*, *weed*, *peel*, *seed*. In the new incongruent rhyme judgement tasks the words sounded alike but looked different, for example, *saw*, *for*, *were*, *more*; or looked alike but sounded different, for example *beak*, *steak*, *freak*, *leak*. As with the other rhyme judgement tasks, the procedures were entirely verbal. The children performed equally well on the incongruent rhyme tasks, and their scores were again well above chance level.

The children were followed in school over the next 3 years and were given the same tests again 1 and 3 years later, when they were 7 and then 9 years old. When Bradley looked to see if the usual relationship between early rhyming ability and progress in spelling and reading was present, she found an interesting pattern. There was a significant relationship between scores on the congruent rhyme tests at age 6 with both spelling and reading at age 9, but the incongruent rhyme scores were only related to progress in reading. To make progress in spelling, the children needed to appreciate the rhyming patterns that both sounded and looked alike, even though they were virtually non-readers when the rhyming tests were given.

Bradley then looked at the relationship between the children's skill at sound categorization (rhyming) and their success on the memory for orthographic spelling task. Careful analysis of the cross-sectional data showed no connection between the two when they were both measured at age 6 or when they were both tested at age 7. Analysis of the longitudinal data, however, did reveal a connection. There was a strong and significant relationship between the children's ability to categorize sounds *as measured by the congruent rhyme test only* at age 6 and their memory for orthographic spelling patterns at age 7, which in turn made a significant contribution to the children's scores on a standardized spelling test when they were 9 years old. Here is convincing evidence that children's early phonological skill, as measured on a rhyming test of words that sound and look alike, is an important factor in the development of memory for orthographic spelling patterns.

Rhymes, Rimes and Spelling

But the phonological skill in question is a specific one—rhyming—a skill that young children can practise for years before they begin to think of spelling. Chukovsky (1956) tells us that it is difficult to think of a more rational system of practice in phonetics than such frequent repetition of all possible sound variations. Children who miss out on this practice because they are late to learn to talk, or lack language experience, are impoverished indeed. For here they discover for themselves the most salient way of organizing words for spelling. When children invent rhyming words in their word play, *easy peasy, teasy weasy*, they naturally segment words into onset and rime, units smaller than the syllable (Mackay, 1972; Treiman, 1985). The onset may coincide with a single phoneme, and learning about phonemic segmentation is vitally important. At the level of the single phoneme we can learn to organize our spelling catalogue alphabetically and work out phonetically regular words one sound at a time. But rimes are particularly important for organizing memory for spelling. They are the key to our filing system for the spelling patterns of hundreds of words that we will never have to learn individually. Because we know that *round* rhymes (rimes) with *sound, bound, mound, pound, ground, found, hound, round, around* and *wound*, we know that these words probably have similar letter patterns. We can also make an informed guess at the spelling of *sounding, grounded, rounder* and many other related words. Is it any wonder that children's ability to make judgements about words that sound and look alike contributes to their developing memory for spellings? Moreover, by having their memory for spelling organized on this basis, children are more likely to have memory capacity available to remember orthographic patterns which cannot be categorized in this way, such as *yacht* and *people*, and to be able to distinguish between homonyms such as *there* and *their*, *so*, *sew* and *sow*, and *steak* and *stake*, which must also be remembered orthographically.

The contribution that sound categorization plays in developing memory for spelling patterns was emphasized by the results of two short training studies also directed by Bradley. The first study included 52 children chosen because they had spelling problems and reading problems. The mean age of the children was 10 years, 2 months, their mean IQ (WISCIR) 105, but the mean spelling age of the group was 7 years, 3 months and the mean reading age 7 years, 8 months (Schonell), 7 years, 11 months (Neale). The children were divided into four carefully matched training groups. The first group received phonological and orthographic training: they were taught to categorize words that sounded alike and helped to discover that these words had similar letter strings using plastic alphabetic letters. They were always given both phonological/letter knowledge and orthographic training in the same training session.

The children in the three control groups received variations of the same training. The second (control) group received the phonological training in one session and were given practice making the same words with the alphabetic letters in alternate sessions, but they were not shown the connection between the two. The third (control) group received phonological (sound categorization) training only, and the fourth (control) group of children had only orthographic training (with the alphabetic letters making words). Each child had 26 individual 10-minute training sessions only, regardless of the type of training.

At the end of the study only the children receiving phonological training had improved on the orthographic spelling test of visual memory for letter strings. The children who received orthographic training making words with alphabetic letters but no training in categorizing these words by their sounds made virtually no improvement on this test (see Figure 20.1). The children who received both phonological and orthographic training and were taught the connection between them made most progress on the standardized spelling test, whereas the children who received phonological training alone made least progress and obviously could have benefited from some orthographic training (Figure 20.2).

As any group of backward readers of this size is certain to be a heterogeneous one, it is particularly important to find that the phonological training in sound categorization was so important for the development of orthographic memory. But the necessity of helping backward readers discover the phonological categorization/orthographic connection was dramatically illustrated by the progress made in reading comprehension (Neale), as shown in Figure 20.3. At the end of the 6-month study the children given orthographic training only had made no progress in reading comprehension at all. Since children's spelling proficiency must eventually be influenced by their meaningful reading experiences, especially for deducing more

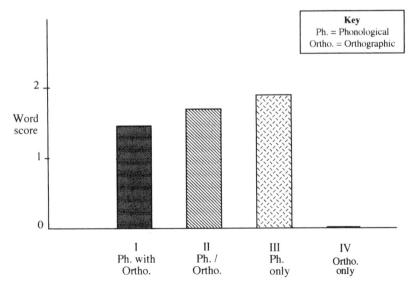

FIGURE 20.1   Improvement on memory for spelling task by backward readers ($N = 52$).

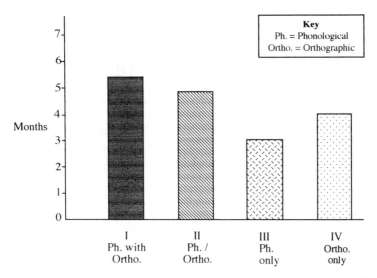

FIGURE 20.2   Improvement on Schonell Spelling Test by backward readers ($N = 52$).

sophisticated spelling rules, this does not augur well for their continuing spelling development (Goswami, 1992).

All children are individuals, and as such will have individual learning styles and strengths and weaknesses. Some of the backward readers in this study had already

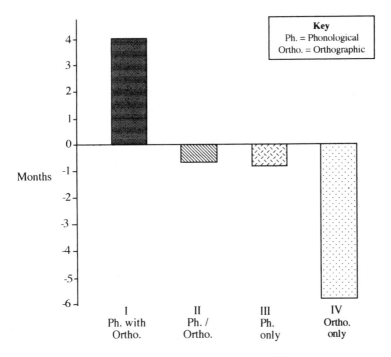

FIGURE 20.3   Improvement on Reading Comprehension (Neale) by backward readers ($N = 52$).

received a lot of phonological training and clearly benefited from the orthographic training. With many young children coming into school the same will apply. Many of them will have had a great deal of practice at sound categorization in their normal language development, but some of them may be meeting the alphabet for the first time. In another short training study organized along exactly the same lines as the one reported above, Bradley looked at the influence of the different types of training on young children beginning school. The main effects of this training study are reported elsewhere (Bradley, 1988), but one trend is particularly relevant here. The three groups given training in sound categorization improved most on the test of orthographic memory for spelling, and were showing an increasing advantage over the orthographic training only group on a standardized spelling test 2 years later.

Children's ability to recognize a relationship between orthographic spelling patterns and phonological patterns in words was also shown in a study by Goswami (1988). Young children, aged 6 and 7 years, were asked to spell words after they had heard and seen priming words. The words to be spelled either shared the beginning three-letter sequence or final three-letter sequence ("rime") of the priming word or had three letters in common but in a different sequence. The children were more likely to spell a word correctly when they were primed with a word which contained the letters in the same sequence, indicating that they were making a connection between the orthographic and phonological sequence of the letters. Furthermore, they spelled more words which shared the rime with the prime word than the beginning sequence of letters. This reinforces Bradley's contention that rhyming is a particularly useful form of categorization for developing spelling skill.

TOWARDS SPELLING PROFICIENCY

Children's memory for orthographic spelling patterns or sequences has recently been investigated by Treiman (1993). She studied a corpus of unaided writing from 43 6- and 7-year-old American children. She concluded that much of the spelling was influenced by phonological and letter name cues, but that there were indications that children were beginning to internalize some orthographic conventions and were also using morphological cues. She gives, as examples, the frequency with which the children used the doubled vowels *oo* and *ee* compared with *aa*, *ii* or *uu* in their attempts to spell words, and emphasizes that double consonants, though not necessarily accurately used, generally followed orthographic convention. She also gives examples of spellings which suggest that the children are beginning to use meaning relations among words from kindergarten, though she has not found this evidence in naturalistic data with children at the earliest stages of spelling as yet.

Marsh *et al.* (1980) tested children on their knowledge of orthography (the qualifying *e* and the correct use of vowels after the letter *c*) and concluded that children begin to make observable progress at around 7 years old. Bradley (1979) also suggested that children bring the strategies together and become much more flexible in their approach at about this time. Children's increasing use of orthographic cues was shown in a study by Waters, Bruck and Malus-Abramowitz (1988). They gave 158 children, aged between 8 and 12 years of age, a spelling test consisting of words which could be correctly spelled by direct phoneme–grapheme correspondence (e.g. *upset*), ambiguous words which could have more than one regular form (e.g. *teeth*) and words and nonwords which required knowledge of an orthographic convention (e.g. *outside*, *groit*). They reported that the fewest errors in all age groups were made on the unambiguous, regular words and that children did equally well on ambiguous words as on those which required knowledge of an orthographic convention. The authors concluded that the children's additional ability to combine phonological and orthographic cues to spell nonwords precludes the possibility that the children were merely using a visual memory strategy to spell.

SUMMARY

Young children can practise sound categorization in their early language play, through nursery rhymes and rhyming word games. They can begin school with an excellent system of categorizing words by the sounds in them before they begin to spell or read. There is evidence that children's early rhyming skill stands them in good stead when they begin to spell using letter knowledge to record their impressions of the way words sound. Children who make the connection between the sound categories that they hear and the orthographic letter patterns that represent them make better progress in spelling. Recognizing rimes is an efficient way of progressing from spelling simple phoneme–grapheme correspondences (e.g. *hen*, *pen*) to spelling more complex orthographic sequences (*light*, *fight*, *sight*, *sigh*, *high*). Children who make these cognitive connections access an efficient way of remembering spelling patterns, and of organizing memory for spelling words in such a way that more memory is available to cater for words which have to be remembered individually.

REFERENCES

Ball, E. & Blachman, B. A. (1991). Does phoneme awareness training in kindergarten make a difference in early word recognition and developmental spelling? *Reading Research Quarterly*, **26**(1), 49–66.

Bertelson, P., Morais, J., Alegria, J. & Content, A. (1985). Phonetic analysis capacity and learning to read. *Nature*, **313**, 73–74.

Bradley, L. L. (1979). Perceptual and cognitive difficulties experienced by able backward readers. Unpublished doctoral dissertation. University of Reading.

Bradley, L. L. (1980), 2nd edition (1984). *Assessing Reading Difficulties*. London: Macmillan. (Latest edition, 1992. Windsor: NFER-Nelson).

Bradley, L. L. (1981). The organization of motor patterns for spelling: an effective remedial strategy for backward readers. *Developmental Medicine and Child Neurology*, **23**, 83–91.

Bradley, L. L. (1985). Dissociation of reading and spelling behaviour. In D. D. Duane & C. K. Leong (Eds), *Understanding Learning Difficulties*. New York: Plenum Press.

Bradley, L. L. (1987). Categorizing sounds, early intervention and learning to read: a follow-up study. Paper presented at the British Psychological Society London conference, December, 1987.

Bradley, L. L. (1988). Making connections in learning to read and to spell. *Applied Cognitive Psychology*, **2**, 3–18.

Bradley, L. L. (1989). Predicting learning disabilities. In J. J. Dumont & H. Nakken (Eds), *Learning Disabilities, Vol. 2: Cognitive, Social and Remedial Aspects*. Amsterdam: Swets.

Bradley, L. L. (1990). Rhyming connections in learning to read and to spell. In P. D. Pumfrey & C. D. Elliott (Eds), *Children's Difficulties in Reading, Spelling and Writing: Challenges and Responses*. Basingstoke: Falmer Press.

Bradley, L. L. & Bryant, P. E. (1978). Difficulties in auditory organisation as a possible cause of reading backwardness. *Nature*, **271**, 746–747.

Bradley, L. L. & Bryant, P. E. (1979). The independence of reading and spelling in backward and normal readers. *Developmental Medicine and Child Neurology*, **21**, 504–514.

Bradley, L. L. & Bryant, P. E. (1983). Categorizing sounds and learning to read: a causal connection. *Nature*, **301**, 419–421.

Bradley, L. L. & Bryant, P. E. (1985). *Rhyme and Reason in Reading and Spelling*. Michigan: Ann Arbor.

Bradley, L. L. & Bryant, P. E. (1991). Phonological skills before and after learning to read. In S. Brady & D. Shankweiler (Eds), *Phonological Processes in Literacy*. London: LEA.

Bruck, M. & Treiman, R. (1990). Phonological awareness and spelling in normal children and dyslexics: the case of initial consonant clusters. *Journal of Experimental Child Psychology*, **50**, 156–178.

Bryant, P. E. & Bradley, L. L. (1985). Phonetic analysis capacity and learning to read. *Nature*, **313**, 73–74.

Bryant, P. E., Bradley, L. L., Maclean, M. & Crossland, J. (1988). Nursery rhymes, phonological skills and reading. *Journal of Child Language*, **48**, 224–245.

Cataldo, S. & Ellis, N. (1988). Interactions in the development of spelling, reading and phonological skills. *Journal of Research in Reading*, **11**(2), 86–109.

Chukovsky, K. (1963). *From Two to Five*. Berkeley and Los Angeles: University of California Press.

Chukovsky, K. (1956). Quoted in Elkonin, D. (1971) Development of speech. In A. Zaporozhets & D. Elkonin (Eds), *The Psychology of Pre-School Children*. Cambridge, Mass: MIT Press.

Clay, M. (1989). *Writing Begins at Home*. Auckland: Heinemann.

Cunningham, A. E. (1990). Explicit versus implicit instruction in phonological awareness. *Journal of Experimental Child Psychology*, **82**, 733–740.

de Hirsch, K., Jansky, J. & Langford, W. (1966). *Predicting Reading Failure: A Preliminary Study*. New York: Harper and Row.

Ehri, L. C. (1985). Effects of printed language acquisition on speech. In D. Olson, N. Torrance & A. Hildyard (Eds), *Literacy, Language and Learning*. Cambridge: Cambridge University Press.

Elkonin, D. B. (1975). USSR. In J. Downing (Ed.), *Comparative Reading: Cross National Studies of Behaviour and Processes in Reading and Writing*. London: Macmillan.

Fernald, G. (1943). *Remedial Techniques in Basic School Subjects*. New York: McGraw Hill.

Fox, B. & Routh, D. K. (1975). Analysing spoken language into words, syllables and phonemes: a developmental study. *Journal of Psycholinguistic Research*, **4**(4), 331–342.

Gentry, J. R. (1981). Learning to spell developmentally. *The Reading Teacher*, **34**(4), 378–381.

Gillingham, A. & Stillman, B. W. (1977). *Remedial Training for Children with Specific Disability in Reading, Spelling and Penmanship*, 7th edition. Cambridge, Mass: Educators Pub. Service.

Goswami, U. (1988). Children's use of analogy in learning to spell. *British Journal of Experimental Psychology*, **6**, 21–33.

Goswami, U. (1992). Annotation: phonological factors in spelling development. *Journal of Child Psychology and Psychiatry*, **33**(6), 967–975.

Huxford, L. M. (1993). The development of phonemic strategies in spelling and reading. Unpublished doctoral dissertation. University of Bristol.

Jansky, J. & de Hirsch, K. (1972). *Preventing Reading Failure*. New York: Harper and Row.

Liberman, I. Y., Rubin, H., Duques, S. & Carlisle, J. (1985). Linguistic abilities and spelling proficiency in kindergarteners and adult poor spellers. In D. B. Gray & J. F. Kavanagh (Eds), *Behavioural Measures of Dyslexia*. New York Press.

Liberman, I. Y. & Shankweiler, D. P. (1985). Phonology and the problems of learning to read and write. *Remedial and Special Education*, **6**(6), 8–17.

Liberman, I. Y., Shankweiler, D. P., Liberman, A. M., Fowler, C. & Fischer, F. W. (1977). Phonemic segmentation and recoding in the beginning reader. In A. S. Reber & H. Scarborough (Eds), *Towards a Psychology of Reading*. Hillsdale, NJ: LEA.

Lundberg, I., Frost, J. & Petersen, O-P. (1988). Effects of an extensive program for stimulating phonological awareness in pre-school children. *Reading Research Quarterly*, **23**(3), 472–475.

Lundberg, I., Oloffson, A. & Wall, S. (1980). Reading and spelling skills in the first years predicted from phonemic awareness skills in kindergarten. *Scandinavian Journal of Psychology*, **21**, 159–173.

Mackay, D. (1972). The structure of words and syllables: evidence from errors in speech. *Cognitive Psychology*, **3**, 210–227.

Maclean, M., Bryant, P. E. & Bradley, L. L. (1987). Rhymes, nursery rhymes and reading in early childhood. *Merrill-Palmer Quarterly*, **33**(3), 255–282.

Marsh, G., Friedman, M., Welch, V. & Desberg, P. (1980). The development of strategies in spelling. In U. Frith (Ed.), *Cognitive Processes in Spelling*. London: Academic Press.

Read, C. (1971). Pre-school children's knowledge of English phonology. *Harvard Educational Review*, **41**(1), 1–34.

Read, C. (1975). Lessons to be learned from the pre-school orthographer. In E. H. Lenneberg & E. Lenneberg (Eds), *Foundations of Language Development: A Multidisciplinary Approach*, Vol. 2. New York: Academic Press.

Read, C. (1986). *Children's Creative Spelling*. London: Routledge & Kegan Paul.

Rohl, M. & Tunmer, W. (1988). Phonemic segmentation skill and spelling acquisition. *Applied Psycholinguistics*, **9**, 335–350.

Share, D., Jorm, A. F., Maclean, R. & Matthews, R. (1984). Sources of individual differences in reading acquisition. *Journal of Educational Psychology*, **76**(6), 1309–1324.

Snow, C., De Blauw, A. & Van Roosmalen, G. (1979). Talking and playing with babies: the role of ideologies of child-rearing. In M. Bullowa (Ed.), *Before Speech*. Cambridge: Cambridge University Press.

Stanovich, K. E. (1992). Speculations on the causes and consequences of individual differences in early reading acquisition. In P. Gough, L. C. Ehri & R. Treiman (Eds), *Reading Acquisition*. Hillsdale, NJ: LEA.

Tizard, B., Blatchford, P., Burke, J., Farquhar, C. & Plewis, I. (1988). *Young Children at School in the Inner City*. London: LEA.

Treiman, R. (1985). Onsets and rimes as clusters of spoken syllables: evidence from children. *Journal of Experimental Child Psychology*, **39**, 161–181.

Treiman, R. (1993). *Beginning to Spell: A Study of First-Grade Children*. Oxford: Oxford University Press.

Trevarthen, C. (1986). Development of intersubjective motor control in infants. In M. G. Wade & H. T. A. Whiting (Eds), *Motor Development in Children: Aspects of Coordination and Control*. Dortrecht: Martinus Nijhoff.

Trevarthen, C. (1987). Sharing makes sense. In R. Steele & T. Treadgold (Eds), *Language Topics—Essays in Honour of Michael Halliday*. Amsterdam: Benjamin.

Vihman, M. (1981). Phonology and the development of the lexicon: evidence from children's errors. *Journal of Child Language*, **8**, 239–264.

Waters, G. S., Bruck, M. & Malus-Abramowitz, M. (1988). The role of linguistic and visual information in spelling: a developmental study. *Journal of Experimental Child Psychology*, **45**, 400–421.

Zhurova, L. E. (1964). The developmental analysis of words into their sounds by pre-school children. *Soviet Psychology and Psychiatry*, **2**, 11–17.

21

The Interface Between Research and Remediation

ELAINE MILES AND T. R. MILES

University of Wales, Bangor

Although the focus of the present book is on problems of spelling, it will not be possible in this chapter to discuss spelling on its own. Specialist teachers in literacy skills are standardly trained to teach reading and spelling together, since each contributes to helping the other. Research that is relevant to the teaching of spelling will therefore also be relevant to the teaching of reading.

We shall begin with the work of Hinshelwood and Orton, because it was they who first studied specific literacy problems and who first put forward ideas for remediation. Next we shall consider the shift to a linguistic approach to these problems; thirdly we shall discuss the need to move away from too close modelling on acquired dyslexia; fourthly we shall discuss studies which use a developmental approach; and finally we shall comment on research which suggests that these children have a basic weakness in dealing with complex or rapidly moving input.

THE TWO PIONEERS: HINSHELWOOD AND ORTON

Both Hinshelwood and Orton were medical doctors, the former an ophthalmologist, the latter a neurologist. The main work by Hinshelwood is his *Congenital Word Blindness* (Hinshelwood, 1917). Orton's writings have recently been collected in a single volume (Orton, 1989) which includes a selection of his papers from 1925 to

---

Handbook of Spelling: Theory, Process and Intervention. Edited by G. D. A. Brown and N. C. Ellis.
©1994 John Wiley & Sons Ltd.

1946 and a work which was first published in 1937 entitled *Reading, Writing and Speech Problems in Children*.

The background to Hinshelwood's work was Kussmaul's (1878) concept of "word-blindness". This term was used by him of patients with acquired injuries whose vision of familiar objects was unaffected but who had difficulty in deciphering text. Hinshelwood postulated that there were a number of separate visual memory centres in the brain, one of them concerned with words and letters. "A lesion on one side of the brain, in the vast majority of cases in the left angular gyrus, will completely obliterate the visual word memories and make the individual word-blind" (Hinshelwood, 1917, p. 11). An article which he wrote in *The Lancet* in 1895 prompted a medical colleague, Dr W. Pringle Morgan, to report on what he thought might be a congenital form of word-blindness (Morgan, 1896). The subject of Morgan's communication was a boy aged 14, named Percy, who had grave difficulty in reading and made some very strange spelling errors, for example *Precy* for *Percy*, *calfuly* for *carefully* and *sturng* for *string*. This paper aroused Hinshelwood's interest, and he set himself "to analyse and explain in detail the symptoms" and "to establish the diagnosis on a scientific basis" (Hinshelwood, 1917, p. 42). This in effect involved clothing some of the symptoms in the language of his theory with regard to the acquired cases. He wished, however, to restrict the term "word-blindness" to cases that were clearly pathological and to describe "slighter degrees of defect" by the term "congenital dyslexia" (p. 81).

With regard to teaching, he makes clear that "no amount of argument can decide the question as to the best method of instruction in these cases. The test of experience alone can settle the point" (p. 107). He believes, however, that the methods which had been successful in retraining those with acquired word-blindness would also be successful, for the same reasons, with the congenital cases. "Such cases are *the exact analogue* of the conditions we have met within acquired word-blindness due to disease. If in these latter cases, where the visual word-centre has been destroyed, we have been able to re-educate such patients and enable them to regain the power of reading, then we have every reason to anticipate with confidence that in congenital cases, *where the same centre is involved*, a similar result will be accomplished by similar methods (p. 91, our italics).

Hinshelwood describes 12 cases, six of them from the same family. Eleven of them had been taught by what he calls the "old-fashioned" method—by which children were taught the letters of the alphabet and then given spelling instruction as an introduction to reading; one, in contrast, had been taught by the method of "look and say", which involves responding to the configuration of the whole word. This was a boy aged 13½. "When I examined him . . .", says Hinshelwood, "I found that the boy had a good auditory memory, and I advised that he should be taught on the old method, beginning with the letters of the alphabet, and as he already knew most of these, he would probably not be long in learning them all. I then advised that he should be taught to spell, and then to read the simple words in a child's first primer, spelling them out letter by letter, and so centres would be trained simultaneously. . . ." (Later) "He had made more progress in the last thirteen months than he had made in the preceding seven years when taught on the 'look and say' principle. The superiority of the old method of instruction over the 'look and say' system was thus strikingly manifested" (pp. 103–4).

He continues: "That method of instruction will, in my opinion, be the best in which a simultaneous appeal is made to other centres beside the visual. This condition is fulfilled by the old-fashioned method of learning to read, in which simultaneous appeal is made to visual centre, auditory centre, and the centre of the memory of speech movements . . . I have often found very great assistance from the use of block letters (i.e. letters cut out in wood) in teaching these children the letters of the alphabet. This was a further application of the method of simultaneous appeal to as many cerebral centres as possible" (pp. 105-6).

There is no reason to doubt Hinshelwood's claim that with the children whom he describes his methods were successful. His reference to "the method of simultaneous appeal to as many cerebral centres as possible" anticipates by several decades the work of Gillingham and Stillman (see below); and the value of such "multisensory" teaching has now been established not only by practitioners but also by systematic research (Bradley & Bryant, 1983, 1985; Hulme, 1981). It is also widely accepted that there should be a structured programme in which words are built from their letters.

The theoretical basis on which he explained his successful results, however, is highly questionable.

In the first place, he appears to have taken a very simplistic view about "cerebral centres". Sir Henry Head, writing in the 1920s, is particularly scathing about "diagram makers" who assume that there must be centres for every conceivable psychological function. In connection with the work of one of his predecessors, Bastian, he refers to "the conception that disorders of speech can be classified as affections of independent centres, or of the paths between them. It inevitably led to the production of a diagram. As each case arose it was lopped and trimmed to correspond with a lesion of some cortical centre or hypothetical path . . . (Bastian's) well known diagram showed not only an auditory and a visual word centre, but also one for the tongue and one for the hand. . . . By the time his book was issued, he and his followers had come to believe so firmly in this form of *a priori* explanation, that in any case of speech defect they thought it possible to foretell the situation of the lesion with perfect assurance" (Head, 1926, p. 56). It is plain that Hinshelwood would have to be ranked among the "diagram makers" whom Head criticized.

Secondly, the use throughout Hinshelwood's writings of "visual" terminology, though understandable in view of the fact that he was an ophthalmologist, has influenced future thinkers, not always for the better. This is a point to which we shall return when we come to discuss the views of Orton.

Thirdly, it is surprising that he believed so many of his cases to be adequate spellers—this despite the evidence in respect of Percy (Morgan, 1896), whose strange spelling errors were clearly on record. His view was that "the auditory memory being unimpaired and sometimes exceptionally good these children have no difficulty in rapidly learning to spell and will be able to spell words long before they have learned to recognise them by sight" (p. 106). One suspects, however, that he may have been quick to latch on to any modicum of ability to spell simple words, to count or to do simple sums, in pursuance of his belief that the centres for these functions were separate; and it is possible that the old-fashioned method of repetition used in class teaching may have made less obvious the additional difficulties which have later come to the fore. From the evidence which he presents it seems that the number of children whom he examined in detail was somewhat limited and that they were mostly of a very low level of literacy. His belief in separate "centres" led him to assume that in "pure" cases the "auditory memory" would be found to be intact. This is clearly mistaken: it is now agreed (to use present-day terminology) that among learning disabled children weakness in the recall of auditorily presented verbal material is extremely common. For all Hinshelwood's greatness as a pioneer, therefore, it must be said that his theorizing restricted the range of topics which he might otherwise have explored.

Between Orton and Hinshelwood there were certain basic points of agreement. They both took the view that these problems were constitutional in origin (Orton, 1989, Chapter 2), that they often ran in families (Orton, 1989, pp. 75–77, 202–217) and that they were more common in boys than in girls (Orton, 1989, p. 76). Both, too, believed that such children could be helped by suitable teaching; both favoured the systematic learning of letter–sound correspondences and both regarded the "look and say" method as unhelpful.

In spite of these similarities, however, there were many differences.

One of the significant things about Orton was the breadth of his experience. He studied carefully "almost a thousand cases" (Orton, 1989, p. 94). These included people of all ages from preschool children to the college student and from all types of school. Besides reading and spelling problems, he was interested in aphasia, apraxia, stuttering and much else. When in 1925 he initiated a study in Iowa which led to detailed examination of 142 children referred by local schools for a whole variety of problems, the survey team included a psychiatrist, a social worker, a psychologist and two graduate assistants (Orton, 1989, pp. 130 seq.). Although he was a creative theorist he was all the time involved in practice—working with children and talking to parents and teachers; and it is clear that he did not let his theories dictate his practical recommendations.

On the theoretical side, what particularly influenced him was the existence of errors which he called "reversals". Wrongly orientated letters (in particular *b* for *d* and *p* for *q*) were described by him as "static reversals", while if there was transposition of letters, for instance *tworrom* for *tomorrow*, he spoke of "kinetic reversals" (p. 90). He postulated that, because of the arrangement of the optic nerves, engrams would be formed in both hemispheres of the brain and that these would be mirror images of each other. In the normal way the engrams in the non-dominant hemisphere would be elided by those in the dominant hemisphere, but he suggested that where dominance is incomplete the elision is imperfect. As a theoretical description of what was happening Orton offered the term "strephosymbolia" (twisting of symbols) (pp. 156–9).

Unlike Hinshelwood, he saw the problem not as a result of cerebral defect but as due rather to a failure in physiological development. In "current neurological practice . . . there has been a change from the older views of an exact, circumscribed, and constant localization of (language) functions" (p. 240). As a result he is critical of Hinshelwood's idea that memories are stored in the left angular gyrus. He points out that when one hemisphere is damaged before speech is learned the other can take over; and he suggests that there would have to be defects in the angular gyrus of both hemispheres to satisfy Hinshelwood's hypothesis—a supposition which he rightly regards as very unlikely. "As our studies of cerebral functioning have progressed, we have been led to discard the older concept of the angular gyrus region as a brain area in which more or less photographic visual memories of words are stored and have come to realise that the process of reading is a much more complex activity requiring the physiological integrity and interplay of many brain areas" (pp. 40–1).

As a result of this approach he was less inclined than Hinshelwood to see the developmental cases as "exact analogues" of the acquired ones. "We feel that the use of the term congenital tends to overstress the inherent difficulty and to underemphasise the many environmental factors, both specific—such as methods of teaching—and more general—such as emotional and social forces—and we therefore prefer the use of the term developmental to congenital since it may be said to include both the hereditary tendency and the environmental forces, which are brought to play on the individual" (pp. 39–40). As a result of this he was led to emphasize the importance of longitudinal studies, in which the same individual is studied over a period of time (p. 230). This is an insight which some subsequent researchers have seemingly failed to appreciate (see later).

He also disagreed with Hinshelwood's division into "pathological" and milder cases (described by Hinshelwood as "dyslexic"). His wide experience led him to the view that there is "a graded series including all severity of handicap" (p. 41).

With regard to teaching, Orton took the view that the use of a particular method in schools could sometimes affect the degree of handicap. Although he estimated that there was, overall, a 2% level of reading disability in the community where he worked in Iowa, he noted that in some areas it was as high as 4%. Although all the schools used "flash" methods (in other words "look and say"), he found that those schools with the 2% incidence had tried phonic methods with the children who were failing (p. 171).

Orton looked upon language as "a complex tripartite associative process in which data of visual, auditory, and kinaesthetic origins are brought into varying relationship" (p. 240). It was this idea which gave rise to the "language triangle" referred to by Gillingham and Stillman (1969) in their teaching manual. Orton had in fact worked in partnership with Anna Gillingham, who was a psychologist, since the 1920s, and it was his concept of "linkages" between the different sense modalities which led to the explicit formulation of the idea of "multisensory teaching". What was needed for the practising teacher was "thorough repetitive drill on the fundamentals of phonic association with letter forms, both visually presented and reproduced in writing until the correct associations (were) built up and the permanent elision of the reversed images and reversals in direction (was) assured" (Orton, 1989, p. 162). Further suggestions—including careful listening to the child's oral language and the breaking down of longer words into syllables—are also made (pp. 258–66). In general, "we find that the best approach and the one which yields the best return for teaching efforts is to find the smallest possible unit which the child can handle and begin a gradual reconstruction of the sequences or series of the smaller units" (p. 298).

It is interesting to note that Orton deplored overstandardization of teaching practices and made an appeal for flexibility (p. 96). This may seem surprising in view of the fact that the Gillingham–Stillman programme has often been criticized on the grounds that flexibility is precisely what it lacks! Anna Gillingham has been described as "forceful" and "demanding" by one who knew her (Slingerland, 1974, p. 55), and although her insistence on a fixed routine has been defended by her successors on the grounds that it gives a pupil a greater sense of security, one may speculate that this was her contribution rather than Orton's.

Despite his criticisms of Hinshelwood, it remains true that Orton's approach was still essentially a visual one. Expressions such as "mirror images" and "reversals" constantly appear in his writings; he was interested in what words *look like* when they are misspelled. This led him to check on whether children whom he saw had any special facility at reading words that were written mirrorwise (p. 141), though his data in this area are not entirely convincing. As far as his recommendations for teaching are concerned, however, it is clear that this particular theoretical preoccupation did not have an undue influence on his practice; his good sense and flexibility seem to have prevented this. He was well aware, for instance, that not all spelling errors could be described as "reversals", in particular, he notes that they were sometimes the result of mispronunciation, as is instanced by the boy aged 17 who "talks of the 'sopperntendnt' of his school and spells it so" (p. 255). He himself believed that all such errors were a secondary result of the confusion caused by reversals, but the care with which he has recorded detail has provided material which later investigators are free, if they wish, to interpret differently.

If we try to take stock of Orton's achievement in general what comes through is the picture of a highly creative thinker who also thought it important to involve himself in the day-to-day work of assessing and teaching children and talking to parents. He was not only an imaginative neurologist; he also had a profound knowledge of language problems and was well informed about teaching methods and practices in schools. Few authorities in the area of medicine and education can have had such a wide range of expertise.

THE SHIFT TO A LINGUISTIC APPROACH

Since the time of Hinshelwood and Orton those with literacy problems which seem at variance with their intelligence level have commonly been called "dyslexic", and this is the word which will be used to describe such individuals during the remainder of this chapter. An exact specification of who exactly should *count* as "dyslexic" need not be given here. (For possible views on this matter see Miles & Miles, 1990, and T. R. Miles, 1993.)

As a result of the work of Orton and Gillingham it became widely accepted that the teaching of dyslexics needed to be multi-sensory. In the years immediately after Orton's death, however, it appears to have been assumed without question that the problem was basically one of orientation and sequencing.

During the 1970s it became increasingly clear that this assumption was incorrect. In a comprehensive review of the evidence available at the time, Vellutino (1979) was able to show that the data could better be explained if one postulated instead a difficulty in linguistic processing. It was in particular the work of Isabel Liberman and her colleagues at the Haskins Laboratories, Connecticut, which caused people to recognize that it was not only the optical features of letters which might cause trouble but also their linguistic function (see in particular Brady, Shankweiler & Mann, 1983; Liberman, 1985; Liberman *et al.*, 1971, 1974). Many other researchers have cited evidence which points in the same direction: in particular, experiments were carried out which suggest that in visual tasks which do not involve linguistic judgements dyslexics perform no differently from controls (Ellis & Miles, 1978; Hulme, 1981; Vellutino *et al.*, 1975). Dyslexics, however, had more difficulty than controls in breaking up words into phonemes and in synthesizing phonemes so that they made words (see Catts, 1989, for sources). They also were found to have difficulty in recognizing rhymes (Bradley & Bryant, 1978, 1985) and in recalling nonsense syllables (Snowling *et al.*, 1986). In terms of the "stages of development" model put forward by Frith (1985), it was suggested that the typical dyslexic is held up at the alphabetic stage; in other words, unless the point is explicitly put to him, he may not notice the relatively consistent relationship between the letters of the alphabet and the sounds which they represent. A commonly used formula was to say that the deficit lies at the *phonological* level, where "phonology" is defined as the science of speech sounds in so far as they convey meaning.

This greater linguistic emphasis had important implications for teaching. It used to be assumed—and even today the assumption is not wholly dead—that children who are "visually weak" should be taught by phonic methods, while those who are "auditorily weak" should be taught by "look and say". However, if the weakness is not specifically visual or auditory but linguistic, then the rationale for such teaching loses much of its justification (compare Liberman, 1985; E. Miles, 1991).

Instead, it became recognized that it is not just the orientation of letters or their correct ordering which has to be taught. It is rather that dyslexic children often fail to master the whole complex relationship between oral language and written language—the fact, for instance, that spoken words can be broken down into phonemes and syllables, the fact that vowels and consonants have a different function, and so on. It was realized that if teaching is to be successful, all these points need to be made explicit.

In addition, the linguistic approach has increased our understanding of what Orton called "reversals". His "kinetic reversals" (for instance *tworrom* for *tomorrow*) are not, strictly speaking, reversals at all since the letters remain the right way round. What is important for teachers is to explain why it is necessary to write the letters in a particular order. In the case of "static" reversals (*b* for *d*, *p* for *q*, etc.), it is now recognized that there are many factors—articulatory, auditory and kinaesthetic—which contribute to the confusions. It is the links between vision, hearing, articulation and writing movements which the teacher needs to emphasize. If a pupil writes *b* for *d* or vice versa he has made an incorrect association; instead of talking about "reversals" it is more helpful to say that he has "written the wrong letter".

The shift to a linguistic approach also made it possible to ask whether—perhaps in subtle ways—dyslexics show deficiencies in oral language and whether they have any symptoms in common with those whose disabilities in oral language are severe. This is an area that has been extensively explored by Paula Tallal.

Her early work, which was carried out in collaboration with Malcolm Piercy, involved the use of operant techniques in the study of developmental dysphasics (Tallal & Piercy, 1973). One of their most important findings was that when tones with a relatively long interstimulus interval (ISI) between them (250 ms) were presented, there were no differences between the dysphasics and the controls in the ability to press the correct panel, but that when the ISI was shorter, for example 15 ms, the dysphasics made many more errors. In some further experiments (Tallal, Stark & Mellits, 1985) it was found that the differences showed themselves in modalities other than hearing, for example when at short ISIs the letter E had to be visually distinguished from the letter K and when two pricks on the cheek or hands were given in quick succession.

When she turned her attention to reading impaired children, Tallal found some interesting similarities. In the case of a large group of them the problem was again that of processing incoming information at speed. She also found that those children who had greater difficulty in responding correctly to rapidly presented non-verbal auditory stimuli tended also to be those who were weak at reading nonsense words (Tallal, 1980a). Her conclusion was that "whereas serious deficits in the rate of processing the acoustic stream may lead to serious developmental language disorders, the more subtle defects found in some of the reading impaired children we studied may be related to inabilities to learn the letter-to-sound correspondences involved in phonic skills" (Tallal, 1980b, pp. 176–177). This is an issue to which we shall return later.

The shift to a linguistic approach had the consequence of encouraging the teacher to see herself as teaching the understanding of language, not just the interplay of sensory modalities. It also set dyslexia in a context of language disabilities, with overlaps with oral language weaknesses, and it therefore became necessary for the teacher to consider how help with oral language could contribute to the child's mastery of written language.

THE RELATIONSHIP BETWEEN DEVELOPMENTAL DYSLEXIA AND ACQUIRED DYSLEXIA

During the 1970s the question was raised as to whether recent knowledge in the area of acquired dyslexia could be used to increase our understanding of developmental dyslexia. (For a review of research in this area see A. W. Ellis, 1994.) We shall argue in what follows that, because of major differences between the two conditions, research based on the subtyping used in acquired dyslexia is of little help to those concerned with the remediation of developmental dyslexics.

These differences can be classified under three heads.

There is good evidence, in the first place, that the neurological basis of developmental dyslexia is quite unlike that of acquired dyslexia. According to recent research (Galaburda *et al.*, 1987), small structural anomalies (ectopias and dysplasias) have been discovered in the brains of the eight dyslexics examined to date; and, perhaps more importantly, it has been found that in every case the two temporal plana are of approximately the same size, whereas in the great majority of brains this is not so. What appears to be important is not damage to a centre or pathway but an unusual balance of skills (Geschwind, 1982; West, 1991). This is in line with the views of Orton rather than those of Hinshelwood. Hinshelwood believed that congenital difficulties were "the exact analogue" of the acquired difficulties; Orton, in contrast, did not consider language disability to be the result of damage to a particular area of the brain but thought rather in terms of physiological anomaly. The work of Geschwind, Galaburda and others gives us increasing confidence that this view of the situation is correct.

In contrast, if a person suffers brain injury as a result of a road accident, a bullet wound or a stroke it may well make sense to ask what area of the brain has been damaged or which "route" or "pathway" has been blocked. It may also be appropriate to construct a diagram of functions and use it to classify the patient as belonging to a particular type ("deep dyslexic", "surface dyslexic", etc.).

In the case of developmental dyslexics, however, if some of them are found, for instance, to have difficulty in reading nonwords, no inference can be drawn about their inability or otherwise to use a particular "route". There is evidence that dyslexics, after teaching, are able to read and write nonwords (Kibel & Miles, 1994); and, indeed, lists of nonwords will be found in the Gillingham–Stillman manual (Gillingham & Stillman, 1969). Those who carry out research in schools which specially cater for dyslexics can therefore expect that many of their subjects will be fairly successful at reading nonwords. This is because it is usually the policy of such schools to teach letter–sound correspondences in a systematic way. If a child has not been exposed to such teaching or has experienced it only for a short time, his ability to read nonsense words will almost certainly be less.

Secondly, it should be remembered that acquired dyslexics, unlike developmental dyslexics, have earlier in their lives accumulated a large store of written language information. Even if as a result of their injury much of what had been learned is no longer available, the loss need not be total. A highly educated adult who reads, say, *fascinating* for *fascinate* (Patterson, 1982) may be searching for memories which are only partially lost, and it is possible that in the past he was exposed to *fascinating* more frequently; however, if a developmental dyslexic were to make a similar error one would infer, not that something had been "lost" but that at this particular stage of his life he had not adequately learned to be sensitive to grammatical morphemes.

Thirdly, there is no "before" and "after" comparison as there is in the case of acquired dyslexics. It is possible that the distinctive strengths and weaknesses of the developmental dyslexic have arisen because in late foetal life or early infancy the normal pruning down of some of the cells has failed to take place (Galaburda *et al.*, 1987); from the point of view of literacy skills, however, there can be no point in asking what a child was like before this happened. The comparison is not with himself as he was before he suffered some injury, but with current norms—with what is expected of children of a particular age and a particular background. By the time these children's reading and spelling are tested—a time which, at least until the advent of the national curriculum, was determined by many different factors and varied from one case to another—they will have been exposed, sometimes over many years, to the pet ideas of their class teachers, to their teachers' attitudes to their failure and additionally, in some cases, to a plethora of remedial methods. They may have attempted their own compensatory strategies, with varying degrees of success; they may have experienced frustration, boredom, self-doubt, and much else.

None of these things has any parallel in the study of acquired dyslexia. Yet some researchers have proposed systems of subtyping which disregard such matters—solely, it seems, because they can be disregarded in the acquired cases. For example, Temple (1986), in one of her research papers, presents data on two 10-year-olds and claims from the different characteristics of their reading and spelling that one was a phonological dyslexic and the other a surface dyslexic. Yet she makes no reference to possible differences in the teaching which they might have received or to differences in temperament or other environment influences—which may, indeed, have been accentuated by the fact that one of the children was a boy and the other a girl. She even says in connection with her control group that "in the sample reported here all the seven-year-olds resemble surface dyslexics rather than phonological dyslexics" (p. 100). It is hard, however, for the practising teacher to understand why she should want to make such comparisons, since the alleged similarity with surface dyslexics must surely have arisen in their case either because of the teaching which they had received or because of the stage of development that they had reached.

Similarly, Seymour (1986, 1987) has reported on one of his research projects in which his selection of subjects and even his definition of developmental dyslexia were determined by his assumption of parallels with acquired dyslexia. It is worth considering his argument in some detail.

The relevant characteristic shared by all acquired dyslexics is poor reading and spelling; this, of course, is not in dispute. It is also not in dispute that details of their history before the injury are largely irrelevant. Quite consistently, therefore, on the assumption of an analogy between the two conditions, Seymour took the view that his task in the case of developmental dyslexics was to investigate a selection of poor readers without any special consideration of their background or educational experience.

These are his own words: "When used in relation to adult neurological patients 'dyslexia' is a general label for disturbances of basic reading functions which may be analysed into various sub-types or syndromes. A more confused situation exists with regard to childhood dyslexia. One reason for this is that attempts have been made to stipulate that 'dyslexia' should be used in a restrictive rather than a general sense" (Seymour, 1987, p. 351).

After explaining that this is done because it is thought that adverse educational or social circumstances are a sufficient explanation for impaired reading development, he goes on: "It is considered that the term 'dyslexia' should be applied only in those cases where such explanations appear not to be applicable. . . . In practice, in adult neuropsychology, the preference has been to apply a descriptive label where an observable deficit exists irrespective of what other impairments may be present. Following the same logic, it would be appropriate to refer to a child as 'dyslexic' if basic reading functions were impaired" (pp. 351–2).

The policy of "following the same logic", however, would have been justified only if the two situations were genuinely analogous. Teachers of dyslexics in the restricted sense do in fact sometimes find themselves called upon to help children who do not present the typical dyslexic picture but who have been socially or educationally deprived, usually with a record of poor school attendance. When this happens their progress is sometimes dramatic—quite unlike the slow and painful progress usually made by dyslexics in the restricted sense. Such children may be "impaired" on Seymour's definition but this is certainly not the normal sense of the word "impair", which according to the *Shorter Oxford Dictionary* implies damage, injury or "making worse''. Yet if these children are not "impaired" there seems little point in looking for analogies with acquired dyslexia.

It is, of course, possible to take a cross-section of a school population and compare normal readers with poor readers, taking account of both age and intelligence, as did Bradley and Bryant (1985). This, however, was not Seymour's procedure: his sample size was 21, and it seems from his account that even these 21 were selected in a somewhat haphazard way. At the time of testing all of them were in their late teens, and by then most were reasonably adequate readers, though many still had spelling problems. In a few cases the level of intelligence was low, and in at least two cases there had been frequent moves with interrupted schooling. As controls he used 13 11-year-olds—despite the fact that they were at an educational stage different from the great majority of the dyslexic subjects (Seymour, 1986). To search for "types" without taking into account these many background differences is a questionable procedure at best and is certainly one which offers little help to the practising teacher.

Overall, therefore, we take the view that "type" classifications which employ models derived from the study of acquired dyslexia are unlikely, at least for the present, to make any significant contribution to remediation.

DEVELOPMENTAL STUDIES

A central weakness in the research described in the previous section is that it involved the making of comparisons between pupils of different ages who, for all one knows, may have been exposed to many different kinds of teaching. A more useful way forward is to try to discover by means of longitudinal studies how children's performances change over time.

The main features of the longitudinal study carried out by Bradley and Bryant are well known (see Bradley & Bryant, 1978, 1983, 1985). From the point of view of remediation the most crucial point in this research was the demonstration of a relationship between the ability to discriminate phonemes at the age of 3 or 4 and subsequently ability at reading and spelling. That the connection was a causal one was demonstrated by a particularly neat design: one of their control groups was trained, not in phonemic awareness but in semantic classification (grouping farm animals together, for instance), and despite similar amounts of attention this group made no greater improvement than an "untreated" group. It is worth noting that the amount of time spent on training each child was very limited—40 sessions of 20 minutes over 2 years—yet Bradley (1990) has reported that the differences between the groups remained apparent many years later.

In a study by Cataldo and Ellis (1988) it was found that it was the score on a phonemic awareness test, not the score on a reading test, which provided the best prediction of subsequent reading ability. Now one obvious way of enhancing phonemic awareness is to give the pupil practice in spelling; and it is widely agreed by teachers of dyslexics that if they concentrate on spelling, particularly on the spelling of phonically regular words, it is likely that the pupil will improve his reading in the process of learning to spell. Class teachers in the past have sometimes provided lists of words-to-be-remembered based on a semantic classification (for instance *currants*, *raisins*, *sultanas*), while there have been educationalists, for example Cripps (1984), who have advocated classifying word families by their visual appearance (for instance *one*, *bone*, *money*). Both these methods are at variance with the principles of multi-sensory teaching.

A further consequence of current research is to call in question the view—still widely influential in educational circles—that the learning of alphabetic skills is not merely unnecessary but positively detrimental to the learning of reading. According to this view, children at the outset need to be given "real books" rather than phonic training. In the case of those who learn to read and spell effortlessly such a policy may be defensible, and it is, of course, not in dispute that children should have the chance to read good literature when they are ready to do so. If, however, a dyslexic is exposed to "real books" before he has achieved an adequate level of phonemic awareness this will clearly not help his spelling, and even if he achieves some success in the recognition of "sight" words the result will simply be that when he is older some other teacher will have to try to teach him the basics of spelling. In contrast, if spelling is systematically taught at the outset the resultant phonological awareness will almost certainly result in improved reading.

An important recent development has been the discovery of the relative ease with which children can segment words into onset and rime (see, for instance, Goswami & Bryant, 1990, Goswami, 1991; Kirtley *et al.*, 1989; Treiman, 1985). The word *cat*, for example, can be divided into the separate phonemes /k/, /æ/ and /t/, but it can also be divided into onset, /k/ and rime /æt/. Now it seems likely from the evidence that children begin to progress in reading and spelling by picking up onsets and rimes rather than by discriminating separate phonemes. Some caution is needed, however, in applying this discovery to the remediation of dyslexic children. In their case, although it may be useful to call attention to rimes—and to the way in which rimes are related to rhymes—it may often be more appropriate for the teacher to work with phonemes. This is because those needing remediation are not normally beginners; they are likely to be older children who are therefore capable, when shown, of more sophisticated analysis of sounds, and the great advantage of teaching grapheme–phoneme correspondence rather than grapheme–rime correspondence is that more generalizations become possible, since more words can be built from combinations of phonemes than from combinations of rimes. Moreover, since the remediator usually works in a context where it is important to try to help the pupil to "catch up" with his peers, it may be necessary for her to "cut corners" by moving straight to phonemic analysis rather than follow the developmental path which is the norm for younger children.

DIFFICULTIES RAISED FOR DYSLEXICS BY COMPLEXITY OF MATERIAL AND TOO RAPID PRESENTATION

A further important advance has been the development of connectionist models (see in particular Brown, Loosemore & Watson, in press). According to this model, "the network learns about associations between pairs of patterns simply by being exposed to the pairs: all the learning takes place by slow modification of connection strengths in the course of 'experience' ''.

An advantage of this kind of model is that it forces investigators to be totally specific about the components of both input and output. As things are, research into current practice often lacks this specificity. Expressions such as "teaching by the phonic method" or "teaching by the look-and-say method", though not wholly uninformative about the overall characteristics of what is being done, nevertheless leave many questions unanswered about the exact nature of the input. In Brown's model these inputs have to be specified to the last detail.

In addition, one is studying the "organism" as it *learns*. One is therefore in effect carrying out a kind of "mini" longitudinal study which provides information about changes in performance over time.

Brown classifies words not simply in terms of "regularity", as has traditionally been done, but in terms of the number of "friends" and "enemies" that each word has. Thus *soap* has no "friends" but a number of "enemies" such as *hope, cope* and *rope*; *luck* has *duck* and *suck* as "friends" but no "enemies", while *bulb* has neither "friends" nor "enemies". He describes how he "lesioned" his model by giving it fewer units with which to work. He suggests that "the difference between normal and dyslexic spelling development can be well characterised in terms of the amount of computational resources devoted to the task. When insufficient resources are allocated to learning the relevant sound-to-space associations, the result is that a lower overall level of performance is achieved at any given stage in learning, but the ordering of the different word types (sc. according to the number of 'friends' and 'enemies') in terms of accuracy is the same". This prediction was strikingly fulfilled when he tested out the model on 25 dyslexic and 132 non-dyslexic children aged between 8½ and 12 years.

It is sometimes assumed that, because of their different physiological organization, dyslexics have a different "learning style" from non-dyslexics. In some circumstances this may be true; for instance in mathematical calculations they may prefer to work the answer out logically rather than rely on their relatively weak memories. In the case of learning to spell, however, what Brown's research suggests is that there is no qualitative difference such as under- or over-reliance on phonic regularities; it is simply that in the case of dyslexics progress is slower and less efficient.

There are, however, some points about the model which the practising teacher may wish to query. In its present form the model does not take into account either word frequency or the existence of silent letters such as the *gh* in *night* or the *b* in *debt*. There are some words which the child meets early in life, such as *have* and *give*, which have few "friends" and many "enemies", and it would be interesting to check whether the absence of qualitative differences between dyslexics and non-dyslexics holds up regardless of word frequency. With regard to silent letters, it is possible that they simply contribute an additional "load" to be remembered; but it is also possible that they are the kind of "dominant detail" which according to Bartlett (1932) is more rather than less likely to be remembered. For the present these possibilities must be regarded as open.

From the work of Tallal (see above) it seems plain that one of the problems for the dyslexic is that of coping with incoming material at speed. This is an idea that has recently been taken up in a very insteresting way by Lovegrove and his colleagues (see Lovegrove, in press). Their research has primarily been concerned with the different pathways by which information is transmitted from the eye to the brain. They distinguish in particular the "transient" subsystem—a channel for processing "high frequency" information, by which the observer is able to appreciate details—from the "sustained" subsystem, which processes low spatial frequency information and enables the observer to receive an overall general impression, for instance of the shape of a word. On the basis of a number of studies (involving contrast sensitivity, responses to flicker, etc.), Lovegrove concludes that it is the transient system which is liable to be deficient in dyslexics. He suggests as a consequence that the accuracy of their reading might be improved if they were presented with "one word at a time". In our view this is an idea which practising teachers should certainly take seriously, provided that, as a consequence, they are not discouraged from teaching the pupil to use contextual information and are not led to suppose that reading consists only of mastering words in isolation.

Lovegrove also considers the possibility that blue light may enhance the processing rate in transient channels. To assess the value of using coloured lenses or coloured filters is too complex a matter for consideration in this chapter (for a recent review of the evidence see Evans & Drasdo, 1991; Stanley, 1994). What seems to us possible is that in the future linguistic/phonological and visual approaches will not be regarded as rival alternatives but rather as complementary to each other. It need not be a case of "either–or . . ." ("*either* a linguistic *or* an optical approach") but rather of "both–and . . .". At the end of his chapter Lovegrove notes how his research may be linked not only with research into phonological processing in general but in particular with the ideas of Tallal (see above).

An interesting development along similar lines has been the publication of a paper by Livingstone *et al.* (1991). Instead of using the words "transient" and "sustained", these authors speak of the "magnocellular" and "parvocellular" systems. "In primates", they write, "fast low-contrast visual information is carried by the magnocellular subdivision . . . and slow, high contrast information . . . by the parvocellular division" (p. 7943). They provide evidence showing that five dyslexic adults, when tested on certain physiological measures (involving visually evoked potentials), responded differently from controls when low-contrast stimuli were presented but did not do so in response to high-contrast stimuli. This suggested that dyslexics might have an abnormality in the magnocellular system. It was then found that in the brains of five dyslexics that had previously been studied post mortem by Dr Galaburda and his colleagues the parvocellular layers were no different from those in the brains of non-dyslexics; in contrast, however, there was considerable disorganization in the magnocellular layers, with the cell bodies appearing smaller. The authors consider the possibility that other cortical systems besides the visual might have a fast and a slow subdivision and that dyslexia specifically affects the fast subdivisions. If this is true of the auditory system the result could be an inability to carry out rapid analysis of speech sounds, and this would account for the many different phonological difficulties which are typically shown by dyslexics. Also, if there is a distinctive limitation in the magnocellular system, this would mean that, despite the many compensatory strategies which dyslexics can learn, there is still a weakness in their ability to process information at speed which no amount of practice can completely overcome (compare T. R. Miles, 1986).

Another interesting new development has arisen from the work of Nicolson and Fawcett (1990). These authors, while recognizing the significance and importance of phonological deficiencies, believe that an explanatory theory of wider generality is possible. In one set of experiments, 23 dyslexic children aged between 12 and 13 years were compared with eight suitably matched control children in respect of their ability to balance on a beam. When this task was carried out on its own there was no difference between the two groups. If a second task was superimposed, however, graded according to the subject's ability—counting backwards in one experiment and pressing one of two buttons according to whether a high or low tone was being sounded in another—the performance of the dyslexics deteriorated whereas that of the controls did not. In interpreting their findings the authors suggest that "unlike the controls, the dyslexic children need to invest significant conscious resources for monitoring balance, and thus their performance is adversely affected by any secondary task which serves to distract attention from the primary task. This need for 'conscious compensation' suggests that for dyslexic children the skill of motor balance is poorly automatized" (Nicolson & Fawcett, 1990, p. 159).

Whatever the future of the "dyslexic automatisation deficit" (DAD) hypothesis which the authors propose, there is one immediate point which is relevant for the practising teacher. The work of Tallal, Livingstone *et al.* and Nicolson and Fawcett is alike in calling our attention to the fact that if a dyslexic is confronted with complex stimuli which follow each other in rapid succession, he will be in considerably more difficulty than a non-dyslexic. The teacher, therefore, may like to consider whether her emphasis might not primarily be on breaking skills up into small units, and integrating them with each other, rather than on teaching phoneme–grapheme correspondences as such as though this were an objective on its own. Above all, of course, she needs to remember the importance of *pacing* and of not presenting material at a faster rate than the pupil finds comfortable.

CONCLUDING REMARKS

What, then, can be said in general about the interface between theory and remediation?

Orton's contribution was highly distinctive. His scientific knowledge coupled with his wide awareness of educational practice enabled him to move effortlessly between the two. The important issue, however, is not whether a particular teacher is competent to understand the technicalities of research or whether a researcher has sufficient educational knowledge to be able to give detailed advice to teachers. What needs to be noted about any teaching situation is that it is always full of extremely complex variables and that normally researchers have deliberately chosen only a few of them for systematic study. There is therefore considerable danger if the researcher is perceived as someone who *prescribes* to the teacher what needs to be done; rather it is for the teacher to apply the new knowledge where it seems relevant.

It should also be remembered that theories can sometimes be misapplied. A well-known example is that of the mother who was told by a psychologist that the best way to stop unwanted behaviour was to make sure it was followed by painful consequences. When her elder son accompanied his request for porridge with some choice swear words she gave him a severe hiding, with her younger son looking on. When she then asked the younger boy what he would like to eat he looked somewhat abashed at the treatment which his brother had received, and replied, "Well, you can bet your fucking arse it won't be the fucking porridge". There is a similar danger in the teaching of literacy. For example, a teacher who has been told that dyslexics are weak at the recall of auditorily presented digits may think that she should give the pupil practice at recall of random digit or letter strings—on the grounds that in so doing she will be "improving his short-term memory". It is more constructive, however, to bear in mind that the pupil will be able to recall a greater quantity of material if he learns to "chunk". Constant repetition of letters or digits may lead to the recall of those particular letters or digits—and can lead to improved recall of telephone numbers!—but this does not mean that it will lead to a "better memory" in general. Similarly, if researchers publish papers saying that dyslexics have difficulty when stimulus material is presented at speed a teacher might be led to assume that gradually increasing the speed of presentation will effect an improvement in all-round speed processing. This is almost certainly not the case.

It does not follow, however, from any of these considerations that researchers and teachers must simply go their separate ways or that neither can legitimately influence the other. The experienced teacher needs to judge whether the findings of researchers are coherent with her own wider—but less systematic—experience. She may well judge, for instance, that a classification of her pupils into "phonological dyslexics", "surface dyslexics", etc., is of no use to her, but that if she thinks about the concepts of "onset" and "rime" or recognizes that spelling skills can be acquired by the recognition of analogies (as is suggested by Brown's work) she may make changes in her teaching procedure which would not have been possible but for the work of researchers.

REFERENCES

Bartlett, F. C. (1932). *Remembering*. Cambridge: Cambridge University Press.
Bradley, L. (1990). Rhyming connections in learning. In P. D. Pumfrey & C. D. Elliott (Eds), *Children's Difficulties in Reading, Spelling and Writing*. Basingstoke: Falmer Press.
Bradley, L. & Bryant, P. E. (1978). Difficulties in auditory organisation as a possible cause of reading backwardness. *Nature*, **271**, 746–747.
Bradley, L. & Bryant, P. E. (1983). Categorising sounds and learning to read: a causal connection. *Nature*, **301**, 419–421.
Bradley, L. & Bryant, P. E. (1985). *Rhyme and Reason in Reading and Spelling*. Ann Arbor: University of Michigan Press.
Brady, S., Shankweiler, D. & Mann, V. A. (1983). Speech perception and memory coding in relation to reading ability. *Journal of Experimental Child Psychology*, **35**, 345–367.
Brown, G. D. A., Loosemore, R. G. & Watson, F. L. (1993). Normal and dyslexic spelling: a connectionist approach. Manuscript in submission.
Cataldo, S. & Ellis, N. C. (1988). Interactions in the development of spelling, reading and phonological skills. *Journal of Research in Reading*, **11**, 2, 86–109.
Catts, H. W. (1989). Phonological processing deficits and reading disabilities. In A. G. Kamhi & H. W. Catts (Eds), *Reading Disabilities: A Developmental Language Perspective*. Boston: Little Brown.

Cripps, C. (1984). *An Eye for Spelling.* Wisbech, Cambs: Educational Software.

Ellis, A. W. (1994). *Reading, Writing, and Dyslexia: A Cognitive Analysis*, 2nd edn. London: LEA.

Ellis, N. C. & Miles, T. R. (1978). Visual information processing in dyslexic children. In M. M. Gruneberg, P. E. Morris & R. N. Sykes (Eds), *Practical Aspects of Memory.* London: Academic Press.

Evans, B. J. W. & Drasdo, N. (1991). Tinted lenses and related therapies for learning disabilities—a review. *Ophthalmic and Physiological Optics*, **11**(3), 206–217.

Frith, U. (1985). Beneath the surface of developmental dyslexia. In K. E. Patterson, J. C. Marshall & M. Coltheart (Eds), *Surface Dyslexia. Neuropsychological and Cognitive Studies of Phonological Reading.* London: LEA.

Galaburda, A. M., Corsiglia, J., Rosen, G. D. & Sherman, G. F. (1987). Planum temporale asymmetry: reappraisal since Geschwind at Levitsky. *Neuropsychologia*, **25**(6), 853–868.

Geschwind, N. (1982). Why Orton was right. *Annals of Dyslexia*, **32**, 13–30.

Gillingham, A. & Stillman, B. E. (1969). *Remedial Training for Children with Specific Difficulty in Reading, Spelling and Penmanship.* Cambridge, Mass: Educators Publishing Service.

Goswami, U. (1991). Recent work in reading and spelling development. In M. Snowling & M. Thomson (Eds), *Dyslexia: Integrating Theory and Practice.* London: Whurr.

Goswami, U. & Bryant, P. E. (1990). *Phonological Skills and Learning to Read.* Hove: LEA.

Head, H. (1926). *Aphasia and Kindred Disorders of Speech.* London: Macmillan.

Hinshelwood, J. (1917). *Congenital Word-Blindness.* London: H. K. Lewis.

Hulme, C. (1981). *Reading Retardation and Multisensory Teaching.* London: Routledge & Kegan Paul.

Kibel, M. & Miles, T. R. (1994). Phonological errors in the spelling of taught dyslexic children. In C. Hulme & M. Snowling (Eds), *Reading Development and Dyslexia.* London: Whurr.

Kirtley, C., Bryant, P. E., MacLean, M. & Bradley, L. (1989). Rhyme, rime and the onset of reading. *Journal of Experimental Child Psychology*, **48**, 224–245.

Kussmaul, A. (1878). Word-deafness and word-blindness. In H. von Ziemssen (Ed.), *Cyclopaedia of the Practice of Medicine*, **14** (Diseases of the nervous system and disturbances of speech). London: Maston, Searle and Rivington.

Liberman, I. Y. (1985). Should so-called modality preferences determine the nature of instruction for children with reading disabilities? In F. H. Duffy & N. Geschwind (Eds), *Dyslexia: A Neuroscientific Approach to Clinical Evaluation.* Boston: Little Brown.

Liberman, I. Y., Shankweiler, D., Fisher, F. W. & Carter, B. (1974). Explicit syllable and phoneme segmentation in the young child. *Journal of Experimental Child Psychology*, **18**, 201–212.

Liberman, I. Y., Shankweiler, D., Orlando, C., Harris, K. & Bell-Berti, F. (1971). Letter confusions and reversals of sequence in the beginning reader: implications for Orton's theory of developmental dyslexia. *Cortex*, **7**, 127–142.

Livingstone, M. S., Rosen, G. D., Drislane, F. W. & Galaburda, A. M. (1991). Physiological and anatomical evidence for a magnocellular defect in developmental dyslexia. *Proceedings of the National Academy of Science, USA*, **88** (September), 7943–7947.

Lovegrove, W. (in press) Visual deficits in dyslexia: evidence and implications. In A. J. Fawcett & R. I. Nicolson (Eds), *Skills and Their Development in Dyslexic Children.* Hemel Hempstead: Harvester Wheatsheaf.

Miles, E. (1991). Visual dyslexia–auditory dyslexia: is this a valuable distinction? In M. Snowling & M. Thomson (Eds), *Dyslexia: Integrating Theory and Practice.* London: Whurr.

Miles, T. R. (1986). On the persistence of dyslexic difficulties into adulthood. In G. Th. Pavlidis & D. F. Fisher (Eds), *Dyslexia: Its Neuropsychology and Treatment.* Chichester: Wiley.

Miles, T. R. (1993). *Dyslexia: The Pattern of Difficulties*, 2nd edition. London: Whurr.

Miles, T. R. & Miles, E. (1990). *Dyslexia: A Hundred Years On.* Milton Keynes: Open University Press.

Morgan, W. P. (1896). A case study of congenital word-blindness. *British Medical Journal*, **2**, 1378.

Nicolson, R. I. & Fawcett, A. J. (1990). Automaticity: a new framework for dyslexia research. *Cognition*, **35**, 159–182.

Orton, S. T. (1989). *Reading, Writing, and Speech Problems in Children* and *Selected Papers*. Austin, Texas: PRO-ED.

Patterson, K. E. (1982). The relation between reading and phonological coding: further neurological observations. In A. W. Ellis (Ed.), *Normality and Pathology in Cognitive Function*. London: Academic Press.

Seymour, P. H. K. (1986). *Cognitive Analysis of Dyslexia*. London: Routledge & Kegan Paul.

Seymour, P. H. K. (1987). Developmental dyslexia: a cognitive experimental analysis. In M. Coltheart, G. Sartori & R. Job (Eds), *Cognitive Neuropsychology of Language*. London: LEA.

Slingerland, B. H. (1974). Memories of Anna Gillingham: a human being like the rest of us. *Bulletin of the Orton Society*, **24**, 55–62.

Snowling, M., Goulandris, N., Bowlby, M. & Howell, P. (1986). Segmentation and speech perception in relation to reading skill: a developmental analysis. *Journal of Experimental Child Psychology*, **41**, 489–507.

Stanley, G. (1994). Visual deficit models of dyslexia. In G. Hales (Ed.), *Dyslexia Matters*. London: Whurr.

Tallal, P. (1980a). Auditory temporal perception, phonics, and reading disabilities in children. *Brain and Language*, **9**, 182–198.

Tallal, P. (1980b). Language and reading: some perceptual requisites. *Bulletin of the Orton Society* (now *Annals of Dyslexia*), **30**, 170–178.

Tallal, P. & Piercy, M. (1973). Developmental aphasia: impaired rate of non-verbal processing as a function of sensory modality. *Neuropsychologia*, **11**, 389–398.

Tallal, P., Stark, R. E. & Mellits, E. D. (1985). Identification of language-impaired children on the basis of rapid perception and production skills. *Brain and Language*, **25**, 314–322.

Temple, C. M. (1986). Developmental dysgraphias. *Quarterly Journal of Experimental Psychology*, **38A**, 77–110.

Treiman, R. (1985). Onsets and rimes as units of spoken syllables: evidence from children. *Journal of Experimental Child Psychology*, **39**, 161–181.

Vellutino, F. R. (1979). *Dyslexia: Theory and Research*. Cambridge, Mass: MIT Press.

Vellutino, F. R., Steger, J. A., Harding, C. & Phillips, F. (1975). Verbal vs. non-verbal paired associates learning in poor and normal readers. *Neuropsychologia*, **13**, 75–82.

West, T. G. (1991). *In the Mind's Eye. Visual Thinkers, Gifted People with Learning Difficulties, Computer Images, and the Ironies of Creativity*. Buffalo, New York: Prometheus Books.

22

From Theory to Practice: Errors and Trials

DAVID MOSELEY

University of Newcastle-upon-Tyne

Applied psychologists have to be pragmatic. There is little point in suggesting changes in the learning and teaching of spelling which are hard to implement in a busy classroom or for which there is little support from field trials or research. The writer has been fortunate in being able to work with educational psychologists, teachers, parents and students over the years in collecting data about spelling and in trialling new materials. This chapter is concerned (a) with data analyses which bear on theoretical issues concerning spelling and (b) with the trialling of modified approaches to the learning of spelling, some of which have led to publication (Moseley, 1988, 1993; Moseley & Nicol, 1986; Moseley & Singleton, 1993). Relevant research evidence will be linked to most of the topics considered.

However, pragmatism does not entail the acceptance of the *status quo*. As an educational psychologist I seek to improve standards of spelling by helping to make learning more efficient and enjoyable, not only for individuals with problems but for all learners. If we are to achieve a more literate society in which almost all people are able to put down in writing whatever they wish to communicate, we need to find ways of overcoming spelling problems. It is not an unreasonable long-term aim that almost all school-leavers should be able to spell at least 2000 words correctly, should be competent in correcting their own misspellings and should seek to build on these competencies. However, evidence suggests that English students face a harder challenge than do those in countries with more regular spelling systems.

Thorstad (1991) and Upward (1992) have in different ways shown that the unpredictability of English orthography is a major barrier to the mastery of spelling.

Handbook of Spelling: Theory, Process and Intervention. Edited by G. D. A. Brown and N. C. Ellis.
©1994 John Wiley & Sons Ltd.

Thorstad compared the dictation accuracy of Italian and English children from similar backgrounds at 6.5 and at 10.5 years. While the younger English children could spell an average of 13 words (23%of the words) in a passage with an English readability level of 13 years, the Italian children had an average of 44 words (79%) correct on the Italian version of the passage, despite the fact that they had only attended school for less than a year before the test was given. At 10.5 years the English children could on average spell only two of the eight hardest words in the passage, while the Italian children averaged nearly eight (*cemento/cement*, *corretto/correct*, *leteralmente/literally*, *percettibile/perceptible*, *permette/permits*, *preparano/preparing*, *speciale/special*, *termometro/thermometer*). The spelling ability of the Italian children was equivalent to their reading ability at both age levels, while the English children at 6.5 years could spell less than half the number of words that they could read.

Upward's study was carried out with English university students of German who wrote in both languages. He found that errors in spelling German words were much less common than errors in English words (by a factor of between 2 and 7, depending on the criteria applied). It was found that 63% of the errors made in English at this level fell under the following categories: (1) silent letters, (2) neutral vowel (schwa) errors, (3) doubled consonants. It is interesting to note that these hard-to-spell features appear many times in the English versions of Thorstad's eight hardest words, but not at all in the Italian versions.

It is clear that English children learn to spell at a rather slow rate, especially in relation to their development of receptive, spoken and word-recognition vocabulary. This is recognized in national attainment targets and is reflected in the structure of standardized spelling tests. An analysis of the word banks in Young's Parallel Spelling Tests (Young, 1983) shows an increase in difficulty in terms of word length and both graphemic and morphemic structure. While 7-year-olds are expected to manage little more than four-letter words, most 9-year-olds have difficulty with words of more than seven letters and it is not until 11 years that the average pupil begins to spell correctly a significant proportion of words of three or more syllables. Unusual graphemes (such as *ph* and *oi*) and neutral vowel spellings like *our* continue to present difficulties to many pupils throughout the secondary phase, as do the more complex morphemic markers.

If we suppose that a competent speller can spell 30 000 words correctly at the age of 15, whereas a less competent speller can manage perhaps 1000, this represents an average learning rate of eight words a day for the former and only two words a week for the latter. The poor speller leaves school with a restricted spelling repertoire of commonly used, short words, the majority with regular spelling patterns and with only the most basic morphemic variations.

Frequency of usage, word length, sound/spelling correspondence and morphemic markers are the main lexical correlates of spelling difficulty.

The cognitive demands imposed by spelling vary with age and with attainment level; they are also a function of different teaching approaches, cognitive profiles and learning styles. For most learners, the more reading and writing that is done, the more spelling improves, largely as a function of print exposure (Cunningham & Stanovich, 1991). Teachers have generally found it necessary to send spelling lists home each week or each night in order to supplement the learning which takes place incidentally through reading and writing. It seems clear that, if little writing is done in school and there is no homework which directs attention to spelling, spelling is unlikely to improve.

Detection and recall of spelling patterns, phonological processing, working memory and the programming of rapid motor output are the main cognitive functions involved in spelling. In good spellers these functions have become automatic and do not interfere significantly with the thinking and feeling aspects of writing.

A great deal of word-specific knowledge has to be accumulated in order to cope with English spelling, and this is a function of interest and application as well as of lexical and cognitive processing variables. When motivation is lacking and writing becomes a chore, ways have to be found of increasing the amount of time spent using and thinking about words and their spellings if the cycle of failure, task avoidance and increasingly negative attitude is to be broken.

Brown (1991) proposed a parsimonious "direct encoding" model of word recognition which he also applied to spelling and to deep, surface and phonological dyslexia. The model relies heavily on a phonological buffer which operates with a hierarchy of perceptual units, mediating both word-specific and intra-word pattern information. Brown's model has intuitive appeal, since spelling proceeds from the spoken word to the written, with visual feedback coming from the written word for a decision as to whether it "looks right".

A similar model and related cognitive psychological research guided the writer when he devised the *ACE Spelling Dictionary*. Users of the dictionary are required to access words on the basis of phonological knowledge, thereby priming the orthographic buffer for recognition of the word. In designing the ACE dictionary, care was taken to structure the page layout so that in searching for a target word, incidental learning of perceptual units or patterns is likely to take place. Morphemic markers are also made perceptually salient. This spelling dictionary is designed to develop phonological awareness as well as word-specific and metalinguistic knowledge, especially when used in conjunction with the *ACE Spelling Activities* (Moseley & Singleton, 1993). "Aurally Coded English" is compatible with all ways of learning spellings which are supported by research evidence, as well as with "process writing" in which spelling is seen as an incidental "clerical" procedure which should not interfere with the construction of meaning. Classroom studies with the ACE dictionary will be described in the final section of this chapter.

SOME CHARACTERISTICS OF GOOD AND POOR SPELLERS

Spelling is not a reliable index of general intelligence, as dyslexics with specific spelling problems often remind us. Crawford (1992) found that spelling test scores and verbal intelligence had only 21% of variance in common and still lower correlation coefficients have been reported in the literature for younger children (Bannatyne & Wichiarajote, 1969) and for retarded readers (Lyle, 1969). In a study of 1254 8–9-year-olds (Moseley, 1972) the writer obtained a Pearson r of 0.45 between receptive vocabulary and spelling. Yet a good speller can spell a great many words, irrespective of spelling regularity and even if a word's meaning is not fully understood. Good spellers can spell new words by analogy, applying a wide range of linguistic principles some of which they may have acquired through using dictionaries. They also make use of word-specific knowledge, which they acquire not only through the application of intelligence but in habitual and repetitive ways.

Logan, Olson and Lindsey (1989) found that champion spellers were intrinsically motivated and highly disciplined, feeling in control of their own learning. They had been interested in words from a very early age and made regular use of dictionaries. They reported making use of visual memory and writing and saying words aloud in order to learn spellings. At undergraduate level Ormrod and Jenkins (1989) found that saying words with exaggerated pronunciation to suit the spelling was an effective learning strategy, while Kreiner and Gough (1990) found that good spellers make use of both rule-based and word-specific information.

Poor spellers typically have limited phonological awareness and working memory skills (Stage & Wagner, 1992), with phonemic segmentation often being a core weakness (Holligan & Johnston, 1991; Rohl & Tunmer, 1988). Batchelor, Kixmiller and Dean (1990) found in their study of 1347 learning disabled children that where reading and spelling problems coexisted, a range of cognitive and motor deficits accompanied those problems, whereas spelling difficulty on its own was often associated with poor visual sequencing.

Levy and Hobbes (1989) studied 51 boys aged 5–11 years who had attention and conduct problems and found that spelling and a vigilance measure were significantly related to the diagnosis of attention deficit disorder with hyperactivity.

Many more boys than girls have problems with spelling and with punctuation (Moseley, 1972, 1974). In a population of 1254 8–9-year-olds in 16 schools there were twice as many boys as girls with spelling quotients of 75 or less, and among those with average or above scores on the English Picture Vocabulary Test (Brimer & Dunn, 1962) five times as many boys as girls were poor spellers.

POSSIBLE CONSEQUENCES OF POOR SPELLING

Poor spellers react in different ways to their difficulties, but attempts to avoid failure are common.

In secondary schools, pupils are introduced to a greatly expanded technical vocabulary in most subject areas (except English) and are frequently provided with handouts and material to be copied. Yet when they do write their own notes, shorter accounts with more repetition and a restricted vocabulary range are more likely to be produced by the weaker spellers.

Moseley (1989a) found that both poor spellers and diagnosed dyslexics differed significantly from good spellers at age 13–15 on a number of quantitative indices. In free writing they:

Used fewer words outside a core 500-word vocabulary
Used more short words
Used more regularly spelled words
Avoided using common hard-to-spell words
Found ways of repeating words in order to "play safe"

Houck and Billingsley (1989) reported similar results concerning word length in a comparison of learning disabled and normally achieving pupils across three grade levels.

Crawford (1992) analysed work produced in Biology and Geography lessons by 51 12–13-year-olds and her data showed that both spelling test scores and spelling error rates were significantly correlated with length of output and with type/token ratio measures. A further finding was that children who thought of themselves as poor writers tended to use fewer words outside a core 500-word vocabulary, even when verbal intelligence was held constant (partial $r = 0.36$, $p < 0.01$).

Poor spelling probably has adverse educational consequences for substantial numbers of pupils, since the belief that good spelling is the mark of the intellectually able and well educated is widespread. Dutter (1986) and Drozda-Sendkowska (1986) found that spelling is a major determinant of composition evaluation by French and by Polish teachers. Inaccurate spelling triggers a heightened sensitivity to other weaknesses in composition. If this happens not only at school but in public examinations, many pupils must be failing to realize their educational potential. The substantial sex difference in the incidence of spelling problems may partly account for the fact that girls achieve much better results than boys in GCSE English. Figures published by the NEA (1992) show that for every seven boys who achieve A–C grades in English Language there are 10 girls.

Apart from the educational implications, there are undoubtedly emotional and social consequences of being "hopeless at spelling". As Crawford found, poor spelling is associated with a poor concept of the self as a writer and it is interesting to read that peer counselling on self-image, locus of control and spelling led to improved spelling, reading and handwriting as well as producing some attitudinal and social gains (James *et al.*, 1991).

As genetic, social and environmental influences interact throughout development, it is implausible to think of educational and social correlates of spelling problems as being always secondary. Stevenson and Fredman's (1990) analysis of data relating to 550 twins aged 13 years showed that genetic factors could explain more than half of the spelling variance, but that maternal criticism was a substantial independent factor. They speculated that children with depressed mothers may acquire attentional deficits. If Stevenson and Fredman are right, the spelling teacher must be careful not to take on the role of the critical mother figure! As one pupil put it, "I am a better speller than I was last year because I haven't got a teacher shouting at me because I missed a letter out in a word in a spelling test".

COGNITIVE CORRELATES OF SPELLING

Cataldo and Ellis (1988), Huxford, Terrell and Bradley (1991) and Foorman *et al.* (1991) carried out separate longitudinal studies which support the view that young children first develop phonological segmentation skills for spelling and then apply segmentation to reading.

The first segmentation skill to develop is the division of a short word into onset and rhyme, but current instructional methods typically deal with single letters rather than with letter strings representing rhymes (or word endings). Children with efficient working memory skills can usually learn by trial and error how to process words in increasingly larger chunks which have some regularity and predictability. However, the slower and less confident will be stuck with a rudimentary letter-by-letter "phonic" approach to spelling, accompanied by the kind of logographic skills which, according to Wimmer and Hummer (1990), are not needed in Germany.

Learning about letter shapes and their sequential arrangement involves some visuomotor activity and is aided by writing the letters rather than typing them or making up words with letter tiles (Cunningham & Stanovich, 1990). In time children come to see and write as units linguistic features of longer and irregular words such as double consonants, consonant cluster onsets, rhyme endings, consonant and vowel digraphs, morphological word endings, roots, syllables and syllable strings. The integration of phonological and visuomotor skills is required here. This is the stage at which children use analogies in their spelling and word recognition, based on familiar letter and word patterns.

The part played by pattern detection, visualization and generation in reading and spelling has not been clearly established by research. Spelling is often said to depend on visual memory or visualization, but we know little about the form in which information is transmitted from the retina to those parts of the left medial extrastriate cortex which are activated by both words and pseudowords which obey English spelling rules (Petersen *et al.*, 1990).

It was to investigate the visuospatial correlates of spelling that the writer devised the POP Spatial Test (Moseley, 1976) and carried out a large-scale study involving 650 boys and 604 girls aged 8–9 years. The POP task is to form a simple pattern by joining up dots and then to find and make an identical pattern in a matrix of dots alongside the model (see Figure 22.1). Many possibilities for making shape, size and orientation errors are available and error categories can be scored separately. The task resembles spelling in that the shapes are made from up to four dots and because it is best to imagine each pattern as a whole before drawing it on the page. The results reported below have not been published previously and include some new analyses of spelling errors in relation to spatial test scores.

The following tests were given to all pupils in the year group (mean CA 9 years, 3 months):

Schonell Spelling Test B (Schonell & Schonell, 1950) English Picture Vocabulary Test POP Spatial Test

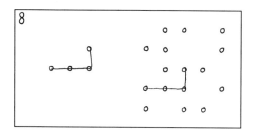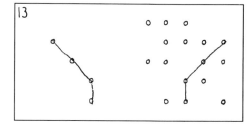

FIGURE 22.1   Two completed POP spatial test items: No. 8 correct and No. 13 showing a L/R mirror image.

Boys and girls differed in overall levels of spelling by as much as 11 months, but as the correlation coefficients between the three variables did not differ significantly by sex, the population was initially treated as a whole. Spelling and vocabulary shared 20% of variance ($r = 0.45$) and spelling and spatial visualization 24% of variance ($r = 0.49$). The multiple r between spelling and the other two test variables accounted for 32% of the variance ($r = 0.57$).

Partial correlation coefficients were computed in order to examine the relationship between spatial visualization and spelling when linguistic measures were held constant. For the population as a whole, 15% of variance was found to be shared when this was done (partial $r = 0.39$). For a subsample of 108 pupils who were seen individually and who were also given a phoneme-blending test (Moseley, 1976), an identical partial r was obtained when both vocabulary and phoneme-blending were held constant.

In order to further elucidate the nature of the association between spelling and spatial visualization at this age level, the POP scores of retarded and advanced spellers (exactly matched on vocabulary scores) were compared. There were 18 boys and 18 girls, all with vocabulary scores in the range 86–100. The retarded spellers had spelling quotients of 75 or less and the advanced spellers had quotients of 110 or more. As expected, the advanced spellers obtained significantly higher POP scores ($t = 3.85$, $p < 0.005$ on a two-tailed test). They were also found to be significantly less prone to mirror-image reversals of the type illustrated in Figure 22.1 ($t = 2.43$, $p < 0.02$, two-tailed).

Separate analyses by sex were then carried out on the above subgroups, since principal component analyses of POP error scores had yielded sex differences. For boys the retarded and advanced spellers were found to differ at the < 0.001 level on a principal component error score which had a high loading on simplification (omission of elements). For girls the two groups differed at the < 0.05 level on a slightly different component, loading on simplification and change of shape.

Having established that poor spellers are likely to make mirror-image, simplification and shape-change errors when visualizing and reproducing simple figures, further comparisons were made in order to see whether particular types of spelling error were associated with spatial visualization. The first 10 misspelled words on the Schonell scripts were scored for letter-shape and letter-order reversals, for upper-case insertions and for misrepresentation of consonant and vowel graphemes. The sample size was larger on this occasion (33 retarded spellers and 36 advanced spellers), as the EPVT vocabulary matching requirement was less stringent (scores in the range 93–107). What emerged was that among the retarded spellers there was a significant tendency for high POP scores to be associated with a higher level of accuracy in spelling consonants than in spelling vowels ($r = 0.49$, $p < 0.01$), while the reverse tendency applied among the advanced spellers ($r = 0.36$, $p < 0.05$). In the case of the good spellers, POP scores were negatively correlated with vowel errors ($r = 0.25$, NS) and positively correlated with consonant errors ($r = 0.35$, $p < 0.05$).

To summarize, it appears that at lower spelling ages (5–7 years) skills of visual analysis and synthesis are applied mainly to consonants, which have to be represented in correct orientation and sequence. Those who are good at representing shapes in correct orientation without omitting parts tend also to be able to apply similar skills in avoiding consonant spelling errors. At higher spelling ages (9–11 years) visual analysis and synthesis may play a part in the spelling of vowel graphemes, but at the same time those who are good at visualizing shapes tend to make more consonant errors in their spelling than those who are less competent spatially.

TEACHING AND LEARNING: MORE OR LESS EFFECTIVE?

Spelling instruction has often been criticized on the grounds that studying lists of words and learning about decontextualized rules are meaningless activities which do little to enhance the quality of creative or other purposive writing. The reactions to this have had one or more of three main aims: (a) to improve traditional approaches, (b) to limit teacher input to what arises naturally through the use of process writing and invented spelling and (c) to facilitate self-correction by means of dictionaries and spellcheckers. In different ways these orientations can each provide engaged learning time during which children can improve their understanding of the orthographic system and can receive feedback on their performance. Positive results have been reported in the literature for approaches to intervention as diverse as direct instruction (Gersten, Keating & Becker, 1988; Lum & Morton, 1984), simultaneous oral spelling (Prior, Frye & Fletcher, 1987; Thomson, 1991) and invented spelling (Cannella, 1991; Clarke, 1988).

Negative results can also be found in the literature, as in Harmes' (1986) evaluation of Gillingham tutorial input with 224 primary and secondary students and a comparison of "whole language" and traditional instruction classrooms by Klesius, Griffith and Zielonka (1991). In such cases one can only speculate about such factors as the pace and motivational value of the programme, the enthusiasm of the teachers and the productivity of the pupils. It is worth noting that traditional and structured approaches may, but need not always inhibit the exploration and enjoyment of writing, while process writing may degenerate into a lax acceptance of children's offerings with insufficient immediate, focused and constructive feedback.

In various combinations the following features can and have been built into innovative projects in the attempt to improve the teaching and learning of spelling:

Individualization (e.g. by developing personal spelling lists)
An emphasis on learning commonly used words
Pupil choice (e.g. of words or of learning strategy)
Increased repetition (e.g. by over-correction or by using games)
Taking some of the tedium out of correcting and learning spellings
Challenge (e.g. demonstrating that "hard" words can be learnt)
Reducing interference (e.g. by learning fewer words)
A multisensory approach or an emphasis on certain modalities
Adjusting learning method to cognitive profile and/or learning style
Presenting and associating words with cues
Encouraging pupils to apply spelling rules
Teaching for generalization (e.g. finding and using similar words)
Providing immediate feedback (e.g. from dictionaries or spellcheckers)
Emphasizing proof-reading skills

Making pupils more aware of error categories
Developing metalinguistic knowledge
Use of competition
Use of social interaction, counselling and cooperative learning

It would be futile to try to obtain a "best buy" from such an extensive list. Teachers can, however, select gift-packs of apparently reliable products and use them as in organic farming on a planned policy of "crop rotation". This approach would avoid the boredom of going through one set of word lists for years on end and might also profitably include some periods of letting the land lie fallow!

Learning Spellings

The idea of learning spellings for regular (often weekly) tests should not be rejected, as there is research evidence which supports the practice and demonstrates that generalization to creative writing can be achieved (e.g. Diaz, McLaughlin & Williams, 1990; Lumley, 1992; Pratt-Struthers, Struthers & Williams, 1983; Watt & Topping, 1993).

Gettinger (1984) provided evidence from well-controlled studies to support the use of reduced unit size, distributed practice and review and training for transfer when working with primary-aged learning disabled students. In a subsequent study (Gettinger, 1985), she added some responsibility for self-directed learning to the experimental procedures. She also evaluated the effect of adding cues (circling a misspelled part of a word in red) to the learning routines and found that student-directed learning with cues was an effective combination. Michael (1986) found that pupils learned as well if not better with self-selected spelling lists as with those supplied by the teacher, and Kapadia and Fantuzzo (1988) found that children with moderate learning difficulties learned to spell more effectively with self-administered spelling tests and reinforcement than with teacher-administered procedures. At the same time, Topping, Scoble and Oxley (1988) combined many desirable features in "cued spelling", including reduced unit size, modelling of learning procedures, choice of words and cues, immediate feedback and praise, regular and frequent practice, fluency-building and testing for mastery. Brierley *et al.* (1989) reported favourably on a study in which cued spelling was used on a class-wide paired learning basis in three mixed ability classes of 9–10-year-olds. Mastery review scores of the words learned yielded average scores of 80%, and 84% of the children felt that they were better spellers after the 6-week intervention. Fenton (1990) also reported high levels of enthusiasm when he set up a modified cued spelling project in his class, made visually stimulating by using pizza slices and turtle shells to cover words when writing from memory. Watt and Topping (1993) achieved mean progress rates on the Vernon test of 2.1 and 3.4 months per month with two groups of 8–9-year-old pupils over 16.5 weeks. The first group of 10 pupils used cued spelling with parent tutors and the second group ($N=4$) with peer tutors. Both groups did much better than a rather ill-matched comparison group and cued spelling pupils wrote longer passages with fewer spelling errors at the end of the project.

Lumley (1992) set up a paired learning intervention for the nine most competent writers in her class of 7–8-year-olds. This involved selecting and writing three words each day from appropriate lists, telling your partner why you had chosen them, adding visual cues to the words so as to aid memory, and learning them well enough to be able to write all three on demand. Weekly tests were completed between partners which showed success rates of between 75% and 96%. All children were including words of up to nine letters in their chosen study sets, with 63% of the words having six or more letters. In free writing produced in similar conditions and of a similar genre there was an overall reduction in spelling mistakes of 32% at the end of the 6-week project.

In both cued spelling and Lumley's approach the interaction between pupils goes beyond checking each other's spelling. For example, Lumley's pupils chose the words to include on learning lists, grouped some of them by meaning and others by spelling pattern, and suggested ways of writing a word so as to make it easier to learn. This discussion between pupils was shown to be important by van Oudenhoven, Wiersma and van Yperen (1987), who compared three instructional methods in a field experiment involving 14 primary schools. Cooperative working in pairs (checking each other's work and discussing the mistakes) was more effective than either individual exercises or such exercises with a partner checking the work in improving the spelling of low achievers.

Crawford (1992) used an A–B–A design over three 6 week periods with two classes of 11–12-year-olds who were above average in cognitive ability (mean verbal IQ 110) and in spelling (mean Young spelling age 12 years, 11 months). Teachers had produced a book containing subject-specific word lists and pupils were encouraged to use it in all subject areas if they needed to check spellings. In the first class the use of this word book constituted the intervention, while in the second class the book was in use throughout and during the intervention phase a weekly learning task was carried out as well. Pupils chose 10 words from the lists to learn each week and were encouraged to copy the words, to identify, highlight and pronounce "tricky parts", with eyes closed to finger-write and say the letter names of "tricky parts", then to write the whole word, first with eyes closed and then using the "look—cover—write—check" routine. Rewards in the form of house points were given for success in learning the words, but there was no check on whether the written guidelines for learning the words had in fact been followed. For both groups the Young Parallel Spelling Tests provided pre- and posttest measures and for subsamples of the poorest spellers writing and spelling performance in Geography and Biology assignments was monitored throughout using quantitative measures of vocabulary range, word length, spelling difficulty and spelling accuracy.

It was found that providing the first class with the subject-specific word book made no difference either to their spelling or to the performance of the poor spellers in their written assignments. However, the second class did make substantial gains on the Young Test (10 months in 4 months), although again there was no evidence of improvement in the written assignments undertaken. The gains in spelling test performance may have been due to the longer period during which the word book was in use or to the weekly learning tasks or to the use of rewards (or to any combination of these). The lack of transfer to spelling in written assignments points to the need to train for such transfer and to reward it when it occurs. In this study there was no planned social interaction either collaborative or competitive and better results might have been obtained had the pupils been more directly involved in compiling the word books, in discussing their contents and monitoring and reflecting on their own learning.

The last study to be described in this section was carried out between October 1992 and March 1993 with pupils in the age range 8–11 years. The intervention was planned by the writer and the learning support teacher of the school concerned. This was a fee-paying girls' day school with class sizes in the range of 13–18 pupils. The ability range was wide, with 61 of the girls in the study having a mean receptive vocabulary score somewhat below average on the admittedly dated English Picture Vocabulary Test (Brimer & Dunn, 1962). Standards of spelling at the start of the project were already high, with none of the girls scoring below an 8-year level. All pupils in five classes participated in the two-term intervention, which was designed as a field trial of daily learning routines using word lists derived from children's writing and teacher nomination for cross-curricular relevance. Except for one class which used the look—cover—write—check procedure, all pupils were shown how to: study—copy—check—highlight—learn. Each girl learned 16–24 words a week, working systematically through one of five graded lists which were allocated according to performance on a pretest. Three classes were assigned specific learning methods, while two were given a choice from the following list:

1. Say the word to suit the spelling
2. Trace and say
3. "Sky-writing"
4. Visualize word and count letters
5. Mnemonic (memory link)
6. Spelling pattern
7. Focus on tricky part(s)
8. Rhyming word

Prior to the project, teachers had regularly provided for their classes lists of spellings to be learned at home, but (except for the one teacher who had already introduced look—cover—write—check) had not discussed ways of learning the words. What was new was not only the idea of differentiated lists (which was intended as a means of providing equal opportunities for successful learning for all pupils), but the idea that the girls should take responsibility for choosing methods of learning which worked for them. One class continued to use look—cover—write—check to provide some form of control, although after the first term this class also increasingly made use of the wider choice of learning routines. Rewards in the form of house points and an entry in the school's *Excellent Book* were available for those who on three occasions obtained full marks on the weekly differentiated tests.

The overall results of the intervention were highly positive, and the assessment tools used allowed many informative analyses to be carried out. The overall mean gain in Vernon spelling age (shown in Figure 22.2) was 19 months over a period of 5 months. This represents an increase from a mean standard score of 108 (SD 14) to 116 (SD 14) and a progress rate of 3.7 months per month. The mean progress rates of different classes varied between 2.2 and 5.6 months per month, and it is perhaps significant that

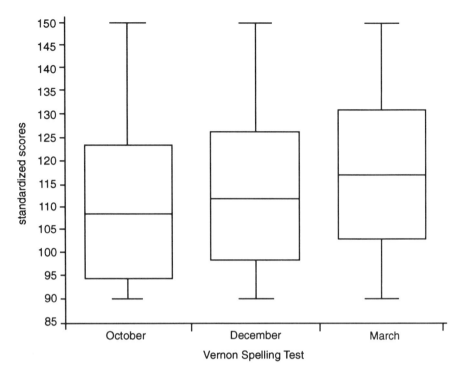

FIGURE 22.2 Box-and-whisker plots (Range and Mean ± SD) showing the progress in spelling of 64 8–11-year-old girls over two terms.

the best class result was obtained by the only teacher who used daily tests to monitor learning. The mean progress rate of the look—cover—write—check class was 3.1 months per months.

The project was largely successful in enabling all pupils to make roughly equivalent gains, irrespective of initial attainment levels. Pearson r coefficients of correlation between initial Vernon scores and gain scores were as follows for the five classes: 0.05, 0.29, 0.69 ($p < 0.05$), 0.05, 0.07. The one class where a significant relationship between initial score and gain score was found was the one where daily tests were used. The weaker spellers certainly made good progress, but the most competent did exceptionally well, four of them improving by more than 2 years.

In two parallel classes of 9–10-year-olds, pupils were allocated at random to the use of learning strategies with a verbal emphasis (1 and 5) or with a visual emphasis (4) and a special version of 7. Both types of strategy were effective, with the visual emphasis having an overall (but statistically insignificant) advantage and proving especially helpful to those who at the start were better at spelling irregular than regular words on the Boder Test (Boder & Jarrico, 1982). During the first term, however, the verbal strategies when used by those were better at spelling regular than irregular words proved to have a statistically significant advantage. The verbal strategies were most effective with those having a verbal rather than a visuospatial cognitive bias, as measured by a ratio score derived from the English Picture Vocabulary and the POP

Spatial Tests. Among eight girls using the verbal strategies, good progress in spelling age was associated with verbal cognitive bias ($r = 0.74$, $p < 0.05$).

Two other classes were given a choice of the strategies 1–7 as listed above. These were demonstrated, practised and discussed with the learning support teacher in two lessons. The girls recorded their strategy choices, choosing between one and four methods. For the younger class (8–9-year-olds with a mean spelling level of 11 years) the two most popular strategies were 7 and 3, focusing on tricky parts and "skywriting". For the older class (10–11-year-olds with a mean spelling level of 11 years, 9 months), the most popular choices were (1) and (5), saying the word to suit the spelling and using mnemonics. For whatever reason, there was a preference among the younger pupils for visually based and mixed strategies and among the older ones for strategies with a verbal emphasis. The mnemonics option was not chosen at all by the younger children; among the older ones it was chosen by all of the pupils with spelling scores below chronological age but significantly less often by the better spellers (chi-square 5.82, $p < 0.02$). In the event, three of the eight girls who made an initial choice to use mnemonics admitted to using it no longer by the end of the first term. Those who used it did just as well if not better than those who did not, but with small numbers no firm conclusion can be drawn. However, the use of predominantly verbal strategies in the older class certainly produced worthwhile gains, with an average progress rate of 4.0 months per month being recorded.

One interesting finding emerged which may have important pedagogical implications if replicated. The verbal/spatial cognitive bias measure was found to be significantly related to outcome across all class groups ($r = 0.31$, $p < 0.02$ between verbal bias and spelling gains for 55 girls). When this relationship was examined separately for stronger and weaker spellers (scoring below and above spelling age 11 years respectively), it was very clear for the weaker spellers ($r = 0.78$, $p < 0.0001$) but not for the stronger spellers ($r = 0.15$, NS). In the case of the weaker spellers ($N = 23$), spelling progress was positively associated with receptive vocabulary ($r = 0.53$, $p < 0.01$) and negatively associated with spatial visualization ($r = -0.60$, $p < 0.002$). Verbal cognitive bias was also found to be significantly associated with good progress in spelling when 23 girls who were (for the sample studied) better at spelling regular than irregular words were considered separately ($r = 0.55$, $p < 0.005$). No such result obtained when 31 girls who were relatively good at spelling irregular words were considered. However, as the proportion of irregular words spelled correctly increased with Vernon spelling age ($r = 0.48$, $p < 0.0001$), the latter group were in fact stronger spellers, with a mean initial score 20 months in advance of those who had relative difficulty with irregular words. Put more simply, it appears that to progress beyond a spelling age of 11 years it is necessary to master irregularly spelled words, and it is easier to do so if you have a good vocabulary and relatively weak spatial visualization skills.

A tentative interpretation is that pupils who are spatially strong may think they can acquire spellings just by taking a quick look at words. In fact, it is probably necessary for them to employ some analytic strategies, applying stored information about linguistic predictability to word parts and finding some way to store the word-specific knowledge required for later recall. This is just what the strategies on offer were designed to achieve, especially (1)—say the word to suit the spelling—and (7)—focus on trickly parts.

If there is a subgroup of relatively poor spellers who have great difficulty with irregular words and who are better at spatial visualization than verbal tasks, they may well share the characteristics of Rourke's subytype 4 (DeLuca, Rourke & Del Doto, 1991). This subgroup had intact reading skills, poor spelling and arithmetic, impulsive behaviour and poor planning and study skills. They were fast at speeded eye–hand coordination tasks, but poor in completing a visual–spatial array on the basis of numerical cues and poor at reproducing visual sequences. They also showed symptoms of depression, lacked verbal fluency, participated little socially and had low tolerance for frustration. It is far from clear how such a constellation of characteristics may be formed, but Feshbach and Feshbach (1987) reported some relevant findings. They found that for 8–9-year-old girls, teacher ratings of empathy, depressive affectivity and aggression predicted reading and spelling attainment 2 years later.

It is highly unlikely that a subgroup of poor spellers with the above characteristics could be identified simply on the basis of an analysis of misspellings. In the study described above, error scores for phonetic accuracy and for relative success with regular and irregular words did not predict spelling gains. Moreover, the ratio of phonetically acceptable to non-phonetic errors was significantly related to spelling age ($r = 0.37$, $p < 0.01$) but not to spelling gains and not independently to the cognitive variables.

Process Writing

There is widespread agreement that teachers who wish to improve the quality of written expression should respond positively and constructively to content rather than negatively and destructively to surface linguistic errors. Yet the habit that many teachers find hard to drop is that of having children write words which are left uncorrected. In the past many teachers greatly reduced the amount of writing young children could do, by writing sentences for them to copy, by having them wait in a queue for the spelling of a single word or by insisting that they should confine themselves to the words in their "Breakthrough" folders. So it is not surprising to find that infant children who are treated as emerging authors respond with more enthusiasm than they did under traditional regimes (Hall, 1989).

The use of invented spelling in the early stages of literacy acquisition has much to commend it in terms of freeing children to write with confidence, to practise letter formation and to explore the alphabetic system. They can understandably feel pride in owning and being in control of what they write. There is also some evidence that word recognition improves as a result. Clarke found that children in invented spelling classrooms could decode regularly spelled words and could recognize high-frequency irregular words better than those in "traditional" classrooms, even though the same basal reading scheme and supplementary phonics programme was used by all the teachers. It is likely that by starting with the spoken word and trying to construct a spelling, children analyse the sound structure of the word and develop their phonemic awareness. This is just the kind of skill which is systematically developed under teacher guidance in the Reading Recovery Programme (Clay, 1979). It is also likely that, as Clay (1975) argued, writing "fosters the development of self-direction in locating, exploring and producing appropriate analysis of printed forms".

Advocates of invented spelling often refuse to tell children how to spell words, but this may be an extreme position and it is perhaps a warning signal that spelling accuracy in the writing samples in Clarke's study fell from a mean of 66% in November to 58% in March. The long-term effects of these early explorations in writing are not known, nor is it clear how best to introduce young children to simple dictionaries and spell-checkers. What does seem to be true is that a *lassez-faire* approach is not the answer. Many English teachers neglected the formal language instruction over the seventies and early eighties and left pupils feeling let down and confused (Austin-Ward, 1986). Students about to enter FE colleges felt that English teachers had contradictory and conflicting attitudes towards grammar, spelling and "correctness".

Bos (1988) found that the process writing approach with older learning disabled pupils did not improve their spelling. In a resource room setting, 14 students aged 9–11 gained in thematic maturity, vocabulary and coherence of writing but made only minimal gains in spelling over a 2-year period. It appears that compiling personal spelling lists and consulting a peer "expert" are ineffective on their own as means of tackling spelling problems. There is here a case for the use of more powerful techniques, such as word-processing (McLurg & Kasakow, 1989) or direct instruction. Working with a large sample of 450 8–9-year-olds, Stevens *et al.* (1987) successfully combined process writing and peer conferences with direct instruction and team practice on language mechanics activities. In this case the "cooperative integrated reading and composition" (CIRC) pupils outperformed controls on reading, spelling, language and writing sample measures.

Using a Spelling Dictionary

Moseley (1988) devised a "Precision Spelling" course for dyslexic and other poor spellers. This was a multi-faceted course in which the *ACE Spelling Dictionary* played an important part. The course consisted of five weekly sessions in which students worked in groups of four with two tutors and two computers. A piece of free writing was prepared for each session and daily spelling activities with and without the ACE dictionary were carried out for at least 10 minutes each day, as agreed in a contract. The writing was valued primarily for its content and the spelling activities were subsequently presented in a positive way through negotiated target-setting.

Fluent use of the *ACE Spelling Dictionary* was developed in the first 2 weeks and the dictionary was then used at home to check spellings in written work. Feedback and guidance were provided to improve proof-reading for spelling errors. A final word-processed version of each piece of writing was prepared.

A personal list of words the writer would like to be able to spell correctly was compiled and a daily learning routine with four words at a time was set up after demonstration and practice. This involved identifying "tricky parts", saying the word so as to fit the spelling, saying the alphabet names of the tricky part/s, visualization and writing with eyes closed and a look—cover—write—check procedure which was applied first to a single word, then to pairs and finally to the set of four words.

Students were also made aware of some rules and spelling patterns, using ideas which have since been incorporated into the ACE Spelling Activities (Moseley & Singleton, 1993). Feedback on progress was provided and suggestions were made for further use of the ACE dictionary and of other books, learning packages, games and computer software.

The first seven students to take the Precision Spelling course made substantial gains in terms of the quantity and quality of their writing. On the Vernon Graded Word Spelling Test (Vernon, 1977), the mean gain was 16 months in 5 weeks.

In a classroom evaluation of the *ACE Spelling Dictionary* (Moseley, 1989b), 10–11-year-old pupils drafted and proof-read all their written work for two terms, using the ACE dictionary to look up suspect spellings before rewriting. It was found that spelling improved at the rate of 1.7 months per month and word recognition at the rate of 2.3 months per month over this period. The five poorest spellers improved at the rate of 3.8 months per month and the five poorest readers at the rate of 3.5 months per month. The quantity of writing produced for similar assignments increased by 41% in the first term. Over the two terms there was a 15% increase in the use of vocabulary outside a basic 500-word list ($p < 0.01$), a 43% increase in the use of hard-to-spell words ($p < 0.02$) and a reduction of 13% in the use of common regularly spelled words ($p < 0.02$). As the children were largely autonomous in their use of the spelling dictionary for correcting their spellings, the teacher was able to use one-to-one conferencing time for discussion of the content and structure of the writing.

Similarly encouraging results were obtained by Hancock (1992), who, as a trainee teacher, visited a primary school 11 times over the summer and autumn terms to work with a mixed-ability group of six 10–11-year-olds. Each visit lasted between 30 and 40 minutes. The children were withdrawn from class to work with the ACE dictionary. They kept records of words found, using a list of 300 commonly misspelled words and a current topic vocabulary list. They also chose six words per week to look up in the dictionary and then to learn using the look—cover—write—check method.

Samples of similar-genre writing were taken before and after the intervention. These showed significant improvements in overall quality (as judged "blind" by an independent evaluator), in spelling (a 50% reduction in error rate), in vocabulary range, in the avoidance of repetition and in the use of longer words. Diary accounts and interviews confirmed the impression of increasing confidence about writing and spelling. Hancock found that all children improved on the criterion measures after the ACE dictionary was introduced and "it was not necessarily the good readers and/or spellers who readily adapted to using the ACE dictionary". One boy with a poor self-image and a negative attitude towards spelling "was extremely enthusiastic to succeed . . . and . . . his small and frequent achievements . . . in areas such as spelling, vocabulary extension and quality of writing . . . did much to boost his confidence and self-esteem". Figure 22.3 illustrates the use of words of nine or more characters in the pre- and posttest writing samples.

Although there were no control groups in any of the above three studies, the amount of improvement greatly exceeded what one would expect to find in response to normal classroom instruction. It is interesting that the weaker spellers made substantial gains, which suggests that the additional print exposure and feedback they received through using the spelling dictionary may even in some cases have produced a reversed "Matthew effect". In the second study the intervention did not involve the regular learning of spellings for tests, but relied on incidental learning and informal help from

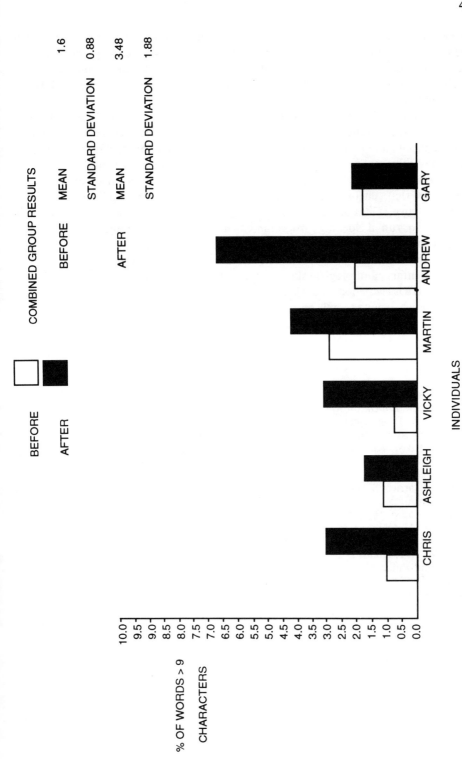

FIGURE 22.3 The use of longer words in the free-writing samples of six pupils before and after work with the *Ace Spelling Dictionary*.

other pupils through the process of checking spellings and redrafting. One is reminded of Jacoby's (Jacoby & Hollingshead, 1990) finding (with undergraduates) that reading correctly and incorrectly spelled words influenced later spelling accuracy for those words, while copying correctly spelled words led to better and faster subsequent spelling.

In all three studies the *ACE Spelling Dictionary* was seen not as an end in itself, but as an adjunct to the process of writing. Aiming to achieve accurate spelling and thinking about sound and spelling units within words need not interfere with creative aspects of writing; indeed, many pupils said that they became more confident as writers after working with the *ACE Spelling Dictionary*. Using a rather different approach, albeit one that encouraged children to discover patterns of sound–symbol correspondence, Cunningham and Cunningham (1992) also concluded that it is beneficial to run a spelling programme which emphasizes phonemic awareness alongside process writing. This writer is working on a simplified version of the ACE system which will allow 5–7-year-olds to access a substantial lexicon on the basis of very rudimentary phonological skills. If from the start children are in control of their spelling, there is every hope that standards of writing will improve and that the richness of the English language will be more widely shared and enjoyed.

REFERENCES

Austin-Ward, B. (1986). English, English teaching and English teachers: the perceptions of 16-year-olds. *Education Research*, **28**(1), 32–42.

Bannatyne, A. D. & Wichiarajote, P. (1969). Relationships between written spelling, motor functioning and sequencing skills. *Journal of Learning Disabilities*, **2**(1), 1–4.

Batchelor, E. S., Kixmiller, J. S. & Dean, R. S. (1990). Neuropsychological aspects of reading and spelling performance in children with learning disabilities. *Developmental Neuropsychology*, **6**(3), 183–192.

Boder, E. & Jarrico, S. (1982). *The Boder Test of Reading–Spelling Patterns*. New York: Grune and Stratton.

Bos, C. S. (1988). Process-oriented writing. *Exceptional Children*, **56**(4), 521–527.

Brierley, M., Hutchinson, P., Topping, K. & Walker, C. (1989). Reciprocal peer tutored cued spelling with ten year olds. *Paired Learning*, **5**, 136–140.

Brimer, M. A. & Dunn, L. M. (1962). *English Picture Vocabulary Tests*. Bristol: Education Evaluation Enterprises.

Brown, P. (1991). DEREK: the direct encoding routine for evoking knowledge. In D. Besner & G. W. Humphries (Eds), *Basic Processes in Reading*. Hove and London: LEA, pp. 104–147.

Cannella, G. S. (1991). Effects of social interaction on the creation of a sound/symbol system by kindergarten children. *Child Study Journal*, **21**(2), 117–133.

Cataldo, S. & Ellis, N. C. (1988). Interactions in the development of spelling, reading and phonological skills. *Journal of Research in Reading*, **11**(2), 86–109.

Clarke, L. K. (1988). Invented versus traditional spelling in first graders' writing: effect on learning to spell and read. *Research in the Teaching of English*, **22**, 281–309.

Clay, M. M. (1975). *What Did I Write? Beginning Writing Behaviour*. Auckland: Heinemann.

Clay, M. M. (1979). *The Early Detection of Reading Difficulties*. Auckland: Heinemann.

Crawford, J. (1992). *An investigation into the relationship between spelling competence, self concept as a writer and the quality of the writing product*. MSc dissertation. University of Newcastle-upon-Tyne.

Cunningham, A. E. & Stanovich, K. E. (1990). Early spelling acquisition: writing beats the computer. *Journal of Educational Psychology*, **82**(1), 159–162.

Cunningham, A. E. & Stanovich, K. E. (1991). Tracking the unique effects of print exposure in children: associations with vocabulary, general knowledge and spelling. *Journal of Educational Psychology*, **83**(2), 264–274.

Cunningham, P. & Cunningham, J. W. (1992). Making words: enhancing the inverted spelling–decoding connection. *The Reading Teacher*, **46**(2), 106–115.

DeLuca, J. W., Rourke, B. P. & Del Dotto, J. E. (1991). Subtypes of arithmetic-disabled children: cognitive and personality dimensions. In B. P. Rourke (Ed.), *Neuropsychological Validation of Learning Disability Subtypes*. New York: Guilford, pp. 180–219.

Diaz, N. D., McLaughlin, T. F. & Williams, R. L. (1990). The effects of practising words in sentences on generalisation of spelling to written work with mildly handicapped students. *Psychology in the Schools*, **27**(4), 347–353.

Drozda-Senkowska, E. (1986). Étude différentielle d'agrégation d'information dans l'évaluation. *Bulletin de Psychologie*, **39**, 305–309.

Dutter, V. (1986). Des critères fonctionnent-ils comme opérateurs cognitifis lors de la saisie d'indices d'évaluation? *Bulletin de Psychologie*, **39**, 311–318.

Fenton, R. (1990). Cued Turtle Spelling. ADE course assignment, University of Newcastle-upon-Tyne.

Feshbach, N. D. & Feshbach, S. (1987). Affective processes and academic achievement. *Child Development*, **58**(5), 1335–1347.

Foorman, B. R., Francis, D. J., Nova, D. M. & Liberman, D. (1991). How letter-sound instruction mediates progress in first-grade reading and spelling. *Journal of Educational Psychology*, **83**(4), 456–469.

Gersten, R. K., Keating, T. & Becker, W. C. (1988). The continued impact of the Direct Instruction model: longitudinal studies of follow-through students. *Education and Treatment of Children*, **11**(4), 318–327.

Gettinger, M. (1984). Applying learning principles to remedial spelling instruction. *Academic Therapy*, **20**, 41–48.

Gettinger, M. (1985). Effects of teacher-directed versus student-directed instruction and cues versus no-cues for improving spelling performance. *Journal of Applied Behavior Analysis*, **18**(2), 167–171.

Hall, N. (Ed.) (1989). *Writing with Reason: The Emergence of Authorship in Young Children*. Sevenoaks: Hodder and Stoughton.

Hancock, R. (1992). An appraisal of the *Aurally Coded English Spelling Dictionary*. BEd project. University of Sunderland.

Harmes, J. M. (1986). A Yankee tutor in Gillingham's court. *Annals of Dyslexia*, **36**, 28–43.

Holligan, C. & Johnston, R. S. (1991). Spelling errors and phonemic segmentation ability: the nature of the relationship. *Journal of Research in Reading*, **14**(1), 21–32.

Houck, C. K. & Billingsley, B. S. (1989). Written expression of students with and without learning disabilities. *Journal of Learning Disabilities*, **22**(9), 561–567.

Huxford, L., Terrell, C. & Bradley, L. (1991). The relationship between the phonological strategies employed in reading and spelling. *Journal of Research in Reading*, **14**(2), 99–105.

Jacoby, L. L. & Hollingshead, A. (1990). Reading student essays may be hazardous to your spelling: effects of reading incorrectly and correctly spelled words. *Canadian Journal of Psychology*, **44**(33), 345–358.

James, J., Charlton, T., Leo, E. & Indoe, D. (1991). A peer to listen. *Support for Learning*, **6**(4), 165–169.

Kapadia, E. S. & Fentuzzo, J. W. (1988). Effects of teacher- and self-administered procedures on the spelling performance of learning-handicapped children. *Journal of School Psychology*, **26**(1), 49–58.

Klesius, J. P., Griffith, P. L. & Zielonka, P. (1991). A whole language and traditional instruction comparison: overall effectiveness and development of the alphabetic principle. *Reading Research and Instruction*, **30**(2), 47–61.

Kreiner, D. S. & Gough, P. B. (1990). Two ideas about spelling: rules and word-specific memory. *Journal of Memory and Language*, **29**(1), 103–118.

Levy, F. & Hobbes, G. (1989). Reading, spelling and vigilance in attention deficit and conduct disorder. *Journal of Abnormal Child Psychology*, **17**(3), 291–298.

Logan, J. W., Olson, M. W. & Lindsey, T. P. (1989). Lessons from champion spellers. *Journal for the Education for the Gifted*, **13**(1), 89–96.

Lum, T. & Morton, L. L. (1984). Direct instruction in spelling increases gain in spelling and reading skills. *Special Education in Canada*, **58**(2), 41–45.

Lumley, J. (1992). *Encouraging independent learning of spelling in competent writers in year two*. ADE course assignment. University of Newcastle-upon-Tyne.

Lyle, J. (1969). Reading retardation and reversal tendency: a factorial study. *Child Development*, **40**, 833–843.

McClurg, P. A. & Kasakow, N. (1989). Wordprocessors, spelling checkers and drill and practice programs: effective tools for spelling instruction? *Journal of Educational Computing Research*, **5**(2), 187–198.

Michael, J. (1986). Self-selected spelling. *Academic Therapy*, **21**(5), 557–563.

Moseley, D. V. (1972). Children who find reading and spelling difficult. In W. K. Brennan (Ed.), *Aspects of Remedial Education*. London: Longman, pp. 58–63.

Moseley, D. V. (1974). Some cognitive and perceptual correlates of spelling ability. In B. Wade & K. Wedell (Eds), *Spelling: Task and Learner*. Birmingham: University of Birmingham Educational Review Occasional Publications, pp. 15–22.

Moseley, D. V. (1976). *Helping with Learning Difficulties*. Course E201, Block 10, Open University, Milton Keynes.

Moseley, D. V. (1988). New approaches to helping children with spelling difficulties. *Educational and Child Psychology*, **5**(4), 53–38.

Moseley, D. V. (1989a). How lack of confidence in spelling affects children's written expression. *Educational Psychology in Practice*, **5**(1), 42–46.

Moseley, D. V. (1989b). Utilisation d'un dictionnaire a codage oral pour l'orthographe et la reconnaissance des mots: une étude en milieu scolaire. *Glossa*, **14**, 14–19.

Moseley, D. V. (1993). *Canadian Spelling Dictionary*. Toronto: Stoddart.

Moseley, D. V. & Nicol, C. M. (1989). *Aurally Coded English Spelling Dictionary*. Wisbech: Learning Development Aids.

Moseley, D. V. & Singleton, G. V. (1993). *ACE Spelling Activities*. Wisbech: Learning Development Aids.

NEA (1992). *Fifth Annual Report 1992*. Manchester: Northern Examination Association.

Ormrod, J. E. & Jenkins, L. (1989). Study strategies for learning spelling: correlations with achievement and developmental changes. *Perceptual and Motor Skills*, **68**(2), 643–650.

Oudenhoven, J. P. van, Wiersma, B. & Yperen, N. van (1987). Effects of cooperation and feedback by fellow-pupils on spelling achievement. *European Journal of the Psychology of Education*, **2**(1), 83–91.

Petersen, S. E., Fox, P.T., Snyder, A. Z. & Raichle, M. E. (1990). Activation of extrastriate and frontal cortical areas by visual words and word-like stimuli. *Science*, **249**, 1041–1044.

Pratt-Struthers, J., Struthers, T. B. & Williams, R. L. (1983). The effects of the Add-A-Word spelling program on spelling accuracy during creative writing. *Education and Treatment of Children*, **6**(3), 277–283.

Prior, M., Frye, S. & Fletcher, C. (1987). Remediation for subgroups of retarded readers using a modified oral spelling procedure. *Developmental Medicine and Child Neurology*, **29**(1), 64–71.

Rohl, M. & Tunmer, W. E. (1988). Phonemic segmentation skill and spelling acquisition. *Applied Psycholinguistics*, **9**(4), 355–350.

Schonell, F. J. & Schonell, F. E. (1950). *Diagnostic and Attainment Testing*. London: Oliver and Boyd.

Stage, S. A. & Wagner, R. K. (1992). Development of young children's phonological and orthographic knowledge as revealed by their spellings. *Developmental Psychology*, **28**(2), 287–296.

Stevens, R. J., Madden, N. A., Slavin, R. E. & Farnish, A. M. (1987). Cooperative integrated reading and composition: two field experiments. *Reading Research Quarterly*, **22**(44), 433–454.

Stevenson, J. & Fredman, G. (1990). The social environmental correlates of reading ability. *Journal of Child Psychology and Psychiatry*, **31**(5), 681–698.

Thomson, M. E. (1991). The teaching of spelling using techniques of simultaneous oral spelling and visual inspection. In *Dyslexia*: Integrating Theory and Practice (M. Snowling & M. Thomson, Eds), London: Whurr, pp. 244–250.

Thorstad, G. (1991). The effect of orthography on the acquisition of literacy skills. *British Journal of Psychology*, **82**, 527–537.

Topping, K. J., Scoble, J. & Oxley, L. (1988). The Cued Spelling Training Pack. Huddersfield: Kirklees Paired Learning Project.

Upward, C. (1992). Is traditionl english spelng mor dificlt than jermn? *Journal of Research in Reading*, **15**, 82–94.

Vernon, P. E. (1977). *Graded Word Spelling Test*. London: Hodder and Stoughton.

Watt, J. M. & Topping, K. J. (1993). Cued spelling: a comparative study of parent and peer tutoring. *Educational Psychology in Practice*, **9**(2), 95–103.

Wimmer, H. & Hummer, P. (1990). How German-speaking first graders read and spell: doubts on the importance of the logographic stage. *Applied Psycholinguistics*, **11**(4), 349–368.

Young, D. (1983). *Parallel Spelling Tests*. London: Hodder and Stoughton.

23

Using Computers to Teach Spelling to Children with Learning Disabilities

BARBARA W. WISE AND RICHARD K. OLSON
University of Colorado

INTRODUCTION: WHY TEACH SPELLING WITH COMPUTERS?

Computer-assisted instruction offers special benefits for children experiencing difficulties with reading. Computer programs can individualize pacing and materials for different levels of ability and interest, can allow repeated practice for mastery and can provide immediate feedback for responses (Cates, 1989). Children can read more difficult material and can read more accurately when computers provide them with speech feedback for difficult words, leading to improvement in reading and attitudes about reading (Olson & Wise, 1992; Reinking, 1987; Wise & Olson, 1993, in press).

Children with reading problems also usually experience problems with other aspects of written language (Bruck, 1988; Olson, in press). Word processors appear to enable these children to write more productively, and the children can use spell-checkers to correct their spellings (Jinkerson & Baggett, 1993). With the wide availability of spell-checkers, the question arises whether spelling should even be taught to children who are experiencing problems in all areas of printed language. If someone is experiencing so many difficulties with printed language, perhaps spell-checkers have eliminated the need to focus on at least one of them. If the only reason to learn spelling were to be accurate in writing, word processors could have eliminated, or at least reduced, the need to learn to spell. But suppose learning to spell provides additional

Handbook of Spelling: Theory, Process and Intervention. Edited by G. D. A. Brown and N. C. Ellis.
© 1994 John Wiley & Sons Ltd.

benefits for reading disabled children. If so, computers may be able to improve that instruction rather than render it unnecessary.

This chapter begins with an overview of the most central deficits in disabled readers and reviews research that suggests why spelling instruction may indeed be helpful for the remediation of these deficits. The second section reviews several studies of computer-assisted spelling instruction. Some of those studies compare typing on a computer with writing for learning to spell. Other studies of computer-assisted spelling show that using computer programs is more advantageous when the programs are designed to be engaging and to take advantage of computers' unique potentials, including some computers' capacity for speech. The third section of the chapter describes research in the Colorado Remediation Project, where we have been trying to improve students' phonological decoding and spelling skills by allowing them to explore print-to-sound relationships in an interactive spelling program. A unique feature of this program is its use of synthetic speech for pronunciations of words and of children's correct or mistaken attempts at spelling those words. The chapter concludes with a summary of what is known so far and what needs to be done next to explore the possible benefits from computer-assisted instruction in spelling.

THEORETICAL BACKGROUND

The children we are most concerned about in our research are those who have significant problems in reading, in spite of normal intelligence, sensory abilities and emotional and educational background. These children are commonly classified as "specific reading disabled" or "dyslexic", and we will use these two terms synonymously as defined above. Although children with specific reading disabilities tend to have problems with all areas of written language, a consensus has been reached that the primary reading deficit is in printed word recognition and the decoding of print to sound. A problem in analytic language underlies this deficit (Olson, in press; Stanovich, 1988; Wagner & Torgesen, 1987).

The analytic language ability underlying reading difficulties is called "phonemic awareness", which is the ability to isolate, order and manipulate speech sounds (phonemes) within spoken syllables. It is often measured by non-reading tasks of blending or segmenting phonemes in spoken syllables. "Phonological awareness" refers to the related, and slightly higher-level, ability to link those speech sounds with print. It is usually measured by tasks that involve decoding novel strings of letters (nonsense words) into sounds (e.g. *niss, ite, vogger, framble*).

Dyslexic children's unique deficits in phonological decoding (nonsense word reading) have been demonstrated in "reading-level-match" (RLM) studies, where older children with reading disabilities are matched to younger controls on a general measure of word recognition (see Rack, Snowling & Olson, 1992, for a review). The older children with reading disabilities in RLM studies are usually substantially worse in nonsense word reading than are the younger controls, despite the fact that their recognition of real words is matched at the same level. For example, an RLM study by Olson *et al.* (1989) found that a group of dyslexic children averaging 15 years of age was substantially lower in nonword reading than a group of normal children averaging

10 years of age. This study also found that the dyslexic group was significantly lower on a non-reading measure of phonemic awareness.

The above pattern of results suggests that problems in phonemic awareness and phonological decoding may be causally related to dyslexics' problems in word recognition. The suggestion becomes stronger when buttressed (1) by evidence suggesting the phonological decoding and phonemic awareness deficits are strongly influenced by common genetic factors (Olson et al., 1989; Olson, in press), (2) by neuroanatomic evidence for differences in brain architecture and function in the language areas of normal and dyslexic readers (Hynd & Semrud-Klikeman, 1989; Larsen et al., 1989), and (3) by studies showing that training in phonemic awareness improves the later reading abilities of children at risk for reading problems (Byrne & Fielding-Barnsley, 1993; Lundberg, Frost & Petersen, 1988; Wise, Lindamood & Olson, 1993; and see Wise, 1991; Wise & Olson, 1991, for a discussion of all these factors).

Deficits in phonemic awareness also cause problems in learning to spell (Bruck, 1988; Lundberg, Frost & Petersen, 1988; Rohl & Tunmer, 1988; Treiman, 1985, 1991). If one cannot analyze and compare the order of sounds in *fist* and *fits*, for instance, then words must be memorized as wholes, making them easily confusable in reading or spelling. Spelling errors of children with reading disabilities tend to reflect the same kinds of problems found in their reading errors: sound omissions, order changes, sound additions, substitutions and repetitions. Lennox and Siegel (submitted) found that children with poor spelling were weaker in phonological and visual strategies when compared to good spellers of the same age. However, when compared to younger normal spellers matched on spelling achievement, the older poor spellers showed worse phonological skills and more reliance on visual similarities. The younger normal spellers' errors were phonologically closer to the words they were attempting to spell. Thus, the poor spellers in the Lennox and Siegel study displayed the weak phonological skill in spelling that appears in the reading errors of children with reading disabilities.

Olson (1985) also found especially poor phonological skills reflected in spelling errors of dyslexic readers. In this study, a group of older disabled readers (mean age 15 yr) was matched to a younger group of normal readers (mean age 10 yr) on the word recognition of the Peabody Individual Achievement Test (PIAT: Dunn & Markwardt, 1970). They turned out to be matched on the spelling recognition test of the PIAT as well. Spelling errors on a different experimental spelling production test were rated for phonological similarity to the target word. "Visual" similarity to the target word was also rated based on the number of letters and maintenance of ascenders and descenders from the target word. Spelling errors of the older dyslexics showed significantly less phonological similarity to the target word than the errors of the younger readers. However, the older dyslexic group scored the same as the younger normal group on the "visual" similarity of their errors to the target words. A phonological decoding task (nonword reading) was also presented to the matched dyslexic and normal groups. As in spelling, the dyslexic group's phonological decoding skills in reading were significantly worse than in the younger normal group.

While phonemic awareness contributes to reading and spelling ability (Calfee, Lindamood & Lindamood, 1973; Stanovich, Cunningham & Cramer, 1984), learning to read also reciprocally improves phonemic awareness (Morais et al., 1979). Some theorists have argued convincingly that learning to spell may be even more strongly implicated than learning to read in developing phonemic awareness. Cataldo and Ellis (1988) describe implicit phonemic awareness as the knowledge about the spoken structure of language that children acquire in learning to talk. They contrast this with the explicit phonemic awareness required to segment spoken words into phonemes. It is this second ability which predicts and correlates with success in reading. Cataldo and Ellis conducted a longitudinal study of learning to read and spell and found that explicit phonemic awareness improved greatly with the experience of learning to spell.

Ehri is another theorist who has argued convincingly for the importance of learning to spell for the development of explicit phonemic awareness (Ehri, 1987, 1989). According to Ehri, the alphabetic strategy needed to translate print to sounds is first used in reverse in spelling, in translating sounds into letter patterns. Ehri and Wilce (1987) found that learning "phonetic cue" spelling helped beginning readers learn to read words. Phonetic cue spelling involves using memory for the names of at least some of the letters in the word (*jail* sounds like *j + l*). Those trained to spell with phonetic cues improved in reading, phonemic segmentation and in spelling similarly spelled words, compared to a group of children who spent a similar time learning individual letter–sound associations.

It seems logical that phonetically based instruction in spelling would also help poor readers improve their deficient phonological decoding skills. DiVeta and Speece (1990) demonstrated this with two learning disabled first-grade boys who improved in phonemic segmentation ability after blending or spelling training of CVC words, even though phonemic segmentation was not explicitly taught.

Uhry and Shepherd (in press) recently demonstrated that spelling training combined with training in phoneme segmentation improves phonemic awareness skill and also improves many reading abilities, even for children at risk for reading disability. They completed an impressive in-class study with 22 first-grade children, seven of whom had been found to be at high risk for reading problems from results of tests of reading and language skills given at the end of kindergarten.

Eleven of the students, in the trained control group, received letter–sound instruction and reading and blending instruction. The other 11, the experimental group, received the same letter–sound instruction, but it was combined with training in spelling and in phoneme segmentation, using blocks to represent phonemes as originated by Elkonin (1963). Spelling instruction included spelling words into a computer and playing spelling games. Children in both conditions studied the same word lists of controlled CVC, CCVC and CVCC items. Children came from two different first-grade classes, with half the children in each group attending each class. Experimenters trained the students in small in-class groups for two 20-minute sessions per week, for about 6½ months.

After this training, students with the spelling/segmentation training performed significantly better than the control group on measures of spelling, nonsense word reading, word recognition and phoneme segmentation. They were marginally better on a test of reading comprehension as well. For reading and spelling, the groups were both at ceiling on CVC items, but the experimental group showed strong and significant advantages on items with consonant blends. Most interesting for our purpose of looking at students at risk for reading problems, the groups almost did not overlap on posttest measures. Only the most precocious high reader in the control group performed better than even the most at-risk child in the experimental group, and both these children were outliers. Otherwise, all children in the experimental group, even the at-risk children, outperformed all children in the control group. Thus, the most important reason for children with learning disabilities to learn to spell may be to improve their reading and writing through improving their phonemic awareness and phonological decoding skills.

Yet besides the potential value from spelling training in improving phonemic awareness and phonological decoding, spelling has some importance in its own right. Spelling difficulties of children with reading disabilities appear to be the most persistent of their difficulties with printed language. A large number of adult dyslexics have learned to read quite adequately by memorizing many whole words in reading. Yet such adults usually still demonstrate an underlying deficit in phonemic awareness and phonological decoding that makes their reading less efficient, and which can be seen in their poor spelling, which typically lasts through adulthood (Lefly & Pennington, 1991).

A certain proficiency with spelling is required for competent writing, with or without spell-checkers. Some spelling and decoding ability is required even to choose among the alternatives offered by spell-checkers. Also, spell-checkers miss errors that match the spellings of other real words but do not match the phonology of the target word (e.g. *hat* for *hate*). Thus, computers do not seem to have eliminated the need to learn to spell. Perhaps they will instead enhance instruction, and help children with learning disabilities to improve their deficient spelling skills, with the potential of also improving their phonemic awareness and phonological decoding in reading.

STUDIES THAT USE COMPUTERS TO TEACH SPELLING

Computers have certain capacities that make them ideally suited to teaching spelling. Computers can motivate most children to practise, provide individualized word lists based on children's error patterns and offer immediate accurate feedback for errors. Computers equipped with speech can also repeat words to be spelled, as often as children want to hear them.

Keyboards or Pencils?

An obvious question arises whether children do learn to spell word lists better when they use computers or when they use traditional pencil and paper methods. No clear answer has emerged from the research on this question.

Cunningham and Stanovich (1990) attempted to isolate and compare the motoric aspects of practising spelling using a keyboard, letter tiles or handwriting. In their study, 14 first-grade children spoke words and their letters out loud while they spelled them, using handwriting, a computer keyboard or letter tiles. The design was within subjects, such that all students used all three methods with different words. The children each studied the same 30 words, which all contained four or five letters. They studied the words in four 30-minute sessions, 15 words on Monday and Wednesday and the other 15 on Tuesday and Thursday. They were tested on the words on Friday.

Cunningham and Stanovich (1990) found that the children learned more words when they wrote than when using the computer or the letter tiles. The advantage for handwriting was maintained even when testing of the words was conducted using the computer or tiles. The suggestion is that at least for first-graders, the motoric involvement of handwriting helped the children remember the correct orthographic patterns for the words they studied. However, in this study, so many words were studied that only 1–3 words were learned per 10-word list. Studying 30 words in one week appears to be rather daunting for first-graders. Bryant, Drabin and Gettinger (1981) recommended studying only three words per session (not 15) for maximal learning. A second problem is that the subjects had not previously learned the positions of the letters on the keyboard, so hunting for each letter probably distracted children from learning to spell.

Vaughn and her colleagues (Vaughn, Schumm & Gordon, 1992, 1993) extended Cunningham and Stanovich's (1990) study to examine whether the results would replicate with first-graders and with older children with learning disabilities, and whether the results would replicate with shorter word lists and sounder educational practices. The first study included 24 first-grade students without learning disabilities (NLD) and 24 older learning disabled (LD) students. The children all had normal range IQs of 90 or above, and the older children scored at least 1½ years below expected grade level in spelling. This study used a pretest to control for previous spelling knowledge, which had not been done in the Cunningham and Stanovich (1990) study. Otherwise, the methods were identical, with the children studying 30 words over 4 days. Cunningham and Stanovich's word lists were supplemented with words chosen from a spelling text, so that a 50-word pretest could be used to generate 30 unknown words per child.

The LD students showed an almost significant trend of learning fewer words than the younger NLD students; average was about 1.2 words per list for the NLD students and 0.45 for the LD students. Another measure reflecting accuracy of smaller units within the words indicated a significant difference favoring the NLD students. However, this study did not replicate any advantage for handwriting over using a keyboard or tiles. The authors speculated that the lower socio-economic status of their subjects may have contributed to the non-replication. Also, the fact that all words were pretested to be unknown by the children may have added to the already difficult task and reduced learning in all conditions to floor levels.

More recently, Vaughn, Schumm and Gordon (1993) extended the study again, hoping to increase the number of words learned by improving the training methods. Vaughn *et al.* based training modifications on some important research findings concerning spelling instruction. These modifications included (1) constructing an individual spelling list for each student and teaching only three words during each instructional setting as recommended by Bryant, Drabin and Gettinger (1981), (2) teaching to mastery, demonstrated by writing the word correctly without a model (Gerber, 1986), (3) including opportunities for students to check their accuracy (Graham & Freeman, 1986), (4) providing clear feedback and error analysis (Gerber, 1984), (5) reducing information gradually in the spelling words until the student could spell the word without a model (Bos & Vaughn, 1991), and (6) extending the training period from 5 to 11 days, to allow for fewer words to be studied per day.

Vaughn, Schumm and Gordon's (1993) students were taught individually for 20 minutes per day. Forty-eight third- and fourth-grade students, half of whom had learning disabilities, again studied 30 unknown words, this time writing the words, tracing them or studying them with a computer. The training method was identical for all three conditions, except for the type of motor response. All three conditions had much teacher involvement concerning discussion of the word's meaning, rehearsal of the spelling, error analysis, studying the word with blanks for vowels or consonants, giving feedback, and repeating the procedures until the student had mastered the word and could spell it correctly without a model.

With these identical and involved instructional methods, it is not very surprising that the motoric conditions made no significant difference in spelling accuracy for either group of children. While the children with learning disabilities learned fewer words in all conditions, no condition proved better overall for either group. Also, the children with learning disabilities forgot words at about the same rate as the other children and showed no advantage for one method over another, even for methods that matched or did not match their self-reported "modality" preference. Interestingly, student interviews revealed that students liked the computer the most but felt they learned more from writing the words by hand. Vaughn, Schumm and Gordon (1993) feel that the motivational aspects of the computer should be considered as an advantage, since all three methods led to equivalent learning when word lists were shortened and reasonable instructional procedures were followed.

Is There More to a Computer than a Keyboard?

Of course, comparing typing and handwriting does not answer whether computers can improve on spelling education. Keyboard use can be taught, in order to reduce the effort needed for children to find the letters they seek. This leaves them with more attentional resources available for learning what they need to learn. Handwriting could be combined with computer use. In addition, computers offer other advantages that may make them extremely helpful for learning to spell.

MacArthur et al. (1990) took advantage of computers' potential for motivating students and individualizing programs. MacArthur was interested in studying whether computers would prove helpful in independent spelling practice, because most spelling practice is accomplished as independent seatwork in special education and regular classroom settings. Forty fifth- and sixth-grade students with learning disabilities studied their spelling words independently using either traditional paper and pencil techniques or a computer. All students had been classified by the schools as learning disabled, and were of normal range intelligence with IQ scores between 85 and 115. Students functioned at least 1½ years below expectation in reading or math, and all of them scored at least 2 years below expectancy in spelling.

The two methods were matched for content, for number of trials and duration of practice, and for teaching time and proximity to peers. Forty study words were selected such that no student knew more than 15% of the words. Students studied the same 10 new words each week. On Monday, the teacher reviewed the 10 spelling words with the entire class, discussing their meanings. Then students practised the words independently for 20 minutes a day for each group, for 4 weeks. For both groups, on Monday, five new words were practised. Students saw the word, a picture and a sentence. They copied the word, wrote it from memory and used it in a sentence completion task. After all five words were presented, the students reviewed them. The other five words were presented on Tuesday, and they practised the words in sentence completions, multiple choice, riddles and scrambled words; there was a memorization task on Wednesday and Thursday. No homework was assigned, and students in the paper and pencil group used the computers for math activities.

Differences in the methods centered around the potential benefits offered by each medium. In the computer group, each word was spelled on the screen at the rate of two letters per second. Students copied the word by typing it on the computer, the word disappeared and the students typed it again. The computer provided immediate feedback and required that the students type the word three times correctly before continuing. In the traditional paper and pencil method, feedback was by self-checking, with delayed feedback by the teacher. To study the words, students were taught to spell the word silently, copy it, cover it and write it from memory, check it, and repeat it till it was correctly spelled three times. However, the materials themselves could not require adherence to this procedure.

Weekly spelling tests and a final retention test showed an advantage for the computer study over the paper and pencil technique. Students in the computer-assisted group were rated as more engaged with the computer-assisted instruction, and this rating of engagement correlated with spelling success. This finding of an advantage for the computer with programs designed to be engaging supports the notion of Vaughn, Schumm and Gordon (1993) that the motivational aspects of using computers may make studying spelling on the computer advantageous for many children.

Van Daal and van der Leij (1992) combined the use of handwriting practice with computer presentation of words in their study. Their program also took advantage of another capacity of some microcomputers: that of high-quality speech support. This study aimed to investigate how practice in reading and spelling difficult words with and without computer support would improve children's reading as well as their spelling.

The computer speech support was quite reasonably expected to reduce demands on working memory during spelling practice because the computer could be asked to repeat the word. The authors also expected this whole-word speech support to reduce children's uncertainty about which particular sound segment should be associated with a given grapheme. However, given what is known about difficulties in phonemic awareness, this conjecture is difficult to justify. Students with problems in phonemic awareness cannot reliably count or order the sounds within a word even when they can hear or can pronounce it themselves. Why would they improve in this ability just by hearing the word pronounced by a computer rather than by themselves or by a teacher? Perhaps, if the computer speech could pronounce the children's spelling attempts so they could compare them to the real word, manipulating the contrasts might help them identify sound order differences. But van Daal and van der Leij's program (1992) uses high-quality digitized speech, which would not have the capability to pronounce novel strings or errors. Nevertheless, the first expectation of reducing memory needs and providing immediate feedback seems likely to be valid and helpful for improving spelling.

Twenty-eight children with written language disorders took part in the study. Their average age was 9 years, 7 months, and their reading achievement averaged 2 years below expectancy by age. Their IQ scores fell in the normal range, between 90 and 110. Students began by taking a computer-assisted reading pretest, and study lists were individualized to include 42 words that had been misread and 12 that had been read correctly. The next day, those words were presented in a spelling dictation task. The students studied about half of the words in 10-minute practice sessions for the next 15 days, with the other portion posttested as untrained control words. The day after training was complete the 54 words were tested for reading accuracy, and on the next day for spelling accuracy.

Two computer-based spelling practice methods and one reading practice were compared. The words were blocked for difficulty and then randomly assigned to one of the three training methods, so that all students used each method. In the reading condition, the student could request speech support up to 10 times per word while it remained on the screen. In the memory spelling method, the written word was presented and the student studied it, with up to five speech support requests available. When the students indicated they were ready to type, the word disappeared from the screen and the students typed it from memory, with speech support available for another five requests per word. In the copying spelling method, the word remained on the screen and the children copied it, requesting speech feedback up to 10 times per word.

Students spent more time per word spelling than reading. Students in the memory spelling condition asked for the most speech support, and took more time in studying the word before typing it. Study time per word decreased over sessions for both spelling conditions and the difference in time between conditions gradually disappeared.

Students improved both in reading and in spelling the words they trained on, and there was no generalization to unpractised words. There were no differences among methods for improving the *reading* of the words. For spelling the words, copying from the computer proved the most successful method and just reading the word was the least helpful method. Writing from memory proved a harder task than copying from the screen in that students made more errors in training and learned to spell fewer words that way. Both before and after training, spelling errors in all conditions reflected problems with grapheme–phoneme correspondences. All the results really show is that copying from the screen is better than writing from memory and that practising spelling helps spelling more than practising reading words, but they do clearly demonstrate this. Particular benefits of speech cannot be ascertained because speech was equally available in all conditions. It cannot be seen from these data whether learning to spell these words improved any phonological skill, except for the null result that there was no improvement in reading or spelling untrained words.

Nicolson, Pickering and Fawcett (1991) used synthetic speech in a spelling program that also utilized a hypercard support environment. Their 23 subjects had participated in their previous studies of dyslexia and had at that time at least an 18-month reading deficit from expectation by age, despite normal IQ and education. While some of these subjects had improved enough in reading so that they no longer qualified as reading disabled by a discrepancy criterion, all remained quite discrepant in spelling achievement.

Nicolson *et al.*'s program required experimenters to type in students' renditions of dictated texts at three different reading levels designed to be appropriate for the varying reading levels of the subjects based on the Schonell reading test. The experimenters dictated the texts in short segments and the students wrote them down. The experimenter typed the student's dictation in, leaving eight of his/her errors in each passage. Each subject then went through three sessions of the program. In the first session, the student and the experimenter created rules or hints for each of the eight errors left in the passage (e.g. one child typed in "U.R. Saturday", to help him remember the *ur* in the middle of the word). In session 2, the experimenter guided the student through the program, encouraging him to use the hints to correct each misspelled word. In session 3, the student did the same thing with minimal help from the experimenter. One month later, the dictation was repeated to see how many words were learned. Speech support was available to pronounce any "choice" button in the program, as well as to pronounce any highlighted word in the text.

After a mean training time of 1 hour, 47 minutes, over two-thirds of the eight studied words were spelled correctly 1 month later. Overall errors were reduced by about one-third with this training, because there was no improvement at all in the untrained words. Questionnaire data indicated the subjects and their parents found the programs enjoyable and valuable. The problem with this study is that there was no control group, and also no way to know how much improvement was due to the computer program itself and how much to the presence and good teaching of the experimenters. But the program is unique in using hypercard, synthetic speech and spelling in context. Its effectiveness in teaching the studied words with gains maintained over 1 month made it seem worthy of mention in this chapter.

THE COLORADO SPELLING STUDIES

Our previous research with computer speech feedback for dyslexic readers has focused mainly on using speech support for word-decoding problems while reading stories (Olson & Wise, 1992; Wise *et al.*, 1989; Wise & Olson, 1993). The reading studies use a high-quality speech synthesizer called DECtalk (Digital Equipment Corporation). Students using the programs have generally improved more in their word recognition, phonological decoding and attitude about reading when compared to similar students reading in the classroom.

We have always been interested in whether speech feedback could be used to remedy the underlying deficit in phonemic awareness and phonological decoding. While group gains in nonword reading have been significant in the reading studies, there has been considerable individual variation in gains that were positively correlated with students' initial level of phonemic awareness at the beginning of training (Olson & Wise, 1992). Therefore, we have been interested in trying other methods to increase the gains for students with poor phonemic awareness. The studies reported earlier linking spelling instruction and phonemic awareness led us to explore spelling training as a means of accomplishing this goal. The goal has been somewhat peripheral to the main thrust of our reading studies, so our research in this area is still rather preliminary. However, recent funding to explore the training of phonemic awareness skills combined with our reading programs is allowing us to develop this research more comprehensively.

Studies already reviewed in this chapter demonstrate that spelling training can improve phonemic awareness and phonological decoding, and that computers can assist in spelling training. We have been interested in what synthetic speech can add to this effort. High-quality synthetic speech has the capacity to provide a unique kind of feedback for improving phonological skills with spelling training. It can pronounce children's misspelled attempts at a word besides being able to pronounce the word to be spelled. Digitized speech, while slightly more intelligible, cannot give feedback for misspelled attempts, since no one could anticipate and prerecord all possible misspellings of a word (Wise & Olson, in press).

DECtalk applies complicated phonological rules to translate into speech any letter string that contains both vowels and consonants, and is nearly as intelligible as recorded human speech for children and adults (Olson, Foltz & Wise, 1986). People make less than one-tenth as many errors identifying words pronounced by DECtalk as compared to two other speech synthesizers used in much educational software (Wise et al., 1989).

We thought it would be interesting to see how children could use the synthesizer to explore print and sound relationships. Some of our programs allow students to compare pronunciations of their own spelling attempts with pronunciations of the word to be spelled, as they change their attempts, as often as they want. The programs also give some orthographic feedback about placement of letters in the spelling attempts. They run on an IBM-XT compatible microcomputer linked to a mouse and to DECtalk. We have conducted two studies with the spelling programs.

The Summer Clinic Study

The first study was conducted during 2 weeks of a summer reading clinic for students experiencing difficulties with reading and spelling (see Wise & Olson, 1992, for the complete description of the study). The study compared behavioral and learning differences when the children could or could not use interactive speech for their spelling attempts. It also investigated whether computerized spelling practice would benefit these children's phonological decoding. Since brief training would be unlikely to cause large gains, we constructed nonwords specifically related in structure to the training words. With structurally related nonwords, children could demonstrate if they had learned about orthographic patterns within the trained words sufficiently to transfer this learning to the reading of related but untrained nonwords.

Subjects included 28 children ranging in age from 7 to 14 years (average 10.9). All students tested at least one grade level below national averages on the Wide Range Achievement Test of spelling (WRAT: Jastak, Bijou & Jastak, 1976). All but three students also tested at least one grade level below the national average on the WRAT reading word recognition test; the ratio of actual reading level to the reading level expected by age by national norms was 0.81 in this group. In Boulder, average students actually test about 1.5 grade levels above national norms in reading (Olson, 1985).

Subjects were pretested on the Wide Range Achievement Tests of Spelling and Reading (WRAT: Jastak, Bijou & Jastak, 1976). Items from both tests were administered first as spelling tests and the next day as reading tests. In addition, a pretest of nonsense word reading was constructed for each subject and given also on the second day of the study. Nonsense words were designed to resemble the misspelled items in word structure (see Appendix): monosyllabic items shared "rime" units (e.g. *then*, *chen*; *edge*, *medge*) and multisyllabic words shared rimes, syllables or morphemes (e.g. *collapse*, *unlapse*; *nature*, *plature*). The child was asked to pronounce each nonword item as if it were a real English word. Items were counted correct by analogy to a real word (e.g. *suth* to rhyme with *truth*) or by phonics rules (e.g. *suth* with the "short *u*" sound as in *such*). Any stress pattern counted correct, and final responses were scored.

Training items were the first 32 items misspelled on the pretests (see Appendix). Even-numbered items were put in the first week's list and odd items in the second week's list to balance the weeks for item difficulty. A "neighbor" training word per item was constructed to resemble the test item, by the same rules used to construct the nonsense words, to give the children extra practice with spelling patterns in the tests words: (e.g. *edge*, *ledge*; *nature*, *future*). Thus, children trained on 32 words in each training condition, 16 of which they had misspelled on pretest and 16 that resembled the tested words in word structure. For each training condition, posttesting consisted of a spelling and a reading test of the 16 trained words, as well as a nonword reading test of the matched nonsense words.

During the first week of training, half the children had orthographic feedback for their errors and speech support only for the target word. The other subjects had speech feedback available for spelling attempts also. Figure 23.1 illustrates the appearance of the CRT screen when the computer first pronounced a word to be spelled (e.g. *plant*). In both conditions, the computer pronounced the word to be spelled, showed the children blanks for the number of letters in the word and the children tried to type in the correct letters. At any point, students in either condition could make the computer repeat the target word by clicking on a "repeat" box with their mouse.

Students in the attempts feedback condition also had a "So Far" box available. As often as they wanted, they could use "So Far" to hear how their spelling attempt in progress sounded. If their attempt did not include a vowel, the computer said, "Please put in an *a*, *e*, *i*, *o*, *u* or *y*, so I can pronounce what you have typed".

$$a \qquad e \qquad i \qquad o \qquad u \qquad\qquad y$$

$$\text{—} \quad \text{—} \quad \text{—} \quad \text{—} \quad \text{—}$$

Repeat ___   **So Far** ___   **Done**___

FIGURE 23.1 Appearance of the screen at the start of Spello.

In both conditions, when satisfied with their attempt, the children selected "Done", which resulted in orthographic feedback. If the child spelled the word correctly, the computer said, "Congratulations! (——) is correct". Otherwise, the computer highlighted any letter in the attempt that was in the real word. It also showed any correctly placed letters below on the next line of blanks. Points were tallied on the screen, with 100, 90 or 80 points added depending on whether the subject correctly spelled the word by the first, second or third request for orthographic feedback. If the student was still not correct after the third "Done", the computer showed the student the correct spelling of the word and requested that s/he type it in correctly.

Students cycled through their list of 16 training items, each one followed by its training "neighbor" (e.g. *edge*, *hedge*). Research assistants sat with the students for about half the time on each session and offered support in using the keyboard or in reminding the children to think about other letters that might sound the same and encouraging them to remember feedback from related words. The goal for the students was to get each word correct with as few requests for orthographic feedback as possible, in order to get as many points as possible per word. But they also got more points per day the more words they spelled correctly each day.

The computer kept track of the number of times each student studied each item, and each subject studied each word at least once in a condition. They studied the new set of words the same number of times when they switched conditions. Older and faster students studied the words two trials each over 3 days of training, while slower students studied each word once in up to 5 days of training. Training sessions averaged about 26 minutes per day, with the remaining clinic time spent on reading programs.

One day after completing the first condition's training, students took posttests. The next week they were switched to the opposite training condition and posttested 1 day after that training was complete. Three or 4 days after the second posttest, all items were readministered as a final test.

The primary study involved the first week of training. The second week of study was called the switched session. Analyses of variance were conducted with each week as a between-subjects' variable because we expected a training order confound and so were primarily interested in the first week's unconfounded results. The first week of training could lead students to learn a strategy that they would tend to use even when the training conditions were reversed. We will try to summarize the main findings from the analyses, and refer the reader to Wise and Olson (1992) for a full description. Many results differed greatly by age, since children ranged from 6 to 14 years old in this study. Therefore, for many analyses, children were divided into three age groups: 9 or below, between 10 and 12, and over 12 years of age.

After spelling training with or without speech feedback for spelling attempts, all children improved in spelling and reading words, and in nonsense word reading, in both weeks. Recall that all children had trained on 32 words, 16 missed on pretest and 16 "neighbors". They were tested on the 16 they had missed on pretest. Younger children learned to spell about one-third of the 16 previously unknown words, while the older children spelled about half of theirs correctly. These spelling gains appear more respectable than some of the earlier studies mentioned that also used long training lists (Cunningham & Stanovich, 1990; Vaughn, Schumm & Gordon, 1992, 1993), but not as strong as the Nicolson and Pickering study with only eight items to be studied in a method with much human interaction and discussion of strategies.

Analyses of word-reading tests showed that younger children read about half of the words that they had not been able to read at pretest correctly. Older children read more than 75% of these words correctly.

For nonword reading, even the younger 7–9-year-old children improved in their ability to read the nonwords, reading about 20% of the (untrained) nonwords which they had been unable to read at pretest. This result is consistent with Goswami's (1986) suggestion that even readers with little experience can profit from rime analogies. Older students gained more in nonword reading, reading about half of them correctly. This result varied quite a bit by feedback condition and by session (first week or second switched week), and will be discussed below. Whether the nonword reading gains would have been as much without the emphasis on orthographic structure in the matched items one cannot know from this study.

The main goal of the study was to see if the children would behave and learn differently when they had interactive speech available for their spelling attempts or not. Recall that the primary goal for students in both conditions, in order to earn points, was to get as many words spelled correctly as possible per day and with as few requests for orthographic feedback as possible. Children certainly did behave differently with speech feedback for spelling attempts than without it. They spent more time on each word when they had speech feedback available for their spelling attempts (94 s vs 73 s, $p < 0.05$). The extra time spent on using the speech feedback was especially strong on the two trials following the first request for orthographic, or spelling, feedback (76 s vs 41 s, $p < 0.01$).

What did the children gain from the use of speech feedback for their spelling errors? The data are not entirely clear. In the primary study, word-reading gains did not differ significantly by condition or for any age group. Children learned to read most of the words they studied in both conditions. This does not seem surprising, given that the children could read (but not spell) many of the items at pretest and that they had about 2 hours of study on them.

In the first week analyzed by itself, children with speech for spelling attempts showed an advantage in learning to spell their unknown words ($p = 0.053$). This was not true in the second week.

The speech support for spelling attempts benefited nonword reading significantly in the first week. This turned out not to be true for the children under 9 years old, but was quite strong in the older children (effect of feedback $p < 0.01$, effect of age $p < 0.05$, interaction $p < 0.01$). Perhaps the young poor readers needed more experience with words and sounds to benefit from the ability to explore phonological relationships (see also Ehri & Robbins, 1992). In the second week, however, the speech feedback did not offer a significant advantage to nonword reading. When the weeks were combined and conditions compared within subjects in a paired t-test analysis, non-significant trends favored speech feedback for improvement in spelling ($p = 0.2$) and nonword reading ($p < 0.1$).

What can one make of the loss of condition effects when the conditions were switched? The groups did not differ significantly on initial measures of age, spelling ability, reading ability or deficit severity. Perhaps the reduced differences when conditions were switched were due to chance factors or perhaps to the order confound. If this were true, one would expect those who had speech for attempts initially to still try a sounding-out strategy, but perhaps less successfully than they had with the speech support. They would make smaller gains than they had initially, but larger than the other group's initial performance. The data fit that picture for the improvement in nonword reading, and the explanation is plausible, but *post hoc*.

The In-School Spelling Study

We recently tried a similar study in a school setting, comparing three forms of feedback during 4 weeks of spelling study. Condition 1 (speech feedback for spelling attempts) and condition 2 (word only support) ran essentially as described in the previous study, except that only two "Done" requests for orthographic feedback were allowed instead of three. Condition 3 was a memorization technique, where the children heard the word and attempted to spell it. If they were correct, the program congratulated them. If they made an error, the program showed them the correct spelling and they typed it in two times correctly while its spelling remained on the screen. The study was designed as between subjects, where subjects remained on one condition for all 4 weeks of the program, with the hope that strategies could be better compared with longer training times.

The study was conducted in two schools in Boulder. Fifty-five children between the ages of 7 and 11 participated in the study, with an average age of 9.8 yr. They took the same pretests as in the summer study, and training and posttest items for neighbors and nonwords were constructed as before. An extra pretest was included, to generate more training words for the longer-term study. Training items were divided such that each week the subject studied four items from each test. Each week the study lists became progressively more difficult.

The first week of the study was devoted to pretesting, scheduling and constructing individualized files and tests. The next 4 weeks were spent on training. The study finished with posttesting in the sixth week.

Students studied 24 words each week, 12 they had misspelled on pretests and 12 items matched to them in orthographic structure. The students spent 20 minutes per day, 4 days per week, using the program during language arts time. Research assistants sat with students about half the time and logged that "monitored time" into the computer so we could check to see that all conditions received equivalent adult attention. At the end of each week, students took a spelling test of the items they trained on. Nonword reading and reading tests were not administered until the sixth week, to save testing time.

Behavioral results indicated the students definitely used the programs in the three conditions differently. Children with speech feedback for errors spent more than twice as much time per word than in either of the other two conditions (conditions 1, 2 and 3 in order: 131 s, 69 s and 49 s, $F(2,48) = 41.65$, $p < 0.0001$). This is also much more time than the students spent in the summer study with the speech feedback for errors (131 s with speech feedback in the school study vs 94 s in the summer clinic).

Since overall study time was held fairly constant for all conditions, these differences in overall time spent studying each word also meant that students in the first condition had far fewer study trials with each word (1.5, 2.7 and 3.5 trials per word respectively in conditions 1, 2 and 3), $F(2,48) = 29.69$, $p < 0.0001$).

Another strong and interesting difference indicated a difference by condition in per trial benefits from the orthographic similarity of trained items to the following neighbor matched in structure. Recall that the student's goal was to spell every word correctly in as few trials as possible, and to spell as many words correctly as possible in each session to get the most points possible. Although all groups spent somewhat and significantly less time on neighbors than on trained items, the difference was significantly greater for condition 1 (difference between trained and neighbor in order: 43 s, 11 s and 8 s, $F(2,48) = 22.47$, $p < 0.0001$, and true also if calculated in terms of the proportion of time spent on neighbors compared to time spent on trained words: 67% vs 85% vs 84%, $F(2,48) = 10.259$, $p < 0.0001$).

Unfortunately, the data in the school study revealed no greater benefits to learning on any posttests from the error feedback from the speech synthesizer. In fact, if one wants simple gains on spelling the studied words, the data indicate that the best way to learn them is to cycle through them as often as possible and memorize them. Children in the memory condition learned the most words on the weekly and the final spelling tests (weekly in order: 45%, 57% and 68%, $F(2,48) = 12.82$, $p < 0.0001$; final: 38%, 49% and 59%, $F(2,48) = 9.29$, $p < 0.001$). When the number of times a word was sent was covaried, these test differences disappeared.

There were no differences among the groups in proportion of previously unknown nonwords or reading words learned. Across all three conditions, students learned 22% of their previously unknown nonsense words and 52% of their previously unknown reading words.

The school study differed in a few ways from the summer study. In the longer-term study, words became progressively more difficult. Only half the subjects completed all 4 weeks of the study, with a quarter dropping out after 2 weeks and a quarter after 3 weeks. Also, students were given one less dose of spelling feedback, which may have made them willing to risk less so that they would not lose points. This suggestion gains support from how much more time students spent in the school study with the speech support than in the summer study. The reading problems of the school subjects were also much less severe. They had a ratio of reading to expected reading score of 0.91, compared to the summer clinic students' ratio of 0.8.

Another big difference in the studies is when the nonsense words were tested—during the same week of study in the summer clinic and after 4 weeks in the school study. The children with speech feedback for errors did learn something about print and sound relationships in terms of the highly significant effect that they spent much less time on neighbor words than the trained item that preceded it, compared to the other groups. However, whatever they learned within the session did not lead to greater benefits than from the other conditions on a test of nonsense word reading 4 weeks later.

Differences in terms of use of the system indicate students do use interactive speech for errors when available to explore how changes in print affect changes in sound. Students in the summer study, who were exposed to programs with and without the feedback for errors, strongly preferred having that feedback available. But it looks as if speech feedback in the program, as currently developed, does not help students use that exploration in a way that benefits them beyond that day's study, as reflected in the shorter time needed for neighbor words, or perhaps that week's study, as conducted in the summer clinic, any more than they could get just from learning to spell the words by memorization or with orthographic explorations.

We must consider the cause of the unexpected advantage for simply typing in words repeatedly and correctly compared to spending time exploring print and sound relationships. Students with the interactive speech feedback actually spent more time spelling the words incorrectly than they did spelling the words correctly. This quite likely caused interference with the correct spellings. Combining the conditions to allow the students to use the synthetic speech to explore phonological relationships, followed by adequate practice to mastery with spelling the words correctly, might provide benefits from both training conditions. It would seem sensible to use information from this and the other spelling studies to try to improve this program so students might be able to obtain greater benefits from the interactive speech feedback for errors.

Improvements one might consider then include suggestions from the research reported earlier as well as from comparisons of the two Colorado studies. Clearly, students should have more practice typing in the words correctly, as the students did in van Daal and van der Leij's (1992) study and in our "memory" condition. Copying the words again by hand seems a worthwhile addition, based on the results of van Daal and van der Leij and on those of Cunningham and Stanovich (1990) and Vaughn, Schumm and Gordon (1992, 1993). Having students study only three to five new words per day has been suggested by Vaughn, Schumm and Gordon (1992, 1993) and by Cates (1989). This would also ensure many repeated trials with a word, which was the strongest predictor of spelling success in our school study. Also, removing words from the study list only as they are learned seems pedagogically more sound than starting a new list when only a third of the old list has been learned. This kind of studying to mastery ensures success and should increase the likelihood of learning strong and generalizable print and sound relations, probably in all conditions. Including one or two more "neighbors" per item would accent generalizable print/sound patterns. Cates also recommends an optimal training time of 15-minute sessions per day.

To gain benefits from the speech feedback *per se*, more "scaffolding" or support may be necessary either from a knowledgeable adult or perhaps from support built into the program itself. Nicolson, Pickering and Fawcett's (1991) program yielded very strong results, but included intense and frequent support from a trained adult.

When adults sit with students on our spelling program, they tend to suggest either ideas about where to listen or other possible ways one might spell a particular sound. This kind of feedback could be built into the program. The "where to listen" feedback is implicit in the spelling feedback of showing that a given letter is in the word but in the wrong place. That feedback could fairly easily be made explicit: for example, "Listen carefully to the ending sounds of the word". Feedback about alternative spelling patterns could also to some extent be accomplished within the program. For instance, when a subject tried *sno* for *snow*, the program could use a window to display "*o-e oa ow* are some good ways to spell *o*. See which one looks the best to you". It would be exciting to try to make a program that takes advantage of children's interest in exploring print and sound with the synthesizer and also provides enough useful support that they could learn generalizable skills from it.

CONCLUSION

A growing body of research, reviewed in the first part of the chapter, suggests that when children learn to spell, they often also improve their phonemic awareness and phonological decoding skills. These language-based skills are uniquely deficient in children with reading disabilities, and causally related to their reading problems.

Researchers of computer-assisted instruction have long focused on reading instruction, but recently some have extended their interest to instructing spelling. Studies reported in the middle of the chapter have demonstrated that children with reading disabilities can improve their spelling with computers, and that many factors can improve the benefits of programs. Programs should be engaging, should probably involve handwriting as well as typing or should teach typing skills, should not teach too many items at a time, should provide correct practice to mastery and should offer good support from a knowledgeable adult or perhaps from the program itself. Computer speech has been successfully used to dictate items for spelling, so that students can hear an item as often as they like.

Synthetic speech would seem to offer extra benefits in terms of exploring print and sound relationships. Students enjoy getting to hear the sounds of their own spelling attempts and to compare their attempt to the word they are trying to spell. In two different studies in Colorado, students spent much more time studying a word when they had speech feedback for their own attempts as well as speech support for the word. They also had greater short-term benefits from orthographic structure with this error feedback than with the other conditions; they required significantly less time to spell orthographic "neighbors" correctly. Students without the speech feedback for errors did not show this difference.

Yet the Colorado programs have not taught students to use the interactive speech feedback in such a way as to get reliable long-term benefits in phonological decoding beyond what they get from learning to spell the words and their orthographic neighbors. Certainly the speech could be left in the program simply because students enjoy it. However, it would seem more sound to try to improve the programs to take better advantage of students' interest and the information in the speech synthesizer. Suggestions in terms of improving the program pedagogically to have fewer items, more neighbors and more practice to mastery were considered, along with ways to provide more informational support within the program similar to what a child could get from a knowledgeable adult.

A few conclusions stand out from the information in this chapter. Teaching spelling to children with reading disabilities is worthwhile, both in order to improve their actual spelling and also in order to improve their phonemic awareness and their knowledge of print and sound relationships. Computer-assisted instruction can benefit this endeavor, because computer programs (1) can be motivating and engaging to these students, (2) can be easily individualized, (3) can provide as much repetition and checking as a student wants, (4) with speech, can repeatedly dictate items to be spelled, and (5) with synthetic speech, can pronounce errors as well as words to be spelled. However, many of the computer-assisted studies reported small gains unless adults were present offering much support. The chapter makes clear, then, that the full potential of computer-assisted spelling instruction has not yet been realized. Better programs will incorporate known ideas about pedagogically valid spelling instruction and computer-assisted instruction, and will utilize the unique capacities computers can bring to the task of spelling instruction.

ACKNOWLEDGEMENTS

We would like to thank Mike Anstett for programming the systems, and Jerry Ring and Laura Kriho for helping to run the studies and set up the analyses. We also thank Bonnie Houkal, Kristi Parisi, Charm Lor, Paul Peters and Lecester Johnson for helping in the summer clinic and in the schools where the Colorado studies were conducted. Research reported in this chapter was supported in part by NICHD grants Nos HD 11683, HD 22223 and HD 27802.

REFERENCES

Bos, C. S. & Vaughn, S. (1991). *Strategies for Teaching Students with Learning and Behavioral Problems*. Boston: Allyn & Bacon.

Bruck, M. (1988). The word recognition and spelling of dyslexic children. *Reading Research Quarterly*, **23**, 51–69.

Bryant, N. D., Drabin, I. R. & Gettinger, M. (1981). Effects of varying unit size on spelling achievement in learning disabled children. *Journal of Learning Disabilities,* **14**, 200–203.

Byrne, B. & Fielding-Barnsley, R. (1993). Evaluation of a program to teach phonemic awareness to young children: a 1-year follow-up. *Journal of Educational Psychology*, **85**, 1–8.

Calfee, R., Lindamood, P. & Lindamood, C. (1973). Acoustic–phonetic skills and reading: kindergarten through twelfth grade. *Journal of Educational Psychology*, **64**, 293–298.

Cataldo, S. & Ellis, N. C. (1988). Interactions in the development of spelling, reading, and phonological skills. *Journal of Research in Reading*, **11**, 86–109.

Cates, W. M. (1989). Research findings applied to software design: computerized instructional spelling programs. *Journal of Computer-Based Instruction*, **16**, 36–45.

Cunningham, A. E. & Stanovich, K. E. (1990). Early spelling acquisition: writing beats the computer. *Journal of Educational Psychology*, **82**, 159–162.

DiVeta, S. K. & Speece, D. L. (1990). The effects of blending and spelling training on the decoding skills of young poor readers. *Journal of Learning Disabilities*, **23**, 579–582.

Dunn, L. M. & Markwardt, F. C. (1970). *Examiner's Manual: Peabody Individual Achievement Test*. Circle Pines, MN: American Guidance Service.

Ehri, L. C. (1987). Learning to read and spell words. *Journal of Reading Behavior*, **19**, 5–31.

Ehri, L. C. (1989). The development of spelling knowledge and its role in reading acquisition and reading disability. *Journal of Learning Disabilities*, **22**, 356–365.

Ehri, L. C. & Robbins, C. (1992). Beginners need some decoding skill to read words by analogy. *Reading Research Quarterly*, **27**, 12–27.

Ehri, L. C. & Wilce, L. S. (1987). Does learning to spell help beginners learn to read words? *Reading Research Quarterly*, **22**, 47–65.

Elkonin, D. B. (1963). The psychology of mastering the elements of reading. In B. Simon & J. Simon (Eds), *Educational Psychology in the USSR*. London: Routledge & Kegan Paul.

Gerber, M. M. (1984). Techniques to teach generalizable spelling skills. *Academic Therapy*, **20**, 49–58.

Gerber, M. M. (1986). Generalization of spelling strategies by learning disabled students as a result of contingent imitation/modeling and mastery criteria. *Journal of Learning Disabilities*, **19**, 530–537.

Goswami, U. (1986). Children's use of analogy in learning to read: a developmental study. *Journal of Experimental Child Psychology*, **42**, 73–83.

Graham, S. & Freeman, S. (1986). Strategy training and teacher- vs student-controlled study conditions: effects on LD students' spelling performance. *Journal of Learning Disabilities*, **19**, 530–537.

Hynd, G. & Semrud-Klikeman, M. (1989). Dyslexia and brain morphology. *Psychological Bulletin*, **106**, 447–482.

Jastak, J. F., Bijou, S. W. & Jastak, S. R. (1976). *The Wide Range Achievement Test*. Wilmington, Delaware: Guidance Associates of Delaware.

Jinkerson, L. & Baggett, P. (1993). Spell checkers: aids in identifying and correcting spelling errors. Paper presented at the annual meeting of the American Educational Research Association, Atlanta, Ga, April 1993.

Larsen, J., Hoien, T., Lundberg, I. & Odegaard, H. (1989). *MRI Evaluation of the Size and Symmetry of the Planum Temporale in Adolescents with Developmental Dyslexia*. Stavanger, Norway: Center for Reading Research.

Lefly, D. & Pennington, B. (1991). Spelling errors and reading fluency in compensated adult dyslexics. *Annals of Dyslexia*, **41**, 143–162.

Lennox, C. & Siegel, L. (submitted). The development of the understanding of phonetic rules in good and poor spellers.

Lundberg, I., Frost, J. & Petersen, O. (1988). Effects of an extensive program for stimulating phonological awareness in preschool children. *Reading Research Quarterly*, **23**, 263–284.

MacArthur, C. A., Haynes, J. A., Malouf, D. B., Harris, K. & Owings, M. (1990). Computer-assisted instruction with learning disabled students: achievement, engagement, and other factors that influence achievement. *Journal of Educational Computing Research*, **6**, 311–328.

Morais, J., Cary, L., Alegria, J. & Bertelson, P. (1979). Does awareness of speech as a sequence of phonemes arise spontaneously? *Cognition*, **7**, 323–331.

Nicolson, R. I., Pickering, S. & Fawcett, A. J. (1991). A hypercard spelling support environment for dyslexic children. *Computers in Education*, **16**, 203–309.

Olson, R. K. (1985). Disabled reading processes and cognitive profiles. In D. Gray & J. Kavanagh (Eds), *Biobehavioral Measures of Dyslexia*. Parkton, MD: York Press, pp. 215–244.

Olson, R. K. (in press). Language deficits in specific reading disability. In M. Gernsbacher (Ed.), *Handbook of Psycholinguistics*. New York: Academic Press.

Olson, R., Foltz, G. & Wise, B. (1986). Reading instruction and remediation with the aid of computer speech. *Behavior Research Methods, Instruments, and Computers*, **18**, 93–99.

Olson, R. K. & Wise, B. (1992). Reading on the computer with orthographic and speech feedback: an overview of the Colorado Remediation Project. *Reading & Writing*, **4**, 107–144.

Olson, R. K., Wise, B., Conners, F. & Rack, J. (1989). Specific deficits in component reading and language skills: genetic and environmental influences. *Journal of Learning Disabilities*, **22**, 339–348.

Rack, J. P., Snowling, M. J. & Olson, R. K. (1992). The nonword reading deficit in developmental dyslexia: a review. *Reading Research Quarterly*, **27**, 28–53.

Reinking, D. (1987). *Reading and Computers: Issues for Theory and Practice*. New York: Teachers College Press.

Rohl, M. & Tunmer, W. E. (1988). Phonemic segmentation skill and spelling acquisition. *Applied Psycholinguistics*, **9**, 335–350.

Stanovich, K. (1988). The right and wrong places to look for the cognitive locus of reading disability. *Annals of Dyslexia*, **38**, 154–177.

Stanovich, K. E., Cunningham, A. & Cramer, B. (1984). Assessing phonological awareness in kindergarten children: issues of task comparability. *Journal of Experimental Child Psychology*, **38**, 175–190.

Treiman, R. (1985). Phonemic analysis, spelling, and reading. In T. Carr (Ed.), *Language, Cognition, and Reading Development*. San Francisco: Jossey-Bass.

Treiman, R. (1991). Phonological awareness and its roles in learning to read and spell. In D. J. Sawyer & B. J. Fox (Eds), *Phonological Awareness in Reading: The Evolution of Current Perspectives*. New York: Springer Verlag.

Uhry, J. K. & Shepherd, M. J. (in press). Segmentation/spelling instruction as part of a first grade reading program: effects on several measures of reading. *Reading Research Quarterly*.

van Daal, V. & van der Leij, A. (1992). Computer-based reading and spelling practice for children with learning disabilities. *Journal of Learning Disabilities*, **25**, 186–195.

Vaughn, S., Schumm, J. S. & Gordon, J. (1992). Early spelling acquisition: does writing really beat the computer? *Learning Disabilities Quarterly*, **15**, 223–228.

Vaughn, S., Schumm, J. S. & Gordon, J. (1993). Which motoric condition is most effective for teaching spelling to students with learning disabilities? *Journal of Learning Disabilities*, **26**, 191–198.

Wagner, R. & Torgesen, J. (1987). The nature of phonological processing and its causal role in the acquisition of reading skills. *Psychological Bulletin*, **101**, 192–212.

Wise, B. W. (1991). What reading disabled children need: what is known and how to talk about it. *Learning & Individual Differences*, **4**, 307–321.

Wise, B. (1992). Whole words and decoding for short-term learning: comparisons on a "talking-computer" system. *Journal of Experimental Child Psychology*, **54**, 147–167.

Wise, B. W. & Olson, R. K. (1993). Computer speech and the remediation of reading and spelling problems. *Journal of Special Education Technology*, **12** (3), 1–14.

Wise, B. W., Lindamood, P. & Olson, R. K. (1993). *Training phonemic awareness: why and how it might be done with computerized instruction*. Part of a symposium at the annual meeting of the American Educational Researchers Association, Atlanta, Georgia, April 1993.

Wise, B. W. & Olson, R. K. (1991). Remediating reading disabilities. In J. E. Obrzut & G. W. Hynd (Eds), *Neuropsychological Foundations in Learning Disabilities: A Handbook of Issues, Methods, and Practice*. New York: Academic Press.

Wise, B. W. & Olson, R. K. (1992). How poor readers and spellers use interactive speech in a computerized spelling program. *Reading & Writing*, **4**, 145–163.

Wise, B. & Olson, R. K. (in press). What computerized speech can add to remedial reading. In A. K. Syrdal, R. Bennett & S. Greenspan (Eds), *Behavioral Aspects of Speech Technology: Theory and Applications*. Amsterdam: Elsevier.

Wise. B. W., Olson, R. K., Anstett, M., Andrews, L., Terjak, M., Schneider, V., Kostuch, K. & Kriho, L. (1989). Implementing a long-term computerized remedial reading program with synthetic speech feedback. *Behavior Research Methods, Instruments & Computers*, **21**, 173–180.

APPENDIX

TESTING AND TRAINING STIMULI IN THE COLORADO
SPELLING STUDIES

WRATread	Neighbor	Nonword	WRATspell	Neighbor	Nonword
cat	hat	gat	go	so	ho
see	bee	vee	cat	mat	dat
red	bed	med	in	pin	stin
to	into	unto	boy	toy	moy
big	pig	vig	and	stand	grand
work	working	worky	will	frill	brill
book	shook	gook	make	lake	plake
eat	meat	deat	him	grim	crim
was	wasn't	twas	say	pray	blay
him	slim	glim	cut	shut	fut
how	row	frow	cook	brook	snook
then	when	chen	light	bright	blight
open	opens	olens	must	dust	nust
letter	better	vetter	dress	press	kress
jar	star	blar	reach	preach	greach
deep	steep	teep	order	ordered	orkered
even	Steven	feven	watch	watching	watchly
spell	smell	pell	enter	center	venter
awake	wake	dake	grown	blown	slown
block	flock	drock	nature	future	plature
size	prize	stize	explain	exclaim	extrain
weather	heather	sweather	edge	hedge	medge
should	could	whould	kitchen	hitching	glitchen
lip	clip	glip	surprise	surmise	survise
finger	linger	minger	result	consult	besult
tray	pray	kray	advice	advise	unvice
felt	belt	delt	purchase	purpose	purpith
stalk	talk	spalk	brief	thief	crief
cliff	stiff	bliff	success	succeed	chucceed
lame	blame	stame	reasonable	treasonable	preasonable
struck	pluck	spuck	imaginary	imagination	imaginate
approve	reprove	deprove	occupy	occupation	occulate
plot	clot	flot	character	characteristic	characting
huge	hugely	chuge	society	presociety	societry
quality	qualify	qualition	official	unofficial	officialization
sour	hour	zour	recognize	recognition	recognify
imply	reply	unply	familiar	familiarize	pamiliar
humidity	rapidity	rumidity	commission	permission	demission
urge	surge	turge	beneficial	beneficiary	beneficious
bulk	sulk	vulk	appropriation	appropriate	preappropriate
exhaust	exhale	exhane	enthusiasm	enthusiastic	enthusify
abuse	refuse	rebuse	criticize	critical	criticipate
collapse	relapse	unlapse	prejudice	precipice	prejupice
glutton	mutton	sutton	belligerent	bellicose	bellition
clarify	scarify	blarify	occurrence	occurring	occurrity

Appendix (*continued*)

WRATread	Neighbor	Nonword
recession	procession	uncession
threshold	threshing	threshment
horizon	horizontal	horizonous
residence	resident	tresidence
participate	anticipate	condicipate
quarantine	quarter	quarant
luxurious	luxury	luxumious
rescinded	rescind	prescinded
emphasis	emphatic	hemphasis
aeronautic	astronaut	agronaut
intrigue	intriguing	untrigue
repugnant	repugnance	impugnant
putative	putatively	rutative
endeavor	endeavoring	mendeavor
heresy	heretic	cheresy
discretionary	discretion	miscretionary
persevere	perseverance	insevere
anomaly	anomalous	anomagy
rudimentary	complimentary	sudimentary
miscreant	miscreate	misdreant
usurp	usurpation	usurpity
novice	novel	noviced
audacious	rapacious	inflacious
mitosis	mitotic	mitosious
seismograph	seismic	seismonaut
spurious	spuriously	spumious
idiosyncrasy	idiosyncratic	idiosynthesy
itinerary	itineration	itinermary
pseudonym	pseudoevent	pseudopod
aborigines	aboriginal	aboriginate

24

Spelling Remediation for Dyslexic Children: A Skills Approach

RODERICK I. NICOLSON AND ANGELA J. FAWCETT
University of Sheffield

The main applied theme of this chapter is an exposition of the "SelfSpell" computer-based environment for children learning to spell. In long-term research on the causes of dyslexia we had built up a panel of dyslexic children, and we developed SelfSpell mainly as a "thank you" to them for their unstinting support of our experimental programme over a period of years. Although SelfSpell was initially developed for this remediation purpose, we later used the system to investigate theoretical issues in spelling.

In writing this chapter we have attempted to bring in as wide a range of theoretical ideas and approaches as seem relevant to the remediation of spelling problems. Consequently, we have gone beyond the traditional confines of linguistic theory and reading analyses and included the much broader literature on skill acquisition and computer-aided skill remediation. This chapter should therefore be seen as complementary to the other chapters in this volume, which typically take a more focused approach to spelling. It should also be stressed that the approach adopted represents only a preliminary attempt at applying a cognitive instructional approach to the analysis and remediation of spelling. We wrote the chapter partly in the hope that readers might be able to develop it further.

The organization of the chapter is as follows. First we review the well-established problems that dyslexic children have in learning to spell, and note briefly the theoretical issues resulting from these difficulties. We then step back, and review the relevant

Handbook of Spelling: Theory, Process and Intervention. Edited by G. D. A. Brown and N. C. Ellis.

literature on acquisition of skill and computer-supported skill remediation, moving towards a specification for a good system for helping children with spelling. The SelfSpell system provides a partial fulfilment of these requirements, and we next present two studies of the use of SelfSpell with dyslexic children. In both studies the children showed significant and lasting improvements in spelling ability, and the second study is of considerable theoretical and applied interest in that dyslexic children with severe spelling difficulties benefited both from a mastery-based approach and from a mnemonic-based approach.

Spelling and Dyslexia

Specific developmental dyslexia is normally characterized by unexpected problems in learning to read for children of average or above-average intelligence. There is still considerable debate over diagnostic methods, but a standard criterion for dyslexia is that provided by the World Federation of Neurologists (1968)—"a disorder in children who, despite conventional classroom experience, fail to attain the language skills of reading, writing and spelling commensurate with their intellectual abilities". A typical estimate of the prevalence of dyslexia in western school populations is 5% (Badian, 1984; Jorm *et al.*, 1986), with roughly four times as many boys as girls being diagnosed. As is clear from the definition, in addition to early difficulties in reading, dyslexic performance is characterized by poor spelling, in particular the production of bizarre errors, based on letter combinations that are not normally found in the English language (see, for instance, Miles, 1983). It is now well established that spelling deficits in dyslexic children typically prove more intractable than the reading deficits on which the original diagnosis of dyslexia is based (Frith, 1985). Relative impairments in reading and spelling may be measured by an "achievement ratio", which charts the improvement in attainment over a year. For non-dyslexic children, on average this ratio is by definition 1.00 (that is, improvement of 12 months in a year), whereas for dyslexic children Thomson (1984) recorded typical ratios of 0.40 for reading and 0.27 for spelling (improvements of only 5 months and around 3 months respectively in any 12-month period). One of the most worrying aspects is that these problems become cumulative, and dyslexic children can get sucked into a vicious circle of deficit and avoidance for written text.

Frith (1985) provided a theoretical analysis of the development of reading and spelling, identifying three stages: namely, the "logographic stage", in which whole words are read as a unit; the "alphabetic stage", in which a word may be decoded using grapheme–phoneme translation rules; and finally the "orthographic stage", in which regularities and spelling patterns are abstracted out as independent (non-phonological) orthographic units and sequences of letters and recognized automatically. The young child who recognizes the word *McDonalds* from the burger packet is in the logographic stage, and can learn a limited number of words from flash cards. Fairly soon, the memory load in the logographic stage becomes too heavy and the child must then progress to the alphabetic stage to make further headway. However, two developments are necessary here: first the child must be able to analyse or segment the word in some way; then he/she must be able to identify each letter or grapheme, supply the appropriate sound and then finally blend the word together into a whole (for example "*c-a-t* that says *cat*"). Frith has argued that the ability to segment and translate graphemes to phonemes and vice versa represents a bottleneck in the development of reading and spelling for dyslexic children. Unfortunately, difficulties at these early stages preclude the smooth transition to the orthographic stage, where the whole word is recognized without the need to break it down phonologically. In fact, Frith (1985) argues that development in reading and spelling involves a reciprocal interaction, and that the attainment of the alphabetic stage in writing must precede its acquisition in reading. She therefore concludes that dyslexic children are blocked at the logographic stage, because they are unable to apply phoneme–grapheme conversion in order to progress to the alphabetic stage.

Despite the current interest in spelling in dyslexic children, there have been surprisingly few comparative studies of the efficacy of training methods. However, in recent evaluations of remedial techniques with dyslexic children with low spelling ages, Thomson (1988, 1991) demonstrated that the traditional methods of "look, cover and check" (visual inspection) are ineffective for the acquisition of consistently misspelled words. In the same series of studies, Thomson also investigated the multi-sensory "simultaneous oral spelling" technique advocated for dyslexic children (e.g. Hulme, 1981). This technique involves saying the word aloud, spelling it, repeating the word, then writing it down, saying each letter individually as it is written, then reading the word, covering it up and spelling it again. He found that the technique was effective for regular words, such as *system, vandal, confirm, turban, nectar*, but with irregular words, such as *biscuit, enough, special, beauty, yachtsman*, the dyslexic children made less progress after 10 daily training sessions than control children matched for spelling age, correctly spelling only 25% compared with the controls' 42%. It appears therefore that the spelling deficits of dyslexic children with low spelling ages are resistant to remediation using either a traditional or a multi-sensory technique.

Much of the research to date on spelling and dyslexia is consistent with Frith's stage framework. However, it should be noted that stage frameworks tend to be descriptive rather than prescriptive (Goswami & Bryant, 1990). To say a child is "stuck in the logographic stage" is not particularly helpful from the point of view of remediation, and indeed one might take it as a counsel for inactivity or avoidance. In this chapter we present evaluation studies of what we consider to be a very promising remediation technique, together with a theoretical interpretation of the results which differs significantly from that of Frith. In contrast to much of the traditional language-based research on spelling and on dyslexia, our approach is based firmly on a general analysis of skill acquisition. Consequently, we first present a brief overview of theories of skill acquisition, taken from the viewpoint of supporting the learning process. Next we review progress in cognate skills, concentrating on early mathematics, which has been the subject of considerable cognitive research. This review prefaces our attempt to provide an initial analysis of the component skills and strategies of spelling, which in turn provides the basis for a preliminary analysis of the support required for a learner speller. First, though, it is important to describe technological developments which permit the development of a new approach to spelling remediation, and which inspired us to try to develop SelfSpell.

Computer-Based Support for Spelling

One promising approach to remedying skills which are resistant to traditional approaches is to use computer-based presentation of material. Unfortunately, dyslexic children tend to suffer from: poor reading; poor spelling; poor working memory; slow processing of written text; and poor motivation with written materials. The specific problems with these enabling skills have made it particularly difficult to provide much computer-based support, since they are the prerequisites for traditional computer-based methods. Thomson (1984) concluded that traditional computer-based learning approaches suffer from a number of disadvantages which render them particularly inaccessible for dyslexic children (Table 24.1). The major problem for poor readers was the method of user interaction. In the absence of audio output, the only method for communicating with the user was visually, and in the impoverished days of the early micro, the traditional method was, at best, "Press RETURN to continue". Therefore, despite the potential of the computer-based approach, early computer-based techniques depended upon skills which were the precise weaknesses of dyslexic children.

The Benefits of Multi-Media Presentation for Dyslexic Children

Educational technology has recently taken a major step forward with the introduction of a new generation of affordable but very powerful micros such as the Apple Macintosh. In particular, the availability of hyper-media and multi-media environments which allow the smooth integration of text, graphics and synthesized or digitized speech, together with capability for interaction using "point and click" rather than keyboard text entry, promise a solution to the problems for dyslexic children noted above. Furthermore, the use of synthesized or digitized speech to present the instructions and give feedback to the children provides the element of fun too often overlooked in the struggle to achieve literacy. Harnessing these unique capabilities can provide a formidable tool for the remediation of even the most intractable difficulties, such as spelling, but the impact of the system will be considerably diminished if it fails to take into account the requirements of the learner as well as the capabilities of the medium.

TABLE 24.1   Evaluation of CAL for dyslexic children (after Thomson, 1984).

Advantages of CAL	Disadvantages of CAL
Provides new motivation	Hard to programme speech
Essential overlearning	Multi-sensory output impossible
Immediate feedback	Limited adaptability to error
Child's own pace	Relies on reading instructions
Non-judgemental and predictable	Lacks human contact
Keyboard avoids handwriting	
Can store and access information	

APPROACHES TO SKILL ACQUISITION

The "classic" account of motor skill development was derived by Paul Fitts (Fitts & Posner, 1967). In brief, he analysed the learning process into three stages: the cognitive stage, in which the basic task requirements are determined; the associative phase, in which a method for carrying out the requirements is worked out; and the autonomous phase, in which the task is carried out more and more smoothly, with less and less need for conscious attention. To take the much used example of learning to drive a car, if one's objective is to select third gear, the cognitive phase includes knowing when to select third gear, what the gear stick layout is, what the function of the clutch pedal is, and so on. The associative phase involves the learning of the sequence—release accelerator pedal, depress clutch pedal, move gearstick up across and up again, release clutch pedal, depress accelerator pedal. However, this process initially needs a great deal of conscious monitoring, to the extent that the beginner actually has to watch the hand movements of the gearstick to the potential peril of those in the vicinity! With extended practice, rather than six sequential actions, the whole procedure becomes a single smooth composite action, requiring little or no conscious monitoring. The skill has become autonomous, or automatic. In a programmatic investigation of the processes of skill, Shiffrin and Schneider (1977) established that with prolonged training an arbitrary cognitive skill could become automatic, but only if the learning conditions were appropriate. In particular, they distinguished between "consistent mapping", in which the required action to a given stimulus remained the same throughout training, and "varied mapping", in which the required action to a given stimulus was varied randomly throughout the training. They demonstrated that consistent mapping was a prerequisite for the development of automaticity, and distinguished between two types of process:

1. Controlled processing. Requires attentional control, uses up working memory capacity and is often serial. It is relatively easy to set up, modify and use in novel situations. It is employed to facilitate long-term learning of all kinds (including automatization).
2. Automatic processing. Once learned in long-term memory it operates independently of the subject's control and uses no working memory resources. It does not require attention and is acquired through consistent mapping. Targets can acquire the ability to attract attention and initiate responses automatically, immediately and independent of other memory loads.

Anderson's ACT* model (1982, 1989) of the acquisition of skill probably represents the most influential current view of cognitive learning, and since it may be traced back directly to Fitts and Posner's (1967) account of motor learning, it forms a reasonable framework for the analysis of both motor and cognitive skill. ACT* suggests that the learning process may be conceptualized as three broad stages. Declarative knowledge (e.g. the task requirements) must be acquired initially. This declarative knowledge must then be "proceduralized" by a "knowledge compilation" process consequent upon successful performance, turning it into a production rule format which can be used to carry out the requirements. The production rules may subsequently be tuned by extended practice, thus making them more efficient. Automatization occurs in this final stage, making the procedures less dependent upon working memory and less susceptible to interference. One of Anderson's achievements was to demonstrate that this theory of learning could be applied not just to "motor" tasks such as studied by Fitts and Posner but also to a range of cognitive skills, including geometrical reasoning, computer programming, development of language and letter recognition.

In skills such as chess, the declarative stage (learning how the pieces move, what their value is, the rules of the game, common openings, etc.) can take years, and is obviously interleaved with the acquisition of procedural skills such as learning to win with rook and king against king. In motor skills such as learning to write a letter *b*, the declarative component presumably comprises the knowledge of the shape of the letter, plus the preferred order of pen strokes. For a skilled writer attempting to write an unfamiliar letter, say a ψ, the necessary sub-skills for writing the individual components are presumably highly learned, and the major difficulty is the declarative learning problem of identifying and remembering what the segments are. It may be seen why studies of learning are so fraught with difficulty. For even a moderately complex task there is a range of possible methods, each involving previously learned skills, each of which may be more or less automatized.

The Conditions of Learning

Theoretical analysis of the different types of knowledge and skill to be learned gives at best half the picture. As Simon (1979, p. 92) has noted: "Generally speaking, textbooks are much more explicit in enunciating the laws of [mathematics] . . . than in saying when these laws might be useful in solving problems". John Anderson (e.g. 1990) has also emphasized that is critically important to explain to a learner how to go about solving problems in addition to merely providing declarative knowledge. In the context of spelling, this viewpoint suggests strongly that telling a child a correct spelling will be of only limited value unless the child understands how to go about reconstructing that spelling for himself/herself. Furthermore, the likelihood of a student acquiring knowledge can be dramatically influenced by the conditions under which the knowledge is made available, and by the learner's attitudes to the learning process. This section highlights some of these applied factors which seem particularly relevant to learning of spelling, and attempts to relate them back to the issue discussed above. It is not possible to do justice to such a huge and well-researched area in a few paragraphs. A recent comprehensive overview is provided by Snow and Swanson (1992). Here we can only take up four of the most important strands, with two—feedback and structure—deriving from the instructional perspective which has inspired much of the computer-aided learning (CAL) approaches to learning, and two—motivation and active learning—deriving from the affective/cognitive approach often seen incorrectly as a competing framework. Any complete remedial system should attempt to integrate both approaches.

Feedback

The importance of feedback in human learning was highlighted by the behaviourist B. F. Skinner (e.g. 1968), whose "programmed learning" technique formed the basis for a generation of CAL programs (see O'Shea & Self, 1983, for a valuable overview and critique of the approach). Skinner argued that the three key requirements for procedural skill learning were:

- The information to be learned should be presented in small steps
- Learners should be given rapid feedback concerning their accuracy
- Learners should learn at their own pace

Despite considerable criticism of the narrowness of Skinner's approach, no-one has seriously criticized these three criteria for effective presentation of instructional material. Indeed, the current connectionist approach to learning (see Brown and Loosemore, this volume, Chapter 16 for an exposition of its application to spelling) might suggest essentially the same approach. Lack, or delay, of feedback is arguably one of the greatest problems in mass educational systems, whether school or university. For many learner spellers, the first feedback will come 10 minutes or even days after the event, and will include feedback on a whole range of mistaken spellings, feedback which is too unfocused and too late to be of much use. It is also important to note that feedback can be just as constructive following an error as a success. Seymour Papert (1980) was one of the first theorists to stress the potential positive value of mistakes as a halfway house to fuller understanding. One of the problems of the British cultural system is that teachers tend to criticize mistakes rather than build on them, with the result that children are brought up to fear making mistakes, whereas one might argue that a child who never errs has never been stretched.

Structured approaches to instruction

Glaser (1976) provided an analysis of the requirements for a theory instruction, distinguishing five essential components of an instructional theory, namely: description of the instructional goals; description of the learners' states before the instruction; explication of the transition processes from initial to desired states; specification of the instructional conditions that facilitate the transition; and assessment of performance and instructional effects.

A related but broader approach to learning and instruction was provided by Robert Gagné (e.g. 1985), and although now somewhat dated, it provides a valuable resource for anyone wishing to explore methods of instruction in greater depth. In brief, Gagné distinguished five key capabilities, namely, information, intellectual skills, cognitive strategies, motor skills and attitude. Gagné's theory of instruction suggests that the overall method for training any skill is first to do a thorough task analysis, determining what the sub-skills involved are, what their prerequisites are, and so on, thus identifying a hierarchical tree of sub-skills that make up the skill. For each sub-skill it is necessary to determine which of the five types of capability it is, and then to devise a method for instruction on that sub-skill. In general, the methods used will depend upon the nature of the skill to be learned, but it is worth highlighting the early stages, which emphasize the need to make clear the objectives of the training plan and remind the learner of relevant information. As noted earlier, there is a consensus in the literature that these early skills should be reasonably well overlearned before subsequent stages can safely build on them.

Motivation

Motivation holds the key to most human learning. It is common to distinguish between intrinsic motivation, in which the topic is interesting in its own right, and extrinsic motivation, in which the motivation derives from some external source (e.g. a course requirement). A series of studies by Malone (1981) showed that motivation was a particularly powerful inducer of learning. A further powerful motivational factor is "ownership", that is, making a problem relevant to one's own interests. If the learner has a personal interest in a topic, motivation and success follow naturally. By contrast, if the learner cannot perceive the point of a topic, it is very difficult to make much headway. A related concept, which is also relevant to type of learning, is that of locus of control. Studies have shown (e.g. Rotter, 1975) that learners who perceive themselves to be in control of their learning situation tend to cope better than those who see themselves as "pawns" in the teaching machine. Furthermore, studies of failure (see Holt, 1984) have often revealed a vicious circle, in which following repeated failures, a learner either adopts a passive learning strategy, or maybe some coping strategy which downplays learning at the expense of some more attainable goal (sport, disruption, etc.). Stanovich (1988) has highlighted this vicious circle for dyslexic children, naming it the "Matthew effect", a biblical reference to the poor getting poorer.

Active learning

Orthogonal to the above analyses are the distinctions between active and passive learning, and between deep and surface processing. One of the best-established facts of instructional psychology is that active learning is better than passive learning, whether for declarative or procedural knowledge. An active learner will try to "make sense" of the information input, attempting to relate it to his/her existing knowledge, and to evaluate and organize it. Active learning is normally associated with deep processing, which means attention to the meaning rather than surface characteristics of the information. Activeness of learning is fragile and can be destroyed by excessive speed of presentation, confusing presentation and fatigue.

Approaches to Instruction in Basic School Skills

It would be otiose to attempt here an exposition of current theoretical approaches to reading, writing and spelling (see the other chapters in this volume, or Goswami & Bryant, 1990). It will be seen, in fact, that most adopt a developmental, psycholinguistic approach, reflecting the major source of theoretical input to the area. Suffice it to say that a learning perspective should also be of use in analyses of reading problems. Consider the conclusions of a recent detailed overview and analysis of the teaching of reading: ". . . Laboratory research indicates that the most critical factor beneath fluent word reading is the ability to recognise letters, spelling patterns, and whole words effortlessly, automatically and visually. The central goal of all reading instruction—comprehension—depends critically on this ability" (Adams, 1990, p. 54). These conclusions reflect closely the expectations of the cognitive skill literature.

Relatively little evidence is available on the skill-based approach to spelling and reading, though a recent series of studies (Yap & van der Leij, 1993) has indicated that dyslexic children do appear to have particular difficulties in automatizing the reading process, requiring a longer exposure time to read words than children matched for reading ability and also showing a slower improvement with practice in tachistoscopic reading than the reading age controls.

Studies of spelling remediation are well described by other contributors to this volume. Elaine and Tim Miles have unrivalled experience of traditional spelling remediation for dyslexic children, and their teaching system (Miles, 1991) provides many valuable suggestions. Peter Pumphrey and Rea Reason (1991) have provided a valuable and comprehensive assessment of all aspects of education for dyslexic children, based on a British national inquiry by a working group of educational psychologists. Barbara Wise and Dick Olson have perhaps the longest experience in computer-based spelling remediation for dyslexic children, having developed their program "Spello", which gives interactive synthesized speech feedback to the child over a period of 5 years or more (see Wise & Olson, 1992, for a recent review of the system). Rather than attempting to duplicate these authors' descriptions of their systems, we turn briefly to analysis of a cognate skill, early mathematics, which develops roughly in parallel with spelling, and which has been extensively analysed from the remediation viewpoint.

Reading 'Riting and 'Rithmetic form the "three Rs" of primary education, the bedrock of further development. Unlike reading and writing, arithmetic is a fully externalizable and rule-based skill, capable of good support even from early generations of computers. Following seminal work by Brown and Burton (1978), it was realized that it should be possible for a computer program—an "intelligent tutoring system" (ITS)—to set questions for a child, and then, by monitoring the responses and comparing them against both the correct method and a "bug catalogue" of faulty methods, to determine whether or not the child misunderstood the principles involved. If so, the ITS should be able to explain what the child was doing wrong and also to "coach" the child in the correct method. Despite very substantial research on these issues, this early ITS research failed to deliver a working schoolroom version for arithmetic, and most ITS development work turned to commercial or higher educational targets. Recently, a complete analysis of the task requirements for an intelligent tutor for arithmetic led to the development of a system (SUMIT) which was designed to fit in with standard classroom practice, working as a teacher's "intelligent tutoring assistant", doing all the routine background work of setting questions, monitoring and correcting answers, explaining where the child was going wrong, and explaining how to do the sum correctly. This support then freed the teacher to concentrate on the things that humans do uniquely, such as explaining the initial ideas, linking them in with related topics such as counting change, and so on. A series of controlled evaluation studies showed that SUMIT was indeed uniquely effective for children of all abilities, leading to a reduction in the estimated required learning time by a factor of around five (Nicolson, 1991). SUMIT is particularly interesting in this context because the principles used to develop SelfSpell were taken from the methodology established for SUMIT. In brief, the principles involved were:

1. Perform a task analysis of the requirements in the skill at each stage in skill development, identifying in particular the problems likely to arise at each stage
2. Perform a cost–benefit analysis of the standard methods of teaching the skill in the class, identifying areas of strength and weakness
3. Consider which of the weaknesses might be suitably alleviated by a computer program
4. Develop a computer program able to support the class teaching process, while being usable also as a support for home spelling
5. Evaluate the effectiveness of the program, and make adjustments as necessary

The outcomes of this methodology are described in the following sections. We start with a preliminary task analysis for spelling.

Stages in Learning to Spell

Even a naive analysis, uninformed by current theory, indicates the formidable problems faced by a child trying to learn to spell. First there is the need to have reasonable familiarity with the "rules of the game", the declarative knowledge that the idea is to use the letters of the alphabet to represent each word, based upon its sound. Next there must be some basic procedural knowledge for how to try to spell a single-syllable word (sound it out then try to identify the first letter (onset), write it down then try to split the remainder (rime) into vowel letter followed by last letter, and so on). In due course the child must learn how to attack a long word (break it down into syllables then try to spell each syllable; or reason by analogy with a similar sounding word whose spelling is known). There must also be procedural knowledge for knowing how to check whether one's attempted spelling is plausible. This entails trying to read out loud one's attempted spelling, and therefore involves grapheme-to-phoneme decoding skills. Once these enabling skills have been grasped, there is no alternative to building the vast declarative knowledge base which makes up lexical knowledge—associating with each word its sound, meaning and spelling—so that rather than a resource-intensive problem-solving exercise, the spelling of a word is a simple automatic "look-up". The lexicon must be built up gradually, but once the enabling skills are learned, together with a critical mass of solid spelling knowledge which can form an anchor for spelling-by-analogy, it seems likely that the process can work by the straightforward process of knowledge accretion. At this level of the reasonably skilled speller, the major problems are not those of general rules but specific confusions—say being unable to remember whether there are one or two cs in the word *necessary*. These confusions are unlike the arithmetic "bugs" described by Brown and Burton, in that the latter are intended to refer to faulty rules, whereas the former are just confusions. Indeed, there is probably no equivalent in the case of arithmetic or chess. We shall distinguish the two categories by use of the terms "rule bugs" and "word bugs". Word bugs typically arise through failure to distinguish between similar but competing spellings (for instance *success* vs *necessary*). Here the problem is that both spellings get strengthened, leading to the presence of alternative high-strength entries in the lexicon. It is here that mere practice is seldom sufficient. Mnemonic strategies (such as the doggerel "Never Eat Cucumbers, Eat Salad

Sandwiches And Remain Young" for the spelling of *necessary*) often prove the answer to this type of word bug.

No doubt a fuller understanding of the linguistic background to spelling (as detailed by the theoretical chapters in this volume) would lead to a more sophisticated analysis, but it is clear that even this common-sense approach provides an analysis rich enough to guide the development of remediation systems. Before turning to a specification for an ideal remediation system, however, it is important to consider the likely problems the learner speller is likely to encounter.

Problems in Learning to Spell

The above analysis suggests a number of likely problems:

1. Lack of understanding of the "rules of the game" and/or absence of "how to" procedural knowledge. The beginning speller may have little or no idea about the purpose of spelling or that words are made of letters each of which is intended to represent that part of the word's sound, with the first letter representing the first sound, and so on. More likely, the learner has not grasped the basic strategy of first deciding the initial letter and putting it down, and then proceeding by sounding out the word. The result of this basic declarative and procedural knowledge is that a child can get trapped in the inappropriate, primitive strategy of attempting to memorize an endless list of "whole-word" spellings, without realizing that there is a key to the spelling system.

2. Lack of mastery of the component sub-skills. Even supposing that a child understands the basic principles of spelling, lack of mastery of the sub-skills involved can essentially prevent learning. It is well established that at the age of around 6 years dyslexic children (that is, children who will shortly be diagnosed as dyslexic) have significant development delays in letter identification, phonological analysis of words, word segmentation and effective working memory. Furthermore, most dyslexic children suffer from significant handwriting problems, so that more concentration than normal is needed merely to write down each letter of the spelling. Each of these problems militates against smooth acquisition of the skill.

3. Resource limitations. For an adult, the component sub-skills in spelling are so well automatized that it is easy to overlook the enormous working memory load involved in learning to spell *cat*. First say it. What's the first sound? That's a *c*. Now what does that look like . . . write it down . . . do I start at the top? Now what? Say it again. What comes after the *c* sound? *at*. Now what does that start with? *a*. What does *a* look like? Write it down, remember to start next to the *c* but higher up so that the bottom lines up . . . Now where have I got to? I've done, what is it, *c* and *a*. What do they make, *ca*. OK, Say *cat* again. Now I've got *ca*, so what does that leave? Yes, *t*. OK, write that down. Now what? I've written *c a t*. Is that it? Yes, I think so." The working memory load is enormous, especially bearing in mind the greater resources required for each of the component skills. For an adult it is perhaps equivalent to mentally multiplying two four-digit numbers. Naturally, the scope for error is very great, leading to a belief that the

task is impossible, together with the danger of acquisition of bad habits, such as putting down the first letter or two and then guessing the rest.

4. Lack of a structured learning environment. Compounding the severe problems above is the unfortunate fact that it is impossible to teach spelling in the structured fashion employed for, say, arithmetic, in which one first masters the basics then introduces the necessary procedures one at a time, slowly building up a large knowledge base in a structured, cumulative fashion. The obvious problems for spelling derive from the enormous domain size, with the large number of words needed even for a fairly basic reading text. Of course, the idiosyncrasies of the English spelling system (even for the most frequent words) mean that it is highly unlikely that the spelling of a particular word will receive the "consistent mapping" needed to allow that word's spelling to become automatized. This in turn leads to a failure to build up "anchoring knowledge" which can be used as bedrock from which to extend one's spelling knowledge by analogy and to check the plausibility of different spelling strategies.

5. Lack of success. This is the near inevitable result of the problems described above. Lack of success has a number of corrosive features in addition to failing to build up a bug-free knowledge base. One cognitive feature is the accumulation of bad habits and random spellings which are difficult to unlearn. More serious, however, is the near inevitable loss of motivation for spelling, and the consequent avoidance behaviour. Most serious of all is the loss of self-esteem, which can have disastrous general effects on the whole attitude to school and life.

Requirements for a Spelling Remediation System

We are at last now in a position to outline what we considered the most important design requirements for a spelling support system. The strategy is twofold: first to consider the established methods of "good practice" for skill acquisition and to try to build in as many as practicable; and second to consider the likely spelling problems discussed above and to try to design into the system a means of minimizing each of the problems. Our initial design requirements for SelfSpell were as follows:

1. Objectives. The program should be *effective* at remedying dyslexic children's most serious difficulties—in particular, spelling problems. Just as important, since motivation contributes crucially to a program's success (e.g. Malone, 1981), it should be *fun* to use!

2. Learning features. It should give immediate feedback—thus offering no opportunity for persistent errors. It should rely on active learning—with the user involved the whole time making active decisions; and it should support a range of forms of learning, including mastery learning. It should incorporate a good deal of positive feedback, making sure that the learner not only has a lot of success but is also aware of the success.

3. Support available. It should include: synthesized speech to supplement text displays; self-selection of materials—adopting the user's own passages, own spellings and own spelling rules. It should be possible to use an alphabetic keypad, so as to

minimize the difficulty in entering the letters. Furthermore, parental support should be encouraged, both for authoring materials and for checking progress.

4. Efficiency features. Automatic training, automatic record-keeping and automatic authoring should be available under program control.

5. Adaptive enhancement. It should be possible to evaluate the effectiveness of the system, and to adapt it as appropriate to further improve its effectiveness and enjoyability.

As a first step to meet this specification, we developed a program within the Apple HyperCard™ multi-media environment, using a Macintosh Classic micro. The intention was that the child should be able to use the system unaided much of the time, but with initial support from a parent or teacher. This support took the form of a multi-media computer environment, SelfSpell, which encouraged the children to construct their own mnemonic rules for the words with which they had difficulty.

A novel feature of SelfSpell was the capability of speaking the instructions, using computer generated synthesized speech. This increased the accessibility of the program for poor readers, thus avoiding many of the problems in computer presentation for dyslexics noted by Thomson (1984). In an initial evaluation study (Nicolson, Pickering & Fawcett, 1991), we demonstrated that the spelling deficits of adolescent dyslexic children were amenable to remediation with appropriate support, in that all the participants showed significant improvement in their targeted errors, extracted from a dictation matched to their reading age. Moreover, both they and their parents reported improvements in motivation following their three sessions of training, which one might speculate contributed to their generalized overall improvement on a second untrained passage. The approach used is described in detail in Nicolson, Pickering and Fawcett (1991) and also in the following section, so here it should suffice to note that it explicitly avoided any use whatever of rote learning, being based on encouraging the child to make up (and store for future use) a rule to help him/her remember each spelling.

The initial study demonstrated clearly that SelfSpell was valuable in the short term for adolescent dyslexic children, but it left three questions unresolved. First, how general were the findings, and in particular, were they peculiar to children who were already able to spell adequately? Second, how robust were the improvements, and in particular, did the approach lead to longer-term benefits? Third, and of key theoretical significance, why was there an improvement, and in particular, was it because of the multi-media presentation technique, the use of mnemonic-based methods, or some combination of the two? A second study (Nicolson, Fawcett & Morris, 1993) investigated these possibilities. We present this study in some detail, as it displays the features of the SelfSpell system well and it also addresses substantial theoretical issues.

TESTING MNEMONIC-BASED VS MASTERY-BASED APPROACHES TO SPELLING REMEDIATION

Participants

The participants in this study were 10 dyslexic children, aged between 10 and 12 years. They had been diagnosed as dyslexic between the ages of 7 and 10, on standard exclusionary criteria (i.e. an 18-month or more deficit in reading age over chronological age, together with normal or above-normal IQ and no primary emotional or neurological problems). Their mean IQ was 112.3 (range 105–128), mean chronological age 11.4 (range 10.0–12.8), with a mean reading age of 8.4 years (range 6.9–9.8) on the Schonell test of single-word reading and a mean spelling age of 6.6 years (range 5.0–9.0) on the Schonell test of regular spelling. It may be seen that, as expected, these children suffered relatively more impairment on spelling than reading, with a mean deficit between spelling and chronological age of 4.8 years. For instance, CE had successfully spelled only *top*, *wet*, *pig*, *peg*, *tub*, *thing*, *belong* and *left*, that is, only eight of the simpler words from the 60 presented in the Schonell test, leading to a spelling age of 5.0 years. Six of the eight had a spelling age of 6.0 or below, and were presumably in the "logographic" stage for spelling. None of the children was familiar with use of the Apple Macintosh.

Experimental Design

In order to compare the mnemonic-based, undirected approach (Nicolson, Pickering & Fawcett, 1991) with a directive mastery learning approach, a mastery learning program (SpellMaster) was written which, following a technique developed by Nicolson (1979), presented each spelling to be learned in a sequence designed adaptively to assist the learning process. Each participant learned 20 spellings, with 10 learned using a mnemonic-based approach and a matched set of 10 learned using a mastery approach. The two training methods are described in detail below.

A pencil and paper pretest on performance was administered by the parents before training began. Three training sessions, each of 20 minutes' duration, were run for each set of 10 words for each child. The order of presentation for the training methods was counterbalanced, so that half started with the SelfSpell rules and half with the Spellmaster. The training took place over the autumn half-term holiday, to ensure that all children would be available to complete three training sessions within a week. One week after the last training session a pencil and paper posttest exactly equivalent to the pretest was administered by the parents. One month after the training tests were completed parents were asked to administer a paper and pencil delayed posttest, to compare the relative long-term benefits of the training approaches.

The Pretest

In order to increase the motivation of these poor spellers, we wanted to train them in words which were of particular significance for them, rather than the limited vocabulary geared to their spelling age. Each parent was therefore asked to identify 20 words with which their child had particular difficulty. We encouraged the parents to choose words that the children used regularly rather than those anyone would find difficult. Having identified the words, the parent dictated them to the child and timed their performance. Parents were asked not to help their child with the spellings during the dictation. Following this baseline test, the parent discussed the words with the child, and helped them to rank them in order of difficulty from 1 to 20. Before the first session the ranked lists were returned to the experimenters and used to produce two sets of words, matched for level of difficulty. Notably, although some of the children spelled one or two of the words correctly, their ranking suggested that they still represented words with which they particularly struggled.

In order to make conditions as close as possible to standard home use, the words were not monitored in any way for regularity or objective ease of spelling. They ranged from complex words such as *dyslexic, persuade, humanities, umbrella* and *grateful* to simpler confusable words such as *there*. The majority of the children demonstrated age-appropriate language usage when selecting their own vocabulary, despite their impoverished reading and spelling skills.

The Training

SelfSpell mnemonic rules

Use of SelfSpell in this study fell into four distinct phases. First (the pretest) the parent dictated the selected words to the child, the child attempted to write down each word, and then ranked them in order of difficulty. Next the experimenter created a passage incorporating the selected words, typed the child's version into the computer and identified all the "bugs", making a bug card for each one. This process is illustrated in Figures 24.1(a) and 24.1(b), where it may be seen that the child has difficulty with many spellings, in particular spelling *might* as *"mintue"*. Next the child went through the passage (helped by the experimenter) identifying all the bugs, and for each one thinking up a rule to help them spell it right the next time (in Figure 24.1(b), the child has typed in the rule "green hero turtles", the title of a popular TV programme, to help him remember the *ght* at the end). In the final phase the child went through the passage unaided, fixing all the bugs, through judicious support from the program (see Figures 24.1(c), (d), (e) and (f)—the latter demonstrates the use of scoring to help with motivation). All the responses were monitored automatically thus allowing easy record-keeping. A novel feature of the program was that all the buttons were programmed to "say" their name if the user "hovered" over them with the mouse pointer, and furthermore there was a "speak" button which used speech synthesis to "pronounce" any words highlighted.

Spellmaster

In addition to the mnemonic-based approach outlined above, a more directive, mastery learning approach is also available under SelfSpell. In this approach a list of words may be typed in (together with their homophone under speech synthesis and an appropriate context description) and each word is then presented individually from time to time until it has been learned. Immediate feedback is used at all times and the correct spelling is displayed immediately following any error. The spellings are introduced cumulatively, first four spellings, then three more when the first four are learned, and so on. The technique employed was that of "overlearning", which is generally considered to be one of the most effective for dyslexic children (see e.g. Thomson, 1991).

An example of the spellings made in the second session for one of the participants using the Spellmaster program is given in Table 24.2. It may be seen that, in effect,

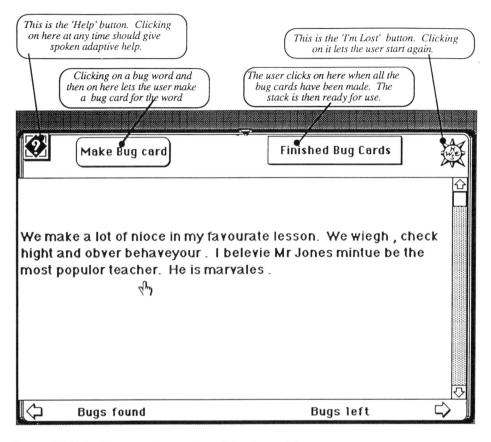

FIGURE 24.1(a)   The computer version of the transcript.

the program requires the user to spell all the words correctly at least three times consecutively and usually more in that even "learned" spellings are retested from time to time.

The children differed somewhat in their approach to this program, dependent on their typing ability. Although some of them tackled typing quite confidently, the less competent children struggled to find the correct letter. Therefore, a method of administration was adopted which allowed the child to type in some of the letters and the experimenter to take over when the child showed signs of tiring. A subsequent version incorporates an on-screen alphabetic keypad.

Results

The results for each child are displayed graphically in Figure 24.2. It may be seen that the children scored few marks on the pretests, but that both approaches led to excellent learning, as evidenced by the high scores on the posttest. The individual results are sufficiently striking to warrant presenting them in full. Note that all these tests were performed using the standard pencil and paper format.

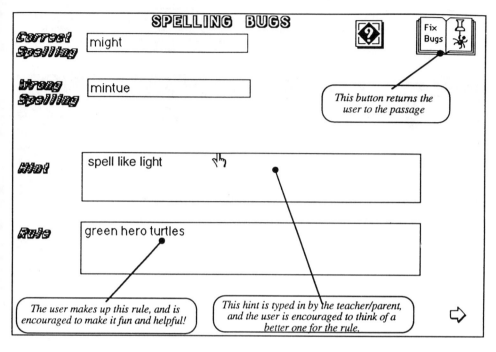

FIGURE 24.1(b)   Making a bug card for *might*.

An analysis of variance was performed on the data with two factors, namely time of test (pre, post and delayed) and training method (mastery or SelfSpell). The analysis indicated that time of test had a highly significant main effect whereas that of training method was not significant ($F(2,18) = 36.8$, $p < 0.0001$; $F(1,9) = 3.2$, NS respectively) and that the interaction was not significant ($F(2,18) = 3.0$, $p > 0.05$). *Post hoc* Tukeys showed that both the posttest and delayed posttest performance were significantly better than the pretest ($p < 0.01$) for both SelfSpell and Spellmaster training. Analysis of the "simple effects" indicated that the Spellmaster training was significantly better than the SelfSpell rules at the posttest ($F(1,9) = 5.7$, $p < 0.05$), but that there were no significant differences between the training conditions at pretest or delayed posttest ($F(1,9) = 0.5$, NS and $F(1,9) = 0.1$, NS respectively).

An informal questionnaire was administered after the training sessions but before the posttest. This established that all the children had enjoyed both the SelfSpell and Spellmaster programs. Preferences for the two programs were equally divided, with half the children preferring the Spellmaster program for the success it engendered and the other half preferring SelfSpell because it was more fun. Interestingly, this could be directly linked to the spelling age of the child. The lowest achievers preferred the Spellmaster, presumably because they typically misspelled even the most basic words. The sole exception was TF, the lowest achiever in the group, who was particularly delighted by the SelfSpell program. Open-ended comments were uniformly favourable.

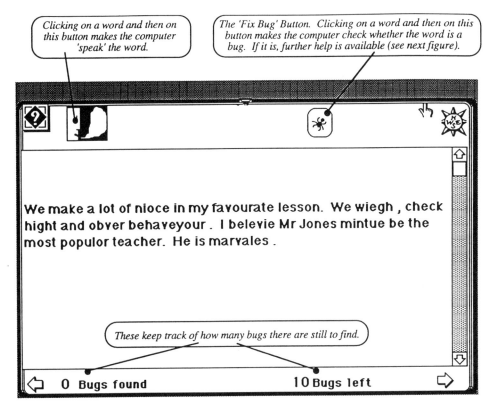

FIGURE 24.1(c)   Child's view of the support environment. Click on a bug.

DISCUSSION

In summary, both the SelfSpell and Spellmaster programs proved effective in remediating the spelling errors of a group of dyslexic children with low spelling ages. Performance on the delayed test showed some decline, but nevertheless was significantly better than at pretest. The Spellmaster program led to significantly better performance on the immediate posttest but performance on the delayed test was equivalent for both training methods.

Let us consider first the three questions which formed the immediate focus of this investigation: would the mnemonic-based approach work with younger children; would it lead to longer-term benefits; and what was the cause of the success of the approach? The first two questions were resolved clearly. The mnemonic-based program proved extremely effective in remediating the spelling problems of younger dyslexics with severe impairments in spelling, even with complex vocabulary far beyond the children's current level of achievement. Moreover, the mnemonic-based method produced lasting improvements for the majority of children. These results therefore replicated and extended the results of our earlier study, demonstrating the short-term and long-term effectiveness of the multi-media SelfSpell approach for dyslexic children of a wide range of spelling

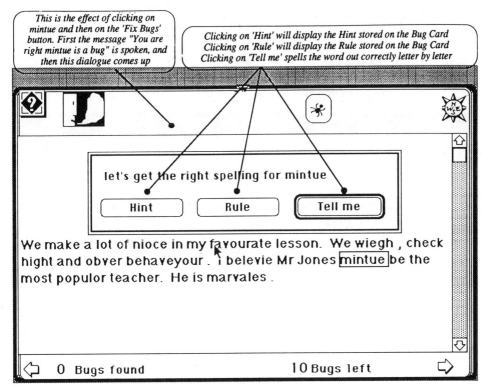

FIGURE 24.1(d)   After selecting *mintue* then clicking on the "bug" button.

ages. Such improvements are particularly striking in view of the typical resistance to remediation found with traditional pencil and paper training (see Thomson, 1991).

Moving to the third issue, the mastery technique was at least as successful as the mnemonic-based approach. This suggests that the mnemonic-based nature of the SelfSpell program was not the only reason for its success and that other approaches can prove equally effective. One might argue that it was the reinforcing nature of the computer presentation, coupled with the immediate feedback and the element of fun, which engendered the success, and that any learning approach which provided a systematic learning method might prove to be of value within such a supportive environment.

It is worthwhile here to consider the theoretical issues underlying the acquisition of spelling in the dyslexic child. Frith (1985) has argued that dyslexic children tend to get locked into the initial, "logographic" stage for reading, in which performance is based on whole-word recognition, and are unable to make the transition to the phonologically mediated alphabetic stage. The child would therefore recognize only the small proportion of words that he/she had previously encountered. Owing to their inability to make connections between the graphemes and phonemes, they would have no mechanism for acquiring new vocabulary unless it was explicitly taught. This would cause particularly severe problems for spelling, which, unlike reading, cannot be

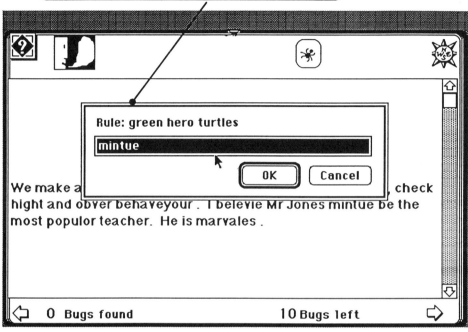

The user has selected 'Rule', so the rule from the Bug Card is displayed. The user should then try to type in the correct spelling into the box below, and then press OK (or the RETURN key).

If the new spelling is correct, the program says 'well done', changes the spelling in the passage, and updates the score counters.
If not it says 'Bad luck' and changes nothing.

Rule: green hero turtles

mintue

OK   Cancel

We make a   , check
hight and obver behaveyour . I belevie Mr Jones mintue be the
most populor teacher. He is marvales .

0 Bugs found   10 Bugs left

FIGURE 24.1(e)   Going for the rule.

TABLE 24.2   Results from spelling mastery.

Word	Spellings on Session 2	Pretest	Posttest	Delay
serious	shrece, sere, serious, serious, serious, serious	seros	serious	serious
certain	srten, sertain, certain, certain, certain, certain, certain	serton	certain	certain
comfortable	comfortable, comfortable, comfortable, comfortable	comfortuble	comfortable	comfortable
grateful	grateful, grateful, grateful, grateful	greateful	grateful	greatful
wearing	wearing, wearing, wearing, wearing	wharing	wearing	wearing
celebrate	slabrat, celebrate, celebrate, celebrate, celebrate	celebrate	celebrate	celebrate
absolutely	apslotly, aberlutly, absorlutely, apsolutely, absolutely, absolutely, absolutely	aberlootly	absolutely	absolutely
receive	resevie, receive, receive, receive	reseve	receive	rese
through	through, through, through, through	throught	though	th
peace	peace, peace, peace, peace	peace	peace	peace

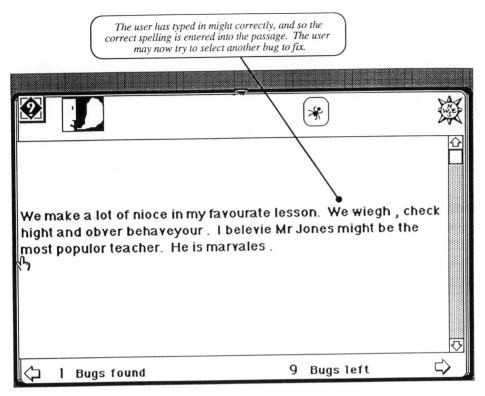

FIGURE 24.1(f)   The result of entering *might*.

facilitated by the use of context. Frith would argue that spelling performance for the younger dyslexic children breaks down in the alphabetic stage—either in the segmentation process, that is, in splitting words down into the individual sounds, or (for the more competent dyslexics) at the stage of phoneme–grapheme translation, that is, producing the correct letter for each sound. This would mean that the child was unable to spell words phonetically, and would explain the bizarre errors which characterize dyslexic performance (such as *mintue* for *might*), where the child is trying to reproduce the shape of the word rather than its constituent sounds.

The good progress of all the children, including those originally with almost no spelling ability, is therefore particularly encouraging, and perhaps rather surprising from the viewpoint of Frith's framework. It is useful here to consider what learning strategy the rule-based and mastery training techniques demand from the learner. The mastery training employs the traditional rote learning approach, and ensures that the speller focuses on both the whole word and its constituent parts, in other words it encourages segmentation. In fact, at the later stages, some of the more able children became overconfident, making simple typing errors, thereby increasing the number of presentations of that word. This feature of the program encouraged the children to proofread their work more carefully, to ensure that it was not marred by careless errors. The SelfSpell program encouraged the speller to focus on both phoneme/grapheme translation and segmentation, emphasizing the number of

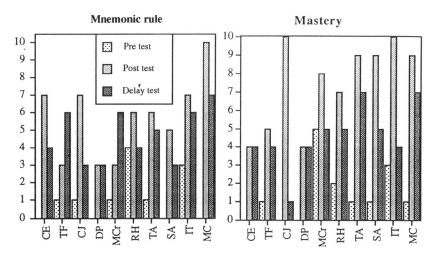

FIGURE 24.2   Correct spellings (out of 10) for rule and mastery training at pre, post and delayed test.

syllables (for example *al-to-get-her* for altogether) and typically using the initials of the missing letter for the clue (an example here might be "insects eat vegetables" for the *ieve* in *believe*).

One interesting possibility is that the design of our experiment, in which mastery techniques were pitted against mnemonic-based techniques but with all the participants exposed to both methods, led unwittingly to the creation of a learning environment which provided support not only for segmentation and for phoneme–grapheme conversion (via the mastery approach) but also for active learning and deeper processing via the mnemonic-based approach. It may be, therefore, that our initial conclusions that either method would prove effective are overoptimistic, and in fact a combination of both methods is needed to cause the improvements, with the mastery method being particularly valuable for helping the younger children learn general word attack skills and the mnemonic-based method proving valuable for learning specific problem words.[1]

Regardless of the precise cause of the effectiveness of the study, it is particularly encouraging to note that all the children in this study seemed able to use the alphabetic principle when given the appropriate support, especially in the light of the discouraging findings of earlier research on spelling remediation, and the theoretical rationale for expecting severe problems in spelling for dyslexic children. It appears therefore that with adaptive support, and given sufficient practice and motivation to succeed, even the most intractable spelling problems can be ameliorated. An interesting parallel

[1]On an applied note, we have now modified the Spellmaster program, in line with the children's comments and the results obtained in this study. Not surprisingly, in fixing the bugs the majority of children preferred to focus on the section of the word where the bug occurred. This meant that they had less practice than the older children in the previous SelfSpell training in deleting and retyping the whole word. Only the more competent spellers in this group were able to cope with this method, despite encouragement from the experimenter to adopt this technique on the final training session. To ensure that the children obtain the benefits of extra practice in typing the whole word, and retain the element of fun, the modified program now has the capability of including the mnemonic rule within a mastery framework.

can be drawn between these results and those of Bradley (e.g. 1988), who demonstrated that early support in phonological processing led to very much better subsequent acquisition of reading. Given early intervention, it seems likely that the initial problems can be substantially alleviated, leading to relatively normal acquisition of spelling skills.

In conclusion, we have argued that multi-media presentation techniques have the potential to provide outstanding support for dyslexic children, using the immediacy and reinforcing effect of computer presentation together with digitized speech available to avoid reliance on textual presentation. The combination of mastery and mnemonic-based techniques was highly motivating and proved very effective at remedying the spelling problems of severely retarded spellers, and the beneficial effects of training persisted over a month later. Most of the participants in the study would be described as in the logographic stage of spelling, with spelling ages of only 5.0–6.0 years. In contrast to the difficulties predicted from Frith's framework, they were by no means blocked in this stage, as evidenced by their rapid learning and good retention using the SelfSpell and Spellmaster instructional programs. These remediation studies highlight the relative poverty of stage frameworks, which typically focus on only one or two aspects of the learning situation, compared with the richness of the cognitive/instructional framework, which considers skill difficulties from the multiple viewpoints of task, learner, resources available and conditions of learning.

REFERENCES

Adams, M. J. (1990). *Beginning to Read: Thinking and Learning about Print*. Cambridge, MA: MIT Press.

Anderson, J. R. (1982). Acquisition of cognitive skill. *Psychological Review*, **89**, 369–406.

Anderson, J. R. (1989). A theory of the origins of human knowledge. *Artificial Intelligence*, **40**, 313–351.

Anderson, J. R. (1990). *Cognitive Psychology and its Implications* (3rd edition). New York: Freeman.

Badian, N. A. (1984). Reading disability in an epidemiological context: incidence and environmental correlates. *Journal of Learning Disabilities*, **17**, 129–136.

Bradley, L. (1988). Making connections in learning to read and to spell. *Applied Cognitive Psychology*, **2**, 3–18.

Brown, J. S. & Burton, R. R. (1978). Diagnostic models for procedural bugs in basic mathematical skills. *Cognitive Science*, **2**, 155–192.

Fitts, P. M. & Posner, M. I. (1967). *Human Performance*. Belmont, CA: Brooks Cole.

Frith, U. (1985). Beneath the surface of developmental dyslexia. In K. E. Patterson, J. C. Marshall & M. Coltheart (Eds), *Surface Dyslexia*. London: LEA.

Gagné R. M. (1985). *The Conditions of Learning* (4th edition). New York: Holt/Rinehart/ Winston.

Glaser, R. (1976). Cognitive psychology and instructional design. In *Cognition and Instruction* (D. Klahr, Ed.), Hillsdale, NJ: LEA.

Goswami, U. C. & Bryant, P. E. (1990). *Phonological Skills and Learning to Read*. Hove: LEA.

Holt, J. (1984). *How Children Fail* (revised edition). Harmondsworth: Penguin.

Hulme, C. (1981). *Reading Retardation and Multi-Sensory Teaching. An Experimental Study*. London: Routledge & Kegan Paul.

Jorm, A. F., Share, D. L., McLean, R. & Matthews, D. (1986). Cognitive factors at school entry predictive of specific reading retardation and general reading backwardness: a research note. *Journal of Child Psychology and Psychiatry and Allied Disciplines*, **27**, 45–54.

Malone, T. W. (1981). Towards a theory of intrinsically motivating instruction. *Cognitive Science*, **4**, 333–369.

Miles, E. (1991). *The Bangor Dyslexia Teaching System*. London: Whurr.

Miles, T. R. (1983). *Dyslexia: The Pattern of Difficulties*. London: Granada.

Nicolson, R. I. (1979). *Identification of stages in learning paired associates*. Unpublished PhD thesis, University of Cambridge.

Nicolson, R. I. (1991). Design and evaluation of the SUMIT Intelligent Tutoring Assistant for Arithemetic. *Interactive Learning Environments*, **1**, 265–287.

Nicolson, R. I., Fawcett, A. J. & Morris, S. (1993). Spelling remediation for dyslexic children: a comparison of rule based and mastery techniques. *Journal of Computer Assisted Learning*, **9**, 171–183.

Nicolson, R. I., Pickering, S. & Fawcett, A. J. (1991). Open learning for dyslexic children using HyperCard™. *Computers and Education*, **16**, 203–209.

O'Shea, T. & Self, J. (1983). *Learning and Teaching with Computers: Artificial Intelligence in Education*. Brighton: Harvester Press.

Papert, S. (1980). *Mindstorms: Children, Computers and Powerful Ideas*. New York: Basic Books.

Pumphrey, P. D. & Reason, R. (1991). *Specific Learning Difficulties (Dyslexia): Challenges and Responses*. Windsor: NFER Nelson.

Rotter, J. (1975). Some problems and misconceptions relating to the construct of internal versus external control of reinforcement. *Journal of Consulting and Clinical Psychology*, **43**, 56–67.

Shiffrin, R. M. & Schneider, W. (1977). Controlled and automatic human information processing II: Perceptual learning, automatic attending and general theory. *Psychological Review*, **84**, 127–190.

Simon, H. A. (1979). Problem solving and education. In D. Tuma & F. Reif (Eds), *Problem Solving and Education: Issues in Teaching and Research*. Hillsdale, NJ: LEA.

Skinner, B. F. (1968). *The Technology of Teaching*. New York: Appleton Century Crofts.

Snow, R. E. & Swanson, J. (1992). Instructional psychology: aptitude, adaptation and assessment. *Annual Review of Psychology*, **43**, 583–626.

Stanovich, K. E. (1988). The right and wrong places to look for the cognitive locus of reading disability. *Annals of Dyslexia*, **38**, 154–177.

Thomson, M. E. (1984). *Developmental Dyslexia: Its Nature, Assessment and Remediation*. London: Edward Arnold.

Thomson, M. E. (1988). Preliminary findings concerning the effects of specialised teaching on dyslexic children. *Applied Cognitive Psychology*, **2**, 19–31.

Thomson, M. E. (1991). The teaching of spelling using techniques of simultaneous oral spelling and visual inspection. In M. Snowling & M Thomson (Eds), *Dylsexia: Integrating Theory and Practice*. London: Whurr.

Wise, B. W. & Olson, R. K. (1992). How poor readers and spellers use interactive speech in a computerized spelling program. *Reading and Writing: An Interdisciplinary Journal*, **4**, 145–163.

World Federation of Neurologists (1968). *Report of Research Group on Dyslexia and World Illiteracy*. Dallas: WFN.

Yap, R. & van der Leij, A. (1993). Skills and their development in children with dyslexia. In A. J. Fawcett & R. I. Nicolson (Eds), *Skills and their Development in Children with Dyslexia*. Chichester: Multilingual Matters.

Name index

Subject index

Wiley titles of related interest

THE DEVELOPMENT OF COMMUNICATION
From Social Interaction to Language
DAVID J. MESSER

An up-to-date advanced text on the development of communication during the first 2–3 years of life. The book provides an authoritative review of the subject while also presenting themes and ideas to provoke discussion and thought.

0-471-94076-3   cloth   352pp   1994

HANDBOOK OF LANGUAGE AND SOCIAL PSYCHOLOGY
Edited by HOWARD GILES and W. PETER ROBINSON

Concerned with the integration of verbal and non-verbal features in communication—how systems work, especially in applied settings and social relationships. It will be essential reading for all social psychologists interested in language and how it functions in communication.

0-471-93875-0   paper   628pp   1993

LANGUAGE, THOUGHT AND REPRESENTATION
ROSEMARY J. STEVENSON

Presents an integrated account of the processes and representations involved in language and thought and the relationship between them. This is achieved by examining a number of topics in language (syntax, semantics, prose, discourse) and thought (problem solving, deduction, hypothesis testing, concept formation).

0-471-93629-4   paper   356pp   1992

HEMISPHERIC SPECIALIZATION AND PSYCHOLOGICAL FUNCTION
JOHN L. BRADSHAW

Cognitive neuropsychology deals with the cerebral organization of, for example, language and speech, reading, recognition of patterns, and perceptual processing. This book discusses recent studies of human cerebral asymmetry, and the effects of certain factors on brain function.

0-471-93118-7   paper   230pp   1991